READINGS IN DEVIANT BEHAVIOR

READINGS IN DEVIANT BEHAVIOR

SECOND EDITION

ALEX THIO

Ohio University

THOMAS C. CALHOUN

University of Nebraska

ALLYN AND BACON

Boston • London • Toronto • Sydney • Tokyo • Singapore

Editor-in-Chief, Social Sciences: Karen Hanson
Editorial Assistant: Sarah McGaughey
Marketing Manager: Judeth Hall
Editorial-Production Service: Omegatype Typography, Inc.
Composition and Prepress Buyer: Linda Cox
Manufacturing Manager: Megan Cochran
Cover Administrator: Brian Gogolin
Electronic Composition: Omegatype Typography, Inc.

Copyright © 2001, 1995 by Allyn & Bacon
A Pearson Education Company
160 Gould Street
Needham Heights, MA 02494

Internet: www.ablongman.com

Library of Congress Cataloging-in-Publication Data

Readings in deviant behavior / [edited by] Alex Thio, Thomas C. Calhoun.—2nd ed.
     p. cm.
   Includes bibliographical references.
   ISBN 0-205-31904-1 (alk. paper)
    1. Deviant behavior.   I. Thio, Alex.   II. Calhoun, Thomas C.
HM811 .R4 2000
  302.5'42—dc21

                                                               00-058271

Printed in the United States of America
10 9 8 7 6 5 4 3   05 04 03 02

Contents

PART ELEVEN
DEVIANT SPORTS   315

PART TWELVE
PUZZLING DEVIANCES   351

PREFACE

In this edition of *Readings in Deviant Behavior,* nearly half of the articles are new. They reflect the current trends in the sociology of deviance. There are now many more studies on noncriminal deviance—including tattooing, stripping, homophobia, and online sex—which represent a significant shift from criminal deviance such as murder and rape. Some of the noncriminal deviances have only recently emerged on the scene, such as the proliferation of cyberdeviance, and others, such as cockfighting and tattooing, have been around for a long time but have only recently become the subject of research by sociologists. On the theoretical front, there is a greater change in emphasis from the positivist to the constructionist perspective. In research methodology, there is a greater use of ethnography at the expense of the traditional use of surveys. All these new developments are showcased in the current edition of this reader.

Like its earlier edition, this anthology has a comprehensive coverage. Unlike many other editors, we have shied away from using only one theoretical approach in selecting articles. Instead, we have chosen a great variety of readings that represent the whole gamut of deviance sociology. We believe that students should know different theories of deviance. They should also know different kinds of data that are collected with different research methodologies.

This reader covers all the major theories in deviance sociology, from the classic, such as Merton's strain theory and Becker's labeling theory, to the modern, such as shaming, phenomenological, and postmodern theories. In addition, this book encompasses a wide range of deviant behaviors. There are articles about deviances that have long attracted sociological attention, such as homicide, burglary, drug abuse, and prostitution. There are also articles on deviances that have in recent years leapt into public and sociological consciousness, such as eating disorders, date rape, cigarette smoking, homophobia, and cyberdeviance. Analyses of these subjects rely on data from theory-informed research that run the gamut from survey to ethnographic studies. All these analyses are multidisciplinary, coming not only from sociologists but also from scholars and researchers in other fields. They all effectively reflect what the sociology of deviance is like today: diverse, wide-ranging, and exciting.

This is also a user-friendly anthology—it has been put together with student needs in mind. The articles are not only authoritative but are also interesting. Many were chosen from different kinds of books, journals, and magazines. Some were solicited from well-known or well-qualified sociologists and researchers. Most important, all these articles have been carefully edited for clarity, conciseness, and forcefulness. Students will therefore find them easy and enjoyable to read while learning what deviance is all about.

We would like to thank all the colleagues who wrote specifically for this book. Our deep gratitude also goes to all those writers whose published works are presented here. Further deserving our thanks are the following reviewers, who have contributed greatly to the preparation of a truly useful and student-oriented reader: Phillip W. Davis, Georgia State University; Jim Thomas, Northern Illinois University; and Kenrick S. Thompson, Arkansas State University. Last but not least, we thank Jefferson Vincent Murphy for finding some of the articles that appear here.

ABOUT THE EDITORS

ALEX THIO

Alex Thio (pronounced *TEE-oh*) is professor of sociology at Ohio University. Born of Chinese parentage in Penang, Malaysia, he grew up in a multicultural environment. He acquired fluency in Mandarin (modern standard Chinese), two Chinese dialects (Fukienese and Hakka), Malay, and Indonesian. He also picked up a smattering of English and Dutch. He added French and German in high school and college.

Professor Thio attended primary school in Malaysia and high school in Indonesia. He then came to the United States and worked his way through Central Methodist College in Missouri, where he majored in social sciences and took many literature and writing courses. Later, he studied sociology as a graduate student at the State University of New York at Buffalo, and he completed his doctorate while working as a research and teaching assistant.

Dr. Thio regularly teaches courses in deviance, introductory sociology, social problems, and criminology. In addition to teaching, he enjoys writing. Aside from this book, he is the author of the popular texts *Deviant Behavior,* Sixth Edition (2001) and *Sociology: A Brief Introduction,* Fourth Edition (2000), and has written many articles.

THOMAS C. CALHOUN

Thomas Calhoun is associate professor of sociology at the University of Nebraska. Born and reared in rural Mississippi, he attended segregated schools and witnessed many civil rights activities in the 1960s. He received his B.A. in sociology from Texas Wesleyan College, M.A. from Texas Tech University, and Ph.D. from the University of Kentucky.

Dr. Calhoun teaches courses in deviant behavior, juvenile delinquency, community-based corrections, and introduction to sociology. He has written a number of articles that appear in journals such as *Sociological Spectrum* and *Sociological Inquiry.* He also enjoys teaching, having won the University's Award given by students at Ohio University and the Outstanding Teacher Award presented by the University's College of Arts and Sciences.

INTRODUCTION

What is deviant behavior? Why ask what it is? Doesn't everybody know it has to do with weirdos and perverts? Not at all. There is, in fact, a great deal of disagreement among people about what they consider deviant. In a classic study, sociologist Jerry Simmons asked a sample of the general public who they thought was deviant. They mentioned 252 different kinds of people as deviants, including homosexuals, prostitutes, alcoholics, drug addicts, murderers, the mentally ill, communists, atheists, liars, Democrats, reckless drivers, self-pitiers, the retired, career women, divorcées, Christians, suburbanites, movie stars, perpetual bridge players, prudes, pacifists, psychiatrists, priests, liberals, conservatives, junior executives, girls who wear makeup, smart-aleck students, and know-it-all professors. If you are surprised that some of these people are considered deviant, your surprise simply adds to the fact that a good deal of disagreement exists among the public about what deviant behavior is.

There is a similar lack of consensus among sociologists. We could say that the study of deviant behavior is probably the most "deviant" of all the subjects in sociology. Sociologists disagree more about the definition of deviant behavior than they do on any other subject.

CONFLICTING DEFINITIONS

Some sociologists simply say that deviance is a violation of any social rule, but others argue that deviance involves more than rule violation—it also has the quality of provoking disapproval, anger, or indignation. Some advocate a broader definition, arguing that a person can be a deviant without violating any rule or doing something that rubs others the wrong way. According to this argument, individuals who are afflicted with some unfortunate condition for which they cannot be held responsible are deviant. Examples include psychotics, paraplegics, the mentally challenged, and other people with physical or mental disabilities. These people are considered deviant because they are disvalued by society. In contrast, some sociologists contend that deviance does not have to be negative. To these sociologists, deviance can be positive, such as being a genius, reformer, creative artist, or glamorous celebrity. Other sociologists disagree, considering "positive deviance" to be an oxymoron—a contradiction in terms.

All these sociologists apparently assume that, whether it is a positive or a negative, disturbing, or disvalued behavior, deviance is real in and of itself. The logic behind this assumption is that if it is not real in the first place, it cannot be considered positive, negative, disturbing, or disvalued. Other sociologists disagree, arguing that deviance does not have to be real behavior for it to be labeled deviant. People can be falsely accused of being criminal, erroneously diagnosed as mentally ill, stereotyped as dangerous because of their skin color, and so on. Conversely, committing a deviant act does not necessarily make a person a deviant, especially when the act is kept secret. It is, therefore, the label *deviant*—a mental construction or image of an act as deviant, rather than the act itself—that makes an individual deviant.

Some sociologists go beyond the notion of labeling to define deviance by stressing the importance of power. They observe that relatively powerful people are capable of avoiding the fate suffered by the powerless—being falsely, erroneously, or unjustly labeled deviant. The key reason is that the powerful, either by themselves or through influencing public opinion or both, hold more power for labeling others' behavior as deviant. Understandably, sociologists who hold this view define deviance as any act considered by the powerful at a given time and place to be a violation of some social rule.

From this welter of conflicting definitions we can nonetheless discern the influence of two opposing perspectives: positivism and social constructionism. The positivist perspective is associated with the sciences, such as physics, chemistry, or biology. It influences how scientists see and study their subject. On the other hand, the constructionist perspective has more to do with the humanities, such as art, language, or philosophy. It affects how scholars in these fields see and study their subject. These two perspectives can be found in sociology; some sociologists are more influenced by the positivist perspective and others by the constructionist. Positivist sociologists tend to define deviance in one way, whereas constructionist sociologists pursue another way. The two perspectives further influence the use of certain theory and methodology for producing knowledge about deviant behavior. The conflicting definitions that we have discussed can be couched in terms of these two perspectives. The definitions that focus on deviance as rule-breaking behavior are essentially positivist, whereas those that center on labeling and power are constructionist. Let us delve more deeply into the meanings and implications of these two conflicting perspectives.

CONFLICTING PERSPECTIVES

The knowledge about deviance basically consists of answers to three questions. The questions are: (1) What to study? (2) How to study it? (3) What does the result of the study mean? The first question deals with the subject of study, the second has to do with the method of study, and the third concerns the data-based theory about the subject. Positivism and constructionism provide conflicting answers to each question.

Subject: What to Study?

Positivism suggests that we study deviance or deviants. The reason deals with the positivist's absolutist definition of deviance. According to this definition, deviance is absolutely or intrinsically real in that it possesses some qualities that distinguish it from conventionality. Similarly, deviants are thought to have certain attributes that make them different from conventional individuals. By contrast, social constructionism suggests that we study law enforcers and other such people who are influenced by society to construct an image of certain others as deviants and then label them as such, or how the process of such labeling takes place and affects the labeled. This is because the constructionist assumes the relativist stance in defining deviance as a socially constructed label imposed on some behavior. Such a definition can be said to be relativist by implying that the deviancy of a behavior is relative to—dependent on—the socially constructed negative reaction to the behavior.

Absolutism: Deviance as Absolutely Real. Around the turn of this century, criminologists believed that criminals possessed certain biological traits that were absent in noncriminals. Those biological traits included defective genes, bumps on the head, a long lower jaw, a scanty beard, an unattractive face, and a tough body build. Because all these traits are inherited, people were believed to be criminals simply because they were born criminals. If they were born criminals, they would always be criminals. As the saying goes, "If you've had it, you've had it." No matter where they might go—they could go anywhere in the world—they would still be criminals.

Then the criminologists shifted their attention from biological to psychological traits. Criminals were thought to have certain mental characteristics that noncriminals did not have. More specifically, criminals were believed to be feeble-minded, psychotic, neurotic, psychopathic, or otherwise mentally disturbed. Like biological traits, these mental characteristics were seen as inherent in individual criminals. Also like biological traits, mental characteristics would stay with the criminals, no matter where they went. Again, because of these psychological traits, criminals would always remain criminals.

Today's positivist sociologists, however, have largely abandoned the use of biological and psychological traits to differentiate criminals from noncriminals. They recognize the important role of social factors in determining a person's status as a criminal. Such status does not remain the same across time and space; instead, it changes in different periods and with different societies. A polygamist may be a criminal in Western society but a law-abider in Moslem countries. A person who sees things invisible to others may be a psychotic in Western society but may become a spiritual leader among some South Pacific tribes. Nevertheless, positivist sociologists still largely regard deviance as intrinsically real. Countering the relativist notion of deviance as basically a social construction in the form of a label imposed on an act, positivist Travis Hirschi argues: "The person may not have committed a 'deviant' act, but he did (in many cases) do *something*. And it is just possible that what he did was a result of things that had happened to him in the past; it is also possible that the past in some inscrutable way remains with him and that if he were left alone he would *do it again*." Moreover, countering the relativist notion of mental illness as a label imputed to some people's behavior, positivist Gwynn Nettler explicitly voices his absolutist stance: "Some people *are* more crazy than others; we can tell the

difference; and calling lunacy a name does not *cause* it." These positivist sociologists seem to say that just as a rose by any other name would smell as sweet, so deviance by any other label is just as real.

Relativism: Deviance as a Label. Social constructionists hold the relativist view that deviant behavior by itself does not have any intrinsic characteristics unless it is thought to have those characteristics. The so-called intrinsically deviant characteristics do not come from the behavior itself; they originate instead from some people's minds. To put it simply, an act appears deviant only because some people think it so. As Howard Becker says, "Deviant behavior is behavior that people so label." Therefore, no deviant label, no deviant behavior. The existence of deviance depends on the label. Deviance, then, is a mental construct (an idea, thought, or image) expressed in the form of a label.

Because they effectively consider deviance unreal, constructionists understandably stay away from studying it. They are more interested in the questions of whether and why a given act is defined by society as deviant. This leads to studying people who label others as deviant—such as the police and other law-enforcing agents. If constructionists study so-called deviants, they do so by focusing on the nature of labeling and its consequences.

In studying law-enforcing agents, constructionists have found a huge lack of consensus on whether a certain person should be treated as a criminal. The police often disagree among themselves about whether a suspect should be arrested, and judges often disagree about whether those arrested should be convicted or acquitted. In addition, because laws vary from one state to another, the same type of behavior may be defined as criminal in one state but not in another. Prostitution, for example, is legal in Nevada but not in other states. There is, then, a *relativity* principle in deviant behavior; behavior gets defined as deviant relative to a given norm, standard of behavior, or the way people react to it. If it is not related to the norm or to the reaction of other people, a given behavior is in itself meaningless—it is impossible to say whether it is deviant or conforming. Constructionists strongly emphasize this relativistic view, according to which, deviance, like beauty, is in the eye of the beholder.

Method: How to Study It?

Positivism suggests that we use objective methods such as survey, experiment, or detached observation. The subject is treated like an object, forced, for example, to answer the same questions as presented to everybody else with the same value-free, emotionless demeanor. This is because positivists define deviance as a largely objective fact, namely, a publicly observable, outward aspect of human behavior. By contrast, social constructionism suggests that we study individuals with more subjective methods, such as ethnography, participant observation, or open-ended, in-depth interviews. With these methods, subjects are treated as unique, whole persons and are encouraged to freely express their feelings in any way they want. This is because constructionists define deviance as a mostly personal experience—a hidden, inner aspect of human behavior.

Objectivism: Deviance as an Objective Fact. By focusing on the outward aspect of deviance, positivists assume that sociologists can be as objective in studying deviance as natural scientists can be in studying physical phenomena. The trick is to treat deviants as if they are objects, like those studied by natural scientists. Nonetheless, positivist sociologists cannot help being aware of the basic difference between their subject, human beings, and that of natural scientists, inanimate objects. As human beings themselves, positivist sociologists must have certain feelings about their subject. However, they try to control their personal biases by forcing themselves not to pass moral judgment on deviant behavior or share the deviant person's feelings. Instead, they try to concentrate on the subject matter as it outwardly appears. Further, these sociologists have tried hard to follow the scientific rule that all their ideas about deviant behavior should be subject to public scrutiny. This means that other sociologists should be able to check out the ideas to see whether they are supported by facts.

Such a drive to achieve scientific objectivity has produced substantial knowledge about deviant behavior. No longer popular today are such value-loaded and subjective notions as maladjustment, moral failing, debauchery, demoralization, sickness, pathology, and abnormality. Replacing these outdated notions are such value-free and objective concepts as innovation, retreatism, ritualism, rebellion, culture conflict, subcultural behavior, white-collar crime, norm violation, learned behavior, and reinforced behavior.

To demonstrate the objective reality of these concepts, positivist sociologists have used official reports and statistics, clinical reports, surveys of self-reported behavior, and surveys of victimization. Positivists recognize the unfortunate fact that the sample of deviants in the studies—especially in official statistics—does not accurately represent the entire population of deviants. Nevertheless, positivists believe that the quality of information obtained by these methods can be improved and refined. In the meantime, they consider the data, though inadequate, useful for revealing at least some aspect of the totality of deviant behavior.

Subjectivism: Deviance as a Personal Experience. To positivists, the supposedly deviant behavior is a personal experience and the supposedly deviant person is a conscious, feeling, thinking, and reflective subject. Social constructionists insist that there is a world of difference between humans (as active subjects) and nonhuman beings and things (as passive objects). Humans feel and reflect, but animals, plants, things, and the others do not. It is proper and useful for natural scientists to assume and then study nature as an object, because this study can produce objective knowledge for controlling the natural world. It may also be useful for social scientists to assume and then study humans as objects, because it may produce objective knowledge for controlling humans. However, this violates the constructionist's humanist values and sensibilities.

Constructionists are opposed to the control of humans; instead, they advocate the protection and expansion of human worth, dignity, and freedom. One result of this humanist ideology is the observation that so-called objective knowledge about human behavior is inevitably superficial whenever it is used to control people. In order for the former white racist government in South Africa to control blacks, for example, it needed only the superficial knowledge that blacks were identifiable and separable from whites. However, to achieve the humanist goal of protecting and expanding blacks' human worth, dignity, and freedom, a deeper understanding of blacks is needed. This understanding requires appreciating and empathizing with them, experiencing what they experience as blacks, and seeing blacks' lives and the world around them from their perspective. We must look at the black experience from the inside as a participant rather than from the outside as a spectator. In a word, we must adopt the internal, subjective view instead of the external, objective one.

The same principle, according to constructionists, should hold for understanding deviants and their deviant behavior. Constructionists contrast this subjective approach with the positivists' objective one. To constructionists, positivists treat deviance as if it were an immoral, unpleasant, or repulsive phenomenon that should be controlled, corrected, or eliminated. In consequence, positivists have used the objective approach by staying aloof from deviants, studying the external aspects of their deviant behavior and relying on a set of preconceived ideas to guide their study. The result is a collection of surface facts about deviants, such as their poverty, lack of schooling,

poor self-image, and low aspirations. All this may be used to control and eliminate deviance, but it does not tell us, in Howard Becker's words, "what a deviant does in his daily round of activity, and what he thinks about himself, society, and his activities." To understand the life of a deviant, constructionists believe, we need to use the relatively subjective approach, which requires our appreciation for and empathy with the deviant. The aim of this subjective approach, according to David Matza, "is to comprehend and to illuminate the subject's view and to interpret the world *as it appears to him.*"

As a result of their subjective and empathetic approach, constructionists often present an image of deviants as basically the same as conventional people. People who are deaf, for example, are the same as those who hear in being able to communicate and live a normal life. They should, therefore, be respected rather than pitied. This implies that so-called deviant behavior, because it is like so-called conventional behavior, should not be controlled, cured, or eradicated by society.

Theory: What Does It Mean?

Positivism suggests that we use etiological, causal, or explanatory theories to make sense of what research has found out about deviant behavior because positivists favor the determinist view that deviance is determined by forces beyond the individual's control. By contrast, constructionism suggests that we go for largely noncausal, descriptive, or analytical theories. Such theories provide detailed analyses of the subjective, experiential world of deviance. Constructionists feel at home with these analyses because they regard most deviance as a voluntary act, an expression of free will.

Determinism: Deviance as "Determined" Behavior. Overly enthusiastic about the prospect of turning their discipline into a science, early sociologists argued that, like animals, plants, and material objects that natural scientists study, humans do not have any free will. The reason is that acknowledgment of free will would contradict the scientific principle of determinism. If a killer is thought to will, cause, or determine a murderous act, then it does not make sense to say that the murderous act is caused by such things as the individual's physical characteristics, mental condition, family background, or some social experience. Therefore, in defending their scientific principle of determinism, the early sociologists maintained their denial of free will. However, today's positivist sociologists assume that humans do possess free will. Still, this assumption, they argue, does not undermine the scientific principle of determinism. No matter how much a person exercises free will by making choices and decisions, the choices and decisions do not simply happen but are determined by some causes. If a woman chooses to kill her husband rather than continue to live with him, she certainly has free will or freedom of choice so long as nobody forces her to do what she does. However, some factor may determine the woman's choice of one alternative over another, or the way she exercises her free will. One such factor, as research has suggested, may be a long history of abuse at the hands of her husband. Thus, according to today's positivists, there is no inconsistency between freedom and causality.

Although they allow for human freedom of choice, positivists do not use it to explain why people behave in a certain way. They will not, for example, explain why the woman kills by saying "because she chooses to kill." This is no explanation at all, because the idea of choice can also be used to explain why another woman does *not* kill her husband—by saying "because she chooses not to." According to positivists, killing and not killing (or, more generally, deviant and conventional behavior), being two contrary phenomena, cannot be explained by the same thing, such as choice. The idea of choice simply cannot explain the difference between deviance and conventionality; it cannot explain why one man chooses to kill when another chooses not to kill. Therefore, although positivists do believe in human

choice, they will not attribute deviance to human choice. They will instead explain deviance by using such concepts as wife abuse, broken homes, unhappy homes, lower-class background, economic deprivation, social disorganization, rapid social change, differential association, differential reinforcement, and lack of social control. Any one of these causes of deviance can be used to illustrate what positivists consider a real explanation of deviance, because, for example, wife abuse is more likely to cause a woman to kill her husband than not. Etiological theories essentially point out factors like those as the causes of deviance.

Voluntarism: Deviance as a Voluntary Act.   To social constructionists, the supposedly deviant behavior is a voluntary act or an expression of human volition, will, or choice. Constructionists take this stance because they are disturbed by what they claim to be the dehumanizing implication of the positivist view of deviant behavior. The positivist view is said to imply that a human being is like "a robot, a senseless and purposeless machine reacting to every fortuitous change in the external and internal environment." Constructionists emphasize that human beings, because they possess free will and choice-making ability, determine or cause their own behavior.

To support this voluntarist assumption, constructionists tend to analyze how social control agencies define some people as deviant and carry out the sanctions against them. Such analyses often accent, as Edwin Lemert has observed, "the arbitrariness of official action, stereotyped decision-making in bureaucratic contexts, bias in the administration of law, and the general preemptive nature of society's controls over deviants." All this conveys the strong impression that control agents, being in positions of power, exercise their free will by actively, intentionally, and purposefully controlling the "deviants."

Constructionists also analyze people who have been labeled deviant. The "deviants" are not presented as if they are robots, passively and senselessly developing a poor self-image as conventional society expects. Instead, they are described as actively seeking positive meanings in their deviant activities. In Jack Katz's analysis, murderers see themselves as morally superior to their victims. The killing is said to give the murderers the self-righteous feeling of defending their dignity and respectability because their victims have unjustly humiliated them by taunting or insulting them. Katz also portrays robbers as feeling themselves morally superior to their victims—regarding their victims as fools or suckers who deserve to be robbed. If robbers want to hold up somebody on the street, they first ask a potential victim for the time, for directions, for a cigarette light, or for change. Each of these requests is intended to determine whether the person is a fool. The request for the time, for example, gives the robber the opportunity to know whether the prospective victim has an expensive watch. Complying with the request, then, is taken to establish the person as a fool and hence the right victim.

SUMMARY AND CONCLUSION

Each of the positivist and social constructionist perspectives consists of three related assumptions, and each assumption suggests a strategy for contributing to the sociology of deviance. For the positivist perspective, the first is the absolutist assumption that deviant behavior is absolutely real. This suggests that we study deviance or deviants. Second is the objectivist assumption that deviant behavior is an objective, publicly observable fact. This suggests that we use objective research methods such as survey, experiment, or detached observation. Third is the determinist assumption that deviance is determined or caused by certain social forces. This suggests that we use causal theories to make sense of research data. With the social constructionist perspective, the first assumption is that deviant behavior is basically a label, mental construct, or social construction. This suggests that we study law enforcers and other labelers, the process of labeling, and the consequences of labeling. The second assumption is that the supposedly deviant behavior is a personal experience. This suggests that we use less objective research methods such as ethnography, participant observation, or open-ended, in-depth interviews. The third assumption is that the so-called deviance is a voluntary, self-willed act. This suggests that we develop noncausal, descriptive theories. (See Table I.1 for a quick review.)

The diverse definitions, theories, methodologies, and data we have discussed reflect many

Table I.1 A Summary of Two Perspectives

POSITIVIST PERSPECTIVE	CONSTRUCTIONIST PERSPECTIVE
Absolutism Deviance is absolutely, intrinsically real; hence, deviance or deviants are the subjects of study.	*Relativism* Deviance is a label, a social construction; hence, labelers, labeling, and the impacts of labeling are the subject of study.
Objectivism Deviance is an objective, observable fact; hence, objective research methods are used.	*Subjectivism* Deviance is a personal experience; hence, subjective research methods are used.
Determinism Deviance is a determined behavior, a product of causation; hence, casual, explanatory theory is developed.	*Voluntarism* Deviance is a voluntary act, an expression of free will; hence, noncausal, descriptive theory is developed.

different aspects of deviant behavior. Although they appear to conflict, they actually complement each other. They may be compared with the different views of a house. From the front, the house has a door, windows, and a chimney on top. From the back, it has a door and a chimney on top but fewer windows. From the side, it has no doors, but it has windows and a chimney on top. From the top, it has no doors or windows, but a chim- ney in the middle. It is the same house, but it looks different, depending on one's position. Taking in the different views on the house ensures a fuller knowledge of what the house actually looks like. Similarly, knowing the different views on deviant behavior ensures a fuller understanding of deviance. This reader is intended to make that possible.

PART ONE

DEFINING AND RESEARCHING DEVIANCE

Charles Farnham is a software writer who has an enormous collection of commercial programs for his computer. Like millions of other people, he has not bought most of the programs; he has simply copied them from his friends' software. Federal law prohibits this kind of behavior, but many computer users who would not steal a library book or cheat on a test have no qualms about copying software illegally. Farnham explains that most software is too expensive and that there is nothing wrong with sampling a program before spending $500 or more.[1]

On the other hand, Aleta Walker, an obese 36-year-old woman, has a different kind of experience. Throughout her life, she has been ridiculed and abused for her weight. What she suffered during childhood and adolescence was particularly poignant. Every day, when she walked down the halls at school, boys would step back and yell, "Wide load!" It was worse at lunchtime. As she said, "Every day there was this production of watching me eat lunch." One day, schoolmates threw food at her. Spaghetti splashed on her head and face, and the long greasy strands dripped onto her clothes. "Everyone was laughing and pointing. They were making pig noises. I just sat there," she said.[2]

Is Farnham deviant for copying software illegally? Some people would say yes, but others would say no. Is Walker deviant for being overweight? Again, some people would say yes, but others would say no. In fact, some would claim that it is her tormentors— the so-called normal people—who are deviant because they are grossly insensitive, nasty, or cruel. Given this disagreement, who determines what constitutes deviance? Stephen Pfohl deals with this issue in the first article here, "Images of Deviance." In the second article, "Defining Deviancy Down," Daniel Patrick Moynihan shows how our society today no longer defines many harmful behaviors as deviant. In Moynihan's words, many people define deviance down by accepting or tolerating a large amount of it as normal, but more conservative Americans define deviance up by demonizing it, condemning it, or advocating harsh penalty for it. In the third article, "Strategies for Researching Street Deviance," Leon Anderson and Thomas Calhoun show how opportunities for researching street deviants—homeless persons and male prostitutes—can be used to maximize the efficiency and quality of field research with deviant populations. Finally, in "Pleasures and Perils in Deviance Research," Erich Goode discusses the benefits and problems that researchers have if they have sex with their subjects.

1. John Markoff, "Though Illegal, Copied Software Is Now Common," *New York Times,* July 27, 1992, pp. A1, C4.

2 Gina Kolata, "The Burdens of Being Overweight: Mistreatment and Misconceptions," *New York Times,* November 22, 1992, pp. 1, 18.

1

IMAGES OF DEVIANCE

STEPHEN PFOHL

The scene is a crowded church during the American Civil War. "It was a time of great and exalting excitement. The country was up in arms, the war was on, in every breast burned the holy fire of patriotism." So says Mark Twain in his short and searing parable—*The War Prayer.* Amidst the clamor of beating drums, marching bands, and toy pistols popping, Twain describes an emotional church service. A passionate minister stirs the gallant hearts of eager volunteers; bronzed returning heroes; and their families, friends, and neighbors. The inspired congregation await their minister's every word.

> And with one impulse the house rose, with glowing eyes and beating hearts, and poured out that tremendous invocation—

> God the all-terrible!
> Thou who ordainest,
> Thunder thy clarion
> and lightning thy sword!

Then came the "long" prayer. None could remember the like of it for passionate pleading and moving and beautiful language. The burden of its supplication was that an ever-merciful and benignant Father of us all would watch over our noble young soldiers and aid, comfort, and encourage them in their patriotic work; bless them, shield them in the day of battle and the hour of peril, bear them in His mighty hand, make them strong and confident, invincible in the bloody onset; help them to crush the foe, grant to them and to their flag and country imperishable honor and glory.

Wars come and go. Words vary. Nonetheless, the essential message of this sermon remains

alarmingly the same: "God is on our side." Before continuing with Twain's story, I ask you to consider a more contemporary version of this age-old narrative—the 1991 Gulf War between Iraq and the United States–led coalition of "New World Order" forces demanding an Iraqi withdrawal from Kuwait. Claiming it to be its moral imperative to repel an act of international aggression, the United States pictured Iraqi President Saddam Hussein as a Hitler-like character bent on world domination. Iraq in turn cited contradictions in the U.S. position (its long-term support for Israeli occupation of Palestinian territories, for example) as evidence of both U.S. hypocrisy and what Iraq alleged to be the true motives for the attack on Iraq—namely, "American" efforts to police the price of oil. Each side in this conflict represented the other as evil, treacherous, and power-mongering. Each side claimed to be righteous and blessed by God. This is typical of societies engaged in war.

Returning to Twain's story, what is untypical about this thoughtful tale is what happens next. It is not only untypical, but "deviant." After the minister completes his moving prayer, an "unnaturally pale," aged stranger enters the church. He is adorned with long hair and dressed in a full-length robe. The stranger motions the startled minister aside and informs the shocked parishioners that he is a messenger from Almighty God. He tells the congregation that God has heard their prayer and will grant it, but only after they consider the full import of their request. In rephrasing the original sermon the mysterious messenger reveals a more troubling side to the congregation's prayer. When they ask blessing for themselves they are, at the same time, praying for the merciless destruction of other humans (their enemies). In direct and graphic language the old man portrays the unspoken implications of their request, as follows:

> help us to tear their soldiers to bloody shreds with our shells;
>
> help us to cover their smiling fields with the pale forms of their patriotic dead;
>
> help us to draw the thunder of the guns with shrieks of their wounded, writhing in pain;
>
> help us to lay waste their humble homes with a hurricane of fire;
>
> help us to wring the hearts of their unoffending widows to unavailing grief;
>
> help us to turn them out roofless with their little children to wander unbefriended the wastes of their desolated land.

The strange old man continues—talking about blighting their lives, bringing tears, and staining the snow with blood. He completes his war prayer with a statement about the humble and contrite hearts of those who ask God's blessings. The congregation pauses in silence. He asks if they still desire what they have prayed for. "Ye have prayed it; if ye still desire it, speak! The messenger of the Most High waits." We are now at the final page of Twain's book. The congregation's response is simple and abrupt. As suggested previously, the old stranger was clearly a social deviant. In Twain's words: "It was believed afterward that the man was a lunatic, because there was no sense in what he said."

The stranger in *The War Prayer* directly threatens the normal, healthy, patriotic, and blood-lusting beliefs of the embattled congregation. Yet it is with ease that they contain and control this threat. They do not have to take seriously the chilling implications of his sermon. Their religious and patriotic senses are protected from his disturbing assault. Why? The reason is as simple as their response. They believe that he is a lunatic. They believe that he is a deviant. By classifying the old man as a deviant they need not listen to him. The congregation's beliefs are protected, even strengthened. The lunatic's beliefs are safely controlled.

The War Prayer is thus a story of how some people imagine other people to be "deviant" and thereby protect or isolate themselves from those whom they fear and from that which challenges the way in which "normal" social life is organized. It is a story of how people convince themselves of what is normal by condemning those who disagree. It is a story of both deviance and social control. . . .

The story of deviance and social control is a battle story. It is a story of the battle to control the ways people think, feel, and behave. It is a story of winners and losers and of the strategies people use in struggles with one another. Winners in the battle to control "deviant acts" are crowned with a halo of goodness, acceptability, normality. Losers are viewed as living outside the boundaries of social life as it ought to be, outside the "common sense" of society itself. They may be seen by others as evil, sleazy, dirty, dangerous, sick, immoral, crazy, or just plain deviant. They may even come to see themselves in such negative imagery, to see themselves as *deviants*.

Deviants are only one part of the story of deviance and social control. Deviants never exist except in relation to those who attempt to control them. Deviants exist only in opposition to those whom they threaten and those who have enough power to control against such threats. The outcome of the battle of deviance and social control is this. Winners obtain the privilege of organizing social life as they see fit. Losers are trapped within the vision of others. They are labeled deviant and subjected to an array of current social control practices. Depending upon the controlling wisdom at a particular moment in history, deviants may be executed, brutally beaten, fined, shamed, incarcerated, drugged, hospitalized, or even treated to heavy doses of tender loving care. But first and foremost they are prohibited from passing as normal women or men. They are branded with the image of being deviant.

When we think of losers in the battle to control acceptable images of social life, it may seem natural to think of juvenile gang members, serial killers, illegal drug users, homosexuals, and burglars. Indeed, common sense may tell us that such people are simply deviant. But where does this common sense come from? How do we come to know that certain actions or certain people are deviant, while others are "normal"? Do people categorized as deviants really behave in a more dangerous fashion than others? Some people think so. Is this true?

Think of the so-called deviants mentioned above. Are their actions truly more harmful than the actions of people not labeled as deviants? In many cases the answer is no. Consider the juvenile gang. In recent years the organized drug dealing and violent activities of gangs have terrorized people living in poverty-stricken and racially segregated urban neighborhoods. Gang-related deviance has also been the focal point for sensational media stories and for social control policies ranging from selective "stop-and-search" police tactics to the building of new prisons and (in Los Angeles) even the criminalization of alleged gang members' parents.

But what about the people most responsible for the oppressive inner-city conditions that lie at the root of many gang-related activities? What about the "gangs" of bankers whose illegal redlining of mortgage loans blocks the investment of money in inner-city neighborhoods? What about the "gangs" of corporate executives whose greed for short-term profits has led to the "off-shoring" of industrial jobs to "underdeveloped" countries where labor is cheap and more easily exploitable? Aren't the actions of such respectable people as costly as, if less visible than, the activities of most inner-city gangs? Yet, there is an important difference: unlike gangs of elite deviants, inner-city youths have little or no real access to dominant institutions in which contemporary power is concentrated.

A related question may be posed concerning serial killers. The violence of serial killers haunts our nightly news broadcasts. Indeed, the seemingly random character of serial killings—although they are most commonly directed against women and children—instills a deep and alarming sense of dread within society as a whole.

Nevertheless, the sporadic violence of serial murderers, no matter how fearful, is incomparable in terms of both scope and number to the much less publicized "serial killings" perpetrated by U.S.-supported *death squads* in countries such as El Salvador and Guatemala. The targets of such death squads are typically people who dare to speak out in the name of social justice. From 1980 to 1991, for instance, approximately 75,000 Salvadoran civilians were secretly killed or made to "disappear" by paramilitary executioners. Why is it that such systematic murders are rarely acknowledged as true serial killings? Why, moreover, do such cold-blooded killings provoke so little U.S. public outrage in comparison to the attention given to the isolated violence of individual murderers, such as Ted Bundy or Jeffrey Dahmer? Is it because the people who authorize them are respectable persons, sometimes even publicly elected officials? Is it because, though we feel vulnerable to other serial killers, we ourselves—at least those of us who are white, male, North American, and economically privileged to live at a distance from the violence that historically envelops the daily lives of others—feel protected from death squads?

Similar questions might be raised about drug users. When we speak of the abuse of drugs, why do we often think only of the "controlled substances" that some people use as a means of achieving psychic escape, altered consciousness, and/or bodily pleasure? True, we as individuals and as a society may pay a heavy price for the abuse of such drugs as cocaine and heroin. But what about other—legal—substances that many of us are "on" much of the time? Some of these drugs are even more dangerous than their illicit counterparts. In addition to alcohol, tobacco, chemical food additives, and meat from animals that have been fed antibiotics and hormones, our society openly promotes the use of prescription and over-the-counter drugs for everything from losing weight, curing acne, and overcoming anxiety to building strong bodies, fighting depression, and alleviating allergies caused by industrial pollution. Certainly many of these substances have their salutary effects and may help us adjust to the world in which we live. However, even legal substances can be abused; they too can be dangerous. The effects can be direct, jeopardizing an individual's health or fostering addiction, or they can be indirect and more insidious. For example, consider the role drugs play in creating and sustaining our excessively image-conscious, age-conscious environment and in promoting our tendency to avoid dealing with personal conflicts and everyday problems in a thoughtful and responsible manner. Also—not to belabor the issue—just think of what we are doing to our planet, to our future, with our use of pesticides, fertilizers, and other industrial products and by-products. To raise such concerns is not to claim that legal drugs are more dangerous than illegal drugs, but simply to suggest that what is officially labeled illegal or deviant often has more to do with what society economically values than with whether the thing is physically harmful per se.

Further consider the actions of sexist heterosexuals. Such persons may routinely mix various forms of sexual harassment with manipulative patriarchal power and an intolerance of alternative forms of sexual intimacy. Despite the harm these heterosexist individuals cause, they are far less likely to be labeled deviant than are gay, lesbian, or bisexual lovers who caress one another with affection. The same goes for corporate criminals, such as the executives recently implicated in the savings and loan scandal. The stealthy acts of such white-collar criminals have cost the U.S. public as much as $500 billion. Yet the elite deviance of the upper echelon of rule breakers is commonly less feared than are the street crimes of ordinary burglars and robbers.

From the preceding examples it should be evident that many forms of labeled deviance are not more costly to society than the behaviors of people who are less likely to be labeled deviant. Why? The answer . . . is that labeled deviants are viewed as such because they threaten the control of people who have enough power to shape the way society imagines the boundary between good and bad, normal and pathological, acceptable and deviant. This is the crux of the effort to understand the battle between deviance and social control. Deviance is always the flip side of the coin used to maintain social control.

2

DEFINING DEVIANCY DOWN

DANIEL PATRICK MOYNIHAN

In one of the founding texts of sociology, *The Rules of Sociological Method* (1895), Emile Durkheim set it down that "crime is normal." "It is," he wrote, "completely impossible for any society entirely free of it to exist." By defining what is deviant, we are enabled to know what is not, and hence to live by shared standards.

The matter was pretty much left at that until seventy years later when, in 1965, Kai T. Erikson published *Wayward Puritans,* a study of "crime rates" in the Massachusetts Bay Colony. The plan behind the book, as Erikson put it, was "to test [Durkheim's] notion that the number of deviant offenders a community can afford to recognize is likely to remain stable over time." The notion proved out very well indeed. Despite occasional crime waves, as when itinerant Quakers refused to take off their hats in the presence of magistrates, the amount of deviance in this corner of seventeenth-century New England fitted nicely with the supply of stocks and whipping posts. Erikson remarks:

> The agencies of control often seem to define their job as that of keeping deviance within bounds rather than that of obliterating it altogether. Many judges, for example, assume that severe punishments are a greater deterrent to crime than moderate ones, and so it is important to note that many of them are apt to impose harder penalties when crime seems to be on the increase and more lenient ones when it does not, almost as if the power of the bench were being used to keep the crime rate from getting out of hand. . . . Hence "the number of deviant offenders a community can afford to recognize is likely to remain stable over time." [My emphasis]

Social scientists are said to be on the lookout for poor fellows getting a bum rap. But here is a theory that clearly implies that there are circumstances in which society will choose *not* to notice behavior that would be otherwise controlled, or disapproved, or even punished.

It appears to me that this is in fact what we in the United States have been doing of late. I proffer the thesis that, over the past generation, since the time Erikson wrote, the amount of deviant behavior in American society has increased beyond the levels the community can "afford to recognize" and that, accordingly, we have been re-defining deviancy so as to exempt much conduct previously stigmatized, and also quietly raising the "normal" level in categories where behavior is now abnormal by any earlier standard. . . .

[In today's normalization of deviance] we are dealing with the popular psychological notion of "denial." In 1965, having reached the conclusion that there would be a dramatic increase in single-parent families, I reached the further conclusion that this would in turn lead to a dramatic increase in crime. In an article in *America,* I wrote:

> From the wild Irish slums of the 19th century Eastern seaboard to the riot-torn suburbs of Los Angeles, there is one unmistakable lesson in American history: a community that allows a large number of young men to grow up in broken families, dominated by women, never acquiring any stable relationship to male authority, never acquiring any set of rational expectations about the future—that community asks for and gets chaos. Crime, violence, unrest, unrestrained lashing out at the whole social structure—that is not only to be expected; it is very near to inevitable.

The inevitable, as we now know, has come to pass, but here again our response is curiously passive. Crime is a more or less continuous subject of political pronouncement, and from time to time it will be at or near the top of opinion polls as a matter of public concern. But it never gets much further than that. In the words spoken from the bench, Judge Edwin Torres of the New York State Supreme Court, Twelfth Judicial District, described how "the slaughter of the innocent marches unabated: subway riders, bodega owners, cab drivers, babies; in laundromats, at cash machines, on elevators, in hallways." In personal communication, he writes: "This numbness, this near narcoleptic state can diminish the human condition to the level of combat infantrymen, who, in protracted campaigns, can eat their battlefield rations seated on the bodies of the fallen, friend and foe alike. A society that loses its sense of outrage is doomed to extinction." There is no expectation that this will change, nor any efficacious public insistence that it do so. The crime level has been *normalized.*

Consider the St. Valentine's Day Massacre. In 1929 in Chicago during Prohibition, four gangsters killed seven gangsters on February 14. The nation was shocked. The event became legend. It merits not one but two entries in the *World Book Encyclopedia.* I leave it to others to judge, but it would appear that the society in the 1920s was simply not willing to put up with this degree of deviancy. In the end, the Constitution was amended, and Prohibition, which lay behind so much gangster violence, ended.

In recent years, again in the context of illegal traffic in controlled substances, this form of murder has returned. But it has done so at a level that induces denial. James Q. Wilson comments that Los Angeles has the equivalent of a St. Valentine's Day Massacre every weekend. Even the most ghastly reenactments of such human slaughter produce only moderate responses. On the morning after the close of the Democratic National Convention in New York City in July, there was such an account in the second section of the *New York Times.* It was not a big story; bottom of the page, but with a headline that got your attention. "3 Slain in Bronx Apartment, but a Baby is Saved." A subhead continued: "A mother's last act was to hide her little girl under the bed." The article described a drug execution; the now-routine blindfolds made from duct tape; a man and a woman and a teenager involved. "Each had been shot once in the head." The police had found them a day later. They also found, under a bed, a three-month-old baby, dehydrated but alive. A lieutenant remarked of the mother, "In her last dying act she protected her baby. She probably knew she was going to die, so she stuffed the baby where she knew it would be safe." But the matter was left there. The police would do their best. But the event passed quickly; forgotten by the next day, it will never make *World Book.*

Nor is it likely that any great heed will be paid to an uncanny reenactment of the Prohibition drama a few months later, also in the Bronx. The *Times* story, page B3, reported:

9 Men Posing as Police Are Indicted in 3 Murders

DRUG DEALERS WERE KIDNAPPED FOR RANSOM

The *Daily News* story, same day, page 17, made it *four* murders, adding nice details about torture techniques. The gang members posed as federal Drug Enforcement Administration agents, real badges and all. The victims were drug dealers, whose families were uneasy about calling the police. Ransom seems generally to have been set in the $650,000 range. Some paid. Some got it in the back of the head. So it goes.

Yet, violent killings, often random, go on unabated. Peaks continue to attract some notice. But these are peaks above "average" levels that thirty years ago would have been thought epidemic. . . . A Kai Erikson of the future will surely need to know that the Department of Justice in 1990 found that Americans reported only about 38 percent of all crimes and 48 percent of violent crimes. This, too, can be seen as a means of *normalizing* crime. In much the same way, the vocabulary of crime reporting can be seen to move toward the normal-seeming. A teacher is shot on her way to class. The *Times* subhead reads: "Struck in the Shoulder in the Year's First Shooting Inside a School." First of the season. . . .

The hope—if there be such—of this essay has been twofold. It is, first, to suggest that the Durkheim constant, as I put it, is maintained by a dynamic process which adjusts upwards and *downwards*. Liberals have traditionally been alert for upward redefining that does injustice to individuals. Conservatives have been correspondingly sensitive to downward redefining that weakens societal standards. Might it not help if we could all agree that there is a dynamic at work here? It is not revealed truth, nor yet a scientifically derived formula. It is simply a pattern we observe in ourselves. Nor is it rigid. There may once have been an unchanging supply of jail cells which more or less determined the number of prisoners. No longer. We are building new prisons at a prodi-

gious rate. Similarly, the executioner is back. There is something of a competition in Congress to think up new offenses for which the death penalty is seen the only available deterrent. Possibly also modes of execution, as in "fry the kingpins." Even so, we are getting used to a lot of behavior that is not good for us.

As noted earlier, Durkheim states that there is "nothing desirable" about pain. . . . Pain, even so, is an indispensable warning signal. But societies under stress, much like individuals, will turn to pain killers of various kinds that end up concealing real damage. There is surely nothing desirable about *this*. If our analysis wins general acceptance, if, for example, more of us came to share Judge Torres's genuine alarm at "the trivialization of the lunatic crime rate" in his city (and mine), we might surprise ourselves how well we respond to the manifest decline of the American civic order. Might.

STRATEGIES FOR RESEARCHING
STREET DEVIANCE

LEON ANDERSON
THOMAS C. CALHOUN

Deviant individuals and social groups have historically comprised a large portion of the field studies conducted by sociologists. A substantial segment of the ethnographic research literature has focused attention on the particular dilemmas that fieldworkers must overcome to study deviant populations. As Douglas, whose writings have addressed these concerns consistently, observes:

> [B]ecause those considered deviant in our society are commonly so distrustful and so concerned with managing their own self-presentations, including hiding their identities, there is great need to analyze and solve the special methodological problems involved [in researching them]. (1972, pp. 4–5)

Specifically, researchers have delineated the particular problems encountered in conducting research with deviant populations and the ways in which these problems can be solved (Carey 1972; Warren 1972; Weinberg and Williams 1972; Humphreys 1975; Kelly 1990). Much of this literature has suggested that the collection of such data is more difficult with deviant populations than more conventional ones. Although a few sociologists have questioned this assumption (Sutherland 1937; Polsky 1967; Douglas 1972), such critical reflections have been made only in passing.

Fieldworkers have failed to address systematically the ways in which field research may be facilitated rather than hampered by characteristics and dynamics associated with deviant populations. A large number of scattered observations consistent with our argument have been made over the past three decades, but these observations have never been pulled together. The goal of this discussion is to examine ways in which ethnographic research can take advantage of special opportunities in conducting fieldwork with those deviant individuals and groups whose deviance occurs largely in public settings, and whose lives are characterized by stigmatization and powerlessness.

METHOD

We explore the facilitative aspects of participant observation with deviant populations by drawing on two field studies. One is a year-long team field study of homelessness in a Sunbelt city conducted in the mid-1980s. Contact was made with homeless individuals almost daily in a variety of settings, such as at meal and shelter lines, under bridges, at day-labor pickup sites, and by following homeless persons through their daily routines. Over a twelve-month period, more than 400 hours were involved observing 168 homeless people in a variety of settings.

The second study, which involved male street prostitutes, was conducted over a three-month period during 1984. The project involved systematic observation on a daily basis in a setting known as "the Block" that served as a pick-up site for hustlers. In addition, interviews were conducted with eighteen male prostitutes between the ages of thirteen and twenty-two.

The researchers engaged in a modified version of the "observer as participant" role (Gold 1958) in which observation is more important than actual participation. The goal was to gather observational data from natural settings and the personal accounts of members, rather than to "learn from doing." This was particularly the case for the study of male street prostitutes, in which observation was limited to hustling activities on the streets, rather than including more intimate illegal acts with "tricks."

Field observations were recorded in the two-stage process described by Lofland and Lofland (1984, pp. 62–68) of compiling mental and jotted field notes, which are elaborated immediately upon leaving the research settings. Both studies utilized inductive filing and coding procedures appropriate for the development of grounded theory (Glaser and Strauss 1967). In keeping with grounded theory techniques, insights from earlier observations were used to set data collection goals in later stages of the research.

FACILITATIVE ASPECTS AND STIGMATIZED POPULATIONS

Four categories were identified in which fieldwork with deviant populations can present strategic research opportunities: (1) access to research settings, (2) establishing relationships, (3) acquisition of information, and (4) researcher interest. Each of these categories is discussed below.

Access to Research Settings

To do field research one must have access to the particular settings in which members conduct their lives (Weppner 1977; Burgess 1984; Lofland and Lofland 1984). Deviant street populations conduct their daily activities in what Lofland (1987) has referred to as the "public realm." By virtue of this, they are often readily accessible for observation. Homeless people live in public space and, therefore, are unable to shelter themselves from probing individuals. In fieldwork with the homeless, initial access was available simply by showing up at the Salvation Army dinner line, observing people, and waiting for conversational openings. Similarly, street hustlers were observed within a public setting that, although restricted, required no special qualifica-

tions to enter. In each case, easy access clearly facilitated the research process.

Establishing Relationships

Perhaps the most widespread assumption regarding deviant populations is that they are suspicious groups with whom it is particularly difficult to establish rapport (Douglas 1972; Kelly 1990). Even though traditional notions of rapport have come under considerable attack in recent years (Johnson 1975; Pollner and Emerson 1983), it is generally agreed that trust is a necessary component of field research in general, and research on deviants in particular. This view is exemplified in Warren's (1972) observation that "trust is necessary to gain access to any world, and particularly necessary in the case of gaining access to a world . . . whose members tend to perceive any alien as a threat" (1972, p. 157).

This assumption is only partially justified. Deviant groups also present special opportunities for developing rapport. Rapport can develop through the researcher's willingness to accept stigma by association, or what Goffman (1963a) referred to as a "courtesy stigma." An example of this stigma was experienced when one of the authors protested the arrest of two homeless men with whom he had been drinking beer under a bridge. When the police offered to let him go, despite the fact that he had been engaged in the same drinking behavior as the other two men, the researcher argued that the other men should be let go as well. The police responded by arresting him. As they walked to the police station one of the officers commented, "This guy isn't very bright, or he wouldn't have argued with us." One of the homeless men replied, "No, he's just a guy who sticks up for his friends." Such experiences strengthen trust in the researcher; the two men ultimately became key informants and introduced the researcher to other homeless individuals.

The second author experienced a similar incident when he was accosted by the police and questioned about a rock-throwing incident that had taken place earlier. When he denied any knowledge about the incident, the police informed him, "You should be careful about being seen in this area because people might get the wrong idea about you." Witnessing this encounter a young hustler said, "I was glad you didn't squeal." The researcher's willingness to accept the courtesy stigma increased the inclination of several street hustlers to share information.

Acquisition of Information

Other aspects of research with deviant populations may facilitate access to members' insider information. Three such aspects are social roles, desire for attention, and opportunities for observing problematic situations.

Social Roles.   Snow, Benford, and Anderson (1986, p. 377) observed that " . . . by virtue of their attendant rights and obligations, [social roles] function as avenues and barriers to other roles and their information bases and perspectives." Two particular roles seem useful with deviant populations: the anonymous stranger and the "wise" person. Paul Cressey, in a posthumously published article (1983) noted that the anonymous stranger role provides an opportunity for gaining information that is difficult for someone who is personally known to the informant to obtain. "The transitory character of contact in the anonymous relationship" (p. 114), Cressey observed, presents no threat of disclosure of potentially damaging information to socially significant others. This anonymous relationship offers informants the opportunity to gain "catharsis and sympathy through impersonal confession" (p. 110).

Most social contexts do not support communication among anonymous strangers (Goffman 1963b, 1971). However, some settings involving stigmatized individuals do support such communication. Alcoholics Anonymous meetings, for example, provide a social setting where individuals are encouraged to share intimate details of their personal lives. While not providing direct sharing among strangers, the homeless subculture entails anonymity and is accepting of intimate revelations shared among strangers as they pass time at soup kitchens, labor corners, and dinner lines. This allowed the gathering of intimate details of many homeless individuals' lives. Often such information was offered during the first or second encounter with a homeless person without probing questions being posed. While these personal narratives must be accepted with caution, since they may contain considerable distortion, they do provide important data.

A second role, the wise person, enhances opportunities for relationships with members of stigmatized populations. Erving Goffman (1963a, p. 28) referred to wise persons as "persons who are normal, but whose special situation has made them intimately privy to the secret life of the stigmatized individual and sympathetic with it, and who find themselves accorded a measure of acceptance." Acceptance evolves largely from the perceived sympathy wise persons have for the stigmatized and the fact that they "are ready to adopt his standpoint in the world and to share with him the feeling that he is human and 'essentially' normal in spite of appearances and in spite of his own self-doubts" (pp. 19–20). The wise individual may be a socially valued commodity, providing deviants with social validation. The wise person also functions as a sounding board for the stigmatized individual's experiences, trials, and tribulations. The social position occupied by the wise person may be useful for those seeking to collect data on many deviant populations, ranging from homosexuals (Warren 1972) to drug dealers (Adler 1985, Adler and Adler 1991).

Need for Attention.   The anonymous stranger and the wise individual roles are of particular utility in field research with deviant populations because they allow the researcher to become a focus of potential informants' needs for attention. As Derber (1979) demonstrated, attention is a fundamental human need that is differentially distributed in society. Attention deprivation is common among such relatively powerless social categories as women and members of stigmatized deviant groups. Some deviant individuals seek attention from almost any available source, thus providing a special opportunity for the responsive and strategic field researcher.

Both research projects presented occasions when informants' desires for attention led to increased opportunities for the collection of both life history data and direct observations, although over-rapport (Miller 1952) had to be avoided. Once street hustlers developed trust, some became so interested in the attention received that they would stop hustling and talk to the researcher. Several began taking the researcher's field schedule into consideration when planning their trips to the cruising area. Socializing became so extensive that it threatened the natural flow of activities in the area and the researcher was forced to randomize visits.

In particular, some subjects want to counter what they view as negative stereotypes about people with their particular stigma. Polsky (1967) noted this potential motivation among criminals, as did Agar (1973) among drug addicts. We observed it as well. For instance, a 49-year-old female who sat on a curb by the Salvation Army reading a newspaper article on the homeless angrily shoved the paper toward the researcher while exclaiming, "Can you believe the way they talk about us transients?" For forty-five minutes she went about "setting the record straight," admonishing the researcher to "be sure to get the truth about us in your book!"

Opportunity in Problematic Situations. In field research analytic insights can be prompted by the fact that the researcher finds the setting and actors new and unusual. In situations where the observed activities are taken for granted by all participants (including the researcher), it may be difficult to discover the socially constructed dimensions of the activity. As Patton (1990, p. 204) observed, "participants in . . . routines may take them so much for granted that they cease to be aware of important nuances that are apparent only to an observer who has not become fully immersed in those routines." Given this, it is understandable why sociological fieldwork has been conducted so often with exotic and deviant populations. Such populations create an analytically productive distance between the researcher and the social world which he or she is investigating. This logic of discovery has at least implicitly guided such works as Goffman's (1961) research on the dilemmas of the self in total institutions and Garfinkel's (1967) study of the construction of a transsexual identity.

One example illustrates how theoretical insights may come more easily in the study of deviant populations. During the early months of fieldwork, the researcher was surprised by the frequency of identity statements by the homeless. These comments were so salient because talk about personal identity seemed to be only weakly related to the essence of homeless existence: physical deprivation. It was difficult for the researcher to understand why individuals who lack such basic survival requisites as stable housing spent considerable time making assertions about who they were. Recognizing this discrepancy between researcher assumptions about homeless life and field observations led to a systematic focus on "identity work among the homeless." The resulting analysis (Snow and Anderson 1987) elucidated the ways in which the homeless fashion and assert personal identities and how those identities change over time. The more focused analysis was relevant to broader social psychological theories as well, in that it challenged some of the prevailing principles of role-identity theory developed by Stryker (1980) and Maslow's (1962) hierarchy of needs.

Researcher Interest

The final aspect of research with deviant groups is in many ways emotional rather than cognitive or social relational. Deviant groups are very compelling populations. The nature of their collective and individual situations may well keep the researcher both emotionally and intellectually interested in research long after his or her interest might have faded in other social groups. As Lofland and Lofland (1984, p. 10) wrote, "Unless you are emotionally engaged in your work, the inevitable boredom, confusion, and frustration of rigorous scholarship will make even the completion—much less the quality—of the project problematic."

One important research activity jeopardized by a lack of interest and emotional involvement in the research topic, Lofland and Lofland note, is the tenacious data logging necessary to produce substantial field notes. Both authors found their experiences in the field to be so powerful that they were motivated to detail their observations in extensive notes. Furthermore, their field experiences made them want to return to the field as soon as possible so as not to miss the action. The compelling character of these groups resulted in more time being in the field and recording more complete field notes than otherwise might have been the case.

CONCLUSION

This discussion has examined facilitative aspects of fieldwork with deviant street populations. Strategic research opportunities were delineated into four areas: access to settings, social relationships, acquisition of information, and the maintenance of researcher interest. As current problems in American society spur a new wave of street ethnography (Kotarba 1990; Calhoun 1992; Koegel, 1992), the foregoing analysis may help to improve the efficiency and quality of street-based fieldwork by enabling researchers to rely less on serendipitous accidents in the field and more on conscious efforts informed by previous experience. Several suggestions for research with deviant street populations that emerge from this discussion are:

1. Access to street deviants in situ tends not to be blocked by powerful official gatekeepers, as is often the case with more formal settings. For this reason, researchers may find it useful to begin their work in these settings directly, rather than by attempting to gain familiarization with street settings and groups through more formal channels such as police departments or social service agencies.

2. Some of the best opportunities for collecting information about street informants are likely to occur in early anonymous encounters before the researcher has established more enduring relationships with the individuals. Researchers need to be aware of this dynamic and prepared to receive a considerable amount of such data in early encounters.

3. Occasional situations in which the researcher has the opportunity to make visible a willingness to accept courtesy stigma may be anticipated and used to enhance rapport.

4. Among street deviants and other stigmatized populations, the researcher is likely to be used by informants to fulfill needs for attention. The researcher should expect to be a confidante for informants and use this role to gather substantial data.

5. The researcher should be particularly attentive to problematic or conflictful situations in the field since these may lead to analytic insights.

6. Within bounds, researchers should welcome the chance to become personally engaged in the social world of their informants, rather than struggling to maximize their emotional distance. Such emotional involvement need not involve a loss of objectivity. In fact, such involvement may well enhance objectivity by eliciting greater rigor and attention to detail in data collection and analysis than would otherwise be the case.

These suggestions obviously do not apply equally to all field research, even with deviant street populations. Indeed, fieldworkers must always assess new settings and groups largely in terms of their uniqueness. Nonetheless, on the basis of the authors' experiences and those of other researchers cited in this paper, the preceding suggestions should be useful in sensitizing those engaged in a street ethnography of deviant populations.

ENDNOTE

An earlier version of this paper was presented at the Qualitative Research Conference in Toronto, Canada, in May 1990. The homelessness research described in this paper was facilitated by a grant from the Hogg Foundation for Mental Health and directed by David A. Snow. The authors wish to thank Mara Holt, Mike Polioudakis, and the anonymous reviewers for helpful comments and suggestions. Editor's Note: The reviewers were J. Kenneth Davidson, Nanette J. Davis, and Joseph Harry.

REFERENCES

Adler, Patricia A. 1985. *Wheeling and Dealing.* New York: Columbia University Press.

Adler, Patricia A., and Peter Adler. 1991. "Stability and Flexibility: Maintaining Relations with Organized and Unorganized Groups." Pp. 173–83 in *Experiencing Fieldwork,* edited by William B. Shaffir and Robert A. Stebbins. Newbury Park, CA: Sage.

Agar, Michael H. 1973. *Ripping and Running.* New York: Academic Press.

———. 1980. *The Professional Stranger.* New York: Academic Press.

Burgess, Robert C. 1984. *In the Field: An Introduction to Field Research.* Boston: George Allen and Unwin.

Calhoun, Thomas C. 1992. "Male Street Hustling: Introduction Processes and Stigma Containment." *Sociological Spectrum* 12:35–52.

Carey, James T. 1972. "Problems of Access and Risk in Observing Drug Scenes." Pp. 71–92 in *Research on Deviance,* edited by Jack Douglas. New York: Random House.

Cressey, Paul. 1983. "A Comparison of the Roles of the 'Sociological Stranger' and the 'Anonymous Stranger' in Field Research." *Urban Life* 12:102–20.

Derber, Charles. 1979. *The Pursuit of Attention: Power and Individualism in Everyday Life.* New York: Oxford University Press.

Douglas, Jack, ed. 1972. *Research on Deviance.* New York: Random House.

Garfinkel, Harold. 1967. *Studies in Ethnomethodology.* Englewood Cliffs, NJ: Prentice-Hall.

Glaser, Barney, and Anselm Strauss. 1967. *The Discovery of Grounded Theory.* Chicago: Aldine.

Goffman, Erving. 1961. *Asylums.* New York: Doubleday Anchor.

———. 1963a. *Stigma.* Englewood Cliffs, N.J.: Prentice-Hall.

———. 1963b. *Behavior in Public Places.* New York: The Free Press.

———. 1971. *Relations in Public.* New York: Harper and Row.

Gold, Raymond. 1958. "Roles in Sociological Field Observation." *Social Forces* 36:217–23.

Humphreys, Laud. 1975. *Tearoom Trade: Impersonal Sex in Public Places.* Enlarged edition. New York: Aldine.

Johnson, John M. 1975. *Doing Field Research.* New York: Free Press.

Kelly, Robert. 1990. "Field Research among Deviants: A Consideration of Some Methodological Recommendations." Pp. 148–56 in *Deviant Behavior: Readings in the Sociology of Norm Violations,* edited by Clifton D. Bryant. New York: Hemisphere.

Koegel, Paul. (1992). "Understanding Homelessness: An Ethnographic Approach," in *Homelessness: A Prevention Oriented Approach,* edited by Rene Jahid. Baltimore: Johns Hopkins Press.

Kotarba, Joseph A. 1990. "Ethnography and AIDS: Returning to the Streets." *Journal of Contemporary Ethnography* 19:259–70.

Lofland, John, and Lyn Lofland. 1984. *Analyzing Social Settings: A Guide to Qualitative Observation and Analysis.* 2nd ed. Belmont, CA: Wadsworth.

Lofland, Lyn, 1987. "Social Life in the Public Realm: A Review." *Journal of Contemporary Ethnography* 17:453–82.

Maslow, Abraham. 1962. *Toward a Psychology of Being.* New York: Van Nostrand.

Miller, S. M. 1952. "The Participant Observer and Over-Rapport." *American Sociological Review* 17:97–9.

Patton, Michael Quinn. 1990. *Qualitative Evaluation and Research Methods.* Beverly Hills, CA.: Sage.

Pollner, Melvin, and Robert M. Emerson. 1983. "The Dynamics of Inclusion and Distance in Fieldwork Relations." Pp. 235–52 in *Contemporary Field Research,* edited by Robert M. Emerson. Boston: Little, Brown and Company.

Polsky, Ned. 1967. *Hustlers, Beats, and Others.* New York: Aldine.

Snow, David A., and Leon Anderson. 1987. "Identity Work Among the Homeless: The Verbal Construction and Avowal of Personal Identities." *American Journal of Sociology* 92:1336–71.

Snow, David A., Robert D. Benford, and Leon Anderson. 1986. "Fieldwork Roles and Informational Yield: A Comparison of Alternative Settings and Roles." *Urban Life* 14:377–408.

Stryker, Sheldon. 1980. *Symbolic Interactionism: A Social Structural Version.* Menlo Park, CA: Benjamin-Cummings.

Sutherland, Edwin, ed. 1937. *The Professional Thief: By a Professional Thief.* Chicago: University of Chicago Press.

Warren, Carol. 1972. "Observing the Gay Community." Pp. 139–63 in *Research on Deviance,* edited by Jack D. Douglas. New York: Random House.

Weinberg, Martin S., and Colin J. Williams. 1972. "Fieldwork Among Deviants: Social Relations with Subjects and Others." Pp. 165–86 in *Research on Deviance,* edited by Jack D. Douglas. New York: Random House.

Weppner, Robert S., ed. 1977. *Street Ethnography.* Beverly Hills, CA: Sage.

4

PLEASURES AND PERILS
IN DEVIANCE RESEARCH

ERICH GOODE

Unlike the practitioners of most other disciplines, sociologists and anthropologists are in an extremely privileged position with respect to autobiography. That is, not only can they write literal autobiographies in the same sense that, say, mathematicians can—that is, they can narrate their life story—they can also tell the story of the intersection of their lives with their work in ways that mathematicians cannot. However, historically, sociologists and anthropologists were supposed to pretend that they had no biography, no self, no experiences relevant to the subject they studied. This was a pose, of course, but it revealed their insecurity on the question of objectivity. Malinowski's posthumously published journals, *A Diary in the Strict Sense of the Word* (1967), should have annihilated that naive notion once and for all. After reading it, one wonders, how could this sensitive, insightful observer have understood the Kiriwina if he harbored such contempt for them? The uproar the publication of the posthumously published diary generated expressed more about the challenge that personal life and feelings posed to social science than about the issue of our right to privacy. If physicists are disembodied observers, analyzing and explaining the mysteries of the universe, perhaps it is a denial of the self that is the key to being taken seriously as a real science. Or so some social scientists believe. Susan Krieger (1991) has argued, to the contrary, that social scientists ought to view the self not as a "contaminant" but as a "key to what we know. . . . The self

is not something that can be disengaged from knowledge or from the research process. Rather we need to understand our participation in what we know" (pp. 29–30).

To specify the matter a bit, for the most part sociological and anthropological researchers have been remarkably coy about what they do on the job. I do not mean by what they "do" the kinds of experiences that form the basis of their research reports. I mean their personal experiences, what does not get written about in their research reports, what goes on behind closed doors, their unauthorized experiences—experiences they are not permitted, whether by informal social convention or professional decree, to discuss; even more important, experiences that, were they to violate these rules, most of their peers would feel they should not have had in the first place.

Even more specifically, social researchers very rarely discuss the subject of emotional and physical intimacy with their subjects, informants, and interviewees, however important it may be to the conceptualization and results of their research projects. Do they avoid the subject because it is unimportant, because it does not impinge on how they think about the issue, what they see, what they write about in their books and articles? How can we ever know this if the topic is hidden from view? The fact is, we are not being given the full story on the actual participation of most social science observers in the behaviors they examine and involvements with the people they study. By that I mean that there is almost certainly a great deal more participation and involvement than is admitted; full self-disclosure tends to be the exception rather than the rule.

SELF-DISCLOSURES OF SEX WITH INFORMANTS

For the most part, sexual practices by researchers tend to be off limits; sociologists hardly ever admit—in print, anyway—that they participated in them while they engaged in their research. Gary Alan Fine (1993) discussed 10 "lies" of ethnography, myths that are widely disseminated in print as true but that insiders know to be false. "Illusions are essential to maintain an occupational reputation," Fine explained (p. 267). Actions that would shatter the illusions "are typically hidden in the backstage regions from which outsiders are excluded" (p. 267). One of these myths is that the researcher is sexually chaste. The reality, Fine asserted, "so secret and so dirty that it is hard to know how much credence to give, is the existence of saucy tales of lurid assignations, couplings, trysts, and other linkages between ethnographers and those they 'observe' " (p. 283). The violent contrast between myth and reality is remarkable, implied Fine. After all, he said, "Humans are attracted to one another in all domains. They look, they leer, they flirt, and they fantasize." And yet, he remarked, the "written record inscribes little of this rough and hot humanity" (p. 284). Although he admitted to no more than "a few looks and thoughts," he said, "others can" (p. 284).

Murray Davis (1983:xxi) claimed that researchers are discouraged from crossing the boundary separating research from participation for fear of "sexual contamination." James Wafer (1996:264), an anthropologist, wrote that one such boundary crosser is Tobias Schneebaum, whose book *Where the Spirits Dwell* (1988) is widely regarded in anthropology "as a dirty joke. As though it were not sufficient provocation to admit that he is gay, Schneebaum breaks the ultimate taboo by being explicit about the fact that he had sex with the natives." One of Wafer's (straight) colleagues

went so far as to say that Schneebaum's main motivation for conducting anthropological research "was to get screwed" (p. 264). To this critic, Wafer added, this was "sufficient reason for dismissing the writer and his work" (p. 264). "But why?" he asked. The researcher is supposed to be "a disembodied" and "asexual" being, Wafer answered.

Ideally, there would not only be no sex in the text, but also no desire. Yet it is hard to imagine that the actual field experience of ethnographers could be so insipid. Surely eros plays as great a role in structuring their relationships in the field as it does in any social context. (p. 265)

There are several major exceptions to the rule of sexual revelation in addition to Schneebaum—nearly all written by anthropologists—and they are extremely instructive.

Paul Rabinow (1977), who conducted field research in Morocco, described a single episode with a Berber woman, a prostitute, in such elliptical terms that the reader does not know for sure whether they even engaged in intercourse. "This woman was not impersonal," Rabinow said, "but she was not that affectionate or open either" (p. 69).

George Lee Stewart, at the time a sociology graduate student and with every intention of writing a book about "the world of the brothel"—apparently it was never published—detailed his first-hand experience with having sex with a prostitute in "On First Being a John" (1972). Stewart described his nervousness, awkwardness, and inexperience and speculated on what his wife would think about the matter.

Charles and Rebecca Palson (1972), two anthropologists, studied comarital "swinging" by exchanging sexual partners themselves. Swingers first, researchers later, for 18 months they engaged in a participant observation study of 136 swinging couples. As they explained, "Most of our important insights into the nature of swinging could only have been found by actually experiencing some of the same things that our informants did" (p. 29). However, aside from informing their readers that they did it, they do not supply any detail about their own experiences.

John Alan Lee (1978, 1979), writing well before the AIDS crisis, studied the social ecology of urban gay sex, that is, the territories, the times, and the social and physical "niches" of homosexual encounters. Sex, Lee claimed, is an "artificially scarce" commodity in Western society; that is, if there were no norms restricting the circumstances under which it takes place, it would be vastly more abundant than it is (p. 175). Gay culture, Lee claimed, subverts the principle of scarcity and provides abundant opportunities "in which individuals may enjoy large number of casual encounters" (p. 177). Having lived "an exclusively heterosexual lifestyle," complete with wife and children, until the age of 32, Lee came out as a homosexual. His participation in the research, he said, was "sometimes as an observer and sometimes for the purpose of personal sexual encounters" (p. 178). The reader gets no more detail than this.

Colin Turnbull (1986) briefly described his sexual relationship with a young Mbuti woman, sent to him by her father, the chief of a tribe. (Apparently, sexual abstinence in young persons is considered abnormal among the Mbuti.) She taught him a great deal about local custom, he explained. Interestingly enough, his relationship with the young woman was not mentioned in his full ethnographic report (1962) but was reported only in a book of readings devoted specifically to the topic of sex, gender, and fieldwork (Whitehead and Conaway 1986).

Joseph Styles (1979) engaged in a study of homosexual bathhouse sexual encounters. Originally, he had resolved to limit himself strictly to observation. "I would go to the baths," he told himself, "see what went on, even talk with the other men—but I wouldn't have sex" (p. 137). In short, initially, Styles said, he would be "a nonparticipating insider" (p. 137). Contact with the action at the baths, however, put an end to that resolve in fairly short order. The first evening "was unremitting chaos," with naked and half-naked men shoving, wandering, crowding, and jamming the hallways; while he stumbled around in the dark, one man tore his towel off his body while a second groped for his genitals (p. 138). He soon

realized that his mere presence in the baths made him "a potential sex object"; moreover, his attempt to strike up a conversation, presumably for research purposes, "was one sign of showing sexual interest in another man" (p. 138).

After talking with several bathhouse insiders, Styles "radically changed" the way he conducted his research. On his return to the bathhouse, rather than rejecting the advances of "a good-looking fellow," Styles thought, "to hell with it!" and "had sexual relations with him" (p. 141). Initially, playing the dual role of observer and participant made him uneasy; hence, he began observing in one bathhouse and participating in a different one. Eventually, however, "the asexual observation became more and more tiresome, more tedious, and more frustrating until," he said, he "gave up observing without sexual intent and plunged fully into the sex life of the baths" (p. 142).

Van Lieshout (1995) conducted an observational study of encounters at a rest stop in the Netherlands that had become well-known in the gay community as a locale for homosexual sex. In this locale, by unspoken convention, Monday evenings were reserved for "leather" and S&M (sadism and masochism) activities. The author explained that his role "became a mixed one"; that is, for some of the time during the evening, he said, "I was an observing participant" and for other times, he was "a participating observer" (p. 25). Van Lieshout explained that his prior experience "in leather bars and cruising areas made it possible to feel at ease almost immediately" (p. 25). It made him, he says, an insider from the moment he surveyed the scene (p. 25). Interestingly, however, in his published account, van Lieshout supplied next to nothing about his own personal experiences. He also explained in a footnote (p. 37) that information obtained from sex partners may be tainted in that the two goals—obtaining sex and supplying information—may work at cross-purposes. For instance, someone may be unwilling to state his actual age for fear of discouraging a potential partner.

Bolton (1992, 1995, 1996) came as close as any ethnographer does to an outright endorsement of sex in the field. To study sexual behavior as it takes place, he said, "We must go beyond the narrow concept of participant observation" (p. 132), that is, mere observation without participation. Indeed, he argued, "Some of the very best cross-cultural work on homosexuality has benefited from insights gained through participation" (1992:132). As for engaging in his ethnography of sexual practices among gay males and how they impact on the transmission of AIDS, Bolton said, "I did not merely observe but participated fully in all aspects of gay life. . . . In my casual sexual encounters with men I picked up in gay cruising situations," he informed the reader (pp. 134, 135), "my approach during sex was to allow my partner to take the lead in determining which sexual behaviors to engage in" (high-risk activities—unprotected anal intercourse—excepted). His activities were consonant with the norms of the gay community he investigated and hence, his sexual activity while engaged in research, he felt, was perfectly ethical.

RESEARCHERS' GENDER AND SEXUAL SELF-DISCLOSURES

Female ethnographers are by no means strangers to sexual activity with informants in the field; a few who have engaged in the experience have even been willing to discuss it in print. Anthropological disclosures of sexual relationships in the field tend to be densely gendered. One gender difference is that women tend to be more vulnerable to male violence; for heterosexual women, while there is pleasure in intimate experiences with men, there is danger as well. This duality assumes prominence in much of the writing of female social scientists who discuss sex in the field. And, although the descriptions of the sexual liasons that both men and women offer are elliptical, sketchy, more implicit than explicit, this might be a bit more so for women than for men. Still, what is so remarkable here is the similarity rather than the difference.

Dona Davis (1986) studied menopausal women in a small fishing village in Newfoundland. Although the norms of her community condemned

sex outside of marriage, in practice couples were expected to pair off sexually before marriage. During her fieldwork, Davis met a hydraulics engineer who lived in a trailer near the village. Far from receiving negative sanctions as a result of her romantic relationship, Davis said, it "seemed to make people a bit friendlier and more at ease around me. . . . I was simply breaking a rule everyone else broke" (p. 254). Note the singular here: one sexual relationship. Note, too, Davis's extremely laconic description of her liason:

> *Local matchmakers arranged a meeting and we became close friends. . . . I often went to his trailer for privacy and some peace and quiet in which to work. . . . One night . . . , there was a severe snowstorm and I was not able to get back to the village. (p. 253)*

Manda Cesara (a pseudonym) engaged in fieldwork among the Lenda (also a fictitious name). The Lenda are an extremely sexually permissive people, discouraging sexual and emotional dependence on a single partner and encouraging a "relatively frequent change of partners" (1982:146). Among the Lenda, sex is regarded as a joyful experience, typically "nonprocreative" and "rejuvenating" (p. 146). In a letter to her mother, Cesara described a man "stepping into my life." (She is married.) He is westernized, has a PhD, spent many years in Sweden, is "bureaucratic, staid, cautious, correct" (p. 147). How, she asked her mother, does one undress in front of such a man? Rather than robbing her of a clear mind and her freedom, as her husband does, her relationship with this Lenda man gives her "freedom . . . , a kind of power over myself" (p. 147). Given her newfound freedom, her anonymity, the intensely personal nature of her book, and the central place of recreational sex in the lives of the people she is studying, it is surprising that Cesara offered virtually no other details about her sex life among them. The reader walks away feeling that this is a deeply gendered book.

Gearing (1995) said that "sex in the field remains a tabooed topic, addressed metaphorically if at all" (p. 188); at the same time, she said, "If we are serious about examining ourselves as researchers, we must grapple with the impact of our sexuality on our fieldwork" (p. 188). Gearing discussed her love affair and marriage with (and eventual divorce from) "E.C.," her best informant. Although in St. Vincent, Gearing's fieldsite, sex is not shameful for women—indeed, an uninhibited view of sex is encouraged—nonetheless, the island "is not a woman's sexual paradise" (p. 189). Gearing described the sexual double standard, "under which the sexual conquest of multiple partners contributes to a man's prestige" (p. 192), whereas for women, there is the ever-present reality of sexual harassment, as well as the ever-present possibility of sexual violence. E.C., she said, was "different." He "was the only Vincentian man I met," she says, "who had not had any children by any previous partner" (p. 199). Moreover, she said, he was willing to do chores around the house.

Gearing's relationship with E.C., she said, gave her a closer, more comfortable relationship with the community she studied. Her neighbors seemed happy that she had a man about the house. Among other things, it demonstrated that she viewed Vincentians as equals and proved she was not a racist (1995:202).

> *Feeling sexually attracted to the people we [ethnographers] live among and study is a much more positive reaction than feeling repulsed by them. As long as we enter relationships honestly and considerately, and are observant of local norms, we should not reject our sexual feelings toward people with whom we work. (p. 203)*

Gearing's (1995) account is predictably scanty concerning the physical details of sex. One understands that her partner has a "sterling character" and "a charismatic charm," is talented at performing a "stand-up comedy routine" (p. 197), and is "tall, well built, handsome, intelligent, funny, charming, considerate, and affectionate" (p. 198). Yet, Gearing's reader must pay close attention to her text to know exactly where her sexual relationship with E.C. begins, since she supplied very little in the way of concrete description about the courtship. Her study is on "gender, kinship, and

household" in St. Vincent, and sexual seduction plays a major role in the substance of her research.

And yet she was almost completely silent concerning her own involvement in this selfsame process.

Few anthropologists have described their fieldwork experience with more sensuality and intensity than Kate Altork. (She is also a published poet and a fiction writer.) Her descriptions of forest firefighters in action (1995) are so vivid that the reader can smell the smoke, see the fire, feel its heat. "My senses were hit with a constant onslaught of sounds and sights, smells and tastes" (p. 123), she wrote, and, when reading her narrative, the reader's senses come alive as well. Altork described her erotic dreams, pointed out the sensual and sexual references in her fieldnotes, quoted men and women firefighters on how sexually arousing fighting fires is, cited approvingly the work of anthropologists who endorse sex in the field, intimated that she may have engaged in sexual activity of a certain sort in the field ("Defining sex in the field: what is it, anyway?"), and told us that "some of the best lovemaking" she has "yet experienced" with her husband took place after her return from "forays into the world of the firefighters" (p. 131).

And yet, nowhere did she get any more sexually explicit than that. The "blind" reading for gender authorship that Callaway (1992) suggested we do for the classic anthropological texts—that is, can we tell from the text itself whether the author is a man or a woman? (pp. 31, 45)—would yield only one conclusion for this piece: The reader never doubts that the author, Kate Altork, is a woman.

> *I am not advocating random and meaningless sexual encounters here, nor am I talking about situations where issues of colonialism and power imbalance enter into the discourse, which may be, in fact, most of the time. . . . The point is not to encourage sensationalistic, National Enquirer–type confessionals from the field, replete with descriptive close-ups and minute details about how a given anthropologist had sex in the field. But we might at least acknowledge that we "did it" if we did (or that we wanted to "do it," even if we didn't), and be open to the fertile possibilities for dialogue about*

*the ways in which "it" changed, enhanced, or de-
tracted from what we felt, witnessed, and interpreted in the field. . . . So. Where does this leave us?
Do we make love in the field or don't we? And, if
we do, how far do we go? How can we untangle the
web of moral and ethical issues involved and explore, as well, the dissonance between the unspoken rules of the academy and our own personal
beliefs and actions? (pp. 121, 131)*

Among personal tales of the field, perhaps no
greater disparity exists between the efflorescence
of emotion and the total absence of raw, concrete
sex than in the writing of Esther Newton (1993a),
who conducted an ethnographic study of Cherry
Grove, a homosexual enclave 45 miles from New
York City (1993b). Newton mentioned that "some
of the people who were objects of my research
were also potential sexual partners, and vice versa"
(1993a:10). She emphasized that the "burden of
being, and being seen as, an erotic creature" (p. 15)
cannot be evaded. She described romantic feelings,
erotic yearnings, sexual urges, physical desire. Yet,
there are no descriptions of sex because in the one
relationship she detailed, there was no sex, no
physical sex at any rate. Newton, a lesbian, describes her "love affair' with Kay, who was 85
years old and confined to a wheelchair. It is almost
inconceivable that a male anthropologist, whether
homosexual or heterosexual, could have had the
experiences Newton had or produced writings
equivalent to Newton's. Unlike the classic ethnographic texts (Callaway, 1992:35, 41), today's narratives are deeply and unmistakably gendered.

Peter Wade (1993) represents an exception to
the rule that few heterosexual men disclose their
sexual relations in the field. Investigating "sexuality and masculinity" in a predominantly Black
area of Colombia, he admitted to "two quite long-
term relationships" with local women (p. 200).
The most gendered aspect of Wade's disclosure is
his motive, which was largely instrumental. "I actively sought a young, single black woman as a
potential partner," he explained, because of the
"desire to transcend the separateness that I received as distancing me from the constructed oth-
erness of black culture" (p. 203). In addition,

Wade said, among the people he studied, "sexual
continence is odd and to be avoided" (p. 205); to
abstain from engaging in sex with women "could
cast doubt on one's masculinity." A small number
of affairs allowed Wade to adopt a "comfortable
gender identity" and "act like a man" (p. 206) and,
hence, be accepted in their culture. His relationships with local women, he explained, made him
less threatening to informants and gave him
greater access to specific sectors of the society, for
instance, to single women. It is difficult to imagine
a woman being, or admitting to being, as instrumental about sex in the field as this.

While granting that racial and class hierarchies were always part of his relationships
(1993:209–210) and acknowledging that much of
the profession regards sex with "native" women
unprofessional and unethical (p. 211), Wade argued that his affairs were mutually gratifying and
located "in the purely personal realm" (p. 212). A
sexual relationship between an anthropologist and
an informant, he said, implies "the same kinds of
ethical and emotional difficulties as any other relationships between these parties" (p. 212).

This brief roster does not exhaust the revelations of researchers who have been forthcoming
about having engaged in sexual behavior among
the people they studied. Lewin and Leap (1996:3)
claimed that revelations of sexual activity (and
fantasies) in the field have nearly always been the
prerogative of heterosexual men. This is most decidedly untrue, for they did not include the revelations in their own volume, *Out in the Field* (1996),
as well as those in *Taboo* (Kulick and Willson
1995), published shortly after their own book went
to press. No matter. In spite of these remarkable
exceptions, the long and short of it is that, of the
thousands of ethnographers who have spent un-
countable hours in close proximity with the people
whose lives they shared and behavior they observed, engaging in almost every imaginable activity with them, only a few dozen have had the
courage to step forward and tell the world about
their more intimate moments. Informal consensus
has it that most ethnographers have remained
chaste in the field, and my guess is that assessment

is correct. But vastly more sexual behavior has taken place than is reported, and that disparity is worthy of discussion. Clearly, then, extremely strong norms exist within the academic community that govern the construction of self-revelations, and they are, for the most part, obeyed.

SEX WITH INFORMANTS: BENEFIT AND RISK

I decided to defy this taboo on sexual self-revelation by writing an account of my intimate experiences with informants in three research endeavors: marijuana use (research conducted in 1967 and that culminated in a book published in 1970), personals-generated courtship (in which I participated for the purpose of dating between 1979 and 1983, and which I studied more systematically in the 1990s), and the National Association to Aid Fat Americans (NAAFA), a kind of "Love Boat" for fat women and men who were sexually and romantically attracted to fat women (where I conducted field research, and dated, between 1980 and 1983).

Was it necessary to have sex with my informants to learn what I found out? Of course not, although at the times when I did so, it seemed perfectly natural; in fact, to have done otherwise would have felt awkward and out of step with everything that was going on. By doing so, I felt a natural and organic part of the tribes I was studying, much as Cesara, Gearing, and Wade did. Does sharing intimate moments with informants lend an authenticity to the researcher's vision that might otherwise have been less authoritative? Discounting the possible social disruption that such experiences may cause, yes, I believe so. Is it worth the risk? That's a separate issue. Manda Cesara (1982) claimed that a sexual and emotional relationship with an informant permits "laying hold of the culture in its entirety through that particular individual" (p. 60).

Many commentators have argued against becoming too involved in the lives of one's informants because it is likely to lead to a loss of objectivity. "Going native" is the term that is commonly used: adopting the way of life of the people

one studies to such an extent that one becomes more an advocate than an ethnographer. In my experience, it's difficult to sentimentalize and romanticize the people you're studying if you are in their face—and they are in yours—all the time. This is especially the case if you engage in intimate relations with them over an extended period of time. The fact is, you are acquainted with details of their lives that range from the spiritual to the mundane, from the way they express their most heartfelt emotions to the way they trim their toenails. For me, unabashed advocacy of my subjects was impossible precisely because I knew too much about them.

In *Gender Issues in Field Research,* sociologist Carol Warren (1988) argued that unless the details of the researcher's sexual experiences in the field are relevant to and illuminate the research experience, they become "gratuitous" (p. 63). In this book, but not in her published account of the research she summarized (1982), Warren cited her own flirtatious behavior toward a judge as a means of gaining rapport and maximizing information gathering (p. 45). In contrast, she said, in that report, she did write about sexual "hustling" of her by male courtroom workers (p. 64). The difference between the sexually toned experiences she revealed in her monograph and those she didn't report, she said, lay mainly in the writing conventions that prevailed when she wrote up her study in the early 1980s. With respect to those incidents she did not write about, she said, "I never thought of it" (p. 64). However, she argued, with most research projects there is no point in bringing the details of the researcher's sexual activities out into the open.

I do not question her assertion that an examination of one's sexual relationship with informants might be irrelevant to some sociological research projects. My guess is, Warren is correct for most research projects, possibly even most participant observation studies. However, it is inconceivable to me that in research contexts in which the field worker lives among informants 24 hours a day the issue of sex between researcher and informant never at least arises, never needs to be resolved.

Certainly the issue of my intimate relations were central to the work I conducted. Permit me to spell out how.

First of all, in all three of my investigations, sex was a centrally relevant topic. In the marijuana research, the conjunction between sex and marijuana use was a major component, and in the personals ad and the NAAFA studies, sex and romance were more or less what they were all about. Ignoring my own sexual experiences during the course of these studies now seems inconceivable to me.

Second, as I've stated above, intimacy generates access to information and usually more information and better information. Sex has a way of riveting one's attention to the matter at hand; what one learns in bed is not likely to be forgotten. At the very least, establishing an intimate liaison with an insider does influence access and rapport, for better or for worse. Moreover, this is likely to be gender related.

Third, having romantic and sexual relations with informants is likely to influence one's view of the reality of the scene or behavior under discussion. One's vision of how things are and how they work cannot but be shaped by sharing one's most intimate moments with an insider, who is likely to see things a certain way.

Fourth, the fact that one has shared an informant's bed necessarily alters how the researcher–author writes up the report. In my case, not only did I change inconsequential details to protect the identity of my sexual partners, I also left out certain details for fear those partners would feel that I had betrayed them, even though their identities were disguised. The very intimacy that grants access to information often results in inhibiting public revelations.

Fifth, sex represented my unconditional entry into NAAFA, and it was sex that proved to be my undoing in it. Only by dating was I seen as a full-fledged member of the organization, and as a result of dating (admittedly, recklessly and promiscuously), I found it impossible to continue my research. Sex was the central fact of my investigation in that setting, and any honest account had to take note of it.

Sixth—and here we come to the issue at hand—sexual intimacy with informants raises a host of ethical questions that demand discussion. At the very least, admissions of sexual liaisons will force researchers to account for their actions as, in the academic environments in which we move, such behavior tends to be frowned on. More on this momentarily.

And seventh: Sexual liaisons present risk, especially for women. For all researchers, they may make a research enterprise less viable, close off avenues of information, and upset and anger participants in a given scene. My own, extremely poorly thought-out involvements in NAAFA made it impossible for me to continue with my research. I have no doubt that for most researchers, sex on the job traverses much of the same landmined territory offered by sex off the job. The wrong partner or partners, too many partners, partners under inappropriate times or circumstances, too much time with one partner or not enough time with another—or, for that matter, spurning someone who wants to be a partner: We all know the perils that lie in wait for us when we make the wrong decision.

For women, these risks are far more perilous, manifold, and painful; in fact, are omnipresent whether they engage in sex or not. In one study, 7 percent of the female anthropologists who responded reported rape or attempted rape against them in the field (Howell 1990); it's possible that was an underestimation. In all likelihood, most of the women in this study were completely celibate. At the same time, it is highly likely that sex with a number of men increases the odds of sexual violence. If a woman becomes known in the community as someone who is sexually accessible to more than a small number of men, she may become a target for unwanted attention, including violence. But again, even if she is celibate, she could become a victim of sexual violence.

In addition, I suspect that most members in most of the communities ethnographers might study would treat a woman who is having sex with one or more of her male informants in a fashion that is likely to be counterproductive, detrimental to the process of gathering information. This is not true of all communities. As we've seen, female researchers studying more than a handful of communities have found informants more relaxed and accessible after their affair with a local became known (e.g., Cesara 1982; Davis 1986; Gearing 1995). Unfortunately, this is atypical.

More common is the experience of Ruth Horowitz (1986), who found that her initial, nonsexual research relationship with male gang members began to slide into one where her informants increasingly regarded her as a "chick," that is, a sexually desirable and available woman. She soon realized that the only role available to her that would permit her to remain on the scene was that of a sexual partner, which was unacceptable to her for both tactical and ethical reasons. As the teasing and flirting escalated, she decided to move her fieldwork into a different social sector—girl gang members. Horowitz did not have the freedom to decide her research role, she argued; her options were extremely limited, constrained by the expectations of her informants. In my opinion, she made the right decision.

Far from endorsing sex between researchers and informants, I am arguing that, under certain circumstances, it is likely to be a terrible thing to do. But under others, it may yield insight. Moreover, I am not arguing that discussing it is a relevant issue in every research project; again, this depends on the study under investigation.

THE ETHICS OF SEX WITH INFORMANTS

To be frank, during none of the three research efforts in which I engaged did I give the matter of the ethics of sex with informants a great deal of thought. In fact, it never occurred to me that sex with informants was ethically improper or methodologically questionable.

In 1967, when I conducted the marijuana interviews, I didn't even know about the existence of "human subjects committees." (In 1967, neither New York University, where I taught during the spring semester, nor the State University of New York at Stony Brook, where I began teaching

in the fall, even had a human subjects committee.) Even if I had, I would have regarded them as yet another hurdle in a gauntlet of bureaucratic restrictions. I had never been told by an academic advisor or older colleague that researchers were required to treat their subjects in specified ways—and must not treat them in specific other ways—as spelled out in a clearly articulated code of ethics. Did the American Sociological Association promulgate a code of ethics before 1967? At the time, I simply had no idea. In fact, the possibility of the very existence of an ethics code never entered my mind. (A little checking reveals that the American Sociological Association did not formulate one until 1968.) Kai Erikson's famous essay on "disguised observation" was published the same year I conducted my marijuana interviews, 1967, but I was not engaged in deception of any kind, I was just smoking dope and sleeping with some of my female interviewees. Truth to tell, I did not read Erikson's classic piece until years later; when I did, I strongly disagreed with its argument (Goode 1996).

It is true that some of the women in these three sites with whom I had relations expressed their disappointment—or anger—after we stopped seeing one another. But I took this as the normal aftermath of relationships gone sour. I never conceptualized my sexual behavior during the entire course of my research as anything other than a freely chosen activity between two equal partners. Did they see things in that way? Today, looking back, it seems clear to me that many did not; at the time, subjectively constructed disparities in power simply did not occur to me.

To me, in interactions with my marijuana informants in 1967, the relationship seemed completely nonhierarchical. In my interviews, it was I who was invading the users' turf, begging them for their time and words. If anything, I reasoned, I was the subordinate party in this transaction, not the other way around. Any intimate relations that fortuitously transpired seemed to me to have nothing to do with my status as a researcher or a university instructor, I figured. It is true that some of the marijuana interviews took place in my apartment (about a quarter), but half were conducted in the interviewee's domicile and the rest were either in the respondent's workplace or in a neutral territory, such as a public place. In the social settings in which I moved, I assumed I was as free as a bird, and so were my informants. In 1967, I gave little or no thought to the ethical, moral, or ideological implications of what I was doing.

The 1960s was a time of love, broadly interpreted anyway, the expression of sensuousness, a garden of earthly delights, party time, each participant celebrating in his or her own personal fashion. Events were washing over us so abundantly and luxuriously that there seemed to be neither the time nor the need to calculate the possible consequences. Music seemed to gush out of nowhere and explode fireworks in our brain, and the right music, at the right moment, with the right partner, under the influence of a drug of choice, was bedazzling, a vortex of ecstasy.

In short, to me it seemed absolutely inconceivable that any single, under-30 researcher—male or female—who was undertaking a naturalistic or an interview study of marijuana use in 1967 would have abstained from either marijuana use or sex with informants. As I saw things at the time, I was simply doing what came naturally, what seemed most comfortable. In fact, it would have been prudish, unseemly, and out of place to have abstained from joining the party, much like refusing to take off one's clothes at a nudist camp. (Adler [1985:24] said something similar in a somewhat different context.) Having conducted fieldwork among an extremely sexually permissive people, Cesara (1982:59) stated categorically that it is inevitable that certain anthropologists would experience sexual relations with informants. I agree. None of this justifies or excuses my behavior, but it does help explain it.

What about the issue of my dating women by using the personal ads (1979–83)? Under "Ethical Standards," subsection 7, "Harassment," the American Sociological Association (1997) stated that sociologists are not to engage in "harassment of any person." Sexual harassment, the ASA

stated, "may include sexual solicitation, physical advance, or verbal or non-verbal conduct that is sexual in nature" (p. 4). (Or it may not. From the wording of this declaration, it's not clear that such actions are by their very nature or by definition sexual harassment.) My behavior could represent a violation of this principle.

Or could it? In answering personal ads, perhaps 90 percent of my motive was for the purpose of dating, and only 10 percent was to gather information. In fact, for all three of these projects, personal and research motives intertwined; I found it impossible to separate them. (I still do.) The politically engaged social scientist informs us that all of us express our ideology in our research, that pure objectivity is a myth, that all science is personal. I'm sure that no one who espouses that position has in mind anything like the sort of behavior I'm detailing here, but drawing a line in the sand between acceptable and unacceptable personal involvements cannot be an easy task.

The fact is, when I answered and placed personal ads, I wasn't certain that I would ever study such behavior more systematically or publish anything from it. In writing about dating via the personals in the 1990s, I was simply drawing on my own biographical experiences to enrich my vision of a given social phenomenon, much the same way an ex-convict (Irwin 1970, 1980), a pool player (Polsky 1969), or a jazz musician (Becker 1963) would have. I'll be blunt about this: I don't see the difference. Riemer (1977) referred to such studies as "opportunistic" research. C. Wright Mills (1959:196) urged us to use our life experiences in our intellectual work. Along with other social scientists, I have taken his advice.

My feelings about my personal and intimate involvements in NAAFA (1980–83) are a great deal more complex and ambivalent than they were for the other two studies. In fact, it is difficult for me even now to put them down on paper, in part because they are too painful and in part because they are partly hidden from my conscious mind. I feel vastly more ambivalent about my efforts in NAAFA than I do about the other two projects because my motives were more mixed; I never clarified for myself or for others exactly what it was I was doing there, what my primary role was. Eventually, I fell off the tightrope because I simply couldn't maintain the dual role I was attempting to play. I do not think that such a role is inherently impossible to maintain. However, I do know that I played it extremely badly. Looking back from the perspective of the better part of two decades, it seems almost redundant for me to admit that I should have handled things quite differently.

Are there sexual actions in the field and revelations of them about which I would be horrified? Of course. Force and sex with minors and those who are mentally incompetent are crimes, crimes of violence, crimes that truly horrify me. Whenever gross disparities in power exist between the researcher and the subject, my sense of ethical disapproval would begin kicking in, sex between faculty and student being the most salient example; in addition, sex between a researcher and welfare moms, heroin or crack addicts, or residents of a battered women's shelter; in short, weak and vulnerable parties. Because the scenes I looked at were inhabited by nonindigent, fairly middle-class informants, to me, none of this seemed to enter into the picture.

CONCLUSIONS

In the first volume of Michel Foucault's *The History of Sexuality,* the reader is told that in Western society, sex is *the* secret. To most of us, sex remains a private sanctuary, a sphere of life over which a veil of secrecy must be drawn. Its enactment is special to us. The rules that govern everyday life seem somehow to be recast when sex is involved. When this veil is ripped away and the doings of one of us is forced into the public consciousness—as we've seen with the sexual doings of U.S. President Bill Clinton, under investigation as I write—the attention of a large portion of the public is simultaneously embarrassed by and riveted on the details.

Sex has played a unique and distinctive role in the study of social life; we have thrown a veil of secrecy around not merely sex but its possible role in social research. "Throughout all the decades of concern with the sex lives of others, anthropologists [and, I would add, other social scientists as well] have remained very tightlipped about their own sexuality" (Kulick 1995:3). Even researchers who have been trailblazers in the systematic study of sexual behavior—Sigmund Freud, Alfred Kinsey, and Masters and Johnson come to mind—have remained extremely reticent about their own sexual behavior. Recent revelations about the sex life of Alfred Kinsey (Jones 1997) argue that this topic is hardly an irrelevancy. Derek Freeman (1991) claimed both that Margaret Mead had affairs with at least one of her male Samoan informants and that this was why her teenage female interviewees lied to her. Commenting on what the researcher is expected—and expected not—to do with subjects, Dubisch (1995:31) pointed out,

> We do almost everything else with our "informants": share their lives, eat with them, attend their rituals, become part of their families, even become close friends, and sometimes establish life-long relationships. At the same time, we "use" them to further our goals, writing and speaking about personal and even intimate aspects of their lives, appropriating these lives for our own professional purposes. Could a sexual relationship be any more intimate, committing, or exploitative than our normal relations with the "natives"? (In some societies, it might even be less so.)

Why? one wonders. Does sex play the same "special" and enshrouded role in the professional lives of social researchers that it plays in the everyday lives of all of us? Is it only sex—that is, this Foucaudian "secret" realm—to them? Or is there something more to it than that?

Is it possible that this veil over the sex life of the researcher is even more crucial for the social scientist than it is for the ordinary man and woman? Might this "secret" to which Foucault referred function to maintain an even deeper secret, the secret of research intersubjectivity? What better means of maintaining the traditional social science fiction of objectivity than to pretend that all ethnographers remain completely celibate when they conduct their research? And what more effective means of emphasizing the fact that sociology and anthropology are deeply social, deeply human, and therefore deeply flawed enterprises than to report, explore, and discuss the subject of sex with the people whose behavior we study?

It is perhaps remarkable that the majority of the ethnographers who have written about the subject of erotic subjectivity in social research through the lens of their own personal experience have been either women (heterosexual or lesbian) or gay men. Kulick and Willson (1995:xiii) found that heterosexual men were not only the most "elusive" about their own sexual activities in the field but were also the ones who discouraged them most emphatically about doing their book *Taboo,* which focuses on that selfsame topic. Why? they ask.

Is it possible, Kulick and Willson (1995) suggested, that such discussion would reveal that not only is sex between male researchers and female informants vastly more common than that between female researchers and male informants, but that it would also cast a bright beam of light on the sexism and racism inherent in such practices and, more generally, that is woven into the very fabric of anthropology (Newton 1993a:xiv)? The "disciplinary silence about desire in the field is a way for anthropologists to avoid confronting the issues of positionality, hierarchy, exploitation, and racism" (Kulick 1995:19).

Once the secret is revealed, the social science pose of objectivity will be more difficult to sustain. How long can we validate the "on stage" pose of ourselves as disembodied, disinterested, and uninvolved social scientists acting out the dictates of a methodology textbook? Is the topic of the researcher's entanglements in the lives of their subjects of study not worthy of discussion? Is a simple admonition "Don't do it!" enough? Contrarily, is the fact that most of us are not entangled in their lives as revealing—and as damning—as the fact that some of us are? Are the implications of erotic subjectivity so obvious and banal as to merit no discussion whatsoever?

I do not see intersubjectivity as inherently poisonous to the task of unlocking the secrets of social life. Like almost everything else in life, intimacy between researcher and subject poses a host of dilemmas. Carefully cultivated, it can be a resource; if permitted to run rampant, it makes the researcher's mission impossible. I fear a too-detached relationship with informants because that means I will remain so utterly out of touch with their lives that anything they say, however fanciful, will seem plausible to me. At the same time, I fear a too-cozy relationship with informants because I want to be free to tell the truth about them. The closer we come to the lives of the people we study, the more we touch them, physically and emotionally, the more we will know about them, yet the greater the likelihood that resentments will be stirred up. There is no way out of this dilemma.

REFERENCES

Adler, Patricia A. 1985. *Wheeling and Dealing: An Ethnography of an Upper Level Drug-Dealing and Smuggling Community.* New York: Columbia University Press.

Altork, Kate. 1995. "Walking the Fire Line: The Erotic Dimension of the Fieldwork Experience." Pp. 107–39 in *Taboo: Sex, Identity, and Erotic Subjectivity in Anthropological Fieldwork,* edited by Don Kulick and Margaret Willson. London: Routledge.

American Sociological Association. 1968. "Toward a Code of Ethics for Sociologists." *The American Sociologist* 3 (November): 316–18.

American Sociological Association. 1997. "Code of Ethics" (pamphlet). Washington, DC: American Sociological Association.

Becker, Howard S. 1963. *Outsiders: Studies in the Sociology of Deviance.* New York: Free Press.

Bolton, Ralph. 1992. "Mapping Terra Incognita: Sex Research for AIDS Prevention—An Urgent Agenda for the 1990s." Pp. 124–58 in *The Time of AIDS: Social Analysis, Theory, and Method,* edited by Gilbert Herdt and Shirley Lindenbaum. Thousand Oaks, CA: Sage.

———. 1995. "Tricks, Friends, and Lovers: Erotic Encounters in the Field." Pp. 140–67 in *Taboo: Sex,*

Identity, and Erotic Subjectivity in Anthropological Fieldwork, edited by Don Kulick and Margaret Willson. London: Routledge.

————. 1996. "Coming Home: The Journey of a Gay Ethnographer in the Years of the Plague." Pp. 147–68 in *Out in the Field: Reflections of Lesbian and Gay Anthropologists,* edited by Ellen Lewin and William L. Leap. Urbana: University of Illinois Press.

Callaway, Helen. 1992. "Ethnography and Experience: Gender Implications in Fieldwork and Texts." Pp. 29–59 in *Anthropology and Autobiography,* edited by Judith Okley and Helen Callaway. London: Routledge.

Cesara, Manda. 1982. *Reflections of a Woman Anthropologist: No Hiding Place.* New York: Academic Press.

Davis, Dona. 1986. "Changing Self-Image: Studying Menopausal Women in a Newfoundland Fishing Village." Pp. 240–62 in *Self, Sex, and Gender in Cross-Cultural Fieldwork,* edited by Tony Larry Whitehead and Mary Ellen Conaway. Urbana: University of Illinois Press.

Davis, Murray S. 1983. *Smut: Erotic Reality/Obscene Ideology.* Chicago: University of Chicago Press.

Dubisch, Jill. 1995. "Lovers in the Field: Sex, Dominance, and the Female Anthropologist." Pp. 29–50 in *Taboo: Sex, Identity, and Erotic Subjectivity in Anthropological Fieldwork,* edited by Don Kulick and Margaret Willson. London: Routledge.

Erikson, Kai T. 1967. "Disguised Observation in Sociology." *Social Problems* 14 (Spring): 366–73.

Fine, Gary Alan. 1993. "Ten Lies of Ethnography: Moral Dilemmas of Field Research." *Journal of Contemporary Ethnography* 22 (October): 267–94.

Freeman, Derek. 1991. "There's Tricks i'th' World: An Historical Analysis of the Samoan Researches of Margaret Mead." *Visual Anthropology Review* 7(1): 103–28.

Gearing, Jean. 1995. "Fear and Loving in the West Indies: Research from the Heart (As Well as the Head)." Pp. 186–218 in *Taboo: Sex, Identity, and Erotic Subjectivity in Anthropological Fieldwork,* edited by Don Kulick and Margaret Willson. London: Routledge.

Goode, Erich. 1996. "The Ethics of Deception in Social Research: A Case Study." *Qualitative Sociology* 19(1): 11–33.

Horowitz, Ruth. 1986. "Remaining an Outsider: Membership as a Threat to Research Rapport." *Urban Life* 14 (January): 409–30.

Howell, Nancy. 1990. *Surviving Fieldwork: A Report of the Advisory Panel on Health and Safety in Fieldwork.* Washington, DC: American Anthropological Association.

Irwin, John. 1970. *The Felon.* Englewood, NJ: Prentice Hall.

————. 1980. *Prisons in Turmoil.* Boston: Little, Brown.

Jones, James H. 1997. *Alfred C Kinsey: A Public/Private Life.* New York: W. W. Norton.

Krieger, Susan. 1991. *Social Science and the Self.* New Brunswick, NJ: Rutgers University Press.

Kulick, Don. 1995. "Introduction: The Sexual Life of Anthropologists: Erotic Subjectivity and Ethnographic Work." Pp. 1–28 in *Identity and Erotic Subjectivity in Anthropological Fieldwork,* edited by Don Kulick and Margaret Willson. London: Routledge.

Kulick, Don and Margaret Willson, Eds. 1995. *Taboo: Sex, Identity, and Erotic Subjectivity in Anthropological Fieldwork.* London: Routledge.

Lee, John Alan. 1978. *Getting Sex.* Toronto: General.

————. 1979. "The Gay Connection." *Urban Life* 8 (July): 175–98.

Lewin, Ellen and William L. Leap, Eds. 1996. *Out in the Field: Reflections of Lesbian and Gay Anthropologists.* Urbana: University of Illinois Press.

Malinowski, Bronislaw. 1967. *A Diary in the Strict Sense of the Term.* Translated by Norbert Guterman. London: Routledge & Kegan Paul.

Mills, C. Wright. 1959. *The Sociological Imagination.* New York: Oxford University Press.

Newton, Esther. 1993a. "My Best Informant's Dress: The Erotic Equation in Fieldwork." *Cultural Anthropology* 8 (February): 3–23.

————. 1993b. *Cherry Grove, Fire Island: Sixty Years in America's First Gay and Lesbian Town.* Boston: Beacon Press.

Palson, Charles and Rebecca Palson. 1972. "Swinging in Wedlock." *Society* 9 (February): 28–37.

Polsky, Ned. 1969. *Hustlers, Beats, and Others.* Garden City, NY: Doubleday Anchor.

Rabinow, Paul. 1977. *Reflections on Fieldwork in Morocco.* Berkeley: University of California Press.

Riemer, Jeffrey W. 1977. "Varieties of Opportunistic Research." *Urban Life* 5 (January): 467–77.

Schneebaum, Tobias. 1988. *Where the Spirits Dwell: An Odyssey in the New Guinea Jungle.* New York: Grove Press.

Stewart, George Lee. 1972. "On First Being a John." *Urban Life and Culture* 1 (October): 255–74.

Styles, Joseph. 1979. "Outsider/Insider: Researching Gay Baths." *Urban Life* 8 (July): 135–52.

Turnbull, Colin M. 1962. *The Forest People: A Study of the Pygmies of the Congo.* New York: Simon & Schuster.

———. 1986. "Sex and Gender: The Role of Subjectivity in Field Research." Pp. 17–27 in *Self, Sex, and Gender in Cross-Cultural Fieldwork,* edited by Tony Larry Whitehead, and Mary Ellen Conaway. Urbana: University of Illinois Press.

Van Lieshout, Maurice. 1995. "Leather Nights in the Woods: Homosexual Encounters in a Highway Rest Area." *Journal of Homosexuality* 29(1): 19–39.

Wade, Peter. 1993. "Sexuality and Masculinity in Fieldwork among Colombian Blacks." Pp. 199–214 in *Gendered Fields: Women, Men, and Ethnography,* edited by Diane Bell, Pat Caplan, and Jahan Karim Wazir. London: Routledge.

Wafer, James. 1996. "Out of the Closet and into Print: Sexual Identity in the Textual Field." Pp. 261–73 in *Out in the Field: Reflections of Lesbian and Gay Anthropologists,* edited by Ellen Lewin and William L. Leap. Urbana: University of Illinois Press.

Warren, Carol A. B. 1982. *Court of Last Resort: Mental Illness and the Law.* Chicago: University of Chicago Press.

———. 1988. *Gender Issues in Field Research.* Thousand Oaks, CA: Sage.

Whitehead, Tony Larry and Mary Ellen Conaway, Eds. 1986. *Self, Sex, and Gender in Cross-Cultural Fieldwork.* Urbana: University of Illinois Press.

PART TWO

POSITIVIST THEORIES

Around 11:15 A.M. on an April day in 1999, Eric Harris and Dylan Klebold, students at Columbine High School in Littleton, Colorado, entered the school's cafeteria, opened fire with semiautomatic rifles, and threw pipe bombs. The gunmen killed two and caused about 500 other students to flee amid the flying bullets and exploding bombs. Then the killers went upstairs and entered the library. Laughing and taunting their victims, they shot 10 more to death, many at point-blank range. Harris and Dylan asked at least two female students whether they believed in God and immediately killed them when they answered "yes." Finally, after murdering 12 students and a teacher and wounding 23 students, the killers committed suicide in the library.[1]

Given such a shocking, monstrous act, positivist sociologists would ask what caused it. For answers, they would look into the young killers' family backgrounds, school experiences, and associations with their peers. Such an investigation might suggest that the causes of the killing could be poor familial relationships, alienation from the school, and association with a violent clique. The focus on the causes of deviance characterizes all positivist theories of deviance.

Positivist theories differ from each other in explaining what causes deviance. The well-known examples are presented in four articles here. In the first, Robert Merton explains how a lack of opportunity to achieve success pressures individuals toward deviance. In the second article, Edwin Sutherland and Donald Cressey attribute deviance to an excess of deviant associations over conventional associations. In the third selection, Travis Hirschi blames deviance on a lack of control in the individual's life. In the final piece, John Braithwaite shows how a lack of reintegrative shaming causes deviance to flourish.

---

1. Glick, Daniel, et al., "Anatomy of a massacre." *Newsweek,* May 3, 1999, pp. 25–31.

5

STRAIN THEORY

ROBERT K. MERTON

The framework set out in this essay is designed to provide one systematic approach to the analysis of social and cultural sources of deviant behavior. Our primary aim is to discover how some *social structures exert a definite pressure upon certain persons in the society to engage in nonconforming rather than conforming conduct.* If we can locate groups peculiarly subject to such pressures, we should expect to find fairly high rates of deviant behavior in these groups, not because the human beings comprising them are compounded of distinctive biological tendencies but because they are responding normally to the social situation in which they find themselves. Our perspective is sociological. We look at variations in the *rates* of deviant behavior, not at its incidence. Should our quest be at all successful, some forms of deviant behavior will be found to be as psychologically normal as conformist behavior, and the equation of deviation and psychological abnormality will be put in question.

PATTERNS OF CULTURAL GOALS AND INSTITUTIONAL NORMS

Among the several elements of social and cultural structures, two are of immediate importance. These are analytically separable although they merge in concrete situations. The first consists of culturally defined goals, purposes and interests, held out as legitimate objectives for all or for diversely located members of the society. The goals are more or less integrated—the degree is a question of empirical fact—and roughly ordered in some hierarchy of value. Involving various de-

grees of sentiment and significance, the prevailing goals comprise a frame of aspirational reference. They are the things "worth striving for." They are a basic, though not the exclusive, component of what Linton has called "designs for group living." And though some, not all, of these cultural goals are directly related to the biological drives of man, they are not determined by them.

A second element of the cultural structure defines, regulates, and controls the acceptable modes of reaching out for these goals. Every social group invariably couples its cultural objectives with regulations, rooted in the mores or institutions, of allowable procedures for moving toward these objectives. These regulatory norms are not necessarily identical with technical or efficiency norms. Many procedures which from the standpoint of particular individuals would be most efficient in securing desired values—the exercise of force, fraud, power—are ruled out of the institutional area of permitted conduct. At times, the disallowed procedures include some which would be efficient for the group itself—for example, historic taboos on vivisection, on medical experimentation, on the sociological analysis of "sacred" norms—since the criterion of acceptability is not technical efficiency but value-laden sentiments (supported by most members of the group or by those able to promote these sentiments through the composite use of power and propaganda). In all instances, the choice of expedients for striving toward cultural goals is limited by institutionalized norms.

We shall be primarily concerned with the first—a society in which there is an exceptionally strong emphasis upon specific goals without a corresponding emphasis upon institutional procedures. If it is not to be misunderstood, this statement must be elaborated. No society lacks norms governing conduct. But societies do differ in the degree to which the folkways, mores and institutional controls are effectively integrated with the goals which stand high in the hierarchy of cultural values. The culture may be such as to lead individuals to center their emotional convictions upon the complex of culturally acclaimed ends, with far less emotional support for prescribed methods of reaching out for these ends. With such differential emphases upon goals and institutional procedures, the latter may be so vitiated by the stress on goals as to have the behavior of many individuals limited only by considerations of technical expediency. In this context, the sole significant question becomes: Which of the available procedures is most efficient in netting the culturally approved value? The technically most effective procedure, whether culturally legitimate or not, becomes typically preferred to institutionally prescribed conduct. As this process of attenuation continues, the society becomes unstable and there develops what Durkheim called "anomie" (or normlessness).

The working of this process eventuating in anomie can be easily glimpsed in a series of familiar and instructive, though perhaps trivial, episodes. Thus, in competitive athletics, when the aim of victory is shorn of its institutional trappings and success becomes construed as "winning the game" rather than "winning under the rules of the game," a premium is implicitly set upon the use of illegitimate but technically efficient means. The star of the opposing football team is surreptitiously slugged; the wrestler incapacitates his opponent through ingenious but illicit techniques; university alumni covertly subsidize "students" whose talents are confined to the athletic field. The emphasis on the goal has so attenuated the satisfactions deriving from sheer participation in the competitive activity that only a successful outcome provides gratification.

Through the same process, tension generated by the desire to win in a poker game is relieved by successfully dealing one's self four aces or, when the cult of success has truly flowered, by sagaciously shuffling the cards in a game of solitaire. The faint twinge of uneasiness in the last instance and the surreptitious nature of public delicts indicate clearly that the institutional rules of the game are *known* to those who evade them. But cultural (or idiosyncratic) exaggeration of the success-goal leads men to withdraw emotional support from the rules.

This process is of course not restricted to the realm of competitive sport, which has simply provided us with microcosmic images of the social macrocosm. The process whereby exaltation of the end generates a literal *demoralization,* that is, a de-institutionalization, of the means occurs in many groups where the two components of the social structure are not highly integrated.

Contemporary American culture appears to approximate the polar type in which great emphasis upon certain success-goals occurs without equivalent emphasis upon institutional means. It would of course be fanciful to assert that accumulated wealth stands alone as a symbol of success, just as it would be fanciful to deny that Americans assign it a place high in their scale of values. In some large measure, money has been consecrated as a value in itself, over and above its expenditure for articles of consumption or its use for the enhancement of power. "Money" is peculiarly well adapted to become a symbol of prestige. As Simmel emphasized, money is highly abstract and impersonal. However acquired, fraudulently or institutionally, it can be used to purchase the same goods and services. The anonymity of an urban society, in conjunction with these peculiarities of money, permits wealth, the sources of which may be unknown to the community in which the plutocrat lives or, if known, to become purified in the course of time, to serve as a symbol of high status. Moreover, in the American Dream there is no final stopping point. The measure of "monetary success" is conveniently indefinite and relative. At each income level, as H. F. Clark found, Americans want just about 25 percent more (but of course this "just a bit more" continues to operate once it is obtained). In this flux of shifting standards, there is no stable resting point, or rather, it is the point which manages always to be "just ahead." An observer of a community in which annual salaries in six figures are not uncommon reports the anguished words of one victim of the American Dream: "In this town, I'm snubbed socially because I only get a thousand a week. That hurts."

To say that the goal of monetary success is entrenched in American culture is only to say that Americans are bombarded on every side by precepts which affirm the right or, often, the duty of retaining the goal even in the face of repeated frustration. Prestigeful representatives of the society reinforce the cultural emphasis. The family, the school and the workplace—the major agencies shaping the personality structure and goal formation of Americans—join to provide the intensive disciplining required if an individual is to retain intact a goal that remains elusively beyond reach, if he is to be motivated by the promise of a gratification which is not redeemed. As we shall presently see, parents serve as a transmission belt for the values and goals of the groups of which the are a part—above all, of their social class or of the class with which they identify themselves. And the schools are of course the official agency for the passing on of the prevailing values, with a large proportion of the textbooks used in city schools implying or stating explicitly "that education leads to intelligence and consequently to job and money success." Central to this process of disciplining people to maintain their unfulfilled aspirations are the cultural prototypes of success, the living documents testifying that the American Dream can be realized if one but has the requisite abilities.

Coupled with this positive emphasis upon the obligation to maintain lofty goals is a correlative emphasis upon the penalizing of those who draw in their ambitions. Americans are admonished "not to be a quitter" for in the dictionary of American culture, as in the lexicon of youth, "there is no such word as 'fail.' " The cultural manifesto is clear: one must not quit, must not cease striving, must not lessen his goals, for "not failure, but low aim, is crime."

Thus the culture enjoins the acceptance of three cultural axioms: First, all should strive for the same lofty goals since these are open to all; second, present seeming failure is but a way-station to ultimate success; and third, genuine failure consists only in the lessening or withdrawal of ambition.

In rough psychological paraphrase, these axioms represent, first a symbolic secondary reinforcement of incentive; second, curbing the threatened extinction of a response through an associated stimulus; third, increasing the motive strength to evoke continued responses despite the continued absence of reward.

In sociological paraphrase, these axioms represent, first, the deflection of criticism of the social structure onto one's self among those so situated in the society that they do not have full and equal access to opportunity; second, the preservation of a structure of social power by having individuals in the lower social strata identify themselves, not with their compeers, but with those at the top (whom they will ultimately join); and third, providing pressures for conformity with the cultural dictates of unslackened ambition by the threat of less than full membership in the society for those who fail to conform.

It is in these terms and through these processes that contemporary American culture continues to be characterized by a heavy emphasis on wealth as a basic symbol of success, without a corresponding emphasis upon the legitimate avenues on which to march toward this goal. How do individuals living in this cultural context respond? And how do our observations bear upon the doctrine that deviant behavior typically derives from biological impulses breaking through the restraints imposed by culture? What, in short, are the consequences for the behavior of people variously situated in a social structure of a culture in which the emphasis on dominant success goals has become increasingly separated from an equivalent emphasis on institutionalized procedures for seeking these goals?

TYPES OF INDIVIDUAL ADAPTATION

Turning from these culture patterns, we now examine types of adaptation by individuals within the culture-bearing society. Though our focus is still the cultural and social genesis of varying rates and types of deviant behavior, our perspective shifts from the plane of patterns of cultural values to the plane of types of adaptation to these values among those occupying different positions in the social structure.

We here consider five types of adaptation, as these are schematically set out in the following table, where (+) signifies "acceptance," (–) signifies "rejection," and (±) signifies "rejection of prevailing values and substitution of new values."

A Typology of Modes of
Individual Adaptation

MODES OF ADAPTATION	CULTURE GOALS	INSTITUTIONALIZED MEANS
I. Conformity	+	+
II. Innovation	+	–
III. Ritualism	–	+
IV. Retreatism	–	–
V. Rebellion	±	±

I. Conformity

To the extent that a society is stable, adaptation type I—conformity to both cultural goals and institutionalized means—is the most common and widely diffused. Were this not so, the stability and continuity of the society could not be maintained. . . .

II. Innovation

Great cultural emphasis upon the success-goal invites this mode of adaptation through the use of institutionally proscribed but often effective means of attaining at least the simulacra of success—wealth and power. This response occurs when the individual has assimilated the cultural emphasis upon the goal without equally internalizing the institutional norms governing ways and means for its attainment. . . .

It appears from our analysis that the greatest pressures toward deviation are exerted upon the lower strata. Cases in point permit us to detect the sociological mechanisms involved in producing these pressures. Several researches have shown that specialized areas of vice and crime constitute a "normal" response to a situation where the cultural emphasis upon pecuniary success has been absorbed, but where there is little access to conventional and legitimate means for becoming successful. The occupational opportunities of people in these areas are largely confined to manual labor and the lesser white-collar jobs. Given the American stigmatization of manual labor *which has been found to hold rather uniformly in all social classes,* and the absence of realistic opportunities for advancement beyond this level, the result is a marked tendency toward deviant behavior. The status of unskilled labor and the consequent low income cannot readily compete *in terms of established standards of worth* with the promises of power and high income from organized vice, rackets and crime.

For our purposes, these situations exhibit two salient features. First, incentives for success are provided by the established values of the culture *and* second, the avenues available for moving toward this goal are largely limited by the class structure to those of deviant behavior. It is the *combination* of the cultural emphasis and the social structure which produces intense pressure for deviation. . . .

III. Ritualism

The ritualistic type of adaptation can be readily identified. It involves the abandoning or scaling down of the lofty cultural goals of great pecuniary success and rapid social mobility to the point where one's aspirations can be satisfied. But though one rejects the cultural obligation to attempt "to get ahead in the world," though one draws in one's horizons, one continues to abide almost compulsively by institutional norms. . . .

We should expect this type of adaptation to be fairly frequent in a society which makes one's social status largely dependent upon one's achievements. For, as has so often been observed, this ceaseless competitive struggle produces acute status anxiety. One device for allaying these anxieties is to lower one's level of aspiration—permanently. Fear produces inaction, or, more accurately, routinized action.

The syndrome of the social ritualist is both familiar and instructive. His implicit life-philosophy finds expression in a series of cultural clichés: "I'm not sticking my neck out," "I'm playing it safe," "I'm satisfied with what I've got," "Don't aim high and you won't be disappointed." The theme threaded through these attitudes is that high ambitions invite frustration and danger whereas lower aspirations produce satisfaction and security. It is the perspective of the frightened employee, the zealously conformist bureaucrat in the teller's cage of the private banking enterprise, or in the front office of the public works enterprise.

IV. Retreatism

Just as Adaptation I (conformity) remains the most frequent, Adaptation IV (the rejection of cultural goals and institutional means) is probably the least common. People who adapt (or maladapt) in this fashion are, strictly speaking, *in* the society but not *of* it. Sociologically these constitute the true aliens. Not sharing the common frame of values, they can be included as members of the *society* (in distinction from the *population*) only in a fictional sense.

In this category fall some of the adaptive activities of psychotics, autists, pariahs, outcasts, vagrants, vagabonds, tramps, chronic drunkards and drug addicts. They have relinquished culturally prescribed goals and their behavior does not accord

with institutional norms. The competitive order is maintained but the frustrated and handicapped individual who cannot cope with this order drops out. Defeatism, quietism and resignation are manifested in escape mechanisms which ultimately lead him to "escape" from the requirements of the society. It is thus an expedient which arises from continued failure to near the goal by legitimate measures and from an inability to use the illegitimate route because of internalized prohibitions.

V. Rebellion

This adaptation leads men outside the environing social structure to envisage and seek to bring into being a new, that is to say, a greatly modified social structure. It presupposes alienation from reigning goals and standards. These come to be regarded as purely arbitrary. And the arbitrary is precisely that which can neither exact allegiance nor possess legitimacy, for it might as well be otherwise. In our society, organized movements for rebellion apparently aim to introduce a social structure in which the cultural standards of success would be sharply modified and provision would be made for a closer correspondence between merit, effort and reward.

THE STRAIN TOWARD ANOMIE

The social structure we have examined produces a strain toward anomie and deviant behavior. The pressure of such a social order is upon outdoing one's competitors. So long as the sentiments supporting this competitive system are distributed throughout the entire range of activities and are not confined to the final result of "success," the choice of means will remain largely within the ambit of institutional control. When, however, the cultural emphasis shifts from the satisfactions deriving from competition itself to almost exclusive concern with the outcome, the resultant stress makes for the breakdown of the regulatory structure.

6

DIFFERENTIAL ASSOCIATION THEORY

EDWIN H. SUTHERLAND
DONALD R. CRESSEY

The following statements refer to the process by which a particular person comes to engage in criminal behavior.

1. *Criminal behavior is learned.* Negatively, this means that criminal behavior is not inherited, as such; also, the person who is not already trained in crime does not invent criminal behavior, just as a person does not make mechanical inventions unless he has had training in mechanics.

2. *Criminal behavior is learned in interaction with other persons in a process of communication.* This communication is verbal in many respects but includes also "the communication of gestures."

3. *The principal part of the learning of criminal behavior occurs within intimate personal groups.* Negatively, this means that the impersonal agencies of communication, such as movies and newspapers, play a relatively unimportant part in the genesis of criminal behavior.

4. *When criminal behavior is learned, the learning includes (a) techniques of committing the crime, which are sometimes very complicated, sometimes very simple; and (b) the specific direction of motives, drives, rationalizations, and attitudes.*

5. *The specific direction of motives and drives is learned from definitions of the legal codes as favorable or unfavorable.* In some societies an individual is surrounded by persons who invariably define the legal codes as rules to be observed, while in others he is surrounded by persons whose de-finitions are favorable to the violation of the legal codes. In our American society these definitions are almost always mixed, with the consequence that we have culture conflict in relation to the legal codes.

6. *A person becomes delinquent because of an excess of definitions favorable to violation of law over definitions unfavorable to violation of law.* This is the principle of differential association. It refers to both criminal and anticriminal associations and has to do with counteracting forces. When persons become criminal, they do so because of contacts with criminal patterns and also because of isolation from anticriminal patterns. Any person inevitably assimilates the surrounding culture unless other patterns are in conflict; a southerner does not pronounce *r* because other Southerners do not pronounce *r.* Negatively, this proposition of differential association means that associations which are neutral so far as crime is concerned have little or no effect on the genesis of criminal behavior. Much of the experience of a person is neutral in this sense, for example, learning to brush one's teeth. This behavior has no negative or positive effect on criminal behavior except as it may be related to associations which are concerned with the legal codes. This neutral behavior is important especially as an occupier of the time of a child so that he is not in contact with criminal behavior during the time he is so engaged in the neutral behavior.

7. *Differential associations may vary in-frequency, duration, priority, and intensity.* This means that associations with criminal behavior and also associations with anti-criminal behavior vary in those respects. "Frequency" and "duration" as modalities of associations are obvious and need no explanation. "Priority' is assumed to be important in the sense that lawful behavior developed in early childhood may persist throughout life, and also that delinquent behavior developed in early childhood may persist throughout life. This tendency, however, has not been adequately demonstrated, and priority seems to be important principally through its selective influence. "Intensity" is not precisely defined, but it has to do with such things as the prestige of the source of a criminal or anticriminal pattern and with emotional reactions related to the associations. In a precise description of the criminal behavior of a person, these modalities would be rated in quantitative form and a mathematical ratio reached. A formula in this sense has not been developed, and the development of such a formula would be extremely difficult.

8. *The process of learning criminal behavior by association with criminal and anticriminal patterns involves all of the mechanisms that are involved in any other learning.* Negatively, this means that the learning of criminal behavior is not restricted to the process of imitation. A person who is seduced, for instance, learns criminal behavior by association, but this process would not ordinarily be described as imitation.

9. *While criminal behavior is an expression of general needs and values, it is not explained by those general needs and values, since noncriminal behavior is an expression of the same needs and values.* Thieves generally steal in order to secure money, but likewise honest laborers work in order to secure money. The attempts by many scholars to explain criminal behavior by general drives and values, such as the happiness principle, striving for social status, the money motive, or frustration, have been, and must continue to be, futile, since they explain lawful behavior as completely as they explain criminal behavior. They are similar to respiration, which is necessary for any behavior, but which does not differentiate criminal from noncriminal behavior.

It is not necessary, at this level of explanation, to explain why a person has the associations he has; this certainly involves a complex of many things. In an area where the delinquency rate is high, a boy who is sociable, gregarious, active, and athletic is very likely to come in contact with the other boys in the neighborhood, learn delinquent behavior patterns from them, and become a criminal; in the same neighborhood the psychopathic boy who is isolated, introverted, and inert may remain at home, not become acquainted with the other boys in the neighborhood, and not become delinquent. In another situation, the sociable, athletic, aggressive boy may become a member of a scout troop and not become involved in delinquent behavior. The person's associations are determined in a general context of social organization. A child is ordinarily reared in a family; the place of residence of the family is determined largely by family income; and the delinquency rate is in many respects related to the rental value of the houses. Many other aspects of social organization affect the kinds of associations a person has.

The preceding explanation of criminal behavior purports to explain the criminal and noncriminal behavior of individual persons. It is possible to state sociological theories of criminal behavior which explain the criminality of a community, nation, or other group. The problem, when thus stated, is to account for variations in crime rates and involves a comparison of the crime rates of various groups or the crime rates of a particular group at different times. The explanation of a crime rate must be consistent with the explanation of the criminal behavior of the person, since the crime rate is a summary statement of the number of persons in the group who commit crimes and the frequency with which they commit crimes. One of the best explanations of crime rates from this point of view is that a high crime rate is due to social disorganization. The term *social disorganization* is not entirely satisfactory, and it seems preferable to substitute for it the term *differential social organization*. The postulate on which this theory is based, regardless of the name, is that crime is rooted in the social organization and is an expression of that social organization. A group may be organized for criminal behavior or organized against criminal behavior. Most communities are organized for both criminal and anticriminal behavior, and, in that sense the crime rate is an expression of the differential group organization. Differential group organization as an explanation of variations in crime rates is consistent with the differential association theory of the processes by which persons become criminals.

7

CONTROL THEORY

TRAVIS HIRSCHI

Control theories assume that delinquent acts result when an individual's bond to society is weak or broken . . . [Elements of the bond are as follows].

ATTACHMENT

It can be argued that all of the characteristics attributed to the psychopath follow from, are effects of, his lack of attachment to others. To say that to lack attachment to others is to be free from moral restraints is to use lack of attachment to explain the guiltlessness of the psychopath, the fact that he apparently has no conscience or superego. In this view, lack of attachment to others is not merely a symptom of psychopathy, it *is* psychopathy; lack of conscience is just another way of saying the same thing; and the violation of norms is (or may be) a consequence.

For that matter, given that man is an animal, "impulsivity" and "aggressiveness" can also be seen as natural consequences of freedom from moral restraints. However, since the view of man as endowed with natural propensities and capacities like other animals is peculiarly unpalatable to sociologists, we need not fall back on such a view to explain the amoral man's aggressiveness. The process of becoming alienated from others often involves or is based on active interpersonal conflict. Such conflict could easily supply a reservoir of *socially derived* hostility sufficient to account for the aggressiveness of those whose attachments to others have been weakened.

Durkheim said it many years ago: "We are moral beings to the extent that we are social beings." This may be interpreted to mean that we are moral beings to the extent that we have "internalized the norms" of society. But what does it mean to say that a person has internalized the norms of society? The norms of society are by definition shared by the members of society. To violate a norm is, therefore, to act contrary to the wishes and expectations of other people. If a person does not care about the wishes and expectations of other people—that is, if he is insensitive to the opinion of others—then he is to that extent not bound by the norms. He is free to deviate.

The essence of internalization of norms, conscience, or superego thus lies in the attachment of the individual to others. This view has several advantages over the concept of internalization. For one, explanations of deviant behavior based on attachment do not beg the question, since the extent to which a person is attached to others can be measured independently of his deviant behavior. Furthermore, change or variation in behavior is explainable in a way that it is not when notions of interaction or superego are used. For example, the divorced man is more likely after divorce to commit a number of deviant acts, such as suicide or forgery. If we explain these acts by reference to the super-ego (or internal control), we are forced to say that the man "lost his conscience" when he got a divorce; and, of course, if he remarries, we have to conclude that he gets his conscience back. . . .

COMMITMENT

"Of all passions, that which inclineth men least to break the laws, is fear. Nay, excepting some generous natures, it is the only thing, when there is the appearance of profit or pleasure by breaking the laws, that makes men keep them." Few would deny that men on occasion obey the rules simply from fear of the consequences. This rational component in conformity we label commitment. What does it mean to say that a person is committed to conformity? . . . [It means] that the person invests time, energy, himself, in a certain line of activity—say, getting an education, building up a business, acquiring a reputation for virtue. When or whenever he considers deviant behavior, he must consider the costs of this deviant behavior, the risk he runs of losing the investment he has made in conventional behavior.

If attachment to others is the sociological counterpart of the superego or conscience, commitment is the counterpart of the ego or common sense. To the person committed to conventional lines of action, risking one to ten years in prison for a ten-dollar holdup is stupidity, because to the committed person the costs and risks obviously exceed ten dollars in value. (To the psychoanalyst, such an act exhibits failure to be governed by the "reality-principle.") In the sociological control theory, it can be and is generally assumed that the decision to commit a criminal act may well be rationally determined—that the actor's decision was not irrational given the risks and costs he faces. . . .

INVOLVEMENT

Many persons undoubtedly owe a life of virtue to a lack of opportunity to do otherwise. Time and energy are inherently limited: "Not that I would not, if I could, be both handsome and fat and well dressed, and a great athlete, and make a million a year, be a wit, a bon vivant, and a lady killer, as well as a philosopher, a philanthropist, a statesman, warrior, and African explorer, as well as a 'tone-poet' and saint. But the thing is simply impossible." The things that William James here says he would like to be or do are all, I suppose, within the realm of conventionality, but if he were to include illicit actions he would still have to eliminate some of them as simply impossible.

Involvement or engrossment in conventional activities is thus often part of a control theory. The assumption, widely shared, is that a person may be simply too busy doing conventional things to find time to engage in deviant behavior. The person involved in conventional activities is tied to appointments, deadlines, working hours, plans, and the like, so the opportunity to commit deviant acts rarely arises. To the extent that he is engrossed in conventional activities, he cannot even think about deviant acts, let alone act out his inclinations. . . .

BELIEF

The control theory assumes the existence of a common value system within the society or group whose norms are being violated. If the deviant is committed to a value system different from that of conventional society, there is, within the context of the theory, nothing to explain. The question is, "Why does a man violate the rules in which he believes?" It is not, "Why do men differ in their beliefs about what constitutes good and desirable conduct?" The person is assumed to have been socialized (perhaps imperfectly) into the group whose rules he is violating; deviance is not a question of one group imposing its rules on the members of another group. In other words, we not only assume the deviant *has* believed the rules, we assume he believes the rules even as he violates them.

How can a person believe it is wrong to steal at the same time he is stealing? In the strain theory, this is not a difficult problem. (In fact, the strain theory was devised specifically to deal with this question.) The motivation to deviance adduced by the strain theorist is so strong that we can well understand the deviant act even assuming the deviator believes strongly that it is wrong. However, given the control theory's assumptions about motivation, if both the deviant and the nondeviant believe the deviant act is wrong, how do we account for the fact that one commits it and the other does not?

Control theories have taken two approaches to this problem. In one approach, beliefs are treated as mere words that mean little or nothing. . . . The second approach argues that the deviant rationalizes his behavior so that he can at once violate the rule and maintain his belief in it. . . . We assume, however, that there is *variation* in the extent to which people believe they should obey the rules of society, and, furthermore, that the less a person believes he should obey the rules, the more likely he is to violate them.

8

SHAMING THEORY

JOHN BRAITHWAITE

Cultural commitments to shaming are the key to controlling all types of crime. However, for all types of crime, shaming runs the risk of counterproductivity when it shades into stigmatization.

The crucial distinction is between shaming that is reintegrative and shaming that is disintegrative (stigmatization). Reintegrative shaming means that expressions of community disapproval, which may range from mild rebuke to degradation ceremonies, are followed by gestures of reacceptance into the community of law-abiding citizens. These gestures of reacceptance will vary from a simple smile expressing forgiveness and love to quite formal ceremonies to decertify the offender as deviant. Disintegrative shaming (stigmatization), in contrast, divides the community by creating a class of outcasts. Much effort is directed at labeling deviance, while little attention is paid to delabeling, to signifying forgiveness and reintegration, to ensuring that the deviance label is applied to the behavior rather than the person, and that this is done under the assumption that the disapproved behavior is transient, performed by an essentially good person. . . .

The best place to see reintegrative shaming at work is in loving families. . . . Family life teaches us that shaming and punishment are possible while maintaining bonds of respect. Two hypotheses are suggested: first, families are the most effective agents of social control in most societies partly because of this characteristic; second, those families that are disintegrative rather than reintegrative in their punishment processes, that have not learnt the trick of punishing within a continuum of love, are the families that fail at socializing their children.

KEY CONCEPTS

Interdependency is a condition of individuals. It means the extent to which individuals participate in networks wherein they are dependent on others to achieve valued ends and others are dependent on them. We could describe an individual as in a state of interdependency even if the individuals who are dependent on him are different from the individuals on whom he is dependent. Interdependency is approximately equivalent to the social bonding, attachment and commitment of control theory.

Communitarianism is a condition of societies. In communitarian societies individuals are densely enmeshed in interdependencies which have the special qualities of mutual help and trust. The interdependencies have symbolic significance in the culture of group loyalties which take precedence over individual interests. The interdependencies also have symbolic significance as attachments which invoke personal obligation to others in a community of concern, rather than simply interdependencies of convenience as between a bank and a small depositor. A communitarian culture rejects any pejorative connotation of dependency as threatening individual autonomy. Communitarian cultures resist interpretations of dependency as weakness and emphasize the need for mutuality of obligation in interdependency (to be both dependent and dependable). The Japanese are said to be socialized not only to *amaeru* (to be succored by others) but also to *amayakasu* (to be nurturing to others).

Shaming means all social processes of expressing disapproval which have the intention or effect of invoking remorse in the person being shamed and/or condemnation by others who become aware of the shaming. When associated with appropriate symbols, formal punishment often shames. But societies vary enormously in the extent to which formal punishment is associated with shaming or in the extent to which the social meaning of punishment is no more than to inflict pain to tip reward-cost calculations in favor of certain outcomes. Shaming, unlike purely deterrent punishment, sets out to moralize with the offender to communicate reasons for the evil of her actions. Most shaming is neither associated with formal punishment nor perpetrated by the state, though both shaming by the state and shaming with punishment are important types of shaming. Most shaming is by individuals within interdependent communities of concern.

Reintegrative shaming is shaming which is followed by efforts to reintegrate the offender back into the community of law-abiding or respectable citizens through words or gestures of forgiveness or ceremonies to decertify the offender as deviant. Shaming and reintegration do not occur simultaneously but sequentially, with reintegration occurring before deviance becomes a master status. It is shaming which labels the act as evil while striving to preserve the identity of the offender as essentially good. It is directed at signifying evil deeds rather than evil persons in the Christian tradition of "hate the sin and love the sinner." Specific disapproval is expressed within relationships characterized by general social approval; shaming criminal behavior is complemented by ongoing social rewarding of alternative behavior patterns.

Reintegrative shaming is not necessarily weak; it can be cruel, even vicious. It is not distinguished from stigmatization by its potency, but by (a) a finite rather than open-ended duration which is terminated by forgiveness; and by (b) efforts to maintain bonds of love or respect throughout the finite period of suffering shame.

Stigmatization is disintegrative shaming in which no effort is made to reconcile the offender with the community. The offender is outcast, her deviance is allowed to become a master status, degradation ceremonies are not followed by ceremonies to decertify deviance.

Criminal subcultures are sets of rationalizations and conduct norms which cluster together to support criminal behavior. The clustering is usually facilitated by subcultural groups which provide systematic social support for crime in any of a number of ways—supplying members with criminal opportunities, criminal values, attitudes which weaken conventional values of law-abidingness, or techniques of neutralizing conventional values.

SHORT SUMMARY OF THE THEORY

The following might serve as the briefest possible summary of the theory. A variety of life circumstances increase the chances that individuals will be in situations of greater interdependency, the most important being age (under 15 and over 25), being married, female, employed, and having high employment and educational aspirations. Interdependent persons are more susceptible to shaming. More important, societies in which individuals are subject to extensive interdependencies are more likely to be communitarian, and shaming is much more widespread and potent in communitarian societies. Urbanization and high residential mobility are societal characteristics which undermine communitarianism.

The shaming produced by interdependency and communitarianism can be either of two types—shaming that becomes stigmatization or shaming that is followed by reintegration. The shaming engendered is more likely to become reintegrative in societies that are communitarian. In societies where shaming does become reintegrative, low crime rates are the result because disapproval is dispensed without eliciting a rejection of the disapprovers, so that the potentialities for future disapproval are not dismantled. . . .

Shaming that is stigmatizing, in contrast, makes criminal subcultures more attractive because these are in some sense subcultures which reject the rejectors. Thus, when shaming is allowed to become stigmatization for want of reintegrative gestures or ceremonies which decertify deviance, the deviant is both attracted to criminal subcultures and cut off from other interdependencies (with family, neighbors, church, etc.). Participation in subcultural groups supplies criminal role models, training in techniques of crime and techniques of neutralizing crime (or other forms of social support) that make choices to engage in crime more attractive. Thus, to the extent that shaming is of the stigmatizing rather than the reintegrative sort, and that criminal subcultures are widespread and accessible in the society, higher crime rates will be the result. While societies characterized by high levels of stigmatization will have, higher crime rates than societies characterized by reintegrative shaming, the former will have higher or lower crime rates than societies with little shaming at all depending largely on the availability of criminal subcultures.

Yet a high level of stigmatization in the society is one of the very factors that encourages criminal subculture formation by creating populations of outcasts with no stake in conformity, no chance of self-esteem within the terms of conventional society—individuals in search of an alternative culture that allows them self-esteem. A communitarian culture, on the other hand, nurtures deviants within a network of attachments to conventional society, thus inhibiting the widespread outcasting that is the stuff of subculture formation.

PART THREE

CONSTRUCTIONIST THEORIES

In 1990 one male couple and two female couples applied for marriage licenses in Hawaii. The applications were turned down on the ground that only a man can marry a woman and vice versa. The couples went to court, charging the state with sexual discrimination. In 1993 the Hawaii Supreme Court ruled that prohibiting same-sex marriage would violate the Hawaii state constitution's guarantee of equal protection under the laws, unless the government could offer some compelling reason to ban such marriage. The case was sent back to Hawaii's First Circuit Court, and, in 1996, its judge ruled in favor of the couples. The key reason is that the judge, after listening to extensive testimony from sociologists and psychologists, found that the state had failed to prove what it believed to be the harmfulness of same-sex marriage on children or somebody else.[1]

This case boils down to whether same-sex marriage—or, by extension, homosexuality—is deviant or not. The Hawaii government apparently considers it deviant in the sense of being harmful. Positivist sociologists hold the same view, which is why they develop etiological theories that point out the causes of deviance. By contrast, the Hawaii Supreme Court, along with the gay and lesbian couples, regard same-sex marriage as similar to conventional marriage—harmless or nondeviant. Social constructionists in sociology agree, which explains why they are more interested in the meaning, rather than causation, of "deviance." They have thus developed theories mostly about how different groups impute conflicting meanings to "deviance" and how these meanings influence human behavior.

This part of our reader features articles about various constructionist theories. In the first article, "Labeling Theory," Howard Becker shows how the meaning of deviance does not derive from the act a person commits but from society's labeling of the act as deviant. In the second selection, "Phenomenological Theory," Jack Katz provides a tour into the experiential world of deviants, revealing how they feel about their so-called deviant activities. In the third reading, "Conflict Theory," Richard Quinney describes what he calls "the social reality of crime." The reality consists of the meanings of such things as criminal laws, enforcement of these laws, their violations by relatively powerless people, and the dominant class' crime ideology about the enforcement of laws against lower-class criminals. In the fourth article, "Feminist Theory," Jody Miller exposes male bias in the sociology of deviance and then presents the feminist understanding of deviance. Finally, in "Postmodern Theory," David and Jessica Friedrichs discuss the major points of the newest constructionist theory in the sociology of deviance.

---

1. James Kunen, "Hawaiian Courtship," *Time,* December 16, 1996, pp. 44–45.

9

LABELING THEORY

HOWARD S. BECKER

A sociological view . . . defines deviance as the infraction of some agreed-upon rule. It then goes on to ask who breaks rules, and to search for the factors in their personalities and life situations that might account for the infractions. This assumes that those who have broken a rule constitute a homogeneous category, because they have committed the same deviant act.

Such an assumption seems to me to ignore the central fact about deviance: it is created by society. I do not mean this in the way it is ordinarily understood, in which the causes of deviance are located in the social situation of the deviant or in "social factors" which prompt his action. I mean, rather, that *social groups create deviance by making the rules whose infraction constitutes deviance,* and by applying those rules to particular people and labeling them as outsiders. From this point of view, deviance is *not* a quality of the act the person commits, but rather a consequence of the application by others of rules and sanctions to an "offender." The deviant is one to whom that label has successfully been applied; deviant behavior is behavior that people so label.

Since deviance is, among other things, a consequence of the responses of others to a person's act, students of deviance cannot assume that they are dealing with a homogeneous category when they study people who have been labeled deviant. That is, they cannot assume that these people have actually committed a deviant act or broken some rule, because the process of labeling may not be infallible; some people may be labeled deviant who in fact have not broken a rule. Furthermore, they cannot assume that the category of those labeled deviant will contain all those who actually have broken a rule, for many offenders may escape apprehension and thus fail to be included in the population of "deviants" they study. Insofar as the category lacks homogeneity and fails to include all the cases that belong in it, one cannot reasonably expect to find common factors of personality or life situation that will account for the supposed deviance.

What, then, do people who have been labeled deviant have in common? At the least, they share the label and the experience of being labeled as outsiders. I will begin my analysis with this basic similarity and view deviance as the product of a transaction that takes place between some social group and one who is viewed by that group as a rule-breaker. I will be less concerned with the personal and social characteristics of deviants than with the process by which they come to be thought of as outsiders and their reactions to that judgment.

The point is that the response of other people has to be regarded as problematic. Just because one has committed an infraction of a rule does not mean that others will respond as though this had happened. (Conversely, just because one has not violated a rule does not mean that he may not be treated, in some circumstances, as though he had.)

The degree to which other people will respond to a given act as deviant varies greatly. Several kinds of variation seem worth noting. First of all, there is variation over time. A person believed to have committed a given "deviant" act may at one time be responded to much more leniently than he would be at some other time. The occurrence of "drives" against various kinds of deviance illustrates this clearly. At various times, enforcement officials may decide to make an all-out attack on some particular kind of deviance, such as gambling, drug addiction, or homosexuality. It is obviously much more dangerous to engage in one of these activities when a drive is on than at any other time. (In a very interesting study of crime news in Colorado newspapers, Davis found that the amount of crime reported in Colorado newspapers showed very little association with actual changes in the amount of crime taking place in Colorado. And, further, that peoples' estimate of how much increase there had been in crime in Colorado was associated with the increase in the amount of crime news but not with any increase in the amount of crime.)

The degree to which an act will be treated as deviant depends also on who commits the act and who feels he has been harmed by it. Rules tend to be applied more to some persons than others. Studies of juvenile delinquency make the point clearly. Boys from middle-class areas do not get as far in the legal process when they are apprehended as do boys from slum areas. The middle-class boy is less likely, when picked up by the police, to be taken to the station; less likely when taken to the station to be booked; and it is extremely unlikely that he will be convicted and sentenced. This variation occurs even though the original infraction of the rule is the same in the two cases.

Why repeat these commonplace observations? Because, taken together, they support the proposition that deviance is not a simple quality, present in some kinds of behavior and absent in others. Rather, it is the product of a process which involves responses of other people to the behavior. The same behavior may be an infraction of the rules at one time and not at another; may be an infraction when committed by one person, but not when committed by another; some rules are broken with impunity, others are not. In short, whether a given act is deviant or not depends in part on the nature of the act (that is, whether or not it violates some rule) and in part on what other people do about it.

Some people may object that this is merely a terminological quibble, that one can, after all, define terms any way he wants to and that if some people want to speak of rule-breaking behavior as *deviant* without reference to the reactions of others they are free to do so. This, of course, is true. Yet it might be worthwhile to refer to such behavior as *rule-breaking behavior* and reserve the term *deviant* for those labeled as deviant by some segment of society. I do not insist that this usage be followed. But it should be clear that insofar as a scientist uses "deviant" to refer to any rule-breaking behavior and takes as his subject of study only those who have been *labeled* deviant, he will be hampered by the disparities between the two categories.

If we take as the object of our attention behavior which comes to be labeled as deviant, we must recognize that we cannot know whether a given act will be categorized as deviant until the response of others has occurred. Deviance is not a quality that lies in behavior itself, but in the interaction between the person who commits an act and those who respond to it.

In any case, being caught and branded as deviant has important consequences for one's further social participation and self-image. The most important consequence is a drastic change in the individual's public identity. Committing the improper act and being publicly caught at it place him in a new status. He has been revealed as a different kind of person from the kind he was supposed to be. He is labeled a "fairy," "dope fiend," "nut," or "lunatic," and treated accordingly.

To be labeled a criminal one need only commit a single criminal offense, and this is all the term formally refers to. Yet the word carries a number of connotations specifying auxiliary traits characteristic of anyone bearing the label. A man who has been convicted of housebreaking and thereby labeled criminal is presumed to be a person likely to break into other houses; the police, in rounding up known offenders for investigation after a crime has been committed, operate on this premise. Further, he is considered likely to commit other kinds of crimes as well, because he has shown himself to be a person without "respect for the law." Thus, apprehension for one deviant act exposes a person to the likelihood that he will be regarded as deviant or undesirable in other respects.

Treating a person as though he were generally rather than specifically deviant produces a self-fulfilling prophecy. It sets in motion several mechanisms which conspire to shape the person in the image people have of him. In the first place, one tends to be cut off, after being identified as deviant, from participation in more conventional groups, even though the specific consequences of the particular deviant activity might never of themselves have caused the isolation had there not also been the public knowledge and reaction to it. . . .Though the effects of opiate drugs may not impair one's working ability, to be known as an addict will probably lead to losing one's job. In such cases, the individual finds it difficult to conform to other rules which he had no intention or desire to break, and perforce finds himself deviant in these areas as well. The drug addict finds himself forced into other illegitimate kinds of activity, such as robbery and theft, by the refusal of respectable employers to have him around.

When the deviant is caught, he is treated in accordance with the popular diagnosis of why he is that way, and the treatment itself may likewise produce increasing deviance. The drug addict, popularly considered to be a weakwilled individual who cannot forego the indecent pleasures afforded him by opiates, is treated repressively. He is forbidden to use drugs. Since he cannot get drugs legally, he must get them illegally. This forces the market underground and pushes the price of drugs up far beyond the current legitimate market price into a bracket that few can afford on an ordinary salary. Hence the treatment of the addict's deviance places him in a position where it will probably be necessary to resort to deceit and crime in order to support his habit. The behavior is a consequence of the public reaction to the deviance rather than a consequence of the inherent qualities of the deviant act.

10

PHENOMENOLOGICAL THEORY

JACK KATZ

The study of crime has been preoccupied with a search for background forces, usually defects in the offenders' psychological backgrounds or social environments, to the neglect of the positive, often wonderful attractions within the lived experience of criminality. The novelty of this [theory] is its focus on the seductive qualities of crimes: those aspects in the foreground of criminality that make its various forms sensible, even sensually compelling, ways of being.

The social science literature contains only scattered evidence of what it means, feels, sounds, tastes, or looks like to commit a particular crime. Readers of research on homicide and assault do not hear the slaps and curses, see the pushes and shoves, or feel the humiliation and rage that may build toward the attack, sometimes persisting after the victim's death. How adolescents manage to make the shoplifting or vandalism of cheap and commonplace things a thrilling experience has not been intriguing to many students of delinquency. Researchers of adolescent gangs have never grasped why their subjects so often stubbornly refuse to accept the outsider's insistence that they wear the "gang" label. The description of "cold-blooded, senseless murders" has been left to writers outside the social sciences. Neither academic methods nor academic theories seem to be able to grasp why such killers may have been courteous to their victims just moments before the killing, why they often wait until they have dominated victims in sealed-off environments before coldly executing them, or how it makes sense to them to kill when only petty cash is at stake. Sociological and psychological studies of robbery rarely focus on the *distinctive* attractions of robbery, even though

research has now clearly documented that alternative forms of criminality are available and familiar to many career robbers. In sum, only rarely have sociologists taken up the challenge of explaining the qualities of deviant experience.

The statistical and correlational findings of positivist criminology provide the following irritations to inquiry: (1) whatever the validity of the hereditary, psychological, and social-ecological conditions of crime, many of those in the supposedly causal categories do not commit the crime at issue, (2) many who do commit the crime do not fit the causal categories, and (3) and what is most provocative, many who do fit the background categories and later commit the predicted crime go for long stretches without committing the crimes to which theory directs them. Why are people who were not determined to commit a crime one moment determined to do so the next?

I propose that empirical research turn the direction of inquiry around to focus initially on the foreground, rather than the background of crime. Let us for once make it our first priority to understand the qualities of experience that distinguish different forms of criminality . . .

A sense of being determined by the environment, of being pushed away from one line of action and pulled toward another, is natural to everyday, routine human experience. We are always moving away from and toward different objects of consciousness, taking account of this and ignoring that, and moving in one direction or the other between the extremes of involvement and boredom. In this constant movement of consciousness, we do not perceive that we are controlling the movement. Instead, to one degree or another, we are always being seduced and repelled by the world. "This *is* fascinating (interesting, beautiful, sexy, dull, ugly, disgusting)," we know (without having to say), as if the thing itself possessed the designated quality independent of us and somehow controlled our understanding of it. Indeed, the very nature of mundane being is emotional; attention is feeling, and consciousness is sensual.

Only rarely do we actually experience ourselves as subjects directing our conduct. How often, when you speak, do you actually sense that you are choosing the words you utter? As the words come out, they reveal the thought behind them even to the speaker whose lips gave them shape. Similarly, we talk, walk, and write in a sense of natural competence governed by moods of determinism. We rest our subjectivity on rhythmic sensibilities, feelings for directions, and visions of unfolding patterns, allowing esthetics to guide us. Self-reflexive postures, in which one creates a distance between the self and the world and pointedly directs the self into the world, occur typically in an exceptional mood of recognizing a malapropism, after a misstep, or at the slip of the pen. With a slight shock, we recognize that it was not the things in themselves but our perspective that temporarily gave things outside of us the power to seduce or repel.

Among the forms of crime, the range of sensual dynamics runs from enticements that may draw a person into shoplifting to furies that can compel him to murder. If, as social researchers, we are to be able to explain more variation in criminality than background correlations allow, it appears that we must respect these sensual dynamics and honor them as authentic. . . .

Approaching criminality from the inside, social research takes as its subject the morally exceptional conduct that the persons themselves regard as criminally sanctionable in official eyes. Since there is an enormous variety of criminal phenomena, how can one demarcate and set up for explanation a limited number of subjectively homogeneous offenses? I suggest that a seemingly simple question be asked persistently in de-

tailed application to the facts of criminal experience: What are people trying to do when they commit a crime?

The resulting topics will not necessarily follow official crime categories. Crimes, as defined in statutes, surveys of citizens, and police records, take definitional shape from the interests of victims and from practical problems of detection and punishment, not necessarily from the experience of those committing the crimes. But if one begins with rough conventional or folk categories, such as hot-blooded murder, gang violence, adolescent property crime, commercial robbery, and "senseless" and "cold-blooded" murder, and refines the concepts to fit homogeneous forms of experience, one can arrive at a significant range of criminal projects: committing righteous slaughter, mobilizing the spirit of a street elite, constructing sneaky thrills, persisting in the practice of stickup as a hardman, and embodying primordial evil.

By way of explanation, I will propose for each type of crime a different set of individually necessary and jointly sufficient conditions, each set containing (1) a path of action—distinctive practical requirements for successfully committing the crime, (2) a line of interpretation—unique ways of understanding how one is and will be seen by others, and (3) an emotional process—seductions and compulsions that have special dynamics. Raising the spirit of criminality requires practical attention to a mode of executing action, symbolic creativity in defining the situation, and esthetic finesse in recognizing and elaborating on the sensual possibilities.

Central to all these experiences in deviance is a member of the family of moral emotions: humiliation, righteousness, arrogance, ridicule, cynicism, defilement, and vengeance. In each, the attraction that proves to be most fundamentally compelling is that of overcoming a personal challenge to moral—not to material—existence. For the impassioned killer, the challenge is to escape a situation that has come to seem otherwise inexorably humiliating. Unable to sense how he or she can move with self-respect from the current situation, now, to any mundane-time relationship that might be reengaged, then, the would-be killer leaps at the possibility of embodying, through the practice of "righteous" slaughter, some eternal, universal form of the Good.

For many adolescents, shoplifting and vandalism offer the attractions of a thrilling melodrama about the self as seen from within and from without. Quite apart from what is taken, they may regard "getting away with it" as a thrilling demonstration of personal competence, especially if it is accomplished under the eyes of adults.

Specifically "bad" forms of criminality are essentially addressed to a moral challenge experienced in a spatial metaphor. Whether by intimidating others' efforts to take him into their worlds ("Who you lookin' at?") or by treating artificial geographic boundaries as sacred and defending local "turf" with relentless "heart," "badasses" and *barrio* warriors celebrate an indifference to modern society's expectation that a person should demonstrate a sensibility to reshape himself as he moves from here to there.

To make a habit of doing stickups, I will argue, one must become a "hardman." It is only smart to avoid injuring victims unnecessarily, but if one becomes too calculating about the application of violence, the inherent uncertainties of face-to-face interaction in robberies will be emotionally forbidding. Beneath the surface, there may be, to paraphrase Nietzsche, a ball of snakes in chaotic struggle. But the stickup man denies any uncertainty and any possibility of change with a personal style that ubiquitously negates social pressures toward a malleable self.

Perhaps the ultimate criminal project is mounted by men who culminate a social life organized around the symbolism of deviance with a cold-blooded, "senseless" murder. Mimicking the ways of primordial gods as they kill, they proudly appear to the world as astonishingly evil. Through a killing only superficially justified by the context of robbery, they emerge from a dizzying alternation between affiliation with the great symbolic powers of deviant identity and a nagging dis-ease that conformity means cowardice.

Overall, my objective is to demonstrate that a theory of moral self-transcendence can make comprehensible the minutia of experiential details in the phenomenal foreground, as well as explain the general conditions that are most commonly found in the social backgrounds of these forms of criminality.

11

CONFLICT THEORY

RICHARD QUINNEY

A theory that helps us begin to examine the legal order critically is the one I call the *social reality of crime*. Applying this theory, we think of crime as it is affected by the dynamics that mold the society's social, economic, and political structure. First, we recognize how criminal law fits into capitalist society. The legal order gives reality to the crime problem in the United States. Everything that makes up crime's social reality, including the application of criminal law, the behavior patterns of those who are defined as criminal, and the construction of an ideology of crime, is related to the established legal order. The social reality of crime is constructed on conflict in our society. The theory of the social reality of crime is formulated as follows.

I.   THE OFFICIAL DEFINITION OF CRIME: *Crime as a legal definition of human conduct is created by agents of the dominant class in a politically organized society.*

The essential starting point is a definition of crime that itself is based on the legal definition. Crime, as *officially* determined, is a *definition* of behavior that is conferred on some people by those in power. Agents of the law (such as legislators, police, prosecutors, and judges) are responsible for formulating and administering criminal law. Upon *formulation* and *application* of these definitions of crime, persons and behaviors become criminal.

Crime, according to this first proposition, is not inherent in behavior, but is a judgment made by some about the actions and characteristics of others. This proposition allows us to focus on the formulation and administration of the criminal law as it applies to the behaviors that become defined as criminal. Crime is seen as a result of the class-dynamic process that culminates in defining persons and behaviors as criminal. It follows, then, that the greater the number of definitions of crime that are formulated and applied, the greater the amount of crime.

II.   FORMULATING DEFINITIONS OF CRIME: *Definitions of crime are composed of behaviors that conflict with the interests of the dominant class.*

Definitions of crime are formulated according to the interests of those who have the power to translate their interests into public policy. Those definitions are ultimately incorporated into the criminal law. Furthermore, definitions of crime in a society change as the interests of the dominant class change. In other words, those who are able to have their interests represented in public policy regulate the formulation of definitions of crime.

The powerful interests are reflected not only in the definitions of crime and the kinds of penal sanctions attached to them, but also in the *legal policies* on handling those defined as criminals. Procedural rules are created for enforcing and administering the criminal law. Policies are also established on programs for treating and punishing the criminally defined and programs for controlling and preventing crime. From the initial definitions of crime to the subsequent procedures, correctional and penal programs, and policies for controlling and preventing crime, those who have the power regulate the behavior of those without power.

III. APPLYING DEFINITIONS OF CRIME: *Definitions of crime are applied by the class that has the power to shape the enforcement and administration of criminal law.*

The dominant interests intervene in all the stages at which definitions of crime are created. Because class interests cannot be effectively protected merely by formulating criminal law, the law must be enforced and administered. The interests of the powerful, therefore, also operate where the definitions of crime reach the *application* stage. As Vold has argued, crime is "political behavior and the criminal becomes in fact a member of a 'minority group' without sufficient public support to dominate the control of the police power of the state." Those whose interests conflict with the ones represented in the law must either change their behavior or possibly find it defined as criminal.

The probability that definitions of crime will be applied varies according to how much the behaviors of the powerless conflict with the interests of those in power. Law enforcement efforts and judicial activity are likely to increase when the interests of the dominant class are threatened. Fluctuations and variations in applying definitions of crime reflect shifts in class relations.

Obviously, the criminal law is not applied directly by those in power; its enforcement and administration are delegated to authorized *legal agents*. Because the groups responsible for creating the definitions of crime are physically separated from the groups that have the authority to enforce and administer law, local conditions determine how the definitions will be applied. In particular, communities vary in their expectations of law enforcement and the administration of justice. The application of definitions is also influenced by the visibility of offenses in a community and by the public's norms about reporting possible violations. And especially important in enforcing and administering the criminal law are the legal agents' occupational organization and ideology.

The probability that these definitions will be applied depends on the actions of the legal agents who have the authority to enforce and administer the law. A definition of crime is applied depending on their evaluation. Turk has argued that during "criminalization," a criminal label may be affixed to people because of real or fancied attributes: "Indeed, a person is evaluated, either favorably or unfavorably, not because he *does* something, or even because he is something, but because others react to their perceptions of him as offensive or inoffensive." Evaluation by the definers is affected by the way in which the suspect handles the situation, but ultimately the legal agents' evaluations and subsequent decisions are the crucial factors in determining the criminality of human acts. As legal agents evaluate more behaviors and persons as worthy of being defined as crimes, the probability that definitions of crime will be applied grows.

IV. HOW BEHAVIOR PATTERNS DEVELOP IN RELATION TO DEFINITIONS OF CRIME: *Behavior patterns are structured in relation to definitions of crime, and within this context people engage in actions that have relative probabilities of being defined as criminal.*

Although behavior varies, all behaviors are similar in that they represent patterns within the society. All persons—whether they create definitions of crime or are the objects of these definitions—act in reference to *normative systems* learned in relative social and cultural settings. Because it is not the quality of the behavior but the action taken against the behavior that gives it the character of criminality, that which is defined as criminal is relative to the behavior patterns of the class that formulates and applies definitions. Consequently, people whose behavior patterns are not represented when the definitions of crime are formulated and applied are more likely to act in ways that will be defined as criminal than those who formulate and apply the definitions.

Once behavior patterns become established with some regularity within the segments of society, individuals have a framework for creating *personal action patterns*. These continually develop for each person as he moves from one experience to another. Specific action patterns give behavior an individual substance in relation to the definitions of crime.

People construct their own patterns of action in participating with others. It follows, then, that the probability that persons will develop action patterns with a high potential for being defined as criminal depends on (1) structured opportunities, (2) learning experiences, (3) interpersonal associations and identifications, and (4) self-conceptions. Throughout the experiences, each person creates a conception of self as a human social being. Thus prepared, he behaves according to the anticipated consequences of his actions.

In the experiences shared by the definers of crime and the criminally defined, personal-action patterns develop among the latter because they are so defined. After they have had continued experience in being defined as criminal, they learn to manipulate the application of criminal definitions.

Furthermore, those who have been defined as criminal begin to conceive of themselves as criminal. As they adjust to the definitions imposed upon them, they learn to play the criminal role. As a result of others' reactions, therefore, people may develop personal action patterns that increase the likelihood of their being defined as criminal in the future. That is, increased experience with definitions of crime increases the probability of their developing actions that may be subsequently defined as criminal.

Thus, both the definers of crime and the criminally defined are involved in reciprocal action patterns. The personal-action patterns of both the definers and the defined are shaped by their common, continued, and related experiences. The fate of each is bound to that of the other.

V. CONSTRUCTING AN IDEOLOGY OF CRIME: *An ideology of crime is constructed and diffused by the dominant class to secure its hegemony.*

This ideology is created in the kinds of ideas people are exposed to, the manner in which they select information to fit the world they are shaping, and their way of interpreting this information. People behave in reference to the *social meanings* they attach to their experiences.

Among the conceptions that develop in a society are those relating to what people regard as crime. The concept of crime must of course be accompanied by ideas about the nature of crime. Images develop about the relevance of crime, the offender's characteristics, the appropriate reaction to crime, and the relation of crime to the social order. These conceptions are constructed by communication, and, in fact, an ideology of crime depends on the portrayal of crime in all personal and mass communication. This ideology is thus diffused throughout the society.

One of the most concrete ways by which an ideology of crime is formed and transmitted is the official investigation of crime. The President's Commission on Law Enforcement and Administration of Justice is the best contemporary example of the state's role in shaping an ideology of crime. Not only are we as citizens more aware of crime today because of the President's Commission, but official policy on crime has been established in a crime bill, the Omnibus Crime Control and Safe Streets Act of 1968. The crime bill, itself a reaction to the growing fears of class conflict in American society, creates an image of a severe crime problem and, in so doing, threatens to negate some of our basic constitutional guarantees in the name of controlling crime.

Consequently, the conceptions that are most critical in actually formulating and applying the definitions of crime are those held by the dominant class. These conceptions are certain to be incorporated into the social reality of crime. The more the government acts in reference to crime, the more probable it is that definitions of crime will be created and that behavior patterns will develop in opposition to those definitions. The formulation of definitions of crime, their application, and the development of behavior patterns in relation to the definitions, are thus joined in full circle by the construction of an ideological hegemony toward crime.

VI. CONSTRUCTING THE SOCIAL REALITY OF CRIME: *The social reality of crime is constructed by the formulation and application of definitions of crime, the development of behavior patterns in relation to these definitions, and the construction of an ideology of crime.*

The first five propositions are collected here into a final composition proposition. The theory of the social reality of crime, accordingly, postulates creating a series of phenomena that increase the probability of crime. The result, holistically, is the social reality of crime.

Because the first proposition of the theory is a definition and the sixth is a composite, the body of the theory consists of the four middle propositions. These form a model of crime's social reality. The model, as diagrammed, relates the proposition units into a theoretical system (Figure 11.1). Each unit is related to the others. The theory is thus a system of interacting developmental propositions. The phenomena denoted in the propositions and their relationships culminate in what is regarded as the amount and character of crime at any time—that is, in the social reality of crime.

The theory of the social reality of crime as I have formulated it is inspired by a change that is occurring in our view of the world. This change, pervading all levels of society, pertains to the world that we all construct and from which, at the same time, we pretend to separate ourselves in our human experiences. For the study of crime, a revision in thought has directed attention to the criminal process: All relevant phenomena contribute to creating definitions of crime, development of behaviors by those involved in criminal-defining situations, and constructing an ideology of crime. The result is the social reality of crime that is constantly being constructed in society.

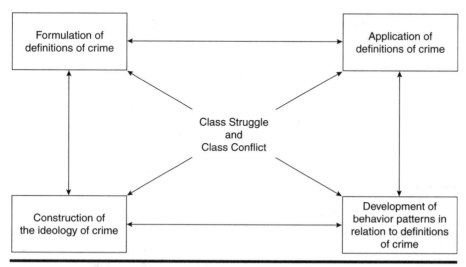

FIGURE 11.1   The Social Reality of Crime

12

FEMINIST THEORY

JODY MILLER

The study of deviance, like other academic disciplines, is largely a male tradition: Male researchers have mostly focused on male "deviants" and built theories to account for largely male activities. Females have typically been ignored. Since the 1970s, however, feminism has emerged to challenge male bias within the sociology of deviance, while providing alternative perspectives on deviant behavior. Here I will discuss some of the major components of feminist perspectives on deviance. First is a critique of male bias in deviance studies. Second is a focus on female "deviants." Third is an insight into sanctions against deviantized females.* Fourth is a sensitivity to how race, class, and masculinity are implicated in the relationship between gender and deviance.

CRITIQUE OF MALE BIAS

According to feminist theorists, the sociology of deviance has developed to a large extent with an exclusive focus on males; when females enter the discussion it has often only been as sexual objects. The exclusion of women from deviance research has inevitably led to the unwarranted assumption that there is virtually no female participation in deviance, outside of sexual deviance. Thus, for example, researchers have long defined gang involvement as a male phenomenon, even though there has always been evidence of female participation even within the earliest works in the field (see Campbell, 1984). Relatively recent studies have further shown that females are any-

where from 10 to 26 percent of gang members (Campbell, 1984; Chesney-Lind, 1993; Klein, 1971; Miller, 1975), that female gang participation may be increasing (Fagan, 1990; Spergel and Curry, 1993; Taylor, 1993), and that in some urban areas, almost one-fifth of girls report gang affiliations (Bjerregaard and Smith, 1992; Winfree et al., 1992).

When women do appear in deviance research, they are often relegated to the periphery of attention, with men given center stage. Thus, in studying female participation in gangs, researchers often have sought information from male gang members rather than from the female participants themselves (Campbell, 1990). Not surprisingly, much of the picture of female deviance reflects male bias instead of reality. Short and Strodbeck (1965), for example, suggested that girls are more likely to become involved in gangs if they are physically unattractive and have not developed adequate peer relations. Rice (1963) also described girls in the gang he studied as "exceptionally unattractive" and "dim." These and other researchers routinely describe gang girls as camp followers whose function is to serve the sexual needs of male gang members.

---

*I will use the phrase "deviantized females" rather than "female deviants" throughout this essay to highlight the labeling process by which individuals come to be seen and defined as deviant actors, a process that is not simply a result of individuals' actions, but a political process shaped by gender, race, and class relations in society, among others. For a similar discussion of the reasoning behind the use of the concept "criminalized women" rather than "female offenders," see Bertrand et al., 1992, and Daly, 1992.

Other marginal, subordinate roles that girls are said to play in gangs include carrying weapons, infiltrating rival gangs, instigating or provoking conflict between male gangs, and engaging in cat fights—fighting one another for the attention of male gang members (for a fuller discussion, see Campbell, 1984, 1990). However, recent studies of female gang members by female researchers have shown that female gang participation is more complex than traditional research indicates, both in the roles that girls play in gangs and in the meanings of their gangs for the girls involved (Campbell, 1984; Moore, 1991).

It is true that some studies have focused specifically on female deviance, but such studies have been rare. Moreover, they reflect the traditional male bias about female participants in deviance. Such studies typically, relate women's deviance to their sexuality, thereby unjustifiably ignoring the social, cultural, and political contexts of their actions (Smart, 1976). Consider Otto Pollack's (1950) highly influential work, *The Criminality of Women.* Pollack theorized that women are just as likely as men to engage in deviant activities but are naturally more able to conceal their deviant acts. Pollack attributed this unusual ability to frequent practice of deceit and manipulation among women, such as hiding their menstrual cycles each month and faking sexual pleasure. Such a condemnatory view of female deviance contrasts sharply with the feminist view.

WOMEN AS DEVIANT ACTORS

Traditional male-biased theory often resorts to biological determinism in explaining women's deviance in terms of their stereotyped sexuality, whereas feminist theorists turn to larger social forces for explanations of female deviance, just as larger social forces have always been used to explain male deviance. In addition, feminists examine gender inequality in society as one of the explanations of female deviance. For illustrations of this point, let us take a look at two feminist analyses, one dealing with female delinquency and the other focusing on female prostitution.

Patterns of Female Delinquency

For the most part, self-report studies indicate that girls participate in various forms of delinquency just as their male counterparts do (Campbell, 1981; Canter, 1982; Chesney-Lind and Shelden, 1992; Empey and Stafford, 1991; Figueira-McDonough, 1985; Sarri, 1983). In a national probability sample of 1,725 juveniles, for example, Canter (1982) found that "males and females generally engage in the same delinquent behaviors." However, arrest rates for girls are higher than for boys for sex-related offenses (such as prostitution) and running away, reflecting a sexual bias within the system in the handling of delinquent girls (Chesney-Lind and Shelden, 1992; Steffensmeier and Steffensmeier, 1980). By contrast, there is evidence of greater male involvement in serious property and violent offenses, as well as in repeated offenses (Canter, 1982). As Canter reports,

> There are significant [gender] differences in the following property items: damaging other property, stealing a motor vehicle, stealing more than $50, evading payment, breaking into a building, and joyriding. . . . Boys are also more involved in the violent crimes of gang fighting, strong-arming students and others, aggravated assault, hitting students, and sexual assault. More generally, the findings point to the substantially greater involvement of males in serious crimes. (1982:337)

The more serious, more violent, and more profitable nature of male delinquency may be attributed to the socialization of boys that encourages them to be more aggressive and masculine than females, in addition to males' greater access to public space resulting from male privilege in patriarchal society.

Even the apparent increase in female deviance over the past two decades reflects the continuing influence of patriarchal society, which places greater limitations on female behavior. For one thing, it is true that female delinquency has increased significantly, but male delinquency has as well. As Canter (1982) reports from studying representative samples of American adolescents, there are "parallel increases" in delinquent involvement among males and females that maintain traditional gender differences in delinquency. It is also true that crime by female adults has increased noticeably, but much of this increase has involved relatively unprofitable, minor crimes such as shoplifting, welfare fraud, and writing bad checks (Steffensmeier, 1981). By all accounts, females are not catching up with males in the commission of traditionally male patterns of violent, masculine, or serious crimes (Chesney-Lind and Shelden, 1992; Empey and Stafford, 1991; Steffensmeier, 1981).

Female Prostitution

For many feminists, female prostitution provides perhaps the clearest example of the oppression of women in patriarchal society. The fact that prostitution flourishes in our culture derives a great deal of support from the sexist view of women as sexual objects that can be sold as commodities for male consumption (Schur, 1988). In addition, economic inequality between women and men leaves prostitution as one of the few viable economic alternatives for some women to earn a decent living. Female prostitutes are subjected to considerable abuse within the male-dominated society.

First, they are stigmatized and punished for breaking the "feminine" norms that prohibit women from having multiple sexual partners. This may explain why Silbert and Pines (1982) found many streetwalkers to be victims of violence: 70 percent of their study sample had been raped by clients, 65 percent reported being beaten by clients, 66 percent were physically abused by pimps, and 73 percent "had experienced rapes totally unrelated to their work as prostitutes."

Second, they suffer abuses in the hands of police officers. These abuses appear in various forms. Most commonly, the women are entrapped by plainclothes police officers or illegally arrested (Carmen and Moody, 1985; James, 1978; Pheterson, 1989). Some police officers use the threat of arrest to get sexual favors from the women (Delecoste and Alexander, 1988). Some officers even arrest the women after having sex with them (James, 1978; Pheterson, 1989).

Many police officers also deny prostitutes their legal rights when victimized by refusing to take any action against the women's attackers (James et al., 1975; Miller, 1993; Pheterson, 1989). Consider the case of Karen, a street prostitute in Fresno, California. A man held an ice pick to her head, raped her repeatedly for three hours, and walked her to a park where he said he was going to kill her. On the way, a friend spotted her and got her away from the man. Later that day, she saw the man again and several friends cornered him, took away his ice pick, and held him for the police. When the police arrived, they let the man go and instead threatened to arrest Karen and her friend for assault, insisting that Karen as a prostitute could not be raped (Delacoste and Alexander, 1988).

THE TREATMENT OF "DEVIANTIZED" WOMEN

According to feminists, many women are labeled "deviants" simply because they do not conform to the traditional expectation that they be feminine, quiet, passive, and the like. As Schur (1984) has noted, women are informally labeled deviants through the use of labels such as "aggressive," "bitchy," "hysterical," "fat," "homely," "masculine," and "promiscuous." These labels "may not put the presumed 'offender' in jail, but they do typically damage her reputation, induce shame, and lower her 'life chances' " (1984). Although numerous women face deviant labeling in everyday life, those who commit crimes suffer greater consequences as "double deviants," for not only violating societal norms against criminal conduct, but also for deviating from normative gender expectations for women (1984).

Not surprisingly, feminists often find that the justice system deals more harshly with female than male offenders, even when their offenses are less serious than those committed by men. This is particularly true in regard to female delinquents who are sexually active or running away from home. Girls have until recently been routinely arrested for committing these status offenses, but boys were left alone for doing exactly the same thing (Chesney-Lind, 1977). Ironically, the harsher treatment of female delinquents has long been carried out under the guise of judicial paternalism, with the judge acting as the girls' father, trying to "protect" them from "sexual temptation" or "immoral activities."

Today girls are less often sent to detention centers for committing status offenses, but the hidden incarceration of delinquent girls through "voluntary" commitments has increased significantly. Private juvenile placement facilities, where youths, without their consent, can be "voluntarily" committed by their parents, are now estimated to have a clientele that is 60 percent female (Chesney-Lind, 1988; Chesney-Lind and Shelden, 1992). Moreover, delinquent girls continue to receive harsher treatment than delinquent boys in some institutional settings such as training schools, detention centers, and treatment facilities (Chesney-Lind, 1978; Chesney-Lind and Shelden, 1992; Gelsthorpe, 1989; Mann, 1979, 1984). One national study, for example, reported that girls are generally allowed less frequent home visits and fewer visiting hours (Mann, 1984).

NEW TRENDS IN FEMINIST STUDIES OF DEVIANCE

The development of feminist deviance studies has been advanced in recent years by an integrated focus on race, class, and gender, rather than an exclusive focus on gender inequality. In discussing female participation in deviance, feminists have sometimes tended to bring a white, middle-class focus to their studies, instead of being attuned to the complexities caused by the intersection with gender of various social positions, such as class and race. Feminists also tend to focus on female deviance, thereby ignoring male deviance. There are, therefore, some feminists who have recently tried to bring the issues of race and class, as well as male deviance, into feminist perspectives.

Race, Class, and Gender

Many of the feminist assumptions about deviantized females and their treatment by the justice system fail to take into account the impact of race or class. Women of color and poor women are effectively ignored. As African American feminist theorist Bell Hooks observed, "When black people are talked about, the focus tends to be on black *men,* and when women are talked about, the focus tends to be on *white* women" (Laub and McDermott, 1985). As a consequence, feminist theories may apply to white, middle-class women but not to women of color or poor women. To take a close look at this problem, let us reexamine the treatment of girls within the juvenile justice system.

Feminists have often used the theory of judicial paternalism to explain the treatment of girls within the juvenile justice system. According to this theory, female offenders are treated more severely than male offenders at all levels of the juvenile justice system, not only because they have violated normative gender expectations, but, more important, because the judge assumes the role of father by trying to protect girls from "sexual temptations and immoralities" (Chesney-Lind, 1977, 1978, 1988; Chesney-Lind and Shelden, 1992). The notion of "paternalism," however, may be relevant to white middle-class women but not to poor women or women of color. This is because protection is often extended to middle-class and white women, to the exclusion of poor and working-class women and women of color. Not surprisingly, poor females and females of color are treated more punitively in the justice system.

In her analysis of police-suspect encounters, Visher (1983), for example, found that "young, black, or hostile women receive no preferential treatment, whereas older, white women who are calm and deferential toward the police are granted leniency." In her study of court decisions, Sarri (1983) also found greater discrimination against women of color: African American females are most likely to be placed on probation, whereas white females have the best chance of escaping sanctions. Other studies have suggested that African American and Latina delinquent girls are increasingly more likely to be sent to overcrowded detention centers and training schools, and their white counterparts are more often referred to their parents or to private treatment agencies (Sarri, 1983; Krisberg et al., 1988).

Masculinity and Deviance

The emergence of feminist deviance studies began with a focus on women. Because women have consistently been ignored and stereotyped within the traditions of the field, the primary focus for quite some time was on building a knowledge base for understanding deviantized females and the sanctions and treatment they face. Increasingly, feminist research is expanding to examine gender not only as it applies to females, but also as it concerns males (Messerschmidt, 1993; Whyte and Dekeseredy, 1992).

Feminists have found a strong link between masculinity and male deviance. Masculinity is a major source of deviance among men and boys, and shapes male participation in crime. According to Messerschmidt (1993), participation in criminal activities is one social resource available for men with which to construct and accomplish masculinity. For example, males who are tough, aggressive, or in possession of other stereotypical masculine traits are more likely to engage in certain violent forms of deviance. This explains why date rape is so common in college fraternities and athletic settings (Martin and Hummer, 1993; Warshaw, 1988).

Race and class shape both masculine ideals and the resources available for constructing masculinity, and these shape the types of deviance males engage in (Messerschmidt, 1993). Participation in street gangs provides an example of how some young men of color from impoverished communities construct a masculine identity. The street gang is especially alluring as a source of masculinity for some young men because they have limited resources available for constructing a masculine identity that fits with the dominant ideal, especially the sense of being able to provide for and take care of their families. The street gang can help them create a masculine identity by offering status, reputation, and self-respect.

Gay-bashing provides another illuminating example of how male deviance involves men seeking masculinity in deviant activities. Gay-bashing is most common among working-class white males. According to Harry (1992), gay-bashing is used to validate the participants' sense of their masculinity, because attacking gay men makes them feel more manly. Gay-bashing can serve this function of validating manliness because patriarchal society associates masculinity with being a male heterosexual. Attacking gay men reaffirms these young mens' sense of themselves as heterosexual.

CONCLUSION

The goal of this essay has been to introduce the reader to feminist perspectives on deviance. It is an expansive and ever-growing field, delving into a wide range of topics, from the critique of mainstream research and theory, to the examination of female participation in deviance, violence against women and children, the treatment of deviantized females, and the ways in which gender is central in any attempt to understand male involvement in deviant behavior. Of course, this brief discussion can in no way cover the full range of topics that feminist perspectives shed light on. Already wide-ranging, the perspective continues to grow rapidly, acquiring many new theories about the relationship between gender and deviance.

REFERENCES

Bertrand, Marie Andrée, Kathleen Daly, and Dorie Klein, eds. 1992. *Proceedings of the International Conference on Women, Law, and Social Control.* Vancouver: International Centre for Criminal Law Reform and Criminal Justice Policy.

Bjerregaard, Beth, and Carolyn Smith. 1992. "Patterns of Male and Female Gang Membership." Working Paper No. 13. Albany: Rochester Youth Development Study.

Campbell, Anne. 1990. "Female Participation in Gangs," pp. 163–182 in *Gangs In America, edited by C. Ronald Huff. Newbury Park: Sage.*

Campbell, Anne. 1984. *The Girls in the Gang.* New York: Basil Blackwell.

Campbell, Anne. 1981. *Girl Delinquents.* New York: St. Martins Press.

Canter, Rachelle J. 1982. "Sex Differences in Self-Report Delinquency." *Criminology* 20: 373–393.

Carmen, Arlene and Howard Moody. 1985. *Working Women: The Subterranean World of Street Prostitution.* New York: Harper & Row.

Chesney-Lind, Meda. 1993. "Girls, Gangs and Violence: Anatomy of a Backlash." *Humanity & Society* 17(3): 321–344.

Chesney-Lind, Meda. 1988. "Girls and Status Offenses: Is Juvenile Justice Still Sexist?" *Criminal Justice Abstracts* 20(1): 144–65.

Chesney-Lind, Meda. 1978. "Young Women in the Arms of the Law," pp. 171–196 in *Women, Crime and the Criminal Justice System,* edited by Lee H. Bowker. Lexington, MA: Lexington Books.

Chesney-Lind, Meda. 1977. "Judicial Paternalism and the Female Status Offender: Training Women to Know Their Place." *Crime & Delinquency* 23:121–130.

Chesney-Lind, Meda, and Randall G. Shelden. 1992. *Girls, Delinquency and Juvenile Justice.* Pacific Grove, CA: Brooks/Cole.

Delacoste, Frédérique and Priscilla Alexander, eds. 1988. *Sex Work.* London: Virago Press.

Daly, Kathleen. 1992. "Women's Pathways to Felony Court: Feminist Theories of Lawbreaking and Problems of Representation." *Review of Law and Women's Studies* 2(1): 11–52.

Empey, LaMar T., and Mark C. Stafford. 1991. *American Delinquency: Its Meaning & Construction.* Belmont, CA: Wadsworth.

Fagan, Jeffrey. 1990. "Social Processes of Delinquency and Drug Use Among Urban Gangs," pp. 183–219 in *Gangs in America,* edited by C. Ronald Huff. Newbury Park: Sage.

Figueira-McDonough, Josephine. 1985. "Are Girls Different? Gender Discrepancies Between Delinquent Behavior and Control." *Child Welfare* 64: 273–289.

Gelsthorpe, Loraine. 1989. *Sexism and the Female Offender. An Organizational Analysis.* Aldershot, England: Gower.

Harry, Joseph. 1992. "Conceptualizing Anti-Gay Violence." *Journal of Interpersonal Violence* 5(3): 350–358.

James, Jennifer, Jean Withers, Marilyn Haft, Sara Theiss, and Mary Owen. 1975, *The Politics of Prostitution.* New York: Social Research Associates.

James, Jennifer. 1978. "The Prostitute as Victim," pp. 175–202 in *The Victimization of Women,* edited by Jane Roberts Chapman and Margaret Gates. Beverly Hills: Sage.

Klein, Malcolm W. 1971. *Street Gangs and Street Workers.* Englewood Cliffs, NJ: Prentice-Hall.

Krisberg, Barry, Ira M. Schwartz, Paul Utsky, and James Austin. 1988. "The Watershed of Juvenile Justice Reform." *Crime & Delinquency* 32: 5–38.

Laub, John H., and M. Joan McDermott. 1985. "An Analysis of Serious Crime by Young Black Women." *Criminology* 23: 81–98.

Mann, Coramae Richey, 1984. *Female Crime and Delinquency.* University: University of Alabama Press.

Mann, Coramae Richey. 1979. "Making Jail the Hard Way: Law and the Female Offender." *Corrections Today* 41: 35–41.

Martin, Patricia Yancey, and Robert A. Hummer. 1993. "Fraternities and Rape on Campus," pp. 392–401 in *Feminist Frontiers III,* edited by Laurel Richardson and Verta Taylor. New York: McGraw-Hill.

Messerschmidt, James W. 1993. *Masculinities and Crime: Critique and Reconceptualization of Theory.* Lantham, MD: Rowman & Littlefield.

Miller, Jody. 1993. " 'Your Life is on the Line Every Night You're on the Streets': Victimization and Resistance among Street Prostitutes." *Humanity & Society* 17(4): 422–446.

Miller, Walter B. 1975. *Violence by Youth Gangs and Youth Groups as a Crime Problem in Major American Cities.* Washington, DC: U.S. Government Printing Office.

Moore, Joan. 1991. *Going Down to the Barrio: Homeboys and Homegirls in Change.* Philadelphia: Temple University Press.

Pheterson, Gail. 1989. *A Vindication of the Rights of Whores.* Seattle: Seal Press.

Pollack, Otto. 1950. *The Criminality of Women.* Philadelphia: University of Pennsylvania Press.

Rice, Robert. 1963. "A Reporter at Large: The Persian Queens." *The New Yorker* 39: 135ff.

Sarri, Rosemary. 1983. "Gender Issues in Juvenile Justice." *Crime & Delinquency* 29: 381–397.

Schur, Edwin M. 1988. *The Americanization of Sex.* Philadelphia: Temple University Press.

Schur, Edwin M. 1984. *Labeling Women Deviant: Gender, Stigma and Social Control.* New York: Random House.

Short, James F., and Fred L. Strodbeck. 1965. *Group Process and Gang Delinquency.* Chicago: University of Chicago Press.

Silbert, Mimi H., and Ayala M. Pines. 1982. "Victimization of Street Prostitutes." *Victimology* 7:122–133.

Smart, Carol. 1976, *Women, Crime and Criminology: A Feminist Critique.* London: Routledge & Kegan Paul.

Spergel, Irving A., and C. David Curry. 1993. "The National Youth Gang Survey: A Research and Development Process," pp. 359–400 in *The Gang Intervention Handbook,* edited by Arnold R. Goldstein and C. Ronald Huff. Champaign, IL: Research Press.

Steffensmeier, Darrell J. 1981. "Crime and the Contemporary Woman: An Analysis of Changing Levels of Property Crimes, 1960–1975," pp. 39–59 in *Women and Crime in America,* edited by Lee Bowker. New York: Macmillan.

Steffensmeier, Darrell J., and Renee Hoffman Steffensmeier. 1980. "Trends in Female Delinquency: An Examination of Arrest, Juvenile Court, Self-Report, and Field Data." *Criminology* 18: 62-85.

Taylor, Carl. 1993. *Girls, Gangs, Women and Drugs.* East Lansing: Michigan State University Press.

Visher, Christy A. 1983. "Gender, Police Arrest Decisions, and Notions of Chivalry." *Criminology* 21: 5–28.

Warshaw, Robin. 1988. *I Never Called It Rape.* New York: Harper and Row.

Whyte, Donald, and Walter DeKeseredy. 1992. "The Homosocial Factor in Male Violence and Masculine Subjectivity." *Men's Studies Review* 9(1):27–31.

Winfree, L. Thomas Jr., Kathy Fuller, Teresa Vilo, and G. Mays. 1992. "The Definition and Measurement of 'Gang Status': Policy Implications for Juvenile Justice." *Juvenile & Family Court Journal* 43: pp. 29–37.

POSTMODERN THEORY

DAVID O. FRIEDRICHS
JESSICA FRIEDRICHS

WHAT IS POSTMODERNISM?

The premise for this article is simple: The student of deviance should have at least some understanding of the meaning of postmodernism and its relevance for the study of deviance. The term *postmodern,* although invoked much earlier, only began to be widely used in the final two decades of the twentieth century (B. Smart, 1993). By century's end a vast literature, cutting across many different disciplines, was adopting a postmodernist perspective in one way or another. A subject search on postmodernism in *Books in Print,* for example, comes up with 839 titles. Accordingly, most if not all readers of this article will have encountered the term postmodern in some form. But to what does this term refer? It does not have a single, fixed meaning. In fact, it has been used in so many ways some scholars have called for its abandonment. Nevertheless, whether we like it or not, postmodernism is surely here to stay, so it makes sense to try to identify some of the principal ways in which the term is invoked. The "post" in postmodernism reflects both the notion of "after" (or a time following the modern) and "against" (in opposition to modern sensibilities and assumptions). The term has also been used in more specific ways. First, postmodernism deals with postmodernity. This term is used to refer to a period in human history that follows the period designated as the modern. The modern era is generally thought to have begun to emerge in the fifteenth or sixteenth century, with the beginnings of capitalism and colonialism and eventually the effects of the En-lightenment period and the Industrial Revolution (Lembcke, 1993). This "modern" way of life accelerated and expanded until about the 1960s. Since then the Western world has undergone a basic transformation and thus entered the postmodern era. In this new era we have seen the collapse of the Euro-American colonial system around the globe, which has left the world without a dominating center and has produced widespread repudiation of the Euro-American value system (Lemert, 1997). In this postmodern era, globalization has also emerged, with various societies powerfully influencing each other and threatening the native culture and way of life in those societies (Benhabib, 1999).

Our postmodern society seems to be changing rapidly in many different ways. Our communities are fragmented, complex, and increasingly "virtual," for example, linking people via the Internet. We are in the heart of a global community, simultaneously transmitting and receiving materials and ideas to and from other societies. Conventional forms of bureaucracy are giving way to more flexible, adaptable "adhocracies," with constant changing of institutional arrangements and roles to fit specific situations. The computer has rapidly been replacing industrial machinery as the core of our technological existence. Mass communication is evolving with almost lightning speed into a form of interactive communication, as exemplified by cable television, the Internet, and home shopping. Growing "fluidity" is taking place in residence and career, with people moving back and forth between different residential locations and in and out of different careers. All these changes inevitably affect deviant behavior and societal responses to deviance. For example, in the increasingly market-dependent economy of our postmodern era, the poor are less and less needed as cheap labor and are turning in growing numbers to criminal behavior (Bauman, 1997). It is therefore important to understand postmodernity in order to understand deviance.

Postmodernism also reflects postmodern thought. This term has been applied to a collection of ideas from a number of late-twentieth-century French philosophers. These ideas include: there is no absolute truth nor stable, fixed meaning in the world; differences of ideas should be celebrated; any attempt to explain the whole of human social existence should be rejected; local action as opposed to collective or centralized action should be used to transform society; and positivism, such as the scientific method, should be repudiated as a means of understanding the human condition (Rosenau, 1992).

Postmodern thought challenges conventional conceptions of the individual or the human subject as a real, independent entity and instead espouses the idea that the individual is knowable only through the language used in interaction with others. Skeptical postmodernists offer a largely negative, hopeless view of the social world with an emphasis on oppression, fragmentation, meaninglessness, vanishing morals, and social chaos (Rosenau, 1992). Some skeptical postmodernists even question the relevance of the social sciences for interpreting the social world, insofar as there is no objective truth about that world. Other postmodern thinkers—affirmative postmodernists—provide a more hopeful, optimistic view, being open to positive action as long as such action is tentative, nondogmatic, and nonideological (Rosenau, 1992). For both strains of postmodernists, language plays a central role in the human experience of reality, so the key to understanding human behavior and events is through an analysis of language.

In sum, college students, including those who study deviance, can benefit from knowing about postmodernism. This does not necessarily mean that students need to undertake a rigorous, intense, and comprehensive study of postmodernism (Friedrichs, 1999). It is, however, an aspect of being culturally literate today to have at least some familiarity with postmodernism. It offers an alternative to conventional perspectives on social reality, including deviance. In the next section we will see how a postmodern criminology has emerged and how it can be applied to the understanding of deviant behavior.

POSTMODERN CRIMINOLOGY AND THE STUDY OF DEVIANCE

Long after postmodern thought had become a significant presence in many areas of intellectual inquiry, it remained little represented in the fields of criminology and deviance (Schwartz and Friedrichs, 1994; Russell, 1997; South, 1997). In the final decade of the twentieth century this began to change. Leading promoters of a postmodern criminology among U.S. criminologists have looked to French postmodern thinkers for inspiration and for perspectives and concepts applicable to crime and deviance. However, their work also reflects the influence of other theoretical perspectives within sociology and criminology, such as conflict, critical, or radical criminology (Arrigo, 1999a; MacLean and Milovanovic, 1997). On the other hand, postmodern criminology does not emphasize the larger issues of social conflict and power. It focuses more on the day-to-day struggles and problems of the human subject, which distinguishes postmodern criminology from conflict or radical theory (Arrigo and Bernard, 1997). In short, postmodern criminology has some parallels and intersecting concerns with other theoretical perspectives but also has its own unique dimensions.

Postmodern criminologists generally have a keen appreciation for human diversity and differences, including those shown by deviants. Compared with other perspectives, postmodernism pays more attention to the outlook and voice of deviants as the marginalized or outsiders of society. Postmodern criminologists challenge the basic claim of the dominant social "discourse" and seek to "replace" that discourse with the voices of those who are different or powerless, such as criminals and deviants. Revolutionaries who fight for a better society, for example, are considered deviants in the dominant discourse, but they can be considered merely different or powerless according to one postmodernist view. The power of language to do harm, such as a school authority who labels hyperactive pupils as troublemakers who need to be punished, is one core thesis of postmodern criminology. Such a criminology focuses on how language is used not only to control but also to destroy those who are different. Language is central, then, to the process of transforming some members of society into deviants, and postmodern criminology is committed to revealing more fully how this transformation works.

At least two postmodern concepts are arguably useful in the understanding of deviance. First the notion of *intertextuality* refers to the idea that there is a complex and infinite set of interwoven relationships, comparable to an endless conversation among different individuals without any prospect of achieving an agreement or final resolution (Bauman, 1990; Graham, 1992). This suggests the need to explore the complex interrelationships among many different forms of deviant behavior—for example, how domestic violence, mental illness, sexual perversion, substance abuse, and corporate crime interact with each other. The concept of intertextuality further suggests that we must attend to the complex ways in which convention and deviation define each other, with ambiguous lines of demarcation between them, so that what is conventional (say, worshiping God) may sometimes be considered deviant (if one is seen as part of a religious cult). The postmodern approach challenges the popular tendency to draw a clear-cut and fixed boundary between convention and deviance.

Another postmodern concept, *hyperreality,* is also useful for understanding deviance (Baudrillard, 1994). We live in a world in which we are inundated with simulations of the real, as can be seen in the pervasive presence of television in our lives. A postmodern, hyperreal world is also perceivable through contemporary advertising, gangsta rap, karaoke, and cybersex (Appignanesi and Garratt, 1995). When we can no longer tell the difference between simulation and reality, when simulation becomes autonomous, and when we are no longer able to verify simulation against reality, then we have entered the realm of the hyperreal. Of course, not everybody is sucked totally into the hyperreal (King, 1998). However, most people cannot escape hyperreality, which inevitably influences many lives to one degree or another. Because the concept of hyperreality usefully captures the erosion of the boundaries between the real and the unreal, it may broaden our understanding of deviance. Consider Las Vegas, America's fastest growing city in the 1990s. In Las Vegas, simulation displaces a reality rooted in the conditions of a natural environment and authentic human experiences. It reeks with the celebration of money as an end in itself (rather than simply as a means), of a world divided into winners and losers, of materialistic excess, of conflict, of sexism and exploitation, of artificiality and inauthenticity, of "amusing ourselves to death," and of excitement over the clatter of slot machine payouts. All these reflect the simulated, unreal quality of human life. Not surprisingly, all manner of deviance, as conventionally defined, thrives in the Las Vegas environment: rates of homicide and suicide in Las Vegas are exceptionally high; sex workers of all types are ubiquitous; substance abuse is a runaway problem; and, of course, compulsive and self-destructive gamblers are all over (Friedrichs, 1996).

On the other hand, hyperreality can also convey a false impression of a totally conventional world with no apparent deviance. Consider Disneyland/Disney World. In sharp contrast with Las Vegas, Disney promotes a wholesome, fun-filled, thoroughly controlled environment where nothing bad or painful happens, where there is no crime or substance abuse or even sex in any recognizable form (Ritzer, 1999). For that matter, some isolated college campuses and college towns have also turned into "unreal" environments vis-à-vis the outside world, but they are not simply similar to Disney World in creating a simulated, unreal, and idealized conventional milieu. They are also similar to Las Vegas in having drinking problems, wild parties, and other deviant activities on campus.

The link between simulation and reality that may lead to deviance also appears in some contemporary films. In *The Truman Show* and *Pleasantville,* idealized simulated communities replace real-life experiences, which raises complicated questions about such experiences. The films *Natural Born Killers* and *Pulp Fiction* explore the complex, interactive relationship between contemporary violence as reality and the media representations of violence. On television, the cult show *Twin Peaks* exemplified the hyperreal phenomena, whereas many television shows create unreal worlds either pervaded with deviance like Las Vegas or reflecting a totally sanitized environment à la Disney World. Video games, too, draw young people into a simulated world in a powerful way. The simulated violence of television and video games tends to lead to violence among troubled teenagers, as has been suggested by a series of school shootings in recent years. This has caused some to ask: Are such teenagers unable to discriminate between the virtual reality of violence and the actual violence in real life that truly hurts people?

Postmodern criminology has quite a number of distinctive strains, but we here consider several that are especially applicable to understanding deviance. One is deconstructionist criminology (Pfohl, 1990; 1994). This suggests that, like crime, deviance can best be understood through deconstruction, or destruction of a conventional way of looking at deviance that is biased by an author's attempt to control powerless deviants. More positively, better understanding can come from analyzing deviance from the perspective of deviants, from knowing what deviants think and feel about themselves and others. A deconstructionist criminology breaks with conventional forms of communicating knowledge by using a multimedia approach with a complex mixture of images and observations.

A second type of postmodern criminology is constitutive criminology (Henry and Milovanovic,

1996). It regards crime (and by extension, deviance) as involving the power to do harm. It further proposes that social beings, such as members of groups and society, as well as social entities, such as groups, institutions, and society, work together in some complex ways to produce crime and deviance. According to constitutive criminology, then, individuals do not by themselves engage in criminal and deviant activities but coproduce what is defined as deviance in the course of their interaction with others. New forms of dialogue, then, can foster greater justice.

A third type of postmodern criminology is cultural criminology (Ferrell and Sanders, 1995). It exposes "crime as culture," emphasizing how crime or deviance can be understood in a cultural context, as a particular way of life, in relation to such forms of behavior as involvement with illicit drugs, posting graffiti, and skinhead violence. The media is viewed as often distorting images of crime and deviance and accordingly promoting inappropriate responses to it. The media generates drug scares and helps foster the image of serial killers as "mythic monsters."

A fourth type of postmodern criminology is postmodern feminist criminology (C. Smart, 1990, 1995). To postmodern feminists, the self does not have a fixed, unchangeable identity but instead varies from one situation to another (Benhabib, 1999; Carrington, 1994). This fluid and changing nature of a woman's self can be applied to deviance: like the woman's self, deviance varies from situation to situation. A postmodern feminist criminology, for example, questions such categories as "wife" and "lesbian"; it suggests more tolerance for ambiguity.

THE CRITIQUE OF POSTMODERNISM

Postmodernist theory has been widely criticized for a variety of reasons. The most common criticism is that the proponents of the theory do not write clearly. As a result, their convoluted, confusing writing often makes the reader unsure of what the postmodernists are talking about. Another criticism is that postmodernists do not have any special training in physics and mathematics and yet some postmodernists try to use quantum mechanics, chaos theory, and other esoteric physical sciences to explain human behavior. Not surprisingly, according to scientists such as Nobel Prize-winning physicist Steven Weinberg (1996), postmodernists get the science wrong and apply scientific concepts incoherently. Most directly relevant to the study of deviance, however, is the criticism that the postmodernist ideas about deviance are not unique or new because they can be found in conflict and symbolic interactionist theories.

Postmodern thought has also been criticized as being inherently conservative and defeatist (Handler, 1992; Taylor-Gooby, 1994). Postmodernism repudiates the assignment of people to categories, but women, minority groups and marginalized deviants (e.g., homosexuals) who are still establishing their "selves" are not necessarily prepared to reject their group identity (Rosenau, 1992). Critics would argue that conditions such as discrimination against homosexuals are best confronted directly, rather than in terms of a postmodernist perspective.

No matter how postmodernism is judged, it does enhance in its own way our understanding of deviance, and reinforces what we already know from other older theories. However, it requires patience to cut through the thick brambles of postmodernist prose to get at what is being said.

THE FUTURE OF POSTMODERNISM

What will the status of postmodernist theory be in the new century? One possible scenario is that postmodernism may be largely discredited, disparaged, forgotten, or written off as a pretentious late-twentieth-century intellectual fad. It could meet the same fate as phrenology (the nineteenth-century pseudoscience that human character could be determined by feeling the bumps on the head), which fell into disrepute in the twentieth century. On the other hand, postmodernism could hypothetically become the dominant form of intellectual discourse, to be hailed as the path-breaking perspective for making sense of the human world, including deviant behavior. The most likely scenario probably falls somewhere between those two extremes. Postmodernist theory will likely evolve, with some of its ideas falling by the wayside and others being refined and becoming more widely accepted. When applied to the study of deviance, postmodernist theory will probably co-exist with other approaches more rooted in traditional and modern thought. But the serious student of deviance should surely be open to the usefulness of some postmodern concepts and metaphors for more fully understanding the production and control of deviant behavior in a rapidly changing world.

APPENDIX: A BRIEF GUIDE TO THE LITERATURE ON POSTMODERNISM

The literature on postmodernist theory is vast, and the original works of the French philosophers who have pioneered this approach are especially difficult. If you are interested in some general guidance on postmodernism and postmodern thought, going beyond what has been provided in this article, you may want to consult works by the following authors, listed in the References section:

Anderson (1995); Appignanesi and Garratt (1995); Crook, Pakulski, and Waters (1992); Dickens and Fontana (1994); Doherty, Graham, and Malek (1992); Grenz (1996); Harvey (1989); Hollinger (1994); Kumar (1995); Rosenau (1992); Sarap (1993); Sim (1999); Barry Smart (1993); and Turner (1990).

ACKNOWLEDGMENTS

The support of a University of Scranton Faculty Research grant is gratefully acknowledged. David Friedrichs would like to thank Martin D. Schwartz, as this article draws significantly from our collaborative work on postmodern criminology. He would also like to note that over the years he has learned much about postmodern criminology from Bruce Arrigo, Stuart Henry, and Dragan Milovanovic, esteemed professional colleagues and friends. Jessica Friedrichs would like to thank Greg Lawless and Matt Fagerberg for helpful discussions. Both David and Jessica Friedrichs thank Jeanne and Bryan Friedrichs for putting up with us while we worked on this article.

REFERENCES

Anderson, Walter Truett, ed. 1995. *The Truth about the Truth: De-Confusing and Re-Constructing the Postmodern World.* New York: Tarcher/Putnam Books.

Appignanesi, Richard, and Chris Garratt. 1995. *Introducing Postmodernism.* New York: Totem Books.

Arrigo, Bruce, ed. 1999. *Social Justice/Criminal Justice: The Maturation of Critical Theory in Law, Crime, and Deviance.* Belmont, CA: ITP/Wadsworth.

Arrigo, Bruce, and Thomas J. Bernard. 1997. "Postmodern Criminology in Relation to Radical and Conflict Criminology." *Critical Criminology: An International Journal* 8:39–60.

Baudrillard, J. 1994. *Simulacra and Simulation.* Ann Arbor: University of Michigan Press.

Bauman, Zygmunt. 1990. "Philosophical Affinities of Postmodern Sociology." *Sociological Review* 38:411–444.

Bauman, Zygmunt. 1997. *Postmodernity and Its Discontents.* New York: New York University Press.

Benhabib, Seyla. 1999. "Sexual Difference and Collective Identities: The New Global Constellation." *Signs: Journal of Women in Culture and Society* 24: 335–361.

Carrington, Kerry. 1994. "Postmodernism and Feminist Criminologies: Disconnecting Discourses?" *International Journal of the Sociology of Law* 22:261–277.

Crook, Stephen, Jan Pakulski, and Malcolm Waters. 1992. *Postmodernization: Change in Advanced Society.* London: Sage.

Dickens, David R., and Andrea Fontana, eds. 1994. *Postmodernism and Social Inquiry.* New York: Guilford Press.

Doherty, Joe, Elspeth Graham, and Mo Malek, eds. 1992. *Postmodernism and the Social Sciences.* New York: St. Martin's.

Ferrell, Jeff, and Clinton R. Sanders, eds. 1995. *Cultural Criminology.* Boston, MA: Northeastern University Press.

Friedrichs, David O. 1996. "Critical Criminology and Progressive Pluralism: Strength in Diversity for These Times." *Critical Criminology: An International Journal* 7:121–128.

Friedrichs, David O. 1999. "Can Students Benefit from an Intensive Engagement with Postmodern Criminology? No." Pp. 159–164 in *Controversial Issues in Criminology,* edited by John R. Fuller and Eric W. Hickey. Boston: Allyn & Bacon.

Graham, Elspeth. 1992. "Postmodernism and Paradox." Pp. 197–211 in *Postmodernism and the Social Sciences,* edited by Joe Doherty, Elspeth Graham and Mo Malek. New York: St. Martin's.

Grenz, S. J. 1996. *A Primer on Postmodernism.* Grand Rapids, MI: Eardmans.

Handler, Joel F. 1992. "Postmodernism, Protest, and the New Social Movements." *Law & Society Review* 26:697–732.

Harvey, David. 1989. *The Condition of Postmodernity.* Cambridge, MA: Blackwell.

Henry, Stuart, and Dragan Milovanovic. 1996. *Constitutive Criminology: Beyond Postmodernism.* London: Sage.

Hollinger, Robert. 1994. *Postmodernism and the Social Sciences.* Thousand Oaks, CA: Sage.

King, Anthony. 1998. "A Critique of Baudrillard's Hyperreality: Towards a Sociology of Postmodernism." *Philosophy & Social Criticism* 6:47–66.

Kumar, Krishan. 1995. *From Post-Industrial to Post-Modern Society: New Theories of the Contemporary World.* Oxford, UK: Blackwell.

Lembcke, Jerry Lee. 1993. "Classical Theory, Postmodernism, and the Sociology Liberal Arts Curriculum." *The American Sociologist* 24:55–68.

Lemert, Charles. 1997. *Postmodernism Is Not What You Think.* Oxford, UK: Blackwell.

MacLean, Brian D., and Dragan Milovanovic. 1997. *Thinking Critically About Crime.* Vancouver, BC: Collective Press.

Pfohl, Stephen C. 1990. "Welcome to the PARASITE CAFE: Postmodernity As a Social Problem." *Social Problems* 37:421–442.

Pfohl, Stephen C. 1994. *Images of Deviance and Social Control,* 2nd ed. New York: McGraw-Hill.

Ritzer, George. 1999. *Enchanting a Disenchanted World: Revolutionizing the Means of Consumption.* Thousand Oaks, CA: Pine Forge Press.

Rosenau, Pauline Marie. 1992. *Post-Modernism and the Social Sciences: Insights, Inroads, and Intrusions.* Princeton, NJ: Princeton University Press.

Russell, Stuart. 1997. "The Failure of Postmodern Criminology." *Critical Criminology: An International Journal* 8:61–90.

Sarap, Madan. 1993. *An Introductory Guide to Post-Structuralism and Post-Modernism,* 2nd ed. Athens: University of Georgia Press.

Schwartz, Martin D., and David O. Friedrichs. 1994. "Postmodern Thought and Criminological Discontent: New Metaphors for Understanding Violence." *Criminology* 32:221–246.

Sim, Stuart, ed. 1999. *Critical Dictionary of Postmodern Thought.* New York: Routledge.

Smart, Barry. 1993. *Postmodernity.* London: Routledge.

Smart, Carol. 1990. "Feminist Approaches to Criminology, or Postmodern Woman Meets Atavistic Man." Pp. 70–84 in *Feminist Perspectives in Criminology,* edited by A. Morris. Buckingham, UK: Open University Press.

Smart, Carol. 1995. *Law, Crime, and Sexuality.* London: Sage.

South, Nigel. 1997. "Late-Modern Criminology: 'Late' as in 'Dead' or 'Modern' as in 'New.' " Pp. 81–102 in *Sociology after Postmodernism,* edited by David Owen. London: Sage.

Taylor-Gooby, Peter. 1994. "Postmodernism and Social Policy: A Great Leap Backwards?" *Journal of Social Policy* 23:385–404.

Turner, Bryan S. 1990. *Theories of Modernity and Postmodernity.* London: Sage.

Weinberg, Steven. 1996. "Sokal's Hoax." *New York Review of Books* August 8 pp. 11–15.

PART FOUR

CRIMINAL DEVIANCE

During the summer before her freshman year in college, Jennifer worked in a bakery, where she met Jack, a coworker. She got pregnant by him and soon they were married, but he turned out to be a heavy drinker who often subjected her to physical violence. Several times, Jennifer moved out, but she returned after Jack showed remorse. Still, the abuse got worse. He would tie her up and vaginally and anally rape her, sometimes burning parts of her body with a lit cigarette. Finally, she bought a gun and killed him after suffering another episode of violence.[1]

There are two broad types of deviance. One is noncriminal deviance, such as binge drinking, cigarette smoking, and cheating at exams. The other is criminal deviance, such as what Jennifer did to her husband and what he did to her, because killing and raping are crimes. Here in Part Four we will read articles about various forms of criminal deviance. One commonly observed fact in the United States is that men are more homicidal than women, presumably because men are concerned about defending their manhood, a problem absent among women. However, are men in other societies as homicidal as U.S. men? Dane Archer and Patricia McDaniel provide the answer in the first article, "Men and Violence: Is the Pattern Universal?" In the second article, "Date Rape on College Campuses," Martin Schwartz discusses the incidence of campus rape, campus reaction to rape, and reasons for sexual violence against college women. In the third reading, "Burglary: The Offender's Perspective," Paul Cromwell enters the experiential world of his subjects to learn how they carry out their crimes. In the fourth selection, "White-Collar Crime," Gilbert Geis deals with the definitional problem of what white-collar crime is, as well as the theories about its nature and causes.

---

1. Walter S. DeKeseredy and Martin D. Schwartz, *Contemporary Criminology* (Belmont, CA: Wadsworth, 1996).

14

MEN AND VIOLENCE: IS THE PATTERN UNIVERSAL?

DANE ARCHER
PATRICIA McDANIEL

Men are more likely than women to commit virtually all types of violent crimes in the United States. This male-female difference is one of the best-known findings in American criminology. On closer inspection, however, this apparently "obvious" finding turns out to be poorly understood. Is the link between gender and violence strictly an American phenomenon, or is the pattern also found in other, very different societies? Also, how well do we understand the *reasons* for the maleness-violence link—does this pattern reflect socialization patterns, cultural factors, or biological differences between the sexes?

Questions about violence have a special urgency in American society. Although violence and aggression are considered important social problems in many societies, the United States leads the industrial world in lethal violence. In any given year, out of every hundred thousand Americans, ten will die from homicide. This homicide rate is 50 times as high as the rate in New Zealand, 30 times as high as the rate in Great Britain, and 10 times as high as the rate in France (Archer and Gartner, 1984). In fact, the American homicide rate is grossly higher than the rate in *any* other industrial nation. This difference is so large that even societies undergoing civil wars—such as the periodic factional strife in Northern Ireland—do not reach the normal, everyday, *average* homicide rate of the United States. Clearly, then, violence constitutes an urgent social agenda for American society.

THEORIES ABOUT GENDER AND VIOLENCE

It is a relatively simple matter to illustrate rival theories about the causes of violence in general, and about gender differences in particular. It is far more difficult to arrive at a conclusive test of which theories are valid. This is because violence, like all complex human behaviors, is undoubtedly determined by a confluence of different factors acting either in concert or contradiction.

Even if researchers were able to establish that a human hormone (e.g., testosterone) was linked to violent behavior, one would still be unable to answer some of the most important questions about *variance* in violence rates. For example, why did the American homicide rate double in the 1960s? Why do Southern states in the U.S. have homicide rates twice as high as the national average and ten times as high as the rates in New England or North Central states? Why is the U.S. homicide rate as much as 50 times higher than the rates found in other industrial nations (Archer and Gartner, 1984).

None of these differences can be explained by a human hormone, which presumably remains constant over time, between North and South, and across international boundaries. Satisfactory explanations about the causes of violence need to be able to account for the extreme variance that characterizes rates of homicide and other violent crimes. Accounting for variations in violence is thus the "acid test" for any theories about the origins of violence and, if strictly applied, it is a test that few theories have been able to pass.

The research literature on violence and aggression is enormous. Any exhaustive review requires a book-length treatment (e.g., Goldstein, 1986), and thus will not be attempted here. Instead, exemplars of different theoretical traditions will be used to contrast the very different perspectives embedded in research on biological, social, and cultural factors that may cause violence and aggression.

Biological theories have provided intriguing but inconclusive findings. For example, Christiansen and Knussman (1987) compared self-ratings of aggressiveness in 117 individuals with actual levels of serum testosterone. The researchers found a positive correlation—that is, individuals with higher self-ratings tended to have higher levels of serum testosterone—but the relationship was not strong. Rada, Laws, and Kellner (1976) compared 52 men imprisoned for rape with a control group of 12 nonviolent prisoners. In general, the two groups did not differ in testosterone levels, but the most violent rapists (those who committed additional, brutal violence during the rape) did have significantly higher testosterone levels.

Other biology-based research has involved animals, using an at best debatable assumption that the complexities of human behavior can be understood by research on creatures that do not use alcohol, shoot firearms, become disgruntled ex-employees, or do any of a thousand other "human" acts that seem to figure prominently in the commission of violent acts. Nonetheless, researchers studying male rats have found that castration at birth reduces the adult aggressiveness of the rats (Connor and Levine, 1969).

Even in animal communities, however, differential parenting may be at least partially responsible for the gender differences one observes in adult creatures. For example, Mitchell and Brandt (1970) studied 16 female rhesus monkeys and their infants. They found that the mothers of males threatened and bit their offspring more than did the mothers of females. Interestingly, the researchers also concluded that the mothers of female monkeys restrained and protected their infants, whereas the mothers of males seemed to prompt greater independence and activity in their offspring.

Unsurprisingly, research on social factors has taken a road quite unlike that traveled by most biological researchers. Nearly a half-century ago, researchers began reporting that parental socialization tended to foster greater levels of aggression in boys (Sears, Maccoby, and Levin, 1957). Parents are more likely to encourage boys to fight back if they are challenged and—at least in American society—this encouragement reflects a widespread parental belief that some aggression is a natural, even desirable aspect of masculinity. The picture is quite different for girls. Parents tend to discourage female aggression, or they simply ignore it. In either case, the net effect is the same: female aggression is simply not reinforced. Research by Bardwick (1971) suggested, though, that although girls were socialized away from using direct physical aggression (the province of boys), they were socialized *toward* other forms of aggression: verbal aggression, subtle interpersonal rejection, manipulation, and so on. Still, it is precisely *physical* aggression that has become urgently problematic. After all, physical aggression—homicide, assault, or rape—wreaks a much greater toll than verbal unpleasantness.

Much of the research sketched thus far reflects American society or, only slightly less narrowly, industrial societies. It is obviously critical to include in our discussion *cultural* factors by asking how aggression and the male-violence link differ across societies. Clearly, there are vast societal differences, including the provocative finding that lethal violence is pandemic in some societies but relatively unknown in others (Archer and Gartner, 1984). Much of the research on cultural differences derives from anthropology. For example, Rohner (1976) coded published ethnographic accounts of children's behavior in 14 traditional societies. He found large intersocietal differences in fostering aggressive behavior among children—for some societies, high levels of aggression were the norm; for others, aggression was relatively unacceptable.

The question of the link between maleness and violence also has cultural implications. It may be that boys and girls are socialized for different adult roles—that is, a sexual division of labor. Perhaps many societies socialize boys for adult roles that require greater levels of aggression, such as hunting or intergroup conflict. This "differential gender socialization" hypothesis has been invoked to account for the higher levels of male aggression observed in many societies studied by anthropologists (Tieger, 1980; Segall, 1983).

The differential socialization hypothesis is not, however, without its detractors. Most notably,

Maccoby and Jacklin (1974) have argued that male–female differences in aggression are too consistent to be the result of the highly variable socialization patterns present in different societies. They further argued that male–female differences are observed as early as age two—too early to be explained by slow, cumulative socialization processes. This argument remains highly controversial, largely because it implies that the maleness-violence link may result, at least in part, from male–female differences that are universal and, perhaps, innate.

NEW CROSS-CULTURAL RESEARCH

Since the late 1980s we have begun a program of work to try to illuminate cultural aspects of violence. The catalyst for this work was the finding by Archer and Gartner (1984) of large, problematic, and intriguing differences in the levels of violence across societies. This new work complements their use of aggregate statistics on national rates of violent crime by examining social psychological differences across cultures. The basic method used in this new research presents individuals aged 16 to 18 with a series of twelve standardized "problem-solving" tasks. Each task involves a different conflict or problem (an unfaithful spouse, a romantic triangle, disciplining a child, a public dispute, a rejected lover, conflict at work, a quarrel between two nations, etc.). The individual is asked to write an imaginative story about how characters in these situations will respond to the conflict.

In each case, potential solutions range from nonviolent to violent. The research focus is on the *quantities and qualities of violence in the stories as a reflection of attitudes toward, expectations about, and justifications for violence as a means of solving conflicts.* The approach can be illustrated here with a conflict situation involving a woman (Mary) and her unfaithful husband (William). The problem is presented to participants, who are asked to write a story about how Mary would respond:

William and Mary have been married for two years. They both leave the house during the day, but they have different schedules. A friend of Mary's tells her that her husband has been seen with another woman while Mary is away from the

house. Mary decides to see for herself. After pretending to leave the house as usual, Mary parks her car half a block from her house. Twenty minutes later, Mary sees a woman drive up to the house. Mary sees William come out of the house. He gives the woman a long, intimate kiss, and they go inside the house together. What will Mary do?

The twelve problem-solving situations used in the study are:

Unfaithful Mary—a husband discovers his wife is unfaithful

Unfaithful William—a wife discovers her husband is unfaithful

Unhappy Ann—a depressed young woman confronts school failure

Demonstrators—an extended protest occurs at a factory

Catherine Leaves James—a young woman tells boyfriend she loves another

James Leaves Catherine—a young man tells girlfriend he loves another

Coworker Dispute—a person steals work and credit from a coworker

Mark the Policeman—a policeman confronts two thieves

Roger and His Son—a father disciplines five-year-old son

Big and Small Nation—two nations are in conflict

Mary Denies Richard—a woman refuses the sexual advances of male friend

John in the Pub—a man is confronted by an aggressive drunk

For each of three of these twelve conflicts (four different test booklets are used, each containing three problems), participants in the study generate an imaginative story about how the characters will respond to or attempt to solve the conflict described. In every case, the problem can be solved by either nonviolent or violent means. For example, the previous problem ("Unfaithful William") generates a wide variety of solutions, including the two examples given here. The first was written by a Swedish high school student; the second by an American high school student.

SWEDISH EXAMPLE (Female Subject, 23095): Mary runs into the house and catches them red-handed.

Mary is very unhappy. She yells at William and runs out of the house. William runs after her. Mary calms down. They decide to talk about it in peace and quiet. The other woman drives home. William and Mary take a seat on the sofa. William explains that he loves the other woman and wants a divorce. Mary says that she agrees. She will not live with a man who does not love her.

AMERICAN EXAMPLE (Male Subject, 01128): Mary feels a sudden surge of anger deep from within her innermost self. Mary vows revenge. She slams the car into gear and races out to the hardware store where she purchases a 33-inch McCulloch chainsaw. When she arrives at the house most of the lights are out, so she creeps around back only to discover that William and his mistress are in back on the deck, dining with fine food over candlelight. Seeing this, Mary pulls the rip cord on her chainsaw. The chainsaw whines to life as William jumps up and screams, "What the fuck is going on?" Mary springs up on to the deck and buries the chainsaw deep into the other woman's head. Her body convulses as blood, flesh, gray matter, and bone fragments fly everywhere. William screams with terror as Mary cuts the motor and pulls the chainsaw out of the shaking lump of flesh which used to be a human. William is cornered as Mary fires up the saw. "Don't Mary, I can explain, please wait, don't!" Mary's eyes are glazed over and she seems possessed. She screams, "Rot in hell you stinking motherfucker!" as she slams the roaring chainsaw into William's mouth.

By themselves, of course, two isolated stories tell us little. The important questions involve the possibility of *general* and *systematic differences* in large samples obtained from different societies. Stories written in response to the twelve problem-solving stimuli were obtained from secondary-level schools in several societies. Data were collected from eleven nations. These nations vary with respect to the prevalence of violence—with some characterized by low rates of violent crime and others by high rates.

Within each of the societies included in the study, efforts were made to identify secondary schools diverse in parental social class, academic ability, and probable educational future. Secondary schools were chosen, rather than colleges and universities, because secondary schools are much more likely to be representative of all levels of class and ability. In most societies, tertiary education is highly stratified, drawing overwhelmingly from the highest financial and ability strata. In each case, a knowledgeable local scholar was asked to identify schools that were likely to draw from populations diverse in social class. In each national sample, approximately 600 to 750 stories were obtained from 200 to 250 individuals—that is, each individual wrote three stories. The general instructions were as follows:

> SOLVING PROBLEMS. In each of the following situations, a specific problem is described. After reading each description, make up a *detailed* story about how the characters in the story will try to solve this problem. In your story, describe *what* the characters do and *what happens* as a result. PLEASE MAKE YOUR STORIES AS *DETAILED* AS POSSIBLE.

A "Violence Code" was created using the method of content analysis to summarize the quantities of violence in the stories from each national sample. Although the Violence Code permits the systematic enumeration of the *quantities* of violence in the stories, qualitative differences between the national samples are also extremely important, because these differences are often subtle and elude simple tabulation. The two methods, quantitative and qualitative, are complementary rather than redundant because they tap very different facets of the data set.*

RESULTS: QUANTITATIVE DATA

A comparison of eleven national data sets reveals large differences in quantities of violence contained in the stories, and these differences are indicated in Table 14.1. These data are for all twelve problem-solving stories combined.

*The methodology is too briefly presented here; a fully detailed description is available from Professor Dane Archer, Department of Sociology, University of California at Santa Cruz, Santa Cruz, CA 95064.

Table 14.1 Levels of Violence in Imaginitive Stories from Different Societies

VIOLENCE TYPE	NATIONAL SAMPLE (n)											MAX/ MIN[a]
	AUST. (596)	CAN. (767)	ENG. (728)	FRAN. (561)	JAP. (693)	KOR. (742)	MEX. (417)	N. ZEAL. (489)	N. IRE. (258)	SWE. (729)	U.S. (1728)	
Any Violence	37.8%	27.2%	28.7%	24.2%	29.0%	18.6%	19.9%	38.7%	32.6%	19.3%	30.2%	2.1
Homicide	12.9	5.7	5.9	4.5	4.0	3.1	4.1	14.4	6.2	5.9	8.7	4.6
2 or more dead	4.8	1.1	0.9	0.6	1.4	0.9	1.7	4.8	2.7	1.2	3.3	8.0
Suicide	4.9	4.6	3.4	3.1	3.8	2.5	1.9	5.9	3.9	2.7	4.3	3.1
Rape	3.5	0.3	2.1	0.4	2.8	3.0	1.7	3.2	3.6	1.0	1.7	12.0
War	4.0	4.1	2.5	5.0	4.6	1.9	1.4	2.9	2.3	3.0	4.6	3.6
Weapon present	16.2	7.2	7.3	8.4	2.6	2.7	4.3	16.4	7.5	6.6	12.4	6.3
Firearms	8.7	5.4	3.0	6.6	1.6	2.0	3.3	7.4	2.0	4.2	7.5	5.4
Handgun	1.0	0.1	0.3	0.0	0.1	0.0	0.7	1.2	0.4	0.1	0.6	12.0
Nuclear weapon	1.5	0.3	0.1	0.0	0.3	0.0	0.0	1.2	0.4	0.3	0.8	15.0

[a]The Max/Min index is the simple ratio of the maximum value to the minimum value. When the minimum is zero, a minimum value of 0.1 is used.

The overall incidence of violence shows low values for the Korean (18.6 percent), Swedish (19.3 percent), and Mexican samples (19.9 percent); much higher values for the New Zealand (38.7 percent), Australian (37.7 percent) and American (29.8 percent) samples. Differences among the eleven samples are even larger for several specific forms of violence, and the eleven-sample range for the incidence of each form of violence is shown by the "maximum/minimum" ratio in Table 14.1. For example, homicide is more than four times as common in the New Zealand and Australian sample as it is in the Korean sample; weapon use varies by a factor of six; and the ratio for rape varies by a factor of twelve.

The eleven national samples can be ranked from high to low in the following order on the frequency of any form of violence in the stories: New Zealand, Australia, Northern Ireland, United States, Japan, England, Canada, France, Mexico, Sweden, and Korea. If one ranks the eleven samples on the other outcomes shown in Table 14.1, most of the rankings correspond closely to this same order. There are a few cases, however, in which a nation's ranking changes by two or more ranks from the overall violence ranking. For example, this is reflected in relatively low incidences of rape in the Canadian stories; relatively high levels of rape in the Korean stories; relatively low levels of war in the New Zealand and Australian stories; and relatively low levels of firearm use in New Zealand. With these exceptions, rankings of the eleven samples generally persist across the different types of violence indicated in Table 14.1.

Gender Differences

Stories written by men are more likely to contain violence than those written by women. This pattern is consistent (1) across all eleven societies and (2) across all twelve problem-solving situations. These gender differences are shown in Table 14.2. A higher proportion of male stories (35 percent overall) contained violence than female stories (22.5 percent) for all eleven national samples. This indicates that male stories were 1.56 times more likely to contain violence than female stories.

The differential for stories containing homicides was even greater; compared with women's stories, men's stories were 2.40 times more likely to contain a homicide. The differential for stories containing firearms was roughly 2.13. It should be noted that these male–female differences were not due to only one or two societies. Consistent male–female differences occurred for 35 of the 36 comparisons (97.2 percent), and for 28 of the 28 significant differences (100 percent) shown in Table 14.2. Independent of the nation studied, therefore, men were more likely than women to write violent stories.

RESULTS: QUALITATIVE DATA

The eleven national data sets vary dramatically not only in the frequency of violent acts—something quantification does a reasonable job of summarizing—but also in the nuances that make the eleven data sets so dissimilar. These nuances defy quantification, and they reflect some of the most important qualities that make the Swedish stories unlike the American stories, and that make both unlike the English stories, and so on. Many themes, patterns, and outcomes found frequently in the stories from one nation were infrequent or even unknown in the stories from another society. Quantification therefore leaves unanswered many subtle questions regarding cultural differences, and a close reading of the stories is required.

With so many stories to choose from, it is possible here only to illustrate some of their diversity and cultural uniqueness. The examples are all from the "Unfaithful William" and "Unfaithful Mary" conflicts. In American stories written in response to these two problems, reactions generally involve anger and rage. When violence takes place in these stories, it is frequently fatal, occurs rapidly in hot blood, and often involves firearms.

Table 14.2 Who Writes More Violent Stories, Men or Women?
(Percentage of Stories with Specified Content)

CONTENT BY GENDER OF AUTHOR	NATIONAL SAMPLE (n)											
	AUST. (596)	CAN. (767)	ENG. (728)	FRAN. (561)	JAP. (693)	KOR. (742)	MEX. (417)	N. ZEAL. (489)	N. IRE. (258)	SWE. (729)	U.S. (1728)	MEAN
Violence												
Male	47.4	31.8	35.9	34.0	32.8	25.5	23.6	43.4	44.6	27.9	37.8	35.0%
Female	28.3	23.0	20.5	18.5	25.0	11.6	18.3	34.3	28.6	15.3	23.9	22.5%
	***	*	***	***	*	***		*	**	***	***	***
Diff.	19.1	8.8	15.4	15.5	7.8	13.9	5.3	9.1	16.0	12.6	13.9	12.5%
Homicides												
Male	20.8	8.1	7.8	9.9	5.6	4.6	6.3	18.1	7.7	10.2	12.4	10.1%
Female	4.8	3.4	3.6	1.4	2.4	1.6	3.0	11.3	5.5	3.7	5.4	4.2%
	***	**	*	***	*	*		*		***	***	***
Firearms												
Male	11.6	6.8	5.9	7.9	3.1	3.5	4.7	9.6	1.5	8.2	9.3	6.6%
Female	5.9	4.4	0.3	5.4	0.0	0.5	2.4	5.8	1.6	2.3	5.8	3.1%
	*	**	***	***	**	**				***	**	***

***p < .001 (at least)

**p < .01

*p < .05

There was a gender difference in the frequency of violence in American stories about "Unfaithful Mary" (36.8 percent of male stories contained violence; 9.6 percent of female stories contained violence) and, to a lesser degree, about "Unfaithful William" (22.6 percent of male stories; 14.6 percent of female stories). The following six examples come from the American sample; the first three were written by men and the next three by women.

American Male, 01049: William waits for three hours. Then finally the man comes out of the house tucking his shirt. By this time, William is outraged, so he starts up his car and drives casually over toward the man and parks right in the way of the man's car. William steps out very casually and reaches under the seat and pulls out his service .45 and chambers a round. In the meantime the man steps out of the car and is walking toward William. William sees him coming toward him so he just points it toward the man and pulls the trigger. The shock of the slug to the man's chest was so great it broke all his ribs and put a hole through him that you could stick a baseball through.

American Male, 03102: First, William hit the dashboard as hard as he could and nearly broke his hand doing so. William starts to get an angry look on his face and all of a sudden, pulls out a .357 Magnum, the most powerful in the world. . . . When William began the third knock, the man answered the door. William asked if Mary was there, the man said that he doesn't know any Mary and so she wasn't there. William then blew off his head and took Mary home and romped on her.

American Male, 12180: William is going to go kick some ass on this dude. First thing William does is wait 15 minutes so he can barge into the house and catch this man fucking the brains out of his wife. Then William fucks this dude up, beats his head in and gets a gun and shoots his ass. Then he goes and fucks Mary's pussy all the rest of the day to make sure she won't want any more dick for a while.

American Female, 12085: William should talk to Mary about what's going on. He should ask her what kind of problem is going on between them, and ask her if there is a problem (and) why she

can't tell him instead of sleeping around with other guys. Maybe they should see a marriage counselor.

American Female, 03106: At the door to the bedroom he stops and listens carefully. His blood is pounding so loudly through his ears that it is hard to hear. Taking a deep breath, he opens the door and stalks into the bedroom. Mary is undressed in bed with a man William has never seen before. She jumps up and the blood rushes from her face. "What the hell is going on here?!" William shouts. Mary breaks down and starts crying as the stranger hurriedly gets dressed and runs out the door. . . . Mary rambles on and on, not seeing what Will is doing, then out of nowhere William pulls out a gun and says, "If I can't have you neither can he!" and with that he proceeds to shoot Mary in the head and, only seconds later, to shoot himself.

American Female, 11012: Mary will probably sit there and think "I want to kill them both." But obviously she won't hurt him. The other woman would yell at him for not getting rid of Mary and the two women will end up fighting and, at the end, the other woman will probably just give up and say something to William like, "You'll be sorry."

The following stories are drawn from some of the other national samples. These examples vary in the quantities and qualities of violence they contain. They also reflect some degree of cultural uniqueness, containing themes and solutions encountered rarely if at all in the American stories.

Swedish Male, 23194: William, a bit sexually frustrated himself, is extremely jealous. He finds however that this jealousy provokes an erotic feeling. His loins tingled as he watched them kiss. His normal uncreative mind starts to burn with new and exciting ideas. He decides to cut loose from his inhibitions and join them. Once in the house, he can hear their laughter in the bathroom. He begins to unbutton his shirt as he approaches the door. As he turns the knob, he can hear the couple gasp. "It's OK," he whispers, "I've come to join you." The couple is noticeably apprehensive but, as he undresses, they begin to relax. Their innovative afternoon has begun.

Swedish Female, 23127: William will go into the house and call for an explanation, (and) ask what the other man is doing in his house with his wife and so on. If it just was a temporary romance, they can be friends again. Or perhaps William will sue for a divorce.

English Female, 28066: After a very hard morning at work, she returns home. William by this time would have gone to work. Mary, in her hunt for evidence, finds an article of the woman's clothing under the bed. Later when her husband returns she confronts him. They don't argue about it but talk sensibly, deciding the best course of action calmly among the two of themselves. Agreeing eventually that she, Mary, is willing to give him a second chance if he gives his word to forget that woman.

English Male, 28015: William sat in his car trying to decide what to do. Should he burst in on them, should he kill them both, should he go to a lawyer or ignore what was happening? William drove up to his house, walked up to the door. He goes inside. Giggles can be heard upstairs. He goes up to the bedroom and Mary and her lover are lying on the bed, semi-naked. Both try to cover themselves up. Mary gets out of bed and tries to calm William down. William pushes her away over a chair. Her lover gets up to defend her and receives a fist in the face. William leaves the house and drives off at high speed to the nearest bar.

Japanese Male, 27007: Mary pretends she knows nothing. Mary then, in the morning and at night, uses these times to see how William feels about her. . . . If William still does not show any affection, Mary will leave the house and will live alone. She will never go out with another man and will never change her feelings about her loving William. In short, she will not revenge, hate or hold a grudge against William loving somebody else. If she ever felt this way, she will condemn her feelings. On the other hand, she will try to understand why men behave in this manner. As a result, they will end in a divorce but she will love William more than she ever had during her marriage.

Japanese Male, 27039: William was angered but, having run to the front of the house, he tiptoed to peek into the window where Mary and the man were. He peeked for a while. Shocked by what Mary and the man were doing, William rushed into the house and shouted at Mary, "Who is this guy?" Mary told excuses but William smacks her. . . .

Australian Female, 26018: Mary is stunned. Slowly she walks to her car and in a daze drives off. Images of the woman kissing her husband flash through her mind. Resolutely, she parks her car near a deserted beach and goes for a walk. She is in a turmoil. Should she confront her husband and demand an explanation or should she bide her time and hope that he tells her himself? Direct confrontation is best, so slowly Mary gets back into her car and drives back home. She is just in time to see the lady leaving. . . . Guilt is written all over William's face as he sees Mary. "It was nothing," he stutters desperately. Mary doesn't say anything. She walks determinedly to their bedroom, pulls out her suitcase and starts packing her belongings. For a moment her eyes fall upon their wedding picture, but she turns away. At the door, she turns one last time to take a look at what was her home and at the man she once loved. Then she turns and purposefully walks toward her car.

Australian Male, 26109: There were noises coming from the bedroom so she moved down the passage slowly and then she peered around the corner. Her friend was right. Then Mary quickly moved to the passage closet and pulled out a handgun. She then returned to the bedroom with the loaded gun, shooting her husband first and then his little playmate. Then turning the gun on herself, after shooting everybody. They had all died instantly.

Korean Female, 25043: Mary investigates their relationship with suspicion. She tries to find out whether their relationship is unclean or just friendship, or has to do with business. If the relationship turns out to be serious (unclean), Mary will suffer deeply from agony and anguish. Since Mary loves William very much, she will leave him for his happiness. Mary's life will be filled with joy thinking that William, the one whom she loves the most, is living a happy life by her sacrifice.

Korean Male, 25149: When William gets home, he asks Mary with a smiling face, "Did you have fun while I was gone?" Mary looks surprised, "How did you know?" If I were William, I'd go to the man and hit him a few times, then give my wife (Mary) to the man.

AN ATTEMPT AT THEORETICAL SYNTHESIS

The large gender differences reported in this paper have implications for three different theoretical explanations that emphasize respectively, biological, social, and cultural factors. Each explanation can be examined in light of the new findings presented here.

First, biology. Given the large and highly consistent gender differences obtained in these data, biological factors cannot in our view be discounted—males wrote more violent stories than women in every national sample and for almost every conflict. In our view, this cross-national finding is apparently consistent with the proposition that gender differences in violence are influenced by biological factors. In the data reported here, the maleness-violence link is both large and apparently universal.

Second, social factors. In all the societies studied here males are consistently more violent than women, but the specific amount of gender difference in violence varies from one society to another. For example, the male–female difference in violence is greater in the United States than in Canada or Japan (see Table 14.2). Similarly, the amount of male violence per se varies from one society to another. Such societal variations can be attributed to socialization, with some societies being more energetic than others in socializing males toward aggression. Socialization does not operate in a social vacuum, though. It seems to work hand in glove with culture.

Third, cultural factors. Gender differences aside, there are dramatic intersocietal differences. Samples from some societies show much higher levels of overall violence and aggression than those from other societies. This finding is consistent with the view that differences in violence are culturally constructed, and that this process varies in significant ways across societies. Standing alone, however, cultural factors appear unable to account for the gender differences found. Given the diversity of cultural practices and variation in child rearing in different societies, universal gender differences in violence and aggression are relatively unexpected.

Again, however, the large aggregate differences across national samples are perfectly consistent with the notion that different cultures produce aggression and violence in different quantities.

CONCLUSION

As noted earlier, there is evident overlap in the predictions implied by social and cultural theories; these perspectives could be referred to collectively as "social-cultural" explanations. Although in this study the surprisingly *consistent* pattern of gender differences (men being more violent than women in all societies) lends apparent credibility to biological explanations, the large *differences* across nations just as strongly support "social-cultural" explanations.

The gender differentials in Table 14.2 are consistent with biological models. Because the pattern of these gender differences is largely the same *within* each of the national data sets, biology—or at least universals that transcend national boundaries—may be implicated. However, the different levels of violence between nations (Table 14.1) are difficult to explain without "social-cultural" models. The enormous differences *between* national data sets in the prevalence of violence in the stories cannot be explained by biological factors and, instead, require consideration of social and cultural variables that vary across these societies. The precise nature of these social and cultural variables remains unknown at this point, but the huge cross-national differences reported here appear to provide a "smoking gun" proving that these variables exist.

The data reported here therefore provide support for the role of very different types of etiological explanations. Both "social-cultural" and biological explanations can claim support in these data because both *differences* (the variation in aggregate violence levels across samples) and *similarities* (the almost universally higher levels of male violence) are found in this cross-cultural comparison.

REFERENCES

Archer, Dane, and Rosemary Gartner. 1984. *Violence and Crime in Cross-National Perspective.* New Haven: Yale University Press.

Bardwick, Judith. 1971. *The Psychology of Women: A Study of Bio-Cultural Conflicts.* New York: Harper and Row.

Christiansen, Kerrin, and Rainer Knussman. 1987. "Androgen Levels and Components of Aggressive Behavior in Man." *Hormones and Behavior* 21:170–180.

Connor, Robert, and Seymour Levine. 1969. "Hormonal Influences on Aggressive Behavior," in *Aggressive Behavior,* edited by S. Garattini and E. B. Sigg. New York: John Wiley and Sons.

Goldstein, Jeffrey. 1986. *Aggression and Crimes of Violence.* New York: Oxford University Press.

Maccoby, Eleanor, and Carol Jacklin. 1974. *The Psychology of Sex Differences.* Stanford: Stanford University Press.

Mitchell, G., and E. M. Brandt. 1970. "Behavioral Differences Related to Experience of Mother and Sex of Infant in the Rhesus Monkey." *Developmental Psychiatry* 3:149.

Rada, Richard, D. Laws, and Robert Kellner. 1976. "Plasma Testosterone Levels in the Rapist." *Psychosomatic Medicine* 38:257–268.

Rohner, Ronald P. 1976. "Sex Differences in Aggression: Phylogenetic and Enculturation Perspectives." *Ethos* 4:57–72.

Sears, Robert, Eleanor Maccoby, and Harry Levin. 1957. *Patterns of Child Rearing.* Stanford: Stanford University Press, 1957.

Segall, Marshall. 1983. "Aggression in Global Perspective," in *Aggression in Global Perspective,* edited by in Arnold P. Goldstein and Marshall Segall. New York: Pergamon Press.

Tieger, Todd. 1980. "On the Biological Bases of Sex Differences in Aggression." *Child Development* 51:943–963.

15

DATE RAPE ON COLLEGE CAMPUSES

MARTIN D. SCHWARTZ

College and university campuses have long been a breeding ground for virtually an epidemic level of felony crime (Hills, 1984; Thorne-Finch, 1992). More than 150 years ago Harvard University was already complaining that students frequently committed "crimes worthy of the penitentiary" (Shenkman, 1989: p. 135). During all these years, because universities have been for the most part reserved for middle- and upper-class white America, campus crime has rarely become a target of the "war on crime." Concern about crime tends to be reserved for the actions of the working class. In recent years, however, a new form of campus crime has created a great deal of publicity. It is date rape, sometimes called "courtship violence."

INCIDENCE

Given their differences in methodology and sampling procedures, various studies on date rape have produced rather different results (Johnson and Ferraro, 1988). The conclusion is nonetheless inescapable that a substantial minority of women on American college campuses have experienced an event that would fit most states' definitions of felony rape or sexual assault (Koss, Gidycz, and Wisniewski, 1987).

Eugene Kanin (1957) first reported more than thirty-five years ago that more than 20 percent of college women had been victims of rape or attempted rape. More recently, Levine and Kanin (1987) found that rates of rape on college campuses have risen substantially since those days. In a survey of sorority members, Rivera and Regoli (1987) found 17 percent of them to

have been victims of completed rape, but in a survey of more than 2,000 students at seven colleges, Makepeace (1986) discovered a significantly higher percentage (23.6 percent) to have been victims of forced sex. In the largest U.S. study, Mary Koss (Koss et al., 1987) distributed a self-report questionnaire to 6,159 students in thirty-two institutions of all types of higher education across the country. More than 15 percent of the women reported that their most serious sexual victimization had been a completed rape, and another 12.1 percent said that their most serious victimization was attempted but uncompleted forced intercourse. In a similar Canadian study of a national random sample of 3,142 women students in forty-four university and community colleges, about 10 percent reported sexual penetration under physical force or threat of force since leaving high school, with about 14 percent reporting attempted sexual intercourse by force or threat (DeKeseredy and Kelly, 1993).

REACTION

How can an injurious act like date rape be so widespread and at the same time be of so little concern to most students, faculty, and administrators? If 15 percent of faculty offices were burglarized, certainly the uproar would be deafening. If 25 percent of college students were the victims of robbery or attempted robbery during their college careers, certainly no campus could avoid massive and high-profile prevention campaigns.

One reason can be found in the enormous feminist literature on rape (e.g., Buchwald, Fletcher, and Roth, 1993; Bart and Moran, 1993). According to these feminist studies, sexism as an ideology encourages men to devalue women and see them as objects to be conquered or used. This sexist ideology, when blended with the catalyst of the American violence ethic, produces at least at the attitudinal level a violent reaction to victims of rape. Thus, we feel that some women, such as flirtatious ones, "deserve" to be the victims of violent sexual crimes, in the same way as annoying people "deserve" to be beaten up or in the same way as countries we don't like "deserve" to be "bombed back into the Stone Age."

This feminist literature for the most part, though, deals with stranger rape. What about the rape of dates or persons well known to the offender? There are few important differences between stranger rapists and date rapists (Belknap, 1989). Most important is that the stranger rapist knows his action to be criminal and makes some effort to hide his identity. The date rapist acts "in public," against someone he knows and may personally like. Thus, the victim of date rape knows the offender. Why, then, are most of the date rapists not brought to the attention of the criminal justice or campus authorities? The answer is that most of the victims do not report the crime. In fact, only 5 percent ever report it to the police, and 42 percent never mention what has happened to anyone at all (Koss et al., 1987).

Why don't the victims report their awful experiences? The answer can be found in the studies by Pitts and Schwartz (1993) and Koss et al. (1987), both of which identify certain women as rape victims in strict accordance with the Ohio Penal Code definition of the crime. Each study discovers that only 27 percent of the women identified as rape victims defined what had happened to themselves as rape. This reluctance to define rape as a crime can be traced to the same popular sexist belief that a woman can be seen as having "deserved" to be the victim of violent sexual attacks and that a woman should bear the brunt of blame for being in the wrong place at the wrong time. However, there may possibly be an additional reason for many women's reluctance to see *date* rape as a crime. That is, many women, including college students, are unsure of the difference between rape and just a horrible thing that happened on a date. This has recently caused some observers to argue that if women are confused about what happened to them, perhaps what happened to them wasn't all that bad after all (Gilbert, 1991; Roiphe, 1993). Whether the women are confused or not may depend on what kind of friends they have. As the data in Pitts and Schwartz' survey suggest, college women whose friends blame them for the sexual assault (being in the wrong place, for example) tend to say that they were not victims of rape, even though the facts of the incident show otherwise. In contrast, those who have supportive friends tend to define their experience as rape.

EXPLANATIONS

We live in a society that can accurately be termed a "rape culture" (Buchwald et al., 1993), where no man can avoid exposure to sexist and pro-rape attitudes. However, some men seem to respond to these pressures more than others. Men who have strong ties to sexist groups seem particularly amenable to peer pressure. This may explain why in a study by Ageton (1983) more than 40 percent of the perpetrators of adolescent sexual assaults had friends who knew about their behavior, and virtually all these friends approved of it or at least expressed indifference. It is true that some researchers such as Heilbrun and Loftus (1986) found that college men who enjoyed sadistic sexual practices were loners and hence unlikely to be swayed by peer pressure. However, most date rapists do not seek sexual sadism at all. They are far more interested in sexual domination, in which the object is "conquest" through obtaining as much sex with as many women as possible. In fact, Kanin (1985) found that date rapists are *not* loners—men who shun campus social activities as well as fail at locating voluntary sexual partners. Instead, date rapists are mostly men who are highly sociable as well as sexually active. Still, their goal is to "score" as often as possible. Moreover, they expect to have so much sex that they often feel frustrated even while engaging in more sex than is typical for the average male student. All this, according to Kanin, can be attributed to a male hypererotic culture, which, through friends' approval and encouragement, pressures members to have sex with as many women as possible, even with the use of force against at least some women.

The hypererotic culture, however, derives much of its support from the widespread sexist attitudes toward women. Otherwise, the hypereroticism of the culture cannot by itself cause woman abuse such as date rape. It is the *sexism* of the culture that contributes to rape. This seems to occur in two ways. First, sexist attitudes fuel the moral ambiguity about whether rape is really a crime or only normal male aggression. Such ambiguity helps neutralize the criminality of rape by making people wonder whether a crime has been committed when a man forces sex on a woman (Fenstermaker, 1989). Such neutralization, which discourages many women from reporting, provides the moral elbow room the date rapist needs to carry out the act. Second, sexist attitudes feed the social support network by convincing its members that sexual aggression against women to the point of using force is acceptable. Thus, men who are part of this sexist network tend to commit date rape.

Such a network seems to characterize many fraternities on college campuses. Not surprisingly, fraternities have been the setting for most known acquaintance gang rapes (Sanday, 1990; Ehrhart and Sandler, 1985). On many campuses with an active Greek life, it is easy to find through the student grapevine at least one recent example of a fraternity in which students engaged in "pulling train" or a "gang bang" (Warshaw, 1988). Given the atmosphere of the sexist moral ambiguity on many campuses, however, not only fraternity men or other college men, but also women students tend to hold the victim re-

sponsible in some way. Even faculty and administrators who have been appointed to oversee fraternities tend to see a lot of "boys will be boys" in forcible rape. They would likely be shocked by the idea that those fraternity goings-on could be a serious crime rather than simply another rules violation. Such an attitude in turn reinforces the sexist moral ambiguity that is conducive to rape on the campus.

There also seems to be something more than moral ambiguity, sexist attitudes toward women, and the hypererotic culture that encourage campus rapes. Researchers have tried to look for that something else. Many feel that sexist men join fraternities, rather than being *made* so by fraternities. However, some researchers have found that fraternities "provide a subculture that insulates their members from the on-going campus climate" (Bohrnstedt, 1969; Wilder et al., 1986). Other researchers have found fraternities to be great promoters of conformity (Hughes and Winston, 1987). Still others have found fraternities causing their members to have less moral concern about social injustice (Miller, 1973). Some researchers observe that the highly masculinist, homophobic views promoted by fraternities, along with their preoccupation with loyalty, a use of alcohol and physical force as weapons for acquiring social domination, and an obsession with competition, aggression, superiority, and dominance, encourage the sexual violation of women (Martin and Hummer, 1993).

Several scholars have recently argued that sexual aggression against women offers an important meaning for some fraternities. Sanday (1990), for example, finds that fraternity rituals provide an important mechanism for eliminating the feelings of dependency on women, which presumably have been inculcated into men through socialization by their mothers. The rituals serve to give fraternity brothers a new readymade self that includes sexist and homophobic attitudes designed for showing virility and dominance over women to cope with feelings of powerlessness. Such attitudes are sometimes effectively proclaimed to the public. Some fraternities would confront Take Back the Night marchers by loudly chanting pro-rape slogans. At Queens University in Ontario, for example, an anti-rape march with the slogan "No Means No" was countered with large banners reading "No Means Now" and "No Means Kick Her in the Teeth" (Thorne-Finch, 1992). Unfortunately, on some campuses the fraternities that, under the advice of their national office, support Take Back the Night marches most strongly are often rumored in the sorority grapevine to have the most actively sexually coercive members.

CONCLUSION

Many scholars talk mainly about athletic teams and fraternities as the organizations that promote attitudes that foster sexual assaults on women, and it is true that some teams and some fraternities do seem to be the locations of an extraordinary amount of problems. Yet others do not. Perhaps the critics are also correct in suggesting that sexually coercive men join with similar men to get approval for their views, picking out the fraternities and sports teams where they would best fit in. If these groups actively promote moral ambiguity toward rape with men already predisposed toward that view, it is easy to see how problems arise.

Further, there are many men who are sexually predatory who are not members of fraternities or athletic teams. An analysis that is limited to these areas is very incomplete. Sexist values as discussed here, friends supportive of taking advantage of women, and attitudes blaming the victim for her own victimization, are all spread throughout society.

REFERENCES

Ageton, Suzanne. 1983. *Sexual Assaults among Adolescents.* Lexington, MA: Lexington Books.

Bart, Pauline B., and Eileen Geil Moran, eds. 1993. *Violence against Women: The Bloody Footprints.* Newbury Park, CA: Sage.

Belknap, Joanne. 1989. "The Sexual Victimization of Unmarried Women by Nonrelative Acquaintances," pp. 205–218 in *Violence in Dating Relationships: Emerging Social Issues,* edited by Maureen A. Pirog-Good and Jan E. Stets. New York: Praeger.

Bohrnstedt, George W. 1969. "Conservatism, Authoritarianism and Religiosity of Fraternity Pledges." *Journal of College Student Personnel* 10:36–43.

Buchwald, Emilie, Patricia Fletcher, and Martha Roth, eds. 1993. *Transforming a Rape Culture.* Minneapolis: Milkweed Editions.

DeKeseredy, Walter S., and Katharine Kelly. 1993. "The Incidence and Prevalence of Woman Abuse in Canadian University and College Dating Relationships." *Canadian Journal of Sociology* 18(2):137–159.

Ehrhart, Julie K., and Bernice R. Sandler. 1985. *Campus Gang Rape: Party Games.* Washington, DC: Project on the Status and Education of Women, Association of American Colleges.

Fenstermaker, Sarah. 1989. "Acquaintance Rape on Campus: Responsibility and Attributions of Crime," pp. 257–273 in *Violence in Dating Relationships: Emerging Social Issues,* edited by Maureen A. Pirog-Good and Jan E. Stets. New York: Praeger.

Gilbert, Neil. 1991. "The Phantom Epidemic of Sexual Assault." *The Public Interest* 103:54–65.

Heilbrun, Alfred B., Jr., and Maria P. Loftus. 1986. "The Role of Sadism and Peer Pressure in the Sexual Aggression of Male College Students." *Journal of Sex Research* 22(3):320–332.

Hills, Stuart. 1984. "Crime and Deviance on a College Campus: The Privilege of Class," pp. 60–69 in *Humanistic Perspectives on Crime and Justice,* edited by Martin D. Schwartz and David O. Friedrichs. Hebron, CT. Practitioner Press.

Hughes, Michael J., and Roger B. Winston, Jr. 1987. "Effects of Fraternity Membership on Interpersonal Values." *Journal of College Student Personnel* 28(5):405–411.

Johnson, John M., and Kathleen J. Ferraro. 1988. "Courtship Violence: Survey vs. Empathic Understandings of Abusive Conduct," pp. 175–186 in *Studies in Symbolic Interaction,* Vol. 9, edited by Norman Denzin. Greenwich, CT. JAI Press.

Kanin, Eugene J. 1957. "Male Aggression in Dating-Courtship Relations." *American Journal of Sociology* 63:197–204.

Kanin, Eugene J. 1985. "Date Rapists: Differential Sexual Socialization and Relative Deprivation." *Archives of Sexual Behavior* 14(3):219–231.

Koss, Mary P., Christine A. Gidycz, and Nadine Wisniewski. 1987. "The Scope of Rape: Incidence and Prevalence of Sexual Aggression and Victimization in a National Sample of Higher Education Students." *Journal of Counseling and Clinical Psychology* 55(2):162–170.

Levine, Edward M., and Eugene J. Kanin. 1987. "Sexual Violence among Dates and Acquaintances: Trends and Their Implications for Marriage and Family." *Journal of Family Violence* 2(1):55–65.

Makepeace, James M. 1986. "Gender Differences in Courtship Violence Victimization." *Family Relations* 35(3):383–388.

Martin, Patricia Yancey, and Robert A. Hummer. 1993. "Fraternities and Rape on Campus," pp. 114–131 in *Violence Against Women: The Bloody Footprints,* edited by Pauline B. Bart and Eileen Geil Moran. Newbury Park, CA: Sage.

Miller, Leonard D. 1973. "Distinctive Characteristics of Fraternity Members." *Journal of College Student Personnel* 14(3):126–129.

Pitts, Victoria L., and Martin Schwartz. 1993. "Promoting Self-Blame in Hidden Rape Cases." *Humanity & Society* 17(4):383–398.

Rivera, George F., Jr., and Robert M. Regoli. 1987. "Sexual Victimization Experiences of Sorority Women." *Sociology and Social Research* 72(1):39–42.

Roiphe, Katie. 1993. *The Morning After.* New York: Little, Brown.

Sanday, Peggy Reeves. 1990. *Fraternity Gang Rape.* New York: New York University Press.

Shenkman, Richard. 1989. *Legends, Lies and Cherished Myths of American History.* New York: Harper & Row.

Thorne-Finch, Ron. 1992. *Ending the Silence: The Origins and Treatment of Male Violence against Women.* Toronto: University of Toronto Press.

Warshaw, Robin. 1988. *I Never Called It Rape.* New York: Perennial Library.

Wilder, David H., Arlyne E. Hoyt, Beth Shuster Surbeck, Janet C. Wilder, and Patricia Imperatrice Carney. 1986. "Greek Affiliation and Attitude Change in College Students." *Journal of College Student Personnel* 27:510–519.

16

BURGLARY:
THE OFFENDER'S PERSPECTIVE

PAUL CROMWELL

*Burglary is easy, man. I've done about 500 [burglaries] and only been
convicted one time.*
—Billy, a juvenile burglar

Why am I a burglar? It's easy money. . . . Beats working!
—Robert, a 20-year-old burglar

These burglars are essentially correct in their appraisal of the benefits and risks associated with burglary. Burglary constitutes one of the most prevalent predatory crimes, with an estimated 5.1 million burglary offenses committed in 1990, resulting in monetary losses estimated to be more than $3.4 billion annually. Yet only about one-half of all burglaries are even reported to the police (Bureau of Justice Statistics, 1991). More alarming still, U.S. Department of Justice statistics reveal that less than 15 percent of all reported burglaries are cleared by arrest. Consequently, burglary has been the subject of a great deal of research in the hope that understanding will lead to the development of effective prevention measures and ultimately to reduction in the incidence of burglary (Lynch, 1990).

THEORETICAL PERSPECTIVE

Here I will report findings from a study of burglars and burglary as seen through the perspective of the offenders themselves. The study addresses several issues critical to the understanding of burglary and

to the consequent development of burglary prevention and control strategies. Among these are: (1) How do residential burglars choose targets? and (2) What determines a burglar's perception of a particular site as a vulnerable target?

Such issues are based on the theory that the commission of a crime is primarily a product of opportunity. Thus, how burglars choose targets and make other relevant decisions has much to do with the opportunity for carrying out burglary. In fact, several researchers have concluded that the majority of burglaries result from exploitation of opportunity rather than careful, rational planning (Scarr, 1973; Rengert and Wasilchick, 1985, 1989; Cromwell, Olson, and Avary, 1991). The assumptions are that offenders develop a sensitivity to the opportunities in everyday life for illicit gain and that burglars see criminal opportunity in situations where others might not. This "alert opportunism" (Shover, 1971) allows them to rapidly recognize and take advantage of potential criminal opportunities. Their unique perspective toward the world results from learning experiences that have sensitized them to events ignored by most. Just as an architect looking at a house notes its functional, technological, and aesthetic qualities, burglars perceive it in terms of its vulnerability to break-in and potential for gain. They do not simply see an open window, but the chance for covert entry and a "fast buck." These perceptual processes are almost automatic and are as much a part of the tools of the burglar as a pry bar or a window jimmy.

METHOD

The Sample

Thirty *active* burglars in an urban area of 250,000 population in a southwestern state were recruited as research subjects (hereinafter referred to as informants) using a snowball sampling procedure. They were promised complete anonymity and a "referral fee" of $50 for each active burglar referred by them and accepted for the study. They were also paid a stipend of $50 for each interview session. The initial three informants were introduced to the researchers by police burglary detectives who had been asked to recommend "burglars who would be candid and cooperate with the study."

The final sample consisted of 27 men and 3 women, of whom 10 were White, 9 Hispanic, and 11 African American. The mean age of these informants was 25 years with the range 16 to 43.

Procedure

The procedure consisted of extensive interviews and "ride alongs," during which informants were asked to reconstruct burglaries they had previously committed and to evaluate sites burglarized by other informants in the study. During these sessions, previously burglarized residences were visited, evaluated, and rated on their attractiveness as burglary targets. Informants were also asked to select sites in the same neighborhood that they considered too risky as targets and to explain why they were less vulnerable than those previously burglarized. At each site informants were asked to rate the "hypothetical" vulnerability of the site to burglary on a scale of 0 to 10. A rating of "0" meant "Under

the circumstances that are present now, I would not burglarize this residence." A rating of "10" meant "This is a very attractive and vulnerable target and I would definitely take steps to burglarize it right now." Informants were told that a rating of "5" was an "average" score. At the conclusion of the study, informants had participated in as many as nine sessions and had evaluated up to thirty previously burglarized and high-risk sites. Four hundred sixty previously burglarized and high-risk sites were evaluated. Each session was tape recorded and verbatim transcripts were made.

FINDINGS

Motivation

Almost every informant used some of his or her proceeds from burglary to buy food or clothing and to pay for shelter, transportation, and other licit needs. However, the greatest percentage of proceeds went toward the purchase of drugs and alcohol and for the activity the burglars loosely labeled "partying." In fact, most informants stressed their need for money to fulfill these needs as the *primary* motivation for their burglaries. Only one informant reported a primary need for money to purchase something other than alcohol or drugs or for partying.

Second in importance was the need for money to maintain a "fast, expensive life." Keeping up appearances was stressed by many as a critical concern. One young burglar reported:

> The ladies, they like a dude that's got good clothes. You gotta look good and you gotta have bread. Me, I'm always looking good.

Katz (1988) has noted that young people may find certain property crimes (joyriding, vandalism, burglary, shoplifting) appealing, independent of material gain or esteem from peers. He categorized these as "sneaky crimes that frequently thrill their practioneers" (p. 53). Similarly, in the present study, almost every informant mentioned excitement and thrills; however, only a few would commit a burglary for that purpose only. Like Reppetto (1974), we concluded that the younger, less experienced burglars were more prone to commit crimes for the thrill and excitement.

Time of Burglary

Rengert and Wasilchick (1985, 1989) found that burglars work during periods when residences are left unguarded. We found the same thing. Our informants stated they preferred to work between 9:00 and 11:00 A.M. and in mid-afternoon. Most organized their working hours around school hours, particularly during the times when parents (usually mothers) took children to school and picked them up after school. Several told us that they waited "until the wife left to take the kids to school or to go shopping." Most stated that they did not do burglaries on Saturday because most people were home then. Only a small number ($n = 3$) of burglars in our study committed burglaries at night. Most preferred to commit their crimes during hours when they expected people to be at work and out of the home. Those who did nighttime burglary usually knew the victims and their schedules or took advantage of people being away from home in the evening.

Inside Information

Burglars often work with "inside men" who have access to potential targets and advise the burglar about things to steal. They may also provide such critical information as times when the owner is away and of weaknesses in security. One female burglar reported that she maintained close contact with several women who worked as maids in affluent sections of the community. She would gain the necessary information from these women and later come back and break into the house, often entering by a door or window left open for her by the accomplice. Others gained information from friends and acquaintances who unwittingly revealed information about potential burglary targets. One told us:

> I have friends who mow yards for people and work as maids and stuff. When they talk about the people they work for, I keep my ears open. They give me information without knowing it.

Information about potential targets is frequently gained from "fences." Because many fences have legitimate occupations, they may have knowledge of the existence of valuable property from social or business relationships. They can often provide the burglar with information about the owners' schedules and the security arrangements at the target site.

People involved in a variety of service jobs (repair, carpet cleaning, pizza delivery, lawn maintenance, plumbing, carpentry) enter many homes each day and have the opportunity to assess the quality of potential stolen merchandise and security measures taken by the residents. Burglars will often establish contact with employees of these businesses for purposes of obtaining this "inside" information. One informant said:

> I know this guy who works for [carpet cleaning business]. He sometimes gives me information on a good place to hit and I split with him.

Occupancy Probes

Almost all burglars avoid selecting houses that are occupied as targets. Only two informants stated that they would enter a residence they knew was occupied. Therefore, it is important that the burglar develop techniques for probing the potential target site to determine if anyone is at home. The most common probe used by our informants was to send one of the burglars to the door to knock or ring the doorbell. If someone answered, the prober would ask directions to a nearby address or for a nonexistent person, for example, "Is Ray home?" The prospective burglar would apologize and leave when told that he or she had the wrong address. A female informant reported that she carried her two-year-old child to the target residence door, asking for directions to a nearby address. She reported:

> I ask them for a drink [of water] for the baby. Even when they seem suspicious they almost always let me in to get the baby a drink.

Several informants reported obtaining the resident's name from the mailbox or a sign over the door. They would then look up the telephone number and call the residence, leaving the phone ringing while they returned to the target home. If they could still hear the phone ringing when they arrived at the house, they were sure it was unoccupied.

Burglar Alarms

In general, burglars agreed that alarms were a definite deterrent to their activities. Other factors being equal, they preferred to locate a target that did not have an alarm instead of taking the additional risk involved in attempting to burglarize a house with an alarm system. More than 90 percent of the informants reported that they would not choose a target with an alarm system. Most were deterred merely by a sign or window sticker stating that the house was protected by an alarm system. As Richard, an experienced burglar, stated:

Why take a chance? There's lots of places without alarms. Maybe they're bluffing, maybe they ain't.

Although several informants boasted about disarming alarms, when pressed for details, almost all admitted that they did not know how to accomplish that task. One informant stated that while she could not disarm a burglar alarm, she was not deterred by an alarm. She stated that once the alarm was tripped, she still had time to complete the burglary and escape before police or private security arrived. She explained that she never took more than 10 minutes to enter, search, and exit a house. She advised:

Police take 15 to 20 minutes to respond to an alarm. Security [private security] sometimes gets there a little faster. I'm gone before any of them gets there.

Locks on Doors and Windows

Past research has been inconsistent regarding the deterrent value of locks on windows and doors. A few studies have reported that burglars consider the type of lock installed at a prospective target site in their target selection decision. Others did not find locks to be a significant factor in the selection process.

The majority of informants in the present study initially stated that locks did not deter them. However, during burglary reconstructions, we discovered that given two potential target sites, all other factors being equal, burglars prefer not to deal with a deadbolt lock. Several told us that they allowed themselves only one or two minutes to effect entry and that a good deadbolt lock slowed them down too much.

The variation in findings regarding security hardware appears related to the burglar's level of expertise and experience. To the extent to which burglars are primarily opportunistic and inexperienced, locks appear to have deterrent value. The opportunistic burglar chooses targets based on their perceived vulnerability to burglary at a given time. Given a large number of potential targets, the burglar tends to select the most vulnerable of the target pool. A target with a good lock and fitted with other security hardware will usually not be perceived to be as vulnerable as one without those items. The professional or "good" burglar chooses targets on the basis of factors other than situational vulnerability and conceives ways in which he or she can overcome impediments to the burglary (such as the target site being fitted with a high-quality deadbolt lock). Thus, to the extent that burglars are skilled and experienced, deadbolt locks have limited utility for crime prevention. However, our findings support the deterrent value of deadbolt locks. Seventy-five percent of the burglaries reconstructed during our research were opportunistic offenses. Many of those burglaries would have been prevented by the presence of a quality deadbolt lock. *It is important to note that nearly one-half of the burglary sites in the present study were entered through open or unlocked windows and doors.*

Dogs

Almost all studies agree that dogs are an effective deterrent to burglary. Although there is some individual variation among burglars, the general rule is to bypass a house with a dog—any dog. Large dogs represent a physical threat to the burglar and small ones are often noisy, attracting attention to a burglar's activities. We found that although many burglars have developed contingency plans to deal with dogs (petting, feeding, or even killing them), most burglars prefer to avoid them. When asked what were considered absolute "no-go" factors, most burglars responded that dogs were second only to occupancy. However, approximately 30 percent of the informants *initially* discounted the presence of dogs as a deterrent. Yet, during "ride alongs," the sight or sound of a dog at a potential target site almost invariably resulted in a "no-go" decision. As Richard said:

I don't mess with no dogs. If they got dogs, I go someplace else.

Debbie reported that she was concerned primarily with small dogs:

Little dogs "yap" too much. They [neighbors] look to see what they are so excited about. I don't like little yapping dogs.

Opportunity and Burglary

The "professional burglars" among our informants tended to select targets in a purposive manner, analyzing the physical and social characteristics of the environment and choosing targets that they knew from experience were ideally vulnerable. But by far the greater proportion of the informants were opportunistic. The targets they chose appeared particularly vulnerable *at the time*. Thus, most burglaries in the jurisdiction studies seem to result from the propitious juxtaposition of target, offender, and situation.

Our findings suggest that a burglar's decision to "hit" a target is based primarily on environmental cues that are perceived to have immediate consequences. Most burglars appear to attend only to the present; future events or consequences do not weigh heavily in their risk-versus-gain calculation. Drug-using burglars and juveniles are particularly oriented to this immediate-gain and immediate-risk decision process. Non-drug-using and experienced burglars are probably less likely to attend only to immediate risks and gains. Our informants, though experienced burglars, were all drug users, and tended to have a "here and now" orientation toward the rewards and costs associated with burglary.

Exploiting opportunity characterized the target selection processes in more than 75 percent of the burglaries reconstructed during our research. Even professional burglars among our informants often took advantage of opportunities when they arose. Chance opportunities occasionally presented themselves while the professional was "casing" and "probing" potential burglary targets chosen by more rational means. When these opportunities arose, the professional burglar was as likely as other burglars to take advantage of the situation.

IMPLICATIONS FOR CRIME PREVENTION

This study suggests burglars may be much more opportunistic than previously believed. The opportunistic burglar chooses targets based on their perceived vulnerability to burglary at a given time. Given a large number of potential targets, the burglar tends to select the most vulnerable of the target pool. The burglar does not, however, choose targets on the basis of situational vulnerability alone. He also considers how to overcome impediments to the burglary.

Programs designed to prevent burglary must be based on valid assumptions about burglars and burglary. Measures designed to combat the relatively small population of high-incidence "professional" burglars tend to overemphasize the skill and determination of most burglars. These measures are expensive, complex, and require long-term commitment at many levels. However, the typical burglar is not a calculating professional against whom complex prevention tactics must be employed. In fact, most burglars are young, unskilled, and opportunistic. This suggests that emphasis should be directed at such factors as surveillability, occupancy, and accessibility. More specifically, dogs, good locks, and alarm systems deter most burglars. Methods that give a residence the "illusion of occupancy" (Cromwell, Olson, and Avary, 1990) deter almost all burglars and are maintained with little effort or cost. Our study suggests that these simple steps may be the most cost-efficient and effective means for residents to insulate themselves from victimization by burglars.

REFERENCES

Bureau of Justice Statistics. October 1991. Criminal Victimization 1990. *Bulletin.* Washington, DC: U.S. Department of Justice.

Cromwell, Paul, James N. Olson, and D'Aunn Avary. 1991. *Breaking and Entering: An Ethnographic Analysis of Burglary.* Newbury Park, CA: Sage.

Katz, Jack. 1988. *Seductions of Crime.* New York: Basic Books.

Lynch, James P. 1990. Modeling Target Selection in Burglary: Differentiating Substance from Method. Paper presented at the 1990 annual meeting of the American Society of Criminology, Baltimore, Maryland.

Rengert, G., and J. Wasilchick. 1985. *Suburban Burglary: A Time and a Place for Everything.* Springfield, IL: Charles C. Thomas.

Rengert, G., and J. Wasilchick. 1989. *Space, Time and Crime: Ethnographic Insights into Residential Burglary.* A report prepared for the National Institute of Justice. (Mimeo).

Reppetto, T. G. 1974. *Residential Crime.* Cambridge, MA: Ballinger.

Scarr, H. A. 1973. *Patterns of Burglary.* Washington, DC: U.S. Government Printing Office.

Shover, Neal. 1971. *Burglary as an Occupation.* Ph.D. Dissertation, University of Illinois. Ann Arbor, MI: University Microfilms, 1975.

17

WHITE-COLLAR CRIME

GILBERT GEIS

The category of "white-collar crime" travels under a number of criminological names. Some prefer the term "upperworld crime," "economic crime," "abuse of power," or "crime in the suites." No matter what they are called, the behaviors being classified are essentially the same: matters such as ripoffs in savings and loan institutions; antitrust violations; health-care frauds; bribery to obtain political favors; misrepresentation of financial statements; offenses against health and safety laws; and unnecessary surgeries or bills for services not rendered by physicians. White-collar offenses can be crimes of violence—hundreds of people die each year from illegally unsafe workplace conditions and from surgeries performed only to collect a hefty fee. More commonly, white-collar crimes involve frauds in which unwitting and unwary customers or consumers are cheated.

The designation "white-collar crime" was introduced into the national vocabulary by Edwin H. Sutherland, a 56-year-old sociologist at Indiana University, in his presidential address to the American Sociological Association in 1939. In his speech, Sutherland deplored the fact that criminology had neglected law breaking by people in positions of power. He argued persuasively that standard explanations of criminal behavior—broken homes, defective intelligence, sociopathic conditions, poverty and slum upbringing, immigrant status—all fell apart when they were brought to bear on the personalities and background of white-collar offenders (Sutherland, 1940).

Sutherland's was a monumental criminological contribution. A *Philadelphia Inquirer* reporter portrayed his audience as "astonished"

when "Dr. Sutherland figuratively heaved scores of sociological textbooks into a waste basket" ("Poverty Belittled," 1939, p. 17). *The New York Times* noted that Sutherland had "discarded accepted conceptions and explanations of crime." The reporter then repeated two of Sutherland's more striking observations: that a larger amount of important crime news could be found on the financial pages of the newspaper than on the front pages and that white-collar crime in many respects was "like stealing candy from a baby" ("Hits Criminality," 1939, p. 12).

Sutherland was the first of many writers to point out that the cost of white-collar crime is much greater than that of street offenses. One bank embezzler in a year typically will steal more than the total taken by all the bank robbers during the same period. Estimates today are that the cost of the savings and loan debacle alone will reach an estimated $1.4 trillion when the final tab is settled in another dozen or so years (Pontell and Calavita, 1993). Such white-collar crime scandals as the Watergate affair and the Iran-Contra imbroglio eat away at public confidence in the country's leaders and in the integrity of their government.

THE DEFINITIONAL DILEMMA

Sutherland defined white-collar crime very loosely, and his imprecision has plagued generations of criminologists seeking to pinpoint exactly what the term means. In the *Encyclopedia of Criminology,* Sutherland depicted the white-collar criminal as "a person with high socioeconomic status who violates the laws designed to regulate his [or her] occupation" (Sutherland, 1949b, p. 511). In his book-length treatise on white-collar crime, he relegated definitional matters to a footnote: "A white-collar crime," Sutherland wrote, "may be defined approximately as a crime committed by a person of respectability and high social status in the course of his [or her] occupation" (Sutherland, 1949a, p. 9). Most scientists avoid such equivocal terms as "approximately" when they seek to clarify the object of their inquiry. But Sutherland, as we will see, believed he had a theoretical explanation for *all* crime; therefore, sharp definitional distinctions among forms of criminal behavior were unimportant to him.

In addition, Sutherland flopped back and forth in his writings on white-collar crime between a focus on real people and one on corporate entities. Note, for instance, his sarcastic putdown of psychiatric explanations of crime:

> We have no reason to think that General Motors has an inferiority complex or that the Aluminum Company of America has a frustration-aggression complex or that U.S. Steel has an Oedipus complex, or that the Armour Company has a death wish or that the DuPonts desire to return to the womb (Sutherland, 1956, p. 96).

Then Sutherland added, "The assumption that an offender must have some such pathological distortion of the intellect or the emotions seems to me absurd, and if it is absurd regarding the crimes of businessmen, it is equally absurd regarding the crimes of persons in the lower economic class" (Sutherland, 1956, p. 96).

There are a number of problems with both of Sutherland's statements. First, he does not demonstrate that the corporations (presumably, he means their officers) do not have the problems he makes fun of; second, he is picking on a straw target in the sense that few, if any, criminologists would support the claim that he is ridiculing; and, third, he is guilty of *anthropomorphism,* that is, of ascribing human characteristics to nonhuman creations, such as business corporations.

Early disputation regarding definitional matters has given way today to general, though still somewhat unsettled, agreement about the nature of white-collar crime. The first major breakthrough occurred in 1973 when Marshall Clinard and Richard Quinney distinguished between (1) occupational criminal behavior and (2) corporate criminal behavior. They defined occupational criminal behavior as the "violation of the criminal law in the course of an activity or a legitimate occupation." Corporate crime for its part was said to consist of crimes committed by corporate officials for their corporation as well as offenses charged against the corporate entity itself (Clinard and Quinney, 1973, p. 189). Laura Schrager and James F. Short, Jr. (1977; see also Ermann and Lundman, 1978) gave further body and differentiation to the second element of the Clinard-Quinney dichotomy, defining what they preferred to call "organizational crime" in the following manner:

> The illegal acts of omission or commission of an individual or a group of individuals in a formal organization in accordance with the operative goals of the organization, which have a serious physical or economic impact on employees, customers, or the general public (Schrager and Short, 1978, p. 408).

Some scholars of white-collar crime, however, take exception to the final phrase of this definition, insisting that the offense need only be against the law, that it is not necessary that it have a "serious" impact. Indeed, they argue that "serious" is a term of art and not of science.

A further distinction among white-collar offenses adds "state-corporate crime" as a separate component of the generic category. Offenses of this nature are defined as follows:

> State-corporate crimes are illegal or socially injurious actions that result from a mutually reinforcing interaction between (1) policies and/or practices in pursuit of the goals of one or more institutions of political governance and (2) policies and/or practices in pursuit of the goals of one or more institutions of economic production and distribution (Aulette and Michalowski, 1993, p. 175).

A 1991 fire at the Imperial Food Products chicken-processing plant in Hamlet, North Carolina, which killed 25 workers and injured another

56, is used to illustrate "state-corporate crime." The state government had encouraged industry to locate in North Carolina by fighting unions with a right-to-work statute and by keeping wages low. As one of the pro-business measures, safety inspections were minimized; as a result, no action had been taken to deal with the illegally locked door at the processing plant that prevented the workers' escape when fire broke out.

A fundamental definitional question remains after the breakdown of white-collar crime into the foregoing subcategories: Should it be the nature of the behavior or the position and power of the offender—or both together—that places the illegal act under the heading of white-collar crime?

The classic Sutherland position was adopted by Albert J. Reiss, Jr., and Albert D. Biderman in their inquiry into the possibility of establishing a data-reporting system (such as we have for murder, robbery, and other traditional offenses) for white-collar crime. They defined white-collar crime as "those violations of law to which penalties are attached and that involve the use of a violator's position of significant power, influence, or trust in the legitimate economic or political institutional order for the purpose of illegal gain, or to commit an illegal act for personal or organizational gain" (Reiss and Biderman, 1980, p. xxiii; see also Geis, 1992).

For Clinard and Quinney, however, position, influence, and significant power are of no concern. If a corporate president fixes prices with competitors or a part-time salesman fudges on his expense account, both are seen as white-collar crimes.

The Clinard and Quinney definitional stance has been adopted in several important studies of the sentencing of white-collar criminals (Benson, Moore, and Walker, 1988; Hagan, Nagel, and Albonetti, 1980; Wheeler, Weisburd, and Bode, 1982; but see Hoyan, Nagel, Albonetti, and Parker, 1985). Because crimes such as fraud and bank embezzlement are included in these studies, as many as half of the violators in some subcategories turn out to be unemployed or to be working in very low-level positions (Daly, 1989), a matter that is a far cry from Sutherland's emphasis on the white-

collar offender's high status. Nonetheless, such an approach democratizes the criminological study of white-collar crime by including everybody who violates a particular law rather than only a select portion of that group.

In a major contribution, Susan Shapiro (1990) has sought to "liberate" the concept of white-collar crime from the definitional shackles she believes have "created an imprisoning framework for contemporary scholarship, impoverishing theory, distorting empirical inquiry, oversimplifying policy analysis, inflaming our muckraking instincts, and obscuring fascinating questions about the relationship between social organization and crime" (p. 362). Shapiro believes that the focus ought not to be on the standing of perpetrators but on the essential nature of white-collar crime—its modus operandi. This, she maintains, involves the violation of trust—of norms of disclosure, disinterestedness, and role competence. As a whimsical example of such misrepresentation, Shapiro relates the story of "Zoogate"—that the Houston Zoo advertised live cobras but displayed rubber replicas, because live cobras could not live under the lights in the area where they would have been kept.

Shapiro grants that her definition would exclude what have been quintessential white-collar offenses such as antitrust violations and violent union-busting. She also admits that it will be difficult to cast aside the Sutherland legacy, which she agrees is "polemically powerful." Whether Shapiro's redefinition of white-collar crime musters adherents undoubtedly will depend on whether it provides more significant understanding of the dynamics of the behavior and whether it offers a sounder framework for research probes.

THEORIES OF WHITE-COLLAR CRIME

His theory of differential association, Sutherland (1949a) believed, provided the proper schema for understanding white-collar crime. As he saw it, all criminal offenders behaved in an illegal fashion because they had learned from others, largely through close personal relationships, to regard law violation more favorably than conformity to legal demands. The theory of differential association, unfortunately, is so imprecise as to be untestable, and it fails to meet the scientific criterion of being able to predict reasonably well who will and who will not become a criminal. Besides, two major early studies of white-collar crime found differential association inapplicable to their findings. For Cressey (1953), embezzlers did not need to learn from others, but already possessed the knowledge of how to cheat; their motive to do so derived from their personal financial need. For Clinard (1952), black-market violations were best understood in terms of the personality characteristics of the offenders. In addition, Sutherland's theory of differential association has rightly been criticized for focusing exclusively on the social psychological process of individual offending and failing to attend to "the far-reaching perspective of [the] power structure" (Thio, 1973, p. 5).

For thirty years after Sutherland, the study of white-collar crime became essentially an atheoretical enterprise, relying largely on a case-study approach (Geis, 1991). The exceptions were studies that sought to relate corporate conditions—form of management, capitalization, market conditions, competitive situation, and similar considerations—to criminal records (e.g., Elzinga and Breit, 1976; Farberman, 1975; Lane, 1953). These, however, essentially have been correlational efforts with only crude theoretical implications.

Recently, however, important strides have been made toward providing white-collar crime with a theoretical framework or, alternatively, incorporating it into a general theory of criminal behavior. James W. Coleman (1987), for instance, sought to tie the social structure and the culture of capitalism to motivations to commit white-collar offenses, but he granted that consideration of the opportunities presented to persons in different social positions also is essential to an adequate understanding of white-collar crime (Coleman, 1987; for a critique see Braithwaite, 1989).

Michael Gottfredson and Travis Hirschi (1990), for their part, have maintained, as did Sutherland, that all crime can be explained by a single theoretical scheme. For them, the key to crime is an absence of self-control in the perpetrator. They insist that lack of self-control accounts not only for crimes—"acts of force or fraud undertaken in the pursuit of self-interest"—but also for accidents, victimizations, truancies, substance abuse, family problems, and disease.

To seek to make their point, Gottfredson and Hirschi single out white-collar crime—the traditional bugaboo for such efforts—for special attention. First, they argue that there is no value in focusing only on the perpetrator's position, asking: "What is the theoretical value in distinguishing a doctor's Medicaid fraud from a patient's Medicaid fraud?" Then they insist that those who commit white-collar crimes, such as frauds, are likely to engage in other forms of law breaking as well, and that the roots of all such activities lie in inadequate self-control.

Gottfredson and Hirschi's position largely is tautological in that they designate acts that by their nature involve absence of self-control and then seek to explain them by this absence. Their attempt to incorporate white-collar crime in their theorizing has been disputed on a number of specific grounds. Steffensmeier (1989), for instance, takes them to task for their focus on fraud and forgery as the basis for their theoretical statement. He observes:

The evidence is quite conclusive . . . that persons arrested for fraud and forgery do not qualify as white-collar criminals, whether that term is used restrictively to refer to crimes committed by persons of high socioeconomic status in the course of their occupation, or if the term is used broadly to refer to crimes committed by an employee (Steffensmeier, 1989, p. 347).

Most arrests for fraud or for forgery, Steffensmeier notes, are not occupationally related but rather involve passing bad checks, credit-card fraud, theft of services, falsification of identification, defrauding an innkeeper, fraudulent use of public transport, welfare fraud, and small con games. Besides, even if Gottfredson and Hirschi's definition is taken at face value, Steffensmeier insists, data indicate that they are incorrect when they claim that the ages of people who commit white-collar crime are much the same as those for ordinary crime: White-collar offenders are significantly older than street offenders. For Steffensmeier, low self-esteem, inadequate self-control, and weak social bonds constitute only partial determinants of some criminal behaviors. For most scholars who study white-collar crime, the idea that low self-control holds the key to such offenses as antitrust conspiracies seems exceedingly farfetched.

After examining the pre-sentence dossiers of 2,462 individuals charged with an array of white-collar offenses (very broadly defined), Michael Benson and Elizabeth Moore (1992) further criticized Gottfredson and Hirschi by maintaining that they largely erred in their conclusion that such offenders are criminally versatile and as prone to deviance as common offenders. They dispute Gottfredson and Hirschi's rejection of motives as important causal forces, and they insist that a more complex causal structure is necessary to account for white-collar offenses.

Gottfredson and Hirsehi's theorizing flies in the face of the persuasive statement offered by Robert K. Merton, a guru of criminological theory. "The decision to encompass a great variety of behaviors under one heading," Merton wrote, "naturally leads us to assume that it is what these behaviors have in common that is most relevant, and this assumption leads us to look for an all-encompassing set of propositions which will account for the entire range of behavior." "This is not too remote," Merton adds, "from the assumption . . . that there must be a theory of disease, rather than distinct theories of disease—of tuberculosis and of arthritis, of typhoid and syphilis—theories which are diverse rather than single" (Merton, 1956, p. 7).

Merton's viewpoint is seconded by Francis T. Cullen (1983), who believes that criminological theory is notably flawed in its failure to adhere to a "structuring tradition," that is, to seek to attend to why an individual chooses to commit one particular kind of criminal offense rather than another. Similarly, John Braithwaite (1985) has maintained that progress in the construction of theories of occupa-

tional crimes probably will have to be confined to specific forms of such offenses, though he believes that more comprehensive interpretive schemes might be useful for understanding corporate crime.

This last category—corporate crime—itself has led to some vigorous recent disputation. In the last piece written before his death, Donald Cressey (1989, p. 32) took criminologists to task for holding to the "erroneous assumption that organizations think and act, thus saddling theoretical criminologists with the impossible task of finding the cause of crime committed by fictitious persons." Corporations do not behave, Cressey insists; their so-called actions are but manifestations of actions by real persons. For Cressey "there can be no social psychology of so-called corporate or organizational crime because corporations have no biological or psychological characteristics" (p. 37).

In rebuttal, Braithwaite and Brent Fisse (1990) maintain that corporations do indeed have distinctive personalities, that they are something other than the sum of the isolated efforts of individuals, and that reasonable theories can be drawn up to explain their illegal actions.

The debate between Cressey and his challengers brought to the surface a related issue that often arises in corporate crime—that of strict liability, in which corporate officers are held criminally responsible even though they were not aware that an offense had been committed. Is it possible to explain such actions in theoretical terms? Cressey would say no; Braithwaite and Fisse would say yes (see also Geis, 1994). This recalls the ancient debate over whether it was possible to explain actions that violated the criminal doctrine of deodand. According to this doctrine, animals and inanimate objects, such as trees, were deemed to be criminally responsible for a death if, for example, they fatally attacked or fell onto a person. Deodands were not abolished until 1846.

CONCLUSION

We have seen various conflicting definitions and theories of white-collar crime. Which one makes the most sense? Consider the illustration offered by Oliver Wendell Holmes, Jr., when he was a U.S. Supreme Court justice:

> The old books say that, if a man falls from a ship and is drowned, the motion of the ship must be taken to be the cause of death and the ship is forfeit [subject to confiscation]—provided, however, that this happens in fresh water. For if the death took place on the high seas, that was outside the ordinary jurisdiction (Holmes, 1881, p. 26).

Will any criminological theory possibly help us comprehend this law breaking? Even in the unlikely event we puzzle our way to such a formulation, how do we satisfactorily differentiate the drowning in fresh water from that on the high seas? Perhaps, in the end, the cynical view of Max Planck, a Nobel Prize laureate in physics, prevails. "A new scientific truth does not triumph by convincing its opponents and making them see the light," Planck wrote, "but rather because its opponents eventually die, and a new generation grows up that is familiar with it" (Crichton, 1988, p. 358).

REFERENCES

Aulette, Judy Root, and Raymond Michalowski. 1993. "Fire in Hamlet: A Case Study of State-Corporate Crime," pp. 171–206 in *Political Crime in Contemporary America: A Critical Approach,* edited by Kenneth D. Tunnell. New York: Garland.

Benson, Michael L., and Elizabeth Moore. 1992. "Are White-Collar and Common Offenders the Same?: An Empirical and Theoretical Critique of a Recently Proposed General Theory of Crime." *Journal of Research in Crime and Delinquency* 29:251–272.

Benson, Michael L., Elizabeth Moore, and Esteban Walker. 1988. "Sentencing the White-Collar Offender." *American Sociological Review* 53:294–302.

Braithwaite, John. 1985. "White Collar Crime." *Annual Review of Sociology* 11:1–25.

Braithwaite, John. 1989. "White-Collar Crime, Competition, and Capitalism: Comment on Coleman." *American Journal of Sociology* 94:628–632.

Braithwaite, John, and Brent Fisse. 1990. "On the Plausibility of Corporate Crime Theory." *Advances in Criminological Theory* 2:15–38.

Clinard, Marshall B. 1952. *The Black Market: A Study of White-Collar Crime.* New York: Holt.

Clinard, Marshall B., and Richard Quinney. 1973. *Criminal Behavior Systems: A Typology,* 2nd ed. pp. 187–223. New York: Holt, Rinehart, and Winston.

Coleman, James W. 1987. "Toward an Integrated Theory of White-Collar Crime." *American Journal of Sociology* 93:406–439.

Cressey, Donald R. 1953. *Other People's Money: The Social Psychology of Embezzlement.* New York: Free Press.

Cressey, Donald R. 1989. "The Poverty of Theory in Corporate Crime Research." *Advances in Criminological Theory* 1:31–56.

Crichton, Michael. 1988. *Travels.* New York: Knopf.

Cullen, Francis T. 1983. *Rethinking Crime and Deviance Theory: The Emergence of a Structuring Tradition.* Totowa, NJ: Bowman & Allanheld.

Daly, Kathleen. 1989. "Gender and Varieties of White-Collar Crime." *Criminology* 27:769–793.

Elzinga, Kenneth, and William Breit. 1976. *The Antitrust Penalties: A Study in Law and Economics.* New Haven: Yale University Press.

Ermann, M. David, and Richard Lundman. 1978. "Deviant Acts by Complex Organizations: Deviance and Social Control at the Organizational Level of Analysis." *Sociological Quarterly* 19:55–67.

Farberman, Harvey A. 1975. "A Criminogenic Market Structure: The Automobile Industry." *Sociological Quarterly* 16:438–457.

Geis, Gilbert. 1991. "The Case Study Method in Sociological Criminology," pp. 220–223 in *A Case for the Case Study,* edited by Joe R. Feagin, Anthony M. Orum, and Gideon Sjoberg. Chapel Hill: University of North Carolina Press.

Geis, Gilbert. 1992. "White-Collar Crime: What Is It?," pp. 31–52 in *White-Collar Crime Reconsidered,* Kip Schlegel and David Weisburd. Boston: Northeastern University Press.

Geis, Gilbert. 1994. "A Review, Rebuttal, and Reconciliation of Cressey and Brathwaite and Fisse on Criminological Theory and Corporate Crime." *Advances in Criminological Theory* 6:321–350.

Gottfredson, Michael R., and Travis Hirschi. 1990. *A General Theory of Crime.* Stanford: Stanford University Press.

Hagan, John, Ilene H. Nagel, and Celesta Albonetti. 1980. "The Differential Sentencing of White-Collar

Offenders in Ten Federal District Courts." *American Sociological Review* 43:802–820.

"Hits Criminality in White Collars." 1939. *New York Times* December 28, p. 12.

Holmes, Oliver Wendell, Jr. 1881. *The Common Law.* Boston: Little, Brown.

Hoyan, John, Ilene H. Nagel, Celesta Albonetti, and Patricia Parker. 1985. "White-Collar Crime and Punishment: The Class Structure and Legal Sanctioning of Securities Violations." *American Sociological Review* 50:302–315.

Lane, Robert E. 1953. "Why Businessmen Violate the Law." *Journal of Criminal Law, Criminology, and Police Science* 44:151–165.

Merton, Robert K. 1956. In *New Perspectives for Research on Juvenile Delinquency,* edited by Helen L. Witmer and Ruth Kotinsky. Children's Bureau Publication No. 356. Washington, DC: Government Publication Office.

Pontell, Henry N., and Kitty Calavita. 1993. "White-Collar Crime in the Savings and Loan Scandal." *Annals of the American Academy of Political and Social Science* 525:31–45.

"Poverty Belittled as Crime Factor." 1939. *Philadelphia Inquirer* December 28, p. 17.

Reiss, Albert J., and Albert D. Biderman. 1980. *Data Sources on White-Collar Law-Breaking.* Washington, DC: U.S. Department of Justice.

Schrager, Laura S., and James F. Short, Jr. 1978. "Toward a Sociology of Organizational Crime." *Social Problems* 25:407–419.

Shapiro, Susan. 1990. "Collaring the Crime, Not the Criminal: Reconsidering the Concept of White-Collar Crime." *American Sociological Review* 55:346–365.

Steffensmeier, Darrell. 1989. "On the Causes of 'White-Collar' Crime: An Assessment of Hirschi and Gottfredson's Claims." *Criminology* 27:345–358.

Sutherland, Edwin H. 1940. "White Collar Criminality." *American Sociological Review* 5:1–12.

Sutherland, Edwin H. 1949a. *White Collar Crime.* New York: Dryden.

Sutherland, Edwin H. 1949b. "The White Collar Criminal," pp. 511–515 in *The Encyclopedia of Criminology,* edited by Vernon C. Branham and Samuel B. Kutash. New York: Philosophical Library.

Sutherland, Edwin H. 1956. "Crimes of Corporations," pp. 78–96 in *The Sutherland Papers,* edited by Albert K. Cohen, Alfred Lindesmith, and Karl Schuessler. Bloomington: Indiana University Press.

Thio, Alex. 1973. "Class Bias in the Sociology of Deviance." *American Sociologist* 8 (February):1–12.

Wheeler, Stanton, David Weisburd, and Nancy Bode. 1982. "Sentencing the White-Collar Offender: Rhetoric and Reality." *American Sociological Review* 47:641–649.

PART FIVE

DRUG USE

David, aged 25, is a successful, extremely well-paid advertising executive. He smokes marijuana every day, usually at night, after work. "I use marijuana to relax," he explains, "to contemplate, and to enjoy myself. It makes me feel good, and I get a lot of insight from it. I'm more able to perceive who the other person is and suspend all of life's petty 'games.' Anyway, I feel good when I'm stoned. That's why I do it. That's why I do it *regularly*. . . . It's fun. Food tastes better; sex is more expressive and enjoyable—yes, pot is an aphrodisiac, at least it is for me. I enjoy music more, I use my imagination more listening to music. . . . When someone asks me, why do I smoke dope, I answer, why not? There are no negatives, only positives. Really. Why not?"[1]

The use of illicit drugs such as marijuana appears to be a widespread problem in the United States. However, the use of *licit* drugs such as alcoholic beverages and tobacco cigarettes is even more prevalent. Not surprisingly, the use of legal drugs causes far more deaths, sickness, violent crimes, economic loss, and other social problems than the use of illegal drugs. For example, every year about 200,000 people in the United States die from alcohol-related diseases and accidents, and more than 430,000 die from smoking, whereas only 5,000 to 10,000 die from illegal drugs. In other words, only two legal drugs—alcohol and tobacco—every year kill at least 60 times as many Americans as all the illicit drugs combined.[2]

Here we will read about both illicit and licit drugs. In the first article, "Drug Use in America: An Overview," Erich Goode describes and explains the past and current status of illicit drug use based on two major surveys. In the second article, "Drug Crisis: The American Nightmare," Elliott Currie discusses the widespread illicit drug problem and explains why some people, particularly the poor, continue to abuse drugs. In the third article, "Cigarette Smoking as Deviant Behavior," Erich Goode probes various aspects of tobacco use, including its nature and prevalence, emerging deviant status, and impact on health. In the fourth selection, "Pleasures versus Public Health: Controlling Collegiate Binge Drinking," Thomas Workman discusses the pleasures of drinking in college and the different approaches to controlling binge drinking on campus.

1. Erich Goode, *Drugs in American Society,* 5th ed. (New York: McGraw-Hill, 1999).
2. Mathea Falco, *The Making of a Drug-Free America: Programs That Work* (New York: Times Books, 1992); *Rethinking International Drug Control* (New York: Council on Foreign Relations, 1997).

DRUG USE IN AMERICA: AN OVERVIEW

ERICH GOODE

The results of drug surveys are media events. Every time the findings of the latest national survey are released, they make the front page. One year, the headline reads "Students Return to Drug Use." The next year, it announces "Illegal Drug Use Declines."

When we read the results of a study on drug use, what's our reaction likely to be? If we are skeptics, we are likely to wonder, *how do they know?* In interviews or with questionnaires, are respondents really completely honest about their consumption of illicit substances? When they are asked questions about the illegal, deviant, or delinquent activities in which they might engage, don't people *lie* a lot? How can we trust the results of studies on illegal drug use?

As it turns out, in studies of deviant behavior, lying is not a major problem—*as long as respondents are convinced that they will remain completely anonymous.* If the people who participate in a study believe their answers will remain confidential, that the researchers will not reveal their names to anyone—that they cannot get into trouble for giving honest answers, no matter what they say—most of them will give candid and truthful answers. Of course, a great many people have imperfect memories. All of us are sometimes wrong about certain facts, but most respondents give fairly accurate answers in an anonymous survey—*to the best of their ability.* However, this generalization may not apply as well to teenagers as to adults, as we will see.

How do researchers know this? It's really quite simple: the process of *triangulation.* Triangulation entails looking at the same thing using different sources of data. We cross-check something someone says with separate and indepen-

dent evidence. If people claim not to have used an illegal drug during the past 48 hours, we test their blood, or urine. If respondents tell us they have never been arrested, we check their arrest records. If interviewees say they were enrolled in a particular drug treatment program, we look up the relevant documents in that program's records.

The fact is, every time a study on drug use, deviance, and delinquency makes these kinds of triangular cross-checks, it finds a strong correspondence between what people say they did and what indisputable evidence shows they actually did (Inciardi, 1986, 1992; Johnson et al., 1985). This correspondence is far from perfect, but for our purposes, it is close enough for us to be able to use answers in surveys as an approximation to real-life behavior. As a result, experts believe we can trust the findings from properly conducted surveys on drug use.

TWO MAJOR DRUG SURVEYS

To get an accurate snapshot of patterns of drug use in general, it is very important that a study be nationally representative. This means that a survey's sample of respondents should look like, reflect, or represent the country as a whole with respect to such crucial characteristics as age, sex, race, social class, region of residence, and so on. Otherwise, we will get a very distorted picture of the behavior that takes place in a society in general because we will be drawing conclusions from a sample that is biased, skewed, or unrepresentative—in other words, that looks like part of the whole rather than the whole. For instance, if we want to find out about the drinking patterns of Americans generally, but we draw our sample exclusively from the state of Utah (which has the lowest rate of alcohol consumption in the country), our *findings* may be accurate but our *conclusions* will be inaccurate and extremely misleading.

Researchers who examine national patterns of drug use have the most faith in two surveys: the Monitoring the Future survey and the National Household Survey on Drug Abuse.

The Monitoring the Future survey is conducted every year by a team of researchers at the Institute for Social Research. This survey is based on self-completed questionnaires in selected schools. It began in 1975 as a study of the drug use of high school seniors. In 1980, it added to the sample college students and young adults who were not in college. In 1991, it began studying 8th and 10th graders as well. This study's sample is huge (between 15,000 and 20,000) and it is representative of the contiguous 48 states. Its response rate is roughly 85 to 90 percent, which is very high. (The nonresponses are made up mainly of absentees.) The Monitoring the Future survey is the best source on adolescent drug use because of the size and representativeness of its sample and because its questionnaires are administered in school rather than at home. Its drawback is that it does not include dropouts and absentees.

A second major data source based on a nationally representative sample is the National Household Survey on Drug Abuse, which has been conducted regularly since 1971. This survey is sponsored and administered by the federal government. Its sample, which is also nationally representative, is drawn from the noninstitutionalized, nonmilitary population older than 12. Interviews are conducted at the respondents' place of residence. The 1998 survey (SAMHSA, 1999) drew a sample of 25,000 persons; the 1999 survey was triple that size. For the purposes of analysis, the National Household Survey divides its respondents into four age categories: 12 to 17, 18 to 25, 25 to 34, and 35 and older. Although the National Household Survey on Drug Abuse is the best ongoing study on the consumption of both legal and illegal substances, one of its drawbacks is that adolescents are inter-

viewed at home, which may influence their answers. Obviously, for adults, this is not a problem.

These two surveys provide the foundation for making generalizations about drug use in the American population during the past 40 years. In fact, one of the early National Household Surveys, conducted in 1979, projected patterns of drug use backward in time to 1960 by calculating age of first use (Miller and Cisin, 1980). Also, because we are able to rely on two data sources rather than one, we can apply the principle of triangulation.

These two surveys, therefore, give us an excellent four-decades-long view of patterns of drug use in the United States. They give us a picture of the rate or magnitude of drug use: what percent of the population uses which drugs, which segments of the population use more than others, and what sorts of changes in drug use have taken place over time. There are many issues these surveys do not explore (for instance, the harm that drug use causes or what the drug experience feels like), but for rates, differences in rates by social category, and changes in rates over time, these studies are both unparalleled and absolutely essential. We simply cannot discuss these issues without consulting these two studies. The figures we obtain from these surveys should not be taken as gospel, of course. For one thing, the National Household Survey on Drug Abuse does not locate or interview people who do not live at a fixed address, such as homeless and street people, whose alcohol and drug use is likely to be higher than the population at large. However, along with the Monitoring the Future survey, the National Household Survey gives us a fairly accurate snapshot of the scope of drug use in America.

DRUG USE IN AMERICAN SOCIETY: A CAPSULE SUMMARY

What do these two studies tell us? To begin with, these surveys reveal what is probably a universal rule in the consumption of psychoactive substances and possibly with respect to human behavior in general. It seems to be a universal rule that *legal* drugs are used by more people, and they are used more frequently, than *illegal* drugs. This is as true in other countries as it is in the United States. Our surveys show us that the two legal drugs, alcohol and tobacco, are used by much higher proportions of the population, and with more frequency, than the illegal drugs. The 1998 National Household Survey—the most recent available at this writing—revealed that a majority of Americans age 12 and older (52 percent) had used alcohol at least once during the past month. Just fewer than two-thirds (64 percent) used alcohol during the past year, and eight in ten (81 percent) said that they had had an alcoholic drink at least once during their entire lifetime. (These figures can be found in Table 18.1.) The figures for tobacco were significantly lower, although still quite substantial: 28 percent of the respondents had smoked during the past month; 31 percent during the past year; and 70 percent at least once during their lives. In comparison, the percentage of Americans who use illegal drugs is much lower than for the legal drugs. In fact, the figure saying that they had used *any* illicit drug using the past month—all illegal drugs added together—was only 6 percent. About one American in ten (11 percent) said that they had used any illegal drug during the last year; and only a third of all Americans (36 percent) had used any illegal drug during their entire lifetime.

Marijuana is by far the most popular illicit drug. It is entirely possible that half of all episodes of use that Americans have with illicit drugs are with marijuana alone. Still, only one American in 20 (5 percent) said that they used marijuana (or hashish) during the past month; one in ten (9 percent) had done so during the past year; and one-third (33 percent) had done so once or more in their lives. The comparable figures for cocaine were: last month, 1 percent; last year, 2 percent; and lifetime, 11 percent. The other illicit drugs were used on a considerably smaller scale than marijuana and cocaine. (Table 18.1 details the rate of drug use in the United States in 1998 for alcohol, tobacco, and several selected drugs, as well as for the use of any illicit drug.)

The exact magnitude of these figures is not the issue, of course, but it is clear that the legal drugs are used on a vastly greater scale than the illegal drugs. In absolute terms, many people do use harmful, dangerous drugs such as heroin and cocaine, and with alarming frequency, in fact, on the order of hundreds of thousands of people. However, in relative terms, that is, expressed both as a percentage of the population and in comparison with the legal drugs—which are harmful and dangerous as well—their use is at a far lower rate.

Table 18.1 Use of Selected Drugs, U.S. Population Age 12 and Older, 1998

	PERCENTAGE OF PEOPLE USING DRUGS			
	Lifetime	*Past Year*	*Past Month*	*Use Ratio*
Alcohol	81	64	52	64%
Cigarettes	70	31	28	40%
Marijuana	33	9	5	15%
Cocaine	11	2	1	8%
Crack Cocaine	2	0.4	0.2	10%
LSD	4	1	0.3	4%
Heroin	1	0.1	0.1	5%
Any Illicit Drug	36	11	6	—

Source: Data from Substances Abuse and Mental Health Service Association, *Summary of Findings from the 1998 National Household Survey on Drug Abuse.* (1999, Rockville, MD: Author), pp. 63–67.

Legal drugs are not only used by more people than illegal drugs, they are also used with greater frequency by those who use them. When we compare use during the past month with lifetime use figures, we get a kind of loyalty or continuance ratio. If for a given drug, most of the people who have ever used are still using (that is, have used during the past month), then its users are very loyal; they stick with that drug, they continue using it over time. On the other hand, if with a particular drug, most of the people who used at one time have discontinued its use (did not use within the past month), its users can be said to be disloyal, that is, they do not stick with that drug. Drugs vary widely with respect to the loyalty of their users.

As a general rule, people are much more loyal to the legal than the illegal drugs; they tend to stick with them longer, they continue using them over a longer period of time. In the United States, slightly fewer than two-thirds (64 percent) of all at least one-time users of alcohol were still using—that is, they had used alcohol at least once during the past month. This is true of only four out of ten (40 percent) consumers of tobacco. In contrast, the loyalty or continuance ratio for marijuana—the "least illegal" of the illegal drugs—is only 15 percent. For cocaine, the continuance or loyalty ratio is 8 percent; for LSD, 4 percent; for heroin, 5 percent; and for crack cocaine, 10 percent. The extent to which users continue using a given drug is the result of a complex mixture of many factors, including the properties of the drug itself—whether it is capable of producing a physical dependency—and the age of its users. Still, a drug's legal status has a great deal to do with user loyalty.

DIFFERENCES IN DRUG USE BETWEEN AGE CATEGORIES

It should come as no surprise that there are extremely large differences in rates of drug use between and among age categories in the population. As a general rule, illicit drug use is low at age 12, rises throughout the adolescent years, reaches a peak in the young adult or 18-to-25-year-old bracket, and then declines throughout the remainder of the life cycle. In contrast, the use of alcohol rises sharply throughout adolescence, but it reaches a plateau in that vast stretch of time between the 18-to-20-year-old bracket and the 40s; in fact, even after the age of 50, its decline is fairly gradual. Clearly, there is something strikingly different about the use of illicit substances; it displays an age-graded pattern that is quite unlike that prevailing for the legal drugs alcohol and tobacco. Deviant or illegal drug use seems to obey a pattern that does not apply to conventional or legal drug use.

The 1998 National Household Survey found an extremely strong relationship between age and illegal drug use. For instance, 10 percent of the 12- to 17-year-olds had used one or more illicit drugs during the past month, 16 percent of the 18- to 25-year-olds, 7 percent of the 26- to 34-year-olds, and only 3 percent of those 35 and older (SAMHSA, 1999, p. 90). Looking at more refined age categories, only 2.9 percent of the respondents who were 12 and 13 years old had used one or more illegal drugs during the previous month, but this figure jumps to 10.8 percent for 14- and 15-year-olds, 16.4 percent for those 16 and 17 years old, and 19.9 percent for the 18- to 20-year-olds. (Let's keep in mind, however, that these interviews were conducted in the respondents' homes, so some teenagers may have kept their use estimates low.) Clearly, between the early to the late teens, illegal drug use skyrockets, But somewhere in the first half of the 20s, it begins to decline. Only 13.5 percent of the respondents in the 21-to-25-year-old bracket said that they had used at least one illegal drug during the previous month. For persons 26 to 29, this declined again, to 7.4 percent. Drug use declines more or less evenly throughout the 30s and 40s, then drops off fairly sharply after 50; less than 1 percent of the respondents who were older than 50 said that they had used an illegal drug during the past month. Pretty much the same picture is revealed when we look at use during the past year. Clearly, age is massively related to illegal drug use.

Many experts believe that the relationship between age and illegal drug use is an example of the more general relationship between age and deviant behavior. Most young people in their early teens live at home and are monitored and supervised—to a greater or lesser degree—by their parents. Their capacity to engage in deviant behavior such as illicit drugs is limited by the fact that their parents exert a strong influence over their behavior. In contrast, by the late teenage years, most young people have the best of all possible worlds: They have not yet assumed adult responsibilities, but at the same time, parental supervision has slackened. By the early 20s, a sizeable proportion of young people are concerned with college, an occupation, and marriage and family responsibilities, and many deviant activities, including the regular consumption of illegal substances, are seen as threats to these valued enterprises. College, an occupation, marriage, and family roles can be thought of as "investments" that might be lost by one's deviant and criminal behavior. Moreover, young people in the 16-to-20-year-old bracket are extremely strongly attached to their peers, more so than at any other age, and as a general rule, young people are more likely to engage in a larger volume of activities that violate conventional, or at least adult, notions of proper behavior. Finally, teenagers are more likely to think of themselves as invulnerable—they are less likely to think of the consequences of their actions—than adults.

All of this adds up to low levels of drug use in the early teens, a rise in the mid-teenage years, a peak in the late teens, and a decline that begins somewhere between the ages of 20 and 25. However, as we will see, some very recent developments have begun to challenge this model of how illegal drug use specifically, and deviant behavior more generally, operates.

DRUG USE OVER TIME: 1975–1998

A commonly believed myth is that illegal drug use was extremely widespread in the 1960s and declined after that. In fact, exactly the reverse is true. Drug use was extremely low in the early 1960s, it increased during that decade, rose sharply in the 1970s, reached a peak sometime in the late 1970s to early 1980s, and declined during the 1980s. During the decade of the 1990s, *adolescent* drug use increased significantly, but *adult* drug use remained more or less stable. For high school seniors, this up-and-down pattern is especially pronounced when we look at the Monitoring the Future survey, whose findings appear in Table 18.2.

Looking at the "any illicit drug" category, we see a rise in use between 1975, when 31 percent of the respondents said that they had used one or

Table 18.2 Drug Use in Past Month by High School Seniors (Selected Years, 1975–1998)

	PERCENTAGE OF PEOPLE USING DRUGS						
	1975	*1979*	*1983*	*1987*	*1991*	*1995*	*1998*
Alcohol	68	72	69	66	54	51	52
Cigarettes	37	34	30	30	28	34	35
Marijuana	27	37	27	21	14	21	23
Cocaine	2	6	5	4	1	2	2
LSD	2	2	2	2	2	4	3
Stimulants	9	10	9	5	3	4	5
Heroin	0.4	0.2	0.2	0.2	0.2	0.6	0.5
Any Illicit Drug	31	39	31	25	16	24	26

Source: For data from 1975 to 1995, Lloyd D. Johnston, Patrick O'Malley, and Jerald G. Bachman, *National Survey Results on Drug Use from the Monitoring the Future Study, 1975–1995*, Vol. 1 (1996, Rockville, MD: National Institute on Drug Abuse), p. 88 for 1998, *Monitoring the Future*, 1999, data downloaded from the Internet.

more illegal drugs during the previous month, and 1979, when this figure reached slightly fewer than four high school seniors in ten (39 percent). However, during the 1980s, illegal drug use declined; by 1991, fewer than half the percentage of 12th graders had used an illegal drug during the previous month (only 16 percent) than was true in 1979. Then, starting in the early 1990s, illicit drug use began to rise once again. In the 1991–1998 period, the percentage of high school seniors who had used at least one illegal drug during the past month rose by ten points, to 26 percent.

In 1991, the Monitoring the Future survey added 8th and 10th graders to its sample. During that year, as with the study's seniors, the percentage of its 8th and 10th graders who used illicit drugs began to rise. In fact, if we look very carefully at this survey's data, something truly remarkable took place during the 1990s. Sociologists refer to a specific age bracket that moves through time as a "cohort." If we follow the Monitoring the Future 1991 8th-grade cohort over time, their rise in drug use is truly astonishing.

In 1991, 5.7 percent of the 8th graders had used at least one illicit drug during the previous month. In 1993, when most of them were in the 10th grade, 14 percent had used one or more illegal drugs. In 1995, when they were seniors, 23.8 percent had used in the previous month, an increase of four times. The comparable figures for marijuana alone are 3.2, 10.9, and 21.2 percent, respectively, which is an increase of six and a half times!

As I pointed out, in the usual pattern, young adults ages 18 to 25 display the highest rates of illegal drugs. In 1991, when 15.4 percent of 18- to 25-year-olds had used an illegal drug during the past month (NIDA, 1991, p. 19), this was also true of 5.7 percent of 8th graders—a ratio of 2.7 times. However, by 1993, the percentages of 18- to 25-year-olds (SAMHSA, 1995, p. 35) and 8th graders who used an illicit drug during the past month were almost identical: 13.5 percent versus 12 percent, almost a ratio of 1:1. By 1994, the use of one or more illicit drugs during the past month by 8th graders (14.3 percent) had actually surpassed that of young adults (13.3 percent). From 1995 to 1998, the young-adult-to-8th-grade 30-day prevalence rate remained more or less stable (Sallett, Goode, and Pooler, 1999). This sudden rise in illicit drug use among very young adolescents to the point that it rivals that of young adults is historically unprecedented.

CHANGES IN HIGH SCHOOL STUDENTS' ATTITUDES TOWARD DRUG USE, 1975–1998

The changes in attitudes toward drug use over the past generation or so are at least as interesting as the changes in drug use itself. In fact, attitudes provide a kind of backdrop to a consideration of deviance. To the extent that attitudes are tolerant toward and accepting of any given behavior, then that behavior is not deviant. In contrast, to the extent that attitudes toward a given activity and its participants are negative, condemnatory, and derogatory, then that activity and those participants must be referred to as deviant.

If we were to posit a relationship between attitudes and behavior over time, common sense would predict that the more negative the attitudes about drug use become, the lower that drug use will be; the less negative the attitudes, the higher the drug use. In addition, it makes sense that forms of drug use that are most strongly condemned tend to be those that are least common. In contrast, forms of drug use that are least strongly condemned tend to be more common. It seems that here, common sense prevails: attitudes and behavior are very closely correlated with one another, and in a predictable direction. The behavioral changes we observed—the rise in use in the 1970s, the decline in the 1980s, and the rise once again in the 1990s—are paralleled by a corresponding attitudinal change. The problem is that we run into a chicken-and-egg situation here: It is not clear which one causes the other. However, it is clear that they are strongly related.

The Monitoring the Future survey makes use of three sets of attitudes toward drug use: whether the recreational use of drugs is perceived as harmful, disapproval of persons who use drugs, and attitudes about the legal status of marijuana. Each of these attitudes expresses disapproval (or approval) of drug use. The more harmful drug use is perceived to be, the greater the disapproval of those who use drugs, and the lower the support for marijuana legalization, obviously, the higher the condemnation of drug use. Contrarily, the less harmful drug use is perceived to be, the less that users are disapproved of, and the greater the support for marijuana legalization, the lower the condemnation of drug use. This is as true when we compare attitudes toward one drug versus another, such as when we compare answers given on a year-by-year basis. Attitudes toward drug use and drug use itself follow one another very closely. Attitudes are more condemnatory toward the use of heroin, cocaine, and LSD than toward the use of marijuana. Moreover, the use of these harder drugs is lower than for marijuana. In addition, during those years when condemnation of drug use is highest, use is lowest; when condemnation is lowest, use is highest.

In the 1970s, the proportion of high school seniors who thought that marijuana use was harmful and who disapproved of its use was relatively low. That percentage increased until the early 1990s, after which it declined again. For instance, the Monitoring the Future survey asked the question, "Do you think people risk harming themselves . . . if they smoke marijuana regularly?" In 1978, only 35 percent of the respondents agreed; in 1991, 79 percent, and in 1998, 59 percent. Disapproval of smoking marijuana "once or twice" followed the same pattern. In 1978, it was 33 percent; in 1991, 69 percent; and in 1998, 52 percent (Monitoring the Future,

1999). Much the same up-and-down pattern is revealed in attitudes toward the legality of marijuana as well as the experimental use of the harder drugs, such as LSD and cocaine. (Attitudes toward the regular use and the legality of the harder drugs is strongly opposed across-the-board.) Clearly, in the sweep of time between the 1970s and the 1990s, significant changes were afoot. The huge decline in marijuana use that took place between the late 1970s and the early 1990s was accompanied by a corresponding decline in attitudinal tolerance for the use of the drug. The later increases in use have gone hand in hand with increases in attitudinal tolerance for the recreational use of drugs, especially marijuana. Once again, attitudes toward experimental use of LSD and cocaine follow much the same pattern, but regular use is opposed in all years.

Which one caused the other? Do changes in attitudes toward drugs cause changes in drug use? Or do changes in drug use cause people to change their attitudes toward the activity? It's not clear. Some observers (Bachman, Johnston, and O'Malley, 1998) argue that attitudes change behavior and that individual lifestyle factors such as school performance, religious commitments, and recreational activities outside the home have relatively little impact on drug use. Whatever the causal arrow, it seems clear that both illegal drug use and relatively tolerant attitudes toward illegal drug use among adolescents are likely to continue for the foreseeable future. As today's young people age, their current behavior and attitudes are likely to continue well into adulthood.

REFERENCES

Bachman, Jerald G., Lloyd D. Johnston, and Patrick M. O'Malley. 1998. "Explaining Recent Increases in Students' Marijuana Use: Impacts of Perceived Risks and Disapproval, 1976 through 1996." *American Journal of Public Health,* 88 (June):887–982.

Inciardi, James A. 1986. *The War on Drugs: Heroin, Cocaine, Crime, and Public Policy.* Palo Alto, CA: Mayfield.

Inciardi, James A. 1992. *The War on Drugs II: The Continuing Epic of Heroin, Cocaine, Crack, Crime,* *AIDS, and Public Policy.* Mountain View, CA: Mayfield.

Johnson, Bruce D., et al. 1985. *Taking Care of Business: The Economics of Crime by Heroin Abusers.* Lexington, MA: Lexington Books.

Johnston, Lloyd D., Patrick M. O'Malley, and Jerald G. Bachman. 1996. *National Survey Results on Drug Use from the Monitoring the Future Study, 1975–1995,* Vol. 1: *Secondary School Students.* Rockville, MD: National Institute on Drug Abuse.

Miller, Judith Droitcour, and Ira H. Cisin, 1980. *Highlights from the National Survey on Drug Abuse: 1979.* Rockville, MD: National Institute on Drug Abuse.

Monitoring the Future, 1999. Data for 1998 Downloaded from the Internet.

NIDA (National Institute on Drug Abuse). 1991. *National Household Survey on Drug Abuse: Population Estimates 1991.* Rockville, MD: Author.

Sallett, Alphonse, Erich Goode, and William Pooler, 1999. "The Death of a Paradigm?: The Onset and Dynamics of an Adolescent Drug Epidemic." Unpublished paper. Stony Brook, NY: State University of New York.

SAMHSA (Substance Abuse and Mental Health Services Administration). 1995. *National Household Survey on Drug Abuse: Main Findings 1993.* Rockville, MD: Author.

SAMHSA (Substance Abuse and Mental Health Services Administration). 1999. *Summary of Findings from the 1998 National Household Survey on Drug Abuse.* Rockville, MD: Author.

19

DRUG CRISIS:
THE AMERICAN NIGHTMARE

ELLIOTT CURRIE

To anyone observing the state of America's cities in the 1990s, it seems devastatingly obvious that we have failed to make much headway against the drug crisis. Americans living in the worst-hit neighborhoods still face the reality of dealers on their doorstep and shots in the night; many fear for their lives, or their children's lives, and sense that their communities have slid downward into a permanent state of terror and disintegration. Even those fortunate enough to live in better neighborhoods cannot pick up a newspaper or watch the news without confronting story after story about the toll of drugs and drug-related violence on communities and families. For most of us, the drug plague seems to have settled in, become a routine feature of an increasingly frightening and bewildering urban landscape.

Yet we also hear official reassurances that, despite appearances, we have made great progress in the war on drugs, or even that victory is just around the comer. The assertion that we are winning the war on drugs is designed to vindicate our present policies: to justify pouring ever-greater resources into what we have already tried, and, in a larger sense, to rationalize our current national priorities. But our visceral reactions are correct, and the cheerleading is premature. The American drug problem remains out of control. It vastly outstrips that of any other industrial nation. And it does so despite an orgy of punishment in the name of drug control that also has no counterpart in the rest of the developed world, or in our own history.

The news is not all bad. Middle-class drug use has declined, and the worst fury of the crack epidemic has abated in many cities. But the first happened in spite of the drug war, not because of it.

And the second, while a welcome gain in the short term, pales beside the profoundly troubling long-term trend. Twenty years after the drug war began in earnest, we are far worse off than when we started. And the outlook for the future is not encouraging.

INTERNATIONAL COMPARISONS

To appreciate the magnitude of the drug crisis in the United States, we need to compare it to the experience of other advanced industrial countries. Most Americans do not realize how atypical we are—in part because that most basic reality is curiously left out, or downplayed, in our national debate on drug policy. There is much discussion of the meaning of short-range fluctuations in drug use in the United States, but little about why we lead the world in drug abuse. Those who wish to minimize the implications of our unhappy leadership often point out that the drug problem has risen *everywhere,* not just in the United States; and there is an element of truth in that. Few countries have been spared some problem with illegal drugs during the last two decades; in some it is serious and increasing. But that should not blind us to the dramatic differences between the United States and otherwise comparable societies.

A revealing study by the Canadian scholars Reginald Smart and Glenn Murray has shown that if the world's countries are divided into those with high, medium, and low drug problems, the United States is the *only* developed country that falls into the "high" category. The others—thirteen in all—are all developing countries: Afghanistan, Bolivia, Burma, Egypt, Iran, Lebanon, Malaysia, Pakistan,

Peru, the Philippines, Singapore, Thailand, and Vietnam. It is sometimes argued that the reason for the peculiar severity of the American drug problem is that we are unusually affluent and excessively tolerant—or as one observer puts it, "richer and more liberal" than other countries with less severe drug problems. But the truth is precisely the opposite; *every* other country with a drug problem on the American scale or greater is a relatively poor country (though not always among the very poorest), and most are also authoritarian and intolerant, often dictatorial. Most are also "source" countries, which grow or manufacture much of the world's supply of heroin and cocaine; in many, the abuse of those drugs has become a crisis of unprecedented proportions, especially among the young. But in the developed world, no other country matches what one British observer has called the "American Nightmare"— or even comes close.

The British, as we will see, have a significant heroin problem which mushroomed in the early 1980s; the German drug problem, which had been relatively stable up through most of the eighties, began to rise again toward the end of the decade; Spain and Italy both have substantial problems with heroin and milder ones with cocaine. Yet none even *begins* to reach our overall levels of drug use; and in only a few developed countries has cocaine in any form, much less crack, made significant inroads.

This is hardly because suppliers are uninterested in the affluent European and Japanese markets; in the late 1980s the American market was so glutted with cocaine that many high-level suppliers began looking to Europe to absorb their surplus product. Yet by the end of the decade there were fewer known cocaine addicts in all of England, for example, than in many urban *neighborhoods* in the United States. There were 677 cocaine-related arrests in France in 1989, and 4900 in the city of Boston. More people died in 1989 of the effects of cocaine abuse alone in Los Angeles than died of *all* drug-related causes in England. As many died from methamphetamine abuse in the city of San Diego as died of *all* drug-related causes in Holland, with fifteen times the population.

Even measured by surveys of high school students—which, as we shall see, *understate* the severity of the American drug problem because they miss our sprawling population of the socially and economically marginal—there are striking differences in the extent of drug abuse between the United States and Europe. Thus, in 1989 something over 10 percent of American high school seniors admitted having tried cocaine—more than five times the proportion turned up by surveys in Germany, Italy, and England (three countries with relatively severe drug problems by European standards) and about *twenty* times the rate in Sweden, Holland, and Norway.

What is true of drug use also holds for its most deadly social and medical consequences. Drug-related violence is by no means absent in European countries, but on the American scale it is simply unknown. There are twice as many drug-related homicides annually in New York City as there are homicides of any kind in all of England, with seven times the population. There were more drug-related killings in the city of Washington, D.C. (population 600,000) in 1988 than there were murders of any type in all of Scandinavia (population eighteen million). No major European city lacks an illegal drug market, but in none of them are entire neighborhoods gripped by Uzi-wielding drug gangs or terrorized by routine drive-by shootings.

The magnitude of the link between drugs and AIDS in the United States is similarly unparalleled in the rest of the industrial world. Nearly 25 percent of the more than 200,000 diagnosed AIDS cases in the United States have intravenous drug use as the only risk factor; another 6 percent involve both IV drug use and homosexuality. The proportion is far higher in some cities—40 percent in New York and 65 percent in Newark, the nation's drugs–AIDS capital. In Sweden, at the end of 1990, there were slightly more than five hundred known AIDS cases, of which only seventeen, or a little over 3 percent, involved IV drugs. In Holland, there were about seventy-five AIDS cases in 1989 in which IV drug use was the only risk factor, or about 7 percent of their total.

Moreover, the American drug crisis, by itself, is responsible for most of the rise in AIDS among *children* in the entire industrial world. In 83 percent of pediatric AIDS cases known by the end of 1990, the children had contracted the disease from their mothers—most of whom bad been infected through contacts with IV drug users. Nationally, about 1.5 out of every 1000 babies are now born to mothers with the AIDS virus (as of 1989); in one hospital in Newark, closer to 40 out of 1000. Mother–child transmission of AIDS is a rare event in most other developed countries (though, again, common in parts of the Third World); in 1989, we had 55 times as many cases as West Germany, 65 times as many as the United Kingdom.

In pointing to these striking differences, I do not mean to idealize the European situation. In some European countries drug abuse is a problem of genuinely troubling dimensions, and in some the AIDS–drugs connection is worsening. But in none of those countries have drugs and drug-related crime rocked the foundations of the social order as they have in the United States, or turned the city streets into urban battlegrounds, or triggered a massive explosion of sexually transmitted disease. . . .

AMERICAN DRUG CRISIS

While it is probably true that the epidemic of cocaine has peaked, both cocaine and heroin are now endemic in America at levels that far surpass those before the start of the drug war. While there is credible evidence that rising health consciousness and growing awareness of the adverse effects of drug abuse have altered the drug habits of the more secure strata of American society, no such evidence exists for the bottom quarter of the population.

Even many who support the thrust of our present drug policies would acknowledge that the drug crisis among "hard-core" users in the more marginal populations is understated by the conventional statistics, and that it has proven remarkably resistant to the conventional tools of the drug war. But they would argue that the declines in *middle*-class drug use prove that the drug war is "on the right track," and that if we only redoubled our ef-

forts we could make it work against the admittedly tougher situation in the inner cities as well.

The trouble with that view is that the conventional drug war had virtually nothing to do with the declines in drug use among the better-off, for it was never *fought* against their drug use. Despite occasional bursts of rhetoric about cracking down on "recreational" drug use in the suburbs, so little did that crackdown actually take place even at the height of the drug war in the late eighties and early nineties that when several University of Virginia fraternities were raided in the spring of 1991—netting, to no one's great surprise, nothing more than small amounts of marijuana and LSD—the story was front-page news in the national press for days. In the Virginia case, law-enforcement officials were reported to have "expressed hope" that the raid would send the message that drug seizures and arrests would no longer "be limited mainly to poor neighborhoods." The drug war has been overwhelmingly targeted at the communities of the poor and near-poor, especially the minority poor. It's possible to argue over whether or not that emphasis is justified; it's not possible to deny that it exists.

Nationally, in 1989, about 40 percent of all arrests for all drug violations were of blacks, who are only 12 percent of the population. The proportion of jail inmates charged with a drug offense who were black or Hispanic rose from 55 percent in 1983 to 73 percent in 1989. The disproportion is even greater in areas where hard-drug use is heavily concentrated: In New York State, over 90 percent of those sent to state prison for drug felonies in 1988 were black or Hispanic, and the figure was even higher—about 95 percent—for the lower-level felonies that made up almost three-fifths of prison commitments for drug offenses. "Measured by jail and prison populations," notes a recent report of the New York State Coalition for Criminal justice, "one can almost say that drug abuse has been legalized for middle-class whites."

In California, only 19 percent of adults and less than 9 percent of juveniles arrested for felony narcotic violations in 1989 were white and non-Hispanic. According to a report from the National Institute of Justice, the drug war was the main reason why the number of black and Hispanic youth held in short-term juvenile institutions nationwide increased by 30 percent between 1985 and 1987 alone—while detentions of non-Hispanic white youth rose by only 1 percent. Minority youth were more likely to be detained once arrested than whites, both for drug sales and possession. They were also more likely than whites to be referred to courts for drug offenses in the first place. The result was a 71 percent increase in the number of non-white youth detained for drug offenses in the space of just two years.

The drug war, in short, has been fought hardest—in some places, almost exclusively—in precisely those communities where drug use remains most severe and most stubborn, barely at all in those where it has fallen. Likewise, it has been fought most fiercely against the *drugs* that remain most stubbornly persistent—heroin and especially cocaine—and barely at all against marijuana, which has undergone the most significant decline and indeed accounts for the bulk of the much trumpeted fall in illicit drug use in the United States. In New York, for example, research shows that the measures taken against crack in the 1980s were far tougher than those for other drugs—including "widespread arrests for sale and possession, more stringent charging decisions, and harsher sentences."

Meanwhile, revealingly, marijuana use declined (according to the self-report surveys) in spite of a very significant *let-up* in the law-enforcement effort against it. Nationally, marijuana possession arrests *dropped* by over 10 percent between 1980 and 1988, while arrests for possession of heroin and cocaine exploded by 600 percent. In California, the pattern was even more extreme: Juvenile felony arrests for marijuana dropped by well over half during the 1980s.

In short, whatever caused the decline in marijuana use among American teenagers in the 1980s, it was certainly not the war on drugs. In most places there *was* no war on marijuana use, and, in some, authorities had officially declared a truce.

What we know from careful analyses of the high-school drug surveys, indeed, is that most of the decline in marijuana use can be attributed to changing perceptions of its dangers to health and well-being—changes which fit well with the long-run trend toward increasing health-consciousness among middle-class Americans, a trend that encompasses declines not only in drug use but in alcohol, smoking, and unhealthy diet, and increased exercise. These changes are all to the good, but they are *not* the result of the war on drugs. (Indeed, to the extent that they are related to specific antidrug strategies at all, they reflect efforts at education and prevention which the last two administrations have systematically slighted.) . . .

ROOTS OF THE CRISIS

"The epidemic areas," [researcher Isidor] Chein concluded, "are, on average, areas of relatively concentrated settlement of underprivileged minority groups, of poverty and low economic status." They were also characterized by low educational attainment and large numbers of disrupted families. Importantly, the data made it clear that race itself was not the overriding factor: low incomes and poor jobs explained most of the link between drug use and race in these neighborhoods. It was not so much that the epidemic neighborhoods were *black* neighborhoods, but that black neighborhoods tended to have large concentrations of low-income people in low-status jobs. . . .

Chein attributed the success of the cohesive family in protecting adolescents against heroin use to its "contribution to a sense of mutuality"—a "sense of human solidarity, a feeling of belonging, respect for the integrity and value of the individual human being, and the long-range motivation of things worth living for"—which was disturbingly rare in the areas of concentrated deprivation in American cities. In interviews, the addicts often expressed "profound pessimism and alienation," agreeing that there was "not much chance for a better world," that "most people were better off not born," and that everyone was "really out for himself: nobody cares." . . . Ideally, a strong, supportive family could shield adolescents against the "prevailing atmosphere of degenerated personal relationships" in these deprived neighborhoods. The catch, of course, was that it was precisely in neighborhoods like these that the family itself was especially vulnerable, as was clear from the high proportion of disrupted and pathological families in them.

As this suggests, Chein's picture of the addicts' backgrounds, personalities, and prospects was generally grim. Young heroin addicts were seen as the most extreme product of a chain of pathologies that began with the economic deprivation of the larger community and were exacerbated by the resulting disintegration or demoralization of many urban families. The boys who became addicted—at least in the white and Puerto Rican neighborhoods—were likely to be those who had suffered the most emotional damage from an inadequate and conflictual family life. But the study was equally emphatic that this was more than just a matter of individual psychopathology. The family's problems were rooted in the larger pathologies of the community—the general bleakness of life, the absence of opportunity, and the breakdown of more supportive cultural values in the American urban environment. . . .

For young people, especially, growing up in these communities, drug use performed a variety of functions which, most observers agreed, reflected ordinary human—and specifically adolescent—needs, but ones which were difficult to fulfill in ordinary ways in these distinctly abnormal circumstances. There were differences of emphasis and specifics, but the serious observers of heroin addiction generally agreed that much more important than the physiological effects of the drug were its uses in helping to build an identity, buttress social status and the esteem of peers, and provide alternative and compelling sources of challenge and purposeful activity for people who were deprived of them through normal channels. In the topsy-turvy world of the shattered communities of the inner city, the very dangers and adversities associated with hard-drug use were transformed into appeals. It was precisely the illegality of heroin use, and the very real danger of arrest and jail, that helped provide the intrigue and "elite-group" identity that observers like Finestone found to be central to the "cat" culture: precisely the high risk of illness, pain, and abject enslavement to addiction that drew the "stand-up cat" to test his mettle against the toughest of drugs. . . .

None of this was to deny that many addicts desperately needed help. But it did shift the perspective on what help should *mean,* in two related ways. First, the research on addiction suggested that what many addicts most needed in the long run was changed lives—broader opportunities for good work and respectable incomes, full participation in the surrounding society. Second, while many addicts did need immediate assistance in the short run, they usually needed a wider range of help than traditional medical or psychiatric treatment offered—help that would enable them to cope with the multiple obstacles they faced in the increasingly inhospitable inner cities. Within this framework, some form of individual treatment could have an important place, but only if it shifted focus, away from the medical model of treating the individual in isolation and toward integration with broader efforts to provide better opportunities and better tools for taking advantage of them.

This view was made explicit in Preble and Casey's classic article. "The ultimate solution to the problem" of lower-class heroin addiction, they argued, "as with all the problems which result from social injustice, lies in the creation of legitimate opportunities for a meaningful life for those who want it." In the meantime, "reparative measures" were necessary. But given their emphasis on the lack of opportunities for good, challenging work as the root cause of the spread of addiction in the inner city, the measures Preble and Casey favored leaned heavily toward "educational and vocational training and placement," rather than chemical treatment with substitute drugs or antagonists, traditional psychotherapy, or group therapy. They proposed a model treatment program that would span a full three years: nine months of intensive vocational and educational training coupled with psychological counseling, and twenty-seven months devoted to "aftercare" in the community, which could involve further training and schooling as needed, along with social and psychological counseling—a "comprehensive social reparation" for those addicts not "too severely damaged by society."

CIGARETTE SMOKING
AS DEVIANT BEHAVIOR

ERICH GOODE

Our guest takes me aside. "Excuse me," he says, "I hope you don't mind, I'd like to go outside for a few minutes for a smoke."

"No problem," I respond, "take your time."

We are in a restaurant. A man at a table behind us is smoking. A woman is sitting to our right. Abruptly, she gets up, walks over to the man with the cigarette. Shoving her face only inches away from his, she announces, "This is a no-smoking area. *Do you mind?*" He stares at her as if she were a bug crawling on a wall, then blows a puff of smoke in her face, snubs out the cigarette on a plate in front of him, and marches out of the restaurant.

It is three o'clock. Two dozen office workers are standing, huddled together, outside the building where they work. It is cold; their shoulders are hunched and some are stamping their feet. All of them are smoking. They seem almost furtive about it, as if they have been caught doing something naughty. Gradually, one by one, they toss their cigarette butts into a bucket filled with sand and drift back into the building.

Today, these are everyday occurrences. They tell us a great deal about the deviant status of cigarette smoking. Such events were rare or nonexistent a generation ago. The history of tobacco consumption is one of the most fascinating tales we might hear. It is also instructive, for from this tale we learn about what it means to be human.

THE NATURE AND PREVALENCE
OF TOBACCO USE

Tobacco contains a drug, a psychoactive or mind-altering substance that is toxic (capable of killing humans in a sufficiently large dose), medically harmful if used over a long period of time, and addicting (capable of producing a physical dependence). More people are killed by the consumption of tobacco than all other drugs combined. Experts at the Centers for Disease Control estimate that roughly 430,000 Americans die *each year* as a result of cigarette smoking, making tobacco consumption by far the country's number one drug problem. Slightly more than one American in four (27.7 percent, to be exact) age 12 and older smoke cigarettes—roughly 60 million people (SAMHSA, 1999, p. 22). Worldwide, the total number of smokers is between one billion and two billion people. According to a report issued by the World Health Organization in 1997, the overwhelming majority of the men—but relatively few of the women—in South Korea (68 percent), Russia (67 percent), China (61 percent), and Japan (59 percent) smoke tobacco cigarettes.

With respect to popularity, in the United States, tobacco is the number two drug, after alcohol. In fact, everywhere, tobacco is used more often than alcohol. In the United States, the level of alcohol consumption among persons who drink averages out to about one and one-half ounces per person per day, the equivalent of two mixed drinks daily. (Most drink less than this, a few drink much more.) In contrast, the typical smoker consumes slightly more than a pack a day; in 1998, this worked out to an average of 22.6 cigarettes daily. This means that more than 10 times as many "doses" of nicotine are consumed by smokers than "doses" of alcohol are consumed by drinkers. Thus, although alcohol is our most widely used drug, tobacco is our most often used drug.

WHAT'S DEVIANT ABOUT THE USE OF TOBACCO?

Why consider the use of tobacco in a book about deviant behavior? What's deviant about smoking cigarettes? Isn't it an activity that is so common it can hardly be regarded as deviant? Isn't it the basis of a respectable, multibillion dollar industry? Doesn't it seem to be stretching the concept of deviance beyond all recognition to regard the consumption of this legal, commonly used substance as a form of deviant behavior? Smoking is instructive to any student of deviance, for two reasons.

First, the deviant status of the use of tobacco has shifted over the years. In European or Western culture, immediately after its adoption from North American Indians (as we'll see shortly), tobacco consumption was denounced and criminalized in no uncertain terms. However, within a generation or two, Europeans had decided to live with it. The use of snuff and chewing tobacco, as well as pipe and cigar smoking, became respectable, at least among men. In the early decades of the twentieth century, cigarettes began to be the method of choice for consuming tobacco, but beginning in the 1960s, a movement gathered strength that redefined tobacco consumption as unacceptable, objectionable, harmful, and an offense against oneself and others—in a word, deviant. The achievement of the goal of discrediting the activity of smoking in all situations and in all social circles is far from complete. Nonetheless, this movement has managed to undermine the respectability of smoking and cast doubt on its validity. The movement's achievement, in the United States at least, is that, although smoking is not a classic form of deviance, its deviant status is partial and growing. The shifting status of tobacco consumption—from deviant to respectable to partially deviant—gives us an insight into the socially constructed nature of definitions of deviance.

Smoking is instructive to the student of deviance for a second reason as well: As we have seen, it represents an activity that is vastly more harmful than almost any other behavior we could imagine. In fact, on a death-for-death basis, it is much more harmful than the use of illegal drugs. The fact that it is only mildly condemned today indicates that there is a huge discrepancy between objective harm and the subjective realm of condemnation. People who engage in many entirely harmless and innocuous activities are considered deviant: Consider the eccentric, the weirdo, the lame, the loser, the person who picks his nose or talks with his mouth full of food. In contrast, politicians who start wars that kill millions of people are rarely condemned by the citizens of their own countries; to the contrary, they are usually considered heroes. Compare the 430,000 people killed annually by tobacco consumption with the country's 18,000 criminal homicide victims per year. Murderers are villains; tobacco executives are respectable, make enormous salaries, and live in fancy houses. What about the village atheist, the lesbian couple who live across the street, the nudists up the block, the recluse who watches the world from half-drawn shades, the bag lady who collects bottles and cans in a shopping cart? Does the behavior of countless other people like them produce a yearly pile of bodies 430,000 corpses high? We don't have to be muckrakers or idealistic reformers to be struck by this discrepancy. The lesson should be clear: Deviance and harm are to some degree independent of one another.

A BRIEF HISTORY OF TOBACCO CONSUMPTION

The tobacco plant is indigenous to the western hemisphere; prior to the 1490s, its use was unknown in Europe and Asia. The native inhabitants of San Salvador, an island in the Caribbean, presented Christopher Columbus with a sheaf of tobacco leaves. A member of Columbus's crew, who went by the name of Rodrigo, returned to Portugal with some leaves—and a tobacco habit as well. When his countrymen saw him blow smoke out of his mouth and nose, they believed him to be possessed by the devil, and he was promptly jailed. By the time of his release, the habit had become widespread in Portugal (Ray and Ksir, 1999, p. 265).

When first introduced into Europe, the practice of tobacco consumption generated a great deal of hostility as well as legislation outlawing the sale and use of this plant product. Some of these laws even called for the death penalty against offenders. In 1604, King James issued a "Counterblaste" condemning the consumption of tobacco. He referred to smoking as "a custom loathsome to the eye, hateful to the nose, harmful to the brain, [and] dangerous to the lung." Within a decade, though, tobacco consumption had become acceptable in Britain. In 1623, the Ottoman sultan ordered that smokers be put to death; by 1655 this effort had been abandoned and tobacco became officially accepted in the empire. In 1634, the czar of Russia ordered the noses of smokers slit as punishment. In China in 1638, decapitation was declared the penalty for tobacco use. In 1614 in Japan, 150 individuals were apprehended for buying and selling tobacco against the emperor's commands. The mogul emperor of Hindustan declared that "as the smoking of tobacco has taken a very bad effect in the health and mind of so many persons I order that no person shall practice the habit" (Home Office, 1968, p. 16). The penalty was to have one's lips slit. Naturally, all of these efforts were a dismal failure (Blum et al., 1969, pp. 87–97).

Interestingly, much of the earliest use of tobacco was medical. Both the botanical names of the plant's genus (*Nicotiana*) and its principal psychoactive or mind-altering ingredient (nicotine) were taken from Jean Nicot, who was the French ambassador to the Portuguese throne. He introduced tobacco to France in 1560. Believing it to be a medicinal herb, Nicot administered tobacco to the queen, Catherine de Medici, wife of Henry II, who suffered from migraine headaches. At the time, the French referred to tobacco as the "holy plant," the "plant against all evils."

The earliest recreational use of tobacco involved inhaling the fumes of the combusted leaf through a tube or a straw. By the 1700s, sniffing or snorting powdered or shredded tobacco snuff became immensely popular in Europe. In the United States in the 1800s, the most popular method of tobacco consumption was chewing. In fact, it was not until the 1920s that the volume of tobacco manufactured for cigarettes outstripped that for chewing. Cuspidors or spittoons—brass receptacles designed to receive chewing tobacco spit—remained in federal buildings until 1945. As late as 1920, three out of four pounds of commercially manufactured tobacco were devoted to cigar and pipe smoking, snuff, and chewing.

Smoking tobacco in the form of cigarettes did not become popular until well into the first half of the twentieth century. In 1900, only 2.5 billion cigarettes were sold in the United States—only 0.5 percent of its present level. In the slightly more than two decades between 1912 and 1935, the number of cigarettes sold in the United States increased from 13.2 billion to 134.4 billion—a tenfold increase. In the decade that followed, until the end of World War II, the number increased by two-and-a-half times, to 340.6 billion. It rose into the 1960s, until it stood at 523.9 billion in 1963, and it continued to grow until 1980, when it reached a high of 631.5 billion. After that, the figure declined; in 1998, 470 billion cigarettes were sold. Of course, these figures do not take into account population increases. More important than the total number of cigarettes sold are the per capita sales—the number sold per person. In 1900, only 54 cigarettes were sold domestically for every person living in the United States age 16 and older. This number increased year by year until 1963, when it hit 4,345. Since that time, the per capita sale of cigarettes has declined year by year. In 1998, it stood at 2,261, only slightly more than half its all-time high. Obviously, 1964 was a watershed year; something happened that year that turned the tide in cigarette sales. What was it?

TOBACCO AND HEALTH

The decline in cigarette consumption since the 1960s can be attributed almost entirely to the widespread acceptance of the view that tobacco consumption is harmful to the smoker's health. In 1964, what is probably the most influential document in the history of the tobacco industry was published: the U.S. Surgeon General's Report, titled *Smoking and Health*. Summarizing the research current at that time, this report argued that the use of tobacco products represented a serious health hazard. The impact of this report was immediate. The 1964 per capita consumption of cigarettes immediately declined slightly and, as we have seen, it continued to fall throughout the twentieth century. In all probability, it will decline well into the twenty-first century.

The many medical studies that have been conducted since the Surgeon General's Report confirm the verdict of that publication: Cigarette smoking is catastrophic to the smoker's health. Nicotine is a poison. If injected directly into the bloodstream, roughly 60 milligrams is the lethal dose that is sufficient to kill a human being. However, because cigarettes are smoked, a substantial portion of the nicotine they contain is dissipated into the air. A cigar contains about 100 to 120 milligrams of nicotine, but its smoke is not inhaled. Nicotine can kill as a result of muscular and respiratory paralysis. Fortunately, not enough of the drug is absorbed during a brief enough period of time for cigars or cigarettes to be lethal (Ray and Ksir, 1999, pp. 281–282).

Perhaps the most noticeable acute or immediate effect of cigarette smoking is that it releases carbon monoxide, which reduces the body's supply of oxygen to the blood, causing shortness of breath and, in more substantial doses, dizziness. A chronic or long-term effect of smoking is that this oxygen deficit will damage the heart and the blood vessels of smokers. The same effect in an expectant mother can damage her fetus and increase the likelihood of birth defects (Goldstein, 1994, pp. 110–111). Nicotine constricts the blood vessels, causing the heart to work harder to maintain a constant supply of blood and oxygen. It also inhibits stomach contractions that are associated with hunger, hence, the belief that if one stops smoking, one may gain weight has some validity. More broadly, the drug does not produce profound behavioral changes or impairment. Nicotine and caffeine are the only drugs passengers do not have

to feel concerned about if their pilot is using them (p. 113). Intellectual and motor ability do not decline significantly under the influence of nicotine. Indeed, at low to moderate doses, they may even improve slightly.

Is nicotine addicting? In the 1980s, Philip Morris, a major cigarette manufacturer, commissioned a study on whether tobacco produces an addiction in rats. The results of this research demonstrated that, according to the criteria of addiction that had been established, nicotine is indeed an addicting drug. However the study was not published. In fact, when company executives reviewed its findings, the researchers were fired and the lab was closed down (Ray and Ksir, 1999, p. 284). In 1994, tobacco executives appeared before Congress and testified that nicotine is not addicting. Today, nearly all pharmacologists, as well as researchers who study the impact of drugs, agree that nicotine is addicting and that it is the primary, and very possibly the only, substance in tobacco that causes this physical dependence.

There are at least six indications that cigarette smoking is addicting or dependency-producing. The first is its frequency; smokers consume an average of 22.6 cigarettes per day in the United States. Second, if we were to plot use during the day with levels of nicotine in the blood, their correspondence would resemble a thermostat. That is, the nicotine level in the smoker's body rises during and immediately after smoking and declines soon afterward. When it falls below a certain amount, the smoker lights up again, elevating that level back to where it was before (Goldstein, 1994, p. 105). A line depicting the presence of nicotine in the smoker's body during the course of a day would resemble a sawtooth pattern, with nicotine rising, falling, then rising again, and so on throughout the day. A truly dependent smoker starts the day with a cigarette. The third indication is, once laboratory animals have been induced to take nicotine regularly, they work extremely hard to continue self-administering it. Exactly this same pattern prevails with heroin and cocaine. If smokers switch to a low-nicotine cigarette, they inhale more deeply or smoke more cigarettes to obtain the same level of nicotine in their body. Fourth, smokers who quit describe feeling a strong "craving" for cigarettes that persists for years after they give up the habit. Fifth, statistics on relapse show that, although many smokers do quit, they do so only with great effort and, usually, after repeated attempts. As many cigarette smokers relapse and return to their drug of choice as heroin addicts. Finally, there are the physical effects produced by nicotine abstention: headaches, fatigue and drowsiness, a shortened attention span, irritability, anxiety, insomnia, hunger, heart palpitations, and tremors (Goldberg, 1997, p. 212). It is virtually impossible to refute the charge that nicotine, the principal drug in cigarettes, is addicting.

Smokers are much, much more likely to die prematurely than nonsmokers. In fact, according to statistics released by the U.S. Department of Health and Human Services and published in *Smoking, Tobacco, and Health: A Factbook,* a nonsmoker is more likely to live to the age of 75 than a smoker is to live to 65. A two-pack-a-day smoker is 23 times more likely to die of lung cancer than a nonsmoker. (The one saving grace of cigarettes—and it is a grim one—is that because smokers are likely to die before 65, society saves a great deal of money on not having to pay their health care, retirement benefits, and Social Security!) For years, cigarette executives claimed that these data were merely epidemiological or correlational. That is, they agreed that smokers were more likely to die of a variety of diseases, but what did that prove? What *caused* these diseases? they asked. Was it the lifestyle of smokers versus nonsmokers? Was it where they lived? Who was to say it was the cigarettes they smoked that caused the differences we observed? What these scientists did not have, tobacco representatives claimed, was evidence pointing to etiological or causal factors in cigarettes indicating that they were directly and actively responsible for these diseases.

In 1996, a team of researchers discovered a chemical in tobacco smoke, benzopyrene, that causes carcinogenic or cancer-inducing genetic mutations (Grady, 1997). In what was probably a carefully crafted public relations move, it was not until 1999 that Philip Morris executives admitted that medical research indicates that smoking causes cancer (Meier, 1999). The fact is, smoking shaves an entire decade off one's life. Moreover, it reduces the quality of life as well, because the last few years of the smoker's life tend to be marred by diseases such as lung cancer, stroke, emphysema, heart disease, and bronchitis. Today, hardly anyone questions the fact that tobacco is seriously harmful to the smoker's life. In fact, the U.S. Environmental Protection Agency estimates that roughly 50,000 Americans die per year as a result of "passive" smoke—smoke inhaled by a nonsmoker from a smoker's cigarette. Also, according to an extensive review of the literature, more than 5,000 infants die as a result of their mother's smoking habit. This does not include an estimated 19,000 to 141,000 spontaneous abortions (or miscarriages) directly or indirectly induced by tobacco smoke (DiFranza and Lew, 1995). The Centers for Disease Control estimates that, in the United States, one out of five deaths can be traced to smoking. Without exaggeration, the consumption of tobacco can be referred to as a holocaust. There is probably no single change that would contribute more to public health worldwide than the elimination of tobacco consumption.

RECENT DEVELOPMENTS

The federal government sponsors two major ongoing surveys of legal and illegal drug use in the United States. Based on extremely large, nationally representative samples, they give us a very good idea of the rate of the consumption of psychoactive substances in the United States. The Monitoring the Future study has surveyed high school seniors every year since 1975, college students and young adults not in college since 1980, and 8th and 10th graders since 1991. The National Household Survey on Drug Abuse has regularly surveyed a sample of the entire population since 1971. Among other drugs, these two surveys ask about the use of cigarettes.

The trajectory of cigarette consumption among adolescents is clear—and disturbing. In

1976, the proportion of 12th graders who had smoked one or more cigarettes during the past 30 days stood at 38 percent. This figure steadily declined through the late 1970s and throughout the 1980s; by 1991, only 28 percent of high school seniors smoked (Johnston, O'Malley, and Bachman, 1996, p. 89). Many public health experts were optimistic that adolescent cigarette smoking would be virtually eliminated by the early twenty first century. However, something strange began to happen in the early 1990s; no one yet has a plausible explanation for this development. Between 1991 and 1998, the proportion of high school students who smoked tobacco cigarettes during the previous month rose from 28 to 37 percent. In 1991, 8th and 10th graders were added to the Monitoring the Future sample. Between 1991 and 1998, 8th-grade smoking rose from 14 to 19 percent, and 10th-grade smoking increased from 21 to 30 percent (Monitoring the Future, 1999). Clearly, a major change took place during the 1990s that brought young people back to the use of cigarettes.

The findings of the National Household Survey on Drug Abuse convey the same message. Table 20.1 tells an astonishing and alarming story. Between the 1970s and the early 1990s, among all age categories, cigarette consumption in the United States declined dramatically. From nearly four Americans out of ten in 1974 (39 percent), the proportion of smokers in the population decreased to a shade over a quarter (27 percent) in 1991. However, after that year, after nearly a three-decade-long decrease, smoking began to rise—but only for adolescents and young adults. Among adults ages 26 to 34, between 1991 and 1998, smoking remained stable at 33 percent, and among those 35 and older, it even inched down a bit, from 27 to 25 percent. In that same period, the proportion of adolescents ages 12 to 17 who smoked increased from 11 to 18 percent, and among young adults ages 18 to 25, the increase was even more dramatic—from 32 to 42 percent (SAMHSA, 1999, p. 79). As these younger persons age, in all likelihood they will carry their smoking habits with them into the older brackets. Given what we know about the health hazards of smoking, we can only view these statistics with alarm.

Between 90 and 95 percent of all adult smokers began their habit before the age of 18. Some experts argue that if we do not begin smoking as teenagers, we are unlikely to smoke at all. Consider, too, the fact that the earlier the habit begins, the greater the likelihood that tobacco will kill the smoker. As reported in the *New York Times* in 1996, experts estimate that, today, roughly 3,000

Table 20.1   Cigarette Smoking in the Past Month by Age, 1974–1998

Age	PERCENTAGE OF PEOPLE SMOKING		
	1974	*1991*	*1998*
12–17	25	11	18
18–25	49	32	42
26–34	47	33	33
35 and older	37	27	25
Total Population	39	27	28

Sources: Data for 1974 from Patricia M. Fishburne, Herbert I. Abelson, and Ira H. Cisin, *National Survey on Drug Abuse: Main Findings 1979* (1980, Rockville, MD: National Institute on Drug Abuse), p. 101, (figure for total population retabulated from sample size, p. 156). For 1991, NIDA, *National Household Survey on Drug Abuse: Population Estimates 1991* (1991, Rockville, MD: Author), p. 91. For 1998, SAMHSA, 1999, *Summary of Findings from the 1998 National Household Survey on Drug Abuse* (1999, Rockville, MD: Author) p. 79.

American teenagers will begin smoking *every day.* Of these, one-third will eventually die of a tobacco-related illness. The Centers for Disease Control estimates that roughly five million Americans ages 17 and younger now smoking will die of one or more diseases caused by cigarette smoking. If the downward trend that began in the mid to late 1970s had continued into the 1990s, perhaps as many as four million of them would not be included in this projection (Feder, 1997).

To many teenagers, cigarettes seem cool, a sign of maturity. To smoke is to be free from adult restrictions, to defy parental authority, to indulge in a slightly wicked pleasure, to celebrate a sensation that is both delicious and dangerous. Perhaps Richard Klein's *Cigarettes Are Sublime* (1993) says it best. He refers to the cigarette as "the wand of dreams," one of "the most interesting and significant cultural products produced by modernity." A man who smokes is seen as virile; a woman who smokes announces that she is sexually available. Campaigns designed to educate young people about the medical harm of smoking, Klein argues, are missing the point. "Warning smokers or neophytes of the dangers [of smoking] entices them more powerfully to the edge of the abyss." Cigarettes offer to smokers a "dark beauty"; they are alluring precisely because they are bad for you, he insists. Every drag haunts smokers with death, tantalizes them with a highwire act that bespeaks daring, bravado, a reckless foolhardiness. Cigarettes are bad, says Klein, and "that is why they are good—not good, not beautiful, but sublime." One need only watch Humphrey Bogart (who died of lung cancer) in *Casablanca,* observe any group of 12-year-olds lighting up, look at a picture of the French writer Albert Camus, a cigarette dangling from his lips, or footage of the 1940s and 1950s newscaster Edward R. Murrow, puffing away while interviewing his subjects, to appreciate the appeal of cigarettes. It is clear from these examples that tobacco has always been associated with decadence, so none of this is new or recent. Even today, adults no less than youngsters associate cigarettes with sinful pleasure. However, for some reason, in the past decade, these alluring associations—which had begun to lose their appeal during the 1980s—are staging an almost explosive comeback among the young.

In 1979, in an article subtitled "Cigarette Smoking as Deviant Behavior," sociologists Gerald Markle and Ronald Troyer predicted "increasingly militant confrontations between pro and antismoking forces, both at the individual and collective level" (1979, p. 611; see also Troyer and Markle, 1983). These were prophetic words. A full-scale battle over cigarettes broke out in the mid 1990s that is likely to continue for decades. A very few landmarks in this war include the following:

- In 1994, a paralegal working in Brown and Williamson (B&W) Tobacco Corporation's Louisville office walked off with cartons full of copies of the corporation's secret internal documents. Since that time, numerous muckraking articles as well as a major book have been written on B&W's unethical sales of a poisonous substance to the public. One of those articles, published in the *Journal of the American Medical Association,* was titled "Looking through the Keyhole at the Tobacco Industry" (Glantz et al., 1995).

- In February 1996, *60 Minutes* broadcast an interview with Jeffrey Wigand, formerly a biochemist with B&W. Wigand's goal was to make a safer, less carcinogenic cigarette. Eventually, he was fired because the company president felt that any mention of a "safer" cigarette would imply that the cigarettes they had been selling were unsafe. Wigand testified to the Justice Department about the harm that cigarettes do and the unethical practices B&W pursued. The smear campaign that B&W launched against Wigand—sending documentation to the *Wall Street Journal* claiming that he was a liar, a wife-beater, a shoplifter, a deadbeat dad, and an embezzler—is dramatized in the 1999 film *The Insider.*

- In 1998, after filing lawsuits against the tobacco industry, 46 states agreed to a $206 billion settlement from the nation's cigarette makers to recover the cost of Medicaid claims spent treating smoking-related illnesses. Many officials had feared that state budgets would become strapped because they pay the major burden of the health care of former smokers suffering from diseases such as lung cancer and emphysema, which are caused in large part by smoking. The settlement resolves all state claims against the industry.

- In 1999, as part of a $100 million public relations campaign, Philip Morris unveiled a new Internet site that stated that there is an "overwhelming medical and scientific consensus that cigarette smoking causes" diseases, including lung cancer, emphysema, and heart disease. It also stated that smoking "is addictive as that term is most commonly used today." The move was widely interpreted as an attempt to reshape its corporate image and to minimize the possibility of future lawsuits against the company.
- In 1994, chief executives for the nation's largest tobacco industry testified before a congressional hearing to the effect that cigarettes are neither addicting nor medically harmful. Immediately, the Democrats in Congress pressed the Justice Department to investigate whether these executives had committed the crime of perjury—in other words, lied under oath. The Justice Department spent five years and millions of dollars investigating the case, but it finally concluded that it could not prove the charge or win the case. In 1999, the investigation was dropped. However, within days of the demise of the case, Attorney General Janet Reno announced a wide-ranging civil suit against big tobacco companies, which seeks to recover billions in smoking-related health care costs. Because the civil court operates under a lower burden of proof than criminal court, observers are more optimistic about this suit than the previous one (Meier and Johnston, 1999).

The conflict between tobacco and its opponents is likely to continue unabated well into the twenty-first century. It is a battle that tobacco cannot win.

REFERENCES

Blum, Richard, et al. 1969. *Society and Drugs.* San Francisco: Jossey-Bass.

DeFranza, Joseph R., and Robert A. Lew. 1995. "Effect of Maternal Cigarette Smoking on Pregnancy Complications and Sudden Infant Death Syndrome." *Journal of Family Practice,* 40 (April): 385–394.

Feder, Barnaby J. 1997. "Surge in Teenage Smoking Left an Industry Vulnerable." *New York Times,* April 20, pp. 1, 28.

Fishburne, Patricia M., Herbert I. Abelson, and Ira H. Cisin. 1980. *National Survey on Drug Abuse: Main Findings 1979.* Rockville, MD: National Institute on Drug Abuse.

Glantz, Stanton A., et al. 1995. "Looking through the Keyhole at the Tobacco Industry: The Brown and Williamson Documents." *Journal of the American Medical Association,* 274 (July 19): 219–224.

Goldberg, Raymond. 1997. *Drugs across the Spectrum.* Englewood, CO: Morton.

Goldstein, Avram. 1994. *Addiction: From Biology to Drug Policy.* New York: W. H. Freeman.

Grady, Denise. 1997. "Study Finds Secondhand Smoke Doubles Risk of Heart Disease." *New York Times,* May 20, pp. A1, A18.

Home Office. 1968. *Cannabis: Report by the Advisory Committee on Drug Dependence.* London: Her Majesty Stationery Office.

Johnston, Lloyd D., Patrick M. O'Malley, and Jerald G. Bachman. 1996. *National Survey Results on Drug Use from the Monitoring the Future Study, 1975–1995.* Rockville, MD: National Institute on Drug Abuse.

Klein, Richard. 1993. *Cigarettes Are Sublime.* Durham, NC: Duke University Press.

Markle, Gerald E., and Ronald J. Troyer. 1979. "Smoke Gets in Your Eyes: Cigarette Smoking as Deviant Behavior." *Social Problems,* 26 (June): 611–625.

Meier, Philip. 1999. "Philip Morris Admits Evidence Shows Smoking Causes Cancer." *New York Times,* October 13, pp. A1, A21.

Monitoring the Future. 1999. Data for 1998 Downloaded from the Internet.

NIDA (National Institute on Drug Abuse). 1991. *National Household Survey on Drug Abuse:* Population Estimates 1991. Rockville, MD: Author.

Ray, Oakley, and Charles Ksir. 1999. *Drugs, Society, and Human Behavior,* 6th ed. New York: McGraw-Hill.

SAMHSA (Substance Abuse and Mental Health Services Administration). 1999. *Summary of Findings from the 1998 National Household Survey on Drug Abuse.* Rockville, MD: Author.

Troyer, Ronald J., and Gerald E. Markle. 1983. *Cigarettes.* New Brunswick, NJ: Rutgers University Press.

21

PLEASURE VERSUS PUBLIC HEALTH: CONTROLLING COLLEGIATE BINGE DRINKING

THOMAS A. WORKMAN

Nancy W. Dickey, M.D., board chair of the American Medical Association, stated on May 20, 1996, "Binge drinking by young people is a major public health problem that we can no longer ignore. When 40 percent of young Americans admit to excessive drinking and 20 percent to binge drinking . . . we must take dramatic steps to safeguard the lives and health of our young people and to protect the society in which they live."

Perhaps you, like many college students, respond to a statement like this a bit defensively. Many of the students I've interviewed have taken great offense to the suggestion that drinking, a "rite" of the college experience, has been painted by authorities and administrators as a public health menace. Some students have criticized the formulation of forced "dry" policies, increased enforcement of legal age, and other restrictions as hypocritical, unfair, and ultimately destructive to college life. On many campuses, a fight has erupted between those who regard alcohol as an important part of the college experience and those who see drinking as a dangerous and deadly practice.

Regardless of personal feelings, the declaration of collegiate drinking as a serious social problem has created a national assault against excessive drinking on college campuses, with a wide variety of programs and approaches, foundation grants and coalitions. *National Lampoon's* fictional Animal House, if it ever existed, has become both the enemy and the target for social reform, because its forms of pleasure are being identified as ultimately killing "the best and the brightest."

Yet, the social problem of collegiate binge drinking, much like the fight against tobacco and other licit drugs, raises a particular tension for a culture that has labeled as deviant those practices that have traditionally evoked, for good or for bad, a deeply held sense of pleasure. The cultural story of drinking in the United States is one of constant tension between guilt and pleasure, morality and control. By looking beyond the debates taking place on campuses across the nation, we can better see the problem of collegiate drinking as a set of tensions between the selling of pleasure in a capitalist society and the controlling of behavior in the public health institution.

This essay explores the collegiate drinking problem as a way of understanding the larger tensions between pleasure and public health. I first outline the history of alcohol's social identity in the United States, and then I examine the conflict between the social function of alcohol for the college-age population and the attempts at reform and intervention being taken to solve the "binge" problem. Finally, I offer a variety of new approaches that emerge to reduce tensions and to find a happy balance between pleasure and control.

ALCOHOL AND SOCIETY: AMBIVALENT PLEASURES AND MORAL PANICS

Alcohol use has been embedded in American culture since the earliest days of the nation. With the inclusion of immigrant groups from a variety of cultures, the United States quickly became a melting pot of customs, rituals, and habits surrounding alcohol. The result is the development of a "historic love–hate relationship with alcohol" that has existed since the days of the early settlers. The love for alcohol, many have suggested, comes not only from the biological reaction of consumption—the legal "buzz" or the out and out "drunk" feeling—but primarily from the marketing of alcohol as a highly useful product. According to Hanson (1995), research continues to indicate that, when used in moderation, the chemical properties of alcohol may be beneficial to health, particularly for males. Don Cahalan, who has spent twenty-five years researching U.S. drinking practices and politics, adds, "Obviously, such a large number of people would not be drinking unless they were getting real or fancied benefits from alcohol as a social lubricant, a picker-upper, the socially approved thing to do, or as a medication for anxiety or depression."

The result is an ultimate feeling of ambivalence for the culture (Hanson, 1995). Alcohol use has been strongly embedded in our culture while at the same time being vigilantly protested as an evil scourge. Hanson (1995) quotes two researchers as concluding that "This culture, much more than others, always behaved with *great* ambivalence toward the idea of alcohol use; . . . its historical record reveals numerous clearly identifiable and constantly changing rules and customs that deal with the reality of use."

Perhaps the most profound attack on alcohol use was the temperance movement that began in 1840 and progressed to a national prohibition of alcohol by 1919. This movement was marked with strongly vilified positions about the use of alcohol; it blamed the substance as responsible for a large host of physical and spiritual problems and moral decay (Hanson, 1995; Straus and Bacon, 1953). Materials by the Prohibition Party and the Women's Christian Temperance Union (WCTU) tried to establish alcohol use as no different than abuse, providing a slanted if not wholly manufactured view of alcohol as morally corrupting, physically harmful, and consistently addictive. Moderation was both rejected as a concept and as a prescription (Babor, 1986). It was impossible,

this discourse claimed, to partake of any alcoholic product without it leading toward drunkenness. One drink would always lead to many, the result of which would be moral, physical, or spiritual death. Rhetoric employed by organizations such as the WCTU established the construction of alcohol as a detrimental substance, regardless of the amount consumed. Heavily distributed tracts and texts blamed alcohol for every possible health problem and social dilemma, from premature death to the destruction of American morality (Gusfield, 1996; Hanson, 1995). The construction of "the alcohol problem" ultimately led to Prohibition, a federal policy that made the consumption of grain alcohol illegal and the United States dry.

Being dry during Prohibition, however, was often seen as both a joke by determined drinkers and a source of frustration for those attempting social control. A number of films, television programs, and histories identify the period as one of reckless abandon, in which speakeasies flourished and bootleggers thrived. Prohibition serves as the backdrop to a cultural understanding of the Roaring '20s that extends beyond the illegal production and distribution of alcohol to include such elements as music, fashion, and entertainment. Advertisers and film producers even glorify the gangster activity that has become a trademark of Prohibition. As historian Alan Jenkins says, "Speakeasies and the Prohibition era itself, nowadays have glamour too." Kenneth Allsop discovered in 1960 a Gaslight Club on North Rush Street in Chicago that was a faithful reproduction of a 1920s speakeasy. Alistair Cooke, in the mid-1950s, visited Princeton, New Jersey, and found a "revive the 20s" cult whose members made their own bathtub gin in the correct manner with distilled water.

From a cultural standpoint, the Prohibition was a period of heightened adventure, adding pleasure to deviancy. Each act of consumption during the era, from bootlegging to attending a speakeasy, served as a form of resistance to the hegemony of social control. Images of raided parties, with the well-dressed and affluent partygoers whisked away in paddy wagons only to receive a wink and nod by a judge, become a symbol of the era. Alcohol scholars such as Hanson and Gusfield argue that the Prohibition actually fueled rather than squelched alcohol consumption because it helped people see it as "forbidden fruit." This continues to drive drinking practices today, particularly for the underage drinker. As Donald Ogden Stuart, a screenwriter alive during the Prohibition, says, "There was an unholy joy in going down some steps to a dingy door, sliding back a panel and saying 'I'm a friend of Bob Benchley's—can I come in?' " (Jenkins, 1974).

Though Prohibition ended with repeal of the federal law in 1933, it has caused American society to stigmatize alcohol today. As Hanson (1995) observes, "Little wonder that even today Americans tend to treat alcohol with the same caution as guns, drugs, and germs, and that many tend to feel guilty when they have even a single drink." This negative view of alcohol can also be found among a variety of researchers and alcohol specialists, who hold what Gusfield (1996) calls "an assumption of malevolence." For example, the results of Wechsler's 1993 survey of collegiate binge drinking, published by the *Journal of the American Medical Association* in 1994, provides only the negative impact of alcohol consumption, in effect blaming alcohol use for date rape, assault, lowered grades, and increased illness and injury (Wechsler, Dowdall, Davenport, and DeJong, 1994). The media, too, consistently misquote statistics compiled from the survey data, heightening the public perception of college students as in a constant state of intoxication, despite alternative findings to the contrary (Borsari & Carey, 1999; Haines, 1996).

By condemning alcohol, U.S. society has made it difficult for people to drink responsibly. People who drink, then, tend to drink for the purpose of getting drunk. The norm for proper ways of drinking has failed to develop. Consequently, as Straus and Bacon observe, "The absence of accepted leadership has been reflected above all in the lack of knowledge about drinking, in the distaste for recognizing problems, and in the failure to present youth with an effective structure of beliefs, compatible with custom, on which consis-

tent, realistic, and confident behavior and attitudes can be based."

DRINKING IN COLLEGE: FUNCTIONAL PLEASURES

What does the Prohibition have to do with today's heavy drinking by college students? Most experts agree that the same motivations—and tensions—that existed at the time of the Prohibition era still endure today, and the college campus is a perfect example of mixed messages and a fight over the control of pleasure.

Alcohol consumption as a part of college life has a long history. Drinking clubs held a consistent presence in America's oldest learning institutions such as Harvard and Yale, establishing long set of traditions for social interaction on campus (Straus and Bacon, 1953). Drinking songs, the use of alcohol at college sporting and social events, and drinking as a form of friendship and bonding were established long before Prohibition and survived long after it. Harry S. Warner, a temperance educator, wrote in 1938 of the "age-old traditions peculiar to colleges, honored and retained here and there, and the outbreaks of enthusiasm moistened with alcohol after big games, at fraternity, alumni, and other group affairs" (p. 38).

Though individual statistics vary, studies on contemporary alcohol use in college indicate that a large percentage of college students get drunk on a regular basis (Carey, 1993; Gross, 1993; Klein, 1994; Slicker, 1997; Wechsler, Isaac, Goodstein, and Sellers, 1994). In one of the most comprehensive studies conducted since the famous Yale Study of 1947–1951, Wechsler and his colleagues determined that at least 68 percent of college students between the ages of 18 and 30 have at least three and as many as six drinks on an average night. In their report to the American Medical Association, they state, "This is . . . a testament to the fact that heavy drinking remains a large part of the young lifestyle" (Wechsler, Dowdall et al., 1994).

Various studies have looked into the motives behind excessive drinking. One study show that students binge drink to (1) have a good time with friends, (2) get drunk, and (3) to celebrate. Similar results were found by Borsari and Carey (1999), Carey (1993), Lichtenfield and Kayson (1994), and Mills, Sirgo, and Hartjes (1993). These studies seem to indicate that students find a social pleasure in alcohol use, follow social pressures toward excessive drinking as the norm, and see drinking as an essential element in recreation, particularly in stressful situations such as exams.

Most interesting, though, is the discovery of a gender difference in drinking behavior. Each study indicates that females are more likely to adopt "adult" drinking behaviors, which tend toward moderation. Likewise, males tend toward more adolescent behavior and are more likely to become drunk more often than females.

In my own ethnographic study of drinking stories in fraternities, excessive drinking accomplished five different cultural functions for young men:

1. *It provides an increased sense of risk, adding excitement and adventure to social events.* We know that risk increases some forms of pleasure—it is why people may enjoy riding the newest roller coaster or engaging in any number of risky sports such as bungee jumping, skydiving, or hang-gliding. Labeled by theorists as "edgework" (Lyng, 1990), risk-taking is heightened by rules and restrictions. The risk comes in "getting away with" something or tempting fate by attempting something that is seen as unsafe. Many of the men engaged in risky behavior were made heroes through drinking stories; their exploits were evidence of defying the odds.

2. *It provides entertainment.* Funny things are always happening around students who are drunk, either through their own actions (puking in a roommate's shoes) or through the actions of others who take advantage of their condition (using a marker to color the face of someone who has passed out). Drinking stories immortalize drinking events as wildly entertaining and as harmless. Often, the most entertaining stories, especially for men, in-

volve some act of aggression, such as a fight or the destruction of property.

3. *It provides an opportunity for physical self-discovery.* Drunkenness offers the perfect opportunity to lower inhibitions and fears, allowing people to comfortably test their own physical abilities and limitations. Many stories involve nakedness in the activity, in which exposure is less self-conscious. Other stories involve physical knowledge: What effect does this substance/quantity/combination have on me? How fast can I recover? What things am I capable of?

4. *It provides opportunities for sexual pleasure, though not always with positive outcomes.* Although many stories include sexual interaction as an outcome of drinking, many of the men used "getting laid" as a source of ridicule, especially if the female involved was not attractive. Many expressed a sense of victimization, believing that less attractive women actually stayed around the party or the house so that they could benefit from "beer goggles."

5. *It is a part of college; it is what students are "supposed" to do.* Almost all the students believed that excessive drinking and drunkenness was a special part of the college experience, one that would make college memorable. They expected to tell their stories to others, and they saw their stories as an expression of privilege (Workman, 1999).

One other important finding in studies of college drinking involves the role of misperceived social norms about drinking. It has been found that in the university setting, students consistently overestimated the amount that other students drink. As Perkins et al. (1999) said, "The abuse of alcohol in student groups and social settings may be recalled more vividly and quickly than actions surrounding abstinence or moderation, thereby getting a disproportionate amount of attention in peer conversation as well as in mass media news and popular entertainment images." The consequence, warn Borsari and Carey (1999), is that students are less likely to question their own behavior if they believe that others also drink excessively and frequently.

All of these norms, functions, and pleasures can be found in the many advertisements for alcohol, because the substance itself is commodified as a key source of social pleasure, particularly for men. Think of a favorite beer commercial, and the stories that are told about drinking through them (even the silly ones, with talking animals or self-mocking advertising executives). The stories are amazingly consistent and almost always involve people of college age. Try to find these themes in television commercials:

1. Alcohol consumption is associated with high levels of social interaction, such as in a crowded bar or a party at which everyone is having a good time and seems connected to others in conversation. One example is the "Coors Silver Bullet" ad, in which the bar is filled with happy, attractive people enjoying themselves while drinking the product as the announcer tells us that Coors Light "won't slow you down." The happiness can last all night.

2. Alcohol consumption is connected to sexual success, where very attractive women are prizes for men who choose the appropriate beer. Men who drink beer are often depicted with attractive women, suggesting that alcohol and sexual pleasure are intricately linked. A classic example is the Keystone Beer commercial, in which the male loses his opportunity to meet a beautiful supermodel due to "bitter beer face." Those choosing the right beer "get" the woman.

3. Alcohol consumption is connected with forms of aggressive and competitive play, such as football, baseball, hockey, soccer, darts, pool, and fighting. Many examples can be found, from the "Bud Bowl" to the commercials in which a beer vendor interviews a fan at a game to ensure the beer "has a good home."

4. Alcohol consumption is a source of male bonding; men can come together without hassles with women. One beer commercial shows a male waiting near a rack of women's clothes, obviously trapped in a shopping trip with his partner. From inside the rack, a hand motions him inside, where other males enjoy beer and a football game, with a significant change in mood.

5. Alcohol is considered an essential commodity, one that is coveted, protected, and chosen over other staples of life. My personal favorite is the commercial in which two young men are at a store, attempting to buy beer and toilet paper. When they learn that the total bill is more than their money, they ultimately buy only the beer, asking for a paper sack and grabbing the receipt.

6. Alcohol is connected to relaxation and recreation, a reward for hard work. "Miller Time" has become a common expression, as advertisements show men ending a long day of work with a stop at the bar, where they perk up, relax, and enjoy the spoils of labor.

That many of these ads employ characters that look, act, and sound like college students speaks volumes about the connection between the commodification of alcohol and the forms drunkenness takes for many college students. Deemed lifestyle advertising (Leiss, Kline, and Jhally, 1997), these commercials create the image of a lifestyle of pleasure. The small snippets of the lifestyle show a one-sided view of pleasure, hiding the potential problems caused by consumption or by the adoption of the lifestyle. How happy will the relationship be with the man and the supermodel if she is his prize? What quality of relationship exists between the man and his girlfriend if he must escape inside a clothes rack? What happens when people lose a game, or find themselves without social interaction, or overconsume—believing that if a little makes for some pleasure, a lot will bring more pleasure? As a social force, advertising may not be the best teacher, but it may be the only training we receive about drinking.

Given the romanticized memories of drinking stories from alumni, older friends, parents, and popular culture, it is not surprising that a population of binge drinkers has emerged in our society.

COMPETING MODELS OF INTERVENTION

The common response to the problem of collegiate binge drinking has traditionally been to treat excessive drinking by college students as a serious threat to public health (Gusfield, 1996). A main reason is the clearly negative portrait of college drinking in the media. Excessive drinking is often presented as having caused physical assault, unwanted sexual advances, the destruction of property, disturbances of the peace, sales of liquor to minors, and worse. Excessive drinking, then, is constructed as an evil student-eating dragon that must be slain (Workman, 1999).

Intervention efforts tend to take a "control of consumption" approach that is reminiscent of Prohibition. Often labeled "environmental change," the control of consumption approach involves the active use of legislation to create stricter laws and policies. Some policies are directed at vendors, including heavy fines for serving underage students, serving intoxicated students, or promoting high-risk drink specials such as penny draws, free drinks, or two-for-one specials. Other policies focus on the students themselves, increasing the penalty for actions taken while intoxicated or requiring some form of alcohol education as a part of disciplinary action.

On the other hand, some universities and colleges have adopted "wet" policies, allowing alcohol to be consumed in some controlled form on campus in order to accomplish the goal of the sociocultural model, which emphasizes the importance of teaching the proper, responsible use of alcohol. Thus students learn codes of behavior in which individuals are held responsible for their actions and must learn how to consume alcohol without creating threats to the health and safety of others.

Today both approaches have met their share of problems and limitations. Control of consumption policies have faced extensive resistance from students, who have constructed themselves as victims of oppressive authoritarianism and who resent the university serving in loco parentis. In 1998, a federal bill allowed universities to contact parents about alcohol violations, overturning a widely held privacy law that kept administrators from involving parents in student drinking problems (Schwartz, 1998). Still, the collective memory of Prohibition continues to lead people to see control policies as ultimately ineffective and to see control itself as the larger problem that leads only to higher adventure, more dangerous attempts at finding pleasure, and a new level of problems.

Perhaps the greatest issue for control of consumption policies, however, lies in the challenge of enforcement. Zero tolerance policies require an extended watch from campus and community police forces, which have been faced with violent and angry protests and riots in a number of university settings. Control of consumption also faces the challenge of unequal enforcement of policy—alcohol consumption is allowed only at campus events involving alumni, faculty, and donors, particularly at sporting events. Many campuses, however, have had to refuse revenue from alcohol sales or to restrict consumption for alumni in order to find a happy medium.

The sociocultural approach has also faced a number of challenges. Campuses that have attempted to allow alcohol find that abuse often results from consumption, despite their best efforts at education. Many universities, therefore, are looking at multiple approaches to solve the problem. Many have developed coalitions that combine the talents and abilities of all segments of the campus and community to deal with issues of policy, education, culture, and individual responsibility regarding alcohol use. Some schools have attempted to provide alternatives to alcohol consumption as ways to seek and receive social pleasure, such as social gatherings without alcohol. Finally, an attempt has been made to differentiate between the binge drinker, the chronic binge drinker, and the early stage alcoholic, with appropriate interventions for each category. Not every student who engages in binge drinking continues a career of problem drinking, and blanketing all students with the label of binge drinkers eliminates the ability of health professionals or concerned friends to identify those who demonstrate a dependency on alcohol. Neither control of consumption nor a sociocultural approach can by themselves isolate and provide assistance for those who demonstrate a real addiction to alcohol.

Although it is too early to tell if these efforts can have any positive effects on the population, the ultimate goal of constructing collegiate drinking as a crisis has produced an active effort to reexamine the role of alcohol in at least one segment of American society.

CONCLUSION

Alcohol has a paradoxical place in the college scene. Drinking—especially binge drinking—is sold to students through a variety of commercial and cultural messages as a source of pleasure, a social lubricant, and an essential part of the college experience. As a result, a number of students have bought in to the belief that getting drunk is a required activity in college. Yet, at the same time, competing messages warn students that excessive alcohol consumption is a public health menace that can destroy lives, derail college careers, and cause a number of negative effects. The media, public health officials, and college administrators have painted excessive drinking as deviant behavior. Because of the tension between the messages of pleasure and the messages of health, it is difficult to prevent students from consuming alcohol or to educate them about low-risk consumption.

REFERENCES

Associated Press. "Lehigh Students Protest Alcohol Program." 1999. November 7.

Babor, T. F. Ed. 1986. *Alcohol and Culture: Comparative Perspectives from Europe and America.* New York: New York Academy of Sciences.

Borsari, B. E., and K. B. Carey. 1999. "Understanding Fraternity Drinking: Five Recurring Themes in the Literature, 1980–1998." *Journal of American College Health,* 48:30–37.

Carey, K. B. 1993. "Situational Determinants of Heavy Drinking among College Students." *Journal of Counseling Psychology,* 40 (2):217–220.

Gross, W. C. 1993. "Gender and Age Differences in College Students' Alcohol Consumption." *Psychological Reports,* 72 (1):211–217.

Gusfield, J. R. 1963. *Symbolic Crusade: Status Politics and the American Temperance Movement.* Urbana: University of Illinois Press.

Gusfield, J. R. 1996. *Contested Meanings: The Construction of Alcohol Problems.* Madison: University of Wisconsin Press.

Haines, M. P. 1996. *A Social Norms Approach to Preventing Binge Drinking at Colleges and Universities.* The Higher Education Center for Alcohol and Other Drug Prevention, U.S. Department of Education. Publication No. ED/OPE/96–18.

Hanson, D. J. 1995. *Preventing Alcohol Abuse: Alcohol, Culture and Control.* Westport, CT: Praeger.

Jenkins, A. 1974. *The Twenties.* New York: Universe Books.

Klein, H. 1994. "Changes in College Students' Use and Abuse of Alcohol, and in Their Attitudes toward Drinking over the Course of Their College Years." *Journal of Youth and Adolescence,* 23 (2):251–270.

Leiss, W., S. Kline, and S. Jhally. 1997. *Social Communication in Advertising: Persons, Products and Images of Well-Being.* London: Routledge.

Lichtenfield, M., and W. A. Kayson. 1994. "Factors in College Students' Drinking." *Psychological Reports,* 74 (3):927–30.

Lyng, S. 1990. "Edgework: A Social Psychological Analysis of Voluntary Risk Taking." *American Journal of Sociology,* 95:851–856.

Mills, J. K., V. I. Sirgo, and D. T. Hartjes. 1993. "Perceptions of Excessive Alcohol Consumption in Stressful and Non-Stressful Situations among Undergraduates." *The Journal of Psychology,* 127 (5):543–546.

Monroe, J. 1996. "Binge Drinking: Alcohol Use among College Students." *Current Health 2,* 22(9):26–29.

Moore, M. H., and D. R. Gerstein. eds. 1981. *Alcohol and Public Policy: Beyond the Shadow of Prohibition.* Washington: National Academy Press.

"New Long-Range Program to Target Youthful Binge Drinking." 1996, May 20. [release]. Chicago: American Medical Association.

Perkins, H. W., P. W. Meilman, J. S. Leichliter, J. R. Cashin, and C. A. Presley. 1999. "Misperceptions of the Norms for the Frequency of Alcohol and Other Drug Use on College Campuses." *Journal of American College Health,* 47, 253–258.

Perlman, S. E. 1997. "Searching for Solutions," *New York Newsday* December 1, p. A23.

Robbins, C. 1993. "Between Paradigms: A Half-Century of Sociological Research on Alcohol." *Contemporary Sociology,* 22 (3):367–369.

Schwartz, D. 1998. "Parental Notification Bill Likely to Become Law," *Lincoln (NE) Journal Star* October 3, p. B1.

Slicker, E. K. 1997. "University Students Reasons for NOT Drinking: Relationship to Alcohol Consumption Level." *Journal of Alcohol and Drug Education,* 42 (2):83–101.

Straus, R., and S. D. Bacon. 1953. *Drinking in College.* New Haven, CT: Yale University Press.

Wechsler, H., G. W. Dowdall, A. Davenport, and W. DeJong. 1993. "Binge Drinking on Campus: Results of a National Study." [Bulletin]. Washington, DC: Higher Education Center for Alcohol and Other Drug Prevention, U.S. Department of Education.

Wechsler, H., G. W. Dowdall, A. Davenport, and W. De-Jong. 1994. "Health and Behavioral Consequences of Binge Drinking in College." *Journal of the American Medical Association,* 272 (21):1672–1677.

Wechsler, H., G. W. Dowdall, G. Maener, J. Gledhill-Hoyt, and H. Lee. 1998. "Changes in Binge Drinking and Related Problems among American College Students between 1993 and 1997: Results of the Harvard School of Public Health College Alcohol Study." *Journal of American College Health,* 47:57–69.

Wechsler, H., and N. Isaac. 1992. "Binge Drinkers at Massachusetts Colleges: Prevalence, Drinking Style, Time Trends and Associated Problems." *Journal of the American Medical Association,* 267 (21):2929–2931.

Wechsler, H., N. Isaac, F. Grodstein, and D. E. Sellers. 1994. "Continuation and Initiation of Alcohol Use from the First to the Second Year of College." *Journal of Studies on Alcohol,* 55:41–46.

Wechsler, H., B. E. Molnar, A. E. Davenport, and J. S. Baer. 1999. "College Alcohol Use: A Full or Empty Glass?" *Journal of American College Health,* 47:247–252.

Workman, T. A. 1999, November. *Constructions from Inside the Drinking Culture: An Analysis of Fraternity Drinking Stories.* Paper presented at the annual meeting of the National Communication Association, Chicago, IL.

PART SIX

HETEROSEXUAL DEVIANCE

Every Saturday night as many as 300 young women line the sides of a seven-mile stretch of a highway from Prague to Berlin in Eastern Europe. On this so-called Highway of Cheap Love, the world's longest brothel, travelers can stop to buy sex from one of those women for $30. Among the women are Czechs, Germans, Hungarians, Romanians, and Bulgarians. Virtually all of them have been forced into prostitution by poverty, which in turn has largely resulted from the collapse of the Soviet empire. Some have entered the sex trade through gangsters, and others through their own parents. On that night, the gangsters can be seen lurking in nearby cars, the fathers sitting in backup automobiles, or the mothers negotiating the deals for their daughters. Every now and then the prostitutes' little brothers appear with sponges and buckets of soapy water, offering to wash the customers' cars for an extra $5. All this is part of the fast-growing, now multibillion-dollar, global sex business.[1]

This kind of prostitution, like any other way for women to sell sex to men, is an example of heterosexual deviance. A closer look at prostitution is provided in the first article here, "Sex Tourism in Southeast Asia," by Jody Miller. The author shows how the global sex business is a gross exploitation and dehumanization of women in developing nations. In the second article, "Mother Sold Food, Daughter Sells Her Body," Marjorie Muecke discusses how Buddhism and village morality contribute to prostitution in Thailand. The next three articles deal with different types of stripping: parade, amateur, and professional. In "Parade Strippers: Being Naked in Public," Craig Forsyth discusses his research on women exposing their breasts at Mardi Gras parades in New Orleans. In "The Naked Body as Site and Sight: The Accounts of Amateur Strippers," Thomas Calhoun and his coresearchers find the reasons why some young men and women take off their clothes in public without pay. In "Strip Club Dancers: Working in the Fantasy Factory," Elizabeth Anne Wood discovers from her research that professional strippers are "interactive subjects" rather than sex objects and that their work involves "impression management" and "emotional labor."

---

1. Margot Hornblower, "The Skin Trade," *Time,* June 21, 1993, p. 45; Michael Specter, "Traffickers' New Cargo: Naïve Slavic Women." *New York Times,* January 11, 1998, pp. 1, 6.

22

SEX TOURISM IN SOUTHEAST ASIA

JODY MILLER

The imperialist West has a long history of exploiting non-Western countries. A traditional form of exploitation involves using people as cheap labor for profit. A new form of exploitation, however, calls for using women as sex slaves for pleasure. This comes in the guise of sex tourism, providing foreign tourists with local prostitutes. Sex tourism is most prevalent in Southeast Asia, especially Thailand.

SEX TOURISM AS A DEVELOPMENTAL STRATEGY

Sex tourism flourishes through the support of developmental policies in Southeast Asia and through the representation of Asian women as sexually exotic. In this article I will focus largely on Thailand. The U.S. military presence abroad has helped stimulate tourism in the Third World. However, far more important, Western developmental policies, with the backing of multinational corporations, have cultivated tourism as a strategy for building the economies of the Third World countries. The promotion of tourism first got its impetus from the United Nations declaration of 1967 as "The Year of the Tourist." Subsequently, international aid programs, such as the World Bank, the International Monetary Fund, and US AID, and multinational corporations have invested in the development of tourist industries in the Third World.

Multinational corporations in particular have found in tourism a lucrative venture through investment in a variety of industries, such as airlines, hotels, tour operations, and travel agencies (Mies, 1986; Truong, 1990). This has created "a division of labor according to which Third World countries, with few exceptions, merely provide the social infrastructure and facilities with little or no control over the process of production and distribution of the tourist-related services at an international level" (Truong, 1990). As a result, the tourist industry greatly benefits multinational corporations, local elites, and international tourists but does little to improve the standard of living or availability of services for the majority of the people living in these regions.

In Thailand, the tourist industry has been a priority within the government's economic plans despite the social inequalities it exacerbates. Thai sex tourism got its boost from U.S. militarization. Although prostitution has a long history in Thailand and other Asian countries, "Southeast Asian women were first turned into prostitutes on a mass scale in the context of the Vietnam war and the establishment of American air and navy bases in the Pacific region" (Mies, 1986). All this began to occur in Thailand in 1967, when the Thai government and the U.S. military signed a treaty to allow U.S. soldiers stationed in Vietnam to come on "Rest and Recreation" leave in Thailand. The immediate consequence was a boom in local and foreign investment in hotels and entertainment establishments (Truong, 1990). When the U.S. military withdrew from Vietnam in the 1970s, there was still considerable incentive for investors to turn to tourism, which had become extremely important in sustaining the Thai economy. By the late 1980s, tourism was "the country's major earner of foreign currency" (Cohen, 1988). In 1986, "Thailand earned more foreign currency from tourism . . . than it did from any other economic activity including its traditional export leader, rice" (Enloe, 1989).

The sex trade is at the heart of this tourism. In the early 1980s, for example, "Bangkok had 119 massage parlors, 119 barbershop-cum-massage parlors and teahouses, 97 nightclubs, 248 disguised brothels and 394 disco-restaurants, all of which sold sexual companionship to male customers" (Enloe, 1989). In addition, hotels participate directly or indirectly in sex tourism. It has been estimated that "between 70 and 80 percent of male tourists who travel from Japan, the United States, Australia, and Western Europe to Asia do so solely for the purpose of sexual entertainment" (Gay, 1985). To meet all this demand, numerous Thai women are forced in one way or another to become prostitutes. The Thai police have estimated their number to be 700,000, "about 10 percent of all Thai women between the ages of fifteen and thirty" (Gay, 1985). Many prostitutes are under age 14, representing about 20 percent of the workers in the Thai sex industry (Ong, 1985).

The majority of those women and girls have migrated from rural areas. A large percentage come from the North and Northeast, the two poorest regions of the country. By not investing in those agricultural regions, Thailand's development policies have worsened the poverty of its rural people. This has forced many poor rural families to rely on individual family members migrating to urban areas as a means of survival. Many of these migrants are young daughters ending up in Bangkok's sex trade.

Sex tourism is an extremely exploitive industry in Thailand. It provides huge profits to tourist businesses and the Thai government. Even the laws that prohibit prostitution are used to control female workers in the industry rather than the owners and managers (Cohen, 1982; Truong, 1990). Because their work is illegal, they are stigmatized and must constantly interact with men "who consider it their right . . . to buy themselves exotic women" (Mies, 1986). They receive only a small percentage of the money they earn, and attempts to unionize have been unsuccessful (Prostitution in Southeast Asia, 1987). One woman sums up what it is like to be a sex worker: "Believe me, if it was not necessary, no one would ever want to work like this. . . . But we have no choice. We must persevere, since we have only ourselves to rely on" (Ekachel, 1987).

THE PROMOTION OF SEX TOURISM

The continuing prevalence of sex tourism depends most heavily on its promotion to Western men. This largely involves presenting Asian women and sex tourism as follows:

1. Asian women are naturally submissive, passive, and willing to cater to men's sexual needs.
2. Asian women have a uniquely "Oriental" sexuality—more intense, sensual, and erotic than Western sexuality, and more animalistic, overt, and indiscriminating.
3. Sex tourism in Southeast Asia is a "fun-filled" form of entertainment, neither exploitive nor inappropriate.
4. Sex tourism in Southeast Asia is a legitimate commodity like any other service in the market economy.

Asian Women as Submissive

Part of Western men's attraction to Asian women springs from the popular assumption that Asian women are more subservient and passive than their Western counterparts. The tourism industry often depicts Asian women as docile and submissive by nature, willing to put male needs ahead of their own. One brochure, for example, describes Thai women as "little slaves who give real Thai warmth" (Kanita Kamha in Truong, 1990). Tourist ads routinely emphasize how easy it is for Western men to find willing and enthusiastic Thai girls in bars and coffee shops.

Moreover, to make Asian women appear sexually desirable, the tourist literature often contrasts their submissiveness with the emancipation of Western women. Bangkok's sex workers are described as "without desire for emancipation," only interested in providing men with their "warm sensuality and the softness of velvet" (in Lenze, 1980). Because their submissiveness is assumed to be sexually desirable, the Asian girls are touted as "mostly young, pretty, gay and a welcome change from the hard-faced crones found in the West" (Thitsa, 1980).

Asian Women's Uniquely "Oriental" Sexuality

When their sexuality is presented to Western men as uniquely "Oriental," Asian women are stereotyped in at least three ways. First, they are said to be unusually adept in sex. Thai women are described in one tourist brochure as the "masters of the art of making love by nature, an art that we Europeans do not know" (Life Travel in Truong, 1990). This image not only appears frequently in tourism materials, it most often occurs in pornographic videos about "Oriental" sex. Such videos highlight "the sexual and exotic characteristics of [Asian] cultures, showing how foreign visitors to these countries can enjoy uninhibited sex" (Truong, 1990). One example is *Live from Bangkok,* an adult video that is presented in documentary style. It shows scenes from massage parlors, dance bars, and sex shows. Viewers are encouraged "to see the stimulating erotic night clubs of Bangkok. The women are beautiful, the sex is extraordinary! It's all here and more. You won't believe your eyes." Similar videos show how Asian women are capable of creating "the most fantastic sensations" for their sex partners.

Another representation of Asian women's supposedly unique sexuality involves portraying them as promiscuous and sexually uninhibited. This is suggested in a Thai business magazine, stating that "Everyone who has ever travelled widely in Thailand knows that indiscriminate love-making goes on in every hotel in the land" (*Business in Thailand* in Truong, 1990). In the *All Asia Guide* (1980), sex shows are described as "actions of astounding dexterity culminat[ing] in a display of sexual gymnastics." In the video *Live from Bangkok,* a woman is shown dancing in a go-go bar and going into a bedroom to have sex with one, then later two, men. The voiceover explains, "after a long night of dancing, performers must wind down by letting loose their extra energy."

Asian women's unique "Oriental" sexuality is also presented in terms of their sexual anatomy. Adult videos often refer to Asian women's vaginas as being tighter than Western women's. Examples of such references include advertisements of Asian girls' legendary "tight pussies," "super tight clits," "super tight snatch," and "Oriental pussies tightly awaiting your cumming attractions."

Sex Tourism as Fun-Filled Adventure

Sex tourism in Southeast Asia is projected as harmless, exciting entertainment. The imagery is devoid of any recognition of exploitation; the language is that of fun, games, and adventure. Sex tourism, Western men are told, must be experienced. "Bangkok is a captivating city, active, even at night . . . and the publicity about the famous massage parlours can only be tried out" (Truong, 1990). Massage parlors are not the only place where Western male tourists can engage in wild, uninhibited sex. Bars also abound where there is "no trouble in going in for a drink, coming out with a gal" (Jacobs and Jacobs, 1979). In some bars, male tourists seated at a table can have bargirls perform oral sex on them. *Playboy* magazine tells its male readers what they can do in such a bar:

> Step into the corner with your buddies, sit down at the famous table for a game of smiles. Drop trousers as you sit. Movement under the table, a girl or two up to no good. And the game of smiles begins. The last one to smile wins (Kluge, 1986).

Numerous prostitutes can be found not only in brothels but also in hotels. Virtually all male tourists are encouraged to participate in sexual adventure, as suggested by the following anecdote described in a travel guide:

> On arrival at an Asian hotel, an official of the World Council of Churches was asked, as men often are, if he wished female companionship for the night. He declined, but the hotel porter persisted in his persuasions, finally asked why he wasn't interested in one of his beautiful young women. "Because I'm a minister of a Christian church," was the reply. The porter left abruptly. Soon came a knock on the

clergyman's door. Enter smiling porter. "Evelything okey-dokey now. Christian woman, she be here soon" (Jacobs and Jacobs, 1979).

Sex Tourism as a Legitimate Commodity in the Market Economy

Sex tourism is regarded as a legitimate commodity because it is part of the market economy where, if there is a need, somebody will always emerge to satisfy it. The sexual commodity in Southeast Asia is easily available for a low price. As a tourist ad says, getting a girl "is as easy as buying a package of cigarettes" (Truong, 1990). According to an American naval officer in the Philippines, "you can fuck a woman up the ass for two apples and a candy bar . . . I would go get a blow job with the same casualness with which I'd buy a six-pack of beer, and for the same money" (Kluge, 1986). Many Western male tourists do not feel guilty for taking advantage of the girls. Instead, they tend to feel that they are doing a favor to the girls and their country by contributing to their economy. The tourist literature plays a role here. As the voiceover in a promotional video explains,

[The girls] come from poor families in country areas to work as sex performers or prostitutes or both. These are not bad girls; in Thailand the whore is as respected as the secretary. Sex is an honorable business, necessary to the economy. The girls send most of their money home to support their families. Some work a few years 'til they've saved enough to go home and open a small business of their own.

THEORETICAL IMPLICATIONS

In short, sex tourism flourishes through the support of developmental policies in Southeast Asia as well as through the representation of Asian women as sexually exotic and through the justification of sex tourism as socially and economically beneficial. All this suggests extreme exploitation of Asian women, without which sex tourism cannot exist, let alone flourish. The exploitation of Asian women as poorly paid sex workers brings substantial profits to business elites in the tourist industry, widening in the process the gap between rich and poor in those Third World countries.

Sex tourism further dehumanizes Asian women, allowing Westerners to see Asian women as less than human. As the wife of an American naval officer in the Philippines says:

I told my husband that as long as he doesn't bring back any diseases, if he goes out there for relief while I'm away in the States, it's all right. If he were with a pretty American girl, or an ugly American girl with brains, I'd be worried. But I've been there, and I know the girls. L.B.F.M.s—little brown fucking machines (Kluge, 1986).

But the dehumanization of Asian women does not appear as such to many Westerners, especially male tourists. This is because, as we have seen, the tourist literature often depicts Asian women as cheerfully submissive.

REFERENCES

All Asia Guide. 1980. Hong Kong: Far Eastern Economic Review, Ltd.

Cohen, Erik. 1982. "Thai Girls and Farang Men: The Edge of Ambiguity." *Annals of Tourism Research,* 9(3): 403–428.

Cohen, Erik. 1988. "Tourism and AIDS in Thailand." *Annals of Tourism Research,* 15(4):467–486.

Ekachel, Sanitsuda. 1987, December. "A Cabaret of Dreams for Bad Girls of Patpong." *ISIS Women's World,* 16:5–6.

Enloe, Cynthia. 1989. *Bananas, Beaches & Bases: Making Feminist Sense of International Politics.* Berkeley: University of California Press.

Gay, Jill. 1985, February. "The 'Patriotic' Prostitute." *The Progressive,* pp. 34–36.

Jacobs, Charles, and Babette Jacobs. 1979. *Far East Travel Digest,* 3rd ed. Palm Desert, CA: Paul, Richmond & Co.

Kluge, P. F. 1986, September. "Why They *Love* Us in the Philippines." *Playboy,* pp. 88–90, 162–164.

Lenze, Ilse. 1980. "Tourism Prostitution in Asia." *ISIS International Bulletin,* 13:6–8.

Mies, Maria. 1986. *Patriarchy and Accumulation on a World Scale: Women in the International Division of Labor.* London: Zed Books.

Ong, Aihwa. 1985, January. "Industrialization and Prostitution in Southeast Asia." *Southeast Asia Chronicle,* 96:2–6.

"Prostitution in Southeast Asia." 1987, January. *Off our backs,* 17 (1):1–2, 7.

Thitsa, Khin. 1980. *Providence and Prostitution: Image and Reality for Women in Buddhist Thailand.* London: Change International Reports.

Truong, Thanh-Dam. 1990. *Sex, Money and Morality: Prostitution and Tourism in Southeast Asia.* London: Zed Books.

MOTHER SOLD FOOD, DAUGHTER SELLS HER BODY: THE CULTURAL CONTINUITY OF PROSTITUTION

MARJORIE A. MUECKE

. . . I am concerned with the question, "Why is the rapid growth of female prostitution not culturally problematic for the Thai?" I argue that beliefs that Thai laity tend to associate with Buddhism and village morality paradoxically support the practice of prostitution in their society. The beliefs provide an ideology that justifies parental and village complicity in and denial of the prostitution of their daughters. . . .

I suggest that the economic rewards of contemporary prostitution have enabled young women to support not only the urban-based profiteers who control prostitution, but more important from a cultural perspective, to remit funds home to their families and villages of origin. Prostitution today is accomplishing what food vending did for the young women's mothers: both of these otherwise disparate endeavors have the effect of conserving norms by which women support the family, village, and other basic institutions of Thai society. The cultural consequences of prostitution for women who do not succeed in it are also examined. I suggest that they, too, conserve traditional norms, in this case, the norm associated with the Buddhist ideology of suffering, and with the common interpretation that women are fated to suffer more than men, as demonstrated in their bodily sacrifices for their children in pregnancy, childbirth, and breastfeeding. The young female body is thus paradoxically the cynosure of beauty and suffering.

The data for this analysis derive from field research, predominantly in Northern Thailand, where I have conducted 5 years of fieldwork in three segments since 1972. Some of the case descriptions are of women who have participated in my longitudinal anthropological study of some 400 urban Chiang Mai families,[1] and others are of women known through the course of related research and scholarly activities in the country. . . .

HISTORICAL BACKGROUND

Thai scholars ascribe the origins of prostitution in Thailand to the early Ayudthia period, which, in the fifteenth century, codified laws that structured society hierarchically and vested authority over women to men, and required men to leave home for extended periods to serve their lords. From the fifteenth century to the late nineteenth century, prostitutes serviced Siamese peasant men when they left their homes for their obligatory annual corvée labor in the service of the king or nobility.[2] Prostitutes also serviced Chinese men who immigrated to Ayudthia as laborers in the seventeenth and eighteenth centuries.[3] The prostitutes were women who had been sold into prostitution by their parents or husbands. Until the late nineteenth century, it was legal for a man to sell or give away his wife or daughter without her consent, as a present to his superior or in payment of his debts; men could also purchase slave women as their lesser wives, and gain Buddhist merit for their generosity in doing so. Thailand is not unique in this history. China and Japan supplied a "vigorous market for prostitutes" with their daughters of poverty in the colonial port towns of Southeast

Asia.[4] Although laws have changed, the historical practice of selling women provides important precedent for the current practice whereby adults, predominantly men, sell family members, particularly daughters, for economic gain.[5]

After World War II, prostitution developed more obviously in cities than in rural areas. The first massage parlor, an imitation of the Japanese steam bath, is reported to have appeared in the Patpong area of Bangkok in 1951.[6] Patpong is now Bangkok's sex entertainment center for international tourists. Although prostitution was outlawed in 1960, massage parlors were legalized in 1966. They quickly became one of the major cover-ups for prostitution in the country. Prostitutes prefer them as worksites over brothels because of their higher class (higher paying) clientele and greater job security.[7]

In the 1980s, prostitution of Thai women mushroomed into an industry of extensive national and international proportions.[8] Its growth parallels that of the economy which has boomed so strongly since 1985 that economists expect Thailand to be "the next Newly Industrialized Country" (NIC). Foreign investments have increased dramatically since 1987, with the bulk of foreign exchange resources being dedicated to the urban infrastructure. This growth has been accompanied by a burgeoning of the middle class of urban consumers, and rural to urban migration of young adults in search of jobs. Meanwhile, the share of agriculture in the economy has fallen from 32.2 percent in 1970 to 24.9 percent in 1980, to 22.3 percent in 1986. In consequence, the income differentials between Bangkok and the rest of the country are increasing: In Bangkok the average annual per capita income in 1988 was estimated as U.S. $2300, in contrast to U.S. $300 for other parts of Thailand, with some areas as low as U.S. $100.[9] The increasing poverty of rural areas relative to urban places contributes to the urban migration of young women to work in the service sector.

Current estimates are that in the Thai population of some 55 million, there are 80,000 to one million women working as prostitutes, plus perhaps some 20,000 girls under the age of 15.[10] An unknown number of Thai women work abroad as prostitutes; estimates for Japan alone are some 10,000.[11] A decade ago, it was estimated that, on a *per capita* basis, twice as many women were prostitutes as men were monks.[12] For Thai Buddhists, this ratio starkly juxtaposes daughters and sons as moral opposites, daughters being of the flesh and "this-worldly," and sons, detached from corporeal desire, so closer to the Buddhist ideal of "otherworldliness."

As large as the above estimates of the number of prostitutes are, they are probably underestimates for several reasons. First, prostitution services are commonly camouflaged in the guise of massage parlors, escort agencies, restaurants, bars, and nightclubs.[13] This is because prostitution is illegal, but creating a site where it is available is not. The figures also minimize the prevalence of prostitution because they exclude both men and women who formerly were involved in the sex trade. Others who profit from prostitution include pimps; procurers; owners (at least some of whom may be highly placed officials or their agents) of massage parlors, escort agencies, bars, and brothels; police and government officials who are given pay-offs to avoid arrest of prostitute employees; and taxi drivers. The figures on prostitution are further biased by the Thai tendency to tolerate polygyny in the form of minor wives (*mia nǫi*).[14] There is little difference between short-term minor wives and prostitutes: "Today's system of prostitution is how traditional polygyny has survived: both provide a man access to the services of more than one woman."[15]

PROSTITUTION IN THE CONTEXT OF CONTEMPORARY BUDDHISM

Theravada Buddhism provides a cultural core for lowland Thai society. As such it shapes the meaning of prostitution and of being a prostitute. Buddhism is linked to prostitution through the concepts of karma (*kam*) and meritmaking (*kaan tham bun*). According to the "law of karma," good actions earn moral merit (*bun*), and wrong actions, demerit (*baap*). The amount of merit and demerit that an individual has earned in past and present incarnations is that person's karma, and determines how much or little suffering that person has in this life. Individuals can change their karma by purposefully making merit. The most common ways to make merit are to give gifts to monks and temples, and to sponsor an ordination of a monk. . . .

Suffering

My Chiang Mai female informants consistently said that the lot of the Buddhist woman is to suffer more because of her greater worldly attachment than man's. . . . The suffering of a prostitute may take a variety of forms, including loneliness, physical abuse and pain, verbal abuse, deception, illness, exhaustion, rejection, uncaring, unsafe abortions, sexually transmitted disease, and the stigma and lethality of HIV infection. Typically, the prostitute's choice was to stay in the suffering of a difficult family or poverty, or to live in the suffering of loneliness, alienation, and personal abuse that goes with being a prostitute. . . .

Women informants who were not prostitutes generally believed that prostitutes suffer because they are mistreated, abused, and exploited, not only, by their "agents," "owners," and clients, but even by parents. A recent university graduate told the story of her friend Noi (pseudonym). Noi's family was poor. She went to Japan to work as a prostitute because she thought she could make more money there than in Thailand. She stayed there for years, working until she saved one million Baht (U.S. $40,600)! Then when she was 25 and getting too old for prostitution, she came home and gave it all to her parents. They took it, took it all, and wouldn't give her one Baht of it. She was very angry. They used it all up on gambling; Noi got none of it. She was so angry she "went crazy." My informant explained that Noi lost not only her money, but also her parents for whose sake she had sold her body for all the years of her life that she could do so profitably. Their keeping the money and using it on gambling rendered the highly moral purpose to which she had dedicated her life immoral. She lost her earnings, her parents, and her morality in one swift swoop; then she lost her sanity.

Merit Making

The Buddhist way to alleviate suffering, either in this or a future life, is to make merit. Monks present themselves as a field of merit for laypersons. By receiving all gifts as if they were given with the intention of making merit, regardless of who contributes them or how they were obtained, the Sanga (Buddhist order of monks) provides a culturally and morally acceptable means for "laundering" of monies that may have been earned through prostitution or other disreputable means.[16] Women in Thai society engage in meritmaking behavior much more regularly than men; they provide food for monks on a daily basis, and frequent the temples on holy days. The work of a prostitute precludes these types of meritmaking, but allows meritmaking that involves money. When making merit, she avoids presenting herself as a prostitute. Merit making is perceived by her and by folk and doctrinal Buddhism as an independent activity in which she is being a good Buddhist.

Prostitutes who work in massage parlors and hotels commonly make merit by inviting friends and clients to participate in a *thɔɔt phaa paa* ritual, an excursion (usually overnight) to a village temple for the purpose of giving money and gifts as a group to the temple.[17] Some prostitutes indicate that they make merit to compensate for the demerit of their stigmatized career and hope it will prevent them from being a prostitute in their next incarnation. Although not so publicized, their donations contribute to building new temple buildings, a major visible impact on poor villages. There is one temple in Bangkok, however, that is named after a woman donor who is widely known to have been a prostitute, Wat Khanikaphol.

Prostitutes generally report feeling pleased that they are able to send remittances home and to make merit at temple ceremonies. . . .

PROSTITUTION AS ECONOMIC AND CULTURAL SURVIVAL

Contrary to belief common in Thailand (and among foreign customers), prostitutes do not cite sexual satisfaction as a major reason for entering or remaining in their jobs. Chief among their reasons are extricating themselves from poverty or from a difficult home life, and earning enough to help the family of origin out of poverty or to build a foundation for their own futures.[18] These reasons reflect failure of the traditional support system of the self-subsistent landed household-family. And they reflect the young women's craving for security, both economic and domestic.

Prostitutes earn different amounts of money depending upon where they work. Those working in unmarked backstreet whorehouses that are heavily patronized by local lower and middle-class men often earn as little as 15 Baht (U.S. $0.60) a trick (with perhaps half going to the house), and typically service at least 10 customers a day/night. In contrast, women factory and construction workers generally earn much less, some 700–1500 Baht (U.S. $28–$60) a month. Prostitutes working in neon-bedazzled massage parlors, nightclubs, or bars earn much more and have fewer customers a night. The most highly paid are those working in restaurants "with special services" or with elite escort services.

After deducting living and job-related expenses (the latter include payments to agents, procurers, and police, and purchase of clothes and cosmetics), it appears that most prostitutes remit funds home to help their families and to make Buddhist merit. A new and substantial house for parents tops the list of purchases, followed by rice fields and electrical appliances: thus, houses and televisions are exchanged for women's bodies.

But the purchases represent more than material goods. They are one of the very few means women have for fulfilling cultural obligations to repay their parents. One 24-year-old described her coworkers:

> *Most have worked some 5–10 years, but they don't have the money they've earned because they sent it home. They sent it home as a way to give the family status* (mii naa mii taa). *Their parents built one house after another* (pluuk baan pen lang lang). *It wasn't just for themselves that the girls worked.*

Many prostitutes pay for younger siblings' education—often to prevent a sister from having to resort to prostitution—others, for parents' medical bills, and some, for a brother's ordination as a monk through which the mother and family can make Buddhist merit and gain in social status. In Northern villages, remittances from prostitutes often mean that parents and siblings do not have to work in the dry season, and have to plant only one rice crop a year. The labor of a daughter-sister who prostitutes herself can spare her family from work as well as provide them with otherwise unattainable consumer goods. Thus, prostitutes invest heavily in the conservation of their families and homes. In doing so, they carry out traditional obligations of women to take care of aging parents and younger siblings.

Thai women have long been responsible for economic maintenance of the household and have held the family's purse-strings. In the middle and upper classes, women are also well represented among owners of large businesses and corporations. Whereas mothers of lower socioeconomic sector families have traditionally sold food to meet their family's subsistence needs, daughters now can sell their bodies to meet the same needs, but, the parents hope and fantasize, on a gratifying grander, almost grandiose, scale. Today's prostitute is upholding the same value her mother did, but constrained to seek more lucrative ways of doing so.

Some prostitutes also conserve family ties by recruiting sisters and cousins to work with them. This mechanism is a major reason that some villages have many of their daughters "working in Bangkok" while others have none. It also reflects the young women's need for the security of social support against the alienation and abuse of their trade. The latter can involve molesting by violent customers, unintended pregnancies and aseptic illegal abortions, drugs to escape the indecencies of the moment ("How else could I get up there all but nude in front of all those strangers and perform in front of them?!" one asked), HIV and other sexually transmitted diseases, and exhaustion from as many as 20 customers a day. Money and sister-cousins as coworkers make it more bearable to be a prostitute.

CONCLUSION

Beliefs that boys are mischievous and men irresponsible, whereas girls are dutiful and women, loyal, run deep in Thai society. Such gender differences are assumed to be innate. But child socialization teaches a double standard: Children are raised with the expectation that real men need sex, and good girls control their sexuality so as not to overcome men with temptation.[19]

The double standard has long stigmatized the female prostitute. Until now. Now a new common sense allows a double standard within the double standard. Although not explicitly labeled as such, there are not only good and bad girls/women but "justified" and "unjustified" prostitutes as well. Those who are "justified" make money, and largely because of their outstanding beauty, make

lots of it.[20] In the streetperson's view, they earn it from foreign clients and send it home to parents and village temples.[21] Remittances and donations tacitly earn them the privilege of hiding their identity as prostitutes from their families and villages.[22] The "blind eye" of the support system back home sanctions the girls' continuing to work as prostitutes. By removing the stigma of prostitution from village daughters in the village, it maintains the bond of security between the young women and those whom tradition and human psychology dictate count most in life. Prostitutes who fulfill the cultural mandate for proper daughters are considered justified. They take care of parents and younger siblings financially, they return home at traditional new years (Songkran) with gifts to receive the blessings of their elders, and they fulfill the Buddhist expectation that women support the Sanga [Buddhist monks] by donating to temples and sponsoring ordinations of their brothers. . . .

NOTES

1. Muecke M. A. "Reproductive success" among the urban poor: a micro-level study of infant survival and child growth in Northern Thailand, Ph.D. dissertation, University of Washington, Seattle, WA, 1976; Muecke M. A. "Thai Conjugal Family Relationships and the Hsu Hypothesis." *J. Siam Society* 73, 25–41, 1983; Muecke M. A. "Make Money Not Babies: Changing Status Markers of Northern Thai Women." *Asian Survey* 24, 459–470, 1984.
2. Skrobanek S. *The Transnational Sex-Exploitation of Thai Women.* M.S. thesis. Institute of Social Studies, The Hague, 1983; Skrobanek S. "Strategies Against Prostitution in Thailand." In *Third World—Second Sex,* Vol. 2 (Edited by Davies M.). Zed Books, NJ, 1987.
3. La Loubere. A New Historical Relation of the Kingdom of Siam. London, 1963 (reprint).
4. Warren J. F. "Prostitution and the Politics of Venereal Disease: Singapore, 1870–98." *J. Southeast Asian Stud.* XXI, 360–383, 1990; Eng L. A. *Peasants, Proletarians and Prostitutes: A Preliminary Investigation into the Work of Chinese Women in Colonial Malaya.* ISEAS, Singapore, 1986.
5. The current prevalence of this practice is, however, unstudied. It is rare enough to be reportable in Thai

newspapers, but sufficiently routine to be part of street knowledge.
6. Wiboon Nakornjarupong. "Patronage and the Night Queens." *Business in Thailand,* pp. 40–52, 1981.
7. Suliman Narumon. Krabuan kaanklaai pen mǫǫ nuat: kǫranii sǔksaa yingbǫrikaan nai sathaan bǫrikaan aab ob nuat [The process of becoming a masseuse: a study of service girls in massage parlors]. Master's thesis, Faculty of Sociology and Anthropology, Thammasat University, Bangkok, 1987; Sulimon Narumon. Krabuan kaanklaai pen phanakhngaan aab ob nuat [The process of becoming a massage parlor staff member]. Paper presented at Chiang Mai University, Chiang Mai, 22 July 1988.
8. Ekachai S. "The Operations of the International Sex Trade Rings." *Bangkok Post Outlook* 44, 261, 1989; Enloe C. *Bananas, Beaches and Bases: Making Feminist Sense of International Politics.* University of California Press, Berkeley, 1990.
9. Pasuk P. Thailand: Miss Universe 1988, in *Southeast Asian Affairs* 1989 (Edited by Ng Chee Yuen), pp. 337, 348. Institute of Southeast Asian Studies, Singapore, 1989.
10. The Ministry of Public Health recently estimated there are 80,000 prostitutes in the country, but "the po-

lice reckon there are at least eight times that number." AIDS? What AIDS? *The Economist,* p. 36, 24 March 1990; Sittitrai W. "Commercial Sex in Thai Society." In *Proceedings of the First National Seminar on AIDS in Thailand.* 1991; Thongpao T. "New Types of Slavery in Thai Society." *Bangkok World* p. 6, 8 October 1986.

11. Haruhi T. "The Japanese Sex Industry: A Heightening Appetite for Asian Woman." *AMPO Japan-Asia Q. Rev.* 18, 2–3, 70–76, 1986.

12. Mulder N. *Everyday Life in Thailand: An Interpretation.* Duang Kamol, Bangkok, 1979.

13. "In 1980 Bangkok had 117 massage parlors which means approximately 20,000–25,000 masseuses. However, masseuses form only a minority of women engaged in prostitution. In addition Bangkok had 94 nightclubs and bars, 269 short-term (that is prostitution-oriented) hotels, 123 second-class hotels where prostitutes are commonly available, and 51 tea houses clustered around the Chinatown area. Besides, a number of whore-houses were believed to operate in moderate or high secrecy, either because they provided virgins who were mostly deceived or forced to receive customers, or because the women were high-class and occasional prostitutes." Hantrakul, Sukanya. Prostitution in Thailand. In *Development and Displacement: Women in Southeast Asia,* p. 20. Monash Papers on Southeast Asia, No. 18. Monash University, Clayton, 1988.

14. A Norwegian natural scientist who traveled in what is now Laos and Northern Thailand in the 1880s reported that "princes and officials who can afford to do so have a number of concubines who can be sold or otherwise disposed of when they are tired of them." Bock C. *Temples and Elephants,* p. 186. White Orchid Press, Bangkok, 1985. (Originally published London 1884).

15. Khin T. *Providence and Prostitution: Image and Reality for Women in Buddhist Thailand,* p. 23. Change International Reports, London, 1980.

16. "Laundering" occurs to the extent that merit accumulated through meritmaking activities balances out the demerit accrued from acts of prostitution. According to both folk and doctrinal Buddhism, wrong actions such as prostitution can be compensated for but not erased.

17. Praphot S. *Meesaa kamsaruan khabuankann ṇng nṇa khṃn thin* [The orchids of the north go home]. *Matichon* 8, 16–17, 1985.

18. Foundation for women. *Khamlaa,* 2nd ed. Bangkok 1988. (In Thai.).

19. See note 1.

20. Narumon reports prostitutes saying that it's better to give up virginity for money than to a boyfriend who drops you anyway and pays nothing.

21. Renu Atthameetr. Women . . . tools of ideals. *Conference on Results of Research of Women in Northern Thailand,* Chiang Mai, 24 August 1988.

22. Mandersen discusses the importance of the daughter-based remittance economy as a strategy of the extended family in island Southeast Asia. Manderson L. (Ed.) *Women's Work and Women's Roles: Economics and Everyday Life in Indonesia, Malaysia and Singapore.* The Australian National University, Canberra, 1983.

24

PARADE STRIPPERS:
BEING NAKED IN PUBLIC

CRAIG J. FORSYTH

This article is concerned with the practice of exposing the female breasts in exchange for "throws" (trinkets and glass beads thrown from floats) from Mardi Gras parade floats in the New Orleans area. It has become so commonplace that the term "beadwhore" has emerged to describe women who participate in this activity. This phenomenon can be compared to other related practices: nude sunbathing, nudism, mooning, and streaking [which many other researchers have studied].

BEING NAKED IN PUBLIC

As a topic for research, being naked in public can be discussed under the broad umbrella of exhibitionism or within the narrow frame of fads or nudity (Bryant 1977). In general, exhibitionism involves flaunting oneself in order to draw attention. In the field of deviance the term exhibitionism may also refer to behavior involving nudity for which the public shows little tolerance (Bryant 1977, p. 100; Bartol 1991, p. 280). This research, however, focuses on a form of public nudity that has a degree of social acceptance.

An extensive sociological study of public nudity was *The Nude Beach* (Douglas et al. 1977). Weinberg's (1981a, 1981b) study of nudists represents another type and degree of public nakedness. Other research has addressed the topics of streaking (running nude in a public area) (Toolan et al. 1974; Anderson 1977; Bryant 1982) and mooning (the practice of baring one's buttocks and prominently displaying the naked buttocks out of an automobile or a building window or at a public

event) (Bryant 1977, 1982). Both streaking and mooning were considered fads. One question considered by sociological research on nakedness is when and why it is permissible, appropriate, or acceptable to be naked in public (Aday 1990). Researchers have also addressed some possible motivations or rationales for public nudity. Toolan et al. (1974, p. 157), for example, explain motivations for streaking as follows:

> While streaking is not in itself a sex act, it is at least a more-than-subtle assault upon social values. Its defiance serves as a clarion call for others to follow suit, to show "the squares" that their "old hat" conventions, like love, marriage, and the family, are antiquated.

Both Bryant (1982) and Anderson (1977) say that streaking began as a college prank that spread quickly to many campuses. As a fad, it still retained parameters of time and place. Bryant (1982, p. 136) contended that it was one generation flaunting their liberated values in the faces of the older, more conservative generation. Anderson (1977, p. 232) said that it embodied the new morality and thus was "perceived by many to be a challenge to traditional values and laws."

Mooning, like streaking, was considered a prank and an insult to conformity and normative standards of behavior. Neither streaking nor mooning had any erotic value (Bryant 1982). Unlike streaking, mooning is still relatively common on college campuses.

Nudism in nudist camps has had little erotic value. Indeed, nudity at nudist camps has been purposively antierotic. Weinberg (1981b, p. 337) believes that the nudist camp would "anesthetize any relationship between nudity and sexuality." One strategy used by nudist camps to ensure this was to exclude unmarried people.

> *Most camps, for example, regard unmarried people, especially single men, as a threat to the nudist morality. They suspect that singles may indeed see nudity as something sexual. Thus, most camps either exclude unmarried people (especially men), or allow only a small quota of them (Weinberg 1981b, p. 337). . . .*

Nude sunbathing incorporates many rationales from voyeurism to lifestyle and in many cases has a degree of erotic value. The sexuality of the nude beach has been evaluated as situational.

> *Voyeurism . . . poses a dilemma for the nude beach naturalists, those who share in some vague way the hip or casual vision of the nude beach. . . . voyeurs have become the plague of the nude scene. . . . The abstract casual vision of the beach does not see it as in any way a sex trip, but the casual vision of life in general certainly does not exclude or downgrade sex (Douglas et al. 1977, pp. 126–27).*

Similar to the nudist in the nudist camp, nude beachers expressed contempt for the "straight" voyeur.

> *Sometimes I really feel hostile to the lookers. Obviously you can't look at people that way even if they are dressed . . . it really depends on your attitude in looking. I've even told a couple of people to fuck off . . . and some people to leave. I was thinking this would be the last time I would come down here . . . there were too many sightseers . . . it sort of wrecks your time to have someone staring at you (Douglas et al. 1977, p. 130). . . .*

[What about parade stripping, the most recent phenomenon of being naked in public, as practiced on Mardi Gras day in New Orleans?]

MARDI GRAS: DEVIANCE BECOMES NORMAL

On Mardi Gras day in New Orleans many things normally forbidden are permitted. People walk around virtually nude, women expose themselves from balconies, and the gay community gives new meaning to the term outrageous. Laws that attempt to legislate morality are informally suspended. It is a sheer numbers game for the police; they do not have the resources to enforce such laws. . . .

The celebration of carnival or Mardi Gras as it occurs in New Orleans and surrounding areas primarily involves balls and parades. These balls and parades are produced by carnival clubs called "krewes." Parades consist of several floats, usually between fifteen and twenty-five, and several marching bands that follow each float. There are riders on the floats. Depending on the size of the float, the number of riders can vary from four to fifteen. The floats roll through the streets of New Orleans on predetermined routes. People line up on both sides of the street on the routes. The float riders and the viewers on the street engage in a sort of game. The riders have bags full of beads or other trinkets that they throw out to the viewers along the route. The crowds scream at the riders to throw them something. Traditionally, the scream has been "throw me something mister." Parents put their children on their shoulders or have ladders with seats constructed on the top in order to gain some advantage in catching some of these throws. These "advantages" have become fixtures, and Mardi Gras ladders are sold at most local hardware stores. It is also advantageous if the viewer knows someone on the float or is physically closer to the float. Another technique is to be located in temporary stands constructed along the parade route that "seat" members of the other carnival krewes in the city or other members of the parading krewe.

In recent years another technique has emerged. Women have started to expose their breasts in exchange for throws. The practice has added another permanent slogan to the parade route. Many float riders carry signs that say "show me your tits"; others merely motion to the women to expose themselves. In some cases, women initiate the encounter by exposing their breasts without any prompting on the part of the float rider.

The author became aware of the term "bead-whore" while viewing a Mardi Gras parade. There were several women exposing their breasts to float riders. I had my 3-year-old son on my shoulders and I was standing in front of the crowd next to the floats. I am also a tall person. All of these factors usually meant that we caught a lot of throws from the float riders, but we caught nothing. Instead, the float riders were rewarding the parade strippers. As we moved away to find a better location, a well-dressed older woman, who had been standing behind the crowd, said to me:

> You can't catch anything with those beadwhores around. Even cute kids on the shoulders of their fathers can't compete with boobs. When the beadwhores are here, you just need to find another spot.

The term was also used by some of the interviewees [in this research].

METHODOLOGY

Data for this research were obtained in two ways: interviews and observations in the field. Interview data were gotten from an available sample of men who ride parade floats ($N = 54$) and from women who expose themselves ($N = 51$). These interviews ranged in length from 15 to 45 minutes. In the interviews with both float riders and parade strippers an interview guide was used to direct the dialogue. The guide was intended to be used as a probing mechanism rather than as a generator of specific responses. Respondents were located first through friendship networks and then by snowballing. Snowball sampling is a method through which the researcher develops an ever-increasing set of observations (Babbie 1992). Respondents in the study were asked to recommend others for interviewing, and each of the subsequently interviewed participants was asked for further recommendations. Additional informal interviews were carried out with other viewers of Mardi Gras.

Observations were made at Mardi Gras parades in the city of New Orleans over two carnival seasons: 1990 and 1991. Altogether, 42 parades were observed. The author assumed the role of "complete observer" for this part of the project (Babbie 1992, p. 289). This strategy allows the researcher to be unobtrusive and not affect what is going on. The author has lived a total of 24 years in New Orleans and has been a complete participant in Mardi Gras many times. Observations were made at several different locations within the city.

FINDINGS

The practice of parade stripping began in the late 1970s but its occurrence sharply increased from 1987 to 1991. During this study, no stripping occurred in the daytime. It always occurred in the dark, at night parades. Strippers were always with males. Those interviewed ranged in age from 21 to 48; the median age was 22. Most of them were college students. Many began stripping during their senior year in high school, particularly if they were from the New Orleans area. If from another area, they usually began in college. All of the strippers interviewed were in one location, a middle-class white area near two universities. Both riders and strippers said it was a New Orleans activity not found in the suburbs, and they said it was restricted to only certain areas of the city. One float rider said:

> In Metairie [the suburbs] they do it rarely if at all, but in New Orleans they have been doing it for the last ten years. Mostly I see it in the university section of the city during the night parades.

Parade strippers often attributed their first performances to alcohol, to the coaxing of the float riders, to other strippers in the group, or to a boyfriend. This is consistent with the opinion of Bryant (1982, pp. 141–42), who contended that when females expose themselves it is usually while drinking. Alcohol also seemed to be involved with the float riders' requests for women to expose themselves. One rider stated:

> Depending on how much I have had to drink, yes I will provoke women to expose themselves. Sometimes I use hand signals. Sometimes I carry a sign which says "show me your tits." If I am real drunk I will either stick the sign in their face or just scream at them "show me your tits."

Data gained through both interviews and observation indicated that parade stripping is usually initiated by the float riders. But many of the women indicated that they were always aware of the possibility of stripping at a night parade. Indeed, some females came well prepared for the events. An experienced stripper said:

> I wear an elastic top. I practice before I go to the parade. Sometimes I practice between floats at parades. I always try to convince other girls with us to show 'em their tits. I pull up my top with my left hand and catch beads with my right hand. I get on my boyfriend's shoulder. I do it for every float . . . I'd show my breasts longer for more stuff and I'll show both breasts for more stuff.

Other parade strippers gave the following responses when asked, "Why do you expose yourself at parades?"

> I'm just a beadwhore. What else can I say?
> I expose myself because I'm drunk and I'm encouraged by friends and strangers on the floats.
> I get drunk and like to show off my breasts. And yes they are real.
> Basically for beads. I do not get any sexual gratification from it.
> I only did it once. I did it because a float rider was promising a pair of glass beads. When I drink too much at a night parade, I turn into a beadwhore.
> It's fun.
> I exposed myself on a dare. Once I did it, I was embarrassed.

Only one woman admitted that she did it for sexual reasons. At 48, she was the oldest respondent. When asked why she exposed her breasts at parades, she said:

> Sexual satisfaction. Makes me feel young and seductive. My breasts are the best feature I have.

One woman who had never exposed herself at parades commented on her husband's efforts to have her participate during the excitement of a parade.

> We were watching a parade one night and there were several women exposing their breasts. They were catching a lot of stuff. My husband asked me to show the people on the float my breasts so that we could catch something. He asked me several times. I never did it and we got into an argument. It seemed so unlike him, asking me to do that.

Float riders often look on bead tossing as a reward for a good pair of breasts, as the following comments show:

> The best boobs get the best rewards.
>
> Ugly women get nothing.
>
> Large boobs get large rewards.

When parade strippers exposed themselves they were not as visible to people not on the float as one would think. Strippers were usually on the shoulders of their companions and very close to the float. For a bystander to get a "good look" at the breasts of the stripper was not a casual act. A person had to commit a very deliberate act in order to view the event. Those who tried to catch a peek but were either not riding the floats or not among the group of friends at the parade were shown both pity and contempt.

> I hate those fuckers [on the ground] who try to see my boobs. If I'm with some people they can look. That's ok. But those guys who seek a look they are disgusting. I bet they can't get any. They probably go home and jerk off. I guess I feel sorry for them too. But I still don't like them. You know it's so obvious, they get right next to the float and then turn around. Their back is to the float. They are not watching the parade. We tell them to "get the fuck out of here asshole" and they leave.

Like a small minority of nude sunbathers who like to be peeped at (Douglas et al. 1977, p. 128), there are strippers who like the leering of bystanders. Our oldest respondent, mentioned earlier, said she enjoyed it. "I love it when they look. The more they look the more I show them," she remarked.

Parade strippers most often perform in the same areas. Although parade stripping usually involves only exposing breasts, three of the interviewees said they had exposed other parts of their bodies in other public situations.

Strippers and their male companions tried to separate themselves from the crowds; they developed a sense of privacy needed to perform undisturbed (Sommer 1969; Palmer 1977). Uninvited "peepers" disturbed the scene and were usually removed through verbal confrontation.

Most strippers and others in attendance apparently compartmentalized their behavior (Schur 1979, p. 319; Forsyth and Fournet 1987). It seemed to inflict no disfavor on the participants, or if it did they seemed to manage the stigma successfully (Gramling and Forsyth 1987). . . .

CONCLUSION

Parade stripping seemed to exist because trinkets and beads were given; for those interviewed, there was no apparent sexuality attached except in one case.

Parade stripping is probably best understood as "creative deviance" (Douglas et al. 1977, p. 238), deviance that functions to solve problems or to create pleasure for the individual. Many forms of deviance, however, do not work in such simplistic ways.

> *Most people who go to a nude beach, or commit any other serious rule violation, do not find that it works [emphasis added] for them. They discover they are too ashamed of themselves or that the risk of shaming by others is too great, so they do not continue. Other people find it hurts them more (or threatens them) or, at the very least, does not do anything good for them. So most forms of deviance do not spread (Douglas et al. 1977, p. 239).*

Some forms of deviance apparently do "work," and parade stripping is one of them. The beadwhore engages in a playful form of exhibitionism. She and the float rider both flirt with norm violation. The stripper gets beads and trinkets and the float rider gets to see naked breasts. Both receive pleasure in the party atmosphere of Mardi Gras, and neither suffers the condemnation of less creative and less esoteric deviants.

REFERENCES

Aday, David P. 1990. *Social Control at the Margins.* Belmont, CA: Wadsworth.

Anderson, William A. 1977. "The Social Organizations and Social Control of a Fad." *Urban Life* 6:221–40.

Babbie, Earl. 1992. *The Practice of Social Research.* Belmont, CA: Wadsworth.

Bartol, Curt R. 1991. *Criminal Behavior: A Psychosocial Approach.* Englewood Cliffs, NJ: Prentice-Hall.

Bryant, Clifton D. 1977. *Sexual Deviancy in Social Context.* New York: New Viewpoints.

Bryant, Clifton D. 1982. *Sexual Deviancy and Social Proscription: The Social Context of Carnal Behavior.* New York: Human Sciences Press.

Douglas, Jack D., Paul K. Rasmussen, and Carol A. Flanagan. 1977. *The Nude Beach.* Beverly Hills, CA: Sage.

Forsyth, Craig J., and Lee Fournet. 1987. "A Typology of Office Harlots: Party Girls, Mistresses and Career Climbers." *Deviant Behavior* 8:319–328.

Gramling, Robert, and Craig J. Forsyth. 1987. "Exploiting Stigma." *Sociological Forum* 2:401–415.

Palmer, C. Eddie. 1977. "Microecology and Labeling Theory: A Proposed Merger," pp. 12–17 in *Sociological Stuff,* edited by H. Paul Chalfant, Evans W. Curry, and C. Eddie Palmer. Dubuque, IA: Kendall/Hunt.

Schur, Edwin M. 1979. *Interpreting Deviance.* New York: Harper & Row.

Sommer, Robert. 1969. *Personal Space.* Englewood Cliffs, NJ: Prentice-Hall.

Toolan, James M., Murray Elkins, and Paul D'Encarnacao. 1974. "The Significance of Streaking." *Medical Aspects of Human Sexuality* 8:152–165.

Weinberg, Martin S. 1981a. "Becoming a Nudist," pp. 291–304 in *Deviance: An Interactionist Perspective,* edited by Earl Rubington and Martin S. Weinberg. New York: Macmillan.

Weinberg, Martin S. 1981b. "The Nudist Management of Respectability," pp. 336–345 in *Deviance: An Interactionist Perspective,* edited by Earl Rubington and Martin S. Weinberg. New York: Macmillan.

THE NAKED BODY AS SITE AND SIGHT: THE "ACCOUNTS" OF AMATEUR STRIPPERS

THOMAS C. CALHOUN
JULIE ANN HARMS CANNON
RHONDA FISHER

Amateur stripping is a contemporary social phenomenon that has undergone limited investigation (Calhoun et al., 1997). We define amateurs as those individuals, male or female, who engage in stripping as a recreational activity rather than as a primary occupation. Why do young men and women, then, take off their clothes in public with no guarantee of financial reward?

Simmel (1950) discusses the ways in which urban life alters individual interactions and the expression of individuality. Specifically, there is a movement from the slower, more predictable pace of rural life to the more stimulating and unpredictable nature of urban existence. This movement creates the need for individuals to capitalize on their uniqueness. Every effort is made to stand out from the crowd. "In order to preserve his most personal core" the individual must overcome the alienating demands of metropolitan life and "exaggerate this personal element to remain audible even to himself' (Simmel, 1950, p. 22).

The need to stand out is an important facet of urban living; however, this task may be particularly difficult for youth. We argue that youth may in fact utilize amateur stripping as a forum for this more personal expression of self which Simmel describes, due to a lack of more publicly available or socially acceptable territories.

Before evaluating the applicability of Simmel's macro level analysis of youth culture and urban life to the study of amateur stripping, we must first identify what is known about professional stripping, particularly as it relates to individual motivations and the use of body territories. To facilitate this analysis we turn to the work of Lyman and Scott (1970).

LITERATURE REVIEW

Motivations

. . . When behavior falls outside normative parameters, individuals are required to account for their actions. . . . Lyman and Scott (1970) identify two types of accounts, "excuses" and "justifications." "Excuses are accounts in which one admits that the act in question is bad, wrong, or inappropriate but denies full responsibility" (p. 114). Justifications differ from excuses. "Justifications are accounts in which one accepts responsibility for the act in question, but denies the pejorative quality associated with it" (p. 114). Lyman and Scott identify several justifications that are contained in the work of Sykes and Matza (1957). Their "neutralization techniques" include: (a) denial of injury; (b) denial of victim; (c) condemnation of the condemners; and (d) the appeal to loyalties.

Two further types of justifications, also identified by Lyman and Scott (1970), have particular relevance for the study of stripping behavior. These include invocations of "sad tales" and descriptions of "self-fulfillment." In a sad tale, the individual talks about a problematic past that contributed to the behavior in question. The self-fulfillment justification is actually a "personal growth" explanation in which individuals claim to gain personal insight from their behavior.

Professional stripping literature has mainly focused on the external rewards of stripping. For professional strippers, male and female, economic gain appears to be the primary motivation for engaging in this behavior (Skipper and McCaghy, 1970; Carey et al., 1974; Dressel and Peterson, 1982b; Peterson and Dressel, 1982; Ronai and Ellis, 1989; Reid et al., 1994a,b). Female strippers typically cite financial crises as the impetus for entering the occupation of professional stripping. For these women, stripping becomes their sole means of economic support (Skipper and McCaghy, 1970).

Interestingly, male strippers offer alternative accounts of their movement into professional stripping. Specifically, male strippers do not typically view stripping as a primary occupation (Dressel and Peterson, 1982b). Rather, they utilize the professional stripping scene as a sexual outlet and source of pleasure (i.e. easy access to women, gifts, and excitement). Further, male strippers often view this extra-occupational venture as a way to move into another form of professional entertainment.

Interestingly, while male strippers endeavor to justify their stripping behavior, female strippers attempt to reduce the stigma surrounding the occupation (Mullen, 1985; Thompson and Harred, 1992). Justification strategies developed by male strippers include: (a) stripping provides liberated women with a social outlet; (b) male stripping provides women with an environment in which they can be sexually assertive; (c) stripping can be viewed as a sexual outlet for women who would otherwise not have partners; and (d) stripping is a unique form of commercial entertainment (Dressel and Peterson, 1982b). In addition to providing a sexual outlet and commercial entertainment, women's justifications

include an instructional aspect. Strippers are often approached by women seeking sexual advice (Boles and Garbin, 1974).

Body Territory and Exploitation

In American society where territorial encroachment affects nearly all members of society, certain segments of the population are particularly deprived, namely, Negroes, women, youth [emphasis added], and inmates of various kinds. (Lyman and Scott, 1970, p. 90).

The establishment of group territories is essential in the formation of specific group identities and the enactment of some rituals or group behaviors which "run counter to expected [societal] norms" (Lyman and Scott, 1970, p. 90). Lyman and Scott identify four types of territories that individuals and groups may claim: (a) public territories; (b) home territories; (c) interactional territories; and (d) body territories.

First, "public territories" are those areas that are available to all individuals and groups for the most part (although restrictions sometimes apply). However, while access is technically unlimited, specific behavioral norms generally apply to all who wish to enter. Public areas are also governed by law, and access is limited at times for specific segments of the population. It is expected that people will follow the established rules and laws in public areas.

Lyman and Scott (1970) note the ambiguous nature of public territories. What appears to be public on the outside may actually be strongly regulated or limited by local custom. Further, status may also be a limiting factor. Those of a particular status group may be turned away from some public territories. Finally, customs or laws may change. A forbidden behavior may become legal or a once legal activity may be prohibited. Currently, it is legal to dance nude in some bars or clubs, although the same behavior would be illegal outside that territory.

A second type of territory designated by Lyman and Scott is the "home territory." Home territories are much more personal in nature than public territories. They are characterized by greater group freedom, control, and intimacy. However, the two territories (public and home) may be confused, because some may be using a space as a home territory while another group uses it as a public territory. As Lyman and Scott (1970, pp. 93–4) note, "It is precisely because of their officially open condition that public areas are vulnerable to conversion into home territories."

"Interactional territories" are identified as a third category by Lyman and Scott. Typically, these include "any area where a social gathering may occur. Surrounding any interaction is an invisible boundary, a kind of social membrane . . . Interactional territories are characteristically mobile and fragile" (Lyman and Scott, 1970, p. 95) because of changes in social status and the intrusion of "newcomers."

Finally, and most importantly for this work, Lyman and Scott explicate the nature of "body territories." Of all territory types, body territories are the most private. A body territory includes "the space encompassed by the human body and the anatomical space of the body" (Lyman and Scott, 1970, p. 96). Accordingly, body space is more sacred than other territory types. Access, in terms of viewing and touching, is quite limited and in many cases regulated by law. However, bodies may be utilized as symbols of individual or group identity. Through specific body alterations, personal space may be used to express "individuality and freedom" (Lyman and Scott, 1970, p. 98).

Although bodies can be utilized as sites for personal expressions of individuality, they can also be exploited. In the case of professional stripping, male and female bodies are not commodified equally. Professional stripping, an occupation that has traditionally been done by women for men, serves as a glaring example of overt sexism in this society. In a move toward pseudo-egalitarianism, women have only recently been allowed access to the world of commercialized sex-related entertainment through the male strip show. Since the mid to late 1970s, more bars and nightclubs have begun to feature male strippers and research has begun to explore the differences (Dressel and Pe-

terson, 1982a,b; Peterson and Dressel, 1982; Margolis and Arnold, 1993).

The primary differences between male and female professional stripping environments can be found in the setting and in the audience. Peterson and Dressel (1982) noted that male strip clubs propagate the notion of the "egalitarian motif:" the opportunity to be like men in terms of aggressive sexual behavior representing a form of equal rights for women.

Margolis and Arnold (1993) challenge the notion of egalitarianism in a comparison of male strip shows and the more traditional ones which feature female dancers. They hypothesize that if the male strip show is a true inversion of traditional gender hierarchy, then "it should be a mirror image of the female strip show with only the sex of the performers and the audience reversed" (p. 335). Margolis and Arnold detail the following factors regarding male strippers, which demonstrate that the role reversal is illusory: male dancers are depicted as sexual aggressors; they interact only as performers and not as waiting staff; their job is one which evokes interest because of its novelty; they are referred to as artistic and sexy versus a whore or a slut; and they are compensated more financially.

Research on stripping has also included a focus on interaction patterns between strippers, customers, managers, bouncers, and announcers, as well as occupational norms (McCaghy and Skipper, 1969; Skipper and McCaghy, 1970; Carey et al., 1974; Dressel and Peterson, 1982b; Peterson and Dressel, 1982; Peretti and O'Connor 1989; Ronai and Ellis, 1989). The types of settings and methods of entertainment determined the interaction strategies and occupational norms of the strippers.

The "homosocial setting" (Peterson and Dressel, 1982), which is typically and frequently mandatory in male strip clubs, is also typical of bars which feature female strippers, and provides a supportive environment for the expression of socially constructed traditional and nontraditional gender roles. For example, in the female stripping environment the audience members (primarily men) are encouraged to play out traditionally masculine gender roles, while in the male stripping environment the audience members (primarily female) are encouraged to transcend traditionally female gender roles and take on sexually assertive behavior which is typically associated with the male gender role (Peterson and Dressel, 1982).

Further, the confirmation of gender roles (traditional or nontraditional) is also demonstrated through the use of exaggerated "heterosexual imagery" (Peterson and Dressel, 1982). Through the use of props and costumes (firefighter, construction worker, Tarzan, Superman, etc.) male strippers seek to magnify and personalize heterosexuality. This heterosexual imagery is a crucial element of the homosocial setting (Peterson and Dressel, 1982).

Treatment of interaction strategies identified in the literature dealt primarily with customer–stripper interactions, where their purpose was to maximize financial gain for the strippers. This is frequently carried out through the manipulation of the body. Financial gain is increased by a strategy labeled "counterfeiting of intimacy" (Boles and Garbin, 1974; Enck and Preston, 1988), in which the strippers pretend to actually care about or desire a relationship with the customer in order to get more money.

For both male and female professional strippers, spatial intimacy or close proximity to the customer tends to be the most lucrative form of interaction. Variations of table dancing appeared to be the most efficient breakdown of social distance between the customer and the stripper (Boles and Garbin, 1974; Peterson and Dressel, 1982; Ronai and Ellis, 1989). However, some strippers are actually interested in maintaining relationships with customers that go beyond the stripping situation (Dressel and Peterson, 1982a,b; Peterson and Dressel, 1982; Ronai and Ellis, 1989). These relationships are usually sexual in nature, and frequently involve prostitution (Barron, 1989).

Given what the literature suggests generally about professional stripping behavior—the factors that influence entry and the interactional patterns between strippers and customers—we are now in a position to assess the applicability of Simmel's theoretical framework in explaining amateur stripping behavior. Specifically, the purpose of this chapter is to broaden our theoretical understanding of amateur stripping behavior framed by Simmel's theoretical presuppositions about youth culture.

METHODOLOGY

Subjects and Setting

Amateur strip night occurs each Thursday at a bar known as Kato's.[1] In this large Midwestern city, Thursday is the main night out for college students. At Kato's there are two contests taking place. The men's competition begins at approximately 10:30 P.M. and the women's competition begins shortly after the men's competition is completed.

During our eight-month investigation we were able to observe, on an average evening, five male and five female participants in the dance contest weekly. Some nights the number of participants in each contest were as high as 11. Only on one occasion did the number of participants fall below three per contest.

The participants in their study are ten men (five white, three African American, one Hispanic, one Asian) and nine women (five white, one African American, one Hispanic, two Asian) who performed in the dance contest at Kato's on at least one occasion, although many perform quite regularly. The age range of the male participants is 21–32, with a mean age of 25. The age range of the female participants is 21–27, with a mean age of 23.

Although we observed many performances during the course of our investigation, the findings are primarily informed by the 19 individuals who agreed to participate in the study. We made numerous attempts to contact dance participants after the competitions; however, many were unwilling to take part in our research. Specifically, women were generally less willing to be interviewed than men. At the initial request, most women were somewhat reticent and had obviously heard a variety of "pick-up lines." Men, however, responded favorably because they believed it was a "pick-up line," yet several men also refused to be interviewed even after numerous attempts were made by the researchers. Although many women agreed to participate after our credentials were confirmed, several women declined immediately due to continued harassment by audience members.

Additionally, several of the participants consider themselves to be "professional" strippers (i.e. they consider stripping to be their primary source of income). Anyone who pays the $2 cover charge upon entry can participate in the competition. Each contest carries a cash prize—$100 for first, $50 for second, and $25 for third place.

The atmosphere at Kato's is quite similar to that of a typical nightclub or disco. The lighting is dim, the music is loud, and the dance floor is the main attraction. Alcohol is available from the beer stand at the main entrance and from bars on the first and second levels. Customers may be seated at tables or booths located on both levels. The dance floor is on the first level, and this is where most customers seek seating (many arrive early to obtain seating closest to the dance floor). The second floor has a balcony overlooking the dance floor and those preferring it, or who cannot find seating on the first floor, sit and look on from above. The activity on the second level is less specifically focused on the contest. It is often difficult to obtain a good view of the competition from this location. Dancing occurs before and immediately following the stripping contests. Finally, customers may play pool at any time during the evening on either floor, even while the dance contest is in progress.

Data Collection and Techniques

The data for this study were collected over an eight-month time period from the population of male and female dancers observed at Kato's. During the beginning stages of the project we engaged solely in observational research. It was essential for us to become "regulars" at Kato's. Although note-taking during the competition was somewhat difficult and often focused a great deal of attention

on our work, we took this as an opportunity to let customers and staff know about the project. Additionally, once audience members, staff, and participants realized what we were doing at Kato's they were more apt to offer suggestions and observational responses that were quite helpful to our research efforts.

Each of the 19 participants agreed to participate by written consent.[2] The participants were given information regarding the nature of the project during the initial contact and at the time of the interview. Participants were also informed that a copy of the research findings would be available at Kato's upon completion of the project.

Because this study is of a potentially sensitive nature, steps were taken to protect the identities of the participants. Participants were informed that no actual individual names would be utilized in the final report of the research findings, and each participant was told that he or she could refuse to answer any question and that the interview could be terminated at any time during the conversation.

Typically, participants were contacted at Kato's after the amateur stripping competition; however, some contacts were made utilizing snowball sampling techniques. Interviews were conducted at a variety of locations, including our offices, participants' and investigators' residences, restaurants, and professional and amateur stripping establishments. Additionally, a few interviews were conducted over the telephone. Data were collected using a semi-structured interview format. Although all interviews were directed by the interview schedule, conversations were not limited to only the scheduled questions. Participants were encouraged to discuss all aspects of amateur stripping that had the potential for the development of future research. All interviews were audiotaped and completely transcribed for future analyses.

Before we assess the appropriateness of Simmel's theoretical framework in terms of amateur stripping behavior, it is necessary that this behavior be evaluated at the micro level, based upon what the scientific literature currently suggests about professional stripping behavior. To frame this discussion we return to Lyman and Scott's

(1970) work on accounts and body territories. Following this discussion, we will turn to Simmel's work on youth culture to examine amateur stripping behavior from a macro perspective.

FINDINGS

Motivational Accounts of Amateur Strippers

As mentioned previously in this work, accounts of stripping behavior have been limited to those offered by professional strippers. Professional strippers document economic need as a primary motivation, while professional male strippers also utilize the profession as a means of achieving future sexual encounters and entertainment career opportunities.

Interestingly, the amateur male accounts are strikingly similar to those offered by professional male strippers. Additionally, amateur women's accounts come closer to the male model, and for the most part do not resonate with the accounts offered by female professional strippers. For this reason, we also present the experiences of a professional female stripper. While amateur women were more likely to use "self-fulfillment" as a justification for stripping, professionals were more likely to utilize "sad tales" (Lyman and Scott, 1970).

Typically, amateur stripping is viewed by male and female performers as a form of recreation or fun. It is also viewed as a form of self-fulfillment. Amateurs generally do not believe that they are harming anyone. Rather, stripping is a way to use the body to receive attention and boost self-esteem. Friends, alcohol, and money often play a role in the decision to strip, but for the most part male and female amateurs claim that the final decision is their own. Additionally, stripping is described as an "adrenaline rush."

Sean, a male performer, discusses how he ended up performing for the first time at Kato's:

INTERVIEWER: Why that particular night?
SEAN: I was down with a bunch of friends and a bunch of girlfriends and they were pretty much coaching me to do it.
I: Did they dare you?

SEAN: Not really. They just kept giving me a bunch of crap about it.

Although Sean claims responsibility for his actions, he justified his behavior because of his allegiance to his friends. In this sense his justification approximates an "appeal to loyalties." Brad offers a similar account of the night's events that led him to strip at Kato's that very first time:

I: The first time you took your clothes off, what was your motivation? Was it a dare, a bet, or did alcohol influence you?
BRAD: I don't know really. Drinking makes you do stuff like that. And it was the first time I'd been to Kato's and I used to go to dance clubs and stuff like Kato's and I just wanted to find out what it was like dancing in front of people.

When asked if he would consider stripping again Brad replied:

Yeah, I'm sure I will but like I said I don't know very much. And I don't go for money 'cause I don't need money. I just go for fun. I mean, I just like it, it's pretty cool.

Although Brad does not justify his behavior through an appeal to loyalties, it is also clear that money is not a primary motivating factor. Brad participates in the contest because it is self-fulfilling and fun.

Kyle had friends with him the night he first performed at Kato's. When asked about his motivation(s), he offered the following account:

I just wanted to do it I guess. The night before I did it at another bar and I did it mostly because it was a fear of mine, getting up in front of an audience.

Similarly to Brad, Kyle finds amateur stripping to be self-fulfilling. He was able to overcome his fear of appearing in public by entering (and winning) the dance contest at Kato's. When asked about how stripping made him feel, Kyle described his participation as an adrenaline rush:

Well, I always compare it to running out before the football game, before all the players run out. 'Cause you're surrounded by the noise.

However, for some, money is the primary motivation. Kevin discusses how money influenced his decision to strip at Kato's that very first time:

> I had just gotten into town and I had some problems with my car and my cousin was like well, "If you need some extra money . . . I'm sure you could probably win." So he told me about it and I went down there and the first time I went I won.

Additionally, as it turns out, Kevin utilizes his exposure at Kato's to help him get offers for professional stripping jobs (e.g. bachelorette parties):

> That's where Kato's came in. I was stripping at Kato's and they saw me there and liked the way I stripped . . . That was kind of like my advertisement. That's why I went to Kato's.

In this way stripping is actually instrumental for both amateur and professional males. Stripping is a means to future employment in the entertainment industry.

Many of the accounts offered by the female amateurs sound quite similar to those offered by their male counterparts. However, amateur women do not appear to utilize stripping as a sexual outlet or avenue for future employment, which is frequently the case for male amateurs and professionals. Rather, stripping is a way to have fun and experience self-fulfillment. Christie describes her motivation to strip at Kato's for the first time:

> All the energy from my friends that were there. They just, were like, "Oh, Christie, you know you want to do it," you know. Because I've done it at private parties before. My mom doesn't have a clue about that. But I've done it for my friends and I wanted to see what it would be like, in what the atmosphere would be like to do it at a bar. You know, in front of a whole bunch of strangers instead of a whole bunch of men that you knew.

Specifically, Christie appeals to the loyalty of her friends and the need for self-fulfillment as primary motivations for participating in the contest. Christie stated that alcohol had nothing to do with her decision to perform that night. She only had one-half of a beer. Additionally, money was not a major motivating factor:

> Oh money, it influences, but, you know, it's not a priority. With me it wasn't anyway. With some people yeah, it might be. You got rent to pay or, you know, have bills to pay. But with me it was just, I wanted to do it. I wanted to have fun.

However, Christie does not believe that she will perform at Kato's again. She stated that "I've fulfilled my curiosity and plus my body is not in the shape that it was." Christie has achieved the self-fulfillment desired from this activity and seemingly has no need to strip again.

Donna has considered professional stripping as a primary occupation and is a regular participant in the amateur contest at Kato's. Her initial motivation to strip had more to do with friends and alcohol rather than money. The first time she participated was on her birthday. She wanted to do something she had never done before:

> I think it was my friends, you know, telling me . . . "You can do it, you can do it." And then I was just sitting there and I was like, "Yeah, I can do this," you know. So I was like, "Okay, yeah, I'll do it."

For Donna, stripping is a way to have fun, please her friends, and feel good about herself.

Tanya agrees with Donna that alcohol makes stripping easier, but argues that it was not the primary motivating factor. Typically, amateur women do not try to excuse their behavior in this way. Rather, alcohol is viewed as a way to manipulate the body in order to lessen personal inhibitions. Tanya states:

> It made it easier to do, but I'd already made my decision to do it. It wasn't one of those things where I get drunk on my birthday and my friends are just sitting there pushing me and the next day I'm bawling.

Tanya also uses stripping to make a political statement about women's beauty expectations:

> I try not to pay attention to the audience any more because they have all negative responses. Because we've thought in America you're not supposed to like yourself, you're not supposed to be sexy. And I'm sorry, but I do. And even though I have low self-esteem, I feel those things about

myself. And being my size [over 300 pounds] in America or in today's society period, you shouldn't do the things I do . . . I like to do what I know people don't think I should do. And that's one of those things I can do.

Stripping is primarily a form of self-fulfillment for Tanya, who argues that stripping is fun. In addition, she performs for reasons other than money:

The money is good, money is fine. It's more fun if you win. But a lot of times it's, I do it because my friends ask me to. My friends beg me to do it, "Come on, we want to see you strip, it's so much fun!"

The accounts offered by those women who strip professionally differ in some ways from those offered by amateur women. Motivational accounts regarding professional stripping correlate with those described in the literature. However, when accounting for their motivations to perform at Kato's, they sound strikingly similar to the women who perform solely as amateurs.

Tammy, a professional dancer, performs at Kato's on occasion. She describes her personal experiences that led her to professional stripping:

You know, when I first started this business I was, to be honest, only 17 years old when I started dancing. I don't know, I was real messed up is what I was. I fucked up a lot. I messed around a lot. I didn't take care of my responsibilities and things I was supposed to do. My money that I had I did not manage well. But at that time I was pretty young and I didn't know what the hell I was doing. But now I'm still young, but I'm older and wiser. I mean I still have a lot more to go in life but I've taken what's been given to me and what I've learned and done something with it.

She evokes a "sad tale" to justify her entrance into professional stripping. However, she describes the satisfaction she gets out of dancing professionally:

It's the money. I also enjoy it. It makes my career. I have my personal, I own my own business now and am doing it. You know, there's nothing wrong with dancing and we've used it to our advantage and I've made a career out of it. It's basically my career. I mean, yeah, part of it is for the money but also I mean it's a big rush getting up on that stage.

People, you know, "Wow," you know. My ex told me it's an adrenaline rush and I think you need that. [Like] rock stars on stage, they drive to that adrenaline rush. It's a type of adrenaline rush. But yeah, the money is good too. I support myself and my two kids very well and I'm very proud of that. And I do it all on my own. It's a big accomplishment.

When asked why she danced at Kato's that night she offered the following account:

I don't know, 'cause nobody could dance that was out there . . . I was having a good time. I was out there partying with my friends, you know, and I was catching a good buzz. I wasn't drunk by any means. I was buzzed but I wasn't drunk by any means. But I mean nobody was really entering. My friend [also a professional stripper] didn't want to enter it and so I just went out there and did it. Nobody could dance so I figured I could place. I mean that may sound very naive, but I figured I could at least place and I would be happy with that.

Again, friends and alcohol play an important role in the decision to perform, but they are not considered primary sources of motivation. Although Tammy dances professionally, her motivation to participate at Kato's corresponds with that of those who perform solely as amateurs.

Amateur Stripping: Body Territories and Exploitation

The key to understanding the "attention" and the "rush" mentioned previously appears to be control. Stripping allows the performer to control the attention he or she receives through the manipulation of the body. As noted by Lyman and Scott (1970), youth have limited access to public territories for the expression of cultural values and beliefs. If they are to enhance self-esteem and individuality, they must find another outlet. For amateur strippers, this outlet is the body.

Again, stripping is a way to utilize the body to receive attention, have fun, and enhance self-fulfillment. Mike offers his opinion as to why performers strip regularly at Kato's:

I think people strip over and over again because once you get in the public eye it's like a cocaine addiction, you just got to do it. I mean when people start yelling for you and you got 25 girls you don't even know yelling your name, you've never even met them or talked to them, it's just a thrill that they want to see you and see you in all your reality dancing. It's ego building, it builds self-esteem. It's just one of these things where you do it once and you get recognition for it, you're going to do it again. If you can get third the first time, second the third time, and first the fifth time, you're going to keep going. And if you eventually get first you're going to keep doing it just because it's a guaranteed hundred dollars. The money is a big part of it.

When asked about why people continue to strip, David also believed that audience attention is an important component in the decision-making process:

Oh you do get a lot of attention. And see, after that I felt like a celebrity. Everybody's like, "Oh, yeah!" The guys are like, "You sly dog you!" Even if you don't win and people just see you they recognize you more afterwards. Then if you're new, you can come into town and break the ice. It's a great way to get to know a few more people. 'Cause you familiarize yourself with people you seen last week.

Further, David discusses the "rush" he gets from performing at Kato's:

When you're dancing and then somebody goes, "Yeah, yeah," so you do "OK." Everybody else is like, "Yeah, alright." You get into it. It's kind of like a high.

Chris identifies several factors that influenced his participation in this activity. He states:

I like to do it and it's fun. And I guess I like a little bit of the attention too, but the attention doesn't play as much of a factor as, well I like to go out there and have fun doing it.

Apparently, in Chris's case, performing provides him with self-fulfillment, attention from others, and increased self-esteem.

Those who performed in the dance contest were also asked if they found stripping to be exploitative, particularly for women. Not surprisingly, accounts of exploitation were almost exclusively limited to women's participation in the amateur stripping contest. These accounts were of-

fered by both male and female performers. Ironically, those who described their motivations to perform in terms of a rush or need for attention and self-fulfillment often described the contest as exploitative of women.

However, men and women alike described amateur stripping as entertaining and fun as noted above. Many argue that individuals have the power to make their own decisions about the event, and that people who make a choice cannot be exploited. Because the element of choice is always present, they argue that no one is *injured* and there are no *victims*. Additionally, strippers discussed this behavior as a form of empowerment or control. Those who are willing to get up in front of a large audience and remove their clothing are looked upon with respect by other strippers. Again, stripping is a way to enhance self-esteem and elicit approval or attention from others. The body is the tool to achieve these outcomes.

Dale, an amateur who has participated on numerous occasions, gives a positive account of amateur stripping:

I: Some people think that stripping is exploitative for both men and women. What do you think about that?

DALE: I think that they don't have enough guts to go out there. That's why they think that. If they were in there and they had that rush and they had that sense of rush, they'd change their minds. I used to think, "I'm never going to do that, it's dumb." Then I did it and I never thought that no more.

I: Do you feel the same about women?

DALE: Yeah. If you've got the guts to do it then go do it. Whether you win or lose, you know, at least you can go out with pride.

Again, this account demonstrates the ways in which strippers utilize the body to enhance individuality while simultaneously achieving fulfillment. Additionally, Dale condemns those who would criticize performers for engaging in this form of deviant behavior. He argues that those who judge others for stripping are actually afraid to use their bodies in this way. According to Dale, strippers should be commended, not condemned for their bravery.

Tanya offers a similar account. However, she describes the tipping transaction as a mechanism of control for both audience members and performers. Through the use of the body, strippers and audience members can manipulate the transaction to their advantage and that increases individual power:

> *Unless somebody is making you do something I don't think you can be exploited. It's really, it's kind of a power thing both ways. Here I am and I want you to get real close to my tits if you put the dollar bill in your mouth, but otherwise I'll keep walking right past you. It's like the guys who feel like they have power 'cause the women are like, "I'm not coming over there unless you have a dollar bill." So I mean it goes both ways. What are you going to say? I wouldn't consider it exploitation. I don't know. I'm not ready to make that kind of judgement call. I think it's a bunch of crap. People are going to do what they are going to do.*

It is interesting to note that many strippers believe that the exploitation is mutual. Audience members and strippers have the ability to control the situation. This is a form of power and personal efficacy according to their accounts, and not exploitation.

Frank also describes the relationship between strippers and audience members as reciprocal in nature. He does not believe that male or female contest participants are being exploited by the management in any way:

> *I don't feel that women are being exploited. I don't treat them like sex objects when I watch these female strippers. I see them as reciprocators. That is, doing something to someone that you also expect someone to do to you. I like it when I do this to women. I like it when they do this to me. That's reciprocation.*

Jon offers an even more complex analysis of performer exploitation. However, rather than viewing the competition as exploitative, he condemns the gender expectations of the larger society. He describes the potential exploitation as follows:

> *At first, I said no, I don't think so. I think that we may define exploitation in many terms. If it was*

only women being paid, different pay than men were, and they were doing the same thing, then I would feel, you know, that they're being exploited. My question of exploitation differs because they both have incentive . . . $100, $50, $25. And they both have a choice. It is not a personal employment because you have been excluded by some institution. But first of all amateur, because you have a lot of young people going there, college people, and it's not necessarily, well they need the income, but it's not necessarily a job. And uh, secondly, when I consider exploitation, I think, it's a different definition for everybody.*

Jon goes on to describe the amateur stripping as empowering or liberating for women. He believes that amateur stripping forces us to redefine gender expectations.

> *But I see the women that are out there as being uninhibited, because we restrict them so much in society. We restrict them to dress wear, to walking styles, to mannerisms, to communication . . . we categorize them in their feminine type atmosphere. But when they are out there doing certain moves, taking charge, taking advantage of what they're doing and not doing, what they show and do not show . . . I think in that sense they're more expressing themselves . . . I think it is different from when we're talking about sexual expectations and norms. We're talking not of economics, but we're talking more [about] sexuality.*

As noted above, some amateurs do describe stripping as exploitative, although they often describe the event as self-fulfilling and fun. Chris describes performing as fun, but also identifies differences in how male and female performers are exploited at Kato's. Specifically, he discusses the differential expectations of male and female performers:

> *The women there, they have to do, like I said, certain things like spread eagle or go up and just grind on the guys or just be real suggestive in order to win there. And I think that exploits them 'cause guys don't really have to do that. I don't know. It's obviously bad, a bad point about the whole thing. There's no fairness at all. I mean girls*

see guys in swimming trunks all the time, you know, like what we have to wear, but guys don't see girls running around naked at the beach and stuff, so I think there's a little bit of unfairness there.

As Chris notes, the body can be used to elicit positive responses from peers, but men and women must utilize this territory, in different ways. Women must be more explicit than men in order to achieve a positive response.

Donna describes her experiences of fun and exploitation, She argues that although dancing is fun and personally rewarding, women also experience negative consequences resulting from their participation in this activity.

I: Some people don't feel that women who participate in the dance contest are being exploited by men. How do you feel about that?

DONNA: Sometimes I believe it's true. But then again, like down there [at Kato's] I don't think that's the case at all.

I: So you don't see women in the dance contest down there as being treated sort of as a sex object?

DONNA: No, not really. I mean because, well no, I have to take that back because I've had a few guys come up to me, you know, and they would talk to me and everything. And then they would just like talk to me totally different after I started doing this.

I: Now, when you say totally differently, what do you mean?

DONNA: Well, like they'll come up and they'll like try to put their arm around me or something and then say, "Oh, what are you doing tonight after the bar closes?" You know, "We could go back to my house and party." And it's just, it kind of bothers me when they do that.

As Donna mentions, the body can be a site of individual expression and self-fulfillment; however, the attention one receives may not be perceived as positive. Audience members and performers may interpret stripping behavior quite differently, and this may negatively impact on the reputation of a female performer.

SUMMARY AND CONCLUSIONS

This study has demonstrated that amateur stripping is in some ways comparable to professional stripping, yet in other significant ways quite different. We sought to investigate those areas that make amateur stripping unique and to ascertain if Simmel's theoretical orientation could be used to enhance our understanding of this aspect of youth culture.

As pointed out in this chapter, the motivations of male and female professional strippers are quite different. Although both see money as a key factor influencing their decision to participate in this occupation, males appear to place greater emphasis on other benefits of the occupation (i.e. greater access to sexual partners, potential for movement into other forms of entertainment, and increased attention based on physical attraction).

Based on our findings, the data indicate that amateur and professional male strippers offer similar accounts to explain their participation in their behavior. The areas with the greatest degree of congruence are: potential sexual outlet; the attention provided by the audience members; an implied adrenaline rush associated with the performance; and personal fulfillment.

There are, however, based on our study, some differences that are central to our understanding of stripping behavior. Where money is a key factor for professional male strippers it is not a primary reason for amateurs. The primary motivating factor for male amateur strippers appears to be the opportunity for the individual to express himself through the body and, further, to individuate himself in the midst of an impersonal audience. Similarly, female amateur stripping behavior is distinct from professional stripping in that money is not the key motivating factor. Rather, self-fulfillment, peer encouragement, and control over their sexuality appear to be more dominant elements in the decision to participate in amateur stripping behavior. For professional female strippers, stripping is viewed as an occupation—thus the emphasis on financial gain—whereas the amateur female stripper is more concerned with entertainment and less with financial gain.

Interestingly, while male and female professional stripping accounts differ dramatically in terms of motivations, male and female amateurs participate in stripping for generally the same reasons (i.e. fun, audience attention, the adrenaline rush, and self-fulfillment). However, while male amateurs often utilize the contest as a vehicle to advance their entertainment careers and to attract potential sex partners, females do not.

Although the comparison of amateur and professional stripping is useful, Simmel's (1950) theoretical framework provides us with the tools necessary for a more complete analysis of amateur stripping behavior. Specifically, urban living allows for the possibility of increased individuality, while simultaneously creating greater anonymity and alienation for individuals. It is for this reason that individuals attempt to distinguish themselves from others. As noted previously, urban youth may have fewer opportunities to individuate themselves due to the lack of appropriate locations for self-expression.

Our analysis of male and female amateur stripping accounts indicates that urban youth utilize the amateur stripping contest as a forum for the expression of individuality through the body. The amateur stripping contest provides the participants with the opportunity to be a part of a larger group, while simultaneously allowing for individual expression apart from the group. Body territories are the sites for this more intimate form of expression. Although encouragement from friends, prize money, and alcohol are all important elements in the decision to strip, the primary motivating factors are individual in nature. Specifically, amateur stripping is utilized by both male and female participants as an entertaining opportunity to achieve self-fulfillment and to express individuality in an urban environment that is typically constraining for youth.

NOTES

Some parts of this work are derived from an earlier article we have written on this subject. See Amateur stripping: sexualized entertainment and gendered fun. *Sociological Focus,* 1997.

1. All names referred to in this work are pseudonyms.

2. One of the male participants agreed to participate over the phone. His verbal consent was audiotaped at this time. Although we sent him a consent form, it was never returned.

REFERENCES

Barron, K. (1989) Strippers: the undressing of an occupation. Unpublished manuscript, Department of Sociology, University of Kansas.

Boles, J. and Garbin, A. P. (1974) The strip club and stripper-customer patterns of interaction. *Sociology and Social Research,* 58, 136–44.

Calhoun, T. C., Fisher, R. and Harms Cannon, J. A. (1997) Amateur stripping: sexualized entertainment and gendered fun. *Sociological Focus,* 30, 50–65.

Carey, S. H., Peterson, R. A. and Sharpe, L. K. (1974) A study of recruitment and socialization into two deviant occupations. *Sociological Symposium,* 11, 11–24.

Dressel, P. and Peterson, D. (1982a) Becoming a male stripper. *Work and Occupations,* 9. 387–406.

Dressel, P. and Peterson, D. (1982b) Gender roles, sexuality, and the male strip show: the structuring of sexual opportunity. *Sociological Focus* 15(2), 151–62.

Enck, G. E. and Preston, J. D. (1988) Counterfeit intimacy: a dramaturgical analysis of an erotic performance. *Deviant Behavior,* 9, 369–81.

Lyman, S. M. and Scott, M. B. (1970) *A Sociology of the Absurd.* New York: Meredith.

McCaghy, C. and Skipper, J. K. (1969) Lesbian behavior as an adaptation to the occupation of stripping. *Social Problems,* 17. 262–70.

Margolis, M. L. and Arnold, M. (1993) Turning the tables? Male strippers and the gender hierarchy in America. In B. D. Miller (ed.). *Sex and Gender Hierarchies.* Cambridge: Cambridge University Press, pp. 334–50.

Mullen, K. (1985) The impure performance frame of the public house entertainer. *Urban Life,* 14(2), 181–203.

Peretti, P. O. and O'Connor, P. (1989) Effects of incongruence between the perceived self and the ideal self on emotional stability of stripteasers. *Social Behavior and Personality,* 17(1), 81–92.

Peterson, D. and Dressel, P. (1982) Equal time for women. *Urban Life,* 11, 185–208.

Reid, S. A., Epstein, J. A. and Benson, D. E. (1994a) Does exotic dancing pay well but cost dearly? Some identity consequences of a deviant occupation. In A. Thio and T. C. Calhoun (eds), *Readings in Deviance.* New York: Harper Collins.

Reid, S. A., Epstein, J. A. and Benson, D. E. (1994b) Role identity in a devalued occupation: the case of female exotic dancers. *Sociological Focus,* 27, 1–17.

Ronai, C. R. and Ellis, C. (1989) Tumons for money: Interactional strategies of the table dancer. *Journal of Contemporary Ethnography,* 18, 271–98.

Simmel, G. (1950) The metropolis and mental life. In K. Wolff (ed.), *The Sociology of Georg Simmel.* New York: Free Press, pp. 409–24.

Skipper, J. K. and McCaghy, C. H. (1970) Stripteasers: The anatomy and career contingencies of a deviant occupation. *Social Problems,* 17, 391–405.

Sykes, G. M. and Matza, D. (1957) Techniques of neutralization: a theory of delinquency. *American Sociological Review,* 22(6), 664–70.

Thompson, W. E. and Harred, J. L. (1992) Topless dancers: Managing a stigma in a deviant occupation. *Deviant Behavior,* 13, 291–311.

STRIP CLUB DANCERS: WORKING IN THE FANTASY FACTORY

ELIZABETH ANNE WOOD

Feminist objections to sex-work tend to be framed in terms of men's objectification of women (Barry 1979, Chapkiss 1997, Griffin 1981, MacKinnon 1987, Roiphe 1993, Phelan 1989, and others). Prostitution, pornography, sex-shows, nude dancing—all are venues for men to gaze at women's bodies. This argument regarding the objectification of women in this way assumes a sort of power wielded by men, against women, that keeps women oppressed, beaten down, submissive or, alternatively, keeps them "buying into" a male dominated system of sexuality and commerce.

Previous sociological research on stripping and strip clubs has focused largely on issues other than gendered power. The most common approach to research on stripping has been framed in terms of "deviant occupation" studies, examining the career paths of strippers and the shared characteristics of strippers as workers in a deviant setting (McCaghy and Skipper 1969 and 1972, Skipper and McCaghy 1970 and 1971, Boles and Garbin 1974a, Carey, Peterson, and Sharpe 1974, and Forsyth and Deshotels 1997 and 1998). This work frames the stripper as a *subject,* not as an object, as argued by proponents of the feminist anti-sex-work perspective mentioned above. A second way to depict the stripper as subject, rather than as object, is to examine the actual lived experience (Ronai 1992). Ronai (1992) places her own *subjectivity* as erotic dancer/researcher in the center of her analysis of the work of stripping.

This article fits more closely into a third approach to the study of stripping, which places the *interaction* between the strippers and customers at the center of analysis (Boles and Garbin 1974b, Gonos 1976, Ronai and Ellis 1989). While descriptive of these interactions, the article's focus is on questions of gendered power, taking issue with the "objectification thesis" of the anti-sex-work feminist characterization. Rather than understanding power as a monolithic social force oppressing women, in this article, power is understood to be a contested, negotiated social resource that is constantly being "enacted" during interpersonal encounters. This power is relational. It is in the service of men, but in a manner more insidious than the power described by the anti-sex-work position of MacKinnon (1987) and others. This article will first describe the characteristics of this power, then will explain how the enacting of this power creates a source of reinforcement for traditional notions of masculinity. Finally it will illuminate the creation and enacting of this "masculine" power (so called because of its connection to traditional notions of masculinity) through specific types of interactions between dancers and customers in strip clubs. These interactions are characterized by two related processes: The first comprises the transformation of dancers into "fantastical subjects" through interaction with customers where the customers might imagine backgrounds and lifestyles for the strippers with whom they interact and the strippers in turn work to anticipate these imagined backgrounds and present an image consistent with them. The second comprises the "impression management" (Goffman 1959) and "emotional labor" (Hochschild 1979 and 1983) on the part of the dancers that makes that subjectification possible.

METHODS

The data for this article were drawn from ethnographic research I engaged in from 1996 to 1998. My primary method of data collection was participant observation: I spent 110 hours as a customer in two New England strip clubs. I participated in interactions with strippers, buying table dances, tipping at the stages, and also in conversations with dancers at my table, where I revealed my interest as a researcher. This afforded me the opportunity to interview dancers as another method of collecting data. Twelve dancers participated in individual open-ended interviews. A third source of data was created as I carried on informal conversations with customers in the clubs. Although no customers I approached would consent to formal, recorded interviews, many were willing to talk to me informally in the club setting. All were informed of my interest as a researcher and all participants of interviews and conversations were assured of their anonymity and the confidentiality of their responses. Data were analyzed in the style of grounded theory (Glaser and Strauss 1967).

A Note on Subjectivity and Research.   Being a clothed woman in a place where women were supposed to be naked, and being a customer in a place where customers were supposed to be men, raised important methodological questions. These questions fall into two categories. The first category contains questions about how the researcher affects the environment she studies. The second category contains questions about how the researcher's identity affects the collection and interpretation of data. An entire article could be devoted to these questions, and here I will only address them briefly.

Women who visit strip clubs where the customers are men and the dancers are women, whether they are researchers or not, affect the environment they have stepped into. During my initial visits to Michael's I realized that my presence drew the attention of customers away from the dancers at times. I discussed this with Diana, a dancer there. She related to me a similar experience of her own:

I checked out Michael's before I worked here and I found that I walked in and they [customers] were looking more at me than at the girls on stage. Because you're there and you're not a dancer, you're more fascinating.

Men who came to the strip club in order to interact with women were also interested in interacting with me. Customers who came to the club only to watch naked women dance, on the other hand, seemed discomfited by my presence. I was not the only woman customer to enter the clubs. Occasionally other women would come in. Some were accompanied by men. Others were friends of dancers. A few came to see feature performers. All seemed to draw a bit of attention from the other customers in the club. I minimized the "intrusiveness" of my presence in two ways. First, I stayed for at least two hours for each visit. I noted that after I had found a place to sit and had been part of the crowd for about an hour, people stopped noticing me. I "blended in." Second, I visited each club frequently. This allowed me to become familiar to the regular customers and to the staff so that my presence was less remarkable. When customers did remark on my presence and interact with me I would answer questions honestly and politely and inform them of my research interest. Several fruitful conversations with customers about their impressions of the clubs were conducted this way.

Addressing concerns about how my identity as a woman-feminist-clothed-researcher-customer would affect my data collection and analysis was stickier. I have confidence in my data and my analysis for the following key reasons. First of all, I encouraged myself to experience what the other customers might have found enjoyable about the setting. I bought table dances and tipped dancers and kept my "sociological imagination" (Mills 1958) open to what was fun or erotic about those experiences. I followed up on these observations by comparing my own responses to those that dancers told me about in interviews. Second, I paid close attention to my personal feelings about the clubs and the people I encountered in them. Whether positive, negative, or neutral, I wrote about these feelings in my field notes and when analyzing my notes I was able to reflect on how my understanding of the research environment might be affected. Third, I allowed my interviews, my observations, and my conversations with customers to all inform each other as I progressed in my research. This provided me with ways to check my own interpretations against those of the dancers and other customers, as well as to check what was reported by dancers and customers against what I witnessed myself in the clubs.

THE "ATTENTION HYPOTHESIS" AND "MASCULINE POWER"

At table-dance clubs, in addition to dancing on stage for tips, dancers sell nude dances performed at the customers' tables but where there is no physical contact between the customer and the dancers. It may seem obvious at the start that the magnet attracting the men to bars that charge more than five dollars for a beer is the sexiness of the "live nude girls." It's pay-per-view where the view is of breasts and hips and legs and bottoms all belonging to sexy women in various stages of undress: perhaps clad in tightly clinging gowns, or sequined bras and panties, or then again, clad only in skin lit by strobes and black lights. Eroticism, however, is only part of what draws the men. Close observation indicates that this eroticism conveys something more: attention. If not for the direct attention a dancer and customer can pay each other, there would be little difference between this type of erotic entertainment and erotic videos. It is the possibility of interaction that sets them apart. The attention, as I watch customers stand a bit straighter when the dancers on stage notice and approach them, seems to be as necessary, perhaps more necessary, than the nudity. The customers have paid money to come in, and pay more money to watch women strip, but they also pay to be seen by the women. They too receive recognition and attention. The following are some of the types of attention routinely given to customers by strippers:

- Several of the dancers lean far forward when receiving a tip, and seem to whisper to the customer, closing out the distractions of loud music and other customers.

- One element of tipping that is very ritualized for many dancers is putting themselves in a position to look up at the customer (she slides her back down the pole to sit on her heels). This not only seems to acknowledge the customer by altering her position to better speak to him but also reinforces his importance by voluntarily putting herself in the "inferior" position.

- Several "missed opportunities" occurred one night where tips were not collected because the stripper failed to notice the customer or where the customer failed to get her attention. In three different instances, customers stood in one place, money in hand, even though the stripper had her back to them, and did not move around to where she could see, despite the fact that she wasn't dancing for another customer at the time. That seems to indicate that it is very important to the customer to have the dancer acknowledge him, rather than having to work to get her attention.

I argue that this attention is most valuable when it allows for two things: first, it must allow for witnesses, that is, it must be visible to the other customers and dancers that fill the social space within the strip club; second, it must allow the customer to imagine the personality and history of the dancer who is attending to him, that is, she must not impede his imagination by telling him details of her life that will jeopardize his ability to see her as a sexy, sensual, and, most importantly, available woman. When these two things occur, they make available more than simple attention. They create a possibility for the enacting of "masculine power."

The term "masculine power" requires both definition and context, as notions of power and of masculinity and femininity are themselves problematic. I use the term to indicate two specific pieces of a socially constructed puzzle that, when assembled according to our cultural expectations, produce a collage of characteristics we most often attribute to men, or that we count as most appropriate or "fitting" when exhibited by men. My usage of this term is consistent with an understanding of gender (the division of human beings into "men" and "women") as being a product of culture and relations of power rather than with an understanding of gender as biologically determined. I do not imply, through calling this power masculine, that it is an *essential* element of being a man (i.e. not all men need possess it, nor does any man need to possess it at all times), nor do I imply that possessing it is *sufficient* to indicate that one is a man (i.e. it might be possessed at times by boys, girls, or women). Terms like "masculinity" and "femininity" are often used to highlight differences between men and women, while at the same time minimizing differences among women and differences among men (Rubin 1976; McCall 1992). Masculine power, then, is power that differentiates men from women, ordinarily being attributed to men, and, when acknowledged in women, is downplayed, de-emphasized or construed as "unfeminine."

That being said, let me now describe these two pieces of that socially constructed masculinity that I have grouped together under the term "masculine power." These two characteristics can best be described as "being desirable to women" and "being able to financially 'take care of' a woman." I emphasize that this power is masculine because it is affirmed for men, by men and women, in a very heterosexist environment that caricatures modern socially constructed standards of masculinity and femininity (i.e. that men should be providers of economic security for women, that they should be desired by women, and that women should be providers of emotional and sexual security and should be desired by men). It is important to recognize that these traits (being desired by women, and having money) are culturally linked, and that this is evident both inside and outside the strip club. Outside the strip club, men might be seen as more desirable to women if they can potentially take care of a family. Likewise, women might be seen as more desirable if they can keep men feeling good about themselves. Strippers who participated in interviews underscored these points. The most sought after customer in the strip club is very

likely going to be the one most willing to spend his dollars. The following passages, taken from interviews with dancers, illustrate the way that they categorize and evaluate customers based on the customers' willingness to spend money:

> Lynne (*describing how dancers warn each other about customers who aren't spending money*): You definitely classify them. If somebody's cheap you say "Those guys are cheap" and you tell the other girls in the dressing room . . . Or "Hey, these guys are tipping me really well, go over there" or "Go talk to these guys. They've got money."

> Becky (*describing the customers she finds most frustrating*): Lately I've been finding a lot that they just come in, just to watch, and they don't tip. I don't know if they don't understand, or if they just don't care, that we're there to work . . . they just want to see what they want to see, and a lot of them don't even pay for it.

The best paid stripper is likely to be the one that is best at creating and conveying feelings of intimacy, interest, and desire for her customers. Strippers I interviewed often conveyed a sense of needing to make customers feel desired in order to sell dances and to keep customers tipping:

> Diana (*discussing her frustration about not making as much as some of the other dancers*): Sometimes I get irritated because some of the other girls do really well and I don't understand why, because I think I have a better body, but . . . it seems like they're better with humoring the customers and eye contact and stuff.

> Lynne (*describing her start at her first table-dance club*): I was watching some of the girls who were not very attractive and they were making killer money and I thought "How do they do that?" and I would ask, and they'd say "You just ask" and I was like "What do you mean 'you just ask'?" and I couldn't comprehend it for awhile, but then I understood that they [customers] want to be approached and asked [for dances], they want you to come to them, they don't want to have to ask you.

> Delaney (*describing how she approaches selling table dances*): I probably walk by and smile and try to engage 'em in a little conversation beforehand, because I realize I'm not the most beautiful

girl in there . . . but I'm flirty and you have to flirt with them and make them feel special and then they're like "wow . . . cool."

"Approaching" customers, "humoring" them and "making them feel special," are all ways that dancers describe their attempts to give customers a sense of being important or desired, and this feeling of being important or desired, according to the strippers interviewed for this study, seemed an important factor in keeping the money flowing.

Several possible criticisms of this "attention hypothesis" seem likely, and I will address them here. At first, it might seem that this affirmation of desirability is undermined by its connection to money. It is the customer's money, not his self, that the dancer desires, and we can see this when we watch a stripper dance for one customer, attend to him, take his money and then move on to the next customer. However, three things keep this relationship between money and attention from devaluing the possible affirmation of power and desirability available through the interaction. First, the giving of money need not be associated with a purchase transaction. Several other ways of framing the situation (Goffman 1974) exist and are used by customers in strip clubs. Dancers I interviewed reported that customers often use reward frameworks ("Here, take this, you deserve it") or gift frameworks ("Here honey, let me help you with your bills/tuition/etc.") as if the fee being paid is not a contractual arrangement, but rather given out of good will. This latter framing mechanism, the gift frame, can also be seen as a sort of "providing" frame: the customer understands himself to be contributing to the dancer's financial security rather than as taking part in a fee-for-service interaction. The second reason this relationship between money and attention is less problematic than might first be assumed has to do with its explicitness. Trade and exchange underlie many types of social interaction between men and women. Often we try to minimize the visibility of these exchanges or frame them in ways to make them seem less strategic. By keeping the exchange visible and explicit, the transaction becomes simply a part of the social setting, taken for granted

and so placed in the realm of social convention rather than in the realm of intentional purchase or sale. Lastly, as indicated above, the giving of money to a woman for something she has provided lends power to that money. Money has value only as long as it can be exchanged for something else. By making the object of that exchange the actions of another person, the money now has not only value, but power. If a customer's everyday interactions with women undermine his sense of financial power (either because he just accepts that his earnings are not sufficient to support himself and his family, or perhaps because the women he meets are self-reliant where money is concerned) then the affirmation of his money's value might enhance the value of the attention he receives, rather than detract from it. The interaction thus provides a two-fold service.

The fact that the dancer moves on to another customer need not detract from the affirmation made available during an individual customer's interaction either. I argue that the power being affirmed is relational, that is, it is created when the attention being purchased is noticed by others and momentarily distinguishes the customer being attended to from other customers who are not receiving the attention of a dancer. After a visit to Dream House[1] one night I made the following note:

Customer in blue shirt, there with two friends, seemed very taken by blonde dancer in red costume. He hadn't approached any other dancers yet and he was gesturing to this one and seemed to be talking about her to his friends. Finally he approached the stage to tip her. She pulled his face into her chest and ran her hands through his hair. She danced in front of him for a few moments, looking in his eyes. He ran his hands along the outsides of her thighs and when he did, he looked over at his friends with his eyebrows raised and his head motioning to the dancer, presumably as if he were proud of his "achievement" and wanted to make sure they saw.

Here, the dancer becomes a symbol that is exchanged with witnesses in return for recognition of the customer's (temporary) desirability and financial power. This "I have her and you don't" (or perhaps "she wants me, not you") argument is in some ways a very micro-level parallel to Bourdieu's (1984) argument about distinctions (in cultural tastes, possessions and displays) as the root of class identification. Rather than illuminating class differences or "one-upmanship," though, my observations of strip club customers illuminate the distinctions made by men on an interactionist level. In the strip club, the symbolic capital being collected and displayed is not the stripper herself but rather the attention of the stripper as she performs for a tipping customer, or does a table dance for a customer who has, or will, pay the fee. Another way to understand the production of status by women for men is suggested by Collins (1992). He argues that wives and girlfriends increase the status of men through the Goffmonian elements of their housework and paid employment when this labor is aimed at creating a designated impression for outsiders (the impression of a clean, orderly home, or a friendly, efficient office for example). Strippers increase the status of men through labor aimed at creating a designated impression for the men themselves—the impression of being interesting, sexy, and desirable.

FANTASTICAL ACTORS

Interviews with strippers, and conversations with strippers while at work at the clubs, have made it clear that from their experience, they believe customers want them to be fantastical subjects. My choice of the word "subject" rather than "object" here is intentional. This means that during the interaction with the customer, the stripper does not so much become a one-dimensional sexual "thing" upon which the customer may act, but rather she becomes, through the customer's assumption of her history, personality, and desires, a fantastical actor whose job it is to turn attention and action toward him. During an evening of observation, Jeff, a customer with whom I talked informally explained that he believed that a lot of dancers lied about why they strip:

> Well, every woman in here has a story about being in school or having a kid or you know, some reason they need to do this, but I think those are just stories.

It was his belief that most strippers "came from troubled homes" and this, he said, caused him to "respect their decisions to be strippers," since they had to deal with adversity from childhood. However, it was also important to him that the strippers be working in the clubs "because they wanted to be." When I asked him what he meant by "wanted to" he explained that they had to like the work. They could not be doing it for primarily economic reasons, or through any sort of "pimping."

It seems that some customers at least need to create an imaginary subjectivity for the stripper (a subjectivity that the stripper helps support), perhaps so they can imagine a life for her without the danger of his imagination being hindered by any obstructing reality. The following excerpt from a conversation with a stripper during an evening of observation illustrates, in her words, the "paper doll" nature of this subjectification:

> "I have a husband. I go to school," says Diana while trying to explain to me her disgust with a certain customer. He had seen her wedding ring (she wears it at work) and had said to her, "You're married? Now I can't even look at you!"
>
> I ask her "Do you think they imagine you exist only within these walls?"
>
> "Exactly," she says. "It's like they think we're paper dolls. We're here to be played with, to be dressed and undressed, and then put away 'til next time . . . other than that we have no lives, nothing outside the club."

Diana's allusion to paper dolls illustrates a sentiment held by many dancers that customers make up their own ideas about the strippers' lives, much as children make up stories about their dolls. Another dancer puts it this way:

> If I tell him I'm married and have a child, he's not going to think I'm sexy anymore. Men come in to see sexy, erotic, women who they think are party-girls. Motherhood they can get at home.

Some elements of a dancer's history are more threatening to the interaction than others. For example, being seen as a mother is not as threatening as being seen as a wife, presumably because mothers can be single and thus available. Jasmine responded to my question about customers' perceptions of dancers by telling me she thought customers assumed the strippers' lives outside of the club mirrored their images inside the clubs:

JASMINE: I think that they think we're pretty wild outside. I think they think we all have a wild life. I don't tell customers that I'm married because I don't want it to affect how they feel. But I always tell them that I have a child. I'm like "Oh yeah, I have a daughter," and I have no problem with them thinking of me in those terms.

INTERVIEWER: Has telling a customer that you have a child ever affected the way he's treated you?

JASMINE: Sometimes it's funny, because if it's someone that's a parent themselves, they want to talk about their kids . . . it brings it more personal and in a very non-threatening sort of way.

Not all dancers experienced the same acceptance of their maternity. Sapphire told me:

I have seen a reaction before, where they seem grossed out when the subject of kids got brought up, and they see you as having no kids at all . . . they really believe that most of the women in there don't have kids and aren't married, but it's even worse about the kids, because they're thinking you're so young and they're fantasizing about your body.

By treating the dancers as "paper dolls" the customer can maintain consistency within his interaction frame. He can construe the dancer's attention as being honest interest, and indicative of potential availability on her part as long as he doesn't acknowledge that she might have somebody waiting at home for her. Men then appear to go to strip clubs to watch the beautiful women of their fantasies swing their naked bodies around brass poles, dance seductively to a deafening beat, caress their breasts and thighs as if in the middle of a very private moment. But they also go to talk to the strippers, to interact beyond simple voyeurism, in a world removed from the reality of complex, multidimensional identities and lives. One of the most

important elements of this fantasy world is that the women occupying it are understood by the men who visit it to be single and thus possibly available. During my own visits to the clubs I witnessed a great many incidents where customers asked strippers out on dates, or offered them money to come back to a home or hotel room after work. It is important that the dancer seem potentially available because then the interest she shows to the customer might seem more personal. Michelle, a stripper, explains by telling me:

If for a moment you can look at him as if he's the only man in the whole room, you can make him think maybe, just maybe, you are really attracted to him. You want him to feel that way.

This might sound exaggerated. After all, surely these men know that the women are simply there to earn money and that none of it is personal. But stripper after stripper, in interviews and in casual conversations, tells me "What do they come in for? They come in because they think they have a chance with you." The following statements, made by three different strippers during individual interviews, demonstrate that they often use this assumption to their advantage by constructing interactions with customers so that the attention they give leads the customer to think that something intimate is happening (or might happen later) between just the two of them:

Michelle: *If you can look at a man in such a way as to suggest that he's got your attention and that there's something going on between the two of you, that it's not just a casual glance around the room and you happened to glance at him . . . you suggest that "I would do anything to be with you," they love that.*

Lynne: *Every day you have to plot and scheme. You have to find that new way to try and make these men think you have an interest in them. They'll say "Oh, you're so nice. Can I take you on a date?" and you say "Well, I don't even know you. I'd have to get to know you first." So you get them to buy a table dance so they can start to get to know you. The key thing is to keep them interested enough to think they might have a chance, but not too much of a chance . . . you've got to be able to string it along.*

Diana was more ambivalent (responding to my question about why men want table dances):

> *I think it's more of an intimate show, that he "has you" for a few songs and that maybe for some men "I can get with her. Maybe I can work her a little bit and get with her," or "Maybe I can get a date or get her to come home with me, give her a little extra money for this or that."*

Ronai and Ellis (1989) note similar strategies used by the table dancers in their research. Dancers used what they imagined to be elements of men's fantasy lives in order to keep them interested in buying dances:

> *By talking "dirty" and acting "like a whore"—for example, telling stories about kinky sex in her life outside the bar—a dancer could keep a customer "going," eager to buy the next dance, ready to believe the dancer might have sex with him later (283).*

The important thing here is not so much *what* the customer wants (sex, a date, etc.) but what he is willing to, or needs to, *believe* in order to see his goal as attainable. Does he need to believe that the stripper is single? Is it enough to know that she engages in "kinky sex?" Strippers present themselves in the ways that they imagine will most meet the customers' expectations. They do this most often by concealing the elements of their lives that would contradict or seem inconsistent with their images as "wild" or as "party girls."

The strippers are not the only parties involved in the construction of these interactions, of course. To suggest that would be to accept the same argument made by feminists about the objectification of women, though operating in the opposite direction: it would be an argument about the objectification of men. The work of stripping is indeed interactive, not unilateral, and so the customers must also play a part in the exchange and impression management that we have been examining. The next section of this article will focus on the tools used by strippers and customers to manage impressions and negotiate interactions—interactions which serve two very different sets of interests and in which the parties' very definitions of the situations are conflicting.

IMPRESSION MANAGEMENT: IDENTITY AND EXCHANGE

For the dancer, impression management involves such elements as costume, makeup, body adornment, choice of music for stage performances, facial expressions, ways of moving, and of course, the information she chooses to share with the customers through conversation. Sometimes these elements present an inconsistent image to the customers. For example, Ronai and Ellis noted that music could interfere with the rest of a dancer's image, where customers were concerned. One customer commented about a dancer: "That girl has a great body, but every time I hear her music [heavy metal] I get the creeps thinking about what she might be like" (Ronai and Ellis 1989, 278). Dancers that I interviewed usually chose music that made them happy, or to which they felt most comfortable dancing. The rationale was that if it made them feel sexy, they'd look sexier or more attractive to the customers. Delaney, a dancer at Jonathan's, explains this in terms of "having a good time":

> *I put on the music I feel comfortable with. I like a lot of reggae and r/b and hip-hop and I'll get up there and I'll get into it because that's "my" music . . . and I'll dance and dance . . . I mean I know a lot of them [customers] are like "what the hell is this music?" but if I'm having a good time, they will too.*

Not all dancers have equal access to the tools of impression management. Each club operated differently regarding some of these tools. At Michael's, dancers were prohibited from wearing jewelry in body piercings anywhere other than in their ears or navels, and tattoos were supposed to be covered (as best they could be) with makeup. The reason for this also involved impression management—by the club owner. He explained to the dancers that he didn't think piercings and tattoos conveyed a "high class image," and since his was a "high class establishment" he wanted the dancers to convey images that were consistent with the image he wanted the club to have. At this same club, a disc jockey selected the music to which the dancers worked. Thus the dancers tended not to associate their self-presentations with the music being played. They focused much more closely on costume, makeup, movement (dancing, posing), and information management, the elements over which they did retain control. At Jonathan's, on the other hand, no prohibition was made on body adornment, and dancers selected music for their sets. Here, however, impression management from the stage had to be accomplished much more quickly as dancers only worked the stage for two songs at a time, where at Michael's, dancers rotated around four stages for a total of five songs before moving to the floor to sell table dances. So while the dancers at Jonathan's had more tools at their disposal with which to create images of themselves for the customers, at Michael's they had more time with which to solidify the images they attempted to create.

In the strip club, the strippers are at first glance the only obvious impression managers. Closer observation shows how the customers also work to manage their self-presentations. In groups of friends, they manage their self-presentations for each other, as well as for the stripper. When alone, they manage their self-presentations for the dancers and for other customers. During an interview, Diana told me about how she learned that the man who pumps her gas invented a story for a dancer he had a lap dance from at Michael's, where Diana works:

> Sunday night, perfect example. I was in there and the guy who pumps my gas every week came in. And he was trying to hide from me but I saw him right when he came in . . . I saw him the whole time. And he was getting a table dance from one of the girls, and when I told her I knew him she said "Is he like a golfer or something?" I was like "No! He fills my gas every week—what kind of story did he tell you?" So when I saw him today I said, "How's that golf tournament?" And he laughed and was like "Real original huh?" And I was like "oh yeah" (rolling her eyes).

The customer's remark that his story might not have been "real original" suggests that he expects story-telling to be part of other customers' interac-

tions with dancers as well. Diana's response (sarcastically saying "oh yeah" and rolling her eyes) confirms that in her experience, customers attempt to create images of themselves for the strippers by giving information that is sometimes false.

At Jonathan's I watched as three young men bought a table dance. All three did a lot of "posing," one tilting his head to the side, one holding his hand to his cheek, in ways that suggested examination or appraisal of the dancer. Posing is a way of intentionally conveying an image to others. There is another way that customers interact with one another that would more readily be considered "showing off," rather than posing or engaging in impression management. An observation at Michael's demonstrated one way in which customers "show off" for each other:

> Two tables of three customers each are seated one on either side of the pedestal stage near the door. They became very competitive about tipping and making noise as the night wore on. It was one of the customers at the table nearest the door that started the noise (hooting and whistling at the dancers) and the table opposite began to get noisy as well. Then the competition for the dancer's attention through tipping started. At one table, a customer would get up and tip and then go back to the table to try and get more money from his friends. At the same time, a customer from the other table would be tipping the dancer. The two groups exchanged looks and even bits of conversation during all of this.

On the other hand, rather than competing to show their enjoyment, or showing off, some customers seem to guard their expressions to keep other customers, or the strippers from thinking they are "enjoying it too much." Sapphire, in an interview noted that:

> If they're even that much more attracted to you that makes them kind of squirm and look around like "someone's going to think I'm enjoying this too much," you know, like "I'm not supposed to be watching her like this."

My observations of customers' impression management indicate that more than relying on dress or body adornment, they depended on conversation, gestures, and facial expressions to try and convey whatever image they wanted to the strippers, or friends, or to other customers. During a table dance, the way a customer looks at the dancer in front of him conveys significant information to the dancer. One dancer explained to me that if a customer doesn't seem to be interested in her body or the music, then she assumes he is displeased with her and that it becomes very difficult to finish the dance. But it might be that the customer is actually trying to show respect for the dancer, or differentiate himself from the other "oglers" by not paying as much attention to her nudity. James, a customer, told me that he "doesn't want to seem like all the other customers who just stare," so he tries to look into the stripper's eyes more than he looks at her body. Tori explained that the way a customer looked at her, and the way she judged his body language during a table dance helped her know how to continue:

> I pay attention to whether or not they look back in my eyes. Whether or not they look at my face. What part of my body they look at, what they want to see more of . . . it kind of tells me whether I need to look them in the face, or whether my smile is important or whether or not they want to see my behind again or whether they just want me to really get down to the music.

Another dancer explained that she thought the most respectful customers were the ones who paid attention, made eye contact, didn't make lewd comments or facial expressions, and openly seemed to be enjoying themselves by smiling at her, nodding to the music, and by tipping. To her, tipping showed a respect for the work involved.

EMOTION WORK: ANOTHER ASPECT OF IMPRESSION MANAGEMENT

Emotional labor involves a specific kind of impression management: the management of feelings. Arlie Hochschild (1979 and 1983) was the first to write about "the commercialization of human feeling." Her research on airline workers, particularly women flight attendants, illustrated the ways in which airlines required flight attendants not only to fit a certain physical image (discrimination suits have ended some of that), but also to create a certain emotional environment for customers. The emotional impression that the airlines want their flight attendants to create for their passengers is one of "being cared for in a convivial and safe place," (1983, 7). The labor that goes into creating this environment is emotional labor not only because its product is emotional but because the process of producing it requires emotional manipulation within the worker herself. Hochschild explains that it "requires one to induce or suppress feeling in order to sustain the outward countenance that produces the proper state of mind in others," (1983, 7). This emotional labor requires the "transmutation of emotional systems" (1983, 19), meaning that workers must take acts that are usually private and employ them in public settings. In the case of strippers, for example, we see the transmutation of sensuality, something that is ordinarily applied to personal interactions, employed in a public setting for work-related purposes.

While the flight attendant's job is to make passengers feel "cared for," the stripper's job is to make customers feel "cared about." The difference between these two emotion-based impressions is that in the first case the intent is to create a feeling of somewhat "maternal" care, that is, having all the mundane details attended (being fed, checked on periodically, being safe) while the intent in the second case is to create a feeling of more sensual attraction. As noted, many customers want not only a "turn on" but also something more personal. In the section above, we saw how strippers manage impressions by leading customers to believe that there was a chance for "something more," something beyond the dances they are paying for. Giving a customer the impression that she is interested in him, the dancer conveys an idea. But there is a feeling, an emotion, that goes along with that idea. The idea is perhaps: "Gee, she seems to like me," or "Maybe she'll go home with me." The corresponding feeling might be better described as something akin to pride, or self-confidence.

Creating this feeling involves more than Lynne's verbal manipulation, "I have to get to know you better." It requires a host of non-verbal cues and gestures. As with Hochschild's flight attendants, smiling and eye contact are among the most important of these. Sapphire told me of a customer who explained to her that eye contact and smiles were important because it made him feel like she "was enjoying the fact that [she's] there for us [customers]." Tori, another dancer, told me during an interview: "I look them in the eye. I smile. Overwhelmingly, people [customers] tell me that it's my smile and my eyes that get them." Adding to the non-verbal nature of these gestures and cues is an even more elusive element, that of seeming "real." That is to say that keeping a smile on her face, or meeting a customer's eyes, isn't enough for either the stripper or the flight attendant. The smile must be convincing. The eye contact must be engaging. Explaining the difficulty of selling table dances, Jasmine told me "you have to be so 'on'." She contrasts being "on" with being "in your own little world." Being "on" means being emotionally and mentally directed toward the customer. Jasmine explains that it is hard to be emotionally directed toward the customer if she is worried about making money:

> I just have to tell myself that it doesn't matter, that I'm just going to work, that it doesn't matter if I have a good night or a bad night. Because if I put that pressure on myself, then I'm tense and that shows. If I'm thinking "I've got to make money," and I'm asking "Would you like a dance?" then it just doesn't work. So I just have to be there and be up and relaxed, it's hard, it's so mental.

This example illustrates the "suppression of feeling" that is part of Hochschild's definition of emotional labor. It takes work for Jasmine to ignore the real reason she is at the club (to make money) and focus on entertaining the customers. While Jasmine talks about the suppression of feeling in her work as a stripper, Sapphire talks about transmuting her private response to nervousness into valuable tools for managing her interactions with customers:

> One of the good things for me is that if I'm nervous or feeling just a little bit uncomfortable or something, I tend to smile or laugh or giggle, so I mean that makes it much easier because when someone's in a good mood and happy and smiling they tend to do a lot better [at selling table dances].

Tori's approach was to use interaction with customers to draw energy for herself on nights when she wasn't feeling "on":

> I just smile more, then I find one person who wants a dance and is really into me and I just take that energy and use that to keep me going.

Emotional work on the part of the stripper is necessary not just to make the customer feel wanted, or attractive, but also to keep him from feeling uncomfortable. A customer reported to Carol Ronai (1992) that "I'm not here to scare the girls. I'm here for the illusion that they like me. When I see a scared new dancer, I feel like the boogie man" (110). It is the dancer's job to look calm, collected, and as if she is enjoying herself, not to look nervous, scared, tired, stressed out, or bored. Delaney, one of the dancers at Jonathan's, felt that customers ought to perform some emotion work as well. By placing some of the responsibility on them to enjoy themselves, she acknowledges the interactivity of creating good feelings. She also acknowledges the ability customers have to make the strippers' work either more or less difficult. Talking about the need for reinforcement from the audience in order to feel good about her dancing she said:

> I get embarrassed if I see other people watching me dance and they notice that no one looks happy. I'd rather have them [the customers at the stage] . . . if they're not tipping I'd rather have them smile and at least pretend they're into it. I think it's embarrassing if they're stone cold.

Delaney's moments of embarrassment are indicative of a *lack* of emotion work on the part of customers. If they wanted to, they could affect a sense of interest in her dancing, or her body, in order to convey to her a feeling of being good at her job. It is possible that one reason that strippers appeal to customers is because it is implicit, through the substitution of money for true emotional obligation, that customers *need not* attend to the emotions of strippers when interacting with them.

Sometimes strippers use emotion work techniques in order to prevent customers from affirming their masculine power. Sapphire discusses using eye contact to make customers feel self-conscious about their participation in interactions with her.

> *You know what's funny? I enjoy making people feel uncomfortable when I'm dancing, I do, cause I kind of giggle to myself when I'm doing it. You know, there are just some men who come in and they're enjoying themselves but they're also uncomfortable because they're kind of embarrassed I'll keep meeting their eyes and they'll keep looking away.*

Some strippers, I've noted, make faces when they turn their backs to customers during table dances. Others roll their eyes. The turning of her back to the customer serves not only to show him her ass, but also to give the stripper a small break from the work of appearing to enjoy the dance. In addition it gives the dancer a chance to demonstrate "role distance" (Goffman 1961) to herself and to the other dancers. It was important to the dancers I interviewed that I know they were not "taken in" by the customers and that while they sometimes honestly enjoyed their work they always framed their interactions with customers as work, not as pleasure.

The Delta flight attendants studied by Hochschild were selling their emotional labor to a company, but directing it toward the passengers with whom they interacted on each flight. The strippers in this study sell their emotional labor directly to their customers. In some ways, that makes the power dynamic in the strip club more complicated. Strippers are, for the most part, independent contractors. They pay the clubs in order to work there. They don't have bosses in the typical sense. Yet to say they are their own bosses would be to underestimate the influence the customers have over them. As noted above this power

is multi-directional. In terms of exchange relationships, the customer has power over the dancer's financial success. He is not obligated to tip except by his regard of strip club conventions and his desire for individual attention from the dancers. The stripper has power over the attention she gives and over the display of her body. Strippers themselves report sometimes feeling sexually or erotically powerful, commanding the attention of the men in the club:

> Sapphire: *Actually, I have fun doing it, most of the time I really do. I like that kind of attention, you know, the spotlight on me, and the money's great, so it kind of gives me what I need . . . I'm kind of sad for when I do get that much older that I can't do it any more.*

Several dancers reported sometimes enjoying the sexual attention they received from customers, telling me that, especially when first starting to strip for a living, the positive attention they got from the customers was "a rush" or "almost addictive." On the other hand, dancers also report feeling that customers in the club have a sort of collective power over the self-esteem of strippers:

> Tori: *I don't see it as female dominance over men, or that they're [strippers] in a power position because they're dancing. I see it as the fact that the women there have their self-esteem affected by the way the customers treat them . . . and in that regard the men do have a lot of power over them, not necessarily as individuals but as a collective in terms of how they relate to them [strippers].*

CONCLUSION

It is notable that in the relationship between stripper and potential customer, rejection almost always happens in one direction: he refuses her dance. In fact, one of the reasons strippers say men come to the clubs is to avoid the potential rejection they face by women at regular bars. If he has money in hand, he will almost certainly be able to secure the temporary attention of a woman in a strip club. Part of this is due to the ordering of interaction within the clubs. Dancers approach customers, asking them to buy dances, and customers approach the stage to give tips and get attention. This alone makes rejection of the customer unlikely, at least as long as his behavior remains within the boundaries of what is allowable in the club. However, if a customer offended a dancer, she might refuse to dance for him again or refuse to sit with him after her dance. Dancers also sometimes avoided approaching certain customers. The "missed opportunities" I described above are possibly incidences of dancers "silently rejecting" customers in a way that avoids the confrontation a verbal rejection could create. Thus, dancers have the power to reject customers but such rejection was usually a reaction to offensive behavior on the part of the customer, and was usually evident in dancers' avoidance of certain customers rather than in outright verbal rejection.

The power discussed in the preceding paragraph is similar to the power in most sales relationships: the customer approaches or is approached by the salesperson and then can accept or reject the product being sold. The customer can influence the salesperson's work environment and financial success while the salesperson can influence the customer's access to the product. However, if we return to the concept of "masculine power" introduced earlier, we see a much more subtle power at work in the strip clubs. Feminist critics of sex-work often claim a general and all-encompassing domination of women by men, a domination that allows no agency on the part of women. I suggest that what actually exists between men and women, and what is evidenced in the interactions between strippers and customers, is a more dynamic and also more insidious power. It is a power that is not *inflicted* by men onto women, but is *enacted* by men and women together primarily for the benefit of men through interactions that affirm cultural notions of masculinity. It is enacted in a setting where the obvious activity is the watching of women by men but where underlying that obvious agenda is the women's attending to their customers. Through the creation and use of fantasy, women simultaneously become "two dimensional paper dolls" (in order to allow the customers to see what they want to see)

while engaging in a significant amount of emotional labor (in order to make believable their attention and interest in the customers). Strip club interactions then, full of ironic twists, create a source of affirmation of customers' masculinity in a very traditional sense, and thus by affirming it, lend power to that masculinity.

One of the ironic twists involves the necessary recognition of the dancers' power to influence customers' experience of affirmation. While the amount of attention a customer receives for his money is the product of often complex negotiation, it is the dancer who retains ultimate control over his access to her smile, eye contact, and further affirmative interaction. Michelle's effort to make her customers feel that they are the "only ones in the room," and that she would "do anything to be with them," indicates the awareness dancers have of their ability to influence the customers' sense of being desired. In addition, Sapphire's use of eye contact to unnerve customers is a vivid reminder that dancers intentionally undermine as well as affirm customers' experience of masculine power.

Finally, customers give dancers a sense of power by being willing to pay for the attention they receive. Dancers told me that one of the dangers of stripping, particularly early on, is becoming "addicted to the money and the attention." They explained that it could "be a rush" to have so many men offering them money to dance, display their bodies, talk, smile, and "be pretty." The dancer gets some elements of her femininity affirmed just as the customer gets his masculinity affirmed. The customer pays for his affirmation with money. The dancer pays for her affirmation in costly though non-monetary ways. Long hours of emotional and physical labor, stigmatization and disdain from outsiders, and having to manage the negativity that customers sometimes direct at dancers are just a few of the costs that dancers balance with the financial rewards and affirmation received through interactions with customers.

This paper paints strip club interactions in the perspective of a feminist interactionism that recognizes nuances not acknowledged by the more mainstream deviant occupations approach on one hand and the more essentialist radical feminist approach on the other. Further research and writing from this perspective would deepen our understanding of sex-work and its implications for the study of gender, of work, and of the construction of emotions, power, and identity.

REFERENCES

Barry, Kathleen. 1979. *Female Sexual Slavery.* New York: Avon Books.

Boles, Jacqueline M. and Albeno P. Garbin. 1974a. "The Choice of Stripping for a Living: An Empirical and Theoretical Explanation." *Sociology of Work and Occupations* 1:110–123.

———. 1974b. "The Strip Club and Stripper-Customer Patterns of Interaction." *Sociology and Social Research,* Jan: 136–144.

Bourdieu, Pierre. 1984. *Distinction: A Social Critique of the Judgment of Taste.* Translated by Richard Nice. Cambridge, MA: Harvard University Press.

Carey, Sandra Harley, Robert A. Peterson, and Louis K. Sharpe. 1974. "A Study of Recruitment and Socialization into Two Deviant Female Occupations." *Sociological Symposium* 11:11–24.

Chapkiss, Wendy. 1997. *Live Sex Acts: Women Performing Erotic Labor.* New York: Routledge.

Collins, Randall. 1992. "Women and the Production of Status Cultures." In *Cultivating Differences: Symbolic Boundaries and the Making of Inequality,* edited by Michéle Lamont and Marcel Fournier. Chicago: University of Chicago Press.

Forsyth, Craig J. and Tina H. Deshotels. 1998. "A Deviant Process: The Sojourn of the Stripper." *Sociological Spectrum* 18:77–92.

———. 1997. "The Occupational Milieu of the Nude Dancer." *Deviant Behavior* 18:125–142.

Glaser, Barney G. and Anselm L. Strauss. 1967. *The Discovery of Grounded Theory: Strategies for Qualitative Research.* New York: Aldine de Gruyter.

Goffman, Erving. 1974. *Frame Analysis.* New York: Harper Colophon.

———. 1961. *Encounters: Two Studies in the Sociology of Interaction.* Indianapolis: Bobbs-Merrill.

———. 1959. *The Presentation of Self in Everyday Life.* New York: Anchor Books/Doubleday.

Gonos, George. 1976. "Go-go Dancing: A Comparative Frame Analysis." *Urban Life,* 189–220.

Griffin, Susan. 1981. *Pornography and Silence.* New York: Harper and Row.

Hochschild, Arlie Russell. 1983. *The Managed Heart: Commercialization of Human Feeling.* Berkeley: University of California Press.

———. 1979. "Emotion Work, Feeling Rules, and Social Structure." *American Journal of Sociology* 85:551–575.

MacKinnon, Catherine. 1987. *Feminism Unmodified: Discourses on Life and Law.* Cambridge: Harvard University Press.

McCaghy, Charles H. and James K. Skipper, Jr. 1972. "Stripping: Anatomy of a Deviant Lifestyle" in *Lifestyles: Diversity in America,* edited by Saul D. Feldman. Boston: Little, Brown and Co.

———. 1969. "Lesbian Behavior as an Adaptation to the Occupation of Stripping." *Social Problems* 17:262–270.

McCall, Leslie. 1992. "Does Gender Fit? Bourdieu, Feminism, and Conceptions of Social Order." *Theory and Society* 21:837–867.

Mills, C. W. 1958. *The Sociological Imagination.* New York: Grove Press.

Phelan, Shane. 1989. *Identity Politics: Lesbian Feminism and the Limits of Community.* Philadelphia: Temple University Press.

Roiphe, Katie. 1993. *The Morning After.* Boston: Little, Brown, and Co.

Ronai, Carol Rambo and Carolyn Ellis. 1989. "Turn-ons For Money: Interactional Strategies of the Table Dancer." *Journal of Contemporary Ethnography* 18:271–298.

Ronai, Carol Rambo. 1992. "The Reflexive Self through Narrative: A Night in the Life of an Erotic Dancer/Researcher" in *Investigating Subjectivity: Research on Lived Experience,* edited by Carolyn Ellis and Michael G. Flahertyn. Newbury Park: Sage Publications.

Rubin, Gayle. 1976. "The Traffic in Women: Notes on the 'Political Economy' of Sex," in *Toward an Anthropology of Women,* edited by Rayna Rapp Reiter. New York: Monthly Review Press.

Skipper, James K., Jr. and Charles H. McCaghy. 1970. "Stripteasers: The Anatomy and Career Contingencies of a Deviant Occupation." *Social Problems* 17:391–404.

———. (1971). "The Stripteaser." *Sexual Behavior* 1:78–87.

PART SEVEN

HOMOSEXUALITY AND HOMOPHOBIA

Kelli Peterson, a 17-year-old senior at East High School in Salt Lake City, had felt lonely as a lesbian student for at least two years. "I thought I was the only lesbian student in East High," she said. "As a sophomore I was really pressured by my friends to date. I came out that year and immediately lost all my friends. I went through the cycle of denial, trying to hide, acceptance, then your friends abandoning you." She and two other gay students formed an extracurricular club called the Gay/Straight Alliance, but this touched off a furor among national conservative leaders, the state legislature, and the local school board. Apparently possessed with the unfounded fear that the club could turn straight students into gays or lesbians, one antigay leader proclaimed: "Homosexuals can't reproduce, so they recruit. And they are not going to use Utah high school and junior high school campuses to recruit." Eventually, a state law was passed banning all gay clubs in high schools.[1]

Such a negative reaction toward lesbians and gays is an example of *homophobia,* prejudice and discrimination against people with the same-sex orientation. Here we will take a closer look at homophobia and homosexuality. In the first article, "Rejecting 'Femininity': Gender Identity Development in Lesbians," Margaret Cooper discusses how the lesbians she interviewed had rejected traditional femininity in their childhood. In the second article, "Radical Gay Activism: A Critical Gay's View," Bruce Bawer argues that gay radicalism, as demonstrated in the Gay Pride Day march, ironically reinforces the antigay stereotypes held by heterosexuals. In the third selection, "Bareback Sex, Bug Chasers, and the Gift of Death," DeAnn Gauthier and Craig Forsyth offer research data to explain why some gays get involved in two, related, new forms of sexual deviance: "barebacking" (engaging in anal intercourse without the protection of condoms) and "bug chasing" (trying to get infected with the deadly AIDS virus through barebacking). In the fourth reading, "The Social Organization of Male Prostitution," Robert McNamara finds from his ethnographic study that male prostitutes have developed a social norm governing their trade and their interactions with each other. In the fifth article, "Homophobia in Schools," Andrew Walters and David Hayes discuss the nature and prevalence of homophobia in educational institutions and offer suggestions on how to combat the problem.

1. James Brooke. 1996. "To be Young, Gay and Going to a High School in Utah." *New York Times,* February 26, pp. A1, B8.

27

REJECTING "FEMININITY": GENDER IDENTITY DEVELOPMENT IN LESBIANS

MARGARET COOPER

The majority of social science research on homosexuality has been on men (see Oberstone and Sukoneck, 1976). Most nonfeminist work on lesbians has been of a quantitative nature, attempting to study the issue of lesbianism numerically. It has not allowed the women's experience to be quoted directly but to be interpreted solely for the reader by the researcher.

This study allows women to speak about their own gender identity development. The difference between "sex" and "gender" should be emphasized since it is a crucial distinction made in this article. Kate Millett (1970, p. 39) wrote of the "overwhelmingly *cultural* character of gender." She, along with others (Stoller, 1968), was active in distinguishing gender from the term "sex," which refers to one's anatomy and physiology. Robert Stoller (1968, pp. viii–ix) wrote that

> gender is a term that has psychological or cultural rather than biological connotations. If the proper terms for sex are "male" and "female," the corresponding terms for gender are "masculine" and feminine"; these latter may be quite independent of sex.

METHODS AND SAMPLE

Martin and Lyon (1972) felt surveys may not even be likely to include the respondents' true feelings, thereby forcing the respondent to fit into a category she or he might not otherwise. They were critical of quantitative methods in the study of lesbianism when they wrote:

> *Experience indicates that the questions are made up generally by heterosexuals and asked of homosexuals who very often find them irrelevant to their particular lifestyle. The questions, for the most part, are unanswerable by the required "yes" or "no" or multiple choice, and their only virtue is that they are easily computerized into instant (misleading) statistic (p. 2).*

With feminist criticism of such studies in mind, a qualitative method, in-depth interviews, was chosen for this article. It allows for respondents to create their own categories rather than merely try to fit into those preconceived by a researcher. The validity of the qualitative method relates directly to the validity of the women's experiences.

Lesbians were identified and contacted through friendship associations. Fifteen women agreed to participate. All respondents were assured confidentiality and assigned pseudonyms. The interviews were conducted and analyzed according to the procedure suggested by Schwartz and Jacobs (1979) and Lofland and Lofland (1984). Rather than utilizing the statistical analyses of quantitative methods, the interview data were examined for emergent patterns of responses and descriptions.

The ages of the respondents ranged from 19 to 38, with the average age of 25.3 years. All of the women were born and reared in small towns and cities in the South and Midwest. All of them currently live in and around cities with a population of 50,000 or less in various towns in the central region of the United States.

Four of the women considered themselves to be feminists. The rest did not. One other woman had recently become involved with the gay rights movement. A few others expressed interest in the gay rights and feminist movements, but not from the standpoint of a participant.

Since the sample size of this study is small, no attempt will be made to say that this sample is reflective of all lesbians. However, this article is an honest account of the experience of the women who did take part in this study.

RESULTS

All of the women interviewed indicated a rejection of traditional femininity. Even as children, some even before they were consciously aware of same-sex attractions, had difficulty fitting into what they saw as the traditional female role. Apparently, even though these women might not have known what they wanted, they knew what they did *not* want. For them, it appears that the female gender role represented more than femaleness. It also represented heterosexuality:

That role is all sex-oriented. It's the dumb house-wife image. If you really look at it, that's just the way it is. (Pat)

I remember as a very young child not identify-ing with the female role because it seemed like, and this was growing up in the sixties, that the fe-male role was strongly attached to your role as a wife and mother and I knew I couldn't do that. So I felt more identified with the male role. When I was a kid, I would play the boy when we played house. And I wanted my mom to buy me "boy clothes." (Kate)

For Kate, this role rejection was directly linked, in her view, to her attraction to other girls. She was aware of this attraction at a very young age and she reported that she developed quite a "macho" image of herself by age seven. She explained it this way:

I used to think, as a kid, that you had to be mascu-line to get a woman. That women liked masculinity and men liked femininity. So I tried to convince every girl on the block that I was a boy. I even took a male name. And of course, it made perfect sense

to me. I never understood when people's parents were flipping out.

The other women's responses fell into three categories: (1) taking the male role (like Kate's ex-ample), (2) being a "tomboy," and (3) rejecting items of dress and play associated with female children. These responses overlapped in all of the interviews.

Taking the male role was seen in both play and fantasy. Cindy said, "Kids would play house; and I was the one, when my cousins would come over, I'd play the boy. I'd always do the boy parts." This led her to believe that she might be gay. This also "concerned" her cousins, one of whom later said to her, "We was all worried about you, won-dering about you because you always wanted to play the guy." Cindy said she wanted to respond by merely saying, "Take a hint." Anita's childhood fantasies often involved taking the male role. She described them by saying:

I might not have known what it was called when I was real young, I can remember going to see "James Bond" and like when . . . my imagination would run wild or I would have some kind of fan-tasy, I'd never fantasize as being one of the women. I was always "James Bond" . . . "Matt Dillon," you know.

Wolff (1971) found that many lesbians, as children, desired to be boys. She found lesbians were five times more likely to have expressed this desire than were heterosexual women. In a study by Fleener and reported by Lewis (1979), 82 per-cent of lesbians sampled had gone through a tomboy phase. In the sample for this article, all fif-teen women told of their "tomboy" experiences as children. Not only did they engage in sports, tree-climbing, etc., many of them chose to play with boys. Robin said, "I was the only girl in my neigh-borhood my age when we moved here, so that was a lot of fun to hang around with the boys . . . I used to be a tomboy really bad." Barbara enjoyed "get-ting out and playing baseball with my brothers or basketball, things like that." This led her to con-clude after some period of time, "I knew I was dif-ferent. I just couldn't put my finger on it." . . .

Lewis (1979, p. 23) called the "rebellion against what is seen as being female and restrictive" that coincides with the desire for "those elements of male identity that carry independence . . . the first rite of passage into lesbian selfhood." The third set of responses involved this "rebellion against what is seen as being female." Carole said that she would "rather take a beating than put a dress on." Barbara not only disliked the frilly dresses her mother bought for her, she also hated the Barbie dolls. "I wanted to burn the Barbie dolls!" she laughed.

During the childhood years, the rejection of the female role is relatively risk-free. This begins to change in adolescence. The world again becomes the dichotomized place of girl/femininity and boy/masculinity, now with an additional imperative: heterosexuality, complete with its emphasis, for girls, on attracting the boys who will become their future protectors of social responsibility (Lewis, 1979). Lewis found that girls then began to lose their desire to be boys. Only 2 percent of her subjects wished to be boys after puberty. Most accepted female identities. However, most did not succumb to tradition, but sought to personally redefine what it meant to be female. As teenagers, sports became an outlet for many of them. Nine of the fifteen women in this study played in sports. This was enough to cause rumors to start. Two women explained it this way:

> I played basketball and stuff, and you know, when you're an athlete and a woman, there's a lot of stereotypes. You know, "she's real bullish!" Or "she can really shoot that hard for a woman." People would say something and my sister heard about it and she'd go home and tell my mom. She would say, "I heard Stella's gay." (Stella)
>
> If you were in athletics at that point in time when I was in high school, you were automatically stereotyped that you were gay because you were a big athlete. . . . You were automatically labeled. (Carole)

For Stella, these rumors were instigators of problems at home. The mere label of "lesbian" proved to be a threat to women. It was a warning that they were stepping outside the lines of accept-

able gender behavior. Carole felt a lot of pressure from peers to disprove the rumors. She said, "It bothered me to a degree . . . it did put a little more pressure on me as to trying to prove myself not being that way as far as dating and stuff like that."

As teenagers, and for some even into adulthood, a rejection of feminine clothing was also a pattern. This rejection ranged from not wearing overtly feminine apparel to dressing in a way that was considered to be "mannish."

> I went through that stage when I had to play a Dyke. Yeah, I had to ride a motorcycle and wear men's pants, men's clothes and I didn't wear women's stuff at all. Men's underwear even, you know. You go through this phase and it's one of those things. (Pat)
>
> I don't know why I'm so butch, why I wear men's clothes. It's not that I want to be a man, because I don't. Because God knows, if I were a man, I wouldn't have been with some of the women that I've been with. (Anita)

For Pat, as with the rest of the women with the exception of Anita and Jennifer, it was just, as she said, a phase. Whether as a child, teenager, or adult, it did seem to serve, as previously stated by Lewis, as a "rite of passage." It is crucial to consider, as Anita articulated, that gay women do *not* want to be men. Instead, they had desired male privilege and access to women. They desired the freedom that men had; and *every* woman in the sample, whether or not she considered herself a feminist, found the female role restrictive.

Since adolescents undergo so much pressure concerning gender conformity, lesbian adolescents might experience confusion, frustration, and ridicule. Sasha Lewis (1979, p. 24) wrote, "The young lesbian realizes that she cannot be a boy, yet she realizes that she cannot be like her female peers and in many cases she feels a sense of intense isolation." Not understanding why such pressure to conform even exists, lesbians then must determine their own paths. For many, as Pat and Kate explained, the lack of role models dramatically increased their problems. The problem was not merely finding good or even adequate role models. It was finding *any* role models. The lack of visibility, on the part of lesbians reinforced their fears of being "freaks."

In what they perceived as a way to escape the constraints of female roles, two of the women had expressed a youthful intention to enter the military. Two more eventually did. Although the army did not satisfy either in her search for identity, both felt their reason for joining involved this rejection of traditional roles. Pat explained:

Why did I join the army? Because it was not a female role. To prove that I was just as good as they (men) were. That I could do anything they could do. . . .

CONCLUSION

While the issue of gender identity in lesbians calls for further research, this study does reveal some important points. Even at an early age, the women in this study were rebels where gender behavior was concerned. Many of them described experiences as "tomboys." They, as children, indicated they had no problem with this behavior but were forced by others to "wear dresses" or "play with dolls." Some did these willingly but rejected traditional femininity when they saw it as representing heterosexuality. Most rejected the traditional female role, because even as children, they could not foresee themselves in the future portraying a heterosexual role. Some, in childhood fantasies, already perceived themselves in lives with women. Many of them saw a need to take the "male role"

to achieve the relation to women that they desired. At the onset of adolescence, much more pressure existed from both peers and adults to abandon "tomboyish" behaviors. . . .

It should be reiterated that the women in this study found the traditional female role to be restrictive and constraining. Beginning as children, they began a journey of self-discovery usually without the assistance of role models or appropriate guidance from those they considered authorities. As adults, each reached her own conclusion on what it meant to be a woman and what it meant to be a lesbian. Risking the labels of "deviants" or worse, these women have chosen roles for which there were no scripts. Consequently, many feminists would consider their androgynous approach to selfhood to be much more well-rounded than those straining to conform to rigidly limited roles. In their paper on the psychological adjustment of lesbians and heterosexual women, Oberstone and Sukoneck (1976) concluded their analysis on gay women with the following:

Are they really more "masculine" in their behavior than their "normal" heterosexual counterparts, or are they more free to develop both their feminine and masculine and, in fact, their human potential? It is possible that, rather than being "masculine," the lesbian woman, by virtue of being an outlaw, has had to develop personality qualities that have been traditionally the domain of the male, such as independence, self-determination, competence, and aggression. (p. 185)

REFERENCES

Lewis, Sasha G. 1979. *Sunday's Women: Lesbian Life Today.* Boston: Beacon.

Lofland, John and Lyn H. Lofland. 1984. *Analyzing Social Settings: A Guide to Qualitative Observation and Analysis.* Belmont, CA: Wadsworth.

Martin, Del and Phyllis Lyon. 1972. *Lesbian/Women.* New York: Bantam.

Millet, Kate. 1970. *Sexual Politics.* New York: Ballantine.

Oberstone, Andrea and Harriet Sukoneck. 1976. "Psychological Adjustment and Life Style of

Single Lesbians and Single Heterosexual Women." *Psychology of Women Quarterly,* I(no. 2): 172–188.

Schwartz, Howard and Jerry Jacobs. 1979. *Qualitative Sociology: A Method to the Madness.* New York: Free Press.

Stoller, Robert J. 1968. *Sex and Gender.* New York: Science House.

Wolff, Charlotte. 1971. *Love between Women.* New York: St. Martin's.

28

RADICAL GAY ACTIVISM:
A CRITICAL GAY'S VIEW

BRUCE BAWER

"The only time I ever feel ashamed of being gay," says a friend of mine, "is on Gay Pride Day."

I know what he means, though my own emotions on that day are, at worst, closer to dismay than to shame. Every June, on the appointed Sunday, I stand on the sidewalk somewhere along Fifth Avenue in midtown Manhattan, sometimes alone and sometimes with friends, and watch the march file past, each group behind its identifying banner: the gay senior citizens, the separatist lesbians, the Dykes on Bikes, the People With AIDS coalition, the recovering alcoholics who call themselves Clean and Sober, the interracial couples who call themselves Men of All Colors Together (formerly Black and White Men Together), the gay and lesbian student organizations from various colleges and universities, the local chapters of direct-action groups like ACT UP and Queer Nation, the disco-blaring floats advertising various bars and dance clubs, the volunteers from Gay Men's Health Crisis and God's Love We Deliver, the Parents and Friends of Lesbians and Gays, the gay Catholics, the gay Episcopalians, the gay Jews, the Gay Fathers, the gays in leather, the gay swimmers. . . .

My feelings are always mixed. There's a certain comfort in being among so many people who have all experienced self-discoveries similar to one's own, and who have all had to deal with the same slights and cruelties that homosexuals have to put up with from people who want to inflict pain or who didn't care or who just don't know any better. The march also provides safety in numbers: no danger of gay-bashing here. And it af-fords a spectacle of quiet heroism: many of the marchers are dying. (In some cases you can tell, in some you can't.) Watching them file past, I know that I'm looking at thousands of untold stories of extraordinary courage.

Yet on that appointed Sunday in June there is always for me, as well, a certain disquiet. Year by year, I find myself increasingly vexed by certain aspects of the march. Part of me doesn't want to attend it. If at its best the event hints at the diversity of the gay population in America, altogether too much of it is silly, sleazy, and sex-centered, a reflection of the narrow, contorted definition of homosexuality that marks some sectors of the gay subculture. On Gay Pride Day in 1991, for instance, I was perplexed to see that among the handful of V.I.P.s on the reviewing stand at Forty-first Street was Robin Byrd, an X-rated movie actress who generally appears in public wearing a string mesh bikini. Byrd's weekly public-access TV program showcases the talents of youngsters, some of them teenage runaways, who work in Times Square strip clubs. Did the organizers of the march, I wondered, really want the world to think that *this* was what being gay was all about?

Byrd may also have been on the reviewing stand a year later, but I didn't see her. On Gay Pride Day 1992 I positioned myself a half-mile or so north of the reviewing stand, near the corner of Fifth Avenue and Fifty-fourth Street. This intersection is three blocks north of Saint Patrick's Cathedral, opposite which a few dozen protesters traditionally congregate behind blue police lines, yelling anti-gay epithets and waving homemade signs on which they have scrawled the usual scriptural quotations. It is customary for marchers passing this group to chant, with rather dignified restraint, "Shame! Shame! Shame!" For some reason, on Gay Pride Day 1992 a group of protesters left their assigned spot while the march was still going by. As they headed up the Fifth Avenue sidewalk past me, toting signs that read "Jesus Forever—Repent," the Queer Nation contingent was about to reach Fifty-fourth Street. The two groups clashed near the northeast corner. "Shame! Shame! Shame!" the Queer Nation members chanted, breaking ranks and heading for the sidewalk as a dozen or so policemen moved quickly to form a human barricade. The Queer Nation marchers and the anti-gay protesters exchanged verbal abuse for a few moments; then the protesters resumed walking up the sidewalk and the Queer Nation contingent peeled away to continue matching down the avenue. Everything seemed in order until one Queer Nation member, a short leathercoat young man with a bushy mustache who was at the moment no more than six or eight feet from me, suddenly stopped and turned around to shriek happily, at the top of his lungs, at the departing protesters: "*Jesus was a faggot!*" I shook my head in disappointment. Now what, I wondered, was the point of *that*?

Apart from that episode, there were the usual sights. Bearded men in dresses. Young men masquerading as Marilyn Monroe, Mae West, Barbara Bush, Joan Collins. Fat men in bathing trunks. Two friends, one dressed as a priest and the other as Jesus. A couple of dozen young fellows in a truck that displayed two banners, one reading "Gay Whore's" and the other "Legalize Prostitution." (I recognized one of the young men from my health club, where he always swims in the fast lane.) There was a float blaring dance music and bearing the name of the radical New Alliance Party, some of whose members marched behind and alongside the float, chanting threateningly with raised fists: "N.A.P! We got to build a New Alliance Movement!" And there were three—count 'em, three—middle-aged members of NAMBLA, the North American Man-Boy Love

Association, two of whom carried the organization's banner while the third held up a sign proclaiming the joys of pederasty.

It must be emphasized that most of the marchers were not at all shocking. There were several times more Gay Catholics than Gay Whores, more men in tennis shorts than in underpants. And NAMBLA was the tiniest group of all. Yet there was plenty to make John Q. Public do a double take—plenty, indeed, that appeared to have been designed to accomplish precisely that. It seemed as if people who wore suits and ties on the 364 other days of the year had, on this particular morning, ransacked their closets for their tackiest, skimpiest, most revealing items of clothing. There were hundreds of bare chests, bare bottoms, mesh pants, nipple rings, leather shorts, and tight designer briefs without anything covering them. Couples who almost certainly didn't go in for public displays of affection on an ordinary Sunday made sure to pause every block or so during their progress down Fifth Avenue to kiss or grab each other's crotches or rub their bodies together in a simulation of sex. There was more sashaying and queeny posing in a couple of hours than one could expect to see in a solid month of gay bar-hopping. Smart, talented people who held down respectable jobs in the corporate world or the fashion industry, on Wall Street or Publishers' Row, seemed to have done their best on this special day to look like tawdry bimbos, bar boys, and beach bums. Time and again, glimpsing this or that unconventionally attired or coiffed or made-up marcher, I found myself feeling momentarily as if I'd stumbled into a private costume party and seen something I wasn't supposed to see. Unfortunately, however, this wasn't a private party; it was a public spectacle.

And therein lay its illogic. The signs that some of the participants carried—signs demanding equal rights, more money for AIDS research, and so on—suggested that the march was intended, at least in part, to be a political statement directed at the heterosexual population. But if this was the case, what could explain the grotesque appearance and vulgar behavior of so many marchers, who were, quite frankly, a public-relations nightmare? The facts of the matter, after all, seemed obvious: The Gay Pride Day march provided a first-class opportunity to exhibit the real face of gay America, to demonstrate that the gay population is in every way a cross-section of the country—black and white, rural and urban, rich and poor. If the gay population put that real face forward on Gay Pride Day, it wouldn't look alien to anyone. But instead, the march represented gay America by means of what seems at times to be a veritable circus parade, a parade that too often underlined the sexual aspect of gay life and underlined the most sordid elements of that sexual aspect. It presented homosexuals less as human beings than as *sexual* beings.

That, indeed, is the hallmark of the gay subculture: The notion that life, for homosexuals, naturally revolves around sex more than it does for heterosexuals. This notion is hardly surprising, given that this particular subculture is the creation of people who are united not by ethnicity, religion, or profession but by sexual orientation; yet one of this notion's unfortunate consequences is an annual march that, instead of giving the world a representative picture of gay life, offers a strange and demeaning caricature thereof. Looking at some of those marchers, I couldn't help thinking that the subculture mentality had worked upon them in such a way that they virtually considered it their responsibility as gay people to reduce themselves to stereotypes every Gay Pride Day; however much they might or might not have to do the rest of the year with the subculture and its ethos, however far they may have grown away from it and into themselves, it was clear from their dress and deportment that, on some level, they had never rejected completely the subculture's definition of what it meant to be gay—and today, apparently, was their Holy Day of Obligation, their day to be as gay as they could possibly be.

Most homosexuals in the New York area, of course, weren't anywhere near the march. Most hadn't even considered coming; they *never* came. Where were they? Well, some were doubtless enjoying a leisurely brunch; some were spending Sunday with their families; some were puttering around the house, or walking in the park, or taking in a movie. I'd seen at least two dozen gay men at church that morning, every last one of them elegantly turned out in suit and tie and polished black shoes, and would be astonished, to say the least, to see any of them in the march. I hadn't mentioned the march to any of them, but I'd talked about it enough with gay friends to have a pretty good idea how they'd react: with a wince, a grimace, a rhetorical question or two: "Who'd want to be part of that tacky display? Why should I participate in something whose sole purpose is to make a dirty joke out of who I am?"

I can't say I felt very differently. I could never bring myself to take part fully in a march that included the likes of NAMBLA. Yet most years I did go so far as to include myself in the ranks of the thousands of spectators who, after the last marchers had passed, tagged along at the end all the way down to Greenwich Village. For I felt that if the image of homosexuals that the march projected was ever to be set right, those of us who were displeased with it in its present form couldn't keep away entirely. We had to do *something*.

That day, as on every previous Gay Pride Day, I found myself reflecting on the march's ramifications. In the evening, people in New York and around the country would turn on their local news and see a few seconds of this or some other gay march. I'd watched enough of those reports to have a pretty good idea what the producers would choose to show: some leathermen, maybe the Barbara Bush and Marilyn Monroe impersonators, almost certainly the young man dressed as Jesus. In the succeeding weeks and months, moreover, long after the young stockbrokers and magazine editors had stowed away their flamboyant Gay Pride Day accoutrements for another year and slipped back into their everyday Brooks Brothers togs, anti-gay propagandists would put together videotapes showing these young professionals looking very, shall we say, unprofessional. These videotapes, featuring the most outrageous parts of this and other recent gay marches, would be advertised in right-wing political magazines and various church publications and would be sold and shipped to purchasers around the country. These purchasers, in turn, would make copies for friends and relatives or show them at neighborhood get-togethers, at church socials, at P.T.A. meetings. From Maine to California, men and women would watch these videotapes and shake their heads in disgust, not only at the individuals portrayed in them but at what they presumably represented. To those men and women, this was the face of homosexuality.

Standing there as the march went by, I didn't have to imagine the reactions of small-town middle Americans to the Gay Pride Day march. This was, after all, a Sunday in June in midtown Manhattan, and there were tourists all over the place. From my spot on the Fifth Avenue curb, I watched one out-of-town family after another hurry across the avenue or up the sidewalk, maps and cameras and shopping bags in hand, on their way from one metropolitan attraction to another. It was clear that the Gay Pride Day march did not figure on these people's sightseeing itinerary but had, rather, taken them by surprise. In every instance, I saw nothing on their faces but shock, revulsion, and a desperate desire to get away from Fifth Avenue as quickly as possible.

One family in particular stands out in my memory: a husband and wife and their tall, gangly, shy-looking son, who was about thirteen and who, it occurred to me, might well wake up one morning four or five years hence and realize he was gay. It distressed me to think that this march would probably shape that family's most vivid image of homosexuality. If the boy did eventually prove to be gay, the memory of this day could only make it harder for him to recognize and come to terms with his homosexuality and for his parents to understand and accept the truth about him. That shouldn't be the way things worked. If the march had any legitimate purpose, it was to make things easier, not harder, for young gay people and their families. Things would be hard enough for them as it was.

That afternoon, on a float for a drinking establishment called the Crowbar, I noticed a sign: "Greetings from the Planet Gay!" The sign, I felt, summed up the whole day: too many of the people involved in the march *did* think of themselves as living on another planet—or, at least, thought of their sexual identity as being something from another planet. They had been provided here with an extraordinary opportunity to educate the heterosexual population about homosexuality, to destroy backward myths, to win friends and supporters for the cause of gay equality; instead, much of the march simply served to reinforce myths, to confirm prejudices, and to make new enemies for homosexuals. If Jerry Falwell or Pat Robertson had wanted to orchestrate an annual spectacle designed to increase hostility toward gays, I reflected, they could hardly have done a better job than this.

It seemed to me, indeed, that the sort of pride on display in the Gay Pride Day march was, in many cases, not so much pride in the sense of "self-respect" or "dignity" than pride in the sense of "arrogance," "conceit," "hubris." Real pride, after all, is a hard-won individual attribute. It doesn't come from being gay, or from belonging to *any* group. It can come, however, from dealing with the fact of your homosexuality in a responsible and mature manner, from not using it as a club to beat other people with or as an excuse to behave irresponsibly or unseriously. The more loudly someone declares his pride, the more it should be suspected; for real pride is not shrill and insistent but quiet and strong. . . .

The marchers who make the Gay Pride Day march embarrassing to many homosexuals and disgusting to people . . . represent the same small but vocal minority of the gay population that has, for a generation, played no small part in shaping and sustaining most heterosexuals' notions of what it means to be homosexual. I've noted that many heterosexuals speak of the "gay lifestyle" as if there were only one way to be gay; but it must also be said that some gays, encouraged by the subculture to think that they are obliged as homosexuals to adopt certain ways and views and tastes, themselves speak of the "gay lifestyle." I've remarked that many heterosexuals think of homosexuality in terms of "practice" or "activity"; but this is at least partly because subculture-oriented gays center their lives on their sexual orientation and because a generation of gay activists have made the right to engage with abandon in certain kinds of sexual activity their principal cause. One day in December 1992, I walked past Saint Patrick's Cathedral in New York during an ACT UP protest presumably connected to the Roman Catholic Church's opposition to pro-tolerance curricula in the public schools. "Teach gay sex!" the signs read—as if

fostering young people's tolerance of homosexuality, or informing them of the existence of gay parents, necessarily involved teaching about bedroom matters. Nothing could be more emblematic of the subculture's view of homosexuality than this reduction of gay identity, gay life, and gay culture to gay sex. I've said that being gay isn't a matter of what one does, in bed or anywhere else, but of what one *is;* too often, alas, the gay subculture acts as if what one does in bed is the *quintessence* of what one is.

BAREBACK SEX, BUG CHASERS, AND THE GIFT OF DEATH

DEANN K. GAUTHIER
CRAIG J. FORSYTH

REVIEW OF THE LITERATURE

Unprotected sex has occurred throughout the AIDS epidemic, as evidenced by the thousands of new infections that occur each year. Since the mid-1980s, AIDS educators have focused primarily on gay men in their campaign to reduce the frequency of barebacking as a route of transmission for the deadly virus that causes AIDS. This strategy seemed to effect real behavioral changes, leading to a marked decline in the proportion of new AIDS cases due solely to male homosexual transmission (Siegel et al. 1989). On the other hand, there continued to be simultaneous evidence that subgroups within the male homosexual community were not effecting behavioral changes (Ames et al. 1995). Whether such activity is actually increasing in frequency, or whether discourse about such activity is only increasing, recent media attention to the subject has been alarmist in tone (McCoy 1997; Peyser 1997; Rotello 1997; Signorile 1997b). In this exploratory study, we argue that the panicked controversy surrounding the recent discussions of bareback sex is a reflection of a larger cultural division over the complex meanings of sexual behavior in the formation and maintenance of personal identities.

Barebacking is considered to be a form of sexual deviance only in certain contexts. If the partners are married heterosexuals, little to no social disapproval occurs. Should the partners be unmarried but romantically involved heterosexuals, social censure increases, but is still relatively mild in the United States of the 1990s. When the behavioral exchange occurs between unmarried heterosexual partners who are not romantically involved, the social censure increases further. But when barebacking involves homosexual male partners, it receives serious social censure, particularly since the identification of this route of transmission for the virus that causes AIDS. What is considered serious deviance, then, often depends on the context in which a behavior occurs more than on the actual content of the acts that comprise that behavior. As West (1987:75) noted, "Many deviant behaviors are merely exaggerated versions of familiar components of ordinary sexuality."

Research has identified three categories of sexual deviance: normal, pathological, and sociological (Forsyth 1996; Gagnon and Simon 1967; Little 1983, 1995). Normal sexual deviance occurs often, and among a large number of participants, thus making it statistically "normal," despite its designation as deviance. This includes such activities as oral sex and masturbation. Although many individuals consider oral sex to be deviant, a majority of adults have engaged in the act (Benokraitis 1996).

The second category of sexual deviance is labeled pathological. Generally, these behaviors are considered to be harmful and are against the law, and few individuals participate. Examples include sexual contact with children, incest, exhibitionism, some forms of voyeurism, and rape (Forsyth 1996; Gagnon and Simon 1967; Little 1983, 1995). This category is similar to the first in one respect: The deviant behaviors exist without the evolution of supportive group structures to maintain participants in the activity.

The third type of sexual deviance is sociological. It consists of precisely those sorts of behavior that generate distinctive forms of social structures that serve to recruit participants, train them, gather people together to perform the act, and/or provide social support for the actor. Examples are pornography, homosexuality, prostitution, swinging, and nudism in nudist camps. Although some individuals develop a homosexual identity without having had contact with other homosexual individuals, most homosexual men engage in, and in many ways depend on, contact with other homosexual men (Forsyth 1996; Gagnon and Simon 1967; Little 1983, 1995). "The social structures engendered by this category of deviance are implicit when one speaks of the homosexual community with its bars, steam baths, publications, organizations, and argot" (Little 1983:29). Such social structures also make use of emerging technology. With regard to sexual deviance, the application of new technology can be seen (among others) in the use of telephones for the phone sex industry, CB radios for the prostitution industry, telescopes for voyeurism, and home video players for the pornographic movie industry (Durkin and Bryant 1995; Forsyth 1996; Luxenburg and Klein 1984). Most recently, the personal computer and the Internet have provided a linking mechanism for individuals interested in identifying like-minded partners for sexual experimentation. Such may be the case with the particular form of barebacking known as bug chasing. Many forms of deviance do not spread (Douglas, Rasmussen, and Flanagan 1977), but those that do, do so because there is a sociological structure to generate or maintain them (Toolan, Ellans, and D'Encarnacao 1974; Weinberg 1981a, 1981b; Forsyth and Fournet 1987; Forsyth and Benoit 1989). Thus,

> On any given night one can log on to the Internet and find lively discussions going on in chat rooms called Bareback M4M or I Like It Raw. . . . A sizeable portion of the poz population (as well as a segment of the negative population) is openly forgoing the use of generally accepted safe-sex practices when engaging in intimate contact with each other. (Bergling 1997:71)

METHOD

Web sites, chat rooms, mailing lists, and personal ads devoted to the subject of barebacking have become part of the Internet landscape in the past few years. The primary data for this project were obtained chiefly from these Internet sources, ultimately constituting an availability sample of men who bareback and others who have information regarding the practice. Secondary data include the scant existing literature on barebacking, especially as expressed in the form of bug chasing, in the popular and academic presses.

FINDINGS

The population of gay male barebackers includes an unknown number of participants, with multiple different key characteristics and motivations. Though many social observers might dismiss some categories of participants as unimportant, each category is intricately related to the others, and therefore should not be dismissed from discussion. For example, bareback sex that occurs between two men who are both HIV positive is (to some) a nonissue. Yet these men comprise part of a community of men who serve as models to one another of acceptable standards of behavior. Their perceptions and definitions of pleasure do not occur in a vacuum and may influence others in their community. In addition, there are real dangers to the HIV-positive partners themselves who are exchanging bareback sex. Specifically, the activity provides routes of transmission for other sexually transmitted diseases, which can burden the immune system, increase viral replication, and hasten death. Finally, there is the danger that unprotected encounters with a different, more virulent strain of HIV could result in coinfection or recombination. Such a scenario has received tentative scientific support (D'Adesky 1997; Robertson et al. 1995; Schoofs 1997) and implies that some individuals currently responding to drug treatment regimens may cease to do so if the recombinant virus is resistant to that particular treatment.

Despite the dangers to self and others, many of these HIV-positive men consider bareback sex with other HIV-positive men to be completely acceptable, as the following statement reveals:

> It's like being thrown into jail for life and then, while serving your time, having the warden threaten to extend your sentence. The threat has no power because nothing can make a life sentence any worse. You can laugh at the threat, even spit in the warden's face. That time I got fucked by another positive guy, I felt I didn't have to fear HIV any longer. I could taunt it, challenge it by taking it into my body without being further hurt. (Gendin 1997:64)

The following statement, from a website dedicated to barebacking, lends further support for this practice:

> For years now, poz men have had to bear a double burden—the burden of the virus itself and the burden of preventing the spread of the disease. Correctly, I believe, many of us have come to the conclusion that within ourselves there is little need to practice this self imposed sexual martyrdom. . . . For us, it's too late. So why shouldn't we party? ("Responses to the Dallas Voice Article" 1997:5)

Another contributor to the same website defended the practice as follows:

> After all, "safer sex" is not hot sex; it's pretend sex. The need for the intimacy of actual skin to skin contact is primal. Condoms are not just a question of sensitivity, they are a barrier to physical, emotional and spiritual communion. ("Responses to the Dallas Voice Article" 1997:6)

Thus, this category of barebackers feels justified in continuing the behavior. Some have acknowledged the risks to self and others but still eschew safe-sex techniques. This can have important consequences for others in the gay community. As one individual noted, "if the larger negative population learned that they could have all the real sex they want, if they are willing to tolerate the risks of being positive," rising infection rates could become problematic ("Responses to the Dallas Voice Article" 1997:6).

Such views are no longer automatically considered as cavalier in the eyes of onlookers, owing to the development of new drug treatment regimens that seem able to check the progression of HIV infections (Rotello 1997; Signorile 1997b). With these medical advances, there appears to be a portion of the gay community that is willing to risk infection to regain the sense of closeness that was lost as a result of safer sex practices. The assumption is that treatment now exists that can make the disease "manageable" over the course of a lifetime rather than an automatic death sentence. As one HIV-negative individual argued, "It's a very manageable disease with the meds today. I'd probably not die from it" (Signorile 1997a:86).

Furthermore, the influence of HIV-positive individuals on HIV-negative individuals should not be underestimated, when considered in context. Though for many years HIV-negative people (both homosexual and heterosexual) have stigmatized HIV-positive people as persons to be avoided (Sandstrom 1994), there is some evidence to support the notion that those who are HIV positive are revered, almost as fighters in a holy war. "if someone has AIDS or HIV, that kind of lionizes them. It's heroic, like fighting the battle. . . . When you get with someone who has HIV, it's like being with someone greater than you are" (Peyser 1997:77). Gay individuals who join the HIV-positive ranks sometimes feel they are entering a selective club, receiving a benefits package that, importantly, includes community sympathy (McCoy 1997). This can be a powerful draw to an already disenfranchised segment of the population. Thus, as only one category of bareback sex, HIV-positive couplings may serve not only as a model for the management of desires but also as a symbol of the rewards that may accrue to those members of our society who possess fatal injuries.

Other categories of barebackers coexist with this first. One category is composed of men of uncertain HIV status who refuse, for a variety of personal reasons, to use safer sex techniques. One often-cited reason is offered in the following statement:

> I would even say that the risks are commensurate with the rewards: [Bareback sex] indicates a level of trust, of cohesion, that I don't think is achiev-

able when both partners are primarily concerned with preventing the exchange of bodily fluids. (O'Hara 1997:9)

In other words, many of these barebackers are convinced that latex simply ruins the intimacy. Some of these individuals have never been tested for HIV, whereas others do so irregularly. HIV status is not a major concern, in themselves or the partners they choose. In fact, some of these barebackers insist on not knowing, acting on the old adage "What I don't know can't hurt me." Since the acknowledgment of the AIDS epidemic, this is the category of individuals who have been most stigmatized (even by the gay community) as pariahs. They were seen to be flirting with suicide, even homicide, in their refusal to incorporate safe-sex techniques into their behavioral schemes. In terms of risk of seroconversion, one might label them passive–aggressive. This group continues to exist today, no less dangerous to themselves or others than they were at the beginning of the epidemic. But they have now been publicly joined by a group of barebackers who do not passively seek HIV infection but, rather, actively "chase" the "bug."

It is possible, even probable, that bug chasers have existed since the beginning of the AIDS epidemic, but that their numbers were extremely small. As the epidemic has progressed, claiming more victims, it is likely that bug chasing increased in frequency owing to a variety of reasons, some of which are articulated below. More important, however, than the speculated increase in frequency of participation in this activity is the certain increase in frequency of public discourse about participation in this activity. In large part, this has occurred because of the evolution and increasing ubiquitousness of computers and the Internet in people's everyday lives. As a means of communication with others of similar interests whom we would otherwise rarely identify, there is no better source. Consequently, bug chasers, in their quest to ascertain interested partners, have simultaneously made very public an activity that heretofore has been virtually unknown by the public at large.

Bug chasing as a form of bareback sex actually involves two categories of participants (though encounters may involve more than two individuals in each of these two categories). There are, of course, the HIV-negative men who seek to become infected with the virus (bug chasers), and there are the HIV-positive men who seek to share the "gift" of HIV (gift givers; Signorile 1997a). Chasers typically advertise for partners with statements such as the following: "Will let you fuck me raw only if you promise to give me all your diseases like AIDS/herpes, etc. Let's do it" (Sheon and Plant 1998:10). Gift givers, on the other hand, typically make comments such as these:

> *Traveling POZ delivery service who prefers other poz guys, but will do it with consenting and sober neg dudes who want to enlist in our ranks. . . . [I plan] to make de-poz-its in eleven cities in four countries between now and October and [am] looking for sex partners at every stop (McCoy 1997:2).*
>
> *Attention neg men! Why stay locked in a boring world of sterile sex when you can join the ranks of the AIDS Freedom Fighters? Let me give you my gift and set you free (Jackson 1997:2).*

Becoming "bug brothers" may occur one-on-one but is just as likely to result at special marathon group sex parties that are held for the purpose of seroconverting as many HIV-negative participants as possible. That individuals would knowingly participate in such events is shocking not only to some members of the gay community but also to the public at large. Especially for this newly informed segment of the population, the practice of bug chasing may seem incoherent, until considered in sociological context.

EXPLANATIONS FOR BUG CHASING

The following explanations are focused particularly on active bug chasers, though many would also apply to the more passive–aggressive barebackers discussed earlier. Four lines of explanation have emerged from the literature and Internet data sources. Although analytically these arguments seem easy to separate, practically they are intricately connected.

Fear and Relief

For some bug chasers, the problem has been that fear of infection inhibited their behavior in the past to such an extent that their perceived quality of life had diminished to unacceptably low levels. "I think about AIDS and the possibility of contracting HIV but that fear is not nearly as strong as the fear of not being with the man I love" (Ames, Atchinson, and Rose 1995:70). These individuals wish for the "relief" of knowing that they are infected. For them, infection is often viewed as "the great inevitable," and thus they wish to merely quicken the inevitable so that they can get on with the business of living out their lives in a more uninhibited fashion, however short that life might be. Some of these individuals, like the HIV-positive men discussed above, believe that HIV is now medically manageable. Consequently, inducing a manageable infection is perceived to be the best route to an increased quality of life.

> In a way it's a relief. I don't have to wonder anymore. That awful waiting is gone. So now, if I do find someone, the relationship can be 100 percent real with nothing in the way. That's what I want: 100 percent natural, wholesome and real. Maybe now that I'm HIV positive, I can finally have my life. (Green 1996:38ff)

Risk Taking as Eroticism

For many individuals, regardless of sexual orientation, the most captivating quality of the sex act is its irrationality. Safe sex, many bug chasers feel, negates that possibility (Gendin 1997). This category of bug chasers defines their behavior as part of an erotic experience filled with excitement and danger. "The thrill of going bareback makes the sex hotter" (Signorile 1997a:2). These individuals perceive heightened sexual satisfaction derived from high-risk sexual encounters wherein they "flirt with death." "Some appear to find a particular sexual charge in the fact that the semen they're receiving is infected" (McCoy 1997:2). Other forms of such high-risk activity include autoerotic asphyxiation and sadomasochistic bondage/torture activities, and even dangerous sporting events

(such as skydiving and bungee jumping) have been linked to "sexual charges" (Lowery and Wetli 1982; McCoy 1997; Myers 1994). Breaking the rules, for some, is simply very exciting.

> Hard as it may be to understand, some gay men have unsafe sex because they want to . . . skate close to the edge. Danger can be erotic, even the threat of contracting a deadly disease (Peyser 1997:77).

Loneliness and Group Solidarity

For other bug chasers, the problem is loneliness. Many HIV-negative gay men feel that they have been left behind as lovers and friends have moved on to a status they do not share. The loss of solidarity and sense of community is overwhelming, particularly for individuals ensconced in a nation already divided along heterosexual–homosexual lines. Now, there is a further split within the homosexual community between those who are HIV positive and those who are HIV negative. The HIV-negative individuals sometimes feel such isolation as a result that they wish to become members of their community again, regardless of the cost. They are willing to commit what is, in essence, suicide in order to maintain their membership in the group. "A lot of gay men feel out of place, put down, worthless. If you're HIV-positive, everybody is generous. There is a sense of community" (Peyser 1997:77). An important component in the makeup of that community is the new emphasis on AIDS as a form of empowerment. "Like the pink triangle that was once used by the Nazis to brand homosexuals and is now a sign of gay pride, gays have sought to transform HIV from a death knell to an empowerment tool" (Peyser 1997:77). The campaign to change the perception of HIV has not occurred to the exclusion of HIV-negative members of the gay community. In discussions focused on stigma-management techniques, invariably there are those present who are not infected with the virus. The messages to which they are exposed resonate a persuasive theme: embracing an AIDS identity can be empowering for HIV-positive individuals (Sandstrom 1994; Tewksbury and McGaughey 1997). For example, in one sample of respondents,

"There is consensus that HIV can bring meaning to life—meaning that would most likely not be experienced by a non-infected individual" (Tewksbury and McGaughey 1997:68). Other HIV-positive individuals have noted that having the virus becomes a transforming experience:

> I now view AIDS as both a gift and a blessing. . . . You go through this amazing kind of transformation. You look at things for the first time, in a powerful new way that you've never looked at them before in your whole life. (Sandstrom 1994:334)

AIDS, then, has become a master status not only in the larger society but in the gay community as well. But within this prominent subculture, the meaning of the status is very different. It is becoming destigmatized, resulting in a change in identity from deviant to charismatic (Warren 1980). Some bug chasers, feeling excluded from full participation in their community, simply wish to be empowered in the same manner as that of their peers in order to obtain the "privileges of membership" (Gendin 1997).

Political Actions

Still other bug chasers behave in this way because they see the behavior as a politically charged action in response to the larger, homophobic culture that has stigmatized gay individuals as a whole and especially HIV-positive gay individuals as outcasts. As one barebacker put it, "Anal sex is my right and damned if I'll do without it!" (Ames et al. 1995:64). The discrimination and moral disdain to which gay men are subjected are viewed by some bug chasers as forces that literally push them to respond in such a politically charged way. To illustrate this line of reasoning, we rely on Lemert's (1951) theory of secondary deviance, where stigmatized individuals come to accept as part of their self-image the public designation of the pejorative label. On acceptance, individuals then go on to fulfill the negative prophecy, strengthening the original stigma against them. Some homosexual men, stigmatized as deviant and disenfranchised from the larger society, may become secondary deviants

through the act of sero-conversion. "A few men believed that [unprotected] anal sex was a 'required' part of truly gay sex and an essential part of coming out. For some of these men, continuing to engage was a political act" (Ames et al. 1995:64).

CONCLUSIONS

This research has examined one form of sociologically unknown sexual deviance: barebackers engaged in bug chasing. This form of deviance has generated much public controversy in recent months, reflecting the larger cultural division in the United States over the complex meanings of sexual behavior. As a form of sexual deviance, bug chasing represents a sociological construct in that it has evolved distinct forms of social structures that help to sustain involvement. Most notably is the Internet forum that has developed to facilitate these behavioral exchanges. Both Forsyth (1996) and Durkin and Bryant (1995) have argued that safe-sex concerns would lead to more virtual sex through the recent advances in computer technology. Our research suggests, however, that sometimes advances in technology may lead to unsafe sex. Thus, computer access to the Internet may encourage discussions of virtual sex (whether these discussions concern voyeurism, pedophilia, or bug chasing), which may in turn lead to dangerous, exploitive, or even unsafe real sex.

We have identified in this research several key reasons why some gay men may engage in unsafe sex, even to the point of seeking infection with a deadly virus. Together, these explanations may be considered as differing expressions of the identity construction and stigma management processes (Coffman 1963). In response to the stigmatization for being either homosexual (by the larger heterosexual community) or HIV-negative (by the HIV-positive community), bug chasers may seek to manage their stigma through any of the varied routes described in this research. In moving from their original role designation of primary deviants to the newly acquired secondary deviant status, many bug chasers seem to have become involved in role engulfment (Schur 1971), where both self-concept and behavior focus largely on the deviant role of homosexual, HIV-negative man. In some sense, these individuals could be described as politicizing the stigma attributed to them through this master status in their bug-chasing response (Schur 1980; Dotter and Roebuck 1988). In terms of individual self-conception, to the extent that the person is able to convert the stigma from that of a personal failing to that of a political issue, a transformation occurs. "The politicized 'deviant' gains a new identity, an heroic self-image as crusader in a political cause" (Humphreys 1972:142). Consequently, the bug chasers gain in self-respect, sense of purpose, heightened group solidarity, and improved perception in quality of life (Schur 1971:323). Both personally and socially, politicizing behaviors such as these can garner considerable rewards.

Because of the exploratory nature of this study, many questions remain unanswered. In particular, the characteristics of the bug-chasing population are unknown. The anonymity provided by the Internet makes identification of these individuals for interviews particularly difficult, and consequently, demographic characteristics can only be surmised from user profiles, which are not always available. Furthermore, because of the potential use of these profiles, many users may have changed important descriptors about themselves in order to remain truly anonymous. Nor are we able to address issues of physical attractiveness among the bug-chasing population. For example, Ames et al. (1995:66) wrote of the possibility that overweight or less attractive individuals may be more willing to risk unsafe sex owing to desperation and a lack of interested partners. To say that this is the case among bug chasers, at this point, would be merely speculative. Future research might seek to address these neglected subjects.

Finally, though we have not yet located any direct comments by bug chasers to this effect, it is possible that guilt motivates some of their behaviors. Many in the gay community speak of "survivor's guilt," but bug chasers may be more willing than others to act in response to that guilt. As Clinard and Meier (1998:457) noted in their discussion of altruistic suicides, the most common form of this type of suicide is that which "represents an attempt to achieve expiation for violation of society's mores" as atonement for perceived wrongs. For some gay men who suffer guilt for remaining HIV negative when all around them their community has been decimated by the fatal virus, the wrong that has been committed is survival. Atonement, for these individuals, may seem to require chasing "the bug."

REFERENCES

Ames, Lynda J., Alana B. Atchinson and D. Thomas Rose. 1995. "Love, Lust, and Fear: Safer Sex Decision Making among Gay Men." *Journal of Homosexuality* 30:53–73.

Benokraitis, Nijole V. 1996. *Marriages and Families.* Upper Saddle River, NJ: Prentice-Hall.

Bergling, Tim. 1997. "Riders on the Storm." *Genre 53* (October):71–2.

Clinard, Marshall B. and Robert F. Meier. 1998. *Sociology of Deviant Behavior.* New York: Harcourt Brace College Publishers.

D'Adesky, Anne-Christine. 1997. "Double Jeopardy." *Out* (October):128–30.

Dotter, Daniel L. and Julian B. Roebuck. 1988. "The Labeling Approach Re-Examined: Interactionism and the Components of Deviance." *Deviant Behavior* 9:19–32.

Douglas, Jack D., Paul K. Rasmussen and Carol A. Flanagan. 1977. *The Nude Beach.* Beverly Hills, CA: Sage.

Durkin, Keith F. and Clifton D. Bryant. 1995. "Log on to Sex: Some Notes on the Carnal Computer and Erotic Cyberspace as an Emerging Research Frontier." *Deviant Behavior* 16:179–200.

Forsyth, Craig J. 1996. "The Structuring of Vicarious Sex." *Deviant Behavior* 17:279–95.

Forsyth, Craig and Genevieve M. Benoit. 1989. "Rare, Ole, Dirty Snacks: Some Research Notes on Dirt Eating." *Deviant Behavior* 10:61–8.

Forsyth, Craig J. and Lee Fournet. 1987. "A Typology of Office Harlots: Party Girls, Mistresses and Career Climbers." *Deviant Behavior* 8:319–28.

Gagnon, John H. and William Simon, eds. 1967. *Sexual Deviance.* New York: Harper and Row.

Gendin, Stephen. 1997. "Riding Bareback." *POZ Magazine* (June):64–5.

Goffman, Erving. 1963. *Stigma: Notes on the Management of Spoiled Identity.* Englewood Cliffs, NJ: Prentice-Hall.

Green, Jesse. 1996. "Flirting with Suicide." *New York Times Sunday Magazine,* September 15, pp. 38ff.

Humphreys, Laud. 1972. *Out of the Closets.* Englewood Cliffs, NJ: Prentice-Hall.

Jackson, Joab. 1997. "Raw as They Wanna Be." http://rampages.onramp.net/~tmikc/xtremesex/brothers_f.html.

Lemert, Edwin. 1951. *Social Pathology: A Systematic Approach to the Theory of Sociopathic Behavior.* New York: McGraw Hill.

Little, Craig B. 1983. *Understanding Deviance and Control: Theory, Research, and Social Policy,* 1st edition. Itasca, IL: F. E. Peacock.

Little, Craig B. 1995. *Deviance and Control: Theory, Research, and Social Policy,* 3rd edition. Itasca, IL: F. E. Peacock.

Lowery, Shearon A. and Charles V. Wetli. 1982. "Sexual Asphyxia: A Neglected Area of Study." *Deviant Behavior* 3:19–39.

Luxenburg, Joan and Lloyd Klein. 1984. "CB Radio Prostitution: Technology and the Displacement of Deviance." *Journal of Offender Counseling Services and Rehabilitation* 9:71–87.

McCoy, John. 1997. " 'Xtreme' Sex: A Return to Anything Goes, or Merely Better Communication about HIV?" http://www5.onramp.net/~tmike/xtremesex/dallasvoice-article.html.

Myers, James. 1994. "Nonmainstream Body Modification: Genital Piercing, Branding, Burning, and Cutting." Pp. 516–31 in *Constructions of Deviance,* edited by Patricia A. Adler and Peter Adler. Belmont, CA: Wadsworth Publishing Company.

O'Hara, Scott. 1997. "Safety First?" *The Advocate* (July 8):9.

Peyser, Marc. 1997. "A Deadly Dance." *Newsweek* (September 29):76–77.

"Responses to the Dallas Voice Article." 1997. http://rampages.onramp.net/~tmike/xtremesex/brothers_fhtml.

Robertson, David L., Paul M. Sharp, Francine E. McCutchan and Beatrice H. Hahn. 1995. "Recombination in HIV-1." *Nature* 374:124–26.

Rotello, Gabriel. 1997. *Sexual Ecology: AIDS and the Destiny of Gay Men.* New York: Dutton.

Sandstrom, Kent L. 1994. "Confronting Deadly Disease: The Drama of Identity Construction among Gay Men With AIDS." Pp. 323–337 in *Constructions of Deviance,* edited by Patricia A. Adler and Peter Adler. Belmont, CA: Wadsworth Publishing Company.

Schoofs, Mark. 1997. "Who's Afraid of Reinfection?" *Poz Magazine* (May):61–3, 78.

Schur, Edwin M. 1971. *Labeling Deviant Behavior: Its Sociological Implications.* New York: Harper and Row.

Schur, Edwin M. 1980. *The Politics of Deviance: Stigma Contests and the Uses of Power.* Englewood Cliffs, NJ: Prentice-Hall.

Sheon, Nicolas and Aaron Plant. 1998, "Protease Dis-Inhibitors? The Gay Bareback Phenomenon." http://www.managingdesire.org/sexpanic/Protease-DisInhibitors.html.

Siegel, Karolynn, Frances Mesagno, Jin-Yi Chen and Grace Christ. 1989. "Factors Distinguishing Homosexual Males Practicing Risky and Safer Sex." *Social Science Medicine* 28:561–69.

Signorile, Michelangelo. 1997a. "In the Company of Men." *Out* (October):86–9, 146–9.

Signorile, Michelangelo. 1997b. *Life Outside: The Signorile Report on Gay Men.* New York: Harper-Collins.

Tewksbury, Richard and Deanna McGaughey. 1997. "Stigmatization of Persons with HIV Disease: Perceptions, Management, and Consequences of AIDS." *Sociological Spectrum* 17:49–70.

Toolan, James M., Murray Elkins and Paul D'Encarnacao. 1974. "The Significance of Streaking." *Medical Aspects of Human Sexuality* 8:152–65.

Warren, C. A. B. 1980. "Destigmatization of Identity: From Deviant to Charismatic." *Qualitative Sociology* 3:59–72.

Weinberg, Martin S. 1981a. "Becoming a Nudist." Pp. 291–304 in *Deviance: An Interactionist Perspective,* edited by Earl Rubington and Martin S. Weinberg. New York: Macmillan.

Weinberg, Martin S. 1981b. "The Nudist Management of Respectability." Pp. 336–345 in *Deviance: An Interactionist Perspective,* edited by Earl Rubington and Martin S. Weinberg. New York: Macmillan.

West, D. J. 1987. *Sexual Crimes and Confrontations: A Study of Victims and Offenders.* Aldershot, England: Gower Publishing Company.

THE SOCIAL ORGANIZATION
OF MALE PROSTITUTION

ROBERT P. MCNAMARA

Historically, male prostitution has taken many forms, including "escort boys," who worked in brothels, and even "kept boys," who served more as companions to clients than as prostitutes (see, for example, Weisberg, 1985). Although research on the subject of male prostitutes is still relatively sparse, there have been a few attempts to examine this population. For instance, the now-classic study by Reiss (1961) found that most of the "boys" view prostitution as a job or simply a means of making money. He also found that many boys limit the scope of their activities, which allows them to retain a sense of identity and control over their lives. Other studies have attempted to identify common characteristics and to describe the various motivations for becoming involved in prostitution (see, for example, Weisberg, 1985; Luckenbill, 1986; West, 1991). Most of the recent research has focused on the risks of AIDS and on the runaway population (see, for example, Ross, 1988; Elifson, Boles, and Sweat, 1993).

However, little is known about the ways in which male prostitutes develop a sense of cohesion as they share similar experiences. Such knowledge can be gained from analyzing my two-year ethnographic study of hustling (male prostitution) in New York City's Times Square, where I had numerous interviews and conversations with the hustlers.

THE MARKETPLACE

Times Square possesses certain characteristics and institutions that facilitate prostitution. The peep shows, porno shops, hotels, bars, and the Port Authority Bus Terminal not only offer a centralized locale for the sex market, but they also provide places for hustlers and clients to meet and carry out their transactions. Additionally, the influx of people who use the terminal and peep shows produces a steady supply of patrons to the market.

Virtually all these organizations are profit making, and the economic benefits they derive from hustling foster their acceptance. This is especially true of the hotels and peep shows, which have strong economic links to the sex trade. Consequently, the nature of hustling is predicated on the existence of these types of organizations as well as the manner in which they allow this type of activity to occur.

Moreover, the Port Authority Bus Terminal provides the market with a diurnal quality. In many ways, hustling is dependent on the work schedule of commuters, and its frequency coincides with rush hours: hustlers are very busy early in the morning, as people make their way to work, and in the early evening, as they return home. There are also a number of older men who reside in the Times Square area who are either retired or living on public assistance. They, too, regularly solicit hustlers and know that the terminal serves as a central meeting place.

Another feature of the hustling market involves the activity's occupational structure. Because the vast majority of hustlers have few, if any, other means of economic support, hustling in Times Square is viewed as an income-producing activity. For most, it is a full-time job. Although some are receiving public assistance, which would normally reduce participation in the trade, these hustlers usually have wives and children to support. Thus, the need to earn a living from hustling remains important.

In this way, hustling can be seen as an occupation for almost all the participants. Another illustration of this occupational role is demonstrated by the fact that most of the hustlers do not reside in the market area. In fact, many live outside Manhattan and, like so many other workers, must commute to Times Square every day. Additionally, part of the market is organized for the hustlers themselves. For instance, there are certain bars or parks where hustlers meet to socialize only with friends and colleagues. As members of the same occupation, they have developed social norms that regulate the trade, their behavior, and various types of social control, which are understood and practiced by everyone involved.

THE HUSTLING LIFE

A typical day for a hustler begins early, often as early as 7 A.M., and ends as late as 2 A.M. or 3 A.M. the next morning. The weekend schedule is different, beginning and ending later and sometimes involving overnight stays with clients. The excitement of the weekend contrasts with the idleness of the remaining days of the week.

The Port Authority Bus Terminal is a special place for many hustlers. Much of the hustling in Times Square occurs either in the terminal or in the peep shows. Both offer anonymity for the client because of the great deal of human traffic through them. The exodus of commuters from the city, for example, especially at rush hour, offers clients the opportunities to lose themselves in the throng of people making their way home and to carry out transactions with hustlers without attracting much attention.

One particular area in the terminal is known among hustlers and clients as the "Meat Rack." This is an area near some of the departure gates

where the majority of hustling takes place. When two parties reach an agreement, they go to a variety of places: the peep shows, a local hotel, the client's apartment or car, or one of the restrooms inside the terminal. However, the latter are now considered less of a sanctuary for hustlers as a result of an aggressive police presence, which includes undercover operations. These areas are now used sparingly or for limited activities.

Hustling activities are marked by their diversity. They may include voyeurism, posing nude, masturbating clients, sadomasochism, and oral and anal sex. Here is an example as told by a hustler:

> A lotta the hustling that goes on here ain't all that bad. I mean you go with a guy, maybe he's a member of the nickel and dime club. Those are the guys who pay you five or ten dollars and they blow you or jerk you off. We call them the nickel and dime club cause they be a lot of lonely old gay guys who are on welfare that come here and pick up guys. It takes maybe ten minutes. Sometimes they get off just watchin' you take off your clothes. Or they suck on your knob for a little bit and then they go.

The frequency with which the boys hustle also varies considerably. Some hustle every day, turning as many tricks as possible, whereas others are satisfied with one or two per day. The deciding factor, obviously, is how much money the boy needs to make. Those with drug habits, especially those addicted to crack, need to hustle as much as possible. Family men need a steady income, but because their income is supplemented by public relief, they usually hustle less frequently than other hustlers. As Lite, a hustler, said, "I hustle at least once a day. The most people I picked up in a day? Seven. I usually pick up like three or four. And if I get like thirty dollars each time, then I chill for the rest of the day. Maybe I don't come back here for two or three days." Obviously, the amount per trick varies according to what the client requires, but the amount can also be determined by the talents of individual hustlers. Some hustlers, such as Apache, are better negotiators and often convince clients to pay more than the usual fee.

Although the terminal is popular, the other primary locations for hustling are the peep shows.

In the basement of many of these shops there are sections that cater to homosexual clients. Virtually every shop has a sign prohibiting hustling, prostitution, drug dealing, and the entry of minors, but one can easily find young men of questionable age standing in the shops' long hallways.

The typical transaction in a peep show involves the hustler entering the peep show first and meeting the client near the booths. The client has already given the boy a few quarters, which gives him a legitimate reason for being there: to watch the movies. This is known as "going for the coins." Each party enters the booth separately, and the "coins" or quarters are then put in the video machine while the sexual act takes place. The managers and clerks of these shops are adamant about not allowing hustlers in their stores, but the boys simply bribe the clerks and the security officers. As long as hustlers are discreet and do not cause trouble, the employees are willing to ignore the illicit activity.

Thus, the peep shows have been, and continue to be, an integral part of a hustler's life. They offer a relatively safe working environment as well as a steady source of income. An added allure of the peep shows is that the shops also sell homosexual porno tapes. According to Apache, a number of boys have participated in the filming of these movies, and it is not uncommon to see posters of them on the walls of the shops advertising their movies.

THE NORMS OF HUSTLING

From the various types of activities to the movie-making ventures, a pattern to hustling exists to which all the participants respond. There are agreed-upon locations, a familiar dialogue, and a roughly established pricing policy for the various activities. This pattern fosters stability in hustling. For the most part, very few problems occur between the hustlers and the clients or among the boys themselves. In the vast majority of cases, the activities are completed without incident.

These patterns of behavior can be seen as a normative system that regulates the boys' behavior. One extremely important norm is that once a hustler and a client begin a conversation, another hustler should never intervene. This serves as a territorial marker that is not to be disregarded. Violation of this norm can lead to severe and violent retaliation. As Flacco explains:

You see that's one thing among hustlers. You don't go and ask nobody—even if you are asking the hustler for money—you don't do it in front of the trick. You don't do that. You don't do that. This one kid caught a serious beat down from me around the corner for that. I had this one trick he was gonna give me $75 just for hangin' out with him, and man, he was about to step off and get into the van to go to New Jersey. This hustler walks up and asks the guy for fuckin' ten dollars, man. In front of me! And I looked at him and said 'Yo you should have never done that.' And the trick got all roust and this and that and he said to me, 'Look I'm sorry, I just don't like people asking me for money.' And he stomped away all pissed off. I turned around and said 'Listen, first of all, you need money you come and see me. But don't you EVER EVER get in front of one of my tricks.' And then I kicked the shit outta him so he would never forget that.

Another related norm involves time and etiquette. There are times when a hustler and a trick cannot complete a transaction, because of price, type of activity, or some other reason. When this occurs, another hustler may offer his services to the trick, if he waits until he is certain the initial conversation has ended. This is often referred to as being a "free agent." Playboy explains:

Yeah well, it's like this. See if Flacco is talking to this guy but they can't work it out, the guy or Flacco starts to leave. As long as he is far enough away so that everybody knows he ain't goin' with him, then he's a free agent and can negotiate whatever deal he wants with anybody else. I can go up to him now and there's no problem 'cause Flacco ain't got no claim on him see? That's what we mean by free agent. But I gotta make sure the guy ain't comin' back to Flacco before I approach him else I'm gonna get my ass kicked. I do that by waitin' until he is far enough away and then maybe I ask Flacco what's up?

Another important norm deals with preserving and enhancing one's reputation within the community. Although one's street reputation is always important in these circles (e.g., being able to handle one's self, showing courage, bravery, etc.), one's hustling reputation is quite important because it has far-reaching implications. A cardinal rule among the boys is to never allow clients to publicly humiliate or insult them in front of their peers. This leads others to believe that particular hustlers are weak (which can lead to a loss of status and a violent retaliation by the group), and it serves as a reminder to other hustlers that they, too, can be treated that way. Additionally, a humiliating incident sends a message to clients that public humiliation of the boys is acceptable behavior. Thus, if a hustler does not respond to a challenge to his reputation, it has serious ramifications for him and his social standing, and it threatens the very structure and social order of the community.

The relationships that exist among the boys also play an important role in the hustling culture. Some, such as Apache, look upon the hustling community as one big family. He says,

It's really like a family here. Everybody knows everybody else; everybody is basically friends with everybody else; and there's kind of a support group, you know. But it's like any big family of boys: You gonna have arguments and fights, and people gonna get pissed off at each other. But basically we all know what we're about, and if somebody needs something and we know them, we help them out. The New Jacks (new hustlers) are different cause we don't know what they about yet. But after you been here a while and you straight up, you added to the family.

Like brothers, hustlers usually pair off and hang out together, sharing drugs, money, or other incidentals. Moreover, a sense of loyalty and responsibility develops between each boy and his partner that causes each boy to try to protect the other. When one goes with a client to a hotel, for example, his partner will usually wait for his companion either outside the room or at the entrance to the hotel.

In some cases, however, a hustler's partner is not always available. In those instances in which a hustler has been picked up by an unknown client, there is an understanding among the members of the community that the boy will not go with him alone. There is usually someone who is hanging out or has just returned from a sexual exchange who will accompany the hustler. What is significant about this norm is that it also includes those situations in which a hustler would sacrifice his own trick to protect his comrade. Although I believe this norm emerged as a result of survival motives rather than altruism, it is an important element in the nature of the trade.

This issue of loyalty also emerges when conflict arises. When fights occur, it is expected and even demanded that a hustler's friends, and, especially, his partner, come to his defense. The issue of who's right is irrelevant; the only concern is how many friends will be fighting alongside him when fists fly. For instance, one day Angel began arguing with another male in front of the bus terminal. As is often the case, the situation escalated into a brawl in a matter of minutes. The other young man had three associates with him, whereas Angel had only one companion, Nelson. Given the high police presence in and around the area, the fight began and ended quickly, yet Nelson failed to join in and support Angel. Raul and I were walking down Eighth Avenue when we saw what was happening. Running to the scene, Raul became furious when he learned Nelson did not react.

The relationships between hustlers have far-reaching effects. Most maintain close ties with one other hustler while being a part of the larger collectivity. The trade norms include personal protection from tricks and other outside threats, and a standing rule involves sharing drugs or money. If a hustler has one or the other, he is expected to share with his friends and associates. This allows everyone to endure and pass the time. Additionally, there is an unwritten "book" about clients. Hustlers will share information on clients in terms of what is expected in payment or any particular preferences the tricks may have.

CONCLUSION

Judging from what the hustlers, clients, and others associated with the trade say, as well as my own observations of events, it seems clear that the sense of cohesion among the hustlers is quite strong. There is a sense of community felt among this population, and this degree of social organization allows the trade to operate with a type of rhythm and flow. As long as everyone understands and abides by the rules, there are few problems.

There is even a mechanism in place to socialize new hustlers to the rules of the trade.

Finally, a clearly defined mechanism of informal social control also operates within the hustler community. The threat of punishment has been a clear deterrent to those who might consider deviating from the norm. In fact, one could even argue that the hustlers of Times Square are a good example of a consensus model of society: As a group and as individuals, the hustlers believe that following the norms of the trade is in everyone's best interest.

REFERENCES

Elifson, Kurt, Jacqueline Boles, and Michael Sweat. 1993. "Risk Factors Associated with HIV Infection among Male Prostitutes." *American Journal of Public Health* 83:79–83.

Luckenbill, David. 1986. "Deviant Career Mobility: The Case of Male Prostitution." *Social Problems* 33 (4):283–96.

Reiss, Albert J., Jr. 1961. "The Social Integration of Queers and Peers." *Social Problems* 9 (2):102–20.

Ross, Michael. 1988. "Social and Behavioral Aspects of Male Homosexuals." *The Medical Clinics of North America* 70 (3):537–47.

Weisberg, Kelly D. 1985. *Children of the Night*. Boston: Lexington Books.

West, Donald J. 1991. *Male Prostitution*. New York: Harrington Park Press.

31

HOMOPHOBIA IN SCHOOLS

ANDREW S. WALTERS
DAVID M. HAYES

Research about homosexuality has flourished in the past twenty-five years. Historical and anthropological inquiry has shown that same-sex attraction and behavior have been expressed in some form throughout history. Sexual arousal and behavior between members of the same biological sex have been reported in nearly all societies and in most nonhuman species. Although recent research has hinted that sexual orientation is rooted genetically or in early prenatal development, homoerotic expression clearly is mediated by the culture and environment to which one is exposed. Regardless of etiological explanations of its origin, research gleaned from the behavioral and biological sciences has shown that homosexuality and bisexuality are neither unusual nor unnatural.

Homophobia—the individual and societal contempt for and prejudice against homosexuals—remains a divisive issue in the United States. Although progress in the last several decades has been made in the reported acceptance of homosexuality, misinformation about and prejudice against homosexuals clearly exist among most Americans.

In fact, homophobia . . . is so ingrained into the American educational and work ethics that many individuals and institutions who express antigay sentiment, impede movements toward equality for gays, and fail to confront blatant forms of homophobia may not identify themselves as biased against homosexuality (Blumenfeld, 1992; Lehne, 1992; Levy, 1971; Stewart, 1994). Thus, for these individuals and institutions, failing to recognize and support the existence and needs of gay/lesbian/bisexual persons is standard proce-

dure. Often, employment and educational settings pressure homosexuals to comply with institutionalized heterosexism by denying their sexual identity—clearly an index of homophobia (see Shilts, 1993, for a detailed chronicle of gay harassment and institutionalized homophobia in the United States military).

Antigay sentiments are prevalent (and often fostered) even at the university level—a cultural institution often accorded the highest respect for advancing social change. In their mission statements, colleges and universities routinely include a commitment to diversifying student enrollment. Recruitment and admissions data suggest colleges and universities seek students in the interest of building a diverse and multicultural campus community. Yet, these very colleges and universities have often failed to provide a safe learning and working environment for homosexual students, staff, and faculty. Over one-half of gay-identified students on a Pennsylvania campus reported fear for their physical safety (D'Augelli, 1989). Actual frequencies of threats and violence toward (perceived) homosexuals may not be reported by individuals on campus (students, staff, or faculty) because many persons suspect that administrations will be unsympathetic and unhelpful. In addition, current policies at most institutions may inadvertently implicate an individual as gay, "outing" him/her to the campus community via public record (e.g., police reports). In fact, in some cases universities have selectively enforced policies against gay students. For example, on October 9, 1995, students at the University of Cincinnati were arrested for writing chalk messages on a campus sidewalk in commemoration of National Coming Out Day. On other occasions, straight students have chalked the very same sidewalks to commemorate other events without arrest or punishment (Long, 1996). Thus, in at least some cases, suspicions among gay individuals that administrations respond differently to them than to heterosexual individuals or heterosexually identified groups are valid.

In addition to institutions of higher education, homophobia has been reported at all levels of the public school system. Although Americans seem to prefer the belief that public school systems provide all students a fair and impartial education (at least within the same school), research has shown that students' race, social class, and gender impact how they are perceived by other students, evaluated by teachers, and relegated into college preparatory or skill-training programs by school counselors (Oakes, 1985; Rist, 1973; Rosenbaum, 1976). Sexual orientation appears to be another factor that prohibits a fair and inclusive education for some students. For example, in one study, 25% of college education majors acknowledged their *inability* to treat a homosexual student fairly. Sears (1992) found that teachers, student teachers, and school counselors in South Carolina reported very high levels of homophobia. Further, few of the educators in Sears's sample intended to expand their knowledge about homosexuality or their experience with gay and lesbian students. In other words, these educators were complacent with their limited understanding of a subject about which they were uncomfortable and uneducated, and were mostly unconcerned about the professional implications of their prejudices.

Students are not alone in the current against homosexuals, however. Instructors and administrators at all levels receive implicit or explicit messages that their sexual orientation is more salient for continued or secure employment than is their competency. Because American education evolved with the primary goal of instilling religious and moral development to youth, the character of teachers as moral examples has been distinctly scrutinized. For example, within varying histori-

cal and cultural contexts, teachers have been prohibited from behavior (e.g., dancing, smoking, marriage, pregnancy) routinely accorded to other adults (Habeck, 1992). Clearly, suspicion or evidence of a teacher's homosexual "proclivities" warranted a swift dismissal from teaching responsibilities; this was, after all, a crime historically punishable by public execution.

Several recent reports suggest that the public wrath against homosexuals continues to result in termination or strong disciplinary action against faculty. In the fall of 1995, a Michigan teacher was nearly fired after acknowledging he had participated in a commitment ceremony with another man. The opinion of many community residents about this instructor's competency as a teacher and his motives for working with students changed within a matter of hours: One day he was a well-liked and adept teacher; the next day he was a prowling pedophile. Within the same month, a teacher in South Carolina was suspended and later reappointed but placed on probation for showing the film *Philadelphia* to her class. Oddly enough, the film was shown as part of a lesson on compassion and humanity. These scenarios—if they are representative of other community and school administration responses—strongly suggest that educators who happen to be homosexual or present material containing themes of homosexuality but with educational value continue to be perceived as a threat to children.

INDIVIDUAL AND CULTURAL PRESCRIPTIONS OF HOMOPHOBIA

Who are the people who report homophobia? Research has consistently found that homonegative [homophobic] individuals express authoritarianism, political conservatism, and strongly endorse traditional definitions of family and sex roles. They are less sexually permissive and more likely to report sexual guilt and erotophobia. Moreover, although they have less personal contact with lesbians and gay men, and hence a predictably confined experience with homosexuality, they believe that homosexuality is a voluntary form of deviancy, and describe homosexuals according to stereotypes.

Religiosity is often cited as a factor contributing to antigay sentiment. Initial research in this area described homonegative individuals as more likely to report strong religious affiliation and frequent attendance of religious services, but also more indifference to and derision for minorities. These studies are consistent with social psychological studies on prejudice and discrimination. For example, active church members and those avouching traditional Christian beliefs express more prejudice than those expressing less traditional beliefs (Batson, Schocnrade, & Pych, 1985; Gorsuch, 1988). . . .

Sadly, cultural prescriptions for homophobia are so endemic that homosexuals themselves are likely to internalize society's contempt of them. For example, in the sexuality courses and professional training seminars that we teach, students' (or professionals') attitudes about homosexuality/homosexuals are assessed using Hudson and Ricketts's (1988) Index of Homophobia (IHP) inventory—a scale widely used by sexuality educators and researchers. At no time has anyone in our courses or training programs reported a complete absence of homophobia (i.e., as measured by a score of zero on the IHP). Thus, all students and professionals—those who are gay, lesbian, or bisexual, and gay "allies" who believe they have overcome their learned homophobia—appear at some level to have internalized our cultural aversion to homosexuals.

HOMOPHOBIA WITHIN SCHOOLS

As social institutions reflecting the values of a dominant culture, schools and institutions of higher education symbolically deny the existence of gay students (e.g., dismissing reports of antigay violence) and resist efforts to implement systematic policies ensuring a safe learning environment for students, staff, and faculty (D'Emilio, 1990; McLaren, 1994). These responses mirror those of society. For example, three Colorado colleges were sued by a student group affiliated with

the Republican National Committee because they required student groups not to discriminate against lesbians and gay men (Long, 1996). These events occurred within the larger, cultural context of Colorado's divisive "No Special Rights" campaign. In this case, students had learned to model the prejudices they witnessed from their larger societal context.

As if rampant homophobia by fellow students were not insult enough, research indicates that few schools/universities systematically train professionals to address the needs of gay students. A number of investigators (e.g., Rofes, 1989; Savin-Williams & Rodriguez, 1993) have reported that schools frequently fail to meet the developmental and social needs of lesbian, gay male, and bisexual youth—or to intercede in the harassment directed at these students. Although some faculty and staff are themselves bisexual, gay, or lesbian, they may fear the repercussions of advocating fair treatment for gay students. Other well-meaning professionals are simply unaware of or unprepared for addressing these issues.

As a consequence, students are often negatively affected by their perception that their sexual orientation must be repudiated or, at the very least, disguised. For example, lesbian, gay, and bisexual adolescents and young adults often lack adequate sources of social support, and as a result, report difficulty in developing a positive psychosocial identity. Developing a positive identity as a gay, bisexual, or lesbian individual is critical, and research indicates that gay and lesbian teenagers report low levels of self-esteem and self-worth. In part, our culturally prescribed heterosexism hinders the formation of supportive social networks for homosexuals. Thus, an indirect effect of our heterosexual bias is the isolation of sexual minorities both from each other and from the dominant group. And, we pay a high price for our failure to support homosexual/bisexual children and students: their feelings of isolation and worthlessness lead them to commit suicide at three times the rate of their heterosexual peers (Center for Population Options, 1992; "Gay Teenagers," 1989).

Considerable controversy has accompanied institutions that both systematically deny or proactively support gay students, staff, and faculty. For example, extending domestic partner benefits has remained an explosive issue between faculty and administrations in higher education, and has resulted in lawsuits at a number of schools (e.g., Rutgers, University of Alaska, University of Vermont). We recognize the possible backlash individual schools, colleges, and universities might experience should they publicly address and support gay students, staff, and faculty. However, we believe that meeting the developmental needs of gay, bisexual, and lesbian students can begin at the individual level. In our experiences training future educators and psychologists/counselors, we have found that while college students and seasoned professionals alike report a range of comfort in addressing the subject of homosexuality (either individually with a student or within curricula), nearly everyone agrees it is an important issue to be addressed.

In order to ensure that homosexual/bisexual students are afforded equal access to education through instruction and counseling, it is necessary to train those individuals who teach, counsel, or administer policy to gay students. Most often, little professional training has been provided in the area of sexuality, and even less on the subjects of homosexuality or the developmental needs of gay students. It is our belief that appropriately training professionals who work with students can result in a more welcoming and supportive environment for gay, lesbian, and bisexual individuals. To this end, the following sections overview several strategies that we use in training college students and professionals about these very issues.

TRAINING COLLEGE STUDENTS

Within secondary schools, textbooks across disciplines exhibit a clear heterosexual bias and routinely omit significant events, themes, or contributions by gay persons (Kielwasser & Wolf, 1994). Thus, presentations of homosexuality are likely to be addressed in health (or, less commonly, sexuality) courses—if they are presented at all. The quality and competence of health/sexuality educators is of vital importance, and often those required to teach human sexuality at the middle-school and secondary level are less than fully qualified for these positions. Training future health and sexuality educators can present a number of challenges, primary among them the fact many individuals are in need of remedial education. In many cases, college students do not complete a course in human sexuality as part of their academic program of study—including those students who will be asked to instruct sexuality education in some form in their teaching positions. In the courses we teach, students cite the limited utility of those content areas typically covered in their collegiate curriculum: anatomy and physiology. Clearly, the biological basis of sexuality is an area in which instructors should demonstrate proficiency. Generally, however, students report greater interest in learning about the social and interpersonal facets of sexuality. Thus, in the absence of an accurate and thorough human sexuality course, the lenses through which professionals-in-training view sexuality as a natural and healthy component of individual development are colored mainly by their own familial, school, and religious experience. To say the least, these experiences may not include exposure to an unbiased discussion of homosexuality or cross-cultural approaches of defining normal versus deviant sexual attractions and patterns of behavior.

It can be a daunting experience for a teacher-trainer to attempt to move reluctant individuals beyond a history of discomfort with sexuality toward becoming competent teachers who are comfortable discussing sexuality. The movement is gradual and the teaching direction often prescribed to target the most stubborn of students. As reviewed above, most students are exposed to a number of cultural forces that reinforce discomfort with homosexuality. It would be highly improbable to assume training participants would revise deep-seated antigay attitudes in an hour's lecture, for example. We believe that involving students/training participants in their own learning is essential in areas such as homosexuality which, for many students, are highly threatening.

As part of students' training, we include both factual information and structured activities/small group discussions about homosexuality. A rational discussion about the factual context of sexual orientation (e.g., etiology, difficulties associated with living in an antigay society versus heterosexual privilege) is often the first time many students hear information presented about homosexuality in a professional context. For example, most education and health promotion majors enrolling in our foundations courses (designed to teach future educators strategies for teaching about sexuality) report having had no formal instruction about homosexuality. Instead, references to homosexuality are usually recalled as negative or pathological (e.g., "I was taught that homosexuals are perverts"). Thus, we structure opportunities for students to discuss their concerns and learn about the intrapersonal dynamics of homophobia. We have found that the tenor of these discussions is usually positive, although some students are quiet or skeptical.

The segment on homosexuality education begins with the question, "Should homosexuality be addressed in public (or private) schools?" In our experience, few students believe homosexuality despite the sensitivity and controversy often associated with it—should be omitted from sexuality-health curricula. Students cite a number of the critical problems facing gay youth (e.g., substance abuse, depression, sexual activity based on motives to prove one's "straight" status). In addition, as students learn more about the difficulties associated with being gay (i.e., runaway and suicide rates), they begin to recognize the disadvantages gay youth brave compared to heterosexuals. It seems clear to us, then, that at some level students are intuitively aware of some of the challenges confronting gay adolescents and young adults.

In summary, students report benefitting from the opportunity to share their attitudes about homosexuality with peers. Structured interventions are particularly helpful in providing students with a fair ratio of challenge versus support, and should be tailored to the group's developmental level.

Again, we fully recognize the improbability of eradicating students' reported homophobia within several class hours. Alternatively, during follow-up class discussions, students have reported feeling better prepared to address homophobia in schools and more importantly, to learn more about how an antigay climate affects themselves and their students.

TRAINING PROFESSIONALS

In contrast to preservice instruction, teachers, school counselors, and mental health providers . . . can share specific examples regarding both teaching about sexual orientation and what they are permitted to address in accordance with school policy. A recent study culling data from the 126 U.S. communities with legal protection against discrimination on the basis of sexual orientation and a random sample of 129 U.S. jurisdictions without such legislation examined the sexual orientation content of school district programs (Rienzo, Button, & Wald, 1996). Results from this study showed that most school districts are not implementing recommended programs to address sexual orientation. Competent instruction about sexual orientation, the existence and support of alliance groups for sexual minority students, and in-service training for counselors and teachers is either absent or inherently flawed by stereotypes and fear at most schools (Rienzo et al., 1996).

Similar to college students, many in-service teachers and counselors in our seminars profess the value of teaching about homosexuality (as well as other subjects that may garner controversy) and serving as allies for gay students. They also indicate that school policy may prohibit such discussions. These reports seem consistent with recent research suggesting sexual orientation is not discussed in health/sexuality education courses—courses students often elect *precisely because* they hope to learn how to integrate sexuality into their lives. Telljohann, Price, Poureslami, and Easton (1995) reported that less than half of their sample of high school teachers included homosexuality in course curricula. Only one in four teachers felt that they were competent to teach about homosexuality, and more than half of the sample indicated that gay/lesbian support groups would not be supported by their school administrations. What appears most disconcerting from the Telljohann et al. (1995) study is that 20% of teachers reported that abusive language was generated by students against homosexuals, and that the teachers were limited in their positions to confront these blatantly violent remarks. Data from the Telljohann et al. (1995) and Rienzo et al. (1996) studies reaffirm the message that gay/lesbian/bisexual students receive in their school tenure: You are alone and unwanted.

In the professional training seminars that we facilitate, exercises or demonstrations that actively involve participants in the learning process are used to facilitate training. Activities have been found to decrease levels of reported homophobia and increase knowledge about the multiple difficulties associated with the coming out process for adolescents and young adults (Walters & Phillips, 1994). These activities engage participants in *discussing* sexual issues. Group discussions allow participants and the facilitator(s) to learn about and empathize with the daily experiences of gay, lesbian, and bisexual individuals—events which faculty, counselors, and administrators can relate to their professional experience. In addition, discussions present opportunities for exploring both the intrapersonal and institutional dynamics of homophobia. We feel that one of the greatest benefits of these activities is that the facilitators are involved only nominally, thereby prompting meaningful discussions and allowing the participants to learn from one another.

Our experience has shown that professionals are amenable to learning how sensitive issues like homosexuality can be used in their positions. In addition, they appreciate both the opportunity to brainstorm new strategies for helping students and participating in low-risk activities that can be modified for their own instructional purposes. . . . At the individual level, educating professionals about the specific needs of lesbian, bisexual, and gay male students often results in a more open—and safe—learning environment. We also attest that many professionals welcome opportunities for how they may better serve students.

CONCLUDING REMARKS

We suggest ample evidence exists that gay, lesbian, and bisexual students are denied the educational opportunities accorded to their straight peers. Research has shown that homonegativism has metastasized to all levels of education and as a consequence, implicitly reinforces homophobia. Cultural forces (e.g., negative attitudes about homosexuality, religiously based polemics damning homosexuals, social norms against legitimizing homoerotic feelings and behavior) are reflected within the academic and social spheres experienced by gay and bisexual students. Recent reports suggest that most schools have failed to implement strategies to ensure the basic physical and psychological survival of gay students as outlined in the Report of the Secretary's Task Force on Youth Suicide (Gibson, 1989). Moreover, faculty and administrations have elected policies that favor a dismissing and inhospitable environment for gay students and colleagues. It is these individuals who choose to ignore homophobic indignities, encourage heterosexism, allow students to be victimized for their (often perceived) homosexuality, and uphold an institutional structure that sanctions the insignificance of gay students.

School and academic personnel are expected to respect racial, ethnic, and religious differences among students, and to encourage students to take pride in their own familial and cultural identity. We argue that sexual orientation is another component of individuals' lives that influences their experience as students (staff, or faculty). Faculty and administrations at all levels are responsible for interrupting violence and harassment against gay students or students taunted by homophobia, and maintaining a learning environment that is free from school-sanctioned victimization. Counselors, mental health providers, and teachers have considerable influence on students. Their demeanor and responses to homophobia can reinforce or dissuade the heterosexual bias absorbed from the dominant society.

Our goal has been to show that the emotional, social, and developmental needs of bisexual, lesbian, and gay male youth are often blighted throughout their tenure on campus. In addition, evidence suggests the working environment is less than receptive for many faculty and staff who identify themselves as gay/lesbian/bisexual, or who work toward affirming the experience of gay students and colleagues. There can be serious risks to challenging the barriers that characterize institutionalized heterosexism. Professionals who are willing to confront homophobia and support gay/bisexual people must be willing to absorb these risks.

Our experience has shown, however, that college students preparing for teaching or counseling positions, as well as seasoned professionals, are often uninformed about the developmental needs of gay students and the positive impact they can have on these individuals. We suggest that training professionals about these issues is a critical first step in ameliorating the experience of gay students and colleagues. Further, training can be introduced . . . at minimal cost, and has been shown to be particularly effective at reducing homophobia among school personnel and university faculty. We have the ability to serve as catalysts for creating an inclusive and positive educational experience for students and colleagues. We believe that it is time to accept this formidable challenge.

REFERENCES

Batson, C. D., Schoenrade, P. A., & Pych, V. (1985). Brotherly love or self-concern? Behavioural consequences of religion. In L. B. Brown (Ed.), *Advances in the psychology of religion.* Oxford: Pergamon Press.

Blumenfeld, W. J. (Ed.). (1992). *Homophobia: How we all pay the price.* Boston: Beacon Press.

Center for Population Options. (1992). *Lesbian, gay and bisexual youth: At risk and underserved.* Washington, DC: Author.

D'Augelli, A. R. (1989). Lesbians' and gay men's experiences of discrimination and harassment in a university community. *American Journal of Community Psychology,* 17, 317–321.

D'Emilio, J. (1990). The campus environment for gay and lesbian life. *Academe,* 76, 16–19.

Gay teenagers and suicide. (1999). Youth Suicide National Report (pp. 16–32).

Gibson, P. (1989). Gay and lesbian youth suicide. In M. R. Feinleib (Ed.), *Report of the secretary's task force on youth suicide: Vol. 3. Prevention and intervention in youth suicide* (ADM 89–1623). Washington, DC: U.S. Department of Health and Human Services.

Gorsuch, R. L. (1988). Psychology of religion. *Annual Review of Psychology,* 39, 201–222.

Harbeck, K. M. (1992). Gay and lesbian educators: Past history/future prospects. In K. M. Harbeck (Ed.), *Coming out of the classroom closet: Gay and lesbian students, teachers, and curricula* (pp. 121–140). Binghamton, NY: Harrington Park Press.

Hudson, W. W., & Ricketts, W. A. (1988). Index of homophobia. In C. M. Davis. W. L. Yarber, & S. L. Davis (Eds.), *Sexuality-related measures: A compendium* (pp. 155–156). Lake Mills, IA: Graphic Publishing Company.

Kielwasser, A. P., & Wolf, M. A. (1994). Silence, difference, and annihilation: Understanding the impact of mediated heterosexism on high school students. *The High School Journal,* 77, 58–79.

Lehne, G. K. (1992). Homophobia among men: Supporting and defining the male role. In M. S. Kimmel & M. A. Messner (Eds.), *Men's lives* (2nd ed.) (pp. 381–394). New York: Macmillan.

Levy, C. J. (1971). ARVN as faggots: Inverted warfare in Vietnam. *Society,* 8, 18–27.

Long, C. D. (1996). For gays and lesbians, it's win some, lose some. *Academe,* 82, 10.

McLaren, P. (1994). Moral panic, schooling, and gay identity: Critical pedagogy and the politics of resistance. *The High School Journal,* 77, 157–168.

Oakes, J. (1985). *Keeping track: How schools structure inequality.* New Haven. CT: Yale University Press.

Rienzo, B. A., Button, J., & Wald, K. O. (1996). The politics of school-based programs which address sexual orientation. *Journal of School Health,* 66, 33–40.

Rist, R. (1973). *The urban school: A factory of failure.* Cambridge, MA: MIT Press.

Rofes, E. E. (1989). Opening up the classroom closet: Responding to the educational needs of gay and lesbian youth. *Harvard Educational Review, 59*, 444–453.

Rosenbaum, J. (1976). *Making inequality: The hidden curriculum of high school tracking.* New York: Wiley.

Savin-Williams, R. C., & Rodriguez, R. G. (1993). A developmental, clinical perspective on lesbian, gay male, and bisexual youths. In T. P. Gullota, G. R. Adams, & R. Montemayor (Eds.), *Adolescent sexuality* (pp. 77–101). Newbury Park, CA: Sage Publications.

Sears, J. T (1992). Educators, homosexuality, and homosexual students: Are personal feelings related to professional beliefs? In K. M. Harbeck (Ed.), *Coming out of the classroom closet: Gay and lesbian students, teachers, and curricula* (pp. 29–79). Binghamton, NY: Harrington Park Press.

Shilts, R. (1993). *Conduct unbecoming: Gays & lesbians in the U.S. military.* New York: St. Martin's Press.

Stewart, J. B. (1994, June 13). Annals of law: Gentleman's agreement. *The New Yorker,* 74–82.

Telljohann, S. K., Price, J. H., Poureslami, M., & Easton, A. (1995). Teaching about sexual orientation by secondary health teachers. *Journal of School Health, 65,* 18–22.

Walters, A. S., & Phillips, C. P. (1994). Hurdles: An activity for homosexuality education. *Journal of Sex Education and Therapy, 20,* 198–203.

PART EIGHT

ACADEMIC AND PROFESSIONAL DEVIANCE

Already swamped with numerous pages to read and study for honors English, anatomy, history, and geometry, high school sophomore Leah Solowsky had hardly enough time to work on her immediate assignment—writing a Spanish essay about healthy diet. She turned on her computer, cruised to the AltaVista search engine, and after a few clicks, she found everything she needed to know about fruits, vegetables, and grains—in flawless Spanish. She downloaded the information, printed it out, and turned it in as her paper the next day.[1]

Cheating in school has recently attracted a great deal of media attention. Although much less publicized, deviance among professors, lawyers, police officers, and other professional people also occurs every now and then. Traditionally, sociologists have shown little interest in deviance among well-educated people like themselves. They assumed that such deviance is virtually nonexistent or too rare to be worth studying. A more likely reason for the lack of interest is the embarrassment that might result from washing dirty linen in public. In recent years, however, many sociologists have started to study academic and professional deviance.

One form of academic deviance involves cheating by college students. In the first article, "Situational Ethics and College Student Cheating," Emily LaBeff and her coresearchers point to studies that estimate the incidence of student cheating to be as high as 50 percent. The researchers found that the major cause of this widespread deviance is the students' ability to use situational ethics to justify cheating. In the second reading, "Criminologists as Criminals," Barbara Zaitzow and Matthew Robinson report their research findings on deviant acts committed by, ironically, criminologists. In the third selection, "Psychotherapists' Accounts of Their Professional Misdeeds," Mark Pogrebin and his colleagues offer data similar to those on student cheating—rationalizing away the deviant nature of professional wrongdoing. Police officers even see much of their professional deviance as necessary, justifiable, legitimate, or acceptable, as discussed in the last article, "Police Lying," by Tom Barker and David Carter.

---

1. Carolyn Kleiner and Mary Lord, "The Cheating Game," *U.S. News & World Report,* November 22, 1999, p. 55.

32

SITUATIONAL ETHICS
AND COLLEGE STUDENT CHEATING

EMILY E. LABEFF   VALERIE J. HAINES
ROBERT E. CLARK   GEORGE M. DIEKHOFF

Studies have shown that cheating in college is epidemic, and some analysts of this problem estimate that 50 percent of college students may engage in such behavior. . . . Such studies have examined demographic and social characteristics of students such as age, sex, academic standing, major, classification, extracurricular activity, level of test anxiety, degree of sanctioned threat, and internal social control. Each of these factors has been found to be related, to some extent, to cheating although the relationship varies considerably from study to study. . . .

In our freshman classes, we often informally ask students to discuss whether they have cheated in college and, if so, how. Some students have almost bragged about which of their methods have proven most effective including writing notes on shoes and caps and on the backs of calculators. Rolling up a tiny cheat sheet into a pen cap was mentioned. And one student said, he had "incredibly gifted eyes" which allowed him to see the answers of a smart student four rows in front of him. One female student talked about rummaging through the dumpsters at night close to final examination time looking for test dittos. She did find at least one examination. A sorority member informed us that two of her term papers in her freshman year were sent from a sister chapter of the sorority at another university, retyped and submitted to the course professor. Further, many of these students saw nothing wrong with what they were doing, although they verbally agreed with the statement that cheating was unethical. . . .

The concept of situational ethics might well describe this college cheating in that rules for behavior are not considered rigid but dependent on the circumstances involved (Norris and Dodder 1979, p. 545). Joseph Fletcher, in his well-known philosophical treatise, *Situation Ethics,* defines it as the notion that any action is good or bad depending on the social circumstances. In other words, what is wrong in most situations might be considered right or acceptable. . . . Central to this process is the idea that situations alter cases, thus altering the rules and principles guiding behavior (Edwards 1967).

[Situational ethics seems to be the core of what Sykes and Matza (1957) call "neutralization," the process of justifying violation of accepted rules. Neutralization takes five forms]: denial of responsibility, condemnation of condemners, appeal to higher loyalties, denial of victim, and denial of injury. In each case, individuals profess a conviction about a particular law but argue that special circumstances exist which cause them to violate the rules. . . .

METHODOLOGY

The present analysis is based on a larger project conducted during the 1983–1984 academic year when a 49-item questionnaire about cheating was administered to students at a small southwestern university. The student body (N = 4950) was evenly distributed throughout the university's programs with a disproportionate number (27 percent) majoring in business administration. In order to achieve a representative sample from a cross-section of the university student body, the questionnaire was administered to students enrolled in courses classified as a part of the university's core curriculum. Freshmen and sophomores were overrepresented (84 percent of the sample versus 60 percent of the university population). Females were also overrepresented (62 percent of the sample versus 55 percent of the university population).

There are obvious disadvantages associated with the use of self-administered questionnaires for data-gathering purposes. One problem is the acceptance of student responses without benefit of contest. To maximize the return rate, questionnaires were administered during regularly scheduled class periods. Participation was on a voluntary basis. In order to establish the validity of responses, students were guaranteed anonymity. Students were also instructed to limit their responses regarding whether they had cheated to the current academic year.

Previous analysis (e.g., Haines et al. 1986) focused on the quantitative aspects of the questionnaire. The present analysis is intended to assess the narrative responses to the incidence of cheating in three forms, namely on major examinations, quizzes, and class assignments, as well as the perceptions of and attitudes held by students toward cheating and the effectiveness of deterrents to cheating. Students recorded their experiences in their own words. Most students (87 percent) responded to the open-ended portion of the questionnaire.

RESULTS

Of the 380 undergraduate students who participated in the spring survey, 54 percent indicated they had cheated during the previous six-month period. Students were requested to indicate whether cheating involved examination, weekly quizzes, and/or homework assignments. Much cheating took the form of looking on someone else's paper, copying homework, and either buying term papers or getting friends to write papers for them. Only five of the 205 students who admitted cheating reported being caught by the pro-

fessor. However, seven percent ($n = 27$) of the students reported cheating more than five times during the preceding six-month period. Twenty percent ($n = 76$) indicated that most students openly approved of cheating. Only seventeen students reported they would inform the instructor if they saw another student cheating. Many students, especially older students, indicated they felt resentment toward cheaters, but most also noted that they would not do anything about it (i.e., inform the instructor).

To more fully explore the ways in which students neutralize their behavior, narrative data from admitted student cheaters were examined ($n = 149$). The narrative responses were easily classified into three of the five techniques [of neutralization] described by Sykes and Matza (1957).

Denial of Responsibility

Denial of responsibility was the most often identified response. This technique involves a declaration by the offenders that, in light of circumstances beyond their control, they cannot be held accountable for their actions. Rather than identifying the behavior as "accidental," they attribute wrongdoing to the influence of outside forces. In some instances, students expressed an inability to withstand peer pressure to cheat. Responses show a recognition of cheating as an unacceptable behavior, implying that under different circumstances cheating would not have occurred. One student commented:

I was working forty plus hours a week and we had a lot to read for that day. I just couldn't get it all in. . . . I'm not saying cheating is okay, sometimes you just have to. . . .

Other responses demonstrate the attempt by students to succeed through legitimate means (e.g., taking notes and studying) only to experience failure. Accordingly, they were left with no alternative but to cheat. One student commented:

. . . even though I've studied in the past, I've failed the exam so I cheated on my last test hoping to bring a better grade.

Another student explained his behavior in the following manner:

> *I studied for the exam and I studied hard but the material on the test was different from what I expected. . . . I had to make a good grade. . . .*

In addition, some students reported accidentally seeing other students' test papers. In such instances, the cheaters chastised classmates for not covering up their answer sheets. As one student wrote, such temptation simply cannot be overcome:

> *I studied hard for the exam and needed an A. I just happened to look up and there was my neighbor's paper uncovered. I found myself checking my answers against his through the whole test.*

Appeal to Higher Loyalties

Conflict also arises between peer group expectations and the normative expectations of the larger society. When this occurs, the individual may choose to sacrifice responsibility, thereby maintaining the interest of peers. Such allegiance allows these individuals to supercede moral obligations when special circumstances arise.

Students who invoke this technique of neutralization frequently described their behavior as an attempt to help another. One student stated:

> *I only cheated because my friend had been sick and she needed help. . . . it (cheating) wouldn't have happened any other time.*

Another student denied any wrongdoing on her part as the following statement illustrates:

> *I personally have never cheated. I've had friends who asked for help so I let them see my test. Maybe some would consider that to be cheating.*

These students recognize the act of cheating is wrong. However, their statements also suggest that in some situations cheating can be overlooked. Loyalty to a friend in need takes precedence over honesty in the classroom. Another student described his situation in the following manner:

> *I was tutoring this girl but she just couldn't understand the material. . . . I felt I had to help her on the test.*

Condemnation of Condemners

Cheaters using this technique of neutralization attempt to shift attention from their own actions to the actions of others, most often authority figures. By criticizing those in authority as being unfair or unethical, the behavior of the offender seems less consequential by comparison. Therefore, dishonest behavior occurs in reaction to the perceived dishonesty of the authority figure. Students who use this technique wrote about uncaring, unprofessional instructors with negative attitudes who were negligent in their behavior. These incidents were said to be a precursor to their cheating behavior. The following response illustrates this view:

> *The teachers here are boring and I dislike this school. The majority of teachers here don't care about the students and are rude when you ask them for help.*

In other instances, students cite unfair teaching practices which they perceive to be the reason for their behavior. One student stated:

> *Major exams are very important to your grade and it seems that the majority of instructors make up the exams to try and trick you instead of testing your knowledge.*

In this case, the instructor is thought to engage in a deliberate attempt to fail the students by making the examinations difficult. Also within this category were student accounts which frequently express a complaint of being overworked. As one student wrote:

> *One instructor assigns more work than anyone could possibly handle . . . at least I know I can't, so sometimes cheating is the answer . . .*

Denial of Injury and Denial of the Victim

Denial of injury and denial of the victim do not appear in the student accounts of their cheating. In denial of injury, the wrongdoer states that no one was harmed or implies that accusations of injury are grossly exaggerated. In the second case, denial of the victim, those who violate norms often portray their targets as legitimate. Due to certain factors such as the societal role, personal characteristics, or lifestyle of the victim, the wrongdoer felt the victim "had it coming."

It is unlikely that students will either deny injury or deny the victim since there are no real targets in cheating. However, attempts to deny injury are possible when the one who is cheating argues that cheating is a personal matter rather than a public one. It is also possible that some students are cognizant of the effect their cheating activities have upon the educational system as a whole and, therefore, choose to neutralize their behavior in ways which allow them to focus on the act rather than the consequences of cheating. By observing their actions from a myopic viewpoint, such students avoid the larger issues of morality.

CONCLUSION

The purpose of this report was to analyze student responses to cheating in their college coursework. Using Sykes and Matza's model of neutralization, we found that students rationalized their cheating behavior and did so without challenging the norm of honesty. Student responses fit three of the five techniques of neutralization.

The most common technique is a denial of responsibility. Second, students tend to "condemn the condemners," blaming faculty and testing procedures. Finally, students "appeal to higher loyalties" by arguing that it is more important to help a friend than to avoid cheating. The use of these techniques of neutralization conveys the message that students recognize and accept cheating as an undesirable behavior which, nonetheless, can be excused under certain circumstances. Such findings reflect the prevalence of situational ethics.

The situation appears to be one in which students are not caught and disciplined by instructors. Additionally, students who cheat do not concern themselves with overt negative sanctions from other students. In some groups, cheating is planned, expected, and often rewarded in that students may receive better grades. That leaves a student's ethical, internalized control as a barrier to cheating. However, the neutralizing attitude allows students to sidestep issues of ethics and guilt by placing the blame for their behavior elsewhere. Neutralization allows them to state their belief that in general cheating is wrong, but in some special circumstances cheating is acceptable, even necessary. . . .

REFERENCES

Edwards, Paul. 1967. *The Encyclopedia of Philosophy, #3,* edited by Paul Edwards. New York: Macmillan Company and Free Press.

Fletcher, Joseph. 1966. *Situation Ethics: The New Morality.* Philadelphia: The Westminster Press.

Haines, Valerie J., George Diekhoff, Emily LaBeff, and Robert Clark. 1986. "College Cheating: Immaturity, Lack of Commitment, and the Neutralizing Attitude." *Research in Higher Education* 25:342–354.

Norris, Terry D., and Richard A. Dodder. 1979. "A Behavioral Continuum Synthesizing Neutralization Theory, Situational Ethics and Juvenile Delinquency." *Adolescence* 55:545–555.

Sykes, Gresham, and David Matza. 1957. "Techniques of Neutralization: A Theory of Delinquency." *American Sociological Review* 22:664–670.

CRIMINOLOGISTS AS CRIMINALS

BARBARA H. ZAITZOW
MATTHEW B. ROBINSON

We were in an airplane on our way back from a recent American Society of Criminology (ASC) meeting, discussing various crime-related issues. We discussed ASC panels, conference papers, and influential speakers. We also talked about the crimes that had recently occurred on college and university campuses, including fatal shootings at the University of North Carolina and Penn State University, a Harvard University student being stabbed forty-five times, and a student setting eighteen fires in one week on the campus of Florida State University. At this exact moment, we overheard, from seats directly in front of us, two criminologists discussing what they had taken (i.e., stolen) from the conference hotel. It made us wonder: Are we criminologists what we study? Do criminologists commit crime or deviance in general? There are reasons to believe that we do.

As noted by Emile Durkheim (1938/1993), "Crime is present not only in the majority of societies of one particular species but in all societies of all types . . . Its form changes; the acts thus characterized are not the same everywhere; but, everywhere and always, there have been men who have behaved in such a way as to draw upon themselves penal repression"(p. 61). Crime is a fact of modern life. Most persons have committed at least one criminal act in their lifetimes, even if the act was relatively minor, and many persons have had the unpleasant experience of being victimized by crime. Criminal behavior represents a heterogeneous collection of acts. Some criminal acts, such as taking an item of little value, are of little consequence in themselves, whereas other criminal acts, such as

spying for a foreign government, can have enormous consequences for many people. Criminality reflects the diverse behavior of diverse people.

Some people commit crimes in connection with their occupations. These offenses occur in all types of occupations and they take many different forms (Geis, 1984). The term *occupational crime* refers to crimes committed through opportunities created in the course of a legal occupation (Sutherland, 1949, 1983). The use of labels such as white-collar crime in the past almost always connoted crimes committed by the rich and powerful. Most criminologists today have broadened the term to refer to crimes committed by persons in a wide range of situations. The focus today is on the nature of the crime and not on the person committing it, thus the term occupational crime. What is not often discussed by criminologists is the extent, form, or nature of criminality or deviant behavior among criminologists themselves. This unexplored area of criminological inquiry is the focus of the present investigation.

OVERVIEW

Deviant behavior in/of the workplace has been a longtime object of sociological interest. The pioneering work of the Chicago School, for example, examined a wide variety of occupational activities that were concomitantly criminal in nature, such as jack-rollers, and "professional" thieves, as well as practitioners of other deviant pursuits, such as taxi drivers and hobos. In 1939, Edwin H. Sutherland suggested the concept of white-collar crime in describing structured criminality in white-collar and commercial work systems. Somewhat later, other researchers articulated additional forms of occupational criminality, including blue-collar crime, blue-coat crime, and khaki-collar crime (Bryant, 1974). The resurgence of ethnomethodological urban studies has focused on a number of deviant and sometimes illegal occupational enterprises, such as stripping (Skipper and McCaghy, 1970; Boles and Garbin, 1974), topless waitressing, being a faith healer, operating exploitive carnival concessionaires (Easto and Truzzi, 1972), and owning underground movie houses and massage parlors.

Deviance does not occur in a social vacuum; it takes place as part of the ongoing process within our major social institutions and their behavioral configurations. Work is such a central institution. A significant proportion of deviant behavior occurs within or as a result of work and occupational speciality. Work organization involves both formal and informal normative structure, so violation of these work norms, such as "rate-busting," the use of forbidden procedures (e.g., shortcut techniques or covering up mistakes of shoddy workmanship), and unethical professional behavior, are in fact deviant behavior. Because certain kinds of work engenders specific routines, pressures, stresses, and problems, some occupational structures and cultures appear to induce, facilitate, and harbor particular kinds of coping behaviors that feed deviance and criminality, such as alcoholism or narcotic addiction.

Similarly, the structure and culture of some conventionally legal work and occupational systems seem to be conducive to characteristic forms of illegal activities. Such work systems possess singular opportunity structures for crime, as well as unique milieus that contribute to the individual motivation for such illicit behavior. Some occupational specialties, although not always defined as illegal, do often transcend the boundaries of propriety and community acceptance, either because of the intent or the nature of the service rendered, and they can accordingly be classified as deviant (e.g., professor–student love affairs). A great many other occupational pursuits are clearly in violation of legal statute even though they provide genuine occupational and career opportunities for the practitioners, and thus they are deviant also (e.g., spending grant money on unauthorized personal expenses).

STATEMENT OF THE PROBLEM

Persistent patterns of deviant behavior in the form of varied, clandestine, and often elaborate illegal practices are found within the social organization of many legal occupational pursuits. Because of a unique opportunity structure and work-related subculture, these illegal activities are often endemic or distinctive to a specific occupational specialty and are therefore characteristic of given work systems. The relationship between work and a particular variety of deviant behavior is not always immediately apparent because the deviant behavioral configurations are frequently buried beneath the surface of occupational structure. Deviant exploitative practices may occur at any status level of the occupational ladder, including the professions. In some instances, a thin line is drawn between nonethical professional behavior and potentially illegal behavior. Even the hallowed halls of ivy are not free of occupational crime.

Howard Becker (1963) observed that, "The career lines characteristic of an occupation take their shape from the problems peculiar to that occupation. These, in turn, are a function of the occupation's position vis-à-vis other groups in society" (p. 102). He illustrated the point with the dance musician, who was caught between a jazz artist's desire to maintain creative control and a structure of opportunities for earning a living that demanded the subordination of this desire to mainstream musical tastes. Musicians' careers were largely a function of how they managed this problem. When the need to make a living predominated, the basis of their self-conceptions shifted from art to craft.

Although Becker applied the same proposition to more deviant occupations, our present investigation was concerned with its applicability to the occupational field of criminology. Specifically, to what extent do criminologists participate in criminal activity (have they in the past or recent present committed a crime), what criminal activities—criminal or deviant—do they participate in, and in the case of detection, what response (formal or otherwise) typically results?

RESEARCH METHODS

Sample.   In order to assess to what degree criminologists engage in such behaviors, we constructed a survey that was mailed to a random sample of 1,500 American Society of Criminology members. Sample selection was obtained from the 1998 membership directory. Surveys from 522 members were returned (*n* = 522), a response rate of 35 percent. This response rate is not surprising given the sensitive nature of the subject matter; moreover, it is comparable to other mail surveys (e.g., see Yu and Cooper, 1983), including those to criminologists (Walsh and Ellis, 1999).

Survey Instrument.   The three-part questionnaire consisted of questions assessing the respondent's demographic characteristics, occupation/career, and criminal/deviant/unethical behavior. The first part of the survey included of occupational/career-related questions (e.g., academic discipline trained in, academic discipline employed in, current position). The second part of the questionnaire was comprised of items that tapped the demographic characteristics of the criminologist sample (e.g., age, race, and education). The third part of the questionnaire included measures of 44 individual forms of criminal, deviant and unethical behaviors and the subsequent formal responses to the behavior (e.g., formal/official response or no response). Many of the types of behaviors included in the survey specifically violate the ASC Code of Ethics, which forbids such acts as: making false, misleading, or deceptive statements; presenting false, misleading, or deceptive claims about one's work; misusing one's position for fraudulent purposes; committing

plagiarism; engaging in reviewer fraud; harassing people on the basis of gender; and coercing or forcing sexual favors from anyone, including those who are under any form of supervision.

FINDINGS

The mean, or average, age of the criminologist respondents was 40 years. The majority of the participants were white (86 percent), male (54 percent), and married (58 percent), and almost two-thirds of the sample (62 percent) had completed a doctorate degree at the time of questionnaire administration.

Most of the respondents (70 percent) indicated they worked in a university setting. There was much variation in the respondents' occupational positions/titles within academia. For example, 25 percent of the individuals were graduate students, 17 percent assistant professors, 13 percent associate professors, 20 percent full professors, and the remaining 26 percent "Other." Almost one-third of the sample (31 percent) responded that they spend their time doing both teaching and research, whereas another third (31 percent) were exclusively involved with research endeavors. Finally (for those who responded to the question), the sample was almost evenly split on tenure, with 29 percent stating they had tenure and another 29 percent who did not have tenure at the time of the study.

Table 33.1 displays a summary of the percentage of respondents who reported they engaged in various criminal, deviant, and unethical behaviors (ever and in the past twelve months). As expected, most of the criminologists reported they had engaged in the most minor of the traffic-related offenses listed. For example, 92 percent and 88 percent reported that they had "intentionally driven at a speed above the speed limit" ever and in the past twelve months, respectively. With respect to the next highest percentage group represented, 66 percent of the criminologist sample had ever "driven while under the influence of a drug, including alcohol," and 35 percent had done so during the past twelve months.

Table 33.1   Percentage of Criminologists Who Admitted to Criminal/Deviant Behaviors Ever and in Past 12 Months ($n = 522$)

	EVER	12 MONTHS		EVER	12 MONTHS
UCR Violent Crime			*Occupational/Economic*		
Assault (Verbal Threat)	36	15	Sold Free Texts	48	12
Battery (Physical Attack)	25	2	Falsify Travel Receipts	20	4
Rape	3	2	Misrepresent Income	18	2
Robbery	2	0	Violate Consulting Rules	12	2
			Used Grant Money for Personal Expenses	11	1
Fraud					
Tax Fraud	19	7	*Occupational/Other*		
Written Bad Check	13	5	Personal Use of Dept. Supplies	84	43
False Statement under Oath	8	2	Obtained Favor for Position	8	4
False Statement for Favor	4	2			
Drug Crimes			*Occupational/Ethical*		
DUI/DWI	66	35	Univ./Coll./Dept. Policy Violation	18	10
Illicit Drug Use	60	27	Avoid Service Responsibilities	9	5
Permitted Drug Use by Minor	43	28	Embellish Vita	9	1
Bought Illicit Drugs	34	17	Exceed Conference Appearance Rules	8	4
Provided Drugs to Minor	26	14	Submit Article to 2+ Journals	5	1
Sold Drugs	11	3	Grant Inflation	8	1
			Review Fraud	5	0
UCR Property Crime			Given Grade for Favors	3	2
Theft	55	7	Represent Work of Others as Own	2	1
Burglary	22	4	Altered Research	1	0
Computer			*Other*		
Accepted Free Computer Programs	66	54	Speeding	92	88
Computer Pornography	15	11	Witness a Crime and Not Report	47	24
Sent Hate E-Mail	5	0			
Computer Hacking	1	0			
Sexual Deviance					
Adultery	23	16			
Made Obscene Calls	9	3			
Prostitution (Pay or Receive)	7	6			
Sex with Student Enrolled in Class	7	5			
Sexual Advances to Someone You Have Authority Over	3	0			

Note: The 44 behaviors were independently coded by two individuals. An estimate of inter-rater reliability of sorting decisions was computed in an effort to ensure the integrity of the categorizations. Of the 44 items that required coding, there were only 2 items in which a coding discrepancy between raters occurred. The resulting 42 agreements were then divided by the sum of the disagreements plus the agreements, thus providing an agreement index. The agreement between the raters was 95 percent.

A surprisingly high percentage of criminologists admitted to committing violent crimes. For example, 36 percent admitted to assaultive behavior ("verbally threatened another person"), with 15 percent indicating participation in the activity during the past twelve months. Twenty-five percent of the respondents admitted to battery ("physically attacked another person"), with 2 percent noting that the behavior had occurred during the past twelve months. Although a small percentage, it is nonetheless alarming that 3 percent of the criminologist sample admitted to ever committing rape ("forced or coerced someone into sexual activity"), with 2 percent noting their involvement in this violent crime during the past twelve months. Similarly, only 2 percent and 0, respectively, admitted involvement in robbery ("taken property from another without permission and with use of force or weapon").

Every category of the UCR Index offenses reveals a possible "maturation effect" with respect to criminologists' subsequent involvement in the activity. For example, although 55 percent of the respondents admitted to the commission of theft ("taken property from another without permission and without use of force or weapon"), only 7 percent admitted to participating in this activity during the past twelve months. Almost one-fourth of the respondents (22 percent) reported that they had committed a burglary ("unlawfully entered another's dwelling; e.g., a house, car, boat, office") at some point in their lives, whereas only 4 percent had done so in the past twelve months.

Nineteen percent of the criminologists admitted to tax fraud ("knowingly made false claims for tax purposes") at some point in their lives, and 7 percent reported that they had done so in the past year. Finally, 13 percent of the respondents admitted to ever having written a bad check ("knowingly issued a check without sufficient funds"); 5 percent in the past year.

When asked if they had ever used illegal drugs ("used illicit or illegal substances"), 60 percent of the sample had, indeed, consumed such substances, with 27 percent admitting to consumption in the past twelve months. Not surprisingly, then, one-third (34 percent) admitted to having purchased drugs ("bought illicit or illegal substances") ever, and 17 percent had done so in the past twelve months. About one in ten (11 percent) admitted to selling drugs ("sold illicit or illegal substances") in their lives, whereas only 3 percent admitted to doing so during the past year. Almost half of the sample (43 percent) had, at some point, permitted drug use by a minor ("permitted alcohol or drug use by minor(s) in your presence"), and 28 percent admitted to allowing such consumption in the past twelve months. One in four (26 percent) reported that they had provided drugs to minors ("bought or provided alcohol or drugs for minor(s)") ever, and 14 percent had done so within the past year.

The only behavior within the acts of sexual deviance category that more than 10 percent admitted to having engaged in was adultery ("had sexual relations while married with a person not your spouse"). One-fourth of the respondents (23 percent) had done so ever, and 16 percent had done so during the past twelve months. Seven percent admitted to ever being romantic with or having sex with a student ("engaged in sexual/romantic relationship with student you were teaching"); 5 percent in the past year.

Sixty-six percent of the respondents admitted they had "accepted a free copy of a computer program from a friend/colleague which was not considered shareware," with 54 percent having done so during the past year. Unfortunately, we cannot say with certainty whether this activity was specifically work- or career-related. After all, people exchange more than word processing and statistical software packages in these days of on-line access. Speaking of easy on-line access, 15 percent of the sample admitted to obtaining computer pornography, with 11 percent admitting that such activity had taken place during the past twelve months. (One cannot help but wonder whether such activity was occurring during or after business/office hours.)

Finally, almost half of the sample (47 percent) reported that they had at some point in their lives witnessed a crime and had not reported it; about one-fourth (24 percent) had done so in the past year. We do not know to which "crimes" respondents were referring here, but we assume that respondents may have witnessed all types of illegal and deviant activities, many at work, committed by colleagues.

Most of the criminologists (84 percent) admitted they had used departmental supplies for personal use, and 43 percent reported that they had done so in the past twelve months. The next most frequent form of occupational deviance by criminologists was the selling of textbooks ("sold free copies of textbooks for money"). Almost half of the respondents (48 percent) had sold textbooks they had obtained for free. Yet, only 12 percent admitted to such behavior during the past year. One in five (20 percent) admitted to having falsified travel receipts in the past ("falsified travel related receipts for reimbursement"), but only 4 percent during the past year. Eleven percent (11 percent) of the respondents admitted to having used a portion of grant monies for personal expenses ("spent grant money on unauthorized personal expenses"), but only 1 percent had done so in the past year.

Criminologists are an interesting occupational group because they seem willing to spend a portion of "obtained" (already-in-hand) grant monies on personal expenses, but they exercise more caution with respect to writing fraudulent grants in which budgets are inflated for personal use. Only 8 percent of the criminologists had reported that they had committed grant fraud ("inflated grant expenses or overcharged a grant agency"), with a mere 1 percent responding that they had perpetrated grant fraud during the past twelve months.

As with any other social group, there are a set of shared norms that guide the behavior of group members. Almost 20 percent of the criminologists violated a job-related rule in the past ("knowingly violated university/college/departmental polices"), and 10 percent had done so in the past year. Fewer than 10 percent reported that they had committed ethical violations categorized within occupational deviance. For example, 8 percent had "exceeded the number of maximum allowable appearances on a conference program," and 5 percent had "submitted an article to two or more journals at the same time." Only 3 percent reported that they had ever given grades for favors ("exchanged grades for favors or given grades for personal reasons"). Two percent had "represented someone else's work as your own," and 9 percent had exaggerated their achievements for gain ("embellished your accomplishments on your vitae or resume—e.g., included a presentation or service activity that you did not complete"). Only 1 percent reported that they had ever "purposely invented or altered research data/findings." Additionally, only 5 percent admitted to ever having engaged in review fraud ("made review decisions for journal articles for personal reasons—e.g., because it did not agree with your stance or beliefs").

CONCLUSION

It is clear that criminologists do participate in varying degrees of criminal, deviant, or unethical behavior. Depending on the type of behaviors involved, many criminologists admit both to having committed them in the distant past and in the twelve months prior to the survey, including many acts classified as "serious" and "harmful" in the criminal law. Such findings should not be considered surprising. After all, who knows more about crime and deviance than criminologists? Criminologists spend years in school acquiring expertise about the subject, and they immerse themselves in studies of free and incarcerated criminal populations. Paradoxically, as criminologists increase their familiarity with crime, they may gain the knowledge needed to successfully get away with committing it; or perhaps past involvement with criminal behavior leads to an increased interest in studying criminology, thus increasing the likelihood of becoming criminologists. Which comes first, the interest in crime or the commission of it? Further research is needed to answer this "chicken or the egg" question.

Because we criminologists are involved in criminal, deviant, or unethical behaviors, any judgments that we pass on criminals, therefore, amount to the "pot calling the kettle black." It is also worth noting that the only behavior that led to a significant likelihood of any type of formal or informal sanction was speeding. The overwhelming majority of the deviant acts among criminolo-gists never came to the attention of the criminal justice system. All this testifies to the influence of one's position within the academic context on one's deviance or criminality and society's response to it.

REFERENCES

Becker, H. 1963. *Outsiders: Studies in the Sociology of Deviance.* Glencoe, IL: Free Press.

Boles, J., and A. P. Garbin. (1974). "Stripping for a Living: An Occupational Study of the Night Club Stripper," pp. 319–328 in *Deviant Behavior,* edited by Clifton D. Bryant. Chicago: Rand McNally.

Bryant, C. D. 1974. *Deviant Behavior: Occupational and Organizational Bases.* Chicago: Rand McNally,

Durkheim, E. 1938/1993. "The Normal and the Pathological," pp. 61–65 in *Deviant Behavior: A Text-Reader in the Sociology of Deviance,* 4th ed., edited by Delos H. Kelly. New York: St. Martin's Press: 61–65.

Easto, P. C., and M. Truzzi. 1972. "Carnivals, Road Shows, and Freaks." *Society,* 9 (5):26–34.

Geis, G. 1984. "White-Collar and Corporate Crime," pp. 137–166 in *Major Forms of Crime,* edited by Robert F. Meier. Beverly Hills, CA: Sage.

Skipper, J. K., Jr., and C. H. McCaghy. 1970. "Stripteasers: The Anatomy and Career Contingencies of a Deviant Occupation." *Social Problems,* 17 (3):391–405.

Sutherland, E. H. 1949. *White-Collar Crime.* New York: Dryden Press.

Sutherland, E. H. 1983. *White-Collar Crime: The Uncut Version.* New Haven, CT: Yale University Press.

Walsh, A., and L. Ellis. 1999. "Criminologists' Opinions about the Causes and Theories of Crime and Delinquency." *The Criminologist* 24 (1):1–6.

Yu, J., and H. Cooper. 1983. "A Quantitative Review of Research Design Effects on Response Rates to Questionnaires." *Journal of Marketing* Research 20:36–44.

PSYCHOTHERAPISTS' ACCOUNTS
OF THEIR PROFESSIONAL MISDEEDS

MARK R. POGREBIN
ERIC D. POOLE
AMOS MARTINEZ

Intimate sexual relationships between mental health therapists and their clients have been increasingly reported in recent years (Akamatsu, 1987). In a survey of over 1400 psychiatrists, Gartell, Herman, Olarte, Feldstein, and Localio (1987) found that 65 percent reported having treated a patient who admitted to sexual involvement with a previous therapist. National self-report surveys indicate that approximately 10 percent of psychotherapists admit having had at least one sexual encounter with a client (Gartell, Herman, Olarte, Feldstein, and Localio, 1986; Pope, Keith-Spiegel, and Tabachnick, 1986). It is suggested that these surveys most likely underestimate the extent of actual sexual involvement with clients because some offending psychotherapists either fail to respond to the survey or fail to report their sexual indiscretions (Gartell et al., 1987). Regardless of the true prevalence rates, many mental health professional associations explicitly condemn sexual relations between a therapist and client. Such relationships represent a breach of canons of professional ethics and are subject to disciplinary action by specific licensing or regulatory bodies. . . .

Since 1988 [in Colorado] sexual intimacy between therapists and clients has been explicitly and formally recognized as one of the most serious violations of the professional–client relationship, subject to both regulatory or administrative and criminal penalties. Yet, between August 1, 1988, and June 30, 1990, 10 percent (*n* = 33) of the 324 complaints filed with the State Grievance Board

involved allegations of sexual misconduct. Given the implications that these sexual improprieties raise for both the client as victim and the therapist as offender, we wish to examine the written accounts submitted to the board by psychotherapists who have had complaints of sexual misconduct filed against them. . . .

METHOD

To the 33 complaints of sexual misconduct filed from August 1988 through June 1990, 30 written responses from psychotherapists were submitted to the State Grievance Board. Twenty-four therapists admitted to sexual involvement with clients; six denied the allegations. In the present study we examine the statements of the 24 therapists who provided accounts for their sexual relations with clients. Twenty-one therapists are men; three are women.

The analytical method utilized in reviewing therapists' accounts was content analysis, which "translates frequency of occurrence of certain symbols into summary judgments and comparisons of content of the discourse" (Starosta, 1984, p. 185). Content analytical techniques provide the means to document, classify, and interpret the communication of meaning, allowing for inferential judgments from objective identification of the characteristics of messages (Holsti, 1969).

The 24 written responses ranged in length from 2 to 25 pages. Each response was assessed and classified according to the types of explanations invoked by therapists in accounting for their acknowledged sexual relations with clients. We employed Scott and Lyman's (1968) classic formulation of accounts (i.e., excuses and justifications) and Goffman's (1971) notion of the apology as conceptual guides in organizing the vocabularies of motive used by our group of therapists to explain their untoward behavior . . .

FINDINGS

Accounts are "linguistic device[s] employed whenever an action is subjected to valuative inquiry" (Scott and Lyman, 1968, p. 46). An important function of accounts is to mitigate blameworthiness by representing one's behavior in such a way as to reduce personal accountability. This involves offering accounts aimed at altering the prevailing conception of what the instant activity is, is well as one's role in the activity. Excuses, justifications, and apologies all display a common goal: giving a "good account" of oneself.

Excuses

Appeal of Defeasibility. In an appeal of defeasibility, one accounts for one's behavior by denying any intention to cause the admitted harm or by claiming a failure to foresee the unfortunate consequences of one's act, or both. . . . In the following account, the therapist claims ignorance of professional rules of conduct governing relations with clients:

> I did not know that seeing clients socially outside of therapy violated hospital policy . . . [I]f I realized it was strictly forbidden, I would have acted differently . . .

In the following example, a therapist admits that she simply misinterpreted her own feelings and did not consciously intend to become sexually involved with her client:

> It was after a short period of time that I first experienced any sexual feelings toward her. I did excuse the feelings I had as something which I never would act on. Unfortunately, I did not understand what was happening at the time.

Similarly, another therapist seeks to diminish culpability by attributing his sexual indiscretion to a misreading of his client's emotional needs:

> I experienced her expressions of affection as caring gestures of our spiritual bond, not lust. And I had no reason to suspect otherwise from her, since I had been so clear about my aversion to romantic involvement. We had sexual intercourse only once after termination. I am not promiscuous, neither sexually abusive nor seductive. . . .

Scapegoating. Scapegoating involves an attempt to blame others for one's untoward behavior. Scapegoating is available as a form of excuse in the professional-client relationship because of the contextual opportunity for the therapist to shift personal responsibility to the client. The therapist contends that his or her actions were the product of the negative attributes or will of the client, for example, deceit, seduction, or manipulation. The therapist in the following example recognizes the wrongfulness of his behavior but deflects responsibility by holding the client culpable for her actions:

> I am not denying that this sexual activity took place, nor am I trying to excuse or justify it. It was wrong. However, the woman who complained about me is a psychologist. She was counseling me as well, on some vocational issues. So if anyone had cause for complaint under the regulations, it seems it would be me.

Another example of an account where the therapist attempts to "blame the victim" for the improper sexual activity reveals the focus on his diminished personal control of the relationship:

> That I became involved in a sexual relationship with her is true. While my actions were reprehensible, both morally and professionally, I did not mislead or seduce her or intend to take advantage of her. My fault, instead, was failing to adequately safeguard myself from her seductiveness, covert and overt.

Here we have a therapist recognizing the impropriety of his actions yet denying personal responsibility because of the client's overpowering charms. The message is that the therapist may be held accountable for an inadequate "self-defense" which left him vulnerable to the client's seductive nature, but that he should not be culpable for the deviant sexual behavior since it was really he who was taken in and thus "victimized." The therapist's account for his predicament presumes a "reasonable person" theory of behavior; that is, given the same set of circumstances, any reasonable person would be expected to succumb to this persuasive client.

Justifications

Sad Tale.   The sad tale presents an array of dismal experiences or conditions that are regarded—both collectively and cumulatively—as an explanation and justification for the actor's present untoward behavior. The therapists who presented sad tales invariably focused on their own history of family problems and personal tribulations that brought them to their present state of sexual affairs with clients:

> Ironically, her termination from therapy came at one of the darkest periods of my life. My father had died that year. I had met him for the first time when I was in my twenties. He was an alcoholic. Over the years we had worked hard on our relationship. At the time of his dying, we were at peace with one another. Yet, I still had my grief. At the time I had entered into individual therapy to focus on issues pertaining to my father's alcoholism and co-dependency issues. I then asked my wife to join me for marriage counseling. We were having substantial problems surrounding my powerlessness in our relationship. Therapy failed to address the balance of power. I was in the worst depression I had ever experienced in my entire life when we began our sexual involvement.

Therapists who employ sad tales admit to having sexual relations with their clients, admit that their actions were improper, and admit that ordinarily what they did would be an instance of the general category of the prohibited behavior. They claim, however, that their behavior is a special case because the power of circumstance voids the defining deviant quality of their actions. This type of account is similar to Lofland's (1969, p. 88) "special justification," where the actor views his current act as representative of some category of deviance but does not believe it to be entirely blameworthy because of extenuating circumstances. One therapist outlines the particular contextual factors that help explain his misbehavior:

> The following situations are not represented as an excuse for my actions. There is no excuse for them. They are simply some of what I feel are circumstances that formed the context for what I believe is an incident that will never be repeated.
> (1) Life losses: My mother-in-law who lived with us died. My oldest son and, the next fall, my daughter had left home for college.
> (2) Overscheduling: I dealt with these losses and other concerns in my life by massive overscheduling.

Other therapists offer similar sad tales of tragic events that are seen to diminish their capacity, either physically or mentally, to cope with present circumstances. Two cases illustrate this accounting strategy:

> In the summer of 1988, my wife and I separated with her taking our children to live out-of-state. This was a difficult loss for me. A divorce followed. Soon after I had a bout with phlebitis which hospitalized me for ten days.

> My daughter, who lived far away with my former wife, was diagnosed with leukemia; and my mother had just died. Additional stress was caused by my ex-wife and present wife's embittered interactions. . . .

Sad tales depict individuals acting abnormally in abnormal situations. In short, their instant deviance is neither typical nor characteristic of the type of person they really are, that is, how they would act under normal conditions. They are victims of circumstance, for if it were not for these dismal life events, their sexual improprieties would never have occurred.

Denial of Injury.   Denial of injury is premised on a moral assessment of consequences; that is, the individual claims that his or her actions should be judged as wrong on the basis of the harm resulting from those acts. Again, the actor acknowledges that in general the behavior in which he or she has engaged is inappropriate but asserts that in this particular instance no real harm was done. This type of account was prevalent among the therapists who had engaged in sexual relations with clients following the termination of therapy.

> *A good therapy termination establishes person-to-person equality between participants. Blanket condemnations of post-therapy relationships also are founded on a belief that such relationships invariably cause harm to the former patient. I defy anyone to meet Gerry, interview her, and then maintain that any harm was done to her by me. . . .*

Apology

. . . Two consequences of an accused wrongdoer's action are guilt and shame. If wrongful behavior is based on internal standards, the transgressor feels guilty; if the behavior is judged on external normative comparisons, the person experiences shame. Shame results from being viewed as one who has behaved in a discrediting manner. In the following three cases, each therapist expresses his remorse and laments his moral failure:

> *I find myself in the shameful position that I never would have thought possible for me as I violated my own standards of personal and professional conduct.*

> *I feel very badly for what I have done, ashamed and unprofessional. I feel unworthy of working in the noble profession of counselling.*

> *I entered into therapy and from the first session disclosed what I had done. I talked about my shame and the devastation I had created for my family and others.*

Schlenker and Darby (1981) observe that the apology incorporates not only an expression of regret but also a claim of redemption. An apology permits a transgressor the opportunity to admit guilt while simultaneously seeking forgiveness in order that the offending behavior not be thought of as a representation of what the actor is really like.

One therapist expresses concern for his actions and proposes a way to avoid such conduct in the future:

> *I continue to feel worry and guilt about the damage that I caused. I have taken steps I felt necessary which has been to decide not to work with any client who could be very emotionally demanding, such as occurs with people who are borderline or dependent in their functioning.*

This account seems to imply that one's remorse and affirmative effort to prevent future transgressions are sufficient remedies in themselves, preempting the need for others to impose additional sanctions. . . .

DISCUSSION

The consequences of deviant activity are problematic, often depending on a "definition of the situation." When a particular definition of a specific situation emerges, even though its dominance may be only temporary, individuals must adjust their behavior and views to it. Alternative definitions of problematic situations routinely arise and are usually subject to negotiation. Thus, it is incumbent upon the accused therapist to have his or her situation defined in ways most favorable to maintaining or advancing his or her own interests. When "transformations of identity" are at stake, such efforts become especially consequential (Strauss, 1962). The imputation of a deviant identity implies ramifications that can vitally affect the individual's personal and professional life. As noted earlier, the negotiation of accounts is a negotiation of identities. The account serves as an impression-management technique, or a "front," that minimizes the threat to identity (Goffman, 1959). If the therapist can provide an acceptable account for his or her sexual impropriety—whether an excuse, justification, or apology—he or she increases the likelihood of restoring a cherished identity brought into question by the deviant behavior.

There is a close link between successfully conveying desired images to others and being able to incorporate them in one's own self-conceptions. When individuals offer accounts for their problematic actions, they are trying to ease their situation in two ways: by convincing others and by convincing themselves. An important function of accounts is to make one's transgressions not only intelligible to others but intelligible to oneself. Therapists sought to dispel the view that their deviation was a defining characteristic of who they really were; or, to put it another way, they attempted to negate the centrality or primacy of a deviant role imputation. The goal was to maintain or restore their own sense of personal and professional worth notwithstanding their sexual deviancy. In a way, laying claim to a favorable image in spite of aberrant behavior means voiding the apparent moral reality, that is, the deviance-laden definition of the situation that has been called to the attention of significant others (Grievance Board) by a victim-accuser (former client).

Goffman (1959, p. 251) maintains that individuals are not concerned with the issue of morality of their behavior as much as they are with the amoral issue of presenting a moral self;

> *Our activity, then is largely concerned with moral matters, but as performers we do not have a moral concern with them. As performers we are merchants of morality.*

The presentation of a moral self following deviance may be interpreted as an attempt by the individual to reaffirm his commitment to consensual values and goals in order to win the acceptance of others (Tedeschi and Riorden, 1981). The demonstration of shared standards of conduct may also be seen as consistent with the wish to redeem oneself in the eyes of others and to preserve self-respect. The desire for self-validating approval becomes more important when circumstances threaten an individual's identity. In these instances an actor will often make self-presentations for purposes of eliciting desired responses that will restore the perception of self by others that he or she desires. If discredited actors can offer a normal presentation of self in an abnormal situation, they may be successful in having their instant deviant behavior perceived by others as atypical, thus neutralizing a deviant characterization.

Individuals seek a "common ground" in accounts of their deviant behavior, explaining their actions in conventional terms that are acceptable to a particular audience. These accounts should not be viewed as mere rationalizations. They may genuinely be believed in. . . .

Finally, it should be noted that, as retrospective interpretations, accounts may have little to do with the motives that existed at the time the deviance occurred. In this case accounting for one's deviant behavior requires one to dissimulate, that is, to pretend to be what one is not or not to be what one is. As Goffman (1959) asserts, social behavior involves a great deal of deliberate deception in that impressions of selves must be constantly created and managed for various others. Thus, it is not logically necessary that one agree with others' moral judgments in order to employ accounts. Even where no guilt or shame is consciously felt, one may offer accounts in the hope of lessening what could be, nonetheless, attributions of a deviant identity. When used convincingly, accounts blur the distinctions between "appearance and reality, truth and falsity, triviality and importance, accident and essence, coincidence and cause" (Garfinkel, 1956, p. 420). Accounts embody a mixture of fact and fantasy. As shown in the accounts provided by therapists, what is most problematic is determining the mixture best suited for a particular situational context.

REFERENCES

Akamatsu, J. T. 1987. "Intimate Relationships with Former Clients: National Survey of Attitudes and Behavior among Practitioners." *Professional Psychology: Research and Practice* 18:454–458.

Garfinkel, H. 1956. "Conditions of Successful Degradation Ceremonies." *American Journal of Sociology* 61:420–424.

Gartell, N., J. Herman, S. Olarte, M. Feldstein, and R. Localio. 1986. "Psychiatrist-Patient Sexual Contact:

Results of a National Survey. I: Prevalence." *American Journal of Psychiatry* 143:1126–1131.

Gartell, N., J. Herman, S. Olarte, M. Feldstein, and R. Localio. 1987. "Reporting Practices of Psychiatrists Who Knew of Sexual Misconduct by Colleagues." *American Journal of Orthopsychiatry* 57:287–295.

Goffman, E. 1959. *The Presentation of Self in Everyday Life.* Garden City, NY: Doubleday.

Goffman, E. 1971. *Relations in Public: Microstudies of the Public Order.* New York: Basic Books.

Holsti, O. R. 1969. *Content Analysis for the Social Sciences and Humanities.* Reading, MA: Addison-Wesley.

Lofland, J. 1969. *Deviance and Identity.* Englewood Cliffs, NJ: Prentice-Hall.

Pope, K. S., P. Keith-Spiegel, and B. G. Tabachnick. 1986. "Sexual Attraction to Clients: The Human Therapist and the (Sometimes) Inhuman Training System." *American Psychologist* 41:147–158.

Schlenker, B. R., and B. W. Darby. 1981. "The Use of Apologies in Social Predicaments." *Social Psychology Quarterly* 44:271–278.

Scott, M. B., and S. M. Lyman. 1968. "Accounts." *American Sociological Review* 33:46–62.

Starosta, W. J. 1984. "Qualitative Content Analysis: A Burkean Perspective," pp. 185–194 in *Methods for Intercultural Communication Research,* edited by W. Gudykunst and Y. Y. Kim. Beverly Hills, CA: Sage.

Strauss, A. 1962. "Transformations of Identity," pp. 63–85 in *Human Behavior and Social Processes: An Interactional Approach,* edited by A. M. Rose. Boston: Houghton Mifflin.

Tedeschi, J. T., and C. Riorden. 1981. "Impression Management and Prosocial Behavior Following Transgression," pp. 223–244 in *Impression Management Theory and Social Psychological Research,* edited by J. T. Tedeschi. New York: Academic Press.

POLICE LYING: "FLUFFING UP THE EVIDENCE AND COVERING YOUR ASS"

TOM BARKER
DAVID CARTER

Lying and other deceptive practices are an integral part of the police officer's working environment. At first blush, you may react to this statement this way: "Police officers should not lie. If you can't trust your local police, who can you trust?" But the matter is not that simple. The police do lie. We will here discuss the patterns of police lying, the circumstances under which it occurs, and its possible consequences.

LEGITIMATE LYING

Certain forms of lying are an accepted part of the police working environment. The lies told are accepted because they fulfill a defined police purpose. Police administrators and officers believe that certain lies are necessary to control crime and "arrest the guilty." In these instances, the organization will freely admit the intent to lie and define the acts as legitimate policing strategies.

The most apparent patterns of "accepted" lying are the deceptive practices that law enforcement officers believe are necessary to perform undercover operations or detect other forms of secret and consensual crimes. Police officers engaged in these activities must not only conceal their true identity but they must talk, act, and dress out of character, fabricating all kinds of stories in order to perform these duties. One could hardly imagine that FBI Special Agent Joseph Pistone could have operated for six years in the Mafia without the substantial number of lies he had to tell (Pistone, 1987). However, the overwhelming majority of undercover operations are not as glamorous or as dangerous as working six years with the Mafia. The most common police undercover operations occur in routine vice operations dealing with prostitution, bootlegging, gambling, narcotics, bribery of public officials, and sting operations.

Much of these undercover operations involve encouraging the target to commit a crime. This may be a legally accepted police practice if the officer acts as a willing victim or the officer's actions facilitate the commission of a crime that was going to be committed in the first place. But this police action can be considered entrapment, which is illegal. According to *Black's Law Dictionary,* entrapment is "the act of officers or agents of the government in inducing a person to commit a crime not contemplated by him, for the purpose of instituting a criminal prosecution against him" (277). It is difficult, though, for individuals with a criminal record to claim that they would not have committed the crime except for the actions of the officer. Nevertheless, the "objective test" of entrapment as advocated by a minority of the Supreme Court focuses on the nature of the police conduct rather than the predisposition of the offender (Stitt and James, 1985). Consider the case of a police organization producing crack for use in undercover drug arrests. According to an Associated Press story, the Broward County Florida Sheriff's Department, not having enough crack to supply undercover officers, has started manufacturing their own. The sheriff's department chemist has made at least $20,000 worth of the illegal stuff. Local defense attorneys have raised the issue of entrapment. As one public defender stated,

I think there's something sick about this whole sys-tem where the police make the product, sell the product, and arrest people for buying the product (Birmingham Post Herald, April 19, 1989:B2).

In short, accepted lies are those that the orga-nization views as having a useful role in police op-erations. The criteria for the lie to be accepted are:

1. It must be in furtherance of a legitimate orga-nizational purpose.
2. There must be a clear relationship between the need to deceive and the accomplishment of an organizational goal.
3. The nature of the deception must be one wherein deception will better serve the pub-lic interest than the truth.

ILLEGITIMATE BUT TOLERATED LYING

A second type of police lies includes those recog-nized as lies by the police but tolerated as "neces-sary evils." Police administrators will admit to deception or "not exactly telling the whole truth" when confronted with the facts. These situational or "white" lies are truly in the gray area of propri-ety and the police can provide logical rationales for their use. When viewed from an ethical stand-point, they may be "wrong," but from the police perspective they are necessary (i.e., tolerated) for achieving organizational objectives. The lies are particularly useful for dealing with the basic prob-lems of police work.

The basic problems confronting the police arise from the mythology surrounding their work: statutes usually require, and the public expects, the police to enforce all the laws all the time; the pub-lic holds the police responsible for preventing crime and apprehending all criminals; the public views the police as being capable of handling all emergencies, and so on (Goldstein 1977). But the police do not have the resources, the training, or the authority to do some of those duties. Thus, the police tend to do things contrary to public expec-tation. One such thing involves discretionary de-cision making or selective law enforcement. For example, in recent years, many politically active

groups such as Mothers Against Drunk Drivers (MADD) have pressured legislators for stronger laws with mandatory enforcement in drunk driving cases. But police officers often make discretionary decisions on D.U.I. offenses even though full en-forcement is their department's official policy. One of us (Tom Barker) learned of an individual who had two D.U.I. offenses reduced, and asked a po-lice supervisor about it.

BARKER: The chief has said that all D.U.I. sus-pects are charged and those over the legal blood alcohol level never have the charge re-duced. In fact, he said this at a MADD meet-ing. Yet, I heard that "so-and-so" had two D.U.I. offenses reduced.

SUPERVISOR: That is true, Tom. However, "so-and-so" is helping us with some drug cases. MADD may not understand but they do not have to make drug busts.

In dealing with disorderly or emergency situ-ations, the police often are forced to reach into a bag of tricks. They may tell noisy teenagers to move along or be arrested even though they have neither the intention nor legal basis for an arrest. They may tell complainants that they will follow up on their complaint or turn it over to the proper agency when they have no intention of doing it. They see such lies as a way of handling "nuisance work" that keeps them from doing "real police work" or as a way of dealing with a problem be-yond their means. The lies are used as a tool of ex-pediency—arguably an abuse of police discretion but one that is tolerated.

Similarly, in domestic disturbances, police of-ficers may have no legal basis for making an arrest. Frequently, there is a misdemeanor for which the officer does not have a warrant, an offense that has not been committed in the officer's presence, or an incident that occurred in a private residence. How-ever, the officer may feel that something must be done. Thus, the officer may lie and threaten to ar-rest one or both combatants, or talk them out to the street or the patrol car to discuss the incident and then arrest them for disorderly conduct or public intoxication when they reach public property.

In interrogating the arrested person, the police also often resort to lying. This is not only tolerated but also taught to police officers. The interrogator is told to put forth a facade of sincerity so convincingly that "moisture may actually appear in his eyes." Another recommended technique of deception requires having a *simulated* evidence case folder on hand during the course of the interrogation if an actual case file does not exist. The interrogator may allude to having a large number of investigators working on the case and producing considerable evidence on the suspect's guilt, even though the interrogator is the only person working on the case (Inbau, Reid, and Buckley, 1986).

It is difficult to say whether these tolerated forms of lying are "wrong." Many investigators would argue that they are not really "lies" but good interrogation methods. It could also be argued in their defense that the end justifies the means as long as the officer's actions are not illegal. However, deception in one context may spill over into other contexts. As a veteran police officer told one of us (Barker) while discussing ways to convince a suspect to agree to a consent search,

BARKER: That sure sounds like telling a lot of lies.
OFFICER: It is not police lying; it is an art. After all, the criminal has constitutional protection. He can lie through his teeth. Why not us? What is fair is fair.

ILLEGAL LIES

A third type of police lying involves violating a substantive or procedural law or some police department rules and regulations. According to noted defense attorney and legal scholar Alan Dershowitz (1983), this serious illegal form of police lying is well known in the criminal justice system. It is part of the "Rules of the Justice Game," including:

> Rule IV: *Almost all police lie about whether they violated the Constitution in order to convict guilty defendants.*

> Rule V: *All prosecutors, judges, and defense attorneys are aware of Rule IV.*

> Rule VI: *Many prosecutors implicitly encourage police to lie about whether they violated the Constitution in order to convict guilty defendants.*

> Rule VII: *All judges are aware of Rule VI.*

> Rule VIII: *Most trial judges pretend to believe police officers who they know are lying.*

> Rule XI: *All appellate judges are aware of Rule VIII, yet many pretend to believe the trial judges who pretend to believe the lying police officers (Dershowitz, 1983:xxi–xxii).*

There are studies to support this observation. One study concluded that "the possibility of police perjury is a part of the working reality of criminal defense attorneys" (Kittel, 1986:20). Fifty-seven percent of the 277 attorneys surveyed in this study believed that police perjury occurs "very often" or "often." In another study, police officers themselves reported that they believe their fellow officers would lie in court (Barker, 1978). An English barrister believes that police officers in his country perjure themselves in about three out of ten trials (Wolchover, 1986).

Lying for Legitimate Reasons

Police officers may engage in perjury or other illegal lying for what they perceive to be legitimate reasons. Thus, they lie because they want to "put criminals in jail," prevent crime, or perform various other policing responsibilities. They believe that they know the guilt or innocence of those they arrest because of their unique experiences in dealing with criminals. But they are forced to lie because necessary elements of legal guilt are lacking, such as no probable cause for a "stop," no Miranda warning, or not enough narcotics for a felony offense. Lying, then, constitutes only supplying the missing elements. As one police officer told one of us, it is often necessary to "fluff up the evidence" to get a search warrant or ensure conviction.

The police rationalize that illegal lying is necessary to ensure that criminals do not get off on "technicalities." A deeper reason is officer frustration. The police are frustrated with the criminal justice system because the court cannot handle large caseloads. They are also frustrated with the routine practice of plea negotiations and intricate criminal procedures, which they may not fully understand. They further sympathize with the victims of crime, having difficulty reconciling the harm done to them with the wide array of due process protections given to defendants. They are, in effect, seeing themselves as doing the "right thing." They cannot see, or could not care less, the fact that their perjury is not only illegal but threatening to civil liberties.

Lying for Illegitimate Reasons

Police officers also often lie for illegitimate reasons, to protect themselves or fellow officers from organizational discipline or civil or criminal liability. Thus, they would lie to cover up their own or others' corruption, an act of police brutality, an injury or death to a suspect, or personal misconduct such as having sex, sleeping, or drinking on duty. Officers may get together to ensure that they tell the same story so as to make the lie look like the truth. This can be illustrated by an experience one of us (David Carter) had. Carter was assisting a police department that was under a federal court injunction related to a long list of civil rights violations involving excessive force and harassment. During one series of inquiries, the following conversation occurred:

CARTER: Did you ever talk to other accused officers before giving your deposition in these cases?

OFFICER: Of course.

CARTER: Did you discuss the facts of the allegation?

OFFICER: Sure. We had to be sure our stories were straight.

Much of the lying does not involve police brutality, though. It has to do with relatively minor violations of departmental rules and regulations. These may include the common practice of eating a free meal, leaving one's beat for personal reasons, not wearing the hat when out of the car, living outside the city limits, and so on. Such violations are extremely common because there are too many rules and regulations, especially in large urban police departments. When a supervisor decides to discipline an officer for violating one of these violations, the officer and fellow officers may resort to lies to protect themselves and each other.

CONCLUSION

Whether police lying is legitimate or illegal, accepted or tolerated, it can have harmful consequences. Lies can and do create distrust within the organization. They encourage police misconduct, including corruption, thereby threatening the department's discipline and viability as a law-enforcement agency. Moreover, when the public learns about police lying, citizen confidence in the police plummets, making it even more difficult for the police to perform their duty. All this inevitably reduces the effectiveness of the criminal justice system as a whole.

REFERENCES

Barker, T. 1978. "An Empirical Study of Police Deviance Other Than Corruption." *Journal of Police Science and Administration* 6:3:264–272.

Birmingham Post-Herald. 1989. "Sheriff's Chemist Makes Crack," April 19:B2.

Dershowitz, A. M. 1983. *The Best Defense.* New York: Vintage Books.

Goldstein, H. 1977. *Policing a Free Society.* Cambridge, MA: Ballenger.

Inbau, F. E., J. E. Reid, and Joseph P. Buckley. 1986. *Criminal Interrogation and Confessions,* 3rd ed. Baltimore: Williams and Wilkins.

Kittel, N. G. 1986. "Police Perjury: Criminal Defense Attorneys' Perspective." *American Journal of Criminal Justice* 11:1:11–22.

Pistone, J. D. 1987. *Donnie Brasco: My Undercover Life in the Mafia.* New York: Nail Books.

Stitt, B. G. and Gene C. James. 1985. "Entrapment: An Ethical Analysis" in Elliston, F. A. and Michael Feldberg (eds.), *Moral Issues in Police Work.* Totowa, NJ: Rowman and Allanheld.

Wolchover, D. 1986. "Police Perjury in London." *New Law Journal,* February: 180–184.

PART NINE

DISABILITIES AND STIGMATIZATION

Disabilities are far more common than popularly believed. In his well-researched book on the subject, Joseph Shapiro discovers that Americans with disabilities are the nation's largest minority, numbering from 3 million to 43 million, more than three times the size of the African American population. In fact, as Shapiro further notes, disability "is one minority that anyone can join at any time, as a result of a sudden automobile accident, a fall down a flight of stairs, cancer, or some serious disease. Fewer than 15 percent of disabled Americans were born with their disabilities."[1]

People with disabilities, particularly the deaf, blind, paraplegic, psychotic, or mentally challenged, differ from most other deviances. Although they are deviant in the sense of being socially disvalued, they cannot be held responsible for their condition. The condition is deviant only as a social construction (or label), rather than deviant in and by itself. Thus people with disabilities have increasingly rejected the implication of the deviant construction that their condition somehow makes them inferior. The rejection makes perfect sense, because people with disabilities appear inferior only when judged in an unfair, prejudiced way—with criteria of competence that are *biased in favor of nondisabled people.* Compare, for example, an average blind person with an average sighted person. Who is more competent in walking from one place to another? If we use the criterion of being able to move about with the eyes *open,* of course the sighted person is more competent. However, if we use the criterion of being able to move about with the eyes *closed,* the blind person is definitely more competent. To better understand the world in which people with disabilities live, we will present several articles about different disabilities and societal responses to them.

In the first article, "How Persons with Mental Retardation See Themselves," Michael Angrosino discusses what it is like be to mentally challenged, as seen from the person's own perspective. In the second selection, "Cross-Cultural Patterns in Eating Disorders," Jennifer Pate and her colleagues review a massive amount of studies, providing a global perspective on anorexia and bulimia. The authors discover, among other things, that eating disorders seem to reflect attempts to deal with the pressure of growing up in a stressful environment. In the next article on the same subject, "Anorexics and Bulimics: Developing Deviant Identities," Penelope McLorg and Diane Taub provide a closer look into the inner, experiential

---

1. Joseph P. Shapiro, *No Pity: People with Disabilities Forging a New Civil Rights Movement* (New York: New York Times Books, 1993), pp. 6–7.

world of mostly female college students with the disorders. In the last article, "The Stigmatization of Persons with HIV Disease," Richard Tewksbury and Deanna McGaughey reveal through research data how victims of AIDS and the AIDS virus are stigmatized and how they cope with the stigmatization.

36

HOW THE MENTALLY CHALLENGED
SEE THEMSELVES

MICHAEL V. ANGROSINO

The study of mentally [challenged] persons in natural settings (i.e., in the noninstitutional communities in which they live and work) was pioneered by Robert Edgerton and his Socio-Behavioral Group at the University of California at Los Angeles. Their work has demonstrated that the conventional wisdom about adults with mental retardation, based as it was on clinical observations, could be enriched by the application of ethnographic methods, including that of the life history.

The life histories of [mentally challenged] persons collected in natural settings have been predicated on the assumption that these people are capable of telling us about their experiences and feelings in a coherent fashion. My own research confirms this assumption but in a somewhat different way. I have not been concerned so much with the verifiable truth value of the content of what my informants tell me (some of which has proven, in fact, to be untrue in the strictly literal sense) but with the ways in which our conversations have created interactive communicative contexts in which their views of the world are revealed in spite of the obfuscations (deliberate or not) in the superficial aspects of the narratives. My concern, then, is to contribute to the literature on naturalistic ethnography among stigmatized people by focusing not on what they say but on their ability to create culturally appropriate metaphors by which to convey their sense of identity to others. . . .

METHOD

I conducted my research at an agency called "Opportunity House" (a pseudonym hereafter termed OH) that provided vocational and academic training to mentally [challenged] men who also have psychiatric disorders and, in most cases, criminal records. OH provided these services at a residential facility in a suburban community, as well as at a multipurpose center in a nearby large city. I had been involved with OH since 1980 as both a volunteer tutor and an officer of its Board of Trustees.

I found that as friendships with some of the long-term clients deepened, material of a life history nature was emerging. I secured permission from the staff to tape some conversations; four of the clients (who were all legally competent) signed release statements allowing me to cite portions of their interviews as long as names were changed and no privileged clinical information was revealed. The interviews did not have the formalized structure of traditional life history interviews (see, e.g., Dollard, 1935; Kluckhohn, 1945; Langness, 1965), but they did yield much that was revealing about the experiences of people whose lives had been in large measure determined by more powerful "others" and who had been characteristically denied the opportunity to speak for themselves. As one social worker told me, "They can't possibly have anything worth saying!"

My role at OH was one of the participant observer. As I had a set of official functions to perform, I could not be simply a neutral "social scientist." It should be kept in mind, however, that my function, while clear to the staff, was rather hazy as far as clients were concerned. It was apparent to them that I was a teacher of some kind, but because I came and went on an irregular schedule, they knew I was not a member of the staff. Moreover, I tried consistently to be minimally disruptive and always deferred questions about agency policy to the responsible staff members. The clients therefore saw me as one with some sort of prestige, but who declined to exercise authority. I was thus to be treated with respect but not necessarily deference, and after a while, I was seen as a confidante—my tapes of our encounters were explicitly for us alone and not for the official records of the agency.

In most interview sessions, I allowed the clients to set the agenda. They seemed to respond very well to this freedom as they were used to being questioned in very strict, clinical formats that allowed them little room for sorting through their thoughts and finding ways to express their feelings. My role as an interviewer was, in part, to guide the discourse back to topics "relevant" to the subjects' lives, although I tried to let them determine relevance. It was more important to be a good listener, a sympathetic audience to encourage and nurture communication. As a result, the life histories tend to ramble more than might be the case in the ethnography of a set of "normal" informants. But, as will be seen, this extremely loose and open-ended interview style by no means yielded random, meaningless chitchat. Moreover, because the interviews were conducted over a period of several years in most cases, they are documents of ongoing and evolving interactions rather than final, retrospective views of life.

It is also worth noting that the life histories under study here represent the mutual efforts of researcher and subject. I cannot claim that the metaphors of self that my respondents chose to convey to me would be those that they would convey to interviewers who presented them with other kinds of feedback. (I *think* my respondents are consistent in their self-images, but depending on the way they interpret others who talk to them, their narrative means might have to be adjusted to communicate those images.) The life histories are thus multivocalic records of encounters between particular people at particular times in their lives. . . .

Given the special nature of my informants and the very small number of texts under study, I could not possibly make a case for using these narratives as sources for generalization about the culture. But I am reluctant to leave them simply as highly personal records of unique individuals in isolated encounters. I therefore suggest that it is possible to make wider sense of such narratives—to see how otherwise inarticulate, deviant, stigmatized people can create meaningful, "shareable," systematic scenarios through which to convey metaphors of their selfhood—by concentrating on the regularities of their forms rather than on the idiosyncrasies of their contents. I further contend that even the brief narratives of mentally [challenged] subjects can demonstrate this sort of formal regularity.

LIFE HISTORIES OF MENTALLY [CHALLENGED] ADULTS

[There are four life histories in the original article; only two are presented here.]

Tyrell Stokes

Tyrell is now 25 years old. He had been a client at OH for three years and then graduated to full independence in the community. He lived on his own for two years but had recently returned. Tyrell grew up in "the Projects," subsidized low-income housing in the city. He never knew either of his parents, having lived as a child with various relatives, none of whom he cares to talk about. He spent time in a juvenile detention facility for purse snatching. After his release, he lived by his wits on the streets and was ultimately arrested on a weapons charge. He spent a brief time in jail (adult status) before being sent to OH. During all that time, he never received special training, and until he came to OH, he had never heard himself referred to as ["mentally retarded"]. He is extremely polished in his social manner and presents a very "cool" face to the world, but he is completely deficient in the most basic academic skills: "I'll tell you how dumb I was. Once I robbed this old lady. She had a bunch of change in her pocketbook. It was a load of pennies—I know that now. But boy! I thought I hit it big! Lookit all that money!" Even after extensive exposure to the OH programs, his academic skills remain marginal. He has also resisted vocational training. Yet he is by far the most articulate of all the clients, the most easily poised in social settings. "Well, you know," he says, "long as I don't have to read and write for nobody they think I'm the baddest dude they ever seen—everybody says I remind them of Eddie Murphy."

Tyrell was eager to graduate. During his first stint at OH, he was openly scornful of the program, although he was grateful for "three hots and a cot." But on his own, he quickly lost his one "honest" job. He fathered a child by the sister of a friend, but he has never assumed a family role, although he still sees the woman and the baby every so often: "Hell, that little baby got enough problems in this world without havin' Tyrell Stokes hangin' around tryin' to be his daddy." He started drinking heavily but always seemed to end up his wanderings in the parking lot of the apartment complex where two other OH graduates were living. They told one of the staffers that Tyrell kept coming around, and she finally convinced him that he had nothing to lose by going back and trying more seriously to learn some real skills.

Since his return, he has stopped drinking but is no more attentive to the training programs. He is terrified at the prospect of going back out on the streets, yet is distressed at the prospect of continuing to rely on OH, where he has to live with "all these weird dudes." He continues to affect a jaunty air, but he is thoroughly frustrated at what his life has become and thoroughly confused about what the future holds.

Tyrell is a classic denier (Zetlin and Turner, 1984). He has only the sketchiest understanding of his handicap and, in any case, will not admit that it has anything to do with his current problems: "I know a whole lotta dudes out on the streets just as stupid as me, but they're all rich. Nice cars, fine women, fancy clothes. It just ain't fair." Tyrell has built this conviction into a consistent philosophy. At first, when I heard him talk about his life and hard times, I assumed that he would be particularly resentful toward White people. I gradually learned, however, that his tormentors were not racially categorized: "Black, White—what the hell? The way I see it, anybody'll get you in the ass if he thinks you can't fight back." I asked him if he thought that I would try to hurt him in some way. "Nah," he said after some reflection. "You're a—what? Teacher? Social worker? Something like that. All you people are losers like me. Never met a 'bad' social worker."

The consistency of this Hobbesian view of society gives Tyrell's autobiography an "oratorical" character (Howarth, 1980). He is always careful to use his reminiscences to prove his central thesis. Despite his casual manner, he rarely says anything off the cuff. He is always trying to make his listeners understand the basic dog-eat-dog nature of the world. Indeed, he began the following story with an explicit instruction to me to make sure that it is accurately recorded:

> You got this story down straight, now? It's like this: Juanita [the girl he got pregnant] never did know nothing about me. How could she know I was poison for her? All she knew was on the surface and that was fine, fine, fine. But I knew what I was, and that's all that mattered. I could tell what she wanted, and I knew she couldn't see me for what I am. So one night I says to her, "Let's go to [the most expensive restaurant in town]." She says, "How on earth?" I says, "Don't worry, baby, you're with Tyrell Stokes now." So she borrows her sister's best dress and fixes her hair and gets done up all like Whitney Houston. I wanted her real bad right then—more than ever. But I had to control it. Me? I show up in cutoffs and some old Nikes I fished out of a dumpster. She didn't say nothing. So we get there and this guy at the door says, "Can't you read? Jacket and tie required, sir." Sir! I says, "No, sir, I can't read. I am too fuckin' bad to read your fuckin' sign." He didn't say nothing. "And what's more, sir, I don't have no money to pay for your fuckin' food even if you do got the balls to let me in." Poor Juanita was crying. But she didn't say nothing. So I says to the guy, "I'll tell you how bad I am. If I feel like it, I'm gonna take a leak right in that fountain!" And I start to go over, but a couple of waiters ran out and tossed me outside. I guess if they didn't, I'd-a have to take that leak for sure! Juanita didn't say nothing, but she called her brother and asked him to pick her up to drive her home. I stood with her till I seen his car comin',

then I took off. I run and run till I just about puked. I didn't even know where I ended up. But she never said a word. But I had to make her see what I was before it was too late.

Although the story itself is wrenchingly emotional, it is introduced with steady calculation. He is also the calculating maker of his own downfall. So eager is he to demonstrate his hypothesis that in this story he deliberately engineers a scenario that could not have ended happily. There is no reason why he could not have taken the young lady on a pleasant, ordinary dinner date, but instead he had to set himself up for a spectacularly humiliating failure lest the poor girl miss the point that things *always* end badly when he is involved.

Tyrell is resignedly tolerant of others, especially OH clients, who do not see life as he does: "They're just dummies, right? What can you expect? I try to tell them the way it is, but it's like nobody's home when you talk to them. Guess they'll have to spend a couple of months in lockup like me before they'll really learn."

Tyrell offers himself as a prototypic victim of an unjust system—despite his good looks and charm, he cannot get anywhere, probably because of the vicious jealousy of the "bad" people out there. Tyrell the paradigmatic martyr is the protagonist in a "self-absolutory" strategy for the mythological rearrangement of his life (Hankiss, 1981). His self-image is negative, but he does not believe that he ever had a chance at something better. He is not speaking specifically of the shortcomings of his own early life; he means more generally the malign nature of society that will always take advantage of a "born loser" like himself.

Nico Petrakis

Nico is 29 years old, although his giggly manner makes him seem more like an adolescent. He was born and raised in a small port town near OH that has long been a center of Greek immigration. Although it has "gone touristy" in the past decade, the town remains a close-knit haven of Greek family, religious, and other cultural values. Nico's re-

tardation was recognized but not given any special emphasis outside school. There were always caring relatives and family friends to help and encourage him, and he was allowed to work in his uncle's dockside café, even earning a small but regular salary there as a cook's helper when he got older. Nico's formal academic skills are good, but he has had a problem matching his behavioral responses to his emotions. He opts to act "silly" rather than try to sort out a more nuanced set of responses to life's challenges.

Nico's particular problem has been dealing with anger. He has decided that it would be "ungrateful" of him ever to admit that things were not to his liking, especially things done by his family. He therefore tended to let his frustrations seethe beneath his giggling exterior. At the flashpoint, he used to retire to his bedroom or to the café storeroom to kick the walls. As he got bigger and stronger, he damaged a fair amount of masonry. His parents were willing to tolerate these outbursts up to the point where they began to threaten the family's very respectable image in the community. They reluctantly agreed to place him in a private supervised boarding home, but after a year's time, they were overcome with remorse and brought him home. Thoroughly confused, Nico got more and more out of control.

Then, after his father heard about OH from a relative who was a high school guidance counselor, he decided that Nico could benefit from the rigorous behavioral training offered there. So Nico was enrolled as a private (i.e., not court adjudicated) client. He spent two years participating in the full program and then graduated to a more lightly supervised apartment program. He is now working at a steady job on the serving line at a busy cafeteria in a big mall. Now that he is "fixed," his family wants him to come back home. Nico does not want to hurt their feelings, but he is afraid that he will relapse if he leaves the care of OH.

Nico is the only one of my main informants with strong and generally positive ties to a community beyond OH, and it is not surprising that he tells much of his story in terms of that community.

He is not as adept as the other three in forming coherent narratives, but he leaves no doubt that he is very proud of his heritage and is eager to tell others about it.

Nico does not, however, have a highly visible concept of self. He always deflects discussions of himself onto his family. If asked, for example, what he did at the café, he will instead launch into a disjointed set of anecdotes about his uncle who owned the café. Nico is a fully engaged member of his community. He is simply more comfortable talking about the group than about his special place in it.

Nico copes by means of passing (Zetlin and Turner, 1984). He is well aware of his deficits but tries to put himself in situations where they will not be noticeable. He often asks, "Am I OK? Do I look right?" He winces when he asks such questions: "Don't wanna hurt these guys' feelings," he explains. "I just don't wanna look like a retard." On the other hand, he is not above using his retardation to get himself out of sticky situations. He tells of once encountering an irate customer at the cafeteria. The man wanted to punch him out for some imagined offense. Nico started giggling hysterically until the bully went away: "Better he think I'm a retard than he beat me up!"

Nico savors his past the way that [the other case histories] do not. But it is very difficult for him to reconstruct it in words; despite his superior academic skills, he is far less articulate than they in ordinary conversation. Nico's autobiography exists as a "text" only because I kept asking him prompting questions, as the following excerpt demonstrates:

[Researcher: Tell me about what you did at your uncle's café.]

Yes, Uncle John. He's a great guy. I really love him.

[R: What did you do there?]

He cooks all his own food. Even bakes. Bread, cakes.

[R: Did you help him?]

He opens every day for breakfast and then he stays open until really late. He never likes to turn people away.

[R: Did you help him in the kitchen?]

Oh yeah. I like to help. He's just like my Pop. They always want to help people. That's why he bought the café when he retired. He wanted to help people. People always need good food, he says.

[R: Tell me about Epiphany.]

Yes. It's our great day. Everybody comes to town, even people from very far away who moved away. They all come back. The Archbishop comes to bless the cross. He throws it in the Bay. The boys dive for it. Who gets it gets good luck all year. There's always a party at the café for the winner.

[R: Did any of your brothers ever win?]

No, but my cousin Al came close one year. The year the Garofalous boy won it. But it's OK—he's like family, too.

[R: What happens at the café on Epiphany?]

Big party. All day long. Sometimes even free sandwiches for the people out on the dock. Singing, dancing. Uncle John never closes down at all on Epiphany.

[R: Did you wait on tables for that big crowd?]

Sure. My brothers and sisters, all my cousins. Everybody helps out. Everybody has something to do. My Mom is a great singer. She sings Greek songs. Italian songs. Even Spanish songs.

[R: Can you sing any Greek songs?]

A little. But my Mom has a beautiful voice. So does my brother Lou. Not my brother Steve. But he's real smart in school, so he don't have to sing, Pop says. He helps out at the café too. He keeps the books for Uncle John. He studies to be a CIA.

[R: Do you mean a CPA, an accountant?]

Yeah, that too. One year he decided he wanted to dive for the cross, but he couldn't swim so good like some of the other guys. He said, "Don't tell Mom." I didn't tell her. He didn't win, but he didn't drown either, so he says it was all worth it.

[R: Did you ever want to dive?]

No. Al's a really good swimmer, though. Later he taught Steve to swim better, but Steve said his diving days were over.

Although it may appear that Nico was not able to respond to me very effectively, he was very pleased to participate and was especially delighted to learn that I had come from an ethnic background that, while not Greek, is similar to it in many ways. He felt that I could understand the mixture of affection and bewilderment that he felt about his community, with its promise of security, and all the potential suffocation that went along with it. Nevertheless, his reminiscences do not have a "shape" independent of our interaction. Nico's is the [more] clearly *dialogic* of the [two] autobiographies.

In spite of this drawback, Nico certainly has worked out his own metaphor. His is a "dynastic" story (Hankiss, 1981). He gives the impression of a man with a very positive self-image. He believes that he is making progress in handling himself appropriately, and he knows that in the eyes of society he is now doing well at a real, adult job. On the whole, he thinks of himself as a well-balanced, happy man with decent prospects. There is even a bride in the offering—a girl "from the Other Side" being sent to him by an aunt. He attributes this fortunate status to his upbringing in the bosom of a large, caring family and the sound traditions of the ethnic community.

This metaphor often takes on an aspect of noblesse oblige. Nico's family taught him to work for what he needed and to take pride in honest work; nevertheless, those who were sick or otherwise unfortunate needed to be helped if they were "family." Thus, Nico treats the other OH clients as a surrogate family, and he is always helping them by lending money or giving them his tapes, clothes, or bicycle. He never refuses to help anyone read or tell time or make change. He is not at all supercilious in these ministrations and appears to be genuinely liked and appreciated by all the others.

CONCLUSIONS

In the material discussed, we can see that there is a suggestive associational relationship between the social coping strategies of deinstitutionalized mentally [challenged] adults (as detailed by Zetlin and Turner, 1984) and the development of consistent self-images. Those self-images are in turn correlated with the adoption of consistent autobiographical forms that convey metaphors of the stigmatized self. Thus, Nico, who has a very positive self-image, chooses to cope by means of strategies that allow him to minimize the effects

of his handicap. He has integrated his retardation more or less comfortably into his self-image and so has no need to deny it; in fact, he can use it for strategic defensive purposes when necessary. On the other hand, Tyrell's self-image is very negative, but his feelings about himself are not solely the result of despair over his handicap—indeed, the handicap hardly figures in his worldview of omnipresent oppression. For him, denial is possible because his retardation is the least important burden that he bears in a world of woe. . . .

My autobiographical research demonstrates the ability of mentally [challenged] people to adopt consistent behavior patterns that enable them to cope in the noninstitutional community. It is therefore a potentially useful addition to the repertoire of ethnographers working among stigmatized and disabled subjects. My contention, however, is that the life history method may not be primarily useful in determining the content of a "culture of deviance," although it can certainly enrich our understanding of what the policy of deinstitutionalization has meant in the lives of its supposed beneficiaries. Rather, it is a way of understanding how deviants manipulate symbolic forms in order to adapt and communicate with the "mainstream" culture in which they must live.

This research reaffirms the implications in the current literature that the adaptive strategies of stigmatized deviants like persons with mental retardation are more than responses of the moment—they reflect a person's preexisting internalized self-image and enhance that image by facilitating social interactions. We may now add that it is possible to encode such self-images in symbolic form, such that when a person tells a life story, meaningful information can be conveyed through the *form* of the story, even when the subject manifests serious linguistic deficits. The autobiography is organized so as to bring to the fore recognizable metaphors of the stigmatized self that resonate with the perceived audience. It is a means to bridge the gap between the "mainstream" and the world of meaning of a heretofore dispossessed and unheard deviant population.

REFERENCES

Dollard, J. 1935. *Criteria for the Life History.* New York: P. Smith.

Hankiss, A. 1981. "Ontologies of the Self: On the Metaphorical Rearranging of One's Life History," pp. 203–210 in *Biography and Society: The Life History Approach in the Social Sciences,* edited by D. Bertaux. Beverly Hills, CA: Sage.

Howarth, W. L. 1980. "Some Principles of Autobiography," pp. 86–114 in *Autobiography: Essays Theoretical and Critical,* edited by J. Olney. Princeton, NJ: Princeton University Press.

Kluckhohn, C. 1945. "The Personal Document in Anthropological Science," pp. 78–193 in *The Use of Personal Documents in History, Anthropology, and Sociology,* edited by L. Gottschalk, C. Kluckhohn, and R. Angell. New York: Social Science Research Council.

Langness, L. L. 1965. *The Life History in Anthropological Science.* New York: Holt, Rinehart Winston.

Zetlin, A. G., and J. L. Turner. 1984. Self-Perspectives on Being Handicapped: Stigma and Adjustment, pp. 93–120 in *Lives in Process: Mildly Retarded Adults in a Large City,* edited by R. B. Edgerton. Washington, DC: American Association on Mental Deficiency.

CROSS-CULTURAL PATTERNS
IN EATING DISORDERS

JENNIFER E. PATE   COLLEEN HESTER
ANDRES J. PUMARIEGA   DAVID M. GARNER

It has been noted that eating disorders (anorexia nervosa, bulimia, and their variants) are unique because they appear to be the only form of psychopathology in which culture appears to play a major role in determining prevalence (Yates, 1990). In the past, it was commonly believed that these disorders were primarily found in young women from achievement-oriented, upper-middle-class families from ethnic backgrounds where food was emphasized as a means of affective expression (Bruch, 1973). For this reason, eating disorders have been considered to be culture-bound syndromes, constellations of symptoms that are restricted to a particular culture or group of cultures (Prince, 1983). However, it appears that the prevalence of these disorders may be increasing dramatically among all social classes and ethnic groups in the United States as well as in a number of other nations with diverse cultures (Jones et al., 1980; Yates, 1989).

Several authors have suggested that changes in cultural values and attitudes may play a significant role in this increase in the development, incidence, and prevalence of eating disorders (Bruch, 1973; Garner and Garfinkel, 1980; Pumariega, 1986). The rise in the prevalence of eating disorders may be a result of the wider adoption of the ideal that thinness has come to symbolize in Western culture; an ideal symbolizing self-discipline, control, sexual liberation, assertiveness, competitiveness, and affiliation with a higher socioeconomic class, as well as the traditional value of attractiveness (Garner et al., 1983;

Nasser, 1988). However, the extent to which this ideal influences the development of eating disorders in non-Western cultures is unclear (Bruch, 1973; Crisp et al., 1976; Nasser, 1988; Prince, 1983). The purpose of the present review of studies from different regions of the United States and other countries is to further clarify possible cultural factors that play a role in the development of eating disorders.

EATING DISORDERS IN DIFFERENT AMERICAN ETHNIC GROUPS

A century ago, Fenwick (1880) observed that anorexia nervosa was more common in the "wealthier classes of society than those who have to procure their bread by daily labor" (p. 107). Bruch (1966) was one of the first modern investigators to suggest a relationship between sociocultural factors and the development of eating disorders. In her series of 43 patients with anorexia nervosa, there were seven Catholics, 11 Protestants, and 25 Jewish individuals. Ten of these individuals came from an upper-class background, 23 from a middle-class background, and six individuals were from a lower-class background. She noted the "conspicuous absence of Negro patients," despite the fact that there were a proportionate number of blacks hospitalized for other problems at the time of her study. She concluded that the main psychological conflicts centered around a struggle for control, a sense of identity, and a sense of effectiveness, with the relentless pursuit of thinness being a final step in this effort. She attributed such attitudes to the strong achievement orientations and psychological insensitivity of the upwardly mobile social and cultural backgrounds of the patients' families.

Rowland (1970), on the other hand, found a high proportion of individuals from lower- and middle-class backgrounds (60 percent and 34 percent, respectively) in his sample. Only 6 percent of his sample was from an upper-class background. Of the 30 patients in his sample, 47 percent were Catholic, 43 percent were Jewish, and only 10 percent were Protestant. Because of the majority of Italian and Jewish individuals (17 of 30) in this study, Rowland (1970) suggested a possible relationship between cultural origin and the importance of food, thus predisposing Jewish, Catholic, and Italian populations to a risk of developing an eating disorder. No black individuals were found in his sample.

Theander (1970) suggested that eating disorders may become more prevalent among all social classes as attitudes about such issues as achievement, appearance, weight, and control become more pervasive throughout all sectors of society.

Although several authors have noted an underrepresentation of black individuals with anorexia nervosa and bulimia in their studies (Garfinkel and Garner, 1982; Gray et al., 1987), there is a growing consensus that the prevalence of anorexia nervosa in the black population is most likely higher than previously thought and is currently on the rise (Hsu, 1987; Pumariega et al., 1984). The reasons for this increase may be attributed to changing referral patterns, greater awareness, and improved case detection, along with increasing use of the health care system by blacks (Crisp et al., 1976; Holden and Robinson, 1988), changing socioeconomic demography with increased exposure to the pressure related to upward social mobility (Andersen and Hay, 1985), and a wider adoption of expectations about body shape and appearance (Hsu, 1987). In other words, it is possible that thinness is becoming as valued by black culture as it is by Caucasian culture (Hsu, 1987). . . .

Very little has been noted about the prevalence and factors associated with eating disorders in Asian-Americans and Native Americans. Kope and Sack (1987) described three cases of anorexia nervosa that were documented in Vietnamese refugees. The three individuals came from middle- or upper-class families that experienced a loss of status concomitant with the Communist takeover that caused them to leave their homeland. Each of these girls had also experienced a major object loss; two of the girls were separated from both parents, and one was separated from her mother.

Yates (1989) has documented cases of anorexia nervosa in adolescent Native American girls who have come from the Navajo community in Tucson, Arizona. The author states that in each instance, these individuals were children of families who had moved off the reservation, were high achieving, and expected their children to succeed. "The painful thinness of these anorexic girls seemed to be a repudiation of the image of the traditional woman on the reservation" (Yates, 1989; p. 816). . . .

Van Den Broucke and Vandereycken (1986) studied fourteen European exchange students who were diagnosed with an eating disorder after coming to the United States. The authors suggested that the experience of encountering a culture clash was one of the possible predisposing or precipitating factors that could play a role in the development of an eating disorder. The authors suggest that in addition to the more usual causes of an eating disorder, adolescent exchange students are confronted with a sudden separation from the family of origin, which may create a serious challenge to the individual's autonomy. Furthermore, the adjustment to new social and familial interaction patterns may lead to unique stresses that can potentiate an eating disorder. Particularly, when exchange students come from upper- or middle-class families with heightened performance expectations, they may be at an increased risk for eating or other adjustment problems.

Few systematic studies have attempted to examine the role of culture and acculturation to American culture in the development and outcome of eating disorders. In a comparative and correlational study of acculturation and eating attitudes in white and Hispanic adolescent girls between the ages of 16 and 18, Pumariega (1986) compared the Eating Attitudes Test (EAT) scores (Garner and Garfinkel, 1979) of Hispanic subjects to those of a group of predominantly white subjects from the southern United States. Although the two groups exhibited similar scores on the EAT, there was a significant correlation between acculturation and higher EAT scores in the Hispanic group. There was also a positive but nonsignificant correlation between socioeconomic status, both current and projected, and higher EAT scores. The author noted that the results supported the hypothesis that cultural factors are related to a higher prevalence of eating disorders. However, he notes that the results fail to fully support a hypothesized relationship between higher socioeconomic status and vulnerability to eating disorders. He suggests that greater adherence to the Western culture may increase an individual's vulnerability toward the development of eating disorders (Pumariega, 1986).

EATING DISORDERS IN CULTURES ABROAD

The psychiatric literature from most countries suggests that anorexia nervosa and bulimia are present but are relatively rare. There is a growing body of literature that indicates at least comparable prevalence in Western-oriented countries and increasing prevalence in developing, Third World nations. The literature from Third World nations does not typically discuss chronic diseases and disorders, because medical professionals are preoccupied with more pressing needs (Dolan, 1991). Nasser (1986) questions the accuracy of Third World findings because of methodological problems, such as the absence of operational criteria to diagnose the syndrome of anorexia nervosa. These disorders have been commonly viewed as manifestations of hysteria or anxiety and not as specific psychiatric entities.

Europe

Several authors have studied anorexia nervosa in European countries, particularly Sweden (Norring and Sohlberg, 1988; Theander, 1970) and Germany (Steinhausen, 1984). Theander (1970) studied 94 individuals in Sweden with anorexia nervosa over a 30-year period. The incidence of this disorder increased throughout the study from 0.24 cases per 100,000 inhabitants during the first decade of the study to 0.45 cases during the last decade of the study (1951 to 1960). . . .

To investigate the incidence of anorexia nervosa over a 20-year period, Willi and Grossmann (1983) reviewed the case histories of females hospitalized in various medical, psychiatric, and pediatric clinics in Zurich, Switzerland, during randomly selected 3-year periods. The authors documented an increase in the incidence of this disorder from 0.38 per 100,000 for 1956 to 1958, to 0.55 per 100,000 during 1963 to 1965, to 1.12 per 100,000 during 1973 to 1975. . . .

Lacey and Dolan (1988) presented the first report of nonwhite, normal body weight bulimics in the United Kingdom. Of the five subjects in this study, one was Pakistani, one was Jamaican, and three were from mixed racial backgrounds (two Afro-Caribbean/English, one African/Indian). All of the subjects were from the same catchment area in southwest London. In a comparison with white bulimic patients from the same area, both groups were similar in clinical presentation. However, the nonwhite subjects reported emotional deprivation that was not encountered by the white subjects. This deprivation included family distress, divorce, separation from their parents at an early age, and incestuous abuse. The five nonwhite subjects in this study all showed a poor response to treatment.

Furnham and Alibhai (1983) compared differences in the perception of female body shapes in individuals of Kenyan Asian, Kenyan British, and British origin to test their hypothesis that social and cultural factors play a dominant role in the perception of one's own and others' body shapes. As the authors predicted, the Kenyan Asians tended to perceive thin female shapes slightly more negatively and fat shapes significantly more positively than a comparable British group. It was also noted that the British Kenyans tended to have more similar perceptions to the British than the Kenyan group.

In an epidemiological study of anorexia nervosa comparing Greek adolescents living in Germany with Greek adolescents living in Greece, Fichter et al. (1983) studied three samples of Greek students between the ages of 13 and 19 years of age. Two samples were composed of subjects living in Greek towns, and the third sample represented Greek subjects residing in Munich. In the first part of the study, the authors recorded the subject's height and weight, obtained details of menstrual history, and administered the Anorexia Nervosa Inventory for Self-Rating. In the second stage of the study, subjects who were suspected of having anorexia nervosa participated in a semistructured interview. The authors noted that there was some evidence that the prevalence of anorexia nervosa was higher in the sample of Greek girls in Germany than in the sample of Greek girls who remained in Greece. This finding may be the result of difficulties that individuals in migrant families encounter when attempting to cope with the new social influences that affect family structure, values, and norms. The authors noted that while the idealization of dieting and slimness was strong for both groups, it was more pronounced for the Greek girls in Greece compared with those living in Germany.

Africa and The Middle East

In a study in northern Sudan, El-Sarrag (1968) noted that it is difficult to determine the exact prevalence of anorexia nervosa, as well as other psychiatric disorders, because many patients either do not seek treatment at all or they are treated by native healers or Zar parties. El-Sarrag (1968) noted that anorexia nervosa is uncommon in this area, suggesting that this may be because people are undernourished. Also, obesity in the female is equated with sexual attractiveness and considered a sign of beauty.

Hooper and Garner (1986) utilized the Eating Disorder Inventory to study a group of black, white, and mixed race schoolgirls in Zimbabwe. The authors noted that binge eating was present within all three groups, with the mixed race showing the strongest tendency toward this behavior. Anorexic or anorexic-like behavior was considerably more prevalent among the white and mixed race schoolgirls than among the black schoolgirls.

In a study of psychiatric morbidity among university students in Egypt, Okasha et al. (1977) documented only two cases of anorexia nervosa of the 1,050 cases that were reviewed. They noted that the clinical picture of these cases was somewhat similar to those described in Western literature, but vomiting was more noticeable than food refusal, and response to therapy was better.

Nwaefuna (1981) reported a case of anorexia nervosa in Nigeria. The individual she described was a 22-year-old black woman with a six-year history of anorexia nervosa that had its onset during the course of her first pregnancy. The author notes that the patient had a history of parental and personal marital separation, was living with her mother, and had a history of precocious physical development that had resulted in her being teased by peers during adolescence. Nwaefuna's observations (1981) are consistent with those reported by Pumariega et al. (1984) regarding the pathogenesis of the disorder. . . .

In a comparative study of abnormal eating attitudes among Arab female students of both London and Cairo universities, Nasser (1986) identified six cases of bulimia nervosa in the London sample of 50, as opposed to none in the Cairo sample of 60 subjects. She attributed this difference to the impact of exposure to Western values.

The Far East

In a study examining the frequency of anorexia nervosa in Malaysia, Buhrich (1981) found 28 female and two male cases of a total of 60,000 psychiatric referrals. It was concluded that the disorder was very rare among Malays compared with Chinese and Indians.

Ong et al. (1982) described seven Chinese females with anorexia nervosa referred to a clinical setting in Singapore. The authors concluded that there is a low incidence of this disorder in Singapore, and it appears to present in a less severe manner than is commonly documented in Western countries.

Several authors have reported a marked increase in the prevalence of anorexia nervosa and bulimia nervosa in Japan (Kamata et al., 1987; Nakane and Umino, 1987). Suematsu et al. (1985) noted that the number of patients seeking treatment for anorexia nervosa had doubled between 1976 and 1981. The clinical presentation of this disorder in Japan appears to be similar to that of Western cultures. . . .

IMPORTANT ASSOCIATED FACTORS

There may be certain factors associated with ethnicity that influence the development of eating disorders.

Socioeconomic status has been documented as a factor that correlates positively with the prevalence of anorexia nervosa and bulimia (Anderson and Hay, 1985). Jones et al. (1980), in their epidemiological survey of anorexia nervosa in Monroe County, New York, found that there was little association between social class and the incidence of anorexia nervosa among children 14 years of age or younger. However, a definite association existed with higher social class in females who were 15 years of age or older, along with a higher prevalence rate. Crisp et al. (1976) reported a difference in the prevalence of anorexia nervosa between school girls attending private and public schools. The incidence of this disorder was 1 per 200 in private school girls versus 1 per 330 in public school girls 16 to 18 years of age. . . .

A number of studies have provided some support for the often made clinical observation of a positive relationship between the competitiveness of the environment (i.e., heightened performance demands) and the prevalence of anorexia nervosa (Boskind-White and White, 1983; Garner and Garfinkel, 1980). For example, female medical students were found to have a 15 percent lifetime prevalence of eating disorders (Herzog et al., 1985). There is a five times greater prevalence of bulimia, and substantially more binge eating symptoms, in university women than among working women (Hart and Ollendick, 1985). However, Garner, Olmsted, and Garfinkel (1983) noted that it is important to distinguish between weight preoccupation and actual clinical eating disorders. For example, certain features of anorexia nervosa, such as dieting and attitudes about shape, occur on a continuum and are commonly reported in subjects who are preoccupied with their weight. However, other characteristic features of eating disorders such as ineffectiveness, interoceptive awareness, and interpersonal distrust, as measured by the Eating Disorder Inventory, are less common in nonclinical samples. The symptomatic expression of anorexia nervosa and other eating disorders appears to represent a maladaptive attempt to cope with the pressure of growing up in a stressed environment. Furthermore, individuals at risk for eating disorders appear to rely excessively on the environment for their sense of self-worth, which makes them more vulnerable to cultural pressures to succeed (Garfinkel et al., 1980; Yates, 1989).

It has also been documented that women who serve as physical ideals or physical role models to other women, such as fashion models (Garner and Garfinkel, 1980), ballet dancers (Garner et al., 1987), cheerleaders (Lundholm and Littrell, 1986), and gymnasts (Calabrese, 1985) are more likely to develop an eating disorder (Yates, 1991). In these groups, the competitive values symbolized by their vocation within a cultural context can contribute to vulnerability to these disorders.

As noted earlier by Bruch (1973), Boskind-White and White (1983) suggest that the female adolescent is vulnerable to the development of an eating disorder, because the cultural message to be slim is constantly being transmitted to her through the family, peers, teachers, books, magazines, and television. In an effort to be accepted, she behaves in a way that is consistent with the beliefs and behaviors of people in the groups to which she aspires to belong. Such messages are particularly powerful within the competitive context discussed above. Boskind-White and White (1983) hypothesize that the conflict between the dual messages of conformity and competitiveness being presented to women in Western societies renders them particularly at risk for these disorders.

Although it has been argued that the clinical presentation of eating disorders has changed since the earliest case reported by Morton (1694), asceticism continues to be an important underlying dynamic in some individuals who develop these disorders (Rampling, 1985; Russell, 1985; Yates, 1991). The aims of ascetic practices, such as dietary restriction, have evolved from the pursuit of religious goals to the fulfillment of more narcissistic needs (Rampling, 1985; Yates, 1991). It has been repeatedly suggested that young women from close, competitive families resort to eating disorders such as anorexia nervosa or bulimia as an attempt to establish a sense of control and autonomy as they struggle to resolve their confusion regarding the female's role in society (Bruch, 1973; Turner, 1984). In addition to eating disorders, it is important to note that this asceticism may also be expressed through culturally accepted behaviors such as obligatory running (Yates, 1991). The paradox is that while asceticism may decline in the general population, it may be accentuated in susceptible individuals who are struggling to establish a sense of control in their lives. . . .

DIRECTIONS FOR FUTURE RESEARCH

Several authors have suggested a risk factor model in summarizing the role that culture plays in the development of eating disorders (Garner et al., 1983; Striegel-Moore et al., 1986). As Western society's influence augments the conflicts over issues such as the female's role in society, physical appearance and attractiveness, and impulse gratification and consumption, the impact on biologically or psychologically susceptible individuals potentially increases. Therefore, the susceptible individual will be more likely to express these cultural influences symptomatically through the development of eating disorders. The specific symptomatology that is demonstrated can also be influenced by cultural variables. Anorexia nervosa and bulimia predominate in the context of an ideology of slimness. However, it is also possible that in other cultural contexts other atypical forms of eating disorders may develop.

There is little question of the importance of cultural factors in the development of eating disorders. Even when material well-being is considered, there appears to be variation in the occurrence of these disorders both among American ethnic groups and between different nationalities. However, there is relatively little systematic empirical research on cross-cultural aspects of eating disorders. Furthermore, many of the reviews of the literature on this topic are not comprehensive and are biased by the author's emphasis on his/her country of origin (Dolan, 1991). A review by an author from a non-Western country may be useful for posing future research problems. It may also be important for researchers in non-Western settings to identify and operationalize criteria for subclinical or atypical forms of eating disorders that are unique to their particular culture. . . .

REFERENCES

Andersen, A. E. and Hay, A. 1985. "Racial and Socioeconomic Influences in Anorexia Nervosa and Bulimia." *The International Journal of Eating Disorders,* 4(4):479–487.

Boskind-White, M. and White, W. C. 1983. *Bulimarexia: The Binge/Purge Cycle,* New York: W. W. Norton.

Bruch, H. 1966. "Anorexia Nervosa and Its Differential Diagnosis." *Journal of Nervous Mental Diseases,* 141(5):555–566.

Bruch, H. 1973. *Eating Disorders: Obesity, Anorexia and the Person Within,* New York: Basic Books.

Buhrich, N. 1981. "Frequency of Presentation of Anorexia Nervosa in Malaysia, Australia, and New Zealand." *Journal of Psychiatry,* 15:153–155.

Calabrese, L. H. 1985. "Nutritional and Medical Aspects of Gymnastics." *Clinical Sports Medicine,* 4:28.

Crisp, A. H., Palmer, R., and Kelney, R. 1976. "How Common Is Anorexia Nervosa: A Prevalence Study." *British Journal of Psychiatry,* 128:549–554.

Dolan, B. 1991. "Cross-Cultural Aspects of Anorexia Nervosa and Bulimia: A Review." *The International Journal of Eating Disorders,* 10(1):67–78.

El-Sarrag, M. E. 1968. "Psychiatry in the Northern Sudan: A Study in Comparative Psychiatry." *British Journal of Psychiatry,* 114:946–948.

Fenwick, S. 1880. *On Atrophy of the Stomach and on the Nervous Affections of the Digestive Organs,* London: Churchill Foster.

Fichter, M. M., Weyerer, S., Sourdi, L., and Sourdi, Z. 1983. The Epidemiology of Anorexia Nervosa: A Comparison of Greek Adolescents Living in Germany and Greek Adolescents Living in Greece, pp. 95–105. In *Anorexia Nervosa: Recent Developments in Research,* eds. P. L. Darby, P. E. Garfinkel, D. M. Garner, and D. V. Coscina, New York: Alan R. Liss.

Furnham, A. and Alibhai, N. 1983. "Cross-Cultural Differences in the Perception of Female Body Shapes." *Psychological Medicine,* 13:829–837.

Garfinkel, P. E. and Garner, D. M. 1982. *Anorexia Nervosa: A Multidimensional Perspective,* New York: Brunner/Mazel.

Garfinkel, P. E. Moldofsky, H., and Garner, D. M. 1980. "The Heterogeneity of Anorexia Nervosa." *Archives of General Psychiatry,* 37:1036–1040.

Garner, D. M. and Garfinkel, P. E. 1979. "The Eating Attitudes Test: An Index of the Symptoms of Anorexia Nervosa." *Psychological Medicine,* 9:273–279.

Garner, D. M., and Garfinkel, P. E. 1980. "Socio-Cultural Factors in the Development of Anorexia Nervosa." *Psychological Medicine,* 10:647–656.

Garner, D. M., Garfinkel, P. E., and Olmsted, M. P. 1983. "An Overview of Sociocultural Factors in the Development of Anorexia Nervosa, pp. 65–82. In *Anorexia Nervosa: Recent Developments in Research,* eds. P. L. Darby, P. and D. V. Coscina. New York: Alan R. Liss.

Garner, D. M., Garfinkel, P. E., and Bonato, D. P. 1987. "Body Image Measurement in Eating Disorders." *Advanced Psychosomatic Medicine,* 17:119–133.

Garner, D. M., Olmsted, M. P., and Garfinkel, P. E. 1983. "Does Anorexia Nervosa Occur on a Continuum?: Subgroups of Weight-Preoccupied Women and Their Relationship to Anorexia Nervosa." *The International Journal of Eating Disorders,* 2(4):11–20.

Garner, D. M., Rockert, W., and Olmstead, M. P. 1987. "A Prospective Study of Eating Disturbances in the Ballet." *Psychotherapy and Psychopharmacology,* 48:170–175.

Gray, J. J., Ford, K., and Kelly, L. M. 1987. "The Prevalence of Bulimia in a Black College Population." *The International Journal of Eating Disorders,* 6(6):733–740.

Hart, K. J. and Ollendick T. H. 1985. "Prevalence of Bulimia in Working and University Women." *American Journal of Psychiatry,* 142:851–854.

Herzog, D. B., Pepose, M., Norman, D. K., and Rigotti, M. A. 1985. "Eating Disorders and Social Maladjustment in Female Medical Students." *Journal of Nervous Mental Diseases,* 173:734–737.

Holden, N. L. and Robinson, P. H. 1988. "Anorexia Nervosa and Bulimia Nervosa in British Blacks." *British Journal of Psychiatry,* 152:544–549.

Hooper, M. S. H. and Gamer, D. M. 1986. "Application of the Eating Disorders Inventory to a Sample of Black, White, and Mixed Race Schoolgirls in Zimbabwe." *The International Journal of Eating Disorders,* 5(1):161–168.

Hsu, L. K. G. 1987. "Are the Eating Disorders Becoming More Common in Blacks." *The International Journal of Eating Disorders,* 6(1):113–124.

Jones, D., Fox, M., Babigian, H. and Hutton, H. 1980. "Epidemiology of Anorexia in Monroe County, New York: 1960–1976." *Psychosomatic Medicine,* 42:551–558.

Kamata, K., Nogami, Y. and Momma, K. 1987. "Binge-eating Among Female Students." *Japanese Journal of Psychiatry and Neurology,* 41(1):151–152.

Kope, T. M. and Sack, W. H. 1987. "Anorexia Nervosa in Southeast Asian Refugees: A Report on Three Cases." *Journal of American Academy of Child Adolescence Psychiatry,* 26(5):795–797.

Lacey, J. H. and Dolan, B. M. 1988. "Bulimia in British Blacks and Asians: A Catchment Area Study." *British Journal of Psychiatry,* 152:73–79.

Lundholm, J. K. and Littrell, J. M. 1986. "Desire for Thinness among High School Cheerleaders." *Adolescence,* 21:573–579.

Morton, R. 1694. *Phthisologia: Or a Treatise of Consumptions,* London: Smith and Walford.

Nakane, A. and Umino, M. 1987. "Psychopathology of Anorexia Nervosa in Young Adolescence." *Japanese Journal of Psychiatry Neurology,* 41(1):153.

Nasser, M. 1986. "Comparative Study of the Prevalence of Abnormal Eating Attitudes among Arab Female Students of Both London and Cairo Universities." *Psychological Medicine,* 16:621–625.

Nasser, M. 1988. "Culture and Weight Consciousness." *Journal of Psychosomatic Research,* 32(6):573–577.

Norring, C. and Sohlberg, S. 1988. "Eating Disorder Inventory in Sweden: Description, Cross-Cultural Comparison, and Clinical Utility." *Acta Psychiatric Scandinavia,* 78:567–575.

Nwaefuna, A. 1981. "Anorexia Nervosa in a Developing Country." *British Journal of Psychiatry,* 138:270–271.

Okasha, A., Kamel, M., Sadek, A., Lotaif, F. and Bishry, Z. 1977. "Psychiatric Morbidity among University Students in Egypt." *British Journal of Psychiatry,* 131:149–154.

Ong, Y. L., Tsoi, W. F. and Cheah, J. S. 1982. "A Clinical and Psychosocial Study of Seven Cases of Anorexia Nervosa in Singapore." *Singapore Medical Journal,* 23:255–261.

Prince, R. 1983. "Is Anorexia Nervosa a Culture-Bound Syndrome?" *Transcultural Psychiatry Research Review,* 20:299–300.

Pumariega, A. J. 1986. "Acculturation and Eating Attitudes in Adolescent Girls: A Comparative and Correlational Study." *Journal of American Academy Child Adolescence Psychiatry,* 25(2):276–279.

Pumariega, A. J., Edwards, P. and Mitchell, C. B. 1984. "Anorexia Nervosa in Black Adolescents." *Journal of American Academy Child Adolescence Psychiatry,* 23(1):111–114.

Rampling, D. 1985. "Ascetic Deals and Anorexia Nervosa." *Journal of Psychiatric Research,* 19:89–94.

Rowland, C. 1970. "Anorexia and Obesity." *International Psychiatry Clinics,* 7:37–137.

Russell, G. F. M. 1985. "The Changing Nature of Anorexia Nervosa: An Introduction to the Conference." *Journal of Psychiatric Research,* 19:101–168.

Steinhausen, H. C. 1984. "Transcultural Comparison of Eating Attitudes in Young Females and Anorectic Patients." *Archiv fur Psychiatrie und Nervenkrankheiten,* 234(3):198–201.

Striegel-Moore, R. H., Silberstein, L. R. and Rodin, J. 1986. "Towards an Understanding of Risk Factors of Bulimia." *American Psychology,* 41:246–263.

Suematsu, H., Ishikawa, H. Kuboki, T. and Ito, T. 1985. "Statistical Studies on Anorexia Nervosa in Japan: Detailed Clinical Data on 1011 Patients." *Psychotherapy Psychosomatics,* 43:96–103.

Theander, S. 1970. "Anorexia Nervosa: A Psychiatric Investigation of 94 Female Patients." *Acta Psychiatry Scandinavia,* 214:1–194.

Turner, B. S. 1984. *The Body and Society,* New York: Basil Blackwell.

Van Den Broucke, S. and Vandereycken, W. 1986. "Risk Factors for the Development of Eating Disorders in Adolescent Exchange Students: An Exploratory Survey." *Journal of Adolescence,* 9:145–150.

Willi, J. and Grossmann, S. 1983. "Epidemiology of Anorexia Nervosa in a Defined Region of Switzerland." *American Journal of Psychiatry,* 140(5):564–567.

Yates, A. 1989. "Current Perspectives on the Eating Disorders: I. History, Psychological and Biological Aspects." *Journal of American Academy Child Adolescence Psychiatry.* 28(6):813–828.

Yates, A. 1990. "Current Perspectives on the Eating Disorders: II. Treatment, Outcome, and Research Directions." *Journal of American Academy Child Adolescence Psychiatry,* 29(1):1–9.

Yates, A. 1991. *Compulsive Exercise and the Eating Disorders: Toward an Integrated Theory of Activity.* New York: Brunner/Mazel.

ANOREXICS AND BULIMICS: DEVELOPING DEVIANT IDENTITIES

PENELOPE A. McLORG
DIANE E. TAUB

Fear of being overweight—of being visually deviant—often leads to a striving for thinness, especially among women. In the extreme, this avoidance of overweight engenders eating disorders, which themselves constitute deviance. Anorexia nervosa, or purposeful starvation, embodies visual as well as behavioral deviation. Anorexics weigh at least 15 percent less than normal weight standards for their age and height. This visual deviation results from a behavioral deviance characterized by self-starvation alone or in combination with excessive exercising, occasional binge-eating, vomiting, or laxative abuse. On the other hand, bulimia nervosa is in most cases only behaviorally deviant. It involves binge eating to be followed by vomiting, laxative abuse, fasting, or vigorous exercising. Bulimics are not visually deviant because their weight is normal or close to normal (Haller, 1992; Schlundt and Johnson, 1990).

Increasingly prevalent in the past few decades, anorexia and bulimia have emerged as major health problems. Approximately 2.5 percent of college students are anorexic, and between 4 and 19 percent are bulimic (Schlundt and Johnson, 1990). Six to 20 percent of anorexics die (Haller, 1992), though bulimia is less life-threatening (Giannini et al., 1990).

Eating disorders are most common among young, white, affluent (upper-middle to upper class) women in modern, industrialized countries (Hsu, 1989; Schlundt and Johnson, 1990). Anorexia occurs most often in two age groups: 13 to 14 and 17 to 18. As for bulimia, the usual age of onset is between 16 and 19 (Mitchell and Pyle, 1988).

Eating disorders have mostly been studied from medical and psychiatric perspectives. Such studies are deficient for obscuring the social facets of the disorders and ignoring the individuals' own definitions of their situations. Thus, in our research reported here, we focus on those two factors, analyzing how they are interrelated, especially the impact of negative societal reaction on the identities and activities of individuals with eating disorders.

METHODOLOGY

We derive our data from a self-help group called BANISH (Bulimics/Anorexics In Self-Help), which met at a university in an urban center of the mid-South. Founded by one of us (Taub), BANISH was advertised in local newspapers as offering a group experience for individuals who were anorexic or bulimic. Thirty people joined the group.

BANISH's demographic profile typifies what has been found in other studies (Schlundt and Johnson, 1990). Members ranged in ages from 19 to 36, with most being 21. All but one were white females. Most were college students; only four were nonstudents, of whom three had college degrees. Nearly all came from upper-middle or lower-upper-class households. The duration of eating disorder ranged from three to fifteen years.

The sole male and three of the females were anorexic; the remaining females were bulimic. Far fewer anorexics than bulimics showed up in this sample because in our society anorexia is less prevalent than bulimia (Schlundt and Johnson, 1990) and anorexics are more likely to deny having an eating disorder (Giannini et al., 1990).

We observed the group's weekly two-hour meetings for two years. During the course of this study, thirty people attended at least one meeting. Attendance varied: ten individuals came nearly every Sunday; five about twice a month; and the remaining fifteen once a month or less, often when seeing their eating problems become "more severe" or "bizarre." At most meetings there were twelve members. Modeled after Alcoholics Anonymous, BANISH encouraged participants to discuss their backgrounds and experiences with others. The group constituted the only source of help for many members, who were reluctant to contact health professionals because of shame, embarrassment, or financial difficulties.

After two years of taking notes at the meetings, we conducted informal interviews with fifteen members, each lasting from two to four hours. Chosen for their longer experience with eating disorders, these interviewees were asked to discuss in greater detail their comments made at the meetings. We were most interested in what led to their eating disorders, how others reacted to their actions, and how they interpreted and dealt with those reactions.

Aside from taking notes at group meetings and individual interviews, we were able to learn more about the subjects in other ways. This is because they visited Taub's office, telephoned both of us, and invited us to their homes or out for coffee. Even among the fifteen who did not attend the meetings regularly, ten contacted us once a month. These informal encounters fostered genuine communication and mutual trust, providing us with greater insight into the lives of anorexics and bulimics.

CONFORMITY

The data suggest that, ironically, conformity to conventional values serves as a precondition for becoming deviant. Like most anorexics and bulimics, our subjects started dieting in their teens. They were merely trying to conform to the cultural norm of thinness. In our society, slim bodies are considered most worthy and attractive, whereas overweight is seen as unhealthy, even offensive or disgusting. This slimness norm is most evident in advertising. Female models in newspaper, magazine, and TV ads are uniformly slender, and ads for diet aids and other similar products suggest that fatness is undesirable (Silverstein et al., 1986). The slimness norm also finds support in the family, where parents socialize children to desire light body weight and slender shape. According to our subjects, their fathers were preoccupied with exercising and their mothers with food preparation. When those subjects dieted and lost weight, they were enthusiastically praised. Because society emphasizes physical appearance as more important for women than men to have, women feel much more pressured to conform to the slimness norm. Not surprisingly, in one survey, of the 56 percent of all women aged 24 to 54 who dieted, 76 percent did so for cosmetic rather than health reasons.

Among these dieters are some who may develop anorexia or bulimia because of their zealous conformity to the ideal of slimness. This specific conformity seems to be part and parcel of a general, overall pattern of conformity to various conventional values. As our data suggest, before our subjects became anorexic or bulimic, they generally did well in school, joining honor societies or academic clubs. They were also "model children" or "the pride and joy" of their parents, to whom they showed strong emotional attachment.

PRIMARY DEVIANCE

Zealous conformity to the slimness norm does not by itself necessarily lead to anorexia or bulimia. At least two other factors must be at work. One is constant failure to achieve or maintain a desired weight through dieting, exercise, or other means. This repeated failure is likely to compel the individual to resort to extreme, deviant ways of achieving weight loss, such as purposeful starvation or bingeing accompanied by vomiting or other purging methods. Another factor in the development of eating disorders is loss of control triggered by a stressful event, such as entering college, leaving home, or feeling rejected by the opposite sex. The extreme weight-loss efforts serve as coping mechanisms, helping the individual to deal with stress.

Initially, the individual succeeds in maintaining a lowered weight and slim appearance. Moreover, friends and family, unaware of the individual's eating disorders, may compliment the individual for losing weight and looking good. Thus, the individual may not see herself or himself as anorexic or bulimic. Such a person is what Lemert (1951) called a *primary deviant,* whose deviant self-image has not emerged despite the exhibition of deviant behavior such as purposely starving or bingeing and purging.

SECONDARY DEVIANCE

Primary deviance, however, usually leads to *secondary deviance,* in which the individual sees herself or himself as a deviant and this deviant self-image affects the individual's social roles and activities (Lemert, 1967). Anorexics and bulimics may begin to see themselves as deviant when they stop receiving compliments for their slimness or weight loss. This is the time when parents or friends become concerned about the anorexic appearing emaciated. The significant others become increasingly aware of the anorexic's compulsive exercising, preoccupation with preparing food but not consuming it, and ritualistic eating patterns (such as cutting food into minute pieces or eating only certain foods at prescribed times). As for bulimics, friends or family members begin to question how they can eat large amounts of food and still stay slim. The significant others may notice telltale marks on the bulimic's hand, which result from repeated inducement of vomiting. Some bulimics may get "caught in the act," bent over the commode.

Given those observations, friends and relatives will likely label the bingeing or purging individual as "anorexic" or "bulimic." Others will label the individual a "starving waif" or "pig." Most significant in this labeling process is society's tendency to turn the individual's deviant status into the individual's *master status* (Becker, 1973). Thus, Nicole, a subject of our study, who had been known as the "school's brain," became known as the "school's anorexic."

This negative societal reaction to anorexics and bulimics produces certain consequences. Initially, anorexics tend to vigorously deny the label. Most of the subjects in our research felt that they were not "anorexic enough," not skinny enough. One subject, Robin, did not regard herself as having the "skeletal" appearance she associated with anorexia. These subjects found it difficult to differentiate between socially approved modes of weight loss, eating less and exercising more, and the extremes of these behaviors. In fact, many of their activities—cheerleading, modeling, gymnastics, aerobics—reinforced their belief that they were normal rather than deviant in trying to be thin. Like other anorexics, Chris felt that she was "ultra-healthy," with "total control" over her body. To Nicole, her anorexic weight was her "true" weight. By rejecting the deviant label, then, anorexics and bulimics remain as primary deviants.

Sooner or later, however, they become secondary deviants by developing a deviant identity, seeing themselves as anorexics or bulimics. Some of our research subjects acknowledged their anorexia after realizing that their eating disorder disrupted their lives. Their inflexible eating patterns unsettled family meals and holiday gatherings. Their regimented life style of compulsively scheduled activities—exercising, school, and meals—precluded any spontaneous social interactions. Compared with the anorexics, the bulimics were quicker to see themselves as deviant, considering their means of weight loss "abnormal" or "wrong and unhealthy." They further regarded their eating disorder as indicative of "loss of control," regretting their self-indulgence, "shame," and "wasted time."

People with eating disorders also exhibit what Schur (1971) calls "role engulfment," centering activities on their deviant role to downgrade other roles. Among our research subjects, the obligations as students, family members, and friends became subordinate to the eating and weight-control rituals. Socializing, for example, was curtailed because it interfered with compulsive exercising, bingeing, or purging. The role engulfment further affects other aspects of the deviant's life. In a social situation, our research subjects often compared their body shapes and sizes with those of others and were sensitized to comments about their appearance. They felt self-conscious around people who knew about their eating disorders. Robin, for example, imagined others "watching and whispering" behind her. While hospitalized, Denise felt she had to prove to others she had stopped vomiting, by keeping her bathroom door open. Other bulimics, who lived in dormitories, were reluctant to use the restroom lest several friends be huddling at the door and listening for vomiting.

People with eating disorders also tend to conceal their deviance from others. Thus, the bulimics in our research tried earnestly to hide their bulimia by bingeing and purging in secret. They felt that others regarded bulimia as "gross" and had little sympathy for the sufferer. It is relatively easy to conceal bulimia, because the bulimic's weight is approximately normal. But it is much harder to conceal anorexia because of the emaciated ap-

pearance. Some anorexics try to hide their problem by wearing large, padded clothes. Others become reconciled to their stigma. As Brian, one of our research subjects, said, "the stigma of anorexia is better than the stigma of being fat."

Finally, both anorexics and bulimics feel isolated or ostracized by others, including some friends and family members. This is because they are often reminded that they are responsible for their eating disorder and that they are able to "get out of it if they try." They further feel discouraged by others' insensitivity to the complexities of eating disorders. In our research, many anorexics reported being told to "just eat more," and bulimics were enjoined to simply "stop eating so much." Not surprisingly, many such deviants find self-help groups like BANISH to be a haven, where they can freely discuss their problems with assurances of mutual understanding, empathy, and support.

SUMMARY

The development of anorexic or bulimic identities involves a sequence of conformity, primary deviance, and secondary deviance. With a background of exceptional conformity to conventional norms, especially the ideal of thinness, individuals subsequently engage in the primary deviance of starving or bingeing and purging. Negative societal reaction, primarily in the form of labeling the individuals as anorexics or bulimics, leads to secondary deviance, wherein they develop the deviant identities with tendencies toward role engulfment, deviance concealment, and feeling isolated.

REFERENCES

Becker, Howard S. 1973. *Outsiders*. New York: Free Press.

Giannini, A. James, Michael Newman, and Mark Gold. 1990. "Anorexia and Bulimia." *American Family Physician* 41:1169–1176.

Haller, Ellen. 1992. "Eating Disorders: A Review and Update." *Western Journal of Medicine* 157:658–662.

Hsu, L. K. G. 1989. "The Gender Gap in Eating Disorders: Why Are the Eating Disorders More Com-

mon among Women?" *Clinical Psychology Review* 9:393–407.

Lemert, Edwin M. 1951. *Social Psychology*. New York: McGraw-Hill.

Lemert, Edwin M. 1967. *Human Deviance, Social Problems and Social Control*. Englewood Cliffs, NJ: Prentice-Hall.

Mitchell, James E., and Richard L. Pyle. 1988. "The Diagnosis and Clinical Characteristics of Bulimia," pp. 267–273 in *The Eating Disorders: Medical and Psychological Bases of Diagnosis and Treatment,* edited by Barton J. Blinder, Barry F. Chaitlin, and Renee S. Goldstein. New York: PMA.

Schlundt, David G., and William G. Johnson. 1990. *Eating Disorders: Assessment and Treatment.* Boston: Allyn and Bacon.

Schur, Edwin M. 1971. *Labeling Deviant Behavior.* New York: Harper and Row.

Silverstein, Brett, Lauren Perdue, Barbara Peterson, and Eileen Kelly. 1986. "The Role of the Mass Media in Promoting a Thin Standard of Bodily Attractiveness for Women." *Sex Roles* 14:519–532.

THE STIGMATIZATION OF PERSONS WITH HIV DISEASE

RICHARD TEWKSBURY
DEANNA McGAUGHEY

In 1963, Erving Goffman applied the term *stigma* to describe the state of people who, because of their bearing undesirable attributes, may be, or have been, disqualified from full social acceptance. Perhaps the most important concept in the study of stigma is its dynamic quality. No attribute is humiliating or celebrated in and of itself (Frable 1993); an attribute becomes a stigma when expectations of what a person should be (virtual social identify) are in conflict with who in fact the person is (actual social identity). Although in most cases the application of a stigma negatively affects the quality of life its bearer maintains, there can be positive consequences of stigmatization as well (Herman and Miall 1990; Gilmore and Somerville 1994; Tewksbury 1994).

Both individuals and groups can be stigmatized. When an individual or group is stigmatized, boundaries are created between mainstream society and that individual or group. Regardless of whether the individual accepts the shame or celebrates his or her difference and deliberately segregates him or herself from mainstream society, the result is the same: The stigmatized person is excluded from full social interaction, and mainstream society maintains its existing normative structure (i.e., the perpetuation of prescribed and proscribed behaviors).

The purpose of this article is to apply the concept of stigma to the study of people living with HIV disease (PLHs). After first discussing the development and functions of HIV-related stigma for mainstream society, discussion focuses on identi-

fying and analyzing two conceptually distinct, but related, varieties of stigma application processes. Drawing on 63 in-depth interviews conducted with PLHs in the Midwest (Kentucky, Ohio, and Indiana), this article details the virtual and actual social identities of PLHs, the indirect and direct experiences of stigmatization experienced by PLHs, the management of HIV-related stigma, and the positive and negative implications of HIV-related stigma.

DEVELOPMENT OF HIV-RELATED STIGMA

HIV disease has physical and social qualities whose interpretations shape society's understanding the disease as a medical and social phenomenon (Conrad 1986; Herek & Glunt 1988; Brandt 1991; Weitz 1991; Tewksbury 1994). The physical qualities include the tendency for the disease to create visible and dehumanizing changes in appearance, the fact that the disease is infectious and incurable, and the fact that its origin is unknown. The social qualities include associations with already marginalized groups (i.e., men who have sex with men and intravenous drug users) and stigmatized activities (i.e., promiscuity and drug use) (Conrad 1986; Herek and Glunt 1988; Weitz 1991; Tewksbury 1994).

In addition to giving meaning to the disease, these qualities are also the conditions whereby PLHs become recipients of stigma (Goldin 1994). The types of stigma Goffman (1963) identified—blemish of character, abomination of the body, and tribal stigma—all may play roles for PLHs. When their infection is believed to be the consequence of participation in socially unacceptable behaviors (for example, drug use or deviant sexual activity), they are assumed to have blemished characters. Because HIV is terminal and has the potential to cause severe physical symptoms (e.g., wasting syndrome, Karposi's Sarcoma, and dementia), PLHs are considered to have abominations of the body. Finally, because HIV is associated with already marginalized groups, those infected may carry a second stigma of group membership, or tribal stigma (Herek and Glunt 1988; Kowalewski 1988; Sandstrom 1990; Cadwell 1991; Tewksbury 1994).

Because of abomination of the body, HIV symbolizes a loss of vitality (i.e., the progressive loss of productivity, physical deterioration, dependence, death). When people are deemed responsible for their own health status, in addition to being stigmatized on the basis of abomination of the body, they are stigmatized on the basis of blemished character and tribal stigma; HIV symbolizes their perceived failing and its consequence. Regardless of attribution of responsibility, all PLHs are potential bearers of stigma on the basis of abomination of the body. When responsibility for the infection is attributed to them, they are potential bearers of stigma on the basis of blemished character in addition to abomination of the body. In the former scenario, HIV is a stigmatized symbol for the loss of vitality (usually accompanying aging). In the latter, HIV is a stigmatized symbol for the consequences of moral decadence.

Although attribution of responsibility has the potential for determining attitudes toward PLHs (King 1983; Bouton et al. 1989; Connors & Heaven 1989; Weiner 1993), the notion of responsibility is not necessary for exclusion from social interaction. Previous research on the experiences of stigma among PLHs has demonstrated that, although blame for infection with HIV disease, in particular infection through same-sex sexual encounters, is central to determining the degree of stigma an individual experiences, fear of contagion is the most salient feature of stigmatizing responses to PLHs (see Triplet and Sugarman 1987;

Bouton et al. 1989; Bishop et al. 1991; Leiker et al. 1995). Because all PLHs are to some degree potentially stigmatized, for the purpose of this paper, *stigma* is defined as a shameful or undesirable difference that has the ability to exclude a bearer from full social interaction.

FUNCTIONS OF STIGMA

When people, as individuals, a group or society, are confronted with a frightening or intolerable situation their response can be to attempt to flee or escape from it; to control it by inactivating or destroying it, or its cause; to deny it; or to displace the fear it engenders such that its impact is eliminated or minimized. (Gilmore and Somerville 1994, p. 1339)

Because currently there is no known cure for infection with HIV, other strategies are used to minimize the danger it presents. Mainstream society can deny the danger it presents to individual members of society through five measures: disidentification, depersonalization, stigmatization, scapegoating, and discrimination (Gilmore and Somerville 1994).

Disidentification "occurs when we separate . . . ourselves from certain other persons, when we create a situation of 'them' and 'us' " (Gilmore and Somerville 1994, p. 1340). Identifying HIV disease with already marginalized groups or persons (i.e., men who have sex with men) or perhaps marginalized "criminals" (i.e., intravenous drug users and prostitutes) provides mainstream society with the attitudes to allow this separation. Depersonalization is regarding the "them" as nonpersons; depersonalization of PLHs occurs when they are defined as entities who are "going to die anyway." Disidentification and depersonalization are internal processes for differentiating and reassuring that " . . . this harm will not befall us, because we are not like 'them' " (Gilmore and Somerville 1994, p. 1340). Stigmatization, by contrast, is both an internal and an external process. Stigmatization involves disidentification and depersonalization in that undesirable attributes are used to designate scapegoats and rationalize discrimination. It also allows the displacement of the negative affect activated by HIV as a deadly, dehumanizing disease.

In sum, mainstream society disidentifies with those carrying, or at risk for, HIV disease. When categories of "us" and "them" are created, those with the disease are not only further marginalized but also dehumanized, or depersonalized. Stigmatization occurs when these internal processes of people in mainstream society are, or have the potential to be, externalized in the form of scapegoating or discrimination. By creating scapegoats and discriminating, people establish boundaries between certain social groups and mainstream society in an attempt to reinforce the separation of perceived differences. Because there is no known cure for HIV disease, instead of acting directly toward the virus, society acts toward those associated with or living with the disease. Stigmatization in this sense, therefore, is a metaphorical "vaccine."

METHOD

The data for this analysis were drawn from a series of in-depth interviews with 63 PLHs in Ohio, Kentucky, and Indiana. All interviews were conducted by the first author between 1991 and 1994. Interviewees were all volunteers who had learned of the project through one of two methods. One method was community service and education organizations that published announcements of the project in newsletters and made announcements at meetings. Most important, the organizations personally referred clients and contacts. The second method was a snowballing technique: At the conclusion of each interview a request was made to refer others to the researcher; several networks of acquaintances were accessed in this manner.

This sample was 87% male, 85% White, and 81% gay. Additionally, the sample was primarily urban, although at least two respondents from each of the three states represented were rural residents.

All interviews lasted between 1½ and 6 hr, with a median length of 3 hr. Each interview fo-

cused on the interviewee's medical condition; social networks; experiences with family, friends, workplace, medical providers, and significant others; and personal, social, and psychological experiences with HIV disease. All interviews were transcribed in full and conceptually coded; analysis followed the procedures of grounded theory development (Glaser and Strauss 1967).

PERCEPTIONS AND EXPERIENCES OF HIV-RELATED STIGMA

Discourse on the perceptions and experiences of PLHs would be incomplete without first addressing how PLHs perceive their virtual and actual social identities (Goffman 1963). The difference between virtual and actual social identity is in how individuals are defined as social beings—hence between the qualities attributed to them and the meanings attributed to those qualities (virtual social identity) and how they identify themselves (actual social identity).

The importance of virtual social identities in discussing the experiences and perceptions of HIV-related stigma is that how PLHs perceive themselves as viewed by mainstream society serves as a measuring rod for interpreting situations as stigmatizing. For example, an individual who believes that mainstream society views him as "contaminated" may identify experiences at a hospital as stigmatizing when personnel wear gloves or gowns. However, a noninfected individual may have similar experiences at a hospital but view the gloves and gowns as simply standard precautions against infection, not as a sign of being viewed as contaminated. In such instances of indirect stigmatization (i.e., those situations when PLHs have not been directly informed or shown that they were being treated differently from anyone else because of their health status), self-perceived virtual social identity is used to determine whether an experience is tainted by stigmatization. Understandably, direct experiences of stigmatization (those instances when PLHs have been directly informed or shown that they were being distinguished because of their health status) are relied upon to confirm indirect experiences of stigma.

VIRTUAL AND ACTUAL SOCIAL IDENTITIES AMONG PEOPLE WITH HIV DISEASE

The most striking feature of how those PLHs seen as responsible for their infection recognize stigmatization is that they see it as arising from both blemished character and abomination of the body. Evoking a sense of value judgment added to their physical condition, they often use terms such as "diseased," "like a leper," "contaminated," and "dirty," to denote their perceptions of others' perceptions.

Some PLHs go so far as to fashion themselves as analogous to rape victims. Like rape victims, these people believe they are viewed as having "asked for" their compromised immunity. Also exemplifying how blemished character and abomination of the body combine to create a perceived virtual social identity is the following statement by George:

> I think the world sees me as this terrible, promiscuous, sex-hungry, drug-using slime of a person. I don't think society or the world sees me as just someone who had a bad break.

As noted above, the physical and social qualities of HIV combine to create opportunities for stigmatization. In the most generic sense, this means that people who are "bad" are punished by both physical deterioration and social marginalization. These same physical and social qualities facilitate the creation of myths surrounding the disease and those with the disease.

> A widely popular HIV/AIDS myth which occurs in several related forms is the morning-after message from the "revenge" infector. Sometimes it is a message written in lipstick or shaving foam in the bathroom by an already departed bedfellow. Other times, it is a message opened on the return flight from the romantic holiday. But the content of the message is always the same: "Welcome to the AIDS Club." (Bloor 1995, p. 2)

Within such myths there are two main characters, a sexually deviant and dangerous villain and an innocent and now manipulated (and infected) victim. Jack, who has been living with AIDS for years, described his view of the virtual identity of people with HIV disease in terms of the "revenge" infector myth:

> You're labeled a pariah. You're avoided. Anytime you're friendly with people they'll claim you're trying to seduce them, and there's that fear that you'll be the Typhoid Mary type.

The actual social identity of people with HIV differs from their virtual social identity. Most persons with HIV can point to the social disdain for the route by which they were infected, such as sexual practices and drug use, but as individuals they do not identify themselves as having done something wrong, merely as having done something unsafe. Frank, a gay man with AIDS, captured the spirit of this belief:

> [HIV] is a disease, not a disgrace. I'm a person. I'm a human. I'm a person living with AIDS.

Among those not infected through stigmatized behaviors, the most attention is devoted to processing labels that denote them as simultaneously helpless and "innocent." These individuals consistently and vehemently oppose the status of victim. Laura, a woman who was infected by her hemophiliac husband, described the reaction she received after having told her story to a local newspaper:

> People have a lot of compassion for me because of the way I was infected, and that upsets me.

Laura explained that she did not feel different from other people living with HIV disease; rather, she felt different from everyone. She went on to state that her response to the status of victim was that although she was not a gay man or an intravenous drug user, that did not mean she had never done anything "wrong." The example she used of "being bad" was that she had had premarital sex. She clearly did not believe that because she had been infected during marriage (as opposed to before) that she should be afforded more dignity than anyone else living with the disease.

Similarly, Trey, a hemophiliac, mirrored Laura's feelings when stating:

I may not deal with the lifestyle of homosexuality, and I may not deal with the lifestyle of IV drug users. . . . But yet, they're things that I am concerned about, and I think a human life is a human life and it's got a great deal of value to it.

Trey continued discussing his feelings on being identified as an innocent victim by stating:

You can't single people out and say this is a victim . . . and these people are guilty. . . . You don't do life that way. . . . We're talking about death here.

Actual social identities of PLHs are incongruent with their virtual social identities in that PLHs perceive themselves as individuals living with a terminal illness, which may be the result of unhealthy activities—as opposed to moral dereliction. In terms of "deserving" their disease, they don't view themselves as any different from any other ill persons, such as those with heart disease or lung cancer.

The importance of understanding the virtual social identities of PLHs is that these identities are used as the foundation for a description of a distinction in the process of stigmatization not previously developed in the literature: indirect versus direct experience of stigmatization. Perceived virtual social identities of PLHs function as filters through which they determine whether uncomfortable experiences are related to their health status.

INDIRECT EXPERIENCES OF STIGMATIZATION

Because PLHs typically disclose their infection to others on a "need-to-know" basis, or when it is determined that they will receive a sensitive response, their experiences of stigmatization—both indirect and direct—can be actively managed. Indirect experiences of stigmatization are those situations when PLHs are not directly informed or shown that they are being discriminated against because of their health. Indirect experiences of stigmatization most often occur at work, in hospitals or with medical practitioners, in the gay community, and in personal relationships. Direct

experiences of stigmatization, on the other hand, are those situations when PLHs are explicitly informed or shown that they are being distinguished because of their health status. Direct experiences of stigmation most often occur when PLHs have discussed their health status widely in society, particularly in the media, and in interpersonal relationships (such as with family or coworkers).

As for indirect experiences of stigmatization at work, many of those in the sample who had disclosed their health status had subsequently experienced a loss of benefits and promotions, or the recommendation that they be demoted. Drake, for example, explained that although when he disclosed his infection at work he received positive and supportive verbal responses, he nonetheless was "unrelatedly" fired.

Trey had also disclosed his status to his employer, because he worked with heavy equipment and feared that he could be injured and risk another person's health. Although he had never before been reprimanded, and in fact had received several promotions and raises previously, since his disclosure he had not received a raise in more than 5 years and had seen numerous others with less seniority than he move into higher positions.

Mack worked with AIDS patients in his field and used this fact as an indication that it would be acceptable for him to disclose his status and his need for time off because of fatigue. Upon his doing so, his employer expressed concern and also advocated a demotion "for his own health," to which Mack was adamantly opposed.

Some PLHs had chosen not to disclose their disease, although their health might be deteriorating, because of the response they believed they would receive. Hector, for example, stated:

If I had cancer, I could go to work and boy, everybody would be behind me, and I know not everybody's going to be behind me because I hear the comments from my employees.

From their perceived experiences of stigmatization these individuals found it difficult, if not impossible, to determine if employees' and coworkers' responses were because of attributions of blemished character or abomination of the body. One gay man, Rick, had had an experience similar to Mack's in that he was fired for "his own good" after taking time off following the death of his partner with AIDS. Rick explained his employer's actions by saying, "I think they looked at me as a liability waiting to happen."

Experiences with medical practitioners are similar to experiences with employers and coworkers in that PLHs do not know whether to classify their stigmatization as related to blemished character or abomination of the body. The predominant feeling of stigmatization the members of this sample reported with respect to medical experiences was that prophylactic measures taken by medical personnel were overdone, resulting in feelings of isolation and filth for people with the disease. Commenting on the preventative measures taken by his dentist, Luke said, "You'd think I was radioactive." Other experiences included a lack of hospital necessities. Ryan described his experience in a hospital after having been admitted for a high fever:

> *I was sleeping on a bed with no linens, in a room with no towels, no personal care stuff, no barf pan, nothing. Just me, on this bed, on a plastic sheet.*

Gay men often note a feeling of discrimination even within the generally sympathetic gay community. Some HIV-positive gay men believe noninfected gays stigmatize them to a greater degree than heterosexuals do. Luke elaborated on this feeling:

> *In the gay community there is still this tendency when somebody gets sick, you let them go away, and it's kind of like an animal, going off into a corner to die.*

Rick also noted the gay community's stigmatizing response:

> *There's a sense of, "Well, I made it through the 1980s, I'm clean, so what did you do?"*

From the remarks of the men in this sample, it is apparent that HIV-positive gay men may perceive stigma emanating even from within what is commonly believed to be a major source of social support—the gay community.

Individual perceptions of stigma occur at work, in the hospital, and within personal relationships. Because PLHs are not explicitly informed that their experiences are because of their health status, it is difficult to determine if the basis for these experiences is a rejection of their health status, a rejection of how others believe they "caused" their disease, or an active attempt to remove and discredit PLHs from full participation in a given setting.

DIRECT EXPERIENCES OF STIGMATIZATION

Direct experiences of stigmatization are those instances when PLHs are informed or shown explicitly that they are being distinguished because of their health status. These experiences are less common than indirect experiences of stigmatization. Because of the virtual identities of PLHs, it is unnecessary for observers to state their reasons for limited contact. In other words, because PLHs "know" that their health status is viewed by others in an undesirable way, any type of exclusion by someone aware of their infection may be construed as stigmatizing.

As mentioned above, direct experiences of stigmatization are most common for those individuals who have discussed their health widely in society. Direct stigma experiences may also be initiated by family members, medical practitioners, and others close to PLHs.

Experiences of stigmatization for those who have gone public include both physical and verbal assaults. Tina, for example, had experienced numerous verbal attacks via telephone and written correspondence. Her children had been assaulted and her lawn strewn with garbage. She said:

> *I've had my car windows broke out, my house windows broke out . . . my whole yard trashed with garbage. . . . They just wanted to make that a garbage dump. That's what the sign in the front yard said. . . . I have a swimming pool, and it's been trashed and the liner ripped . . . my children jumped and beat up.*

In addition to these incidents, Tina had had bomb threats and been asked not to return to her church. Someone had tried (unsuccessfully) to have the one child who was living with her removed from her home. When she married her present husband, it was front-page news. About one incident, she recalled:

> One man [called and] threatened to come over and "F" my brains out and then blow my brains out, and I said, "Well, be sure to bring a condom . . ." and he hung up on me.

In the same vein, Richard, a gay man with HIV, had received letters after an article about him appeared in a local newspaper. Included in these letters were comments such as:

> It's hard to believe that anyone could be such a disgrace to humanity to bring down so much shame on yourself, your family, your community. . . . Go somewhere else. . . . Keep your face out of the newspapers and off the TV. Leave this country and let your family live!

> Your lifestyle is a queer [sic] and what is wrong with you. No one is borne [sic] to be that way. You must be missing something in the head to even think about laying down with another man. . . . if you had not laid around being a man hore [sic], you would not have your problem with AIDES [sic].

> Too bad suicide didn't work. You better go back in the closet, in a closet and stay.

When coworkers discovered that Henry's wife had died with AIDS, his work equipment was vandalized with derogatory references to AIDS. When he confronted his boss with the equipment, Henry was told, "It's not my job to babysit." At about the same time, Henry was sitting in his car at a fast food restaurant when one coworker approached him,

> . . . wearing surgical gloves. POW! . . . just blindsided me. Broke my glasses. . . . He said, "I'll tell you something. . . . The only way you're getting back in that warehouse is fight your way back. We don't want you here anymore."

Finally, after he left work one afternoon to pick his daughter up from school, the brakes went out on Henry's new car. The dealer found that the brake lines had been cut.

Stigmatizing experiences initiated by family members or close associates are predominantly centered around religious beliefs. The belief that HIV infection is God's punishment for immoral sexual behavior is a common theme to these stigmas. When Blake disclosed his status to his mother, referencing his gay lifestyle, she stated, "I told you you'd get punished for it." Jordan had the same experience upon disclosure to his parents; his pronouncement was met with a lecture from his father, who quoted heavily from a Bible in his hands. Abigail had a baby-sitter find out about her status and subsequently confront her about her sin of premarital sex; HIV, she was told, was God's retribution for premarital sex.

Stigmas can also come from PLHs, in part because they too are members of society, exposed and responding to the same messages and socializing agents as all others. It is only logical for some negative perceptions to be internalized. Upon the birth of her child, Abigail was unsure as to whether the baby was infected; therefore, both because she feared her own future loss and because of her fear and loathing of the disease, she actively rejected her newborn child:

> When [the baby] was born it was real hard for me to get close to [the baby]. I didn't want [the baby] in my room. . . . I didn't want to think the thought of getting close to [the baby] and losing [the baby].

Obviously, Abigail wasn't limiting contact with her baby because she believed the baby caused its own infection, or because she feared becoming infected. She did, however, limit contact with the child because of abomination of the body.

MANAGEMENT OF HIV-RELATED STIGMA

When a person is diagnosed with HIV disease, he or she begins an often long and painful process of adjusting the physical and social meanings of the disease to his or her existing sense of self. In other words, the construction of a new actual social identity that integrates one's diseased status into an existing actual social identity begins. For HIV status to be integrated effectively, accommodations to the new virtual social identity must be integrated into one's behavioral repertoire. Actual and virtual social identities are contingent on one another in determining the quality of life: "Who we are, both to ourselves and others, determines the opportunities with which we will be presented and prevented" (Tewksbury 1994, p. 337). It is through the management of HIV-related stigma that PLHs determine "who they are" in relation to this disease.

Management of HIV-related stigma involves adjusting the distinctive features of the disease into one's personal life. The major strategies are information control and embracement (Sandstrom 1990). The strategy employed is determined primarily by disease status and progression, and secondarily by route of transmission and demographics such as race, gender, and sexual orientation.

Information Control

Information control refers to limiting the visibility of one's health status by controlling disclosure or interactions with others. Included as techniques of information control are passing, covering, isolation, and insulation (Goffman 1963; Sandstrom 1990; Weitz 1991; Herman 1993).

Passing with HIV disease predominantly occurs during the early stages of the illness when physical limitations are rare and minimally encumbering. An individual is capable of passing simply by not disclosing his or her health status to anyone. Marcus, for example, passed for healthy by completely suspending interactions with his family:

I was so afraid and ashamed to call home, I didn't call home for about 3 or 4 years.

The most common method of passing during the early stages of HIV disease, however, is selective disclosure (Sandstrom 1990) or concealment (Herman 1993). Selective disclosure or concealment "can be defined as the selective withholding or disclosure of information about self perceived as discreditable" (Herman 1993, 308). For PLHs in

particular, information is withheld from those who are perceived as being insensitive toward HIV-related issues or biased against those persons with the disease. Gay men, for example, generally tend to use the virtual identities of other gay men as a measuring rod for acceptance. If an individual (either the PLH himself or another gay man) is responded to negatively when disclosing a gay identity, there is an assumption that his HIV status will also receive a negative response. Mack illustrated:

My family I did not tell, because when I told them I was gay, they didn't speak to me for 4 years.

Rick decided not to disclose his health status to his family when, upon his disclosure of his partner's hospitalization for complications from AIDS, his mother, instead of inquiring into his partner's status, asked if Rick himself had AIDS.

Passing becomes increasingly difficult as HIV disease progresses. As a consequence, many PLHs find it necessary to modify their management strategy. Covering is used to manage interactions where there are physical cues that a PLH is unhealthy. Covering usually involves identifying oneself as having a less stigmatized disease, such as cancer or tuberculosis (Sandstrom 1990). Some HIV-positive persons transfer their medications to differently labeled or unlabeled containers. Blake covered for an extended hospital stay by telling people that he had been admitted for a nervous breakdown. George covered himself by controlling the amount of knowledge about AIDS he delivered. George explained:

I don't want to implicate myself by telling as much as I know. . . . Some people might suspect just knowing my living arrangements.

Hector covered his diseased status by "leading a straight life." It is common for gay men to pursue a cover by obscuring their association with a gay lifestyle—in effect, trying to pass as heterosexual.

When HIV disease produces limitations on a bearer that cannot be covered, the PLHs may begin isolating or insulating themselves from interaction. At this point, the PLHs are liminal; they are "not only separated from [their] previous social anchorages, but [they] are not clearly linked to any new ones" (Sandstom 1990, p. 277). It is at this point of identity construction that new social networks are created that facilitate living "normally" with HIV disease. Mack described how the physical manifestations of the disease had disrupted his existing social relationships, in particular with his HIV-negative partner:

> He likes to go to the beach and play in the sun and all that, and with KS, I can't. I don't want to go to the beach and put on a bathing suit and have people look at my purple spots.

Isolation and insulation are the final techniques of information control. To reiterate, it is at this stage that PLHs have to integrate the physical limitations of the disease into their actual social identities. Passing and covering become increasingly difficult, if not impossible, and new social networks must be created to accommodate the limiting effects of HIV disease while at the same time affording meaningful relationships. Many PLHs begin establishing primary relationships with other PLHs they meet through support groups or other AIDS services, and it is not uncommon for the relationships a PLH has to consist almost entirely of relationships with other PLHs.

Embracement

Embracement is the second major strategy for managing HIV-related stigmatization. Embracement occurs when an individual adopts and gives meaning to his or her AIDS identity. According to Weitz (1991, p. 134),

> As their illness progresses, both the concerns of persons with HIV disease and the resources available to them shift. Stigma becomes less of a critical issue, as their interactions with others necessarily become more limited and they develop a supportive, if narrower, circle of friends, relatives, and health care workers.

Participation in support groups is the most common form of identity embracement. Within these groups, PLHs generally both give and receive support in regard to the medical and social aspects of their lives. Other aspects of embracement include ideological embracement (i.e., taking up a sense of purpose) and identity embracement, (i.e., calling oneself a "person with AIDS" as opposed to an "AIDS victim").

The importance of virtual social identities for stigma management is that mainstream society, in determining the virtual identities of PLHs, defines HIV-related stigmas. When virtual identities become less restricting, such as when members of mainstream society do not impose strongly negative attributes on PLHs, or when PLHs segregate themselves from society, stigma management becomes a decreasingly important aspect of daily life.

NEGATIVE AND POSITIVE IMPLICATIONS OF HIV-RELATED STIGMA

Because stigma functions to limit social interaction and social interaction is a salient feature of actual identity, stigmas are most commonly regarded as restricting and negative. However, there are also positive aspects to stigmatization (Herman and Miall 1990; Gilmore and Somerville 1994; Tewksbury 1994). Commonly, positive consequences accompanying social isolation include an emancipation of expression.

The negative implications of stigmatization on PLHs are the shame accompanying the disease, invalidation as persons, and isolation. Regarding the shame of living with the disease, when PLHs do not wish to be segregated from society the stigma management techniques they employ tend to increase their feelings of "difference" and isolation. Discussing passing as healthy, Andy explained:

> That tells you right there, there is shame. That also helps me internalize it as shame to my disease.

Andy also described his fear of people finding out about his status because he believed, "that would invalidate all that I was able to do, that I did well." As Goffman (1963) noted, when one is stigmatized, one is potentially "spoiled" as a complete person.

In addition to shame and invalidation, PLHs describe the fear of isolation as a negative implication of stigma. Jordan expressed his fear of dying alone:

Life with this disease, it's living with fear. Everyday I wake up scared. I'm afraid of losing my family. I'm scared of losing my lover, of losing my friends. I'm scared of losing everything around me and dying alone.

The positive implications of HIV-related stigmatization are the various forms of emancipation of expression. Emancipation of expression refers to a modified prioritization of values. No longer are achievements in work and other mainstream activities top priority; they are replaced by an appreciation for the basic elements of life. Tina illustrated this sentiment when she stated:

When you're terminally ill, your plants can be dead and your curtains can be crooked. You just don't care. You want to live. . . . That's the way a person that's looking at limited time faces life.

Regarding emancipation from superficial relationships, Edward, a 47-year-old man living with AIDS, explained:

The nice thing is that you know that the people who are your friends and who stick by you and who demonstrate compassion and care are the kind of friends that you need. . . . That was the good that came out so soon after I was sick, because it got rid of the trash.

Similarly, Bill suggested that he might be a better friend as an HIV-positive person, for two reasons: He did not take the need for social support for granted, and the uncertainties accompanying HIV had led him to recognize the potential imminence of death.

Shawn's change in priorities moved him from a focus on external sources of gratification to a sense of empowerment:

I do a lot more for myself now than I used to. . . . I can get a little more selfish, I think. . . . If I want something, I go out and buy it. Why not? I may not get the opportunity to do it for myself in the future,

so I do it now. . . . I don't subject myself to the bullshit anymore. . . . I think you get this sense of empowerment and courage and think, "What can you do to me? I've faced the worst and I came through that. Hit me with your best shot."

Although PLHs universally argue that the negative consequences of HIV disease far outweigh the benefits of stigmatization, there is a consensus that HIV can bring meaning to life—meaning that would most likely not be experienced by a noninfected individual.

CONCLUSION

This research has added to the understanding of how individuals—here, people with HIV disease—experience the effects of stigmatization. The examination of direct and indirect stigma applications has revealed how such experiences are highly contingent on one's virtual social identity as a PLH. People living with HIV commonly believe that society perceives them as burdens and/or derelicts. These perceptions, however, are incongruent with actual social identities insofar as PLHs identify themselves as similar to persons living with other categories of terminal illness.

Normatively, both direct and indirect stigmatization arise within and from only very limited contexts. This is a function of selective disclosure, which allows PLHs to retain their predisease virtual and actual social identities. However, accompanying disease progression are physical limitations requiring an integration of PLHs' objective health status with their sense of self. In other words, as the physical qualities of HIV limit the activities of an individual, he moves from being "John Doe," to being "a person with HIV disease." When an individual evolves an actual social identity in which HIV is central, stigma management techniques evolve from an emphasis on information control to embracement.

Negative implications of HIV-related stigma are fairly clear; but stigma may also yield positive consequences for individuals and classes of individuals. For PLHs in particular, the major positive implication of HIV-related stigma is the accompanying emancipation of expression, as is evidenced most notably in a heightened appreciation of the basic elements of life, such as friendship and other social relationships. However, the majority of consequences are, in fact, negative for recipients and remain the manifest function of stigmatization—marginalization of those perceived as different or socially less valuable.

REFERENCES

Bishop, G., A. Alva, L. Cantu, and T. Rittiman. 1991. "Responses to Persons with AIDS: Fear of Contagion or Stigma?" *Journal of Applied Social Psychology* 21: 1877–1888.

Bloor, M. 1995. *The Sociology of HIV Transmission.* Thousand Oaks, CA: Sage.

Bouton, R., P. Gallaher, P. Garlinghouse, T. Leal, L. Rosenstein, and R. Young. 1989. "Demographic Variables Associated with Fear of AIDS and Homophobia." *Journal of Applied Social Psychology* 19: 885–901.

Brandt, A. 1991. "AIDS and Metaphor: Toward the Social Meaning of Epidemic Disease." pp. 91–110 in *In the Time of Plague,* edited by A. Mack. New York: New York University Press.

Cadwell, S. 1991. "Twice Removed: The Stigma Suffered by Gay Men with AIDS." *Smith College Studies in Social Work* 61: 236–246.

Connors, J., and P. Heaven. 1989. "Belief in a Just World and Attitudes toward AIDS Sufferers." *The Journal of Social Psychology* 130: 559–560.

Conrad, P. 1986. "The Social Meaning of AIDS." *Social Policy* 17: 51–56.

Frable, D. 1993. "Being and Feeling Unique: Statistical Deviance and Psychological Marginality." *Journal of Personality* 61: 85–107.

Gilmore, N., and M. Somerville. 1994. "Stigmatization, Scapegoating and Discrimination in Sexually Transmitted Diseases: Overcoming 'Them' and 'Us.' " *Social Science and Medicine* 39: 1339–1358.

Glaser, B., and A. Strauss. 1967. *The Discovery of Grounded Theory.* Chicago: Aldine.

Goffman, E. 1963. *Stigma: Notes on the Management of a Spoiled Identity.* New York: Simon and Schuster.

Goldin, C. S. 1994. "Stigmatization and AIDS: Critical Issues in Public Health." *Social Science and Medicine* 39: 1359–1366.

Herek, G. N., and E. K. Glunt. 1988. "An Epidemic of Stigma." *American Psychologist* 43: 886–891.

Herman, N. J. 1993. "Return to Sender: Reintegrative Stigma-Management Strategies of Ex-Psychiatric Patients." *Journal of Contemporary Ethnography* 22: 304–321.

Herman, N. J., and C. Miall. 1990. "The Positive Consequences of Stigma: Two Case Studies in Mental and Physical Disability." *Qualitative Sociology* 13: 251–267.

King, P. 1983. "Attribution Theory and the Health Belief Model." Pp. 170–186 in *Attribution and Theory: Social and Functional Extensions,* edited by M. Hewstone). Oxford, UK: Basil Blackwell.

Kowalewski, M. 1988. "Double Stigma and Boundary Maintenance: How Gay Men Deal with AIDS." *Journal of Contemporary Ethnography,* 17:211–228.

Leiker, J., D. Taub, and J. Gast. 1995. "The Stigma of AIDS: Persons with AIDS and Social Distance." *Deviant Behavior* 16: 333–351.

Sandstrom, K. 1990. "Confronting Deadly Disease: The Drama of Identity Construction among Gay Men with AIDS." *Journal of Contemporary Ethnography* 19: 271–294.

Tewksbury, R. 1994. " 'Speaking of Someone with AIDS. . . .': Identity Constructions of Persons with HIV Disease." *Deviant Behavior* 15: 337–355.

Triplet, R., and D. Sugarman. 1987. "Reactions to AIDS Victims: Ambiguity Breeds Contempt." *Personality and Social Psychology Bulletin* 13:265–274.

Weiner, B. 1993. "AIDS from an Attributional Perspective." Pp. 287–309 in *The Social Psychology of HIV-Infection,* edited by J. B. Pryor and G. D. Reeder. Hillside, NJ: Lawrence Erlbaum.

Weitz, R. 1991. *Life with AIDS.* New Brunswick, NJ: Rutgers University Press.

CYBERDEVIANCE

Six years ago Christopher Klaus, then only 19, started his company, Internet Security Systems (ISS), out of his grandmother's house. By now he has earned well more than $200 million. He and his young employees help numerous corporations ward off hackers who try to break into their computer systems. The Internet security provided by ISS and other similar companies has become a highly profitable business because the security measures in most computers are so "laughably inadequate" that they "often fail to stop intruders armed only with the most rudimentary skills." Not surprisingly, as indicated by a recent survey, even in top corporations and government agencies, 30 percent said their systems had been penetrated by outsiders and 55 percent reported unauthorized access by insiders.[1]

There is no way to know how many hackers exist in cyberspace, but there are clearly enough to attract the attention of law enforcement. Most hackers are relatively innocent and harmless; they break into various computer systems strictly for the challenge and will notify system administrators how they broke in. A few are downright criminal, and they are called "crackers." Crackers use their computer skills for malice, such as disabling a telephone company's computer network to knock out the phone service for an entire city. Law enforcers, due to their lack of computer knowledge, often confuse harmless hackers with destructive crackers. As a result, many hackers end up being treated like criminals. In the first article here, "The Social Construction of Hackers as Deviants," Paul Taylor explains in greater detail how and why hackers are often labeled as deviants or criminals in today's society.

Hackings and crackings are some of the byproducts of the computer revolution. The same revolution has also brought about other kinds of cyberdeviance. In "Let Your Fingers Do the Talking," Diane Wysocki shows how the computer network has lured some people into the chat room for sexual purposes. In the next reading, "On-Line Accounts of Unrepentant Pedophiles," Keith Durkin and Clifton Bryant reveal how the Internet has made it possible for pedophiles to spread their view that pederasty is harmless or acceptable behavior.

---

1. Brendan I. Koerner, "Can Hackers Be Stopped?" *U.S. News & World Report,* June 14, 1999, pp. 46–52.

THE SOCIAL CONSTRUCTION OF HACKERS AS DEVIANTS

PAUL A. TAYLOR

Wherever rules are created and applied, we should be alive to the possible presence of an enterprising individual or group. Their activities can properly be called moral enterprise, for what they are enterprising about is the creation of a new fragment of the moral constitution of society, its code of right and wrong . . . Social groups create deviance by making the rules whose infraction constitutes deviance, and by applying those rules to particular people and labeling them as outsiders. From this point of view, deviance is not a quality of the act the person commits, but rather a consequence of the application by others of rules and sanctions to an "offender." The deviant is one to whom that label has successfully been applied; deviant behavior is behavior that people so label. (Becker 1963, pp. 9, 145)

The study of hackers, or the computer underground (CU), provides excellent evidence that a true appreciation of deviancy reveals much more than a simple case of *them* and *us:* the "normal" labeling the "deviant." Instead of being based upon fixed meanings, the deviant status of hackers is shown to be achieved only as part of an essentially contested process and antagonistic social terrain. This paper explains how society's response to hacking has evolved from initially benign tolerance to a much more punitive attitude exemplified by the passing of anti-hacking legislation. This evolution in attitude can be seen in the computer security industry (CSI) and law-enforcement agencies' active construction of a deviancy status for hackers. A crucial, underexamined aspect of this deviancy construction process is the way in which it provides a group identity for those doing the labeling. In addition, the deviant status of hacking is rather flexible at times. We see how on some oc-casions the CSI and CU share fundamental characteristics and how, in certain officially sponsored circumstances, hackers are viewed as a societal benefit rather than a problem. Computer crime thus provides a useful illustration of deviancy as a social construction rather than a moral absolute.

HACKING AS A CONTESTED TERM

In its original technological sense, the word "hacker" simply connoted a computer virtuoso. That is still the meaning enshrined in the 1994 edition of the *New Hacker's Dictionary,* which defines such a person as someone "who enjoys exploring the details of programmable systems and how to stretch their capabilities; one who programs enthusiastically, even obsessively."

The meaning of the term *hacking* has gone through several changes, from its original dictionary definition of "cut or chop roughly, mangle, cut (one's way) through thick foliage etc., manage, cope with" to its present definition of "gain unauthorised access (to data in a computer)" (*The Concise Oxford Dictionary,* 8th edition.) The term was coined at MIT during the 1960s to denote the highly skilled but largely playful activity of academic computer programmers searching for the most elegant and concise programming solution to any given problem (Levy, 1984). What is now considered deviant behavior was once benignly tolerated high jinks. Levy describes three generations of hackers who exhibited to various degrees qualities associated with the hacking's original connotation. The pioneering computer aficionados at MIT's laboratories in the 1950s and 1960s formed the first generation of hackers, defined as those who were involved in the development of the earliest computer programming techniques. The second generation includes those involved in bringing computer hardware to the masses with the development of the earliest personal computers (PCs). The third generation refers to the programmers who became the leading lights in the advent of computer games architecture. Hacker is now almost exclusively used to describe an addition to this schema: the fourth generation of hackers, who illicitly access other people's computers.

To members of the current CU, hacking still refers, in the first instance, to the imaginative and unorthodox use of *any* artifact. However, the media and CSI have largely succeeded in reducing hacking's connotations to solely computer-based activities, and the currently accepted meaning of hacking has solidified around the notion of the unauthorized access to, and subsequent use of, other people's systems. This reduction in possible meanings is a reflection of the processes that must take place before hackers— once viewed as merely mischievous—can gain deviant status. This status of hackers as deviants only occurs because it becomes most widely accepted out of the contested and competing meanings of the word hacker. Because the dominant, prevailing connotations of hacker are now pejorative, its evolution requires explanation, and for

this we turn to the reasons and enabling conditions that underlie the construction of hacking as a deviant activity.

THE CONSTRUCTION OF DEVIANCY: *THEM* AND *US*

> It is an interesting fact that most scientific research and speculation on deviance concerns itself with the people who break rules rather than with those who make and enforce them. If we are to achieve a full understanding of deviant behavior, we must get these two possible foci of inquiry into balance. We must see deviance, and the outsiders who personify the abstract conception, as a consequence of a process of interaction between people, some of whom in the service of their own interests make and enforce rules that catch others who, in the service of their own interests, have committed acts that are labeled deviant. . . . We can describe the perspectives of one group and see how they mesh or fail to mesh with the perspectives of the other group: the perspectives of rule-breakers as they meet and conflict with the perspectives of those who enforce the rules, and vice versa. But we cannot understand the situation or process *without giving full weight to the differences between the perspectives of the two groups involved.* (Becker, 1963, pp. 163, 173)

Too often in discussions of computer crime, the hackers are discussed in isolation from their nemeses, the law enforcers. There needs to be much more effort put into understanding the *them* and *us,* the conflictual relationship that exists between the two groups. In order to understand a social group labeled as deviant, we have to pay due attention to its ongoing interaction with those labeling it:

We can construct workable definitions either of particular actions people might commit or of particular categories of deviance as the world (especially, but not only, the authorities) defines them. But we cannot make the two coincide completely, because they do not do so empirically. They belong to two distinct, though overlapping, systems of collective action. One consists of the people who cooperate to produce that act in question. The other consists of the people who cooperate in the drama of morality by which "wrongdoing" is discovered and dealt with, whether that procedure is formal or quite informal. (Becker, 1963, p. 185)

The conflict between the computer underground and its opponents not only provides a good illustration of Becker's analysis of deviancy but gives an additional intriguing exemplar of how social practices dynamically emerge within technological environments.

CULTURE LAG: FEAR, IGNORANCE, AND VULNERABILITY

The cops, and their patrons in the telephone companies, just don't understand the modern world of computers, and they're scared. "They think there are masterminds running spy rings who employ us," a hacker told me. "They don't understand that we don't do this for money, we do it for power and knowledge."

Telephone security people who reach out to the underground are accused of divided loyalties and fired by panicked employers. A young Missourian coolly psychoanalyzed the opposition. "They're over-dependent on things they don't understand. They've surrendered their lives to computers." (Sterling, 1991, p. 4).

Although the allegedly criminal aspects of hacking alone would seem enough to fuel its deviancy status, the act also contains a mysterious technological element manifested in the non-

technical person's uninitiated awe of computers' complexities and capabilities: The "black magic" allegedly practiced by the deviants of Salem has its contemporary manifestation in the mysteries of the black box of technology. Our sublimated fear of technology has strong cultural roots ranging in time from Mary Shelley's *Frankenstein* (1818) to movies such as the duo of *Terminator* films (1984 and 1989) and *The Matrix* (1999). Thus despite potential reasons for us to welcome their maverick spirit, hackers also serve to remind us of our technological vulnerability or ignorance, and the act of stigmatization often proves easier than seeking to understand them. This has come across in the problems of law-enforcement officials and legislators in their encounters with the CU, and in this sense hackers are perhaps a specific illustration of some of the wider problems society faces as it struggles to assimilate new information technologies into existing social structures. This is a phenomenon Marshall McLuhan calls *culture lag.*

As a consequence of culture lag, there have been various cases of alleged overreactions to computer security incidents by law-enforcement agencies. In the E911 case, for example, a member of the hacker group *Legion of Doom*, Craig Neidorf, was accused of threatening the safety of residents throughout the United States by copying a document containing details of the telephone emergency 911 system. When the case came to trial, federal prosecutors were embarrassed when it was proven by the defense team that the allegedly sensitive document valued at $80,000 was in fact available to the general public for $13. Authorities' often dramatic response to hackers and their activities was perhaps most vividly manifested in a series of police raids (code-named *Operation Sun Devil*) on the homes of hackers by gun-carrying U.S. law-enforcement officers. The officers were accused of overreacting to the physical threat posed by hackers in their homes by entering with their guns drawn. The officers were also accused of removing excessive amounts of computing equipment unrelated to their specific investigations. A British perspective on overzealous law enforcement is provided by the father of the 16-year-old London-based hacker Richard Pryce, who was accused of hacking into the computer systems of U.S. military bases:

It was around 7 P.M. and I was watching TV when about eight cars pulled up and people started banging on the door. When I answered it, the officers came filing in . . . there were so many of them, I thought he must have killed someone. They burst into his room and pulled his hands away from his computer keyboard. They then stripped his room. When I went up the stairs he was sitting there in shock while they were ripping up his floor-boards. They searched his room for 5 hours. (The Express, 1, 4).

Although such responses can be interpreted as exhibiting the displaced fear of the law enforcer, they can also be viewed as part of a deliberate strategy to simultaneously reduce the offenders' self-esteem and increase their deviancy status in the eyes of the law enforcer:

Where the target of the raids is an individual, usually at his or her own home, this simple approach to raid and seizure is . . . entirely appropriate and very effective. Hackers and pedophiles in particular are used to dealing with people and problems by means of remote connections; suddenly to be faced by a veritable army of (in the U.S., gun carrying) officers is usually sufficient to persuade total—indeed, often abject*—cooperation. (Barrett, 1997, p. 157, emphasis in the original)*

The idea that such overreactions are a form of displaced fear is backed by the case of convicted hacker Kevin Poulsen, whose attorney Paul Meltzer said: "It's ludicrous, it's absurd . . . They can't decide if they've got a kid playing in his garage or [the infamous spy] Julius Rosenberg" (Fine, 1995). Meltzer adds that he was "very disturbed by the inability of federal prosecutors to distinguish between assault with a deadly weapon and assault with a computer. I mean, c'mon, the guy's nonviolent." Poulsen's own words are also instructive:

The trouble began before I was released. I planned on living with my parents when I got out of prison, until I could find employment and live on my own. My probation officer anticipated this a month before my release-date, and visited my parents. He was shocked to find that they had recently purchased an IBM compatible computer, and he warned them that they must get rid of it before I moved in. They didn't have a modem, mind you, but as a notorious hacker I might easily fashion a modem out of ordinary household appliances. . . . It got even more interesting when I was released. When I reported to my probation officer, he explained to me that, not only could I not use any computer, with or without a modem, but that I couldn't be in the same room as a computer . . . Judge Real declined to second-guess the decisions of the probation officer, and specifically rejected the contention that I should be allowed to obtain employment that allows access to computers without modems, noting, "Who knows what a computer can do?" (Poulsen, n.d.).

Justin Peterson (alias *Agent Steal*) reinforces the involvement of culture lag in the relationship between hackers and law enforcers. Peterson spent forty-one months in federal prison for hacking into a bank's computer and transferring funds. While serving his sentence, he met another hacker, Chris Lamprecht, alias *Minor Threat*. He describes what happened:

The prison officials were terrified of us. They became obsessed as they read our mail, screened our magazines, listened to our phone calls, and sent informants to try and infiltrate our little group of technophiles. The only conclusion they could come to was that they had no idea what we were up to. When the computer at the prison industries plant crashed, Chris was promptly fired from his job there. It wasn't his doing, but unbridled paranoia spreads far and wide among bureaucrats. (Peterson [Agent Steal], 1997).

Hacking's predominantly nonphysical character and its accompanying air of mystery tend to heighten its potential for creating fear and anxiety. Its anonymity mixed with its illicit nature make it easier for the media to portray the actions of hackers, who are rarely seen in the flesh, in deviant terms. According to the convicted hacker Kevin

Poulsen, "Criminal cases involving suspected unauthorized computer access, or 'hacking,' are frequently subject to wild, unsubstantiated, and often bizarre claims by prosecutors and investigators."

HOSTILITY

Mostly they seem to be kids with a dramatically underdeveloped sense of community and society. (Cosell, e-mail interview)

Somewhere near vermin, i.e. possibly unavoidable, maybe even necessary pests that can be destructive and disruptive if not monitored (Zmudsinki, e-mail interview).

Electronic vandalism (Warman, e-mail interview).

I am for making the penalties for computer trespass extremely painful to the perpetrator. . . . Most administrators who've had to clean up and audit a system of this size probably think that a felony rap is too light a sentence. At times like that, we tend to think in terms of boiling in oil, being drawn and quartered, or maybe burying the intruder up to his neck in an anthill. (Johnson, 1991).

A general social atmosphere of vulnerability in the face of complex technology is translated by key stigmatizing figures, or *moral entrepreneurs* (Becker, 1963), into hostile but nonspecific and moralistic language that supports the construction of hackers' deviant status. The act of hiring a hacker has been compared to "hiring a confessed arsonist to install fire alarms, or hiring an admitted pedophile as a teacher" (Taylor, 1999, p. 106). Although a potentially useful byproduct of hacking activity is technical insights into the security flaws of computer systems, such benefits become subordinate to the need to express opprobrium against the morality of the actions themselves. The language of blame and morality is consistently used by hawkish members of the computer security industry in a process of *blame displacement:* These law enforcers label hackers as deviants as a means of deflecting any responsibility and blame for security breaches from those who own and maintain the systems.

System owners or system administrators . . . are very remiss in their duty, they couldn't care less and therefore at least, there is quite an understandable tendency to blame the penetrator rather than blaming themselves for not having taken at least adequate counter measures, in fact in some cases counter measures have not been taken at all . . . if it is proved to you that you haven't done your homework, then you almost automatically go into a defensive attitude which in this case, simply amounts to attacking the hacker, blaming him morally, heaping opprobrium on his head . . . yes, the fear factor is involved. (Herschberg, e-mail interview)

In addition to fear, hostility and subsequent stigmatization of hackers play useful roles in helping to professionalize the still relatively immature CSI.

THE PROFESSIONALIZATION PROCESS

The story of the creation of this "social menace" is central to the ongoing attempts to rewrite property law in order to contain the effects of the new information technologies that, because of their blindness to the copyrighting of intellectual property, have transformed the way in which modern power is exercised and maintained. (Ross, 1991, pp. 80–81)

In the sense that groups reaffirm their own identities by marginalizing others, deviancy labeling techniques are used to exclude hackers from influence within the computing world. At the same time, they help to develop a consistent ethical value system for "legitimate" security professionals. In an additional twist, however, this marginalization of "bad guys" is needed because the two purportedly antagonistic groups, in fact, are quite alike: both hackers and security professionals are driven by the same need to explore and test technical limits. Similarly, there is the case of Clifford Stoll's investigation of an intrusion into the University of California, Berkeley, computer laboratories, which he subsequently described in the best-selling book, *The Cuckoo's Egg*. Reviewing Stoll's book, Jim Thomas of the *Computer Underground Digest* points out:

> Any computer undergrounder can identify with and appreciate Stoll's obsession and patience in attempting to trace the hacker through a maze of international gateways and computer systems. But, Stoll apparently misses the obvious affinity he has with those he condemns. He simply dismisses hackers as "monsters" and displays virtually no recognition of the similarities between his own activity and those of the computer underground. This is what makes Stoll's work so dangerous: His work is an unreflective exercise in self-promotion, a tome that divides the sacred world of technocrats from the profane activities of those who would challenge it; Stoll stigmatizes without understanding. (Thomas, 1990)

What makes Stoll's behavior even less understandable is that throughout the book he recounts in detail how he himself engages in the same kind of activities that he criticizes others for indulging in. His activities included borrowing other people's computers without permission and monitoring other people's electronic communications without authorization. In labeling hackers as "monsters," Stoll participates in a degradation ritual that aims at redefining the social acceptability of a group by using assertion and hyperbole in the place of reasoned argument. Thus Stoll refers periodically in his book to hackers as "rats, monsters, vandals, and bastards" (Thomas, 1990).

The hacker Craig Neidorf (alias *Knight Lightning*), in his report on a CSI conference, argues that what mostly distinguishes this group from his own is the form, rather than content, of the knowledge they seek to utilize. For example, articles written by hackers usually contain the same types of material found publicly in other computer and security magazines.

Bernie Cosell, a commercial systems manager who was one of the most vociferous of the CSI opponents to hackers encountered during the study, compared hacking to joyriding in cars: "Assuming you come out to the parking lot and your car is JUST where it was left, except maybe the engine feels a bit warm. How is this different than discovering that someone had logged into your computer?" (Cosell, e-mail interview). Crucially however, despite the force of his moral view, he also admitted that he:

> had to do this sort of thing once or twice over the years. I recall one incident where I was working over the weekend and the master source hierarchy was left read-protected, and I REALLY needed to look at it to finish what I was doing, and this on a system where I was NOT a privileged user, so I "broke into" the system enough to give myself enough privileges to be able to override the file protections and get done what I needed [at which point I put it all back, and told the system administrator about the security hole]. (Cosell, e-mail interview)

The fact that hackers and law enforcers can have fundamentally similar qualities reflects a general ethical indeterminacy in the field of computer security. There is often a lack of agreement even among computer professionals about what constitutes the correct procedures with which to confront certain research and educational issues. This can be seen in the debate that accompanied the publication of computer expert Fred Cohen's article, "Friendly Contagion: Harnessing the Subtle Power of Computer Viruses" (1991). In the article, Cohen suggests that the vendor of a computer-virus prevention product should sponsor a contest encouraging the development of new viruses, with the provisos that the spreading ability of the viruses should be inherently limited and that they should only be tested on systems with the informed consent of the system owners.

In reply, another expert responded with the charge that:

> *For someone of Dr. Cohen's reputation within the field to actually* promote *the uncontrolled writing of any virus, even with his stated stipulations, is to act irresponsibly and immorally. To act in such a manner is likely to encourage the development of yet more viruses "in the wild" by muddling the ethics and dangers involved. (Spafford, 1991, p. 3).*

Given such ethical indeterminacy, we now turn to the processes whereby hackers come to be labeled as deviant.

WITCH-HUNTS AND HACKERS

> *The kinds of practices labeled deviant correspond to those values on which the community places its highest premium. Materialist cultures are beset by theft (although that crime is meaningless in a utopian commune where all property is shared). The correspondence between kind of deviance and a community's salient values is no accident . . . deviants and conformists both are shaped by the same cultural pressures—and thus share some, if not all, common values— though they may vary in their opportunities to pursue valued ends via legitimate means. Deviance . . . emerges exactly where it is most feared, in part because every community encourages some of its members to become Darth Vader, taking "the force" over to the "dark side." (Dougan and Gieryn, 1990, p. 4).*

Dougan and Gieryn (1990), like Meyer and Thomas (1990), have examined the deviancy aspects of computer crime by comparing its boundary formation processes within computing with the historical examples of witch trials. Witch hunts tend to occur in periods of social transition in which

there are significant levels of anxiety; a relatively modern manifestation was the McCarthy hearings conducted in the U.S. Congress during the height of the Cold War. The computer revolution has created conditions of large-scale social and technical transition that, in the eyes of some commentators, have led to hackers being made the scapegoats of the accompanying social unease. Dominant social groups initially mythologize and then stigmatize peripheral groups that do not share their value structure. We have seen how the initial awe and even respect with which hackers were originally viewed as " technological wizards" has given way to the more frequent hawkish perception that they are instead "electronic vandals."

Part of the cause of the witch-hunt mentality, as it has apparently been applied to hackers, is the increasing tendency within society toward the privatization of consumption. John Perry Barlow identifies the hacker as the latest such scapegoat of modern times in a series that includes Communism, terrorism, child abductors, and AIDS. He sees post–Cold War feelings of vulnerability and the information/generation gap as constitutive factors in the approach of the witch-hunt:

> *More and more of our neighbors live in armed compounds. Alarms blare continuously. Potentially happy people give their lives over to the corporate state as though the world were so dangerous outside its veil of collective immunity that they have no choice. . . . The perfect bogeyman for modern times is the Cyberpunk! He is so smart he makes you feel even more stupid than you usually do. He knows this complex country in which you're perpetually lost. He understands the value of things you can't conceptualize long enough to cash in on. He is the one-eyed man in the Country of the Blind. (Barlow, 1990, p. 56)*

THE PARLIAMENTARY DEBATE
AS DEGRADATION RITUAL

> *The prototype of the rule creator . . . is the crusading reformer. He is interested in the content of rules. The existing rules do not satisfy him*

*because there is some evil which
profoundly disturbs him. He feels
that nothing can be right in the world
until rules are made to correct it. He
operates with an absolute ethic; what
he sees is truly and totally evil with no
qualification. Any means is justified to
do away with it. The crusader is
fervent and righteous, often self-
righteous. (Becker, 1963, p. 148)*

This section uses the debates held in the
United Kingdom's parliament on the 1990 Computer Misuse Act to illustrate how anti-hacking legislation can display qualities of a degradation ritual.
This parliamentary stigmatization can take two
closely related forms. In the first, the motivations
of hackers are impugned, and in the second, the du-
bious nature of hackers' motives is highlighted by
a group-bonding process that emphasizes the
"them and us" scenario.

The following is an example of the first form,
presented by Lewis Moonie, member of Parliament
(M. P.), concerning the motivations of hackers:

*The motive . . . is simple to understand—human
greed. Although we do not condone theft, we can
possibly understand the need or personal circumstances which may drive someone to commit that
act. That is not the case with the kind of computer
misuse that we are discussing. Very often the people involved are educated professional people and
they have the wherewithal to afford to carry out
such behavior. . . . Although we may not accept
greed, we can understand it. The motive for malice
is more difficult to comprehend. . . . There are
many kinds of people involved and most, although
not exclusively all, are men. Although I have never
professed to have espoused the cause of Freud in
my psychiatric work, I believe that a profound sexual inadequacy is often related to such behavior.
(Hansard, 1990, p. 1156)*

The second aspect of the stigmatization
process, the construction of the them and us scenario, involves, first, reinforcing group identity by
underlining those qualities that produce the *us,* and
second, contributing to perceptions of the alien nature of *them.* An example of the former is the way

in which Powell "proves" the potential menace of
hacking by referring to the social position of a figure calling for legislation to deal with hacking:

*Yesterday I received a letter from a constituent who
is a leading official in one of the world's leading
banks. He asked me to support the Bill, and I am
happy to assure him that I do so with enthusiasm. . . . When such an important official troubles
to write to a Member of Parliament about a specific piece of legislation, knowing the background
of his career I have not the slightest doubt that the
menace of hacking and its consequences is widespread. (Hansard, 1990, p. 1147)*

An M. P. attempts to make the difference in
personal qualities between such a constituent and
those of the CU culture starkly apparent by quot-
ing directly from the latter:

*To show the sort of twisted culture that the Bill is
trying to stamp out, I have an extract from a bulletin board . . . stating: "who's seen the news in the
'sunday Times' . . . page A5 . . . about hacking . . . and freaking Mercury . . . they also want restrictions on BBS's . . . it's that stupid cow . . . the
Devon MP "computer expert" [Emma Nichol-
son] . . . dont make me laff . . . could be bad news
tho . . . maybe someone should assassinate her?"
Did somebody suggest that hacking is a harmless
culture? All that I can say is that it is a privilege
and I am honored to join my hon. Friend on the
hackers' hit list. (Hansard, 1990, p. 1137)*

Once the sense of the *us* has reinforced a sense
of group identity, the process to establish unequivocally "who we are not" begins. Colvin continues
by relating how he hoped "that the debate will dispel any lingering belief that the computer hacker is
some sort of Raffles of the microchip" (Hansard,
1990, p. 1142). Another M. P., Nicholson, describes
in detail various salacious and potentially destabi-
lizing aspects of hacking activity ranging from proliferation of pornography on bulletin boards to
interest being shown by political groups such as the
Greens, Anarchists and those behind the "Elec-
tronics and Computing for Peace Newsletter." She
seeks to distance herself from "people who believe
that they have a right of access to all knowledge
and that everything should be out in the open—and

should specifically be open to them." Nicholson proceeds to relate reported incidents of hackers who have allegedly "tried to kill patients in hospital by accessing their drug records and altering their prescriptions on computer" (Hansard, 1990, pp. 1151, 1153). Finally, she advocates legislation against hackers because:

> *It is no good saying that people must increase their protection, because hackers are very clever. They will find a way around every form of protection that one buys or creates. That is what they are there for. They make a great deal of money out of it and the German hackers, at any rate, support a drug-based lifestyle on their activities. I was about to say, "enjoy," but I should certainly not enjoy a lifestyle based on drugs. Because drugs are expensive, hackers need to make a great deal of money to support their lifestyle. (Hansard, 1990, p. 1154)*

Nicholson fails to give any corroborating evidence for many of these assertions. Her association of German hackers and drugs is possibly a reference to the case of Pengo, the hacker Stoll tracked down in *The Cuckoo's Egg,* but that individual case does not seem to warrant the status of being generally applicable to the whole German hacking scene. This example of lack of specific evidence underlines the information gap surrounding computer crime that policy makers face. Nicholson further exemplified the degradation ritual's tendency for reliance on rumor rather than empirical facts by referring to an unsubstantiated case that Scottish poll-tax computers had had details of those eligible to pay the tax corrupted with information about dead people. Another M. P., Waller, demonstrated the role "guestimates" play with his observation that 80 percent of the computers in Hong Kong have been infected with at least one kind of virus. The disproportionate reliance upon the "casual empiricism" of rumor and guestimates ironically increases pressure to legislate against hacking because of the higher levels of fear the lack of statistics may produce. As Waller said, "while we are aware of the tip of the iceberg, we do not know how much lies beneath the surface," (Hansard, 1990, p. 1161).

CONCLUSION: MIT AS ALCATRAZ?

There has been an evolution in the way in which hacking activity is viewed by society. Although the idiosyncratic behavior of the early hackers of MIT was benignly tolerated, hacking is now subject to legal prosecution, which in a way threatens to turn MIT into Alcatraz. By exploring the nature of this evolution, this paper has illustrated Becker's point that deviancy is a flexible label rather than an absolute judgment. What distinguishes hacking in terms of deviancy construction, however, is its added complicating element of technology. Unlike most other groups labeled deviant, hackers retain knowledge and expertise that is potentially invaluable to society at large and even those carrying out the labeling.

Society is challenged by the need to find ways in which hackers' knowledge can be co-opted for productive purposes. The construction of deviancy risks becoming an excuse for not confronting head-on the implications of our information age's culture gap. There seem to be two options: "We can either treat it as healthy and provide a venue for it, or turn our children into criminals by criminalizing their normal behavior" (Fred Cohen, e-mail interview). Cohen further explains,

> *When I was younger, I knew many "hackers" who went after systems, and none of them were malicious. Now I know some malicious ones, but they are generally malicious because of family or financial problems, not because they are "criminals." In every case I have seen, these people need friends and legitimate ways to explore. They need guidance and moral interpretation from someone they respect, not jail time with rapists and thieves in some stinking cell. . . . As the group ages . . . people begin to cross the line between explorer and pirate. Unfortunately, many of these latter-day Fagins corrupt young people who, in their quest to explore, are not given legitimate venues, and are thus drawn into illegitimate activities. . . . The reason most of these people are drawn into the "dark side" is because they are abandoned by the "good guys." I, for one, will not abandon our youth to criminal activities.*

In the confusing and rapidly changing world of technology, there is a need to find a workable *third way* between overly benign tolerance and the unthinking stigmatization of hackers. This will inevitably be difficult, but failure threatens severe implications for the ways in which our society fosters and rewards technological curiosity and ingenuity.

REFERENCES

Barrett, N. 1997. *Digital Crime: Policing the Cybernation.* London: Kogan Page.

Barlow, J. P. 1990. "Crime and Puzzlement." *Whole Earth Review,* (Fall): 44–57.

Becker, H. S. 1963. *Outsiders: Studies in the Sociology of Deviance.* New York: Free Press.

Dougan, W., and T. Gieryn. 1990. "Robert Morris: Worm? Virus? Hero?" Unpublished paper, Sociology departments of UCLA and Indiana universities.

Fine, D. 1995. "Why Is Kevin Lee Poulsen Really in Jail?" [on-line] Available on Internet: http://www.com/user/fine/journalism/jail.html

Hansard. 1990. United Kingdom Parliamentary Debates, House of Commons, February 9.

Johnson, B. 1991. "What the Laws Enforce." *RISKS* (electronic digest) (March):11:32.

Levy, S. 1984. *Hackers: Heroes of the Computer Revolution.* New York: Bantam Doubleday Dell.

Meyer G. R., and J. Thomas. 1990. "(Witch)Hunting for the Computer Underground: Joe McCarthy in a Leisure Suit." *The Critical Criminologist* (September 2nd): 225–253.

Peterson, J. [Agent Steal]. 1997. "Everything a Hacker Needs to Know about Getting Busted by the Feds" [on-line]. Available on Internet: http://www.grayarea.com/agsteal.html

Poulsen, K. n.d. "Recidivism Explained" [on-line]. Scales-O-Justice website available on Internet: http://catalog.com/kevin/returns.html

Ross, A. 1991. *Strange Weather.* London: Verso.

Spafford, E. H. 1991. *Three Letters on Computer Security and Society* (Technical Report, CSD-TR-91-088). West Lafayette, IN: Purdue University.

Sterling, B. 1991. "CyberView 91 Report" [on-line]. Available on Internet: http://www.eff.org/pub/Net_culture_Bruce_Sterling/cyberview_91.report

Taylor, P. A. 1999. *Hackers: Crime in the Digital Sublime.* London: Routledge. *The Express,* March 22, 1997.

Thomas, J. 1990. "Review of *The Cuckoo's Egg.*" *CuD* Vol 1.06, File 4 of 5.

LET YOUR FINGERS DO THE TALKING: SEX ON AN ADULT CHAT LINE

DIANE KHOLOS WYSOCKI

Interpersonal relationships have changed at a dramatic rate during the late twentieth century, with the advancement of technology and the emergence of the "information society" (Ryan, 1997). The increased availability of technological products such as computers, modems, computer bulletin boards (BBS), and the Internet, along with their declining prices, have had a dramatic effect on social life as we have known it. While in the comfort of home or office, social networks have increased, new on-line communities have emerged, individuals have met their spouses or partners, and even fulfilled their deepest sexual fantasies.

The purpose of this paper is twofold: to examine how and why individuals participate in sexually explicit computer bulletin boards; and to see if sex on-line is a way of *replacing* face-to-face relationships or a way of *enhancing* them. This analysis focuses on the social construction of love and sexuality and uses a sexually explicit computer BBS that I have called *Pleasure Pit* as the source for contacting individuals who combine their technological abilities with their sexual desires. Specifically, this project focuses on how one sexually explicit BBS operates, what types of people use it, what kinds of activities are available for the participants, why individuals participate in *sex* on-line and how those sexual behaviors are accomplished without face-to-face interaction.

SEX ON-LINE

It has been suggested in the mass media that the computer, via e-mail, chat mode and BBS is *the*

place to go for on-line "sexual" relationships. Sex via the computer can develop through the interactive sharing of fantasies, looking at sexually explicit photographs and/or sharing similar sexual interests (Bright, 1992; Childs, 1994; Bloom, 1995; Hamman, 1996; Brophy, 1997). According to one source more than 50 percent of all on-line communication is related to sex (Childs, 1994) and sexually explicit BBS with names like *Kinknet, ThrobNet* and *StudNet,* are geared to all kinds of variations of sexual pleasure. On the Internet, the lists of sexually explicit BBS are extensive, have active user participation and are very lucrative, with one service making over $500,000 a month (Anonymous, 1997). Similarly, in one web site the chat (or Internet Relay Chat—IRC) rooms were separated into those rated G—for users of all ages; R—not recommended for those under 18; and X—for those who are over 18. The site has between 800 and 1000 users on it at any given time. Within each of the sections there are different chat rooms for people to meet other individuals. The G-rated section has 7 chat rooms, the R-rated has 16 chat rooms, and the X-rated was the most active with 41 chat rooms that included *The House of Pain* for those interested in bondage and S & M, *The Sex Shop* for those interested in sex toys, and *The Locker Room* for gay men (Personal observations, Feb. 1998).

In *net.sex,* Nancy Tamosaiti (1995: 2), a journalist who writes about electronic communications and who spent time investigating sexual BBS, states that "cybersex" refers to "looking for a partner to exchange erotic e-mail with, or to meet live for steamy sessions on the IRC (Internet Relay Chat) area." Finding people who participate in cybersex is not difficult and Tamosaiti found that individuals who use sexual BBS report they are more comfortable telling secrets on-line, having on-line sexual encounters, and "cheating" on their spouses with someone they have "met over the BBS." Similarly, John Richards (1994) states it is impossible to tell how many sexually explicit BBS there are; however, in a poll by *Boardwatch Magazine,* the second and third choices of best BBS are sexually explicit and geared towards adults.

In October 1995, an on-line sexual survey was created by the InterCommerce Corporation. By June 1997, a total of 20,791 respondents had participated in the survey and reported that being on-line *enhanced* their sexual behaviors (InterCommerce Corporation, 1996). The top reasons respondents gave for participating in sex on-line was that it was "a benign outlet for sexual frustration. . . . It has made me more open-minded. . . . Promotes honest communication. . . . Promotes safe sex . . . [and] has improved my sex-life." Other respondents believed cybersex helped their marriage and discouraged adultery. While information about the exact number of people who use the computer for sexual activities and information changes constantly, it is becoming recognized that if you want sex . . . it is only a keyboard away.

PLEASURE PIT: A SEXUALLY EXPLICIT COMPUTER BULLETIN BOARD

Gaining Access to *Pleasure Pit*

In order to learn about the sexual relationships people have developed over computers, I located the name and telephone number of a BBS through a computer newspaper offered free of charge in a computer store. The BBS was located in a Midwest US city and called *Pleasure Pit.* Previous research has suggested that gaining entry to a new research setting could be difficult. Gaining access to this BBS however was easy with the help of *gatekeepers* or in this case the systems operators (SYSOP) (Berg, 1998). Originally I logged onto

Pleasure Pit and explained to the SYSOPs that I was a sociologist interested in using *Pleasure Pit* to collect data. I was unprepared for the enthusiastic response I received and was invited to meet the SYSOPs and learn how the BBS was run.

When an individual first signed onto *Pleasure Pit* they were required to give their correct name, address, and phone number to the SYSOPs. Before the user was given full access to the BBS, the SYSOPs checked to make sure the individual trying to gain access was not a minor by calling the home telephone number. If the number given by the user was not correct, BBS access was denied. That first night, even as I was learning about the BBS, one of the SYSOPs wrote a message for all users to see that said:

> There will be a female here at the Pleasure Pit *office to do interviews with anybody who happens to be online . . . she is doing research on BBS relationships and is interested in what happens to your inhibitions when your[1] on the key board (we know what happens to them). Watch for more info on her activities. I may call you voice to set up a voice interview with her. If you volunteer you will be first called and you husband-types (with spouses not into this) be sure to let me know that you do or don't want a call . . .*

During that same evening I placed my questionnaire onto *Pleasure Pit.* Using a doorway questionnaire program, each question gave the respondent the option of either choosing one of the multiple-choice answers or writing text if they wanted to give a more detailed answer. When the respondent completed a question and hit "enter," the program automatically moved to the next question. The *Pleasure Pit* programmer made it very easy for me to collect the data from my home computer. Every few days I would call *Pleasure Pit* from my home and then download the answers given by the respondents. At that time I would separate the respondent's name from the questionnaire and then give each questionnaire a number to ensure confidentiality.

---

[1]I have decided to leave the quotes in their original form and have not changed the original spelling.

The SYSOPs and I tried a few more approaches to gain more involvement in my study. First, the SYSOPs told users once again that there was a questionnaire on-line from a sociologist who needed help and told them how to locate the questionnaire. Second, my presence was advertised on *Pleasure Pit* when people first signed on and there was also a flashing notice saying I was the CO-SYSOP of an on-line relationship conference. Respondents—predominantly males—began to contact me immediately. In order to attract more women, the SYSOPs sent a notice from me to the 122 registered females and couples on *Pleasure Pit*. The note said:

> *To All Female Users of Pleasure Pit BBS.*
>
> *I am a graduate student at UC Santa Barbara. I am doing my Ph.D. dissertation on the relationships people develop over computer bulletin boards. I have placed a questionnaire in the Questionnaire menu (it is number 6) and I am CO-SYSOP in Conference 36. People have been responding, however, I haven't heard from many women. Please help me by taking the time to answer my questionnaire. If you have any questions contact me on this board. Just address it to Diane. Or you can contact me on the Internet (address given) or Prodigy (address given). All of your answers are confidential. Thanks Diane*

Women began to contact me immediately and were quite willing to help by answering my questions.

Interviewing subjects on-line was very easy. *Pleasure Pit* users saw my requests for respondents and contacted me. If they were willing, we would get into chat mode on *Pleasure Pit* where we could type back and forth to one another in real time. Otherwise, I would e-mail some questions to the respondent, who would then e-mail the answers back. The best part about doing "interviews" on-line was that I could capture what was being written and I would automatically have it transcribed. Many of the respondents were more than willing to answer my questions and truly liked the idea of being "interviewed on-line" and talking about their cybersexual experiences.

Who Uses *Pleasure Pit?*

A total of 133 usable questionnaires were collected in this study. Questionnaires were discarded only if the respondents did not answer the demographic questions or if I had reason to believe they were not serious. I discarded two questionnaires because, after I examined them, I found they were from children who managed to gain access to the BBS.

The amount of time the *Pleasure Pit* respondents had been using on-line bulletin boards of any kind varied from the first time to 15 years with a mean of 2.61 years. The hours each respondent spent on any BBS each day ranged from 1 minute to 12 hours a day, with a mean of 1.63 hours, with the majority (97%), having spent 5 hours or less a day on-line. This is consistent with other projects that have found users to spend 3 or more hours a week (Anonymous, 1997) on-line. The respondents who used *Pleasure Pit,* and who communicated with other people on-line, said they talked with up to 100 different people each week for pleasure, but on average they communicated on-line regularly with 13.31 people in a week. The majority (72%), communicated with less than 20 different people.

The individuals who used *Pleasure Pit* were predominantly male (77%), which might be expected because, overall, more men use computers than women (Sanz et al., 1994). The respondents ranged in age from 19 to 62 years, and were relatively young with the average age of all of the respondents being 35.2 years, and the majority (94.30%) under the age of 50. Reported ethnicity was mostly white (89.9%). Regarding religion, 22 percent said they were Catholic, 25 percent said they were Christian, 4 percent said they were Jewish and the rest did not answer the question. Over 50 percent of the respondents stated religion had no influence in their lives. About half of the respondents were married, 30.28 percent stated they were single, and over 51 percent reported having up to three children. A total of 71 percent stated they were heterosexual, 22 percent reported they were bisexual, and only 4 percent stated they were homosexual. Only 3 percent reported themselves to be transgendered or transsexual. Most of the respondents worked, with 70 percent having a full-time job. Only 2 percent were retired and the rest worked part-time, were students, unemployed, homemakers, or volunteers. The majority of the respondents in this sample reported having had a college education. Only 18 percent reported a high school education or less. Of the *Pleasure Pit* users in this sample, 22 percent declined to say how much money they made, but the majority (52%) of these respondents stated they made $39,999 or less a year. The respondents in this study were similar to the respondents in other sexual studies on-line (Tamosaitis, 1995; InterCommerce Corporation, 1996).

MOTIVES FOR ON-LINE SEXUAL ACTIVITY

Five basic reasons were reported by the respondents of this study for using sexually explicit BBS. As shown in Figure 41.1, the reasons most commonly given for taking part in sex on-line were due to the need for anonymity, time constraints in their personal life, the ability to share sexual fantasies with other people, to participate in on-line sexual activity, and to meet other people with similar sexual interests.

Anonymity

As expected, respondents stated they participated in sexually explicit BBS because they were able to take on whatever persona they liked from within the comfort of their own home or office. According to Stone (1995: 84):

> our commonsense notion of community and of the bodies from which communities are formed take as starting points, among others, that communities are made up of aggregations of individual 'selves' and that each 'self' is equipped with a single physical body . . . [however, computers] place the 'I' without whose coupling to a physical body there can be no race or gender, no discourse, no structure of meaning . . . [it is] about negotiating realities.

In other words, individuals using computer BBS have the opportunity to be whoever they want to be because the computer "provides ample room for individuals to express unexplored parts of themselves" (Turkle, 1995: 185). The users can take on a different identity and portray themselves as that person or persons. If they are too shy and/or are unable to be comfortable meeting people face-to-face, the computer provides the physical barrier and anonymity which enables the users to meet new people and communicate from a distance. For instance, a 29-year-old female, states that

> they [other BBS users] can get to know me, faults and all, and vice versa, without too much pressure. It is also a great way to weed out the scary ones [individuals] . . . no one can hide behind their words for long . . . I have met more people on-line than through traditional methods.

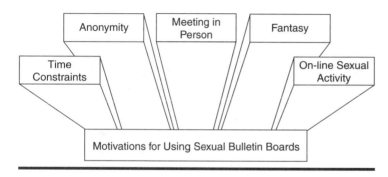

FIGURE 41.1 Motivations for Using Sexual Computer Bulletin Boards

According to Goffman (1963), when individuals possess attributes that discredit them in the eyes of others, it can greatly affect their self concept of themselves and the way they interact with other people. The anonymity of the BBS is one way in which individuals can conceal themselves in order to avoid receiving the negative reaction of others. The computer provides the perfect shield against stigma. A single male wrote that since he was shy, e-mail "provided a curtain to hide behind." Similarly, Fred stated he has had more opportunities to talk to people on-line than he does off-line. In fact, he said:

> I am a little more shy face-to-face, but I'm working on it. On-line, you can talk to someone without worrying about how you are dressed or undressed, what you look like. All the other person can see is what you want them too. I'm very open on the boards [BBS] . . . for some it's just a fantasy life and the people aren't usually anything like they are in person. I am, I'm just the same, just a little more shy in person.

Some respondents, especially women, mentioned they felt they were fat and undesirable in person. On the BBS, they stated they felt completely different; they felt young, wanted, slim, and sexual.

Too Many Time Constraints

Another reason respondents stated they used sexually explicit BBS was due to the many time constraints in their lives. Some mentioned they had very little time in their busy schedules to pursue friendships or sexual contacts on a face-to-face basis. Traditional face-to-face relationships of any kind develop through a pool of "eligibles" who are involved in close proximity to one another (Michael et al., 1994). However, there are many constraints to finding a person with similar sexual ideas and desires within close social networks. According to Michael et al. (1994: 153) it is "difficult to find a sexual partner who, right off the bat, has the same sexual preferences as you have. If you desire anything but vaginal sex or, perhaps, oral sex, it will be hard to find a partner with your

tastes." The respondents in this study stated the same thing. They believed it took too much time and was almost impossible to meet people with similar sexual interests and therefore the computer was the best way to handle this dilemma. A 41-year-old married man said he uses e-mail and BBS to meet people for sex because of the "immediacy of sexual conversation. Real life sexual relationships require a lot of small talk first." Paula, a single female who said she was in a face-to-face relationship with a man, considered the BBS as the "preliminary foreplay leading to real sex with swinging heterosexual couples who are real and sensitive." Paula was interested in trying new sexual behaviors, such as having sex with other couples, engaging in sex with women, and watching other people having sex. Paula believed she would not have found couples who shared her similar interests if she had not been on-line looking for sexual sharing.

Sharing Sexual Fantasies

The views most commonly held about sex are formed at a very early age and are dependent upon the dominant views held by groups we associate with and society as a whole (Rubin, 1990). Any sexual activity that is not heterosexually oriented and geared towards reproduction traditionally has been considered to be against the *ideal* norms of society (D'Emillio and Freedman, 1988), which makes it difficult for some to share sexual fantasies and interests with those in the *face-to-face* world. David stated he would never be the type to go to bars hoping to find some kind of (sexual) action, but wanted a friend with whom he could talk and have sex. He also said he had some sexual fantasies he was unwilling to share with his wife and had found the BBS was a safe way to ask for what he was really interested in. David was very specific about what he was looking for:

> I want a special woman who can understand and handle it when I want to wear nylons, panties, etc. . . . one who would not mind strapping on a dildo and say giving me a work-out . . . one who would let me watch her please herself as well as

watch me put on a show for her . . . also a male who would like to try a few safe fantasies together . . . no strings attached . . . just pure pleasure . . .

A bisexual male stated that his:

on-line friends are safe and we should all be able to have fun with no guilt feelings . . . if people have fantasies and their spouse doesn't want to hear them or do them . . . well what's the harm if we do it on the BBS . . . we are all adults.

Of the 72 percent of respondents who stated they had a spouse or significant other, only 20 percent had told their partner about their use of sexually explicit BBS. Often the users stated they *would not* or *could not* tell their significant other about their sexual fantasies. *Pleasure Pit* provided an outlet for them that they could keep private from those closest to them.

It has been found that fantasy and role-playing are a very pleasurable addition to sexual activities (Benjamin, 1983; Bright, 1992; Michael et al., 1994; Hamman, 1996), which has made the sexually explicit BBS attractive to its users. In order to assess the types of sexual fantasies that were common to the respondents, each respondent was asked to answer questions about 10 different fantasies which were as follows:

1. Bisexual Fantasy: having sex with both males and females
2. Lesbian Fantasy: two women having sex
3. Gay Fantasy: two men having sex
4. Being Submissive: also known as masochistic— enjoying being dominated
5. Being Dominant: also known as domination— being in control
6. Transvestism: wearing the clothing of the opposite sex
7. Water Sports: sexual excitement from contact with urine
8. Threesomes: sex with more than one other person
9. Group Sex: sex with a group of people
10. Sex Outdoors: sexual activities outdoors

For each of the fantasies described, the respondents were able to pick one of the following answers: (1) No interest at all; (2) Some interest;

(3) I am interested, would try this under the right circumstances; (4) Have tried this, did not like it; and (5) Have tried this, plan on trying this again.

The majority (55%) had already tried and liked the outdoor sex fantasy and 14–23 percent had tried and liked Bisexual, Dominant, Submissive, Threesome, and the Group Sex Fantasies. The fantasy that rated the lowest among the respondents was the Transvestite fantasy, where only 4 percent said they had tried and liked it and only 1 percent said they were willing to try this fantasy at all. This supported the data that showed less than 3 percent of all respondents claimed to be transgendered. Between 22 and 49 percent of respondents stated they would be willing to try all of the fantasies except for the Transvestite and the Gay and Lesbian fantasies. The reason gay and lesbian fantasies rated so much lower than the other fantasies could be due to the fact that there were numerous BBS geared to gay and lesbian interests. BBS users who stated they were gay or lesbian could be more comfortable on those BBS than on *Pleasure Pit,* which seemed to attract mostly heterosexuals. The answers also suggested the individuals who signed onto *Pleasure Pit* had particular sexual interests, some of which they have tried and others they were hopeful of finding someone to try them with. While some of the respondents have thought about these particular fantasies, and would try them if the opportunity arose, many also stated they had tried them and liked them. No one needed me to explain what I meant by any of the fantasies and most of the respondents did not have any to add to my list, which suggested I covered most fantasies. However, the responses of the individuals in this project suggested that they came to sexually explicit BBS because of their unfulfilled fantasies.

On-Line Sexual Behavior

Sexually explicit material, such as videos, books, or magazines, are just a few of the outlets for people to find out about new sexual acts and develop new fantasies and ideas. Traditionally, this material has been geared towards the heterosexual male and has included scantily dressed or nude women in all kinds of poses or sexual acts; now sexual material has been made available for people with all kinds of sexual interests. Reading stories and looking at sexually explicit pictures typically has been known as "material to masturbate by." Whereas masturbation used to be considered dangerous and apt to "destroy both the body and the mind" of the individual (D'Emillio and Freedman, 1988:69), it is currently taught as an accepted practice and takes place on a regular basis for many individuals (Michael et al., 1994).

With all this in mind, it should be no surprise that computers, e-mail, and various BBS have provided outlets for people interested in fulfilling their sexual fantasies. It is easier than meeting someone face-to-face and trying to decide if that person would experience the same sexual interests. For instance, if two people meet on a BBS conference for bondage, they already know that each has some interest in that kind of sexual activity and are able to divulge their fantasies early in the "relationship." If they like one another, they could then act out their sexual fantasy on-line.

On *Pleasure Pit,* one of the most common ways sex on-line happened was that the individuals went into chat mode and in "real time" typed out a fantasy with each other or a group of people. The sex act was accomplished by typing out in detail what each person could be doing to the other. Nate, a man who is getting married and whose significant other knows about his on-line escapades, stated he had sex on-line and "loved it." It began with "me and this lady talking and she then called my computer, and we told each other what we looked like and then we started with . . . well, what we wanted to do with each other and then acted it out with words." Nate said he didn't masturbate during this because he "loves the real thing, but it was fun to role play."

Most often the act of having "sex" on-line involved masturbation for the users and ended usually in an orgasm. One female stated that she had "sex" on-line quite frequently and she said:

> I love it when the guy gets off . . . it starts with teasing and flirting . . . leads to more . . . I usually rub my clit and we eventually get off . . . I most often

> am wearing a mini skirt or nude and it goes from there . . . it is planned sometimes, most often not . . . usually the men are on-line for a hot chat and wanting to cumm [sic] . . .

However, a female stated that sex on-line for her was both good and bad: "one time was VERY good, had 3 orgasms! One time I fell asleep (really) the rest were just like masturbating to a magazine/book, but OK." A 28-year-old male, who describes himself as single and heterosexual, stated that sex on-line is: "interesting . . . made my floppy drive into a hard drive: . . . [and is] good practice for the 'real' world." Some commented they learned more about what their cyber partner wanted sexually, because they were more willing to talk about their sexual needs and desires than with their face-to-face partners. Sex on-line, therefore, provided a place to practice what could be done later on in person.

Meeting the Sexual Fantasy Person of Your Dreams

Meeting the perfect sexual partner is not always easy. If individuals were looking for someone who could fulfill their sexual fantasies off-line, they needed to be able to meet someone who expressed similar sexual interests. It was also difficult for most people to discuss sexual fantasies with someone face-to-face because it meant risking rejection (Culbert, 1968). Normally when individuals meet each other face-to-face, the meeting follows a fairly straightforward path. At the initial face-to-face meeting, physical characteristics, such as gender, class, ethnicity, and age are shown because the individuals are in close spatial proximity and the bandwidth is greater. These characteristics have been found to be very important variables in the continuation of face-to-face relationships (Cameron et al., 1977). If the relationship is continued, then the individuals involved take their time learning about the internal characteristics of one another while often putting on a *facade,* or *frontstage* appearance that could mask their true problems, feelings, or emotions (Goffman, 1959), thus making the sharing of sexual desires difficult.

On the other hand, relationships that develop over BBS appear to be much easier for people. They are able to get to know one another without inhibitions and share their sexual fantasies with their on-line partners. They meet on "conferences" where they are more likely to have similar sexual interests. Sexually explicit BBS discussions tend to move very quickly since both people divulge their fantasies early in the "relationship." The main difference between the greater and narrower bandwidth is that the individuals can create detailed images as part of their interaction with one another (Stone, 1995). If they like one another, they can act out a sexual fantasy on-line while typing in detail the images they are trying to portray about their sexual situation. In this way, the users also acquire clues about the individual backgrounds by way of their writing, grammar structure, and the internal characteristics. In other words, their *backstage identity* is shown at a much faster rate (Goffman, 1959).

After meeting on-line and finding they have similar sexual interests, the individuals decide whether to meet one another face-to-face. If they meet, the physical characteristics are then revealed and the individuals decide whether to continue or discontinue the relationship based on the physical characteristics they display. If they decide not to meet one another on a face-to-face basis, they still have the option of continuing to correspond via computer. The computer BBS ultimately gives individuals more options than face-to-face meetings and the respondents in this study who have met one another in person say that when they got to know one another by their internal characteristics first, then physical characteristics did not matter as much. In other words, finding someone who in fantasy is sexually compatible can be more important in the relationship than looks, age, sex, and ethnicity.

Many of the respondents stated they were quite willing to meet and have sex with another willing partner either over BBS or in person if the chance arose. Over 57 percent stated they had already met someone face-to-face with whom they became involved as a result of meeting through

Pleasure Pit. Most stated the experiences went well for them. A single man who claimed to be bisexual went to the park and met his on-line friend, but said "nothing happened" after that. A woman, who was married and claimed to be heterosexual stated that she met "many nice couples and single males." Another male who stated he was bisexual and married met people from the BBS and "had at one time a bi encounter . . . that was great [and] would do it again with the right person . . . would like to meet an understanding female for special encounters." Another single female found that "2 guys were WONDERFUL! nice, good-looking, funny, friendly, great." However, she also found "two guys were fat, lied about [their] looks, shy, 1 of them is obsessed with me and the rest (8 or 9) are normal, everyday nice people." One married woman, who was bisexual and whose husband knew about her on-line relationships stated: "We, my husband and I, meet people all the time as we like to meet new people and make new friends, not all the people we have met have stayed friends, and some have become lovers." Fred stated he met many women on-line and some have worked out well:

> . . . the last woman I met from a BBS was from GA. She lives there still, but is thinking of coming out here. We seem to be falling in love with each other. The one before her, I met through a Denver BBS . . . we chatted many times before we got the chance to meet . . . she was very nice, I came to love her, but there wasn't that spark that said she was the right one for me. We are still very close friends.

Lady had face-to-face contact with numerous people she met over the BBS. She said:

> I expected nothing but friendship when I met them and that is exactly what I got . . . most of these people I met over lunch . . . one of them ended up being a date and then later a lover but as I said before nothing was different than what I expected since I really didn't expect anything but friendship in the first place.

For Don, actually meeting a person face-to-face was the ultimate goal of finding on-line relationships and he appeared to be "selling" himself by advertising the things he was willing to do sexually for a woman.

Meeting on-line makes telling fantasies much easier and people were able to "experience" what they had only been fantasizing about. One married man, who considered himself heterosexual, stated he had an interest in cross-dressing and submission and met some males on-line as well as females. When he met a man who shared his interest in cross-dressing he stated:

> . . . *both of us had always wanted to meet someone (guy) and be dressed up with garter belts, nylons, panties and then to see what happened. . . . Last year we met and went back to my place, undressed from our clothes, he was watching a XXXX movie I had in the VCR while he was playing with his cock, well I couldn't stand it anymore so I made the 1st move, yes I knelt in front of him and proceeded to give him my first blow-job . . . after awhile he had me position myself so I was fucking his mouth, then we both decided to do the 69 bit . . . so on the floor we went with me on my back and him slowly riding my mouth . . . he stopped because he didn't want to cum in my mouth, we finished the session by both of us jacking off onto my stomach. . . . I do want to do it once again only for the other guy to shoot his load into my mouth . . . this same guy has not wanted to meet because now all he wants is to jack-off, not into any bi stuff . . . but he has asked me to meet with him and his wife, yes his wife wants a big dick as well as two men doing her . . . right now I'm just waiting to hear from them.*

Sometimes, when individuals have met face-to-face after spending time in cyberspace, there was disappointment, which usually was the result of one or both parties not having told the truth about themselves. Most often the lies were about physical appearance. One male respondent stated that some people he had met had not been completely honest and:

> *tell you how good of shape their [sic] in . . . you know like 38-22-36 and 128 LB . . . when you get there they are more like 180 or so . . . or they will tell you things like yes, I want to do this or that and when you meet it is different . . .*

David looked forward to meeting a woman face-to-face, stated he really did not care too much about her personal appearance and said:

> . . . *yes, sounds like we are going to finally meet and if the mail was any promise as to what we both are going to do or want . . . we better call the fire house now and have them stand by . . .*

One single man, who had met with people off-line, said he had one sexual relationship that "was a bust if you will forgive the choice of words." Another man who now is divorced found "a couple of the people just weren't my type for whatever reason!" but never really said what his type was. One man was very uncomfortable when meeting his on-line friend because she brought her child to the meeting. Regardless, disappointment does not seem to stop these respondents from trying once again to meet someone with whom they may be sexually compatible.

OTHER RELATIONSHIPS

Significant Others and On-Line Sex

Although most spouses or partners knew their significant other had been using the computer, very few knew exactly what their partners were doing and that the computer was being used as a sexual outlet. One respondent stated he communicated with other people sexually at work or when his wife was not at home. Others logged on after their partners went to bed at night. Another respondent stated he had a laptop and "unless you're looking straight at it is hard to see." This same respondent said he was "hoping to get lucky and of course I don't want her to know." Yet another respondent said he "does all my BBS work at the office . . . don't want the headaches of explaining my fantasies to my wife."

Other times, the significant other knew their partner was on-line, but not that so much time and money was being spent on the X-rated BBS. One respondent stated his wife and he

> *were married young and no matter what we really haven't been able to relax with each other . . . I'm*

always told she has no fantasies and she has never masturbated. I've tried a couple of times to relax her and masturbate her, but it just seems like it can't be . . . I'm sure its not what I'm doing cause I've done this with other women and both have enjoyed it . . . also phone sex with my wife . . . we used to do it when I was gone or working the all day shifts, but that too has stopped . . . she is going through a lot of changes and guess maybe I am also . . . but the bottom line is that I do need and want sex, either on phone or in flesh with a special friend . . .

Jan, a 30-year-old married female, stated:

just access the BBS when he [her husband] is not here or sleeping, Why? Because of our relationship. I don't want him to have the access to the email. I have little sexual contact with my husband. I want to look at pics of naked men for some stimulation.

The mass media commonly has stories about love and lust on-line and about couples who have gone off to live happily ever after (Kerr, 1993; Edwards, 1994). However, the other side of these stories is that some individuals spent endless amounts of time on-line, withdrew themselves from communicating at home, and became involved in a cybersexual romance with someone other than their partner. Some respondents stated they were having trouble with their face-to-face relationships because of their sexual computer use. One man stated his ex-wife met some friends on *Pleasure Pit,* and then their relationship broke up. Similarly, the SYSOPs of *Pleasure Pit* stated they knew of many more relationships that had broken up as a result of one spouse who became involved in an on-line relationship.

Women and Sex On-Line

Men tended to outnumber women on-line (Morgan, 1993; InterCommerce Corporation, 1996), because sometimes women felt they had been reduced to sex objects, degraded, or sexually harassed (Kantrowitz, 1994; Sheppard, 1995). However, women stated they felt comfortable when they participated in on-line sexual activities. In this study, I found women become involved in sexual

BBS for reasons similar to those of the men. There seemed to be two distinct groups of women: those who were on-line to meet someone for sexual purposes and those who were on-line just for safe sexual discussions or encounters. One single woman said she "met more people on-line than through the traditional methods." Lady, who stated she is bisexual, started off by telling me she was not a "typical woman, nor your typical BBS using female either." She explained:

. . . I don't do much of the things most women do . . . my values and morals are much different than most women . . . and as far as the BBS goes I actually tell the truth about who I am and what I look like . . .

Other women stated they were on-line because they considered themselves "bi-curious" which means they wanted to have sex with another woman and have come to the BBS to find exactly what they are looking for. Over 61 percent of the women stated they had previously been interested in or had already had a bisexual experience. One woman who is married said: "I am really interested in trying a bi-female relationship and the BBS given me protection and a chance to meet someone in a safe environment before I meet her face to face." Ann, who is a single woman with a boyfriend, stated she was "looking for an entry into the swinging scene. We are new, interested, and willing to learn and would like to meet other heterosexual swinging couples and go to swinging parties."

The second group of women who participated in sex on-line were those who came to the BBS only for fantasy within the safety of their own computer. One woman, Katie, who was "happily married to a really great guy" stated she came on-line looking for:

sex hot chats . . . it provides me a way to be a bit freer sexually than in real life and yet still meet friends . . . [I am] a lot more open on-line and able to be nastier and sexier [than off-line].

Katie added that one of the reasons she was on-line was because she had fantasies she felt she couldn't and wouldn't act out in real life, but could act out on-line. Another single woman stated she felt much safer having sex and being involved with people on-line "because I will most likely never meet these people so I can say and be anything I want."

Some of the women in this study said they were attracted to the impersonal aspect of sexual BBS. The computer gave a "sense of anonymity" (see also Wysocki, 1996) which enabled the individuals to be more open and direct with one another. Many stated they could say things to other people they would not think of saying face-to-face or even to their spouse or significant other. Computer BBS seemed to make self-disclosure much easier.

The women stated that one advantage to being in a relationship with someone on-line was they had no commitment to the individuals they became involved with and they did not feel they had to take care of them. For instance, one woman who was divorced stated that on the BBS there was "no laundry, no cooking, no putting up with some man's crap when they live with you." She was able to be in cyberspace and have cybersex when she wanted to and only when she wanted to. There were no demands put on her. Another woman suggested that "the person [on-line] doesn't know you so you can say virtually anything." And someone else said the BBS "sometimes provides you with a sense of security and no questions." A married woman who stated she had little sexual contact with her husband, had tried computer sex but found it "too difficult to be into it when typing . . . phone sex is better, you don't have to use both hands to talk with."

Women were on-line for many of the same reasons as men. They were looking to fulfill specific fantasies and wanted to eliminate the wasted time looking for people with the same interests off-line. While some of the people who responded claimed to be in good strong relationships and just looking for added excitement, other women were looking to obtain fulfillment that was not happening in their off-line relationships. Most of the women who answered this survey knew exactly what they were looking for and were very specific. They did not appear to want to play games which failed to meet their needs and found comfort in the fact that if they did not like the sexual activity on-line, all they had to do was hang up.

DISCUSSION

In conclusion, this study of adult sexual relationships over a sexually explicit BBS found people used it for many different reasons. The most common reason given was that the respondents had specific fantasies and desires that were not being fulfilled in their relationships off-line. Some of the respondents stated they did not have the time it took in off-line relationships to get to know one another and see if they had similar sexual interests. It became much easier to go to a "conference" set up for specific pleasures, such as S&M, and know that the people participating in that "conference" have some interest in the subject or they probably would not be there.

The anonymity of the BBS also seemed to be an attraction to many of the users. They felt they could be more open and direct without having face-to-face interactions. Many stated they could say things to other people about their sexual needs and fantasies that they would not think of saying to someone they knew face-to-face or even to their spouse or significant other. Computer BBS just seemed to make self-disclosure much easier, and therefore reversed the order of the relationship. When people first meet in face-to-face relationships they look at the character of the individual to see how they are displayed (clothing, ethnicity, class) and then they decide whether to continue. In on-line relationships, the order is reversed. Once the BBS users had developed a relationship on-line, even if it was relatively new, the people involved sometimes met to have "real" sex. Ultimately individuals got to know each other much better and quicker, based on actual characteristics. Rather than face-to-face relationships being replaced by computers, the computer BBS has worked as a way of enhancing the face-to-face relationships in some cases.

Often the ultimate goal of meeting on-line for many individuals on this BBS was to meet in person. Therefore, the BBS and face-to-face encounters work together in a common enterprise to enhance interpersonal relationships.

ACKNOWLEDGEMENTS

I wish to thank Beth Schneider, Harvey Molotch, Bruce Straits, and Gary Marx for their support and encouragement and also Jill Williams, Annetta Wright, Ken Plummer, and the reviewers at *Sexualities* for making comments on this paper. I am especially grateful to the owners of the *Pleasure Pit* who spent endless hours making computer adjustments so I could collect data and to the many computer bulletin boards users who answered my questions and allowed me to play voyeur. Finally, thanks to George Wysocki for patiently teaching me the technical aspects of computers and for spending endless hours listening to me talk about my on-line friends and my research.

REFERENCES

Anonymous (1997) "Internet Sex Sells," *Computerworld* 31(9): 59.

Benjamin, Jessica (1983) "Master and Slave: The Fantasy of Erotic Domination," in Ann Snitow, Christine Stansell and Sharon Thompson (eds) *Powers of Desire: The Politics of Sexuality*, pp. 280–99. New York: Monthly Review Press.

Berg, Bruce (1998) *Qualitative Research Methods for the Social Sciences*. Boston, MA: Allyn and Bacon.

Bright, Susie (1992) *Susie Bright's Sexual Reality: A Virtual Sex World Reader*. California: Cleis Press.

Cameron, Catherine, Oskamp, Stuart and Sparks, William (1977) "Courtship American Style: Newspaper Ads," *Family Coordinator* 26(1): 27–30.

Childs, Matthew (1994) "Lust Online," *Playboy* (April): 94–6, 152–3.

Culbert, Samual Alan (1968) *The Interpersonal Process of Self-Disclosure: It Takes Two to See One*. New York: Renaissance Editions.

D'Emillio, John and Freedman, Estelle (1988) *Intimate Matters: A History of Sexuality in America*. New York: Harper & Row.

Edwards, Cliff (1994) "Computer Dating: New Bar Scene in Your Own Home," *Santa Barbara News Press* (23 Jan.): D4.

Goffman, Erving (1959) *The Presentation of Self in Everyday Life*. New York: Doubleday.

Goffman, Erving (1963) *Stigma: Notes on the Management of Spoiled Identity*. Englewood Cliffs, NJ: Prentice-Hall.

Hamman, R. B. (1996) "The Role of Fantasy in the Construction of the On-line Other: A Selection of Interviews and Participant Observations from Cyberspace," [Online]: *http://www.socio.demon.co.uk/fantasy.html*.

InterCommerce Corporation (1996) "Sex Net," [Online]: *http://www.survey.net/sexlr.html*.

Kantrowitz, Barbara (1994) "Men, Women & Computers," *Newsweek* (16 May): 48–55.

Kerr, Robert (1993) "Digital Age Couples Meet Via On-line Dates," *Rocky Mountain News* (16 Nov.): 5D.

Michael, Robert, Gagnon, John, Laumann, Edward and Kolata, Gina (1994) *Sex in America: A Definitive Survey*. New York: Warner Books.

Morgan, Curtis (1993) "Cybersex," *The Miami Herald*, (22 Aug.): A1, A4.

Richards, John (1994) "Editor's Notes," *Boardwatch Magazine* (April/May): 8.

Rubin, Lillian (1990) *Erotic Wars: What Happened to the Sexual Revolution*. New York: Farrar, Straus & Giroux.

Ryan, Alan (1997) "Exaggerated Hopes and Baseless Fears: Technology and the Rest of Culture," *Social Research* 65 (3): 1167–91.

Sanz, Cynthia, Shaw, B. and Young, S. (1994) "Where Love Has Gone," *People* (21 Feb.): 40–43.

Sheppard, Nathaniel (1995) "Cyber Jerks," *Denver Post Magazine* (26 Mar.): 6–7.

Stone, Allucquere Rosanne (1995) *The War of Desire and Technology at the Close of the Mechanical Age*. Cambridge, MA: MIT Press.

Tamosaitis, Nancy (1995) *net.sex*. Emeryville, CA: Ziff-Davis.

Turkle, Sherry (1995) *Life on the Screen: Identity in the Age of the Internet*. New York: Simon & Schuster.

Wysocki, Diane Kholos (1996) "Somewhere over the Modem: Interpersonal Relationships over Computer Bulletin Boards," unpublished PhD dissertation, Department of Sociology, University of Santa Barbara.

ON-LINE ACCOUNTS
OF UNREPENTANT PEDOPHILES

KEITH F. DURKIN
CLIFTON D. BRYANT

Adults who engage in sexual activity with children, or possess such a sexual orientation, are considered to be among the most serious deviants in our society. Such contacts are illegal everywhere in the United States. Pedophiles, unlike some other varieties of deviants, enjoy almost no social support. None of the 2,753 respondents to a recent national survey indicated that they believed it was "normal" or "all right" for adults to have sexual contact with children (Janus and Janus 1993). The prospect of adults engaging in sexual activity with children "inspires an innate disgust in most people" (Finkelhor 1979:693). Pedophiles are "considered to be among the most degenerate" of all deviants (Bryant 1982:332). In fact, they are even disvalued by other deviants. In prison, "pedophiles occupy the lowest rung of the inmate social system" (Heitzeg 1996:325). The especially strong societal condemnation of pedophilia raises an important sociological question: How do pedophiles manage such a disvalued identity?

Currently, there is a growing societal concern over the use of the Internet by pedophiles. These individuals are using this computer network to transmit child pornography, to locate children to molest, and to communicate with other pedophiles (Durkin 1997). There have also been reports of adult men masquerading as children and entering computer chat rooms that are frequented by youngsters to engage in sexually oriented discussions or "cybersex" with these children (Lamb 1998). Although the use of the Internet by pedophiles presents serious social problems, it also

provides new possibilities for sociological investigations of pedophilia.

Pedophilia has been the topic of a plethora of studies conducted by psychologists, psychiatrists, sociologists, sexologists, and criminologists. However, this previous research has been widely criticized on methodological grounds. Critics have pointed to the fact that not even a single investigation has used a potentially representative sample of pedophiles (Okami and Goldberg 1992). These studies typically used samples of individuals who were incarcerated for committing sexual offenses or who were receiving mental health treatment. However, those samples are biased and lack generalizability. The subjects included in those studies constitute "at most a very tiny and unrepresentative sample" of all pedophiles (Finkelhor 1986:138). Therefore, there are a large number of pedophiles about whom little is known.

The data for this study were gathered from a Usenet discussion group composed of pedophiles, alt.support.boy-lovers. Scott and Lyman's (1968) classic formulation of accounts served as the conceptual framework for this study. The guiding research question was this: How do pedophiles who use the Internet account for their deviance? The accounts framework affords an effective conceptual tool for examining pedophiles and the attitudes that they hold in regard to their deviant orientation and behavior. Accounts reveal a certain way of viewing the world and, thus, can be considered as an indicator of the deviant's cognitive structure. Mayer (1985:21) noted that "one striking characteristic of the pedophile is the ability to minimize or rationalize his activities." Many pedophiles "have an entire set of beliefs that they feel justify sex between a child and an adult" (Abel, Becker, and Cunningham-Rathner 1984:89). Their distorted belief systems manifest themselves in the explanatory statements they offer for their orientation and behavior. A conceptual examination of pedophiles' accounts offers the prospect of substantially advancing the development of theories about individuals who sexually abuse children. Scott and Lyman (1968:62) argued that "the study of deviance and the study of accounts are intrinsically related, and a clarification of accounts will constitute a clarification of deviant phenomenon." Consequently, an understanding of the accounts offered by pedophiles who use the Internet will augment and extend our understanding of the general nature of pedophilia.

ACCOUNTS

The notion of accounts was first advanced by Marvin Scott and Stanford Lyman (1968). They defined accounts as "socially approved vocabularies that neutralize an act or its consequences when one or both are called into question" (p. 46). There are two categories of accounts.

The first . . . is *excuses*. When an individual offers an excuse, he or she admits that the behavior in question was wrong but denies full responsibility for the act or its consequences. Excuses cite "circumstances mitigating or entirely eliminating the everyday requirement of accountability" (Rothman and Gandossy 1982:451). A successful excuse may reduce the tendency of others to hold the actor responsible for the behavior in question or to make negative inferences about the actor's character (Michner, DeLamater, and Schwartz 1986). There are four types of excuses: appeals to defeasibility, appeals to accidents, appeals to biological drives, and scapegoating.

Justifications are the second category of accounts. Justifications are accounts "in which the individual or group accepts responsibility for the deviant behavior or belief but denies the pejorative or stigmatizing quality of it" (de Young 1989:114).

This usually involves some "attempt to change the audience's perception of the act" in question (Riordan, Marlin, and Gidwani 1988:496). Deviants who use justifications seek "to make a normally immoral act moral" or, at the very least, not as aberrant as it is typically considered (King 1987:220). There are several types of justifications: denial of victim, denial of injury, condemnation of condemners, appeal to loyalties, the sad tale, a claim of self-fulfillment, and basking in the reflected glory of related others.

Furthermore, Nichols (1990) observed that accounts can be extraordinarily complex. He argued that there is a distinction between monothematic and polythematic accounts. Monothematic accounts use only one defensibility, whereas polythematic accounts draw on two or more defensibilities. Although there is virtually no discussion of polythematic accounts in the extant literature, examples of this phenomenon can be found nonetheless. For example in their research on convicted murderers, Ray and Simons (1987:65) discovered an example of an account that can be conceptualized as polythematic: "Some respondents maintained that a series of stressful events had driven them to use intoxicants as a way of numbing their psychological pain. They contended that in this stress-motivated intoxication, they acted irrationally [and committed murder]."

[This] account combines a sad tale (i.e., a series of stressful events) with an appeal to defeasibility (i.e., stress-induced intoxication).

ACCOUNTS AND PEDOPHILIA

There is currently a relatively limited body of literature dealing with the excuses and justifications of pedophiles. The majority of this information comes from research conducted on, and observations made regarding, pedophiles in clinical and correctional populations.

It appears [from this research] that these particular deviants tend to offer two types of excuses for their behavior—appeals to defeasibility and scapegoating. In his classic paper on child molesters and drinking, McCaghy (1968) documented an excellent example of the former type of excuse. He found that convicted child molesters frequently attributed their sexually deviant behavior to alcohol. A second type of excuse used by these individuals is scapegoating. Mayer (1985:21) noted that adults who have sexual contact with children often "try to place the blame on the child for seductive behavior." Moreover, Lanning (1987:27) observed that a child molester who has been apprehended by authorities "may claim that he was seduced by the victim, that the victim initiated the sexual activity, or that the victim is promiscuous or a prostitute."

Pedophiles also offer justifications for their deviant orientation and actions. The relevant academic literature has indicated that they attempt to offer three types of justifications for their deviance: denial of injury (including the claim of benefit assertion), condemnation of condemners, and an appeal to loyalties. Many molesters argue that their actions were not harmful to the child involved (Finkelhor 1979; Mayer 1985). In fact, clinical reports reveal that many child molesters believe that such activity will not harm a youngster unless force is used (Stermac and Segal 1989; Pollock and Hashmall 1991). Such fallacious assertions contradict the voluminous body of scientific literature that indicates that children who are molested often suffer a variety of physical, psychological, and social damage because of their victimization (see Conte and Berliner 1988; Green 1988; Fuller 1989; McLeer et al. 1994; Jumper 1995). An extension of the denial of injury justification involves a claim of benefit (Friedman 1974). This entails the assertion that the behavior in question not only lacks injurious qualities but is actually beneficial. There have been reports of pedophiles offering this specific justification for adults engaging in sexual activity with children (Abel et al. 1984; Barnard et al. 1989). For instance, Stermac and Segal (1989:582) found that "men who have sexual contact with children differ from other men in the types of cognitions and beliefs that they have regarding the salutary consequences of this behavior on children." Pedophiles also offer condemnation of condemner's justifica-

tions. This particular type of account is featured prominently in the literature of pedophile organizations such as NAMBLA (de Young 1989). Law enforcement officers and social workers are typically the targets of diatribes that accuse them of engaging in a variety of unscrupulous and incompetent practices such as "brainwashing" children and engaging in a draconian witch hunt against pedophiles. A final type of justification proffered by these individuals is an appeal to loyalties. The central allegiance claimed by pedophiles is the so-called "rights" of children. Such arguments have been advanced by the pedophile organization NAMBLA (Leo 1983; de Young 1989). This type of justification typically involves the claim that "the repression of childhood and adolescent sexuality is damaging to minors and therefore society." As part of the liberation of children and adolescents free sexual expression is encouraged. This sexual expression includes the "right" of children and adolescents to be sexual with adults (Gonsiorek 1994:29).

Although the previous work dealing with the accounts of pedophiles has been informative, most of it suffers from the same methodological problems that plague pedophile research in general. For instance, McCaghy (1968), Stermac and Segal (1989), and Pollock and Hashmall (1991) all used subjects who were drawn from clinical or correctional populations. Similarly, the observations made by Barnard et al. (1989) and Lanning (1987) regarding the excuses and justifications of pedophiles were based on their respective experiences in clinical psychology and law enforcement. Because pedophiles in clinical and correctional settings do not constitute a representative sample, the generalizability of these research findings and observations are limited. De Young (1989) conducted a study of the accounts that appeared in NAMBLA publications. However, it is unclear how generalizable the results of her research are as these accounts are a product of an organization rather than of individual pedophiles. Consequently, the information obtained from an investigation of the accounts of pedophiles who use the Internet will serve as a useful supplement to this extant body of literature on the excuses and justi-fications of pedophiles.

METHOD

The data were gathered from a Usenet newsgroup composed of pedophiles, alt.support-boy.lovers. Users of this newsgroup can read and post mes-sages. These postings are organized in an archival fashion. These messages can be downloaded to a personal computer and sent directly to a printer. Consequently, messages can be printed for content analysis. There are approximately 5 to 10 new mes-sages posted daily. There are between 150 and 200 messages posted to the newsgroup each month. These postings range in length from several sen-tences to several paragraphs.

We performed content analysis on all of the postings to the Usenet newsgroup alt.support.boy-lovers for a period of one month. There were a total of 154 postings from 80 individuals that ap-peared on the newsgroup during this time period. Ninety-three of these postings were contributed by 41 users who are admitted pedophiles. These 93 postings constituted the data that were analyzed for this undertaking. Slightly more than half (51 percent) of the individuals who posted to the newsgroup during the month were admitted pe-dophiles. These individuals contributed 60 percent of the postings for this time period. The unit of analysis for this undertaking was the individual pedophile (i.e., the posters). The postings of each of the admitted pedophiles were examined to de-termine the presence or absence of themes that corresponded to the respective variable of interest. The coding categories were based on the following operational definitions of the respective variables:

Account offered—the posting contains some type of explanation offered in defense of pedophilia or adults having sexual contact with children.

Condemnation of condemners—the poster at-tempts to shift the focus from pedophiles and their behavior to the actions of those who condemn them. Targets of condemna-tion may include law enforcement officers, social workers, psychologists, psychiatrists, and others.

Denial of injury—the poster claims that adults engaging in sexual contact with chil-dren does not cause harm to children. It may involve a claim of benefit assertion.

Claim of benefit—this particular account is an extension of the denial of injury account. The poster goes a step beyond simply as-serting that adult–child sex does not harm the child and claims that such behavior is actually beneficial for the child involved.

Appeal to loyalties—the poster attempts to justify pedophilia and adult-child sex by claims of an allegiance to "children's liber-ation" or "children's rights."

[Basking in reflected glory of others]—the poster makes the assertion that "great men" have also been pedophiles.

Polythematic account—the posting contains an appeal to more than one defensibility. It includes any combination of the following accounts: condemnation of condemners, appeal to loyalties, denial of injury, and [basking in reflected glory of others].

RESULTS

The number and percentage of pedophiles in this sample who offered each of the various accounts are reported in Table 42.1. Slightly more than one half (53.7 percent) of these 41 pedophiles proffered some type of account in defense of pedophilia or adults engaging in sexual activity with children. The most common type of account offered by the pedophiles in this sample was denial of injury. Thirty-nine percent provided this type of account which consisted of the assertion that sexual contact with adults does not cause harm to children. For in-stance, one poster, who was speaking of his sexual relationships with boys, wrote, "The experiences were always mutual and I don't feel/think those [boys] were mentally damaged by this as many people believe." Another pedophile asserted that: "I don't see anything wrong with a teenager having

Table 42.1 Number and Percentage of Pedophiles Offering Each of the Various Types of Accounts

ACCOUNT	NUMBERING OFFERING	PERCENTAGE OFFERING
Any type of account	22	53.7
Denial of injury	16	39.0
Condemnation of condemners	13	31.7
Polythematic account	10	24.4
Basking in reflected glory	6	14.6
Claim of benefit	4	9.8
Appeal to loyalties	2	4.9

a sexual relationship with an adult providing both are consenting and that there is some sort of friendship for this closeness to be based on."

The next most popular account, condemnation of condemners, was offered by nearly one third (31.7 percent) of the pedophiles in this sample. This involved shifting the focus from pedophiles to those who would condemn them, such as law enforcement officers, social workers, mental health professionals, and parents. Interestingly, gay men were also the target of condemnation. Some of the pedophiles who use this newsgroup had apparently argued that they were an oppressed sexual minority similar to homosexual men. They had made these claims on computer newsgroups dedicated to discussions of homosexuality. In response, several gay men had posted messages on alt.support.boy-lovers claiming that the behavior of pedophiles is aberrant and has nothing to do with homosexuality. One of the pedophiles responded,

> Oh wow, you're a good homosexual. You should be accepted by society. And in many countries you will indeed. You might even find yourself integrated in society as being a homosexual.
>
> No, you don't want to be classified in the same category as those nasty, tasteless, and horrible pedophiles. You don't like the young boys so you don't even want to think about those pedophile bastards. Come on you guys! What was the situation about half a century ago? Homosexuals were in the same position as pedophiles are nowadays. People looked upon homosexuals as being nasty, tasteless, and horrible bastards. Now YOU are

> doing the same towards another group. You're right: pedophiles aren't in the same group, but a little bit of understanding is the least pedophiles could expect from previously repressed groups.

Another target of condemnation was people who had contributed postings to the newsgroup that expressed opposition to pedophiles. For instance, one individual, who claimed he had found this newsgroup by accident, argued that pedophiles were mentally ill and should seek psychiatric help. In response, one pedophile remarked, "Most likely that's because you have the brain of a chimpanzee and are just as brainwashed by the mythologies of your culture as the other 90% of your putrid country."

Approximately 15 percent of the pedophiles in the sample offered a ["basking in reflected glory"] account. This involved the claim that great men have also been pedophiles. For example, one poster wrote,

> A favorite pastime of boy lovers is collecting pictures of boys, and those boy lovers who have no desire to break the law usually make excellent photographers. An example is the German photographer Hermann List, who is internationally renowned as one of the finest photographers of the first half of this century.

Another maintained,

> some of the more famous lovers of boys throughout history include the following: Alexander the Great. The Greek philosophers Socrates and Plato.

Plato was 13 when the two met. The Greek poets Anacreon, Alcaeus, Meleager, Strato, and many others far too numerous to mention . . . Oscar Wilde, commonly thought to be the "father of the modern gay movement." In fact, he loved boys, not men. Allan Ginsberg, the beatnik poet of the '60s, and his literary guru William S. Burroughs (of "Naked Lunch" fame).

The claim-of-benefit account, which consisted of the contention that sexual contact with an adult is beneficial to children, was offered by 9.8 percent of the pedophiles in the sample. This justification is an extension of the denial of injury account. Speaking of the boys that he was sexually involved with, one pedophile remarked,

In all cases the boys had a noticeable improvement in their self-esteem, their grades in school went up, they became more stable emotionally, and in one case I pulled a boy back from the drug/school dropout scene and he is now an officer in the Army.

Another poster wrote, "I feel that a consensual intergenerational relationship can be a learning experience for people that want to get involved in one."

The least popular account among these pedophiles was an appeal to loyalties, which was only offered by 4.9 percent of the sample. One pedophile briefly spoke of his support for the "sexual rights of minors" in a posting. Another individual always concluded his posting with the statement "in liberation," which was obviously an allusion to the so-called "children's liberation movement."

Nearly one quarter (24.4 percent) of the pedophiles in this sample offered a polythematic account that appealed to more than one defensibility. They included some combination of denial of injury, condemnation of condemners, [basking in reflected glory], and appeal to loyalties. Some of these accounts were quite lengthy and presented detailed arguments. For example, one pedophile contributed a polythemtic account that combined a denial of injury account with a condemnation of condemners account:

A child is a sexual being. Therefore, children should have the right to explore any aspect of sexuality they desire to engage in. Why do parents,

politicians, and police (the 3 p's) feed guilt into children that are sexually active? The guilt and shame put on the child's senses does a major amount of damage to the child. The majority of damage comes when the parents press charges and the boy lover goes to jail and the boy has to deal with the fact that the relationship which was consensual has put this guy away for a long time. There is no doubt that children can and do have the ability to decide for themselves what they want. . . . Children that are sexually active should be left to themselves to decide who should be their sex partner. . . . Consensual sex is justified in all forms, so there should not be a tag of criminal placed on intergenerational sex.

Caution should be exercised in the interpretation of these results. First, these findings cannot be generalized to the entire population of pedophiles who use the Internet with any certitude. They are reflective of admitted pedophiles who participate in the Usenet newsgroup alt.support.boy-lovers. There is no way to know how the users of this particular group are similar to or different from pedophiles who participate in other computer forums (e.g., America Online). Second, these findings are probably not generalizable to pedophiles in the general population. Pedophiles who use this newsgroup are probably of higher socioeconomic status than other pedophiles because they have the resources necessary to access expensive computer and telecommunications equipment. Although there are some limitations associated with the generalizability of the results of this research, this study has significant import nonetheless inasmuch as it represents the first substantive data on pedophiles who use the Internet. Furthermore, a major problem associated with previous research on pedophiles is the fact that the samples used were drawn from clinical and correctional populations. Accordingly, the current undertaking can serve as a useful supplement to the extant body of knowledge on pedophilia.

The overall tone and demeanor of this newsgroup may contribute to the management of the deviant identity of pedophile. Semantic manipulation would appear to be a major mechanism of both self- and public image enhancement. In the context of this newsgroup, pedophiles are referred to as "boy lovers." In fact, this newsgroup is named alt.support.boy-lovers. Sex between adults and children is called "love." However, in the context of the larger society, pedophiles are referred to with such pejorative appellations as *pervert* and *child molester.* [Sociologists have] observed a similar tendency in some occupations. They noted that trash collectors call themselves *sanitation engineers,* undertakers refer to themselves as *funeral directors,* and dog catchers use the term *animal control officer* in a self-descriptive fashion. This technique has implications not only for the self-concept of the practitioners of these occupations but also for the public perceptions of these vocational endeavors. Although it is highly unlikely that the use of the term boy lover will have any impact on public perceptions of pedophiles, it nonetheless may have important implications for the self-concept of pedophiles. Rather than conceiving of themselves as child molesters or perverts, these pedophiles can more comfortably conceptualize themselves as adults who have a "romantic" interest in boys.

CONCLUSION

The purpose of this research was to examine how pedophiles who use the Internet account for their deviance. These pedophiles make extensive use of accounts. Two specific accounts, denial of injury and condemnation of condemners, were particularly popular among this group of pedophiles. The ["basking in reflected glory"] account figured prominently in the accounting systems of some of these pedophiles. This is a noteworthy finding as there has been little previous documentation of deviants who use this particular account. The results of this research also indicate that accounts have a greater complexity than is normally indicated in the literature. This is an especially significant oversight as accounts can be extraordinarily complex in the real world (Nichols 1990). Nearly one quarter of the pedophiles in this sample offered polythematic accounts. Therefore, it is extremely important that sociologists involved in the study of accounts take this into consideration. The re-

sults of this research, along with the relevant academic literature on the topic of pedophilia, indicate that there are several readily identifiable accounts that pedophiles offer for their deviant orientation and behavior.

These computerized accounts may very well have import beyond neutralizing deviance for the respective individuals who offer them. Although pedophiles have traditionally used accounts, the Internet provides a highly effective mechanism for the aggregation and dissemination of accounts. As Durkin and Bryant (1995:194) observed, the computer can function as a "germination and distribution mechanism for sexual deviancy." The pedophiles who use the computer newsgroup alt.support.boy-lovers are in effect advertising and propagandizing their ideological position. The fact that a substantial number of these pedophiles are offering accounts may lead to the generation of a consolidated body of accounts. In turn, this may help the scores of pedophiles who read this newsgroup to justify or legitimate their deviant orientation and behavior. [Some sociologists have observed a] similar phenomenon occurring in the various sadomasochistic organizations they studied. They noted that an important function of those groups was the development and communication of various justifications and apologia that allow the members to accept their deviant behavior as being perfectly normal.

Currently, there is a great deal of societal concern regarding pornography in cyberspace. Recently, the federal government attempted to enact legislation to ban indecent communication on the Internet. Unlike other research on the topic of sexual deviance in cyberspace (e.g., Durkin and Bryant 1995; Lamb 1998), the current investigation found little in the way of pornographic materials. Consequently, it is difficult to address issues surrounding governmental censorship of the Internet on the basis of this study's results. However, the findings of this research appear to have implications for one particular matter related to governmental intervention in the use of the Internet. Recently, it has been suggested that the computer access of pedophiles who are on probation and parole be restricted (L. Davis, McShane, and Williams 1995; Durkin 1997). The logic behind this argument is that exposure to the pornography available on the Internet, as well as the supportive environment that this computer network affords pedophiles, may be detrimental to rehabilitation efforts and consequently encourage reoffending. The results of the current undertaking indicate that the computer newsgroup alt.support.boy-lovers provides a highly sympathetic milieu for its users. This finding provides additional support for the recommendations made by L. Davis et al. (1995) and Durkin (1997) to restrict the computer access of pedophiles as a condition of their probation or parole.

Sociologists also need to examine other forms of deviant behavior that rely on the computer. Durkin and Bryant (1995:197) noted that

> what seems to be conspicuously lacking are investigative efforts to document, explore, and analyze the newly emerging socially deviant uses of computers, founded on the unique capabilities, characteristics, and applications of computer communication, especially the evolution of non-white-collar deviant and criminal behavior patterns.

Given the diversity of deviants who are using the Internet, this certainly appears to be a significant oversight. For instance, pedophiles are not the only sexual deviants who are using the Internet. There are computer forums dedicated to nearly every conceivable form of sexual deviance, including bestiality, coprophilia, sadomasochism, and transvestism, to mention but a few. Moreover, hate groups, such as White supremacy and Holocaust denial groups, are using the Internet to proselytize and organize. A former Ku Klux Klan official who runs a racist site called Stormfront claimed "we're reaching tens of thousands of people who never before had access to our point of view" (Kanaley 1996:05). Furthermore, there have been reports of cults, such as Heaven's Gate, using the Internet to recruit new members and disseminate their groups' deviant ideologies (see Lacoyo 1997). Finally, there have been reports of some individuals "becoming addicted to the Internet in much the same way that others became addicted to drugs, alcohol, or gambling" (Young 1996:899). There is a compelling need for sociologists to be more attentive to the novel configurations of deviant behavior that rely on the computer. The mass media is beginning to provide glimpses into the use of the Internet for deviant purposes, but the topic still awaits systematic research by sociologists.

REFERENCES

Abel, Gene G., Judith V. Becker, and Jerry Cunningham-Rathner. 1984. "Complications, Consent, and Cognitions in Sex between Children and Adults." *International Journal of Law and Psychiatry* 7:89–103.

Barnard, George W., Kenneth Fuller, Lynn Robbins, and Theodore Shaw. 1989. *The Child Molester: An Integrated Approach to Evaluation and Treatment.* New York: Brunner/Mazel.

Bryant, Clifton D. 1982. *Sexual Deviancy and Social Proscription: The Social Context of Carnal Behavior.* New York: Human Sciences Press.

Conte, Jon R., and Lucy Berliner. 1988. "The Impact of Sexual Abuse on Children: Empirical Findings." Pp. 72–93 in *Handbook of Sexual Abuse on Children,* edited by Lenore E. A. Walker. New York: Springer.

Davis, Laura, Marylin D. McShane, and Frank P. Williams. 1995. "Controlling Computer Access to Pornography: Special Conditions for Sex Offenders." *Federal Probation* 59(2):43–8.

De Young, Mary. 1989. "The World According to NAMBLA: Accounting for Deviance." *Journal of Sociology and Social Welfare* 16:111–26.

Durkin, Keith F. 1997. "Misuse of the Internet by Pedophiles: Implications for Law Enforcement and Probation Practice." *Federal Probation* 61(3):14–8.

———— and Clifton D. Bryant. 1995. "Log On to Sex: Some Notes on the Carnal Computer and Erotic Cyberspace as an Emerging Research Frontier." *Deviant Behavior* 16:179–200.

Finkelhor, David. 1979. "What's Wrong with Sex between Adults and Children?" *Journal of Orthopsychiatry* 49:692–97.

———. 1986. *A Sourcebook on Child Sexual Abuse.* Beverly Hills, CA: Sage.

Friedman, Norman L. 1974. "Cookies and Contests: Notes on Ordinary Occupational Deviance and Its Neutralization." *Sociological Symposium* 11:1–9.

Fuller, A. Kenneth, 1989. "Child Molestation and Pedophilia: An Overview for the Physician." *JAMA: Journal of the American Medical Association* 261:602–6.

Gonsiorek, John C. 1994. "A Critique of Current Models in Sexual Abuse." Pp. 21–36 in *Male Sexual Abuse: A Trilogy of Intervention Strategies,* edited by John C. Gonsiorek, Walter H. Bera, and Donald LeTournea. Thousand Oaks, CA: Sage.

Green, Arthur H. 1988. "Overview of the Literature on Child Sexual Abuse." Pp. 30–54 in *Child Sexual Abuse: A Handbook for Health Care and Legal Professionals,* edited by Diane H. Schetky and Arthur H. Green. New York: Brunner/Mazel.

Heitzeg, Nancy A. 1996. *Deviance: Rulemakers and Rulebreakers.* New York West.

Janus, Samuel, and Cynthia Janus. *The Janus Report on Sexual Behavior.* New York: John Wiley & Sons. Jumper, Shan A. 1995. "A Meta-Analysis of the Relationship of Child Sexual Abuse to Adult Psychological Adjustment." *Child Abuse and Neglect* 19:715–28.

Kanaley, Fred. 1996. "Hate Groups Using the Internet to Proselytize, Organize." *Morris County Daily Record,* July 7, p. O5.

King, Kim M. 1987. "Normative Contingencies: Charity and Moderation." *Current Perspectives in Social Theory* 8:215–37.

Lacayo, Richard. 1997. "The Lure of the Cult." *Time,* April 7, Pp. 44–46.

Lamb, Michael, 1998. "Cybersex: Research Notes on the Characteristics of the Visitors to On-Line Chat Rooms." *Deviant Behavior* 19:119–33.

Lanning, Kenneth V. 1987. *Child Molesters: A Behavioral Analysis,* 2nd ed. Washington, DC: National Center for Missing and Exploited Children.

Leo, John. 1983. "A New Furor over Pedophilia." *Time,* Jan. 17, p. 47.

Mayer, Adele. 1985. *Sexual Abuse: Causes, Consequences and Treatment of Incestuous and Pedophilic Acts.* Holmes Beach, FL: Learning.

McCaghy, Charles H. 1968. "Drinking and Deviance Disavowal: The Case of Child Molesters." *Social Problems* 16:43–9.

McLeer, Susan V., Marian Callaghan, Delmina Henry, and Joanne Wallen. 1994. "Psychiatric Disorders in Sexually Abused Children." *Journal of the American Academy of Child and Adolescent Psychiatry* 35:313–19.

Michner, H. Andrew, John D. DeLamater, and Shalom H. Schwartz. 1986. *Social Psychology.* New York: Harcourt Brace Jovanovich.

Nichols, Lawrence. 1990. "Reconceptualizing Social Accounts: An Agenda for Theory Building and Empirical Research." *Current Perspectives in Social Theory* 10:113–44.

Okami, Paul, and Amy Goldberg. 1992. "Personality Correlates of Pedophilia: Are They Reliable Indicators?" *Journal of Sex Research* 29:297–328.

Pollock, Nathan L., and Judith M. Hashmall. 1991. "The Excuses of Child Molesters." *Behavioral Sciences and the Law* 9:53–9.

Ray, Melvin, and Ronald L, Simons. 1987. "Convicted Murderers' Accounts of Their Crimes: A Study of Homicide in Small Communities." *Symbolic Interaction* 10:57–70.

Riordan, Catherine A., Nancy A. Marlin, and Catherine Gidwani. 1988. "Accounts Offered for Unethical Research Practices: Effects on the Evaluation of Acts and Actors." *The Journal of Social Psychology* 128:495–505.

Rothman, Mitchell L., and Robert P. Gandossy. 1982. "Sad Tales: The Accounts of White-Collar Defendants and the Decision to Sanction." *Pacific Sociological Review* 25:449–73.

Scott, Marvin B., and Stanford Lyman. 1968. "Accounts." *American Sociological Review* 31:46–62.

Stermac, Lana E., and Zindel V. Segal. 1989. "Adult Sexual Contact with Children: An Examination of Cognitive Factors." *Behavior Therapy* 20:573–84.

Young, Kimberly S. 1996. "Addictive Use of the Internet: A Case That Breaks the Stereotype." *Psychological Reports* 79:899–902.

DEVIANT SPORTS

Cockfighting is a widely popular sport in the Philippines. There are about 1,500 cock-pits across that island nation. Cockfighting is an industry consisting of breeders, feed-ers, handlers, owners, "cock doctors," bookmakers, and gamblers. The average annual income in the Philippines is only about $1,200, but bets of $2,000 to $3,000 are com-monplace. Cockfighting is indeed a mass obsession. Suggestions of cruelty to the ani-mal are thus incomprehensible to most Filipinos. Instead, there is widespread admiration for the bravery of the chicken. As a businessman who enjoys cockfighting says, "You get one with his intestine hanging out and he'll still fight. They're very brave." The cock-fight is always deadly because a three-inch razor blade is strapped to the left leg of each bird.[1]

Although cockfighting is legal in the Philippines, it is not in the United States ex-cept in a few places in the South. Nonetheless, some Americans like to indulge in the savage pleasure of watching a cockfight and the thrill of betting on the outcome. Gen-erally, when something is illegal, it tends to cause individuals to engage in some de-viant activities. Thus the illegality of cockfighting can be expected to encourage cheating and other related deviances. However, in the first article here, "Cockfighting: The Marketing of Deviance," Donna Darden and Steven Worden find in their ethno-graphic study of cockfighting that "cockers" strive to establish their reputation for hon-esty and trustworthiness.

A similar paradox can be found in the second article, "The World of Dogfighting," by Rhonda Evans and Craig Forsyth. Here we see that despite the deviant status of dog-fighting, the "dogmen" consider themselves respectable and endeavor to make their transactions with each other appear as respectable and legitimate as conventional busi-nesses. In the third selection, "The Techniques of Neutralization among Deer Poach-ers," Stephen Eliason and Richard Dodder show how deer poachers try to deal with the illegality of their deviant sport by justifying their action as if they had done nothing wrong. Finally, in the fourth reading, "Hints of Deviance in Bingo," by Constance Chap-ple and Stacey Nofziger, we can also discern a similar paradox in another kind of de-viant sport: Although bingo is popularly considered respectable because it is associated with churches and charities, it does have certain elements of deviance, such as being a form of gambling.

1. "The Politics of Fighting Cocks," *The Economist,* March 15, 1997, p. 40.

COCKFIGHTING:
THE MARKETING OF DEVIANCE

DONNA K. DARDEN
STEVEN K. WORDEN

Then one day I was driving through a small town . . . and I noticed one of the nicest set-ups for gamefowl that I have ever seen. I stopped . . . and gazed. . . . About that time an old man came out of his house and started towards me. . . . He said he remembers seeing me . . . buying fowl off a friend of his. The same man who got me started in this sport. . . . I was talking to probably the toughest, most honest and complete rooster man alive today, at least I think so. Anyway, we introduced ourselves and he told me about how he had tried to locate me about a year ago. I asked Sal why he tried to find me of all people and he said because he needed a partner. Well, when he said that, I about fell out of my shoes. Sal then explained that he had just moved to Oklahoma a few years ago and that he wanted someone who was a beginner in this sport, willing to learn what fifty years of cockfighting had taught him. (Whitney, 1991, p. 150)

Prus (1989a, 1989b) has shown us the close relationship which can exist between sociology and much of marketing. [That is,] the ethnographic study of marketing in action—the observation of salespeople selling, for example—can add to our knowledge of sociology. Here, we use a qualitative approach to the marketing of game fowl and the sport of cockfighting to illuminate problems which may be common in the deliberate spread and diffusion of other deviant activities, and we note the gamefowl world's attempts at solutions.

Cockfighting is a hobby and sport for all of its practitioners, and a business venture for the many who sell gamefowl and accessories. Like any small business person, the entrepreneurial cockfighter faces a different set of problems from those that General Motors and IBM contend with, yet he too must work within a set of forces which shapes his activities. We look here at the market forces which affect entrepreneurial cockfighters and the solutions they find as they and their consumers construct the marketing of a deviant sport and the fighting cock as a commercial object. After a brief description of cockfighting, we will describe our research and discuss how cockfighters market their questionable sport. We will show how marketing deviance differs from more conventional marketing.

COCKFIGHTING

Cockfighting is a very old sport—some even claim "the oldest" (Dundes, 1994, p. vii). In 386 Saint Augustine used a description of a cockfight in his "De Ordine" to illustrate evil in the world.

Although cockfighting is not universal, it may be the closest to a universal sport, occurring almost everywhere that chickens live. There are cultural nuances to the fights which occur in different places, some differences larger than nuances (bare-spurred versus the "slasher" fights, for example, see below), but the elements are fairly standard, owing to the inherent elements of pitting two roosters against each other to fight.

A cockfight consists of several rounds of putting weight-matched pairs of specially bred roosters against each other in a pit. Depending on the circumstances, they usually fight until one is dead. The birds are often brightly colored, and, again depending on the circumstances, a fight may be awesomely savage and, in its way, beautiful, although bloody. Spectators usually make bets on the birds, in any of several fashions, frequently calling out bets even as the fight progresses. Birds may fight bare-heeled (rarely) or with knives ("slashers") or gaffs (slender, pointed spurs) attached. The knife fight is quicker and bloodier, and more rounds are held during a session. During the gaff fight, it is normal for both birds to be wounded and exhausted but still living, so they may be dragged to a pit where they lie near each other. One or the other will usually rise up one last time to peck at the other, evidencing the quality of "deep gameness," and winning the fight. They may stay in the drag pit for an hour or more. During that time, other birds are fighting in the main pit. Most of the people involved in cockfighting are men, although there are some women involved. The settings for the fights are usually rural, and range from the informal fight in a farmer's yard to the formal, specially constructed pits in a few areas of the country such as the Neighbors Game Club in Cibola, Arizona, which seats 350 people.

Most often, a cockfight is like other rural small town events, such as a rodeo or a high school ballgame. Although as Bryant and Capel (1974) have pointed out, cockfights attract people from all levels of the stratification system, our data show that people from the high-end of the social hierarchy are underrepresented: rural poor, construction workers and agriculturists predominate at most cockfights. People wear levis, overalls, camo outfits, and the occasional sport shirt. They generally sit on wooden benches or mill around. There is often a sign posted saying, "No Profanity, Alcohol, or Gambling." During daylight fights, there is usually gambling, but the alcohol and profanity are less obvious than they are at night fights, which can go on all night. Behavior at these fights can get rough, so that there may be as much fighting in the stands as in the pits. During daylight fights, children run around, men stand around and tell tales, women talk. There is little unanimity in the crowd. For a person who does not have money riding on a particular fight, the scene can grow boring. The fighting of the roosters often looks more like a pair of robins arguing over turf in one's front yard than a WWF scene, a lot of wing flapping and little more. If the ground is red clay, such as in the area we studied, and the birds both brightly colored, one may see little or no blood, just a lot of dust. The smells and sounds resemble a rodeo more than anything else. The atmosphere is rather like that of a secret club. Cockers do not believe that outsiders and those who oppose the sport know anything about it, but they do not want video pictures taken or newspaper accounts given. They feel like they are "in on something."

Referees are usually cockfighters themselves, men who are not fighting birds at this particular event. They are chosen and paid by the house, and ratified by the people in attendance. If people do not trust them, they will not return to that pit. Most are trusted by the crowd; Worden attended one fight where a referee's wife was fighting, but everyone believed him to be impartial. Referees are most important when the birds are dragged to the pit; they may be accused of counting fast or slow at these occasions.

BACKGROUND

Like marrying your cousin, cockfighting is illegal in most states in this country and frowned upon in the rest. Schiff (1995) called it a "degraded gladiatorial spectacle," categorizing it with professional wrestling, a comparison students often made for us in classroom discussions, except that students ranked it much lower than wrestling, in a league sometimes with wife-beating. There can be no arguing its disvalued status in much of our society. How do people get involved in such a disvalued activity, especially one that is inherently social, shared with others, rather than a type of secretive deviance? Some cockfighters got into their sport through the propinquity that must also assist people in falling in love with their cousins, as the novelist Harry Crews describes in a short story:

> [I been a cocker] all my life. My daddy given me my first chicken when I was twelve year old. Most rooster men that's any good been in it that long. It don't take but a lifetime to learn it. (Crews, 1979, p. 35)

One informant, for example, told us that before he knew about organized cockfighting, he used to shut two roosters in his bathroom and let them fight it out. Cocks do fight each other without human intervention, and people do fall in love without social approval and sanction. However, most cockfighters do not learn the sport from watching their chickens.

Most cockers get involved with the sport through deliberate diffusion instigated by the entrepreneurial cockers. The informant who fought chickens in his bathroom later introduced a friend to the sport this way. The friend, now a cocker too, said that he had not even known that chickens fought before watching in the bathroom pit. Tales such as the archetypal anecdote about Sal with which we begin this article, about how old men pick young men, beginners, give them their first birds, and train and encourage them in the sport of cockfighting and the care and raising of fowl, are quite common. Obituaries are usually written by sons, protégés, and admirers of the men who have died, rather than colleagues and peers. As we will show, old men recruit new ones in order to promote the sport and to ensure their own immortality, and young men turn to old ones as the only trustworthy people available in an ambiguous, probably disreputable, world. This gives a distinc-

tively gerontocratic aspect to both the sport and the marketing efforts.

In order to continue the sport, old cockfighters must market it, recruit new cockfighters, sell or give them birds, and encourage them in the sport, and they must do so in a relatively covert manner because of the widespread disvalued nature of the sport and the illegality of it in most parts of the country. In order to sell chickens, they must establish their reputations as honest and knowledgeable old men engaged in an illegal activity, whose only vested interest seems to be in continuing the sport for its own sake.

METHOD

This paper is based upon research into cockfighting which began in the spring of 1989 and continued intensively for about three years. The data were obtained through participant observation, intensive interviewing, and analysis of secondary materials. Our naturalistic study took place along the border region of Eastern Oklahoma and Western Arkansas. Worden did the primary research and observation, with Darden's role mostly limited to locating respondents and secondary research. This is not a sport where middle class female college professors are warmly greeted and introduced to the nuances of meaning and behavior. Although there are a few women cockers, some men's wives attend some fights, and "sew-up girls" may repair injured birds, this is a mostly male world. The editor of *The Gamecock,* however, is a woman.

Worden has observed formal and informal cockfights at varied settings. Interviews with main informants and informal conversations with many different participants were carried out over a period of nineteen months. Finally, an informant (who has since died, allegedly shot by his ex-wife's new boyfriend) read and commented on some of our material and corroborated its major conclusions, as well as our interpretations of supporting data.

For this study, we also concentrated on 24 issues of magazines devoted to cockfighting: *The Gamecock* (various issues ranging from May 1967 to May 1991), *Grit and Steel* (several issues from 1991), and *The Feathered Warrior* (several from 1991). For comparison, we read the June 1992 and January 1993 issues of *Bird Talk,* a magazine devoted to exotic bird keeping, and talked with a number of owners of such birds and one former breeder. Darden also attended the 1993 Annual Rattlesnake Roundup in Whigham, Georgia, and we looked closely at the program from that event.

MARKETING DEVIANCE

Since we are talking about marketing, it is useful to use paradigms established in that discipline to shape our discussion of the spread of cockfighting and selling gamefowl. Kotler's (1991) version of marketing is one of the most used and best accepted; we will adapt his major concepts for our project. While the models of the conventional marketing process that Kotler (1991) and others present may describe the processes by which mass marketers and many smaller businesses operate, we wonder if they work for the entrepreneur engaged in marketing dangerous or illegal activities: marketing deviance? When, for example, the environment is more than merely hostile, and threatens to arrest the seller and destroy his product and production facilities, can one of these models explain that situation and help the seller to make decisions? How do you sell something illegal, to people who know it is illegal?

Studies of drug sales, prostitution, and other vices help in this connection, but only to an extent. Many studies (Adler & Adler, 1983) have described the various techniques of drug-dealing. Two major differences between drug-dealing and cockfighting are the relative ephemerality of drug dealing compared to cockfighting and chicken-raising, and the relative visibility of the contraband which the owner must hide or disguise.

Although the small, local drug dealer may continuously maintain possession of a large enough amount of drugs to send him or her to prison, the bigger dealer usually maintains possession for a very limited amount of time, if any, before distributing the product to others who will merchandise it

in smaller amounts to others. People who grow chickens, however, have committed themselves to several years' worth of labor, possession, and visibility. An airplane full of illegal drugs is extremely visible, but it is also portable and soon emptied. A pound of cocaine or marijuana will fit in an easily carried container. A couple of acres of loud and brightly colored roosters tied to little sheds is also very visible, not portable, and relatively permanent. Law enforcement uses specially trained animals to sniff out drugs, but anyone who knows what to look for can spot a rooster yard.

Prostitutes face the visibility problem from a slightly different perspective. Call-girls, masseuses, and others at the higher end of the profession may have normal, conventional marketing problems, but the street hooker has to be out and available to customers without attracting the attention of law enforcement. This is a tricky act, with various solutions. Some women rely on the portability idea, moving frequently, from corner to corner, which makes repeat sales difficult. Some believe (wrongly) that they can hide or deny their activity by "passing" as dates if they do not mention money first. Some rely on pimps or other forms of word-of-mouth, and likely others pay law enforcement people to ignore them. Again, though, the chicken farmer's size and visibility present problems which prostitutes can handle with relative ease.

Still, cockfighters have not thought of themselves as outlaws, but as little guys who have fallen victims to big guys, little guys who are maintaining a noble tradition with a long and respectable history, including George Washington and Abraham Lincoln, and other notable chicken men of their times—in face of terrific odds. These odds include not only "the many crazy laws that are trying to be passed" (Abacherli, 1991, p. 171) and the animal rights activists, but the "big money men" who fight in the knife fight variation which runs costs up beyond the reach of the average little guy. In this form of cockfighting matches are over rapidly and many more cocks are destroyed (Worden & Darden, 1992).

How do these people continue to think of themselves as embattled practitioners of a noble sport which is illegal? Most believe that the birds will fight anyway, that birds just do fight. Many say that birds do not feel pain, owing to their simple nervous systems. Heame (1994) would likely disagree with this point. In her essay on "Parrots and Philosophers," for example, she says, ". . . even a cat isn't as good at keeping control of a conversation as a parrot is" (1994, p. 4). Barber (1993) would definitely disagree with the notion that birds are too simple to feel pain. In his book *The Human Nature of Birds,* he demonstrates that birds are intelligently aware. While breeders of exotic birds generally take a position somewhere between Barber's and that of cockfighters, owners of pet exotics emphatically agree with Barber, finding their pets not only intelligent but cuddly, lovable, and loving. Cockers, of course, may admire their birds and love their sport, but they do not love their birds. It is a rare rooster who even gets a name. Exotic bird breeders usually leave the naming of birds to the people who will buy and love them, as do dog breeders. Some particularly courageous and game roosters do get names. Pigeons are never named; they all receive numbers and are identified by their numbers only (Worden, 1992).

In defending their sport, cockers also point out that nature itself is bloody. If a poultry farmer has 100 chicks, for example, and eight live, the farmer is doing well. For the cockfighter, who has watered, fed, trained, and tended these birds for at least two years, the argument is simple: these birds get treated better than do those raised for food, and they may die with the dignity that nature intended for them, in a fight. Others ignore the whole question of animal rights by believing that chickens are fowl, not animals. The illegality issue they nullify by saying that the government is overreaching itself, getting into issues that are none of its concern, that the government has no right to regulate a group of gentlemen making wagers.

With the outlawing of the sport, however, and the often highly publicized efforts of both law enforcers and animal rights activists, cockfighting has in recent years attracted adherents who do think of themselves as outlaws. "Just tell me

something is illegal, and I'll do it," one informant said. While the "fraternity of cockers," as they often call themselves, probably contains no armed robbers or hit men, many cockers probably grow and sell marijuana on some scale or own illegal weapons. The story circulated among some of our informants that two men had tried unsuccessfully to set up a "clean" pit, and when it failed, they sold out to people rumored to be big drug-dealers in the area. It is likely that at least some drug money is laundered through cockfighting, since cash is the usual standard of exchange.

Kotler uses several core concepts of marketing to look at the processes of conventional marketing, and we will adapt these to look at our data and describe the selling of deviance. These concepts are: needs, wants, and demands; product; value; exchange; and market (1991, p. 4).

Needs, Wants, and Demands

According to Kotler, needs are basic and biological. Wants are ways of satisfying needs, and demands are elaborated satisfiers. Consider food, bread, and croissants. While the idea of needs is a little too psychological and too motivational for us, we are willing to talk about wants and desires/ demands here. Conventional marketers protest, perhaps rightly, that they engage in satisfying existing wants rather than creating new ones. The case of gamefowl is largely an exception, as the established chicken men must depend on finding new chicken men and getting them to want chickens. Cockfighters talk about wanting entertainment and wanting to continue the traditions of the "great sport" of cockfighting. The novice and the more experienced chicken man who buy chickens want to win money in the pits.

Although marketers usually consider sellers' long-range goals to be the obvious financial profit, those who sell chickens have an additional long-range goal. The epitome of the sport consists of becoming a legend whose fighting record is attested to by having his name attached to the stock which will be preserved by those who come after him.

Sandy Hatch may well not recognize the fowl that bear his name today as having much of a connection with the fowl that he had way back when. The important thing would be that he would be so extremely proud that his name and legend had lived on and was passed down to today's fowl, who contain little true old-time Hatch blood. His name is synonymous with the tenacious, game, powerfully enduring fowl for which his fowl were known for. The qualities of endurance and power liken today's hatch type fowl to those from the hands of the originator himself. (Warbird, 1991, p. 29)

Most cockers want to become trustworthy old men who can choose younger men to train and entrust with their fowl (Prus 1989b, p. 102–130). Inmortality is the ultimate desire/demand of the chicken man, seller and buyer. In the short run, this reputation as a trustworthy old man helps to sell chickens, too, and it is often a deliberate construction on the part of the seller.

Products

Product includes services, and refers to satisfying needs, wants, and desires. Here, the major product is a chicken. Since fighting the chickens is illegal in most states, and shipping animals across state lines for the purposes of fighting is against federal law, most sellers sell brood stock, and the buyers experiment with crossbreeding the fowl to produce battlecocks for fighting. As with drugs and prostitution, there is no product stability or standardization with chickens. The best breeding chickens are usually considered to be the pure lines with the original breeders' names attached.

I continue to read with interest the arguments against pure this or pure that. Well, if anyone is so shallow or nitpicking as to condemn such a practice by those of us that purchased fowl under this premise, whether we think them to be pure as the original breeder bred them or not, it still remains our right to call them what we want! If anyone wants to nitpick such a trivial difference with you, then tell them to stick it and walk away. You will have done yourself a favor. (Warbird, 1991, p. 29)

If there ever were pure lines of chickens, the resurgence of cockfighting in this country after World War II probably ended them. Whether there once were or not, the establishing of a chicken as a pure breed today is a social constriction. One cannot look at a chicken and know from its physical characteristics that he is a Hatch or a Kelso. Color, comb size, leg color, and other features once distinguished the various breeds, but they no longer do. There are many arguments over the ostensible breeds of specific chickens. The chicken that is sold as a "White Hatch" is a socially constructed product in that only through the claims that the breeder makes and the breeder's reputation and fighting record can the buyer form any idea of what he is purchasing. The features of a bird which breeders and buyers stress are things such as muscle and the quality of his conditioning. A desirable bird has just the right amount of muscling in his legs. Too much muscle makes a bird unable to act: he can't "cut" (is too slow and cannot aim). A bird that can "cut" can aim his gaff or knife, a skill which comes from an inbred instinct, cockers believe. The bird that cannot cut just flails away in the direction of his opponent. Superb conditioning results in rock-hard strong legs and wings. A bird with "bottom," probably a genetic feature, is one that can sustain punishment. "Gameness" is the key to a superior bird, that ability to persevere in the face of obstacles, to peck his opponent with his last dying gasp, to "hang in there" until the end. Stories are told about cockers who come with birds in polished wooden cages, put their birds in the pit with those of guys who bring their birds in paper bags, with mites crawling all over them, and lose to the mite-infested bird that is "deep game." A bird that is ready to fight, genetically superior and in condition, will swagger and cut his wings side to side before a fight. Handlers say that they can feel the tension in the birds and tell when the birds are ready. They also believe that the birds can feel the confidence and courage that the good handlers impart to them through holding them before a match. They also say that a good handler can feel the electricity go out of a bird during a match, when the handlers separate the birds. Advantages that some handlers are said to use include strychnine, which can cause a bird to attack even his handler, and steroids. Such chemicals are considered invasions on the pure sport by most cockers.

The cheapest fowl probably come from Mexico or the Philippines, but most American and Spanish cockers currently prefer to "Buy American," particularly fowl from the Arkansas–Oklahoma area where it is believed that the cold winters produce birds with fewer parasites and the "ground" is superior. The ground refers to just that, the portion of earth the chicken uses, but it has become a bit mystified among cockers and includes in its meaning the climate and weather, the other living things which share it, such as parasites, and other uncontrollable forces of nature. There is a fad element to choosing birds, in that at various times and places, one breed will be "in" and others "out." Being in results from winning, or being thought to win, at derbies and other fights. Instability of the chicken as product also results from biological factors. Genetics and breeding are always a gamble and when the birds are kept outside, available to predators and other natural elements, with parentage often unknown, the risks become quite high. A breeder may find his "nick," the absolutely best fowl, in a set of brothers, but may never be able to reproduce them. It takes two years to raise, train and fully test a battlecock. By the time a breeder is certain that he has a superior battlecock, the parents (if he knows which birds they were) are two years older, a long and significant time in the breeding life of a chicken. The care, feeding, and training also matter, so that genetic perfection may not prove out in the pits for an inexperienced owner. This product instability makes the breeder's reputation as a trustworthy, winning old man even more critical and problematic. Sellers offer services, too. A typical display ad in *The Gamecock* offers:

SPECIAL—With the purchase of fowl you may spend 1 week at my expense seeing how we take care of our fowl and go to a derby with us to watch our roosters perform. (Think about it.) SPECIAL CONSIDERATION GIVEN TO BEGINNERS!!!

Videotapes, magazines, books, personal phone calls, all back up the chicken seller and offer advice on feeding, training, keeping, and handling birds. Often these include strange advice: "A ounce of cure is worth a pound of remedy" according to Long Spur (1991, p. 77). This follow-up service is particularly crucial because the young guys are thought not to know what they are doing. Like new guys in any endeavor, new guys, beginners, in cocking must pay their dues (thus enabling the old guys to fleece them from time to time), but not to the point of driving them out:

To misinform beginners or purposely mislead someone can probably do more harm to this sport than some other more often talked about enemies. (Roberts 1991, p. 24)

His customers are experienced cockers that know ace battlecocks. Not beginners that don't know a good cock from a bad one. (Fulldrop Jr., 1991, p. 136)

In closing, I have a word for all the beginners out there. Keep with it and be as strong-willed as the gamest cock alive! So often I read short articles about beginners being involved in raw dealings. I have been very fortunate in not being involved in many. I would just like to tell you there are plenty of experienced cockers that are willing to guide and help the beginners. The beginner only needs one prerequisite, to be strong-willed. (Whitehackle Haven, 1991, p. 87)

If they do not recruit and keep the young guys, the sport will not continue and there will be no one to trust with their immortality. More importantly, they cannot make money in the pits. Much of the money that changes hands in the pits goes from beginners who bet without sufficient knowledge of the real variables—the trainers and handlers—to the more knowledgeable, experienced men.

There is other equipment available for breeding and fighting birds. Breeding equipment is pretty basic and seldom used by cockfighters. Incubators for hatching eggs, for example, are expensive and not thought to be worth the money. Medications are sold as for any other kind of livestock, so that one bypasses the veterinarian as often as possible. Worming medications, feed supplements, and other sorts of medications are usually as much related to lore passed down and around as to any sort of scientific research that a veterinarian may have access to and charge a lot of money for. In contrast, *Bird Talk,* a magazine for exotic bird keepers and breeders, has a column written by a veterinarian. Other paraphernalia, such as tie-downs, are also sold. Some breeders tie each rooster to his own little shed, to keep the birds from fighting with each other, wandering away, or getting into any other kind of trouble. Tied-down birds cannot be carried away by predators such as hawks.

The equipment for fighting the fowl, the knives and gaffs, is probably, next to the birds themselves, the single most important item available to the cocker (Worden & Darden, 1992). The world of cockers is divided into those who fight with the gaff, the traditionalists, and those who fight with the more deadly knife. A large variety of these instruments is available, as are cases for containing them. Some men make their own elaborate wooden cases. Attaching the gaff to the bird is considered an art by many, and is often done in secret. It involves wrapping the gaff with tape to attach it to the bird's heel.

The chicken, then, is the major product, other than the sport itself. As we have suggested, the chicken may represent a man's hopes for financial gain and even immortality, but he remains basically a chicken. He is not a pet. He is not beloved, although he may be admired. He is not cuddled or named, only trained, tended, and bred. Pictures of winners with trophies are published in cockfighting magazines, whereas *Bird Talk* pictures pets with Santa Claus and with favorite toys. He is a product.

Values, Cost, and Satisfaction

Values are "the consumer's estimate of the product's overall capacity to satisfy his or her needs" (Kotler, 1991, p. 6), and are usually expressed in terms of price.

There is very little price competition among gamefowl sellers. The value of chickens at the time of sale is established by the breeder's record in the pits and his reputation.

> *I have to put in a good word for Papa Buck. Both Tom Johnson and myself have gotten the Brown Reds from Buck. Both of us have had the very best success with them. They are not only agile and able fighters, but have the bottom to hang in there just as long as it takes and then some . . . not a trait for which Brown Reds are known for. (Warbird, 1991, p. 30)*

Because the line of chickens a man produces does not stop at the man's death, especially if he has passed his stock and lore on to a younger man, his obituary may even become part of his reputation and of someone else's promotional material. Probably for these reasons, the obituaries in the magazines tell more about a man's chickens than about the man and his life; perhaps, in this instance, his chickens are his life:

> *MSGT. Milton M. Hall, U.S. Army Air Corps, born July 24, 1915, died March 23, 1990. Services were held at Cochran Mortuary in Wichita, Kansas. A veteran of World War II, he passed away at home. He was known for his Canadian Mugs, which he had won numerous derbies at different pits in Kansas. Before his death he tied a 33 derby at BJ's in Ponca City, Oklahoma. Winning a hack and four in a row. He leaves a wife, son, and daughter. We will miss him. (Bert White, 1991, p. 214)*

In conventional market arenas, where a buyer can rely on sellers' reputations, histories, credit ratings, and so forth, buying still involves "uncertainties, risks and dilemmas" (Prus 1989a, p. 135).

> *Despite attempts to make purchasing more "professional" . . . buying remains a gamble. Not only does buying entail strategies and gaming, trust and cooperation, and deception and competition, but buying activity takes place within a setting of shifting uncertainties and reflects dependencies on others outside the immediate transaction. (Prus, 1989a, p. 139)*

Buyers of fighting chickens, quite naturally, fear "phony chicken-peddlers." The real secret to obtaining value in buying chickens lies in the old man who spots a promising youngster, what Prus

(1989a) describes as a "seeker," and gives him his chickens. All other deals are suspect:

> Mr. KinCannon is the only major breeder that I know that does sell super blood lines (when he does sell fowl). His word is his bond and he sells out every year to repeat customers. (Fulldrop, Jr. 1991, p. 136)

Many informants asked, "Why would a guy sell his best chickens to someone he may meet later in the pits?" Their answer is that most will not, leaving anyone who offers fowl for sale open to the charge of being a "phony chicken peddler." "However a small percentage [of beginners] get hooked up with an *honest cocker* and tries to learn and goes ahead to make an excellent cocker," according to RWN (1991, p. 30). Sometimes people buy out of state, figuring that a seller who lives at a distance might be willing to sell good chickens, but they know that sellers often fight out of state, too, so they cannot depend on that method of finding a trustworthy seller. The second best method is to buy from a pure line (in conventional marketing, an established brand), but you can never be sure that you are doing that. Our observations confirm the dubiousness of the pure line; on several occasions Worden watched a breeder stroll through his yard, pick up eggs and put them unmarked into his pocket, so that he had no way of knowing which chickens produced which eggs.

Some deny the importance of the brood fowl, saying that the stock is less important than the regimen of care and training.

> I'm sure many of you cockers have read this best selling book on nutrition and I'm going to try to emphasis to you as a game fowl feeder that it is just as important to fowl as it is to a human being. I think we under emphasize feed and proper nutrition and over emphasize the importance of paying large amounts of money for a trio. (Dutcher, 1991, p. 148)

These people offer their secrets, again backed up by pit records and reputations, either free through letters and columns in the magazines or by purchase as books, pamphlets, or video tapes:

> The purple powder is a strong grease cutting biodegradable detergent that you can buy at a wholesale outlet store for around $2.50 to $3.00 a gallon. If you can find the orange powder, it is the strongest (Long Spur, 1992. p. 76)

Customer satisfaction is defined very simply: "When you don't kill 'em." Chickens are usually sold with the admonition. "If you do not like them, kill them." Sellers do not want buyers to give away unsatisfactory chickens, because doing so might dilute the purity of the blood lines. Chickens can be battletested, i.e., pitted against each other unarmed in controlled circumstances to observe their parent abilities as fighters, at 6 months as "baby stags," and at one year as stags. If owners are not pleased by the chickens' performances at these ages, they usually kill the chickens. (And, of course, the full-grown 2-year-old or older battlecock who loses in the pit usually dies, too.) A man who keeps the chickens he has bought, then, is a satisfied customer, as is, obviously, a repeat customer.

Exchange, Transactions, and Relationships

This refers to obtaining products we want, offering resources in exchange for them. The epitome here is "relationship marketing," wherein the seller tries to build up long-term trusting relationships with customers (Bigus, 1972; Prus & Irini, 1988). Advertising, promotion, sales force training, distribution, and repair service are all methods of effecting exchange and developing relationships in conventional marketing.

Word-of-mouth is still the most effective means of advertising and promoting in all forms of marketing. For the cockfighter/chicken seller, this extends to winning in the pits and constructing and maintaining a reputation as a good chicken man: usually honest, religious, sometimes considerate and caring, a man of integrity.

> Maybe the most important thing, by all means, be honest in all your dealings. This is probably the most important as you can get a bad reputation much quicker than an honest one. I have birds, thru friendship and small amounts of cash, that wasn't for sale at any price. (Cogburn, 1991, p. 158)

Personal sales, where the buyer and seller jointly define the chickens as breeders of potential winners from proven lines, without any or much third-party intervention, account for most sales. Cantrell and Brannan, Ohio cockers, invite potential buyers to "bring two of the best cocks you have or can acquire and we will be more than glad to show you [ours] in action" (Whitney, 1991, p. 18). Many people buy mail-order chickens, a process which most chicken men agree is absurd. The idea is to find those honest chicken sellers who will sell good chickens out of state and not have to face those chickens in a nearby pit. Most mail-order buyers are disappointed.

The major third-party intermediary or facilitator in the marketing of fighting chickens is the magazine. Although professionally printed, all three seem to be the results of desktop publishing of one sort or another. *The Gamecock* reports a circulation of 13,000. Spelling, grammar, and punctuation vary from poor to awful, as does the quality of photographs and their reproduction. The content is about 50% advertising, much of it informal and folksy in tone. The editorial content is about 40% letters and 60% columns, articles, and notices. Most of the editorial content is informational, about choosing and caring for chickens. There are some letters asking for help, but most letters are gratuitous offers of expert information from old cockers with secrets to share, what Prus (1989a, p. 205) might call "cultural entrepreneurship." These likely have the effect, and perhaps the intention, of boosting the writer's reputation:

> After several requests, I have written a Cocker's Guidebook. . . . I hope it will be helpful to many cockers, especially beginners. . . . I have been so blessed in my life that I feel the least I can do is share with those less fortunate. (Roberts, 1991, p. 24)

The information is welcomed by all of the cockfighters we know.

> I thank The Feathered Warrior people for publishing a fine magazine, month after month, for the benefit of many. Good information is there to read each month. It seems that it is getting better as time

goes on. The many pictures published each month are appreciated by cockers worldwide. (Roberts, 1991, p. 24)

These are the only magazines many cockers read, although some also read *Field and Stream,* and, interestingly, *The Pigeon Journal.* Most readers relate to the magazine very personally, as if they knew the editor, the authors, and the other readers.

> I enjoy your magazine and the articles by Bill Roberts. He is one good man and doesn't mind helping you in any way he can, and also Sleepy. I went to see him and his better half, they are just as nice as can be. I enjoyed the coffee and chicken talk. They make you feel welcome and at home, and ask if there is any way he can help you. (Trull, 1991, p. 156)

Many of the authors use only their nicknames: Long Spur, Whitehackle Haven, the Traveller. The magazines form the core of a community for most cockers. The relationship is so intense and personal for many that we heard comments such as, "I'm gonna cut his [the editor's] balls off for letting that guy advertise his phony chickens."

Relationships among cockfighters show a great deal of respect and deference. Good friends will tease and interact informally, using nickname, but acquaintances call each other "Mr." Mr. is usually an honorific, implying an older, respected, experienced man. The articles in the magazines use Mr. and use specific names only when they have something good to say about a person. Perhaps in response to the possibility of slander or castration, an author who has something bad to say about another person usually avoids mentioning that person's name.

> Many of the ads in the magazines play on the "old man" theme:
> After 31 years of raising, selling and fighting gamecocks, I am ready to slow down a little and take it easy. (Whitney, 1991, p. 34)

The story among our informants is that one man ran the same ad saying he was old and ready to retire for 20 years.

The idea of vicarious competition is implicit in much of the magazine content and in cockers' conversations. Many cockers are rural, poor, aging athletes, disabled, and overweight—they cannot themselves compete physically, so they enjoy the competition among their birds. Although it is perhaps peripheral, it is worth noting that in every society in which men fight gamecocks, at least one word referring to the birds is also a slang reference to the penis. (Dundes, 1994)

Another theme obvious in the magazines and conversations is death. Fighting birds is about death, equanimity in the face of death, stoicism, physical courage, and an unflinching acceptance of pain. These are old agricultural and masculine values, so it is not surprising to find them here. These values combine easily, too, with the theme of the God-fearing older man who is the hero of the sport and of most of its stories.

Markets

For chicken sellers, the potential market is mostly younger guys, beginners, since older guys usually have their stock or will know whose stock they want and often get it free. The younger guys are seen as naive if not stupid, and in need of a lot of help and advice. The market is crucial, of course, as it always is, but perhaps even more so because it also offers posterity, the ultimate reason many of the chicken men are in the sport.

Kotler (1991) presents the model in Table 43.1 of the relationships among the various factors in the conventional market:

This overall picture shows that marketing deviance differs considerably from conventional marketing. Instead of being an example of one of Kotler's two contrasting strategies (the marketing concept or the selling concept), selling gamefowl appears to be a hybrid of the two, the deviant marketing concept (shown in Table 43.2). There are fewer steps in the process of marketing deviance. The factory, as Dutcher (1991, p. 149) says, is often the producer. The product is unstable and unstandardized. The producer is the seller, who has only the one intermediary/facilitator (the magazines) to worry about. There are no wholesalers or sales forces. Distribution is usually from one hand to another, although occasionally interstate shipments are made, which legally limits the kinds of fowl which can be sold. Word-of-mouth is a strong determinant of sales and is highly dependent on building a reputation as an honest competitor; but the seller as competitor is suspect. Marketing efforts are so uncoordinated as to be fragmented. Profits are made in an ancillary fashion through betting in the pits and through taking advantage of the people the trustworthy old man must convince of his trustworthiness. And this entrepreneur works within a particularly hostile environment (not so hostile, perhaps, as the drug-dealer or the prostitute, who may be killed): given the size of the setup required to keep and raise chickens, and its obvious signs, the gamecock breeder's operation is extremely visible and relatively permanent. In some places there is probably collusion with authorities,

Table 43.1 Kotler's Models of Conventional Marketing Processes

STARTING POINT	FOCUS	MEANS	ENDS
Factory	Products	Selling and promotion	Profits through sales volume
	(a) The selling concept		
Market	Consumer	Coordinated needs marketing	Profits through satisfaction
	(b) The marketing concept		

Table 43.2 The Deviant Marketing Concept

STARTING POINT	FOCUS	MEANS	ENDS
Producer as factory	Reputation of product	Word of mouth, uncoordinated activities	Profits through side activities (i.e., gambling), immortality

since a drive down many secondary highways in this country yields the obvious signs of fighting chickens being kept.

The threat to destroy the product is particularly harsh for the chicken man, since his product is also his factory. While the drug-dealer may face huge financial loss if his or her stock and other possessions are confiscated, these things can be replaced. Most arrests for prostitution result in fines, some in jail terms; either way, the prostitute has lost only time and money, not her product. When the law destroys the last of Mr. Smith's Hatches, however, there are no more. And Mr. Smith loses his shot at immortality.

CONCLUSIONS

We have described the processes involved in the marketing of a deviant activity, cockfighting. Cockfighting is illegal in most states in this country, and yet the breeding and selling of fighting chickens is legal, and the traditions and history attached to cockfighting maintain that the sport is old, honorable, and gentlemanly, descended from such figures as George Washington and Abraham Lincoln. We have found that those engaged in marketing the sport and its paraphernalia, including the chickens, must conduct their activities in ways which differ from the marketing activities of more conventional businesses, as described in the marketing literature. We have found that there is an apparent paradox involved, in that while the participants usually consider themselves fine, upstanding citizens, they trust each other only slightly, knowing that they may well end up pitting their birds against each other. This results in the necessity for establishing one's reputation as an honest, trustworthy person

who is engaged in illegal and stigmatized activities. Since the organization of the marketing efforts is very loosely structured, with no sales force and only one third-party medium for advertising, the most effective form of advertising and marketing is word-of-mouth, which can spread rapidly through this community of mostly rural people who communicate through their magazines and through face-to-face encounters at fights and in informal meetings. Having winning birds and winning honestly, without taking advantage of neophytes, is the best method of establishing one's reputation for honesty and trustworthiness. Winning, however, can sometimes come at a cost of the honesty reputation.

The marketing of fighting chickens, because of this deviant nature and stigmatized tradition, has a distinctly gerontocratic aspect. As the stories, perhaps myths, of the old man giving his chickens and his blessing to the promising youngster demonstrate, a chicken man can never trust an opponent. Yet, in order to keep the sport going, to insure that there is a history for a man to go down in, chicken people must recruit new chicken people, who become opponents. The only trustworthy person is the old man who no longer competes (cf. Adler & Adler, 1983). As Whitney (1991, p. 150) concludes:

> So to all you other beginners out there, when your driving around and see some old man out tending his birds, stop and introduce yourself. Maybe you're what he's looking for. If not then, good luck.

Does this gerontocratic aspect characterize the marketing of other deviant activities? It probably does to a greater degree than researchers have noticed. The smart drug buyer, for example, tries to maintain an established, trustworthy source: prostitution is stratified in terms of trustworthi-ness. This gerontocratic aspect of the marketing of deviance deserves further attention.

REFERENCES

Abacherli, L. (1991, May). Defense Fund Committee. *The Gamecock,* 172.

Adler, P. & Adler, P. (1983). Relationships between dealers: The social organization of illicit drug transactions. *Sociology and Social Research, 67,* 260–278.

Barber, T. X. (1993). *The human nature of birds.* New York: Penguin.

Bigus, O. (1972). The milkman and his customers. *Urban Life and Culture,* 1, 131–165.

Bryant, C. & Capel. W. (1974, November). Profiles of the American cocker. *Grit and Steel,* 33.

Cogburn, R. (1991, May). Letter to the editor. *The Gamecock,* 157–8.

Crews, H. (1979). Cockfighting: An unfashionable view (pp. 35–41). *Florida frenzy,* Gainesville, FL: University Presses of Florida.

Dundes, A. (1994). *The cockfight: A casebook.* Madison: University of Wisconsin Press.

Dutcher, M. (1991, May). You are what you eat! *The Gamecock,* 148–149.

Fulldrop, Jr. (1991, May). Super bloodlines part 2. *The Gamecock,* 136–137.

Hearne, V. (1994). *Animal Happiness.* New York: HarperCollins.

Kotler, P. (1991). *Marketing management.* Englewood Cliffs, NJ: Prentice Hall.

Long Spur (1991, May). Bubblefoot cure. *The Gamecock,* 76–77.

Prus, R. (1989a). *Pursuing customers: An ethnography of marketing activities.* Newbury Park: Sage.

Prus, R. (1989b). *Making sales: Influence as interpersonal accomplishment.* Newbury Park: Sage.

Prus, R. & Irini, S. (1988). *Hookers, rounders, and desk clerks: The Social organization of the hotel community.* Salem, WI: Sheffield.

Roberts, B. (1991, May). Tools of the trade. *The Gamecock,* 68–69.

RWN, (1991, February). Beginners only. *Grit and Steel,* 30.

Schiff, S. (1995. April 5). Geek shows. *The New Yorker,* 9–10.

Trull, J. (1991). Letter to the editor. *The Gamecock,* 156.

Warbird. (1991, July). A few thoughts. *The Feathered Warrior,* 29–30.

White, B. (1991, July). Obituary for M. M. White. *The Gamecock,* 214.

Whitehackle Haven (1991, May). Reminiscence of Doc Tuttle. *The Gamecock,* 86–87.

Whitney, R. (1991, May). Beginner's luck. *The Gamecock,* 150.

Worden, S. & Darden, D. (1992). Deviant behavior. Knives and gaffs: Definitions in the deviant world of cocking. *Deviant Behavior,* 13, 271–289.

Worden, S. (1992). *Fighting chickens and racing pigeons: Animalistic extensions of identity.* Mid South Sociological Association, Chattanooga, TN.

44

THE WORLD OF DOGFIGHTING

RHONDA D. EVANS
CRAIG J. FORSYTH

The act of baiting animals against one another, for entertainment, has existed throughout history. . . . Although the baiting sports had faced opposition throughout their existence, which stemmed largely from their competition with the church and the theater for public audiences, it was not until the upper class completely withdrew its support that they became subject to legislative reform (Matz, 1984). In 1835, the following baiting sports were declared illegal in England: bear baiting, bull baiting, and dogfighting (Atyeo, 1979; Matz, 1984; Semencic, 1984; Vesey-Fitzgerald, 1948). During this period the upper class had shifted its support to cockfighting, which soon became their dominant form of entertainment.

It is believed that dogfighting was transported to the United States by European dog breeders who were looking for a new market for their product and by the Irish immigrants who had also enjoyed a long tradition of baiting sports in their homeland (Atyeo, 1979). There is evidence that baiting sports were being practiced in this country as early as 1726, if not earlier.

The baiting sports faced opposition in the United States, much like they had in Europe. Early laws pertaining to baiting sports varied from state to state and often from county to county within the states. New York passed legislation in 1856, which made dogfighting, cockfighting, and ratting illegal (Matz, 1984).

The most formidable opponent that the baiting sports encountered, in the new world, was Henry Bergh (Matz, 1984). He came onto the scene in 1866 with a version of the Society for the Prevention of Cruelty to Animals and prepared to

do battle with the baiting sports. Prior to this time, animal humane laws pertained primarily to horses and cattle and did not specifically include dogs. Bergh's efforts, paradoxically, contributed to the spread of dogfighting rather than to its demise. Bergh's failure to eliminate dogfighting can be contributed in part to upper class patronage of this event, which continued into the 20th century in the United States (Enquist and Leimar, 1990).

The next serious attempt to stop dogfighting did not emerge until 1976 when the federal government passed legislation making it a felony to transport dogs across state lines with the intent to fight them (Atyeo, 1979; Semencic, 1984). This legislation was in part a reaction to efforts by Humane Societies to bring baiting sports to the attention of the general public by use of the media. Despite continued efforts at legislative reform, not to mention the ever increasing social stigma associated with dogfighting, participation continues. Dogfighting is now illegal in all 50 states and a felony in at least 36 states.

METHODOLOGY

This article examines the world of dogfighting, through the use of thick descriptions (Geertz, 1973). The data, for this study, were obtained through field research, using interviews with and observations of people who fight dogs. Our technique was to let the responses speak for themselves, thus presenting the world of dog fighting in full vivid detail and then to offer both summarization and interpretation. This method, which is called interpretative interaction (Denzin, 1978), is concerned with the study and imputation of meaning, motive, emotion, intention, and feeling as life events are experienced and organized by interacting individuals. This method is in stark contrast to thin description, which consists solely of statistical explanation and abstraction. Our purpose was to capture the essence of dogfighting from those who have experienced it.

Interviews were conducted with 31 individuals who fight and breed pit bulls. All of the participants had been involved in dogfighting for several years. Three interviews were conducted with former breeders and fighters of pit bulls who no longer participate in the sport. Interviews ranged from 2 to 4½ hours. These interviews were conducted at the pre-fight meetings, at the fights or at the homes of dogfighters. Several informal interviews were also conducted with spectators and the wives of men who participate in dogfighting. Additional data were obtained from interviews with SPCA officials, veterinarians, and local sheriff's officers. Observations took place at 14 formal dogfights. Spectators were represented by all races, ages, and both sexes. In the United States, formal dogfighting is a sport dominated by White men. Although the participation of Black males is on the rise, they make up only a small percentage of the participants within the sport. Women for the most part are there as spectators, but do have an active role in gambling. Women rarely handle dogs. The research took place in several parishes of Louisiana and counties in Mississippi. The authors also examined newspaper accounts of dogfighting.

The goal of this research was to describe the world of the dogfighter so that subsequent researchers will be able to recognize its components and proceed with their own research based upon knowledge gained from this study. This is, indeed, the test of validity of qualitative research (Forsyth, 1986).

Both of the authors have relatives who are engaged in dogfighting. Additional respondents were identified through a snowball method. Each respondent was questioned regarding several aspects of dogfighting: the reasons they engage in dogfighting and how they started dogfighting; techniques of breeding and training; the negotiation of

a contract; the fight, the setting, and the choice of a setting for the fight; the types of dogs in general and great fighting dogs of the past; changes in dogfighting; and the career of a fighting dog. Additional questions were intended to elicit responses regarding the rationalizations and motivations used by dogmen for their continuance in these illegal activities, and their confrontations with residents, law enforcement and/or humane society officials, or other dogfighters.

In our interviews with dogmen they continually referred to themselves as a fraternity. McCaghy and Neal (1974) also used the term fraternity in describing the informal association of cockfighters. We will also use the term fraternity in describing dogmen. All the names of dogmen used are pseudonyms.

FINDINGS

Breeding

Breeding [pit bulls] to participate in the sport of dogfighting is the most crucial function within the fraternity of dogmen. It is the facet on which every other element within the sport is based and without it the sport could not exist. Thus, breeders hold the most prestigious positions within the fraternity.

The following responses were from experienced dogmen regarding the importance of breeding and the various techniques employed in breeding.

> . . . *Now you got certain bloodlines, if you're a breeder you just don't choose dogs at random. They've got to have a background behind them. Sometimes you have athletes that come up that are just freaks. Those idiots that don't know anything about breeding they start breeding into them. He's not the one who made that fighting dog; it's his daddy and his mama. Hell the people don't know that, they want to breed to that dog because he's a good dog. That's not where it's at. If it's not a line of production of good dogs I don't want him. (INTERVIEW)*

> *It's the bloodline you go by. Just cause a dog won't fight doesn't mean he won't throw good dogs. The genes are still in that dog. (INTERVIEW)*

As indicated in these statements . . . breeding is perhaps the most important aspect of dogfighting. Another critical facet of the game is the training of the dog.

Training

When these dogs reach a certain age, anywhere from a year old to 18 months, they are rolled (briefly put against a proven dog) a few times to test their ability and gameness. If the owner determines that the dog is ready for the pit, he then puts out a wager that is open to anyone. The amount of the wager is usually anywhere from a couple hundred dollars to as much as $100,000.

Once the wager is accepted and a contract is drawn up it is time to prepare for the fight. The dogs undergo from 6 weeks to 3 months of rigorous training to prepare for the fight. They must be brought down to their pit weight, which is considered the optimal weight at which a dog can fight. This training seeks to build wind and stamina in the dogs so that they can fight for long periods of time if need be.

Various methods are used in the conditioning of a dog such as a treadmill, flirtpole and sometimes even swimming, The dogs are also fed special lean diets at this time. The following responses were from accomplished dogmen regarding the relevance of training and the sundry of methods utilized.

> It takes a lot of time and money to get these dogs ready for the pit. They don't just throw their dogs into the pit and hope for the best. They go through a lot of trouble to make sure their dogs are in the best condition possible for the fight. They invest in all kinds of equipment to aid in the conditioning of the dogs. They have treadmills, flirtpoles, and turntables that are made just for the dogs. As a matter of fact, there's a man out in Scott, LA that makes dog treadmills, for a living . . . The object is to make sure that your dog can go the distance in the pit. If your dog is not conditioned properly he won't be able to maintain his wind in the pit. Hell, these fights can last anywhere from 30 minutes to 4 or 5 hours. That's why the conditioning is so important. (INTERVIEW)

> Around 19 months to 2 years old, if his attitude is right then I will school him out. I'll roll him a few times with different types of dogs to teach him different types of fighting. I'll do that 4 or 5 times. I decide how far to push the next time by what he shows me at each roll. The last time I roll him, I would game check him by putting some time on him and a better dog on him. You let him see the bottom. You make sure he gets some of the worst end of the deal. A lot of people put 2 or 3 dogs on him, one after the other. I find it easier to put him on a jenny or a mill and blow all his air out of him and then put a dog on him for 30 minutes. You see what kind of attitude he has then. When you match a dog he will never have to fight against more than one dog. He only has to whip one dog at a time. (INTERVIEW)

As demonstrated in these accounts, experienced dogmen are very cognizant of the significance of proper training. Matches sometimes continue for 4 hours (there is no time limit). Dogs must be trained so they will have the stamina to endure the match. Individuals who place bets also put a lot of weight on the reputation of the dog's trainer.

Negotiating a Contract

When a member of the fraternity has a dog he is ready to fight, he puts out his conditions such as the weight of the dog, sex of the dog, and the amount he wants to bet on the fight. These facts are advertised either in the underground journals or by word of mouth. Once another dogman accepts the conditions and the wager a contract is drawn up.

The process of matching dogs has become a normative process. The owner "puts out a weight," which means they have a dog at a particular weight that they wish to fight.

> First thing people do is put a weight out there. They agree upon a weight, like 46 lb. male. They agree on a purse and a forfeit. A forfeit means that if a dog comes in over weight his owner must pay the other owner the agreed upon amount and negotiate a new contract. A match is set at a specific amount of money, let's say three thousand dollars, that is the purse. The forfeit will be set at let's say five

hundred dollars. If your dog comes in over weight, you have to pay a $500 forfeit then negotiate a new contract. The first fight was canceled. The man with the dog that was over weight will lay odds. He might agree to pay $3,500 because his dog is over weight, which puts the other dog at a disadvantage. (INTERVIEW)

Although not as critical to the fight itself as training and breeding, and not as monetarily important as the contract, planning and selecting the location is critical. Because dogfighting is illegal, participants are very secretive about the date and location of the event.

Planning and Selecting the Location of the Fight

Dogfights are most commonly staged in secluded rural areas such as barns or fields. There is a national network, consisting of members of the dogfighting fraternity, which facilitates the planning of locations for these events. When a contract is drawn up for a fight, the participants decide on a central location. They then contact a dogman in that area to make arrangements to have the fight at a location that he provides. The following are comments about finding a location.

The location of the fight is usually kept secret until the afternoon of the fight with only the two owners and the man providing the location knowing where it will take place. This is done in order to protect themselves against possible raids. When the time arrives for the event to take place everyone is then informed of the location. The people leave the initial location at separate times so as not to attract attention and all meet at the location of the fight.

When Rick and L. G. agreed to fight their dogs, they called Mike to help them plan a location for the event. They wanted to meet somewhere in between Florida and Arizona so Mike agreed to have the fight here in North Louisiana. There's a whole network of dogmen who aid one another in finding locations for the fights. They're the only three people who actually know where the fight will be. They keep the location a secret until the night of

the fight in order to avoid raids. Once Mike lets everybody know where the fight will take place, we leave his house one vehicle at a time so as not to attract attention. We have to be careful these days with the Humane Society breathing down our necks and pressuring the cops to bust up dogfighting. I don't know why those damned people don't just mind their own business. They act like we're hard core criminals or something. We're not hurting anybody and the dogs love to fight, so what's the harm. (INTERVIEW)

Dogmen realize that keeping this veil over the circumstances of the fight, until immediately before the event, is necessary for the survival of dogfighting. A successful raid can push those marginal dogmen and spectators out of the sport. Dogmen face fines, confiscation of dogs, and in some states prison time. A sport supported by such a small fraternity cannot afford to lose any peers.

The Meeting of Dogmen and Dogs

The Pre-Fight.   On the day of the fight the participants and the spectators, usually members of the fraternity, which tends to be almost exclusively male, meet at a dogman's house near the location where the fight will take place. Here they will converse for hours before the fight about such things as the history of champion bloodlines, recent fights that they have attended, breeding and conditioning practices, and a vast array of other issues pertaining to their sport. This gathering of the fraternity before the event is a very important element of the dogmen subculture. It is at this time that the social status of the fraternity members is most evident. In these conversations the old timers do most of the talking and the newcomers listen like obedient students eager to learn all that they can. It should be noted that even though dogfighters are seen as deviant by society, they did not have deviant self-concepts.

The following is both a vivid description and summarization of the meeting before a dogfight took place. The fight had been planned for months, The following interview took place during the trip in a car to the pre-fight meeting.

We're almost there now . . . just a little further up the road. Everyone who is anyone, in the dog game, will be at the fight tonight. They've been planning this event for months and people from all over the country will be there. Most of the old timers will be there. Man, they are awesome. They can teach you anything you want to know about the game and the dogs. They know all the champion bloodlines and every champion dog that ever walked on the face of this earth. Well hell, they're the ones that put most of the champion dogs on the ground. Those guys know what the hell they're talking about when it comes to anything having to do with dogfighting. It's important that you listen to them and show them the respect they deserve. If those guys don't accept you, you are not going anywhere in this game. They decide who is going to move in this circle, so don't piss them off. (INTERVIEW)

The following interviews took place at the pre-fight meeting that was held in the home of a dogman.

Dogfighting is just like anything else, you've got to start at the bottom and work your way up. If you're lucky, someone who is already established in the game will take you under his wing and teach you everything he knows. Man, I owe everything I know to Ron. He's the one who got me started in the game. Once I was able to convince him that I was serious about the game, he let me buy into his bloodline, brought me with him to some really big fights, and introduced me to all the right people. I would have never been able to gain acceptance without his backing. He's highly respected in the game, for both his bloodline and always bringing good dogs to the pit. That's the way it works here. These people don't like strangers and they are always worried that newcomers might be undercover cops. But, if one of the old timers brings someone to a fight, they know he's all right, just remember it's all about who you know and what you know. (INTERVIEW)

We'd better head over to Norman's place; we don't want to miss the beginning of the fight. When we get there, park as close as you can to the road and turn your car facing the road. You never know when we might need to make a fast get away. Just remember if the cops ever show up at a fight, always be prepared to leave fast. If they ever catch you, you didn't see or hear anything about dogfighting. Always be loyal to the fraternity and don't

ever rat out anybody else. If they catch you they'll try to get a confession out of you. Don't give it to them. (INTERVIEW)

These pre-fight comments reveal the loyalty of dogmen to their sport. Their need for secrecy and loyalty is why the ranks of dogmen are difficult to invade. Although the viewing of these fights was certainly more stirring, the pre-fight meetings were more informative. At these meetings one learns about all aspects of the dogmen and their pit bulls.

The Fight. There are two types of dogfights: formal and informal. The informal fight is when two dogs are fought without any contract. There may be only a few people present, it may take place in the streets, is usually engaged in by teenagers and arises spontaneously. Formal fights are defined as organized events in which a contract exists (stating the terms of the fight—amount of the wager, the weight at which the dogs will be fought, the amount of the forfeit and the sex of the dogs). In addition, there is a subculture that maintains it. Our research was only concerned with the formal dog fight. Formal fights were classified as either conventions or private matches.

There used to be conventions, now it's turned into private matches. A convention you might have up to 6 or 7 fights that night. At private matches the most you will have is 2 fights and with the same people . . . at conventions there were up to 300 people. The fights may go on all night into the morning. Law enforcement could catch us at conventions because there are so many people there and you cannot check them all out. In a private match the owner of the place where the fight takes place checks everyone out before they get there. (INTERVIEW)

Prior to the fight the dogs are weighed in and washed to make sure they are free of any noxious substances that could interfere with the dogs' ability to fight.

They're weighing in the dogs now. Snow weighs in at 38 pounds and Black weighs in at 37 pounds. They are very well matched. It's all going to come down to the conditioning and gameness of the dogs. Now they are washing the dogs. They do that to make sure that their opponent didn't put any chemicals on the dogs that could interfere with the fight. If one of the opponents is still suspicious after they wash the dogs, they have the option to taste their opponent's dog. If one of the opponents does try something like putting chemicals on his dog, the ref will rule foul play and the dog will be disqualified. Then that person will have to pay his opponent the forfeit fee. It looks like everything is fair and square here. (INTERVIEW)

The dogfight is a staged event in which two dogs are placed into a pit, much like a boxing ring, and fight until one opponent either quits or dies, at which time the other is declared the winner. There is a referee and two handlers present in the pit with the dogs and many spectators viewing the event. The fight begins when the referee tells the handlers to pit their dogs; at which time the dogs are released and attack one another. Once the fight begins the spectators begin placing bets with one another on which dog will win. The dogs continue fighting until one of them makes a turn, which is defined as turning the head and shoulders away from his or her opponent. Once the referee calls the turn the handlers then handle their dogs when they are out of holds, which means they are not biting each other, and the dog that made the turn must scratch to his opponent. Scratching is defined as crossing the scratch line, which is drawn in the center of the pit, and attacking one's opponent within a specified amount of time, usually 10 to 30 seconds. If a dog fails to scratch, his opponent is declared the winner. If the scratch is successfully completed the fight continues. From this point on the dogs are only handled when they are out of holds and they are required to scratch in turn. At any time in the fight if a dog fails to scratch in turn he is declared the loser.

It's almost time for the fight to start. We'd better go on into the barn. They're charging $20 per person tonight. That seems like a lot of money but think about the risk that Norman is taking having the fight on his property. I don't much mind paying. After all, this is the big event that we've been

waiting for months to see and it's finally here. It's going to be one hell of a fight. (INTERVIEW)

The owners are bringing the dogs to their corners of the pit. Tile pit is about 20 feet by 20 feet, and this one is surrounded by 3-feet-tall wooden sides. Both of the dogs look eager to fight.

Norman says sternly, "gentlemen pit your dogs." The handlers release their dogs and Snow and Black lunge at one another. Snow rears up and overpowers Black, but Black manages to come back with a quick locking of the jaws on Snow's neck. The crowd is cheering wildly and yelling out bets. Once a dog gets a lock on the other, they will hold on with all their might. The dogs flail back and forth and all the while Black maintains her hold. It looks like Black is hung up so Norman motions for the handlers to separate the dogs. They approach the dogs and L. G. pries Black's mouth open with a breaking stick. The dogs are returned to their corners and sponged down with water. Once again Norman calls for the dogs to be pitted. This time Snow must scratch to Black and make contact with her within 10 seconds. Snow races toward Black and is not going to let Black get the best of her. Snow goes straight for the throat and grabs hold with her razor sharp teeth. Almost immediately, blood flows from Black's throat. Despite a severe injury to the throat Black manages to continue fighting back. They are relentless, each battling the other and neither willing to accept defeat. This fighting continues for an hour. Finally, the dogs are out of holds and Norman gives the okay for them to be handled. He gives the third and final pit call. It is Black's turn to scratch and she is severely wounded. Black manages to crawl across the pit to meet her opponent. Snow attacks Black and she is too weak to fight back. L. G. realizes that this is it for Black and calls the fight. Snow is declared the winner

Rick collects his money. L. G. then lifts Black from the pit and carries her out back. Her back legs are broken and blood is gushing from her throat. A shot rings out barely heard over the noise in the barn. Black's body is wrapped up and carried by her owner to his vehicle.

There are four possible ways in which the fight may end: a dog's failure to scratch, the owner calling the fight (this is analogous to the manager of a boxer throwing the towel into the ring that signals that the fighter has quit), the death of one or both dogs, or one of the dogs jumping the pit.

The failure to scratch is described as an opponent's failure to cross the scratch line and attack his opponent upon command of the referee and is the most common way in which fights will end. A less common ending is the death of one of the opponents.

> *Well I've been in it [dogfighting] for 14 years and I've only seen one dog die in the pit. A fight normally ends when one of the dogs fail to scratch. It's very hard to get a game dog. A dead game dog is one that always goes back even if he is beat down. (INTERVIEW)*

The least common ending is for one of the dogs to jump the pit, which means they literally jump out of the pit in order to escape their opponent. This is very rare because a dogman will not bring a cur dog (coward) to a fight at the risk of facing humiliation. If a dog does jump the pit it will surely result in his death at the hands of his owner.

Within the dogfighting fraternity, the most admirable quality is gameness, that can be described as continued willingness to fight and never stop fighting as long as one is physically and mentally able to continue. The canine opponents employed in these dogfights are expected to show this quality of gameness as long as there is breath left in their bodies. A dog that exhibits this quality in extreme measures is considered to be dead game (some call this a killer dog) and therefore he will be seen as the ultimate canine warrior. So important is this quality that it is the goal of every dogman to own a dog who is dead game.

DISCUSSION

The sport of fatal fighting (Enquist and Lelmar, 1990) in America primarily involves two animals: the fighting cock and the pit bull dog. There is very little literature on dogfighting and little academic interest in the topic. The literature that does exist on fatal fighting is primarily concerned with the fighting cock (Bryant, 1982; McCaghy and Neal, 1974; Worden and Darden, 1992). The efforts of law enforcement have taken their toll on the dogmen fraternity. In the past, large meets called conventions took place, now these events have been reduced to private matches.

As deviant transactions (Best and Luckenbill, 1980) increase in complexity, deviants are more likely to be seen as accountable for their behavior. Consequently, efforts of social control agents increase and the range of reactive tactics of deviants expand. These endeavors act to organize deviant transactions. Secrecy about operations and identities of participants construct a central theme of the deviant organization. Dogmen have developed norms that govern conduct between their deviant associates, therefore planning and precautions have assumed law-like importance to them. The organization of dogmen, although deviant and secret, resembles respectable transactions. The dogfight has become an ordered, yet deviant activity, by respectable people.

When one views a staged dog fight between pit bulls for the first time, the most macabre aspect of the event is that the only sounds you hear from these dogs are those of crunching bones and cartilage. The dogs rip and tear at each other; their blood, urine, and saliva splatter the sides of the pit and clothes of the handlers. This is the American Pit Bull Terrier at work in a role they have been performing for over a century. The emotions of the dogs are conspicuous, but not so striking, even to themselves, are the passions of the owners of the dogs. Whether they hug a winner or in the rare case, destroy a dying loser, whether they walk away from the carcass or lay crying over it, their fondness for these fighters is manifest. Whether it produces admiration or disdain, you will be overwhelmed by the game and the connection between the true dogman and his fighting dog.

The meaning that this sport has for these men can only be gotten from listening to the accounts of dogmen who are willing to share several generations of knowledge and experience. The loyalty and secrecy are important components of subcultural maintenance. This article has conveyed these subcultural pieces so that the reader will better understand the complete world of the dogmen. This world is indeed much more than a dogfight. More research is needed into this much-maligned arena of sport. Hopefully this research will serve as a heuristic device for further study on this topic.

DOGFIGHTING: VICTIMLESS CRIME?

There are two broad research perspectives in the understanding of deviant behavior. Understanding deviance involves studying both those who make the rules and those who break the rules (Becker, 1963; Little, 1995). These two perspectives are both evident if we look at cases of deviance in which there is objective rule breaking but there is not consensus in society, as to the deviance of the act. In other words, there is a law against the behavior but many times when the law is broken the rule breaking is treated as though it were not deviant at all (Little, 1995). Becker (1963) called such behavior secret deviance, meaning that it is so well hidden nobody sees it and if it is seen nobody seems to do anything about it. Closely related to this category of deviance in some respects is the idea of victimless crime. Victimless crimes (Schur, 1965) refer to the willing exchange among adults of goods and services. These goods and services are legally proscribed, but are strongly demanded by the adult public. Homosexuality, illegal gambling, drug misuse, abortion, prostitution, and pornography are examples of victimless crimes. The primary characteristics of so called victimless crimes is a transaction between two participants, both of whom choose to enter into a relationship. Because neither individual in the relationship desires to make a complaint, laws against these exchanges are difficult to enforce. Most activities of this sort go on with little intrusion from law enforcement (Little, 1995). Although authors have tended to label several crimes as victimless, they are not all equally deserving of the label. The violation of blue laws may be without victims, but the labeling of other crimes such as prostitution (Yablonsky and Haskell, 1988), pornography (Durham, 1986) and abortion (Goode, 1997) as victimless has caused considerable debate. The question in regard to these types of crimes is the following: are there victims and are they disruptive to members of our society (Vito and Holmes, 1994)?

The impediment to these victimless events comes from moral entrepreneurs. The presumption is that they serve the community by protecting its virtue and its members. Dogfighting involves two forms of deviance: gambling and the violation of animal protection laws. Because gambling is widely accepted in the areas where dogfighting takes place (horse racing, casinos, lottery), it is not this aspect that has brought on the concern of moral entrepreneurs. Dogfighting has been labeled as deviant because moral entrepreneurs consider the dog a victim. Dogmen and their supporters see it as a victimless crime. In addition, dogfighting is in conflict with the new environmental sensitivity. Animals have arisen as a highly visible and logical subset of this new environmental awareness/sensitivity and greater respect is accorded them as a somewhat incidental beneficiary in this cultural wave of animal rights (Palmer and Forsyth, 1992). Dogfighting agitates this cultural swell, hence dogmen can expect a persistent storm of moral challenge.

REFERENCES

Atyeo, D. (1979). *Blood and guts, violence in sports.* New York Paddington Press.

Becker, H. S. (1963). *Outsiders.* New York: Free Press.

Best, J., & Luckenbill, D. F. (1980). The social organization of deviants. *Social Problems, 28,* 14–31.

Bryant, C. D. (1982). Cockfighting in sociohistorical context: Some sociological observations on a socially disvalued sport. *The Gamecock, 45,* 65–70, 80–85.

Denzin, N. (1978). *The research act.* New York: McGraw-Hill.

Durham, A. (1986). Pornography, social harm, and legal control. *Justice Quarterly, 3,* 95–102.

Enquist, M., & Leimar, O. (1990). The evolution of fatal fighting. *Animal Behavior, 39,* 1–9.

Forsyth, C. (1986). Sea daddy: An excursus into an endangered social species. *Maritime Policy and Management: The International Journal of Shipping and Port Research, 13,* 53–60.

Geertz, C. (1973). *The interpretation of cultures: Selected essays.* New York: Basic Books.

Goode, E. (1997). *Deviant behavior.* Upper Saddle River, NJ: Prentice-Hall.

Little, C. B. (1995). *Deviance and control.* Itasca, IL: Peacock Publishers.

Matz, K. S. (1984). *The pit bull fact and fable.* Sacramento, CA: De Mortmain Publishing.

McCaghy, C. H., & Neal, A. G. (1974). The fraternity of cockfighters: Ethical embellishments of an illegal sport. *Journal of Popular Culture, 8,* 557–569.

Palmer, C. E., & Forsyth, C. (1992). Animals, attitudes, and anthropomorphic sentiment: The social construction of meat and fur in postindustrial society. *International Review of Modern Sociology, 22,* 29–44.

Schur, E. (1965). *Crimes without victims.* Englewood Cliffs, NJ: Prentice-Hall.

Semencic, C. (1984). *The world of fighting dogs.* Neptune City, N.J.: T. F. H. Publications.

Vesey-Fitzgerald, B. (1948). *The book of the dog.* Los Angeles and Toronto: Borden Publishing.

Vito, G. F., & Holmes. R. M. (1994). *Criminology.* Belmont, CA: Wadsworth.

Worden, S., & Darden, D. (1992). Knives and gaffs: Definitions in the deviant world of cockfighting. *Deviant Behavior, 13,* 271–289.

Yablonsky, L., & Haskell, M. (1988). *Juvenile delinquency.* New York: Harper & Row.

THE TECHNIQUES OF NEUTRALIZATION AMONG DEER POACHERS

STEPHEN L. ELIASON
RICHARD A. DODDER

This study uses neutralization theory as a theoretical framework. It was introduced to the sociological literature over 40 years ago by Sykes and Matza (1957). Rogers and Buffalo (1974:318) defined neutralization as "a method whereby a person renders behavioral norms inoperative, thereby freeing himself to engage in behavior which would otherwise be considered deviant."

In their original formulation of neutralization theory, Sykes and Matza (1957:667–69) identified five techniques of neutralization: *the denial of responsibility, the denial of injury, the denial of the victim, the condemnation of the condemners,* and *the appeal to higher loyalties.*

Five additional neutralization techniques were subsequently introduced by others—including Minor (1981), *the defense of necessity;* Klockars (1974), *the metaphor of the ledger;* and Coleman (1994), *the denial of the necessity of the law, the claim that everybody else is doing it,* and *the claim of entitlement*—so that there are currently a total of 10 neutralization techniques at the present time in the literature (Collins 1994).

A number of empirical studies on traditional delinquency and serious crime have provided support for neutralization theory (Rogers and Buffalo 1974; Minor 1981). Studies examining neutralization theory have not been limited to traditional delinquency. For example, Levi (1981) examined strategies used by professional hit men to carry out their duties as hired killers.

Also, Brennan (1974) examined neutralization techniques in relation to abortion. Neutraliza-tion theory has also been examined in relation to marijuana smoking (Priest and McGrath 1970) and religious dissonance (Dunford and Kunz 1973). More recently, it has been applied to the study of genocide (Alvarez 1997).

The purpose of this research is to examine neutralization theory as it relates to poaching behavior and to provide a descriptive account of the specific neutralization techniques used by deer poachers.

METHOD

In the first phase of the research project, we conducted a random sample survey among individuals in the state of Colorado who were cited for illegal deer possession from 1990 to 1996. Letters requesting assistance in identifying subjects for the project were mailed to the director of the Division of Wildlife of eight western states. Four of the states did not send a reply, two of the states sent summaries of yearly wildlife offenses and poaching information or literature, and one state sent a letter indicating that it would not be able to assist with the request for information. Colorado was the only state that agreed to assist with this study.

The Colorado Division of Wildlife furnished the names and addresses of individuals cited for illegal deer possession in the state from 1990 to 1996. A sample consisting of 875 of the most recent individuals (all individuals cited between 1991 to 1996 and a random sample of those cited in 1990) were sent a questionnaire in the mail asking them to describe some of their attitudes and activities regarding hunting laws and other issues.

Because the main focus of this study was to examine the techniques of neutralization used by deer poachers, the questionnaire also contained a series of 10 items developed by us that measured the extent to which subjects justified or rationalized their illegal hunting behavior by subscribing to the 10 techniques of neutralization discussed in the previous section. Statements were designed to measure each neutralization technique in the context of illegal deer hunting.

Each subject received an eight-page survey as well as a cover letter that described the purpose of the study. Also enclosed was a business reply envelope addressed to us so that there would be no cost to return the survey. Because of the high cost of first-class mail and our limited budget, we decided to send the surveys using third-class postage. The envelopes were metered, however, to give them the appearance of being first-class postage as much as possible. However, some of the surveys did go out first-class. Officials at mailing services claimed that this was because addresses or ZIP codes that are "nonautomatable" cannot handle third-class mail.

Two months after the surveys were mailed, 42 completed surveys were returned ($N = 42$), which yielded a response rate of 4.8 percent. However, it should be noted that 72 of the surveys that were mailed first class were returned to us by the post office because subjects did not reside at the address on the envelope. Thus, the response rate is higher if only those who received the survey are taken into account. The postal service does not return letters that are mailed third class, making it impossible to know exactly how many of the individuals actually received the survey.

In addition, 10 subjects did not return the survey but instead sent letters or comments in an attempt to explain their situation and/or vent their hostility to the researchers about receiving the survey. Many of these letters and comments suggested individuals' attempts to neutralize their actions and were thus used as data in the Findings and Discussion section along with those comments written by subjects who completed the survey.

The second part of the research project consisted of in-depth interviews with poachers. Ethnographic data obtained from interviews was used to clarify and elaborate the information obtained from the survey. They are reported in the Findings and Discussion section along with letters and comments that were received regarding the survey. Of the 42 subjects who returned a completed survey, 15 agreed to be interviewed over the telephone and 13 in-depth interviews were conducted with these individuals.

In addition, we conducted interviews with three of the individuals from Colorado who were sent a questionnaire and who responded to us by means of letter or telephone (but who did not return the questionnaire), as well as with four other individuals who had poached but had not been apprehended. These four individuals were personal contacts of the first author. Subjects ranged from 20 to 72 years of age.

Five game wardens from Idaho, Utah, and Wyoming were interviewed to provide additional information from the law enforcement perspective on the poaching problem in the western United States. They also provided important information about the neutralization techniques that poachers use when they are apprehended. Game wardens who were interviewed were identified by personal contacts of the first author and the snowball method of selection.

The five game wardens who were interviewed ranged from 40 to 50 years of age. They also had a great deal of experience on the job. Indeed, the wardens had a combined 86 years of wildlife law enforcement experience, which amounts to an average of 17.2 years of experience each in dealing with offenders.

We conducted a total of 25 in-depth interviews with poachers and game wardens. Interviews took place from April to October 1997 and lasted from approximately 30 minutes to 3.5 hours. Poachers were questioned about the incident they committed, if the offense took place during open or closed season, the sex and size of the deer, and their feelings toward game wardens. Game wardens were questioned about the extent of the poaching problem, changes in poaching over the years, rationalizations poachers use when they are apprehended, and social characteristics of poachers. . . .

FINDINGS AND DISCUSSION

Many individuals were offended because they received a survey, and some of them did not hesitate to vent their anger. Indeed, one unanticipated result from the Colorado sample was that several of the poachers took the time to explain their behavior by including a letter with the completed survey, by providing extensive written comments on the survey, or by sending a letter without the questionnaire.

For example, the following comments were written by a resident hunter on the back of a survey that was mailed in but not completed:

> I almost didn't answer this, I had to leave it lay for several days in order to calm down some. I am very proud of my almost 40 years of hunting and fishing in Colorado. For someone to put me in the same category with poachers, as far as I am concerned that puts them in the same category with antihunting groups. If that's an injustice it can't be a bigger injustice than what you did [to] me. I made a mistake once, and a young hothead game warden tried to take advantage of it to boost his arrest record point system. I misread some very complicated regulations. They write them more complicated every year to try to boost their "fine" income.

The next comments were provided by a nonresident hunter who wrote them on the front page of an uncompleted survey that was returned:

> I find both your letter and your survey to be insulting—you presume facts not proven in both. I have hunted for over 50 years and have never intentionally hunted illegally and neither has anyone with me. I suggest you get a life.

The term *poacher* seemed to be offensive to these individuals, most of whom wrote comments suggesting that they were decent, upstanding sportsmen in spite of the fact that they had broken the law. One game warden said, "You should have used the phrase 'I'm conducting a study of illegal deer hunting' " instead of " 'I'm conducting a study of poaching' " in the cover letter. This is because many offenders do not consider themselves poachers and find this word offensive.

Another warden said that the term poacher is a very negative label because in the hunting community a poacher is someone who is despised. He said that these individuals would be likely to "take a swing at you" if you suggested they were poachers.

Poaching is a generic term that is used to refer to the illegal taking of wildlife in various forms. It encompasses not only flagrant closed-season violations but also applies to activities that are illegal and that occur during the open hunting season as well. Many violations occur during the legal hunting season. . . . However, the fact that many individuals do not consider offenses that occur during the open hunting season as actually constituting poaching explains why many individuals were offended by receiving a survey dealing with poaching behavior.

Indeed, deer poaching simply involves the illegal taking of deer. It may occur during the legal season or out of season and it may involve a single animal or multiple animals. A person may poach once in his or her lifetime or on a regular basis. Some of the poachers in this study had been apprehended only once and claimed that it was their first time poaching; others were multiple offenders and acknowledged a long history of poaching behavior.

Interviews with poachers revealed that they had been cited for a variety of offenses that constituted illegal possession. Many of the offenses took place during the legal deer hunting season. For example, a couple of subjects said that they were apprehended for trespassing because they shot a deer on public land and it jumped over a fence onto private land. A couple of other individuals committed the violation of shooting deer that did not have the sufficient number of antler points to satisfy the antler point restriction for the particular unit that they were hunting on. Some of the individuals who were nonresidents were charged with purchasing resident hunting licenses.

One hunter shot a deer for his friend (party hunting). Another had a doe permit but killed a buck deer. One hunter had a doe permit but killed two buck deer and abandoned them. One poacher took a doe during the rifle season when he had a buck tag. Another poacher claimed that he had already harvested and tagged a deer the day before and was out in the field with his buddies when a wounded deer came stumbling by him, so he shot it to put it out of its misery. He left it and was turned in by two hunters who witnessed the incident.

Some of the poachers illegally took their deer during the closed season. For example, one poacher said that he and his buddy had been drinking beer and decided to kill a small buck they happened to see while driving around. Another poacher said that he and a friend had been target shooting on a relative's property and came across a herd of about 30 deer, so they decided to kill a couple of does.

The majority of game wardens said that practically all of the individuals they apprehend for poaching offer justifications for their misdeeds. When it comes to hunting violations, it is very rare for individuals to assume responsibility for their illegal actions. A couple of the officers said that they would find it refreshing if the poachers they apprehend would simply admit that they took a chance and got caught instead of denying that they did it and attempting to mitigate it with all kinds of excuses. One game warden stated the following in this regard, "There's damn few times I've ever contacted someone who didn't have a rationalization. Sometimes it may be comical. It is very rare that they are upfront with you and say 'I took a chance and I got caught.'" There were some situations, however, in which offenders were not likely to offer excuses to game wardens. For example, one officer said that shooting deer on winter range well after the legal hunting season has ended usually does not generate excuses. Rather, he said, offenders exhibit a "flight, then fight" reaction in which they first attempt to evade the officer and then challenge the charges in court.

Another officer said that when he catches individuals in the act of using a spotlight to hunt deer at night they usually do not offer reasons.

One game warden who deals with a lot of poaching cases involving trophy animals said that most of the individuals he apprehends do not attempt to rationalize until their case goes to court. This is illustrated by the following statement: "The biggest majority now don't say anything. Most of them just lawyer up. I think that's in reference to the penalties being much stiffer than they used to be. Rationalizations are brought up in court for defense."

Four types of neutralization techniques appeared most frequently from interviews and written comments in this study. These included *the denial of responsibility, the metaphor of the ledger, the defense of necessity,* and *the condemnation of the condemners.*

The Denial of Responsibility

Many of the poachers denied responsibility for killing deer illegally by claiming the situation for which they were cited was a mistake or an accident. Indeed, the denial of responsibility was the most common neutralization technique identified and was evident in many of the comments and interviews.

For example, one subject in the study had been hunting and killed a three-point buck. He was dragging it down the mountain to his vehicle when a game warden drove up and checked his license. The subject had the deer tagged with his uncle's tag and was cited for the offense. He attempted to neutralize his actions through the denial of responsibility, claiming he did not know that the law prohibited party hunting in Colorado.

The following written comments from individuals indicate how they attempted to deny responsibility for killing deer illegally:

> My license was for the area [where] I shot the deer. It did not state that only part of the area was open to hunt as the warden stated. If licenses and regulations were written clearly this would not have happened. Even the game warden said he could clearly

tell I did not do this purposely when he talked to me. Of course I was guilty until proven innocent.

My husband told me he got me a doe license—it was a buck license.

My one illegal deer was because I was shooting for a legal doe and it was a buck. Its horns were below the ears and it was dusk and I couldn't see them.

I do not hunt illegally. It was an accident.

My incident was a totally honest mistake—[I] turned myself in to [the] local agent after dressing game in [a] suitable fashion (and packed [the] meat out). . . . In my own clear mind [this was] the honest thing to do and [I] was fined $750. 99.999% [of hunters] would leave a mistaken kill to rot—after this incident I would give the same some thought.

The game wardens who were interviewed for this study said they are more likely to use discretion if they can determine that a situation was in fact an accident and if hunters turn themselves in and are cooperative with them. This may take the form of writing a letter to the judge asking for leniency or it may simply result in a warning being issued instead of a citation. Game wardens were not likely to use discretion when offenders denied committing an act of poaching or else were unwilling to talk about it. Indeed, Forsyth and Marckese (1993b) found an offender's demeanor to be a crucial factor in whether a game warden is likely to use discretion. More specifically, he found that individuals who do not show respect to the game warden are more likely to be cited or arrested. However, a couple of the poachers said that poaching is not an accident and believed that one should be held responsible for one's own hunting behavior. This is illustrated by the following comments: "A person shooting a gun should <u>KNOW</u> his target, any mistake is permanent." "Accidental animal killing is not done with a gun."

The Metaphor of the Ledger

Individuals also attempted to neutralize with the metaphor of the ledger technique. The following letter was received from an individual who returned the business-reply envelope but did not return the survey. Stapled to the letter was a cover letter for the survey that had been torn from top to bottom and then sealed back together with tape.

> . . . In the 40 years of hunting all sorts of game and in as many states I have never broken the laws of any state except for one occasion. That happened to be in Colorado in 1991. I chose to shoot a deer very close to the end of the day and the game warden chose to cite me for the violation.
>
> It was a very costly and embarrassing experience and one that I will never forget or repeat.
>
> I [have been] an NRA and NMLRA member for many years and teach hunter safety classes to civilians as well as law enforcement officers. I believe if you do the crime you should do the time.
>
> I find your questionnaire offensive and misdirected. I do not believe that you will get a response from the poaching community, but then I could be wrong. Good luck in your survey.

This illustrates an attempt by this individual to demonstrate that he is a good person in spite of having poached and that all of his positive qualities such as teaching hunter education classes and being a member of national firearms organizations should somehow make up for the one instance in which he broke the law.

Another individual, who was a nonresident and was cited for purchasing a resident license, also used the metaphor of the ledger technique to justify his actions. He was apprehended at a check station after harvesting a large deer and was not only angry about receiving a large fine for his violation but also about how Colorado Division of Wildlife officers confiscated his large buck deer. While interviewing him, he stated . . . that he was a decent, law-abiding citizen. . . .

The Defense of Necessity

Game wardens said that in the field hunters rarely use the defense of necessity to justify poaching. Yet, some wrote comments about the necessity of poaching deer if a person needs the meat. The following examples from written comments illustrate the defense of necessity:

> Hungry kids and no welfare makes a man do what he can for his family.

> I was fined for taking a deer that did not meet the Colorado Division of Wildlife's point restrictions. I shot a spike deer and according to the rules for the season it had to be [a] two point or better. I hunt only and solely for meat. I feel I should be able to do that at any time any place. I have always had a current license when I hunt. I had a buck tag when I shot the spike. Like the regulations that Roosevelt's alphabet soup government writes it is solely for revenue to the state or federal government. The people of this country are taught ignorance in school—that is why we have their stupid money-grubbing minority . . . government in power. I will follow a law— but regulations are not right.

> I have taken one animal illegally some years ago and I am not proud of it but I was laid off, my wife was between jobs, and in a resort town there are no soup lines and not very many [people] who want to help.

As previously mentioned, game wardens said that in the field they rarely hear the "I needed the meat" or defense of necessity excuse. The financial consequences (i.e., gun and vehicle forfeitures, fines) of illegally taking a deer are simply too great for the benefits that are derived from it (50–60 pounds of meat from an average deer). It appears to be more socially acceptable among hunters and the public to claim that one needs the meat than it is to claim that a deer was illegally taken for other purposes.

Indeed, an in-depth interview with [a] subject . . . yielded the following statement in which he attempted to reaffirm the social acceptability of illegal hunting for the meat while at the same time acknowledging that poaching for other reasons, especially a trophy, is completely unacceptable:

> I killed a doe, and it was for the meat only. I've only hunted illegally once in my life. It's wrong to poach, but it's wrong for a family to go hungry as well. Hunting builds strong bonds between people that last forever. It teaches respect for animals and the forest. Poaching for a rack is unacceptable. There should be leniency for people who need meat. What's the bigger crime: killing deer or burning down for-est for new ski slope runs? This loss of habitat hurts more deer and elk than poaching ever does.

The Condemnation of the Condemners

In regard to the condemnation of the condemners technique of neutralization, some of the subjects strongly believed that game wardens sometimes hunt deer illegally. One subject bluntly wrote "I know of three that do." Some subjects also had very negative attitudes and great hostility toward game wardens and the Division of Wildlife as well, as the following written comments from one individual suggest:

> Hunting in the state of Colorado is all dirty, dirty politics. You must be a prick to become a game warden in the state of Colorado. It helps in their point status.

Other individuals simply had very negative attitudes toward game wardens; these are illustrated by the following comments: "The area game warden is an ass." "I have a real hatred for them. I wouldn't trust them. I think a lot of them are assholes." "The game warden is a horse's ass deluxe!"

The game wardens also said that some of the trophy poachers they apprehended had teenage children with them. These poachers were thus socializing their own children into the illegal act of trophy deer poaching, lending support for differential association theory. Although it does not explain everything, the impact of early socialization experiences cannot be ignored when searching for the roots of deviant behavior. This is consistent with findings of Curcione (1992), Green (1990), and Forsyth and Marckese (1993b), who reported that the majority of individuals in their studies were introduced to poaching by a family member. Through the socialization process, individuals learn not only the appropriate methods and techniques for taking game illegally but also the rationalizations that are used to justify participation in such activities.

Indeed, the meanings that are acquired by children during social interaction with significant others play an important role in the development of deviance. Regarding fishery violations, Curcione (1992:53) stated "the meanings acquired early on in the biographies of these poachers gave rise to a general orientation that favorably disposed them toward certain fishery violations when the opportunities arose."

CONCLUSION

In our society, there is a stereotype of a poacher as someone who goes hunting during the closed season, often at night, and displays a wanton disregard as he recklessly shoots animals or anything that moves. And although it is true that this type of poaching does occur, it is not an entirely accurate representation of the continuum of activities that constitute poaching behavior. Indeed, although out-of-season trophy poaching has received great publicity during the past decade, the most common form of poaching violation is related to opportunity and occurs during the legal hunting season. The following statement from a game warden illustrates this:

> A lot of poaching situations are opportunistic. Guys don't go out intending to break the law, but an opportunity presents itself. The percentage of trophy poachers is small, but it is more publicized. Most hunters understand there is a risk. There are only a few 35–40 inchers out there, and a few poachers could wipe them out. These trophy deer are in high demand by hunters. Trophy poachers remove the most desirable animals and the public doesn't have the opportunity to harvest them. Compared to overall violations, out-of-season trophy poaching has very few cases.

Game wardens generally felt that poaching did not have an effect on the deer herd in terms of overall numbers but believed that it did have an impact on the number of trophy animals that were available. They also reported that other factors had a greater negative impact on the deer herd than poaching did. The following comments from game wardens illustrate this:

> Poaching is a big problem, but not in terms of overall numbers. It is a problem because of the type of animals that are taken. This area has big bucks and bulls.
>
> It does reduce the number of trophy animals. Poaching does not affect the overall deer herd. The

> biological impact is riot high, but it is very significant socially because of the social impact or publicity that it creates. The weather and hunting seasons can have a much larger impact on the resource. On this 30-mile stretch of highway we lose 300 to 500 deer a year.

This is consistent with the findings of Forsyth and Marckese (1993a:25), who reported that the game wardens they interviewed also believed that poaching was not as detrimental to wildlife as some other activities were, such as the loss of habitat through logging and farming practices.

This study provides support for neutralization theory. The overwhelming majority of individuals in the study believed that illegal deer hunting is wrong and tended to be committed to the dominant normative system of society.

Nearly all of the subjects used neutralization techniques to justify their participation in this activity. Thus, when it comes to hunting offenses the use of neutralization techniques as a mechanism for reducing guilt appears to be very common. Some neutralization techniques were reported more often than others. The most common techniques of neutralization that subjects used to justify participation in this particular type of activity were the denial of responsibility, the metaphor of the ledger, the defense of necessity, and the condemnation of the condemners.

One thing is clear from this study—the term poaching means different things to different individuals. Indeed, many of the poachers did not consider themselves poachers or their deviant activities as actually constituting poaching behavior.

Illegal deer hunting is most often committed by men. Women do not participate in recreational hunting to the extent that men do, and possibly as a result there are very few women in relation to men who commit this type of offense.

Most poaching offenses tend to be opportunistic in nature and take place during the legal deer hunting season. Trophy poaching is not as common, but it receives considerable publicity when it does occur. It is hoped that this study will generate additional interest among scholars in the sociology of poaching.

REFERENCES

Alvarez, Alexander. 1997. "Adjusting to Genocide: The Techniques of Neutralization and the Holocaust." *Social Science History* 21:139–68.

Brennan, William C. 1974. "Abortion and the Techniques of Neutralization." *Journal of Health and Social Behavior* 15:358–65.

Coleman, James W. 1994. *The Criminal Elite: The Sociology of White Collar-Crime.* New York: St. Martin's Press.

Collins, Michael D. 1994. "Neutralization Theory: An Empirical Application and Assessment." PhD dissertation, Oklahoma State University, Department of Sociology, Stillwater.

Curcione, Nicholas R. 1992. "Deviance as Delight: Party-Boat Poaching in Southern California." *Deviant Behavior* 13:33–57.

Dunford, Franklyn W. and Phillip R. Kunz. 1973. "The Neutralization of Religious Dissonance." *Review of Religious Research* 15:2–9.

Forsyth, Craig J. and Thomas A. Marckese. 1993a. "Folk Outlaws: Vocabularies of Motives." *International Review of Modern Sociology* 23:17–31.

———. 1993b. "Thrills and Skills: A Sociological Analysis of Poaching." *Deviant Behavior* 14:157–72.

Green, Gary S. 1990. "Resurrecting Polygraph Validation of Self-Reported Crime Data: A Note on Research Method and Ethics Using the Deer Poacher." *Deviant Behavior* 11:131–37.

Klockars, Carl B. 1974. *The Professional Fence.* New York: Free Press.

Levi, Ken. 1981. "Becoming a Hit Man: Neutralization in a Very Deviant Career." *Urban Life* 10:47–63.

Minor, W. William. 1981. "Techniques of Neutralization: A Reconceptualization and Empirical Examination." *Journal of Research in Crime and Delinquency* 18:295–318.

Priest, Thomas B. and John H. McGrath. 1970. "Techniques of Neutralization: Young Adult Marijuana Smokers." *Criminology* 8:185–94.

Rogers, Joseph W. and M. D. Buffalo. 1974. "Neutralization Techniques: Toward a Simplified Measurement Scale." *Pacific Sociological Review* 17:313–31.

Sykes, Gresham M. and David Matza. 1957. "Techniques of Neutralization: A Theory of Delinquency." *American Sociological Review* 22:664–70.

46

HINTS OF DEVIANCE IN BINGO

CONSTANCE CHAPPLE
STACEY NOFZIGER

In U.S. society, gambling has long been seen as a "bad habit" that "undermined the work ethic and embodied the danger of addiction" (Burnham, 1993, p. 146). Throwing away hard-earned money and seeking easy payoffs were once seen as signs of depravity and immorality. Today, Americans tend less to see gambling as deviant, unless it is compulsive gambling. As suggested by Smith and Preston's (1984) study, a few people continue to see gambling as deviant because it involves wagering hard-earned money for the elusive goal of monetary profit. However, most people do not consider gambling deviant because they see it mostly as "play, leisure, and recreation."

As a form of gambling, bingo is also socially constructed or defined as both deviant and nondeviant. Some people consider bingo deviant because they associate it with casino and "back alley" gambling, but most regard it as acceptable or even respectable, probably because they associate it with church, charity, and sociability. Here in our research we try to find out how bingo players themselves view their game.

RESEARCH METHODS

Data was collected in ten different bingo sites in southern Arizona over a six-month period in 1996. Most of our information regarding bingo playing times and locations came from a national periodical for bingo players. This publication, known as the *Bingo Bugle,* lists a considerable number of local clubs and organizations that offer bingo throughout the week. Although this investigation did not cover every bingo location available, the nine sites we selected represented a good cross section of bingo activities in southern Arizona.

A team approach was used for this research. On most occasions two researchers were present simultaneously collecting data. The data was collected in three different steps. First, we engaged in pure participant observation. We entered each location as players, bought the required bingo cards or sheets, purchased a variety of "daubers" (paint pens used to mark off the numbers on the sheets), played the games, watched other players around us, eavesdropped, and sometimes even won. Much of the activity in which we were interested took place before play began and between sessions of play. It was during this time that people socialized, read, knitted, and played games. Although we were participating fully in the activities associated with playing bingo, we were openly taking notes and would tell any interested observers who inquired that we were doing a "project" on bingo.

In the second step of our research we conducted informal interviews with players. These interviews were undertaken whenever the opportunity arose. Although bingo halls are typically structured for people to be seated in close proximity, various bingo norms of silence during play and larger cultural, privacy norms made lengthy interviews difficult. However, given short breaks in play, waiting in line for food or to use the restroom, and one or two locations where talking during play was more acceptable, we were able to conduct long, informal, unstructured interviews.

The interviews took the form of casual conversations. Although the topic of the interviews varied, we typically attempted to discover the history of the players' involvement in bingo and their reasons for playing. In total, we have fourteen women who acted as informants in our study. The length of each casual interview depended on personal proximity and the informant's willingness to engage in conversation with us. In an hour-long interview, for example, the informant was seated across from us, was interested in our "project," and most importantly, was very willing to answer our questions and keep the conversation running throughout the bingo play. Many interviews occurred because an informant happened to sit near a researcher or was next to the researcher in a food or bathroom line. Most interviews lasted only a few minutes, although our conversations normally resumed at various times later. The average interview lasted fifteen to twenty minutes.

The final part of our research consisted of an examination of the printed materials about bingo. These materials included information sheets from the different locations. They often explain rules of the game, the different games scheduled for each session of play, and the prizes offered. We further consulted five editions of the local *Bingo Bugle*. The *Bugle* is published once a month. It is distributed across town to most locations offering bingo and to several grocery stores. The *Bugle* lists the days, times, places, and addresses of the bingo locations, pictures of past bingo winners, and various articles related to bingo. The *Bugle* also lists bingo competitions and bingo vacations offered nationally, so interested players can connect with other players from around the country. This data provided a larger view of the activities associated with bingo and gave valuable information on the local bingo schedules and the general demographics of players.

RESULTS

With one notable exception, all of our informants were middle-aged and older women. The majority were white. On some locations we encountered greater numbers of Hispanic and African American players, but their proportion never exceeded one fourth of the players. Although most of the bingo workers (callers, ticket takers, and floor workers who sell bingo sheets) were men, we saw very few men playing bingo. The popular perception of bingo as an "old ladies" game held true for our informants. Not surprisingly, for example, three informants, "Mom," "Curly," and "Frosty" (pseudonyms rather than real names), told us that they never played bingo when they were younger because they considered it an "old lady game." Because these players are seemingly harmless or respectable, the game does not project a deviant image.

The informants in our study generally did not see bingo as deviant either. Instead, they viewed the game as a "fun way to spend the afternoon." The majority had become bingo players through friends or family members. Regardless of how they started playing bingo, most expressed their reasons for continuing to play in terms of relationships to other people. As several informants told us, they were bored most of the time and bingo gave them the opportunity to socialize with others. Some informants even described their bingo playing as a social gathering of friends. Playing with friends, then, placed emphasis on fun and social time instead of gambling and winning. One woman, "Plum," told us that she and another bingo player split their winnings equally because they were there simply to have fun. Two other informants, "Frosty" and "Silky," revealed that they had a long-standing, weekly get-together with five or six other women who play bingo. The members of this group would bring all kinds of food to share with each other, and they would chat and laugh throughout the evening of bingo.

This emphasis on social time and fun was also evident in several informants' choices of where to play bingo. They preferred smaller clubs and churches instead of casinos. According to one informant, in a casino, which has more people, bingo was played with more seriousness and competitiveness; there were fewer opportunities for socialization, talking was more often discouraged, and no one was allowed to bring in food. In contrast, the smaller clubs or churches allowed outside food to be brought in. These places were also decorated to render a "homey" atmosphere for the bingo players.

Another dimension of bingo that prevents the game from being seen as deviant is its association with charity. Our informants often justified their play by emphasizing the charitable nature of the game's proceeds. They knew that a large percentage of the proceeds from bingo are given to local churches, charities, and other non-profit organizations.

Nevertheless, there are some hints of deviance in bingo. Many of the bingo players we observed were surprisingly versatile in their involvement in what Arneklev and his coresearchers (1993) call "imprudent acts." According to these researchers, any behavior that ignores long-term consequences for short-term gratification can be considered imprudent behavior. A prime example is gambling of various forms, and along with gambling, two other examples of imprudent behavior often occur among bingo players, namely drinking and smoking. Indeed, we found that wherever drinking was allowed, large numbers of bingo players drank, even though it was still in the early afternoon during the workweek. Past research indicated that bingo playing may prevent alcohol consumption by offering an alternative social pastime away from bars (King, 1987). However, our research shows that these two activities can, and do, coexist.

An even more common manifestation of imprudent behavior in bingo players is smoking. Nearly all the locations we visited allowed smoking, and one of the two places that banned smoking advertised a special "smokers' game" to allow smokers to go to a special area to smoke during the middle of a game. Other locations offered "non-smoking sections," a euphemism at best, in the form of a single or two rows of tables directly adjacent to the chain-smoking players at the smoking tables. In one club, there were so many smokers puffing away that there was a thick haze of cigarette smoke hanging in the air that ultimately forced us to cut short our observations in this location.

Finally, several informants openly admitted that they frequently engage in various other forms of gambling, including gambling at the casinos. One informant, a middle-aged, white woman, told us that she is a "big-time gambling freak." Another informant said that "playing bingo is no different from gambling at the casino, because it was very addicting." Some others admitted to playing the Lotto or going on cruises in which they can play bingo as well as gamble at slot machines and poker games.

SUMMARY AND CONCLUSIONS

Our findings indicate that, for the most part, bingo players play bingo for fun and profit. Numerous informants told us that if it were not fun, they would not come back to play. The fun typically derives from meeting other players with similar interests and backgrounds. However, not one informant told us that they play for fun alone. Profit is an equally important attraction for playing bingo. It is the potential for financial gain, or the thrill that winning brings, that ultimately brings them back time and again. Every informant told us that if they never won, they would stop coming back to play bingo. It is this aspect of bingo as gambling that makes the game appear deviant to the players and others. It also encourages such deviant behavior as other kinds of gambling, drinking, and smoking.

Our research suggested that the demographics of bingo players contribute to the social definition of the game as a harmless leisure activity. Because the majority of the players are older, retired women, the image of bingo as a grandmotherly game makes it difficult to view the players and the game as deviant. The location of bingo further helps influence the social construction of the game as deviant or nondeviant. The bingo in casinos is more likely to be seen as deviant because their players are more likely to be men and relatively young, when compared with players in smaller clubs, social halls, and local churches.

Finally, the organizational atmosphere in which bingo playing occurs also helps shape the social construction of bingo as deviant. Bingo playing in the churches and social halls appears less deviant because the atmosphere is clearly more "homey." There are greater opportunities for friendly interaction, including the sharing of food and other refreshments, among bingo players and the bingo workers. Such socializing, however, does not occur in the casinos, so the bingo at those places tends more to be seen as deviant.

REFERENCES

Arneklev, Bruce J., Harold G. Grasmick, Charles R. Tittle, and Robert J. Bursik Jr. 1993. "Low Self-Control and Imprudent Behavior." *Journal of Quantitative Criminology,* 9(3):225–247.

Burnham, John C. 1993. *Bad Habits: Drinking, Smoking, Taking Drugs, Gambling, Sexual Misbehavior, and Swearing in American History.* New York: New York University Press.

King, Kim M. 1987. "Normative Contingencies: Charity and Moderation." *Current Perspectives in Social Theory,* 8:215–237.

Smith, Ronald W., and Frederick W. Preston. 1984. "Vocabularies of Motives for Gambling Behavior." *Sociological Perspectives,* 27:325–348.

PART TWELVE

PUZZLING DEVIANCES

In the afternoon of December 2, 1997, 15-year-old Kenny White took his father's pistol, aimed it at his head, and pulled the trigger. He had lived his short life in a small town in South Dakota. The day he killed himself, he had not shown to others any sign of suicide in the making: He had eaten lunch with his school buddy, ridden around town in a pickup truck, and bought Christmas presents with his pocket money. Yet he had apparently planned to take his own life. Next to his slumped body in his bedroom was a note he had scribbled: "I really don't know what to say in these dam things, but I want you to know that I love you mom and dad. I'm not in English class so my spelling doesn't have to be perfect." He also asked his mother to quit smoking and his parents, separated for ten years, to remarry. He further wrote his will, bequeathing his baseball cards, BB gun collection, and Minnesota Twins jersey to various friends.[1]

Like Kenny White, about 30,000 Americans die by their own hand every year. As a cause of death, suicide ranks eighth among adults, but second among adolescents. There is something ironic about suicide. In a highly individualistic society, we are supposed to be more concerned with ourselves than others, to like ourselves more than others. Yet every year we are far more likely to kill ourselves than others, as indicated by the fact that the U.S. suicide rate is more than 50 percent higher than the homicide rate.[2] Equally puzzling to the general public is why African Americans, who generally have a tougher life than their white peers because of racial prejudice, have a much lower, rather than higher, suicide rate. The answer is available in the first article here, " 'It's a White Thing': An Exploration of Beliefs about Suicide in the African-American Community," by Kevin Early and Ronald Akers.

As puzzling to the general public as suicide are other forms of deviance that we will read here. One is why it strikes fear into many parents' hearts that their teenage children like to listen to heavy metal and rap music. In the article, "Media Depictions of Harm in Heavy Metal and Rap Music," Amy Binder attributes to the media the parents' fear that the loud music is dangerous and harmful to their youngsters. In the next article, "Tattoos Are Like Potato Chips . . . You Can't Have Just One," Angus Vail offers insight into a form of deviant behavior over which the general public often scratches its head and asks why would anyone deface their body with so many tattoos. Finally, many people find it hard to understand how panhandlers can survive by passively depending on others to give them small change. In his article, "Panhandlers: Overcoming the Nonperson Treatment," Stephen Lankenau shows how panhandlers are far from passive; instead they actively manipulate others into offering them enough money to survive.

1. Pam Belluck. 1998. "In Little City Safe from Violence, Rash of Suicides Leaves Scars." *New York Times,* April 5, pp. 1, 21.
2. U.S. Census Bureau. 1999. *Statistical Abstract of the United States.* Washington, DC: Government Printing Office.

"IT'S A WHITE THING": AN EXPLORATION OF BELIEFS ABOUT SUICIDE IN THE AFRICAN-AMERICAN COMMUNITY

KEVIN E. EARLY
RONALD L. AKERS

The low black suicide rate is well documented. There has been an increase in black male suicides in the past two decades, but until the mid-1980s that was matched by an increase in suicides among white males. The differences in suicide between younger black and white males has never been large and may be getting smaller. Nevertheless, overall the white suicide rate is nearly double the black suicide rate. The ratio of white male to black male suicide rates is 1.75:1, and the suicide rate among white women is more than double the rate for black women (see Department of Health and Human Services, 1992). It is this persistent difference in rates of suicide across racial groups that has been the focus of sociological interest in suicide in the black community. The question raised by this difference is, Why is there relatively little black suicide? . . .

The answer most frequently given in the literature is a general "buffering hypothesis." This hypothesizes that black suicide is lower, in part, because of the role played by religion and the family in the African-American community in ameliorating or buffering social forces that might otherwise promote suicide. Billingsley (1968), Stack (1974), Allen (1978), Martin (1978), and McAdoo (1981) all look at the family, church, and social support systems they believe help insulate African Americans from suicide. This perspective is also adopted by Rutter (1985), who used the term protective factors. Woodford (1965) pro-posed that experiences with urbanization, segregation, and racism have helped to buffer African Americans from suicide by producing adaptability. Davis hypothesized that:

> *For blacks, the stresses and anxieties that might lead to suicide have often been off-set by strong family and communal ties. Effectively denied all other mechanisms to compensate for rejection and abuse, blacks have in the past used their families, communities, and institutions (i.e., churches, social clubs, fraternal organizations, etc.) to develop positive and functional forms of response to recurrent stressful social situations. The black community, in effect, has functioned as a protective society, providing participation and purpose, a sense of belonging, and the possibility of cooperative and self-help approaches to problems. (Davis, 1980, p. 228)*

As stated in the literature the hypothesis remains nonspecific as to just what it is about the church, family, or other institutions in the African-American community that has provided or could provide suicide buffering. We propose that there are both social and cultural dimensions to any suicide buffering effect that may be found. The social dimension relates to the extent to which social relationships and responsiveness to one another provide social support countering suicide situations and motivations. The cultural dimension refers to the normative climate, the values and norms shared by the church, family, and other institutions in the African-American community.

Research has not yet identified the empirical content of either of these dimensions.

The purpose of this reading is to report an exploratory, qualitative investigation of the content of the cultural/normative dimension. The study was designed to find what, if any, religious beliefs there are in the African-American community that might serve a suicide-buffering function. Specifically, we report a study of normative views of suicide, contrasted with views of other deviant acts such as drug abuse and crime, reported by religious leaders in one community. The study did not have comparative data from the white community and therefore was not an effort to directly test the buffering hypothesis or to explain differences in white and black suicidal behavior. Rather, the study attempted to identify the content of religiously based antisuicide beliefs to gain a greater understanding of black cultural perceptions of suicide. . . .

METHODOLOGY

The study was conducted in 1991 in a southeastern standard metropolitan statistical area (SMSA) of about 84,000 with 21 percent African Americans. The data were collected by the first author in face-to-face interviews with black pastors. There are a total of 37 black churches located in the area, and 30 pastors agreed to take part in the study. The pastors were interviewed as informants, as persons strategically located in the community to provide information, insight, and contacts within that community. Therefore, they were asked their own opinions and were asked to comment on beliefs about suicide in the general community.

The interviews were loosely structured and undisguised, lasting about 1½ hours each. The interviews were divided into two main sections. The first section covered: (1) The pastor's views as leader of the church and the stated position of his or her church on suicide; (2) The pastor's assessment of the role of the church and religion in the African-American family and community; (3) The extent to which the pastor teaches and preaches on suicide-relevant topics; and (4) The definition and meaning of suicide and its causes and assessment

of why there are few suicide deaths in the African-American community. The second part of the interview asked the pastors to respond to two vignettes depicting cases of suicide and attempted suicide. . . . Each vignette was succeeded by four to seven follow-up questions that were designed to elicit pastors' judgments and attitudes about several issues related to the nature of suicide depicted in the vignettes and the role that the black church could play or had played in dealing with these social issues.

None of the pastors reported direct experience with cases of suicide, and therefore assessment of actual cases could not be used. The vignettes allowed us to explore what the stated reactions and assessments would have been if the pastors had encountered such cases. . . .

FINDINGS

Not surprisingly, the pastors offer strong support for the contention in the literature iterated above that the church serves unifying and leadership functions in the black community. They point to the black church as an institution that has provided social and cultural integration for black Americans and has interacted with the black family to provide resiliency under stressful conditions. . . .

Beliefs about Suicide

The pastors' perceived significance of the church in the community does not guarantee that its stand on suicide is widely shared in the black culture, and our research did not include a community survey. However, as we have seen, the literature strongly supports this perception, and it seems reasonable to assume that the norms and attitudes expressed by the pastors are reflected to some extent in the larger community. Those norms, as articulated by the pastors in this study, condemn suicide on religious grounds and define it as so alien to the black experience, religious and secular, that willingness to commit suicide runs directly counter to all that is implicit in what it means to be African American. . . .

In the view of the pastors, the black church unequivocally condemns suicide as unforgivable sin. "Man is not the giver of life. Hence, man has not the authority to take life." "The Lord giveth and only the Lord taketh away."

> [Interview 08269010] We don't condone suicide. We condemn it to the maximum. We believe that most people that commit suicide never [get the chance before dying] to ask for forgiveness.

> [Interview 07289001] God did not put us here to determine our own conclusion of life and taking it upon ourselves to make quick exits. That, Biblically, is not an approved act of God. It's unpardonable sin. One who commits suicide goes to hell and is unpardoned for their sin. . . .

This definition of suicide as a sin that is unpardonable is combined with the view that suicide runs counter to black "soul." The soul represents the gift of life. The soul is tied to the black experience not only spiritually, but has worldly, cultural, and traditional dimensions. If one is to ensure one's soul a proper place in heaven after death, it is important to live life as productively as possible despite life's many obstacles. Obstacles should not be a deterrent to life, but an encouragement to struggle. To struggle with the help of God is believed to enhance the quality of life and to make the individual resilient to pressures that would otherwise cause suicide. The soul belongs to God and is entrusted to the individual who is ultimately held accountable. To the extent that this norm of accountability for one's own life and soul is transmitted in both sacred and secular versions throughout the community, it could act as one of the normative suicide buffers.

Suicide Is a "White Thing"

The pastors were asked directly why they believed that suicide is less of a problem for the African-American community and why suicide occurs infrequently. Their explanations for black suicide are . . . that the person committing suicide has experienced a breakdown in religious and family ties and stress associated with the assimilative effects of racial integration that is seen as undermining the internal integration of the black community. As we have seen, the specifically religious norms on the unexcusable and inexplicable nature of suicide may be one element buffering against these suicide-inducing pressures.

But the pastors' responses reflect a fusion of these religious norms with secular norms. The message in their assessments is that suicide, in addition to being unholy and sinful, is almost a complete denial of black identity and culture. It is assumed that suicide is outside the black experience. It is simply not done. In the revealing words of the first pastor interviewed, which inspired the title of this paper, "suicide is a white thing."

Suicide is viewed as a white thing not simply because of its recognized greater statistical frequency among whites. Rather, the phrase captures the idea that suicide is antithetical to black culture. This was communicated to the interviewer and first author, who is black, not only by the first pastor but by several others in subsequent interviews. They insisted that he should not even have to ask questions related to blacks and suicide because suicide is a white thing, not a black thing. "As a rule blacks don't kill themselves . . . you should know this already." "Well, being black you should know that black people want to live." "You should know that suicide is somethin' that occurs over there, on the other side of the tracks." "We want to live, son . . . we want to get there . . . you should know this."

All of the pastors presented the view that there are unique features of black culture that render some of the same difficulties and problems that might lead to suicide by whites less of a suicide threat for African Americans. The belief is that having to deal historically and currently with economic, political, and social deprivation has made black Americans more resilient against these problems. Indeed, one of their worries was that racial integration, in spite of all its other benefits, may break down some of that resiliency because it may foster blacks taking on white culture and attitudes about suicide. . . .

[Interview 09049013] I think in this case it goes back to our culture. We have been taught down through the years that we as a people don't do these kinds of things . . . committing suicide. As a boy growing up I never knew anything about blacks committing suicide until integration came about and I believe black America then began to take on the traits, if you will, of white America.

[Interview 09229020] We as a race have always been used to hardships. We are more used to hardships than whites. Suicide was always more prevalent among whites than it was blacks. I personally believe that if black folks are killin' theyself it's because of the integration. We've gotten where we're communicating closer with whites every day. . . .

The pastors portrayed blacks as being a more religious people than their white counterparts. Additionally, blacks were described as being able to endure more hardships and not succumb to the despair and despondency that leads to suicide. The black experience in America is one of struggle. Survival represents hope and the promise of a better life after death. The church unifies black Americans around a common tradition shaped out of suffering. The church is a source of strength, identity, coping skills, and a reason for living. Thus, the pastors identified secular as well as religious norms forming a cultural buffer against suicide in the black community to keep suicide from having become a black thing. Suicide is excluded as contradictory to what it means to be black. Whites may do it, but blacks do not.

SUMMARY AND CONCLUSIONS

The most common explanation for the relatively little black suicide proposed by scholars is that the black church and family ameliorate social forces that might otherwise lead to suicide. We have referred to this as the buffering hypothesis and noted that it leaves unspecified what it is that does the buffering. The principal goal of this study was to investigate what some of these buffers might be.

Thirty pastors in one community in a southeastern state were interviewed to elicit their observations and views on suicide in the black community. . . . According to the pastors, the church is a refuge, problem-solver, and moral voice of the black community. They describe the church as central to the black experience, which is consistent with what sociologists of race and ethnicity have been saying for a long time. Assuming the importance of the black church in the larger community as asserted by these pastors and as stated in the literature, we have tentatively identified religiously based beliefs with the potential for countering suicide.

The pastors condemned suicide as an unpardonable sin. Theologically, they defined it as an unpardonable sin "against God's perfect will." Suicide does nothing for the "soul" except place it in peril of eternal damnation. The church recognizes no justification for suicide. . . .

Our research has uncovered another dimension of the pastors' beliefs about suicide to which future research should pay particular attention, namely the perception of suicide as inherently contradictory to the black experience and a complete denial of black identity and culture. The pastors reasoned, "Why talk about suicide? [Not concentrating on suicide in sermons] is not an oversight, it just is not a problem." Problems that might lead to suicide by whites do not pose a threat to black Americans. Blacks have developed an apparent resilience to direct self-destructive behavior. To struggle and endure hardships toughens one to withstand sorrows, and religious faith offers hope and the promise of a better life. Suicide is seen as peculiar to white America "across the tracks." Black Americans may get involved in crime and drug abuse, but "to our credit at least we don't kill ourselves. That's a white thing." . . .

Other factors in black suicide beyond buffering of moral norms and values are not examined in this study. Therefore, there is no claim to have provided a test of the buffering hypothesis. However, the study has provided evidence of a religiously influenced social meaning of suicide as unacceptable, perhaps even unthinkable, for the vast majority of black Americans. This permits us to go beyond the general hypothesis of the suicide-buffering function of the religious institution in the black community found in the literature to propose the following specific hypothesis: The condemnation of suicide as wrong and as an unthinkable contradiction of black culture is sufficiently pervasive in the black community that it helps to keep the rate of suicide low.

REFERENCES

Allen, Walter. 1978. "Black Family Research in the United States: A Review, Assessment and Extension." *Journal of Comparative Family Studies* 9:168–189.

Billingsley, Andrew. 1968. *Black Families in White America.* Englewood Cliffs, NJ: Prentice-Hall,

Davis, Robert. 1980. "Suicide among Young Blacks: Trends and Perspective." *Phylon* 41:223–229.

Department of Health and Human Services. 1992. Statistical Series, annual data, 1990. Series E-21. *Vital Statistics of the United States,* Vol. II, Mortality, Part A. Washington, DC: Public Health Service, National Center for Health Statistics.

Martin, Elmer P. 1978. *The Black Extended Family.* Chicago: University of Chicago Press.

McAdoo, Harriette. 1981. *Black Families.* Beverly Hills: Sage Publications.

Rutter, Michael. 1985. "Resilience in the Face of Adversity." *British Journal of Psychiatry* 147:598–611.

Stack, Carol. 1974. *All Our Kin.* New York: Harper & Row.

Woodford, J. 1965. "Why Negro Suicides Are Increasing." *Ebony* 20:89–100.

MEDIA DEPICTIONS OF HARM
IN HEAVY METAL AND RAP MUSIC

AMY BINDER

In September 1985, a group of politically well-connected "Washington Wives" calling themselves the Parents' Music Resource Center (PMRC) was invited to testify before the U.S. Senate Committee on Commerce, Science, and Transportation. Led by Tipper Gore (wife of then Senator Al Gore of Tennessee) and Susan Baker (wife of then Treasury Secretary James Baker), the group's objective was to reveal to committee members the current state of rock music lyrics—particularly the lyrics of heavy metal music. The PMRC and its expert witnesses testified that such music filled youthful ears with pornography and violence, and glorified behaviors ranging from suicide and drug use to occultism and anti-patriotic activities. The mass media covered the hearing in great detail, provoking debate in the national press over the alleged harmfulness of rock music lyrics and whether the proposed labeling of music lyrics constituted censorship.

Almost five years later, another event again focused the nation's attention on music lyrics—the lyrics in rap music. In June 1990, a U.S. District Court judge in Fort Lauderdale, Florida, found the 2 Live Crew album *As Nasty as They Wanna Be* to be obscene in the three counties under his jurisdiction. This was the first recording ever declared obscene by a federal court (*New York Times* 17 June 1990). During the following week, authorities from one of those counties' Sheriff's Department— Broward County—arrested a local record store owner who had continued to sell the album and took into custody two members of the 2 Live Crew band when they performed material from the album at an adults-only show in the area. The arrests and impending trials again galvanized heated public debate over whether the lyrics in contemporary music harmed listeners and warranted restriction.

These two widely publicized debates about contemporary music, both of which concerned "harmful" lyrics and occurred within five years of each other, provide comparative cases for examining how the mass media serve as an ideological vehicle. In both cases, writers in the mainstream press expressed concern about the harm that could result from exposure to lyrics containing sexual and violent themes, and called for action against such content. Despite these similarities, however, the substance of media arguments changed significantly as the controversy shifted from heavy metal music to rap music. Foremost among these differences was the change in emphasis regarding whom the music was harming: the individual listener or society as a whole.

I suggest that two factors drove the changes in the media discourse surrounding the dangers of heavy metal music versus rap music. One factor is the difference in the content of the lyrics themselves. In general, the controversial rap lyrics were more graphic than their heavy metal counterparts, and discussions in the media reflected this variation.

Second, the broad cultural context in which the "white" music and "black" music were being received also significantly affected changes in the discourse. Rather than asserting a simple reflection model (i.e., the media only mirror "what's out there"), I argue that the pronounced shift in the discourse about lyrics cannot be explained by differences in the cultural objects alone. Instead, the shift reflects opinion writers' perceptions of the populations represented by these two musical genres. Writers who were concerned about heavy metal lyrics and rap lyrics did not address the content of the music alone; embedded in their discussions were reactions to differences in the demographic characteristics of the genres' producers and audiences—music made by and for working and middle-class white youth versus music they perceived as predominantly by and for urban black teenagers. In a cultural landscape marked by divergent perceptions of black youths versus white youths, different concerns emerged in the mainstream media about the impact of each group's form of cultural expression. I show that rap music—with its evocation of angry black rappers and equally angry black audiences—was simultaneously perceived as a more authentic and serious art form than was heavy metal music, and as a more frightening and salient threat to society as a whole than the "white" music genre.

METHODOLOGY

I examine the national discourse surrounding the harmfulness of music lyrics by analyzing nationally distributed mainstream publications that target a range of audiences. Demographic profiles as of 1991 provided by these publications show that readerships varied along socioeconomic lines: the *New York Times* and *Time* magazine have the wealthiest and most highly educated readers, *Newsweek* and *U.S. News and World Report* represent an intermediate socioeconomic level, and the readership of the *Reader's Digest* has low levels of annual income and education. The publications also vary politically: the *New York Times* is considered one of the most liberal large newspapers, the *Reader's Digest* is considered conservative, and the other three publications fall somewhere in between.

For comparison to this mainstream debate, which was written for a "general" (primarily white) American readership, I also examined the discourse in two popular middle-class publications that serve a predominantly black readership: *Ebony* and *Jet* (hereafter referred to as black or

African-American magazines). The articles in these African-American magazines were coded to determine if the race of the readership made a difference in how the music genres were framed.

The articles published in the five mainstream publications and the two black magazines were located in the *Reader's Guide to Periodicals* and the Lexis/Nexis data bank. Between 1985 and 1990, these publications printed more than 1000 news and opinion articles that concerned heavy metal music or rap music. Of these, 108 of the mainstream articles and 10 of the black magazines' articles were opinion pieces that specifically addressed the lyric content of the music. . . . In the African-American magazines, all 10 articles were written about rap music. Although all of the roughly 1000 articles were read, for methodological and theoretical reasons I limited coding and analysis to these 118 opinion articles.

The 118 opinion pieces were content-analyzed using coding categories constructed by the author. This first reading generated 68 categories, which were collapsed into nine frames. This set of nine frames accounts for the total discourse surrounding the issue of harm in lyrics in these publications from 1985 to 1990. Each article was then read again to determine which of the nine frames were used in each piece. The mean number of frames per article was 1.6.

Frames are "schemata of interpretation that enable individuals to locate, perceive, identify, and label" events they have experienced directly or indirectly (Snow, Rochford, Worden, and Benford, 1986, p. 464; see also Goffman, 1974, p. 21). Frames help receivers make sense of social occurrences because they organize events into recognizable patterns and help individuals understand what actions they can then take in light of these events. The nine frames that were used in the 118 articles analyzed here to depict heavy metal and rap music are of two types. The "music is harmful" frames include corruption, protection, danger to society, and not censorship. The other, "music is not harmful" frames comprise no harm, threat to authorities, generation gap, and important message/art (see Table 48.1).

Table 48.1 Percentage Distribution of Frames by Type of Frame, for Mainstream Publications and African-American Publications and Type of Music, 1985–1990

TYPE OF PUBLICATION AND FRAME	TYPE OF MUSIC		
	PERCENT HEAVY METAL	PERCENT RAP	PERCENT HEAVY METAL AND RAP
Mainstream Publications[a] *(Chi-square = 72.1, 16 d.f., p < .01)*			
"Music Is Harmful" Frames			
Corruption	34	0	31
Protection	31	14	23
Danger to society	13	64	38
Not censorship	22	21	8
Total	100	100	100
Number of frames	32	14	13
"Music Is Not Harmful" Counterframes			
Freedom of speech	18	14	27
No harm	39	22	16
Threat to authorities	4	1	21
Generation gap	25	3	5
Important message/art	14	60	21
Total	100	100	100
Number of frames	28	65	19
African-American Magazines[b] *"Music Is Harmful" Frames*			
Corruption	0	0	0
Protection	0	0	0
Danger to society	0	0	0
Not censorship	0	0	0
Total	0	0	0
Number of frames	0	0	0
"Music Is Not Harmful" Counterframes			
Freedom of speech	0	6	0
No harm	0	24	0
Threat to authorities	0	6	0
Generation gap	0	17	0
Important message/art	0	47	0
Total	0	100	0
Number of frames	0	17	0

[a]The *New York Times, Time* magazine, *Newsweek, U.S. News and World Report,* and *Reader's Digest.*
[b]*Ebony* and *Jet.*

HARMFUL OR NOT HARMFUL: FRAMING MUSIC LYRICS

Popular music has always been denigrated by adult society. Musical genres like the blues, jazz, and early rock and roll and dances like the jitterbug, samba, and rhumba provoked complaints from the older generation about the perversion and general corruption of its children (Peterson, 1972; McDonald, 1988; Rosenbaum and Prinsky, 1991). Thus, the controversy that made its way into the limelight in the late 1980s to early 1990s was one episode in an ongoing debate.

But to understand the specific nature of the controversy surrounding the lyrics in heavy metal music and rap music, it is necessary to examine the two defining events that shaped this media discourse: the Senate hearing in 1985 and the arrests and trials of rap musicians and record store owners in Florida in 1990. The data in Table 48.1 indicate that these events focused the media discourse first on heavy metal music (in 1985, 13 of 15 mainstream articles addressed heavy metal) and later on rap music (in 1990, 33 of 48 mainstream articles addressed rap). In the intervening years, 1986 to 1989, mainstream media attention was more evenly split between the two music genres.

The Senate Hearing and Its Aftermath

Considered the "hottest ticket in town all year" (Gore, 1987), the 1985 standing-room-only Senate hearing launched a maelstrom of media debate about music lyrics. The competing arguments introduced at the hearing were generally used to discuss heavy metal for the duration of the five-year debate.

One of the most frequent arguments made about heavy metal music throughout the five-year controversy was introduced in 1985 by members of the PMRC and its witnesses. This argument, which I call the *corruption* frame, stated that explicit lyrics—whether glorifying suicide, anti-authority attitudes, or deviant sexual acts—have a

negative effect on children's attitudes. This frame emphasized the music's corrupting effect on young listeners rather than on the effects such listeners might have on the society at large. A five-minute speech delivered to the Senate Committee by PMRC witness Joe Steussy illustrates this frame:

> *Today's heavy metal music is categorically different from previous forms of popular music. . . . Its principal themes are, as you have already heard, extreme violence, extreme rebellion, substance abuse, sexual promiscuity and perversion, and Satanism. I know personally of no form of popular music before, which has had as one of its central elements the element of hatred. (U.S. Senate Hearing Before the Committee on Commerce, Science, and Transportation 1985, p. 117)*

The *corruption* frame also appeared frequently in the national press. In an article titled "How Shock Rock Harms Our Kids," one writer argued, "lyrics glamorize drug and alcohol use, and glorify death and violent rebellion, ranging from hatred of parents and teachers to suicide—the ultimate act of violence to oneself" (*Reader's Digest* July 1988, p. 101). The idea that children's values were corrupted by music received considerable play inside and outside the Capitol.

Like *corruption*, the *protection* frame was also introduced around the time of the Senate hearing and was prominent in references to heavy metal music throughout the five-year debate. Similar to the rhetoric found in *corruption*, this frame argued that parents and other adults must shield America's youth from offensive lyrics. Reflecting on her campaign against graphic lyrics, Tipper Gore (1987) wrote:

> *We feel as we do because we know that children are special gifts, and deserve to be treated with love and respect, gentleness and honesty. They deserve security and guidance about living, loving, and relating to other people. And they deserve vigilant protection from the excesses of adult society. (p. 46)*

While opinions varied over how best to protect children from the dangers of lyrics (some thought that lyrics should be labeled, while others thought laws should be enacted against harmful music), the underlying theme infusing this argument invoked adult responsibility, particularly as exercised by caring parents. In his discussion of heavy metal, William Safire wrote:

> I am a libertarian when it comes to the actions of consenting adults, and hoot at busybodies who try to impose bans on what non-violent grown-ups can say or read or do. With complete consistency, I am anti-libertarian when it comes to minors. Kids get special protections in law . . . and deserve protection from porn-rock profiteers. (New York Times 10 Oct. 1985, sect. 1, p. 31)

Danger to society was a third theme that emerged around the time of the Senate hearing, although arguments containing this frame were used infrequently in relation to the "white" music genre. In contrast to the *corruption* frame, which warned of harm to the individual, the *danger to society* frame warned that when lyrics glorify violence, all of society is at risk. As applied to heavy metal music, the argument focused largely on the satanic influences inherent in some heavy metal music, and warned that vulnerable youths under the music's spell might wreak havoc on innocent citizens. Paul King, a child and adolescent psychiatrist who testified at the Senate hearing on behalf of the PMRC, stated:

> One of the most pathological forms of evil is in the form of the cult killer or deranged person who believes it is OK to hurt others or to kill. The Son of Sam who killed eight people in New York was allegedly into Black Sabbath's music. . . . Most recently, the individual identified in the newspapers as the Night Stalker has been said to be into hard drugs and the music of the heavy metal band AC/DC. . . . Every teenager who listens to heavy metal certainly does not become a killer. [But] young people who are seeking power over others through identification with the power of evil find a close identification. The lyrics become a philosophy of life. It becomes a religion. (U.S. Senate Hearing Before the Committee on Commerce, Science, and Transportation 1985, p. 130)

In addition to cult-like violence, this frame—when it was used vis-à-vis heavy metal—suggested that violence against parents, teachers, and sometimes women could also result from listening to this music.

Of course, the serious charges brought against music lyrics by the PMRC and supportive media writers did not go unanswered, either at the Senate hearings or in the media. Music industry executives, outraged musicians, and media writers hastened to defend the content of contemporary music and the artistic integrity of its creators. These arguments appeared in the counter-frames that were produced in this debate.

Frank Zappa, John Denver, and Dee Snider (of the heavy metal band Twisted Sister) kicked off the attack against PMRC activities and concerns when they served as opposing witnesses at the Senate hearing, where these counterframes first widely appeared. One common argument, termed the *no harm* frame, argued that lyrics were not harmful to young listeners. Covering a variety of ideas around this central theme, this frame claimed that youthful audiences know that the cartoonish lyrics are not meant to be taken seriously, that songs with explicit lyrics represent a small minority of music, that music lyrics are a negligible part of the culture's barrage of sexual and violent images in the media, and that there is no causal connection between music and behavior. This last point was picked up by the media—one writer suggested that "the social impact of a heavy metal concert is belching" (*Time* 30 September 1985, p. 70). The *no harm* frame was often used in this sarcastic manner, where the writer argued that music was safe and belittled the concerns of the opposition.

Opponents of the PMRC also suggested that opposition to heavy metal's lyrics could be explained by the generation gap between Gore and her allies, and the youths they sought to protect. The *generation gap* frame was used at the Senate hearing and subsequently to point out that vulgarity, parental anxiety, and censorship are all perennial concerns, and that outrage expressed about music lyrics bespeaks a generation gap between parents and their children. Although this frame's rhetoric is clearly a subset of the *no harm* frame (e.g., the music isn't harmful, parents just perceive it as harmful), it differs from the *no harm* frame by making explicit the role of parents in the controversy surrounding lyrics. In an article that appeared two weeks after the Senate hearing, Russell Baker picked up the theme of misplaced, but predictable, parental concern:

> Stirred by the [PMRC] alarmed mothers, my mind began playing back the full repertory of bawdy, off-color, and just downright dirty songs it had gathered during years when my mother would have cringed if I let on that I knew a more emphatic way of saying "gosh darn it all to the dickens." (New York Times *13 Oct. 1985, sect. 6, p. 22)*

The *threat to authorities* frame, which is closely related to the *generation gap* frame, suggested that people in positions of political power felt most threatened by contemporary music. Using this argument to ridicule a competing critic's attack on music, one writer complained:

> [Mr. Goldman, a writer for the National Review] hallucinates rather luridly: "You needn't go to a slasher film to see a woman being disemboweled in a satanic ritual—just turn on your local music video station." No example is named. Such notions have been a right-wing staple for decades, and they'd be as risible as Mr. Goldman's article if legislators hadn't begun to take them seriously. (New York Times *26 Mar. 1989, sect. 2, p. 24)*

Here, the conservative right, which traditionally has caused trouble for youth culture, is blamed for the condemnation of music.

Witnesses at the Senate hearing and media writers frequently disparaged the concerns of the PMRC and its supporters by arguing that they advocated censorship. In one of the most colorful exchanges during the hearing, Frank Zappa charged that "the complete list of PMRC demands reads like an instruction manual for some sinister kind of toilet training program to housebreak all composers and performers because of the lyrics of a few" (U.S. Senate Hearing Before the Committee

on Commerce, Science, and Transportation 1985, p. 53). The *freedom of speech* frame maintained that labeling albums, printing lyrics on album covers, and encouraging musicians to use restraint restricted artists' First Amendment right to freedom of speech and created a "chilling effect" on expression. By arguing that "the real danger is presented not by rock music, but by those who want to control what should or should not be heard," this frame minimized the perceived threat of graphic lyrics by focusing on the dangers of abridging musicians' freedom of speech (*New York Times* 8 December 1985, sect. 11, p. 40).

In a vivid example of how this discourse about music was a media dialogue, the *freedom of speech* counterframe spawned a countercounterframe from media supporters of the PMRC, who claimed that they did not favor censorship. Writers sympathetic to the PMRC used the *not censorship* frame to defend their positions against accusations of censorship and presented themselves as providers of consumer information (to parents), not as enemies of free speech. Tipper Gore said:

> We do not and have not advocated restrictions on [freedom of speech]; we have never proposed government action. What we are advocating, and what we have worked hard to encourage, is responsibility. (Newsweek *29 May 1989, p. 6)*

Rap to the Fore: Framing 2 Live Crew

While most of the frames applied to heavy metal music were also applied to rap music, new concerns emerged as writers turned their attention to the "black" music genre. Some of these concerns were expressed in a frame new to the five-year debate, while others were voiced using frames already developed for heavy metal music.

For example, the *danger to society* frame was frequently used to talk about rap music following the arrests of 2 Live Crew in Florida. However, the concerns about the *types* of danger contained in rap lyrics differed sharply from the concerns about heavy metal. Rather than focusing on the dangers of one-in-a-million devil-worshipping mass killers, the *danger to society* frame as applied to rap much more pointedly emphasized that rap music created legions of misogynistic listeners who posed a danger to women, particularly because rap music depicted rape and other brutality. Providing a short inventory of women-harming abuses, one writer argued, "What we are discussing here is the wild popularity (almost 2 million records sold) of a group that sings about forcing anal sex on a girl and then forcing her to lick excrement. . . . Why are we so sure that tolerance of such attitudes has no consequences?" (*U.S. News and World Report* 2 July 1990, p. 15).

One counterframe that was specifically instituted for rap (although it later was occasionally applied to heavy metal) was the *important message/art* frame, which was used most dramatically around the time of the government actions against rap music in Florida.

The *important message/art* frame, which argued against the "harmful" position, asserted that rap lyrics have serious content. The frame includes statements about the important messages and concerns of rap music, the artistic expression contained in the music, the lyrics as a reflection of urban reality, and the fact that rappers were positive role models for young black listeners. Foreshadowing arguments that appeared four months later in the trial over 2 Live Crew lyrics, one media writer stated:

> In its constantly changing slang and shifting concerns—no other pop has so many anti-drug songs—rap's flood of words presents a fictionalized oral history of a brutalized generation. (New York Times *17 June 1990, sect. 4, p. 1*)

This frame argued that the music itself is worthy of serious contemplation, and that all people—black, white, young, old—could benefit from its important messages.

With the injection of new concerns in the *danger to society* frame and the emergence of the *important message/art* counterframe largely for rap, the set of frames used to analyze the discourse surrounding these two genres of music in the years 1985 through 1990 is complete.

RACIAL RHETORIC: MAPPING THE SHIFT IN FRAMES

The top half of Table 48.1 presents a percentage distribution of types of frames applied to heavy metal and rap music genres in mainstream publications. Mainstream media writers used certain frames about equally in their discussions of heavy metal and rap, suggesting that some frames were applicable to both genres. The *freedom of speech* and *not censorship* frames, for example, were about equally frequent in the discourse about both music forms. Both frames were used in 1985 in reference to heavy metal and continued to characterize the discourse about rap. Other frames, however, were applied primarily to one genre and not the other.

"Music Is Harmful" Frames

A pronounced shift occurred in the frames used to construct the "harmful" discourse in the mainstream media: Frames that were used most frequently to describe the dangers of heavy metal—*corruption* and *protection*—were rarely used to describe the harmfulness of rap music; conversely, the *danger to society* frame was prominent for rap music but not for heavy metal music. Thus, the frames used most often to decry heavy metal music were less salient for rap music, while the frames used most often to condemn rap music were less relevant for heavy metal music. The arguments represented by these frames may have been based on different referent images, given their disparate concerns.

The *corruption* frame, which accounted for more than one-third of all frames supporting the harmfulness of heavy metal music, concerned the music's effects on young listeners' values and behavior (e.g., the lyrics may lead some listeners to indulge in "self-destructive" activities). A corollary to this frame, the *protection* frame, urged parents and other adults to care enough about society's youth to get involved in activities that would guarantee their children's welfare. The *corruption* and *protection* frames together accounted for two-thirds of all "music-is-harmful" frames used in the mainstream press' discussion of heavy metal music.

The power of these frames derived from the referent images they evoked. Articles in which the *corruption* frame appeared often referred to the writers' own children (or children like theirs) being exposed to this dangerous material and the potential suffering because of it. Writer Kathy Stroud reported:

> *My 15-year-old daughter unwittingly alerted me to the increasingly explicit nature of rock music. "You've got to hear this Mom!" she insisted one afternoon . . . , "but don't listen to the words," she added, an instant tip-off to pay attention. The beat was hard and pulsating, the music burlesque in feeling. . . . Unabashedly sexual lyrics like these, augmented by orgasmic moans and howls, compose the musical diet millions of children are now being fed at concerts, on albums, on radio and MTV.* (Newsweek *6 May 1985, p. 14*)

And in another article titled "What Entertainers Are Doing to Your Kids," the following passage was one of many that charged that decent children were being exposed to obscene lyrics so that the music industry could profit:

> *President Reagan stepped into the fray in mid-October, venting outrage over music's messages. "I don't believe our Founding Fathers ever intended to create a nation where the rights of pornographers would take precedence over the rights of parents, and the violent and malevolent would be given free rein to prey upon our children," the President told a Republican political meeting. According to growing numbers of critics, irresponsible adults in the entertainment business are bedazzling the vulnerable young with a siren song of the darker sides of life. Violence, the occult, sadomasochism, rebellion, drug abuse, promiscuity, and homosexuality are constant themes.* (U.S. News and World Report *28 October 1985, p. 46*)

The frame's implicit message to the reader was that even privileged children from good homes were at risk from the lyrical content of heavy metal music. These arguments contended that *our own kids* were endangered by this music, a message that was absent from the frames used to discuss rap.

While the *corruption* and *protection* frames clearly emphasized the music's harmful effects on individual listeners, writers using these frames expressed little concern that the lyrics would have an unfortunate effect on other members of society. Except for a few references to satanic murders and abusiveness to women, articles using these two frames rarely mentioned the possibility that young listeners might violently direct their new-found rebellion, anti-authority sentiment, and heightened sexuality on the society at large.

The *danger to society* frame argued that changes in attitudes and behaviors stemming from lyrics endangered society as a whole (i.e., listening to lyrics that extol violence and the brutalization of women and police would lead to rape and murder). Nearly two-thirds of the "harmful" frames applied to rap music were the *danger to society* frame, compared to about one-tenth of the frames applied to heavy metal music.

It might be expected that in turning their attention from heavy metal to rap, media writers would have continued using the *corruption* frame and would have argued that rap lyrics harmed young black listeners by spreading messages that would lead to self-destructive behaviors. Because most writers considered rap lyrics to be even more explicit than the heavy metal messages, rap lyrics should have been framed as even more harmful to their young audience. Yet, rather than warning the American public that a generation of young black children was endangered by musical messages, the writers argued that the American public at large would suffer at the hands of these listeners as a result of rap music. Clearly, the listener's welfare was no longer the focus of concern.

Unlike the referent images of "my daughter" and "our own kids" that appeared in articles about heavy metal, the prominent rap frames referred to a very different young listener: a young, urban, black male, or more often a group of urban, black male youths. George Will, drawing on the same images, invoked in the Summer 1990 trial of the alleged Central Park rapists, wrote:

Fact: some members of a particular age and social cohort—the one making 2 Live Crew rich—stomped and raped [a] jogger to the razor edge of death, for the fun of it. Certainty: the coarsening of a community, the desensitizing of a society will have behavioral consequences. (Newsweek 30 July 1990, p. 64)

An article called "Some Reasons for Wilding," which appeared approximately one year before Will's, used the same referent image of the Central Park rape. In this article, Tipper Gore and Susan Baker stated:

"Wilding." It's a new word in the vocabulary of teenage violence. The crime that made it the stuff of headlines is so heinous, the details so lurid as to make them almost beyond the understanding of any sane human being. When it was over, a 28-year old woman, an investment banker out for a jog, was left brutally beaten, knifed, and raped by teenagers. . . . "It was fun," one of her suspected teenage attackers told the Manhattan district attorney's office. In the lockup they were nonchalantly whistling at a policewoman and singing a high-on-the-charts rap song about casual sex: "Wild Thing." (Newsweek 29 May 1989, p. 6)

In this passage, the teenagers—who from media accounts were known to be black and Hispanic—"nonchalantly" whistle and sing rap lyrics following their alleged crime spree. The image of listeners here (minority, urban youths) differs dramatically from the listeners portrayed in articles about heavy metal (white, middle-class teenagers). Furthermore, the referent images of the threats posed by these two groups of youths also changed. Whereas "our kids" listening to heavy metal lyrics might stray off their expected social tracks because of their incited disrespect for authority or early interest in sex, listeners to rap music were lamented not because their self-destructive activities were of great importance or concern, but because they would probably travel in packs, rape women, and terrorize society.

"Music Is Not Harmful" Counterframes

The arguments proclaiming that music was not harmful also shifted as the discussion turned from heavy metal to rap. While the *freedom of speech* and *threat to authorities* frames were used about equally for heavy metal and rap, the mainstream press used the three remaining frames (*generation gap, no harm,* and *important message/art*) differently for the two genres. The *generation gap* frame, which derided parents for following the age-old tradition of disliking their children's music, made up 25 percent of the "not harmful" frames applied in the discourse about heavy metal, but only 3 percent of the frames used in the discourse about rap. Thus, writers on the "not harmful" side of the debate also detected the *parental* concerns that infused the debate about heavy metal—concerns that were largely absent in the debate about rap. That mainstream writers on the "not harmful" side rarely used the *generation gap* frame to defend rap against parental assaults is another indication of invisibility of "parents" and "our kids" in the discourse about rap music.

Just as the *generation gap* frame was used disproportionately to defend heavy metal, so the *important message/art* frame was used asymmetrically by the mainstream press to defend rap. Led by the *New York Times,* 60 percent of the "not harmful" frames used for the "black" genre were the *important message/art* frame, compared to only 14 percent of the frames used for the "white" music form. Mainstream opinion writers described heavy metal music as exaggerated, cartoonish buffoonery that posed no danger to listeners (the *no harm* frame) while they legitimated rap as an authentic political and artistic communication from the streets (the *important message/art* frame). Variously described in the media as "folk art," a "fresh musical structure," a "cultural barometer," and "a communiqué from the underclass," rap was valorized as a serious cultural form by the *New York Times, Newsweek,* and *Time* (but not *U.S. News and World Report* or *Reader's Digest*). As suggested by other authors (Bourdieu [1979] 1984; Thompson 1990), elites, such as writers and readers of the *New York Times,* seem to have exerted a pervasive effort to adopt rap as an "authentic" cultural form (just as jazz, country music, and comic books had been adopted previously), but to dismiss heavy metal as inconsequential—the politically empty macho posturing of white males.

The *important message/art* frame also received considerable play in the two African-American magazines, *Ebony* and *Jet*. Of the 10 articles published about music lyrics in these magazines from 1985 to 1990, all were about rap (presumably the "white" genre was not of concern to black readers' children), and all argued that music was not harmful to children or society. Eight of the ten articles contained the *important message/art* frame.

Articles in *Ebony* and *Jet* consistently valorized rap music, assessing its lyrics as harmless and containing only positive and important messages from and for black youths. The African-American magazines also argued that the older black generation could learn something from rap: By listening to the lyrics of the music, black adults could comprehend the daily lives of their own children. . . .

CONCLUSION

I argue that media writers use frames selectively to represent the stories they tell. They choose from a set of social-cultural images to make their accounts convincing, compelling, and familiar to themselves and to their audiences. Although there are many different icons and memories that could be used to catch readers' imaginations, writers choose the same cultural images and memories over and over again to relate their concerns about an issue. This repeated use of certain images produces recognizable patterns of frames, which media writers use to comment on socially important issues.

In the discourse surrounding the harmfulness of music lyrics from 1985 to 1990, media writers in the mainstream press invoked different frames to address the "white" genre of heavy metal music than they used to discuss the "black" genre of rap music. They constructed images of race and adolescence to tell separate stories of the dangers lurking in the cultural expressions of the two distinct social groups. In doing so, they called upon memories of historical events and cultural icons to demonstrate the detrimental effects of these objects on their audiences and on society as a whole. These racially charged frames were most powerful when they built on the stated or unstated fears and anxieties of readers and tapped into their audience's understandings of what white youths and black youths were like.

Finally, in using these frames, writers provided audiences with a map for understanding what was wrong with the younger generation—whether it was their "own kids" or urban, poor, black kids. This map portrayed a causal relationship between music and behavior and explained phenomena like teen suicide, sex, and violence as consequences of explicit lyrics. These explanatory frames made no reference to such existential conditions as teens' feelings of hopelessness or powerlessness, or to material concerns like diminishing economic prospects. . . .

REFERENCES

Bourdieu, Pierre. [1979] 1984. *Distinction: A Social Critique of the Judgement of Taste.* Cambridge, MA: Harvard University Press.

Goffman, Erving. 1974. *Frame Analysis.* Cambridge, MA: Harvard University Press.

Gore, Tipper. 1987. *Raising PG Kids in an X-Rated Society.* Nashville, TN: Abingdon Press.

McDonald, James. 1988. "Censoring Rock Lyrics: A Historical Analysis of the Debate." *Youth and Society* 19:294–313.

Peterson, Richard. 1972. "A Process Model of the Folk, Pop, and Fine Art Phases of Jazz," pp. 135–151 in *American Music: From Storyville to Woodstock,* edited by C. Nanry. New Brunswick, NJ: Transaction Books.

Rosenbaum, Jill Leslie, and Lorraine Prinsky. 1991. "The Presumption of Influence: Recent Responses to Popular Music Subcultures." *Crime and Delinquency* 37:528–535.

Snow, David, E. Burke Rochford, Steven Worden, and Robert Benford. 1986. "Frame Alignment Processes, Mobilization, and Movement Participation." *American Sociological Review* 51:464–481.

Thompson, John. 1990. *Ideology and Modern Culture.* Palo Alto, CA: Stanford University Press.

U.S. Senate Hearing before the Committee on Commerce, Science, and Transportation. 1985. *Contents of Music and the Lyrics of Records.* Washington, D.C.: U.S. Government Printing Office.

TATTOOS ARE LIKE POTATO CHIPS . . . YOU CAN'T HAVE JUST ONE

D. ANGUS VAIL

The *Hartford Courant* (1997) recently reported the results from an American Business Information, Inc., survey listing the top six growth businesses in 1996. Along with the expected high-tech entries such as Internet service, a decidedly unexpected industry made the list: Tattooing. Similar attention has come to tattooing by way of recent *New York Times, New York Post,* and "All Things Considered" stories on the recent legalization of tattooing in New York City after a 37-year ban. In the following pages, I discuss how those who are largely responsible for tattooing's growth become "collectors"—heavily tattooed.

INTRODUCTION

People learn how to become deviant. How each individual learns his or her particular brand of deviance depends on the kind of deviance in which she or he participates. Professional thieves learn their trade from other professional thieves (Sutherland 1937), marijuana users learn how to smoke marijuana and how to interpret the drug's effects from other marijuana users (Becker 1963), and tattoo collectors learn how to interpret tattoos from those who wear them (Vail 1997).

That deviance is a learned process is well documented. Deviance theories have explained many expressions of deviance. One form of deviance not yet examined in the sociological literature, however, is tattoo collecting. In the following pages, I examine how tattoo collectors learn to become collectors.

In discussing how one becomes a tattoo collector, I discuss how collectors learn about aesthet-

ics appropriate for their body suits, what motifs appropriately and accurately convey their ideas, iconographies appropriate for those motifs, and how to choose artists to complete their collections. I frame this discussion in Matza's (1969) theory of affinity, affiliation, and signification and the phenomenology of Alfred Schutz (1962, 1967).

METHOD

Data for this article were collected through several ethnographic and auto-ethnographic methods. I conducted most interviews at a recent four-day tattoo convention in the southeastern United States. I conducted in-depth, semi-structured interviews with tattoo collectors and artists at the convention site. I also conducted formal interviews with artists and collectors in California and Connecticut.

Informal field conversations with tattoo artists and collectors (from Austria, Australia, France, Japan, Switzerland, California, Connecticut, Michigan, New Jersey, New Mexico, Ohio, Oregon, and Texas), participant observation at tattoo conventions, participation in the tattoo subculture for the past 12 years, and over 150 hours getting tattooed have all provided me with preliminary data on which to base my suppositions. The data taken from these "less formal" observational techniques have been recorded in ethnographic field notes over the past four years.

I collected further secondary interview data from videos focusing on prominent "fine-art" tattoo artists from the San Francisco Bay area (Stearns 1988, 1990).

BECOMING AND BEING A COLLECTOR

Becoming a tattoo collector is a transformative experience in more ways than one. This transformation is physical (i.e., one actually alters skin pigmentation), psychological, and subcultural. Becoming a collector involves not only changing the way that light reflects off one's skin, but also the way that others view that skin and the person inside it. The images one chooses and the ways one combines them say a lot, not only about the person who has chosen them, but also about who has influenced those choices. For example, Ch_, an arborist, describes his collection as follows.

CH_: For my arm-band, I went out in the woods and cut a piece of branch with bittersweet around it . . . because . . . I climb trees and work outdoors . . . a lot doing tree removals and pruning and shit like that. . . . And this one over here . . . is sort of like . . . a protector. That's my climber line with my protecting dragons on either end. And then the third one [is] my back. . . . That design [a graphic depiction of a bare tree] came from . . . my belt buckle. . . . T_r did both of these pieces [on the lower legs]. This one here, I said, "I want some leaves in it. I want the Polynesian design, [Celtic] design, a band around by calf, but I want leaves in it." What he did was put in unfolding springtime ferns.

. . . American fine-art tattooing is, in many respects, a melting pot of motifs and aesthetics. The current tattoo renaissance encompasses such diverse styles as photorealism, cybertech, traditional Japanese style, neotribalism, and any number of combinations of the above. Artists have also made profound technical advances.

Although the meaning of specific tattoos is inherently individual, people learn how to build their collections from other people. It takes a great deal of research for one to become intimately familiar with a particular motif and the iconography appropriate to use within it. It takes still more comparative research to figure out what styles and/or motifs one will use in building one's collection.

Some do this research using tattoo magazines and some learn through symbolic interaction with other collectors and artists. In the end, however, collectors learn how to become collectors.

Learning to Become a Collector: Affinity

Matza (1969) discussed the process of becoming deviant. Although tattoos are less a statement of deviance than they once were, becoming heavily tattooed still stands outside social norms. Becoming a collector requires devotion to a lifestyle that is more marginal than that associated with fraternities or "tasteful" flowers. In short, one must want to become a collector. This desire is what Matza (1969:90–100) called *affinity*. "[Affinity] may be regarded as a natural biographical tendency borne of personal and social circumstance that suggests but hardly compels a direction of movement" (P. 93). In essence, affinity refers to a person's *desire to become deviant*. Comments like the following were common among respondents both in formal interviews and in informal field conversations.

CH_: My wife's been collecting for about 20 years, off and on, small pieces. And I've always wanted one, I just, y'know, never came across the right idea or the right person to do it.

Ch_ is not alone in having always wanted a tattoo. However, not everyone who gets one tattoo becomes a collector.

To make the jump from having tattoos to being a collector, one must first have an affinity for being a collector. Here, I mean not only wearing tattoos (often, but not necessarily, many of them), but conceiving of oneself as tattooed.

Several of the people that I just talked to discussed becoming collectors in terms of starting with just one tattoo and building their collections from that starting point. The experience of getting several small, bad tattoos as a start seems to be a common one. It is only after they start to conceive of themselves as collectors, however, that they . . . begin to visualize their collections as conceptual and stylistic wholes. This becomes apparent by start-ing their collections by covering their old, small tattoos. This cover work tends to evolve in either geographic (i.e., specific areas of the body) or con-ceptual patterns. (field notes)

This excerpt from my field notes speaks to how people express themselves differently once they have conceived of themselves as tattooed as opposed to wearing tattoos. The tattoos with which they started are pictures in their skin. The collections that they have started to build represent a new self-image: that of the tattoo collector. Part of what allows the collector to fully realize this transition is what Matza (1969) called *affiliation*.

Learning to Become a Collector: Affiliation

"Affiliation describes the process by which the sub-ject is *converted* to conduct novel for him but al-ready established for others" (Matza 1969:101). This process has also been analyzed by Sutherland (1937, 1939) as "differential association." Accord-ing to both Sutherland and Matza, deviance is taught in symbolic interaction with successful de-viants. "[Sutherland's] method of affiliation harbors an idea of conversion. . . . Unless one always was deviant, in which case little illumination is required, *becoming deviant* [emphasis added] depends on being converted" (Matza 1969:106–7). Thus, the collector learns how to feel good about becoming a collector, as well as learning where to place his or her tattoos. She or he learns how to become a col-lector *from other collectors and tattooers.*

As previously mentioned, for this conversion to be successful, one must want to be converted. Hence, affinity and affiliation work together in creating both deviance and deviants.

Respondents typically talked about tattooing as a desirable experience, the quality of which af-fected the perceived quality of the tattoo more than the crispness of lines or the boldness of the shad-ing. In this way, collectors and artists alike see be-coming collectors in terms of recruitment.

L_: What goes into a great tattoo is, I guess, is the experience, because it's like a personal album

or something. . . . It's like a montage of your life. That's why the Japanese said I got tat-tooed for memories, and he got tattooed for a story. Some stupid fucking Japanese, Orien-tal story, he got tattooed for, y'know?

The pejorative "some stupid fucking Japanese, Oriental story" shows how L_ views the appropri-ate way to become tattooed. For L_, collectors should get tattooed to hold on to their memories. For him, the Japanese notion of getting tattooed for a story is inappropriate.

Other collectors view tattoos as a means of expression of personal spirituality and, thus, a moral enterprise.

SH_: For me to do a tattoo on somebody that runs against the grain of my philosophical life, it's impossible, it's just not going to happen. Y'know, if somebody comes to me and says "I want a tattoo of dismembered babies" and whatever, I'm like, "Sorry."

In this statement, Sh_ shows how he goes about recruiting select people into his philosophical ap-proach to tattooing. He not only is concerned with expressing himself artistically, he is concerned with teaching people that tattoos should be a means of positive self-expression. By turning away work that he finds indicative of destructive tendencies, he is not only strengthening the re-solve of those he tattoos, he is also telling those whom he refuses to work on that their notion of what is acceptable for tattooing is flawed. In essence, he is recruiting "the right kind of people" into the tattoo world.

Sh_ also recruits through means other than tat-tooing or showing his collection. The following ex-change shows how his beliefs of the appropriate reasons for becoming tattooed run counter to com-mon misconceptions about the exhibitionistic ten-dencies of tattoo collectors. In essence, becoming a collector involves learning how to act like one.

DAV: Do you ever exhibit your collection?
SH_: No. Because they're real personal, my tattoos. I always get asked to take my clothes off, but I never do. And the line that I always give . . . is

that when you start taking your clothes off, nobody listens to what you have to say. You lose credibility real fast.

Both tattooers and collectors teach other collectors about appropriate "use of the [body as a] canvas." Fine-art tattoos take into account musculature, size, shape, and texture of a given area of the collector's body. Fine-art "backpieces," for example, incorporate the breadth of the collector's shoulders and narrowness of his or her waist in the design. Another example is Filip Leu's watershed color portrait of Jimi Hendrix (Bannatyne 1992:52), done on my right thigh in 1992. Because the thigh is roughly the same size as a face and follows similar outlines (roughly oval), the portrait used all of the canvas, and used it appropriately.

[A] collector, Sa_, learned about appropriate use of the canvas [body] from her husband (a tattoo collector and motorcycle mechanic). Her collection, still in its initial stages, is of gargoyles.

Currently, she has four gargoyles, all of similar size and style. They begin on her left shoulder and descend down the center of her back. Eventually, they will finish on her right hip, connected by vines. She was not ready to get a full back piece, but she had seen other women's backs, tattooed in the same basic shape, in tattoo magazines. As she described it to me, the contours of the string of gargoyles accent her figure. Also, the design leaves two fairly large open canvases. (field notes)

Hence, Sa_ has learned about appropriate use of the canvas and has shown respect for its shape and possibilities. She learned about use and respect for the canvas from other collectors (her husband and collectors in tattoo-oriented publications) and from her artists.

These interviewees were recruited, and continue to recruit others, by learning and sharing what makes a tattoo (and/or a tattooer) good. Although every respondent talked about the artistic ability of his or her tattooer(s), 75 percent said that technique was less important than rapport. In a sense, then, collecting is based more on feeling a connection with an artist than acquiring "fine art." Now that they see themselves as collectors, they

are going to make this self-applied label work for them. This is the final element of Matza's (1969) process of becoming deviant: *signification*.

Learning to Become a Collector: Signification

After one learns the techniques of being deviant, one often reconceptualizes one's life in terms of that deviance. In discussing "indication," Matza (1969:165) elaborated on this notion of identity building among professional thieves.

Quite different from consequence, indication points the subject to a consideration of himself; to the question of the unity of meaning of the various things he does and the relation of those things to what he conceivably is. To consider the possibility that the theft was important in the sense of being indicative of him puts the subject well into actively collaborating in the growth of deviant identity by building its very meaning.

In essence, once deviants have internalized their deviant labels, they reconceptualize their actions in terms of being appropriate for people who are "like that." Tattoo collectors see collecting as *appropriate for tattooed people*. This can have profound effects on how they view their collections as well as appropriate ways to display them.

As I said in the section on affiliation, once collectors begin to think of themselves as collectors, they often begin to plan how each new tattoo will work within the canvas. An aspect of collecting that exhibits signification is working around public skin. Co_ illustrates this point nicely.

Co_ is working on a full body suit, accompanied by facial piercings and satyr-horn implants on either side of his widow's peak at the hairline. The following excerpt from field notes shows how Co_ has planned his suit, at various stages, to *combine his tattooed identity with one that is acceptable to those outside the subculture.*

[Before] he became a full-time tattooer and piercer . . . his crew chief wouldn't let him work with any . . . tattoos showing. So, he had to get long-sleeved t-shirts to cover the tattoos that went to his elbow. He [has subsequently covered his

arms] down to the wrists and is now going on to the tops of his hands. He said that he . . . is thinking about leaving the collar untattooed and, that way, he can take out the facial piercings and put on a hat and go out in public with a long-sleeved shirt and still look somewhat respectable.

Thus, even though Co_ is obviously devoted to body modification, he still is concerned with getting along in normative society. By leaving open canvas at the collar, he will be able to pass (Goffman 1963; Garfinkel 1967) more easily. Other collectors are less concerned with passing than with planning their remaining space.

L_'s collection has been complete for about 20 years, but in the following excerpt from our interview he recalls when he realized what he had to do to finish the collection.

L_: Well, yeah. You look at yourself and you just, y'know, you see that there are these spaces that just need to be filled up. It's not that you're comparing yourself to someone else, or some kind or image, it's just that those spaces aren't complete. It's like you're on a course and you've gotta finish it. . . . Most tattoo suits fit within standard barriers. Some people go above and beyond, but the prescribed cover job is like, a neck band, ankle bands, wrist bands, put a cargo net underneath your nuts and then just fill the rest of it up. So when it's done, you can tell.

Thus, L_ completed his collection within "standard barriers." He filled his canvas from those barriers into the body of the suit.

CONCLUSION

Collecting tattoos is both an individual and a collective journey. Collectors must choose their own designs for their own reasons. Yet, they learn how to incorporate those designs into collections from others who have been successful in building collections. Some have attempted to explain what these collections mean. I believe this is a fruitless endeavor. However, studying the tattoo collection process sheds light on several broader sociological and phenomenological issues.

Tattoo collecting incorporates all three of Matza's (1969) stages of becoming deviant (i.e., affinity, affiliation, and signification). As becoming a collector involves both considerable financial commitment and physical and stigmatic discomfort, it requires devotion to the process. In short, a collector's affinity must be strong.

Collectors must also learn how to become collectors. They must learn how to evaluate tattoos and tattooers. This involves learning how to evaluate technique and how to build rapport. Collectors must also learn how to best represent the tattoo subculture. This involves learning techniques of passing (Goffman 1963; Garfinkel 1967) and consensus building. They learn these things through affiliation with other collectors.

Finally, collectors, learn how to [confirm] their new master statuses (Becker 1963) as collectors, not just as people with tattoos. They begin to view their collections in the future-perfect tense (Schutz 1962, 1967), as collections that will-have-been-completed. This process of navigating signification from both within and without the tattoo world involves respecting the canvas as it is and as it will be.

In becoming tattooed, the collector learns not only how well-established members of the tattoo world conceive of "proper" use of form and iconography in building a collection, but also how to see him- or herself as a tattooed person. Although some may consider the distinction between those who have tattoos and those who are tattooed a semantic one, semantics, in this case, are important.

In discussing those who have tattoos, the analyst (be that person a sociologist, anthropologist, or psychologist) assumes a possessive relationship between the person and the dermographic embellishment that she or he has purchased. In essence, this person's tattoos are no different than the car she or he drives or the hair style she or he sports on any given day. Like these adornments, tattoos represent possessions that can be considered with or without the individual who wears them.

The collector, on the other hand, sees him- or herself as tattooed, not just as the owner of the pigments residing in the first layer of his or her dermis. The images that adorn the collector's canvas are, as L_ so colorfully stated earlier in this article, his or her memories made physical. To the collector, tattoos are not something one owns. Rather, they are a part of him or her, no less important than the color of his or her hair or skin and no more easily removed from his or her identity than his or her deepest beliefs, most profound concerns, or idiosyncratic sense of humor. In short, the collector does not see himself as John who has tattoos but as John who is tattooed.

Because, for the collector, tattoos represent a master status, all of his or her actions, beliefs, fears, and hopes can be seen in his or her collection. How those personal characteristics become part of the collection only the collector knows.

That they are there, however, is irrefutable. The fact that they are there affects not only the ways that collectors see themselves, but also the ways that others see them. In short, their tattoos have profound effects on their interactions with intimates and nonintimates alike.

The recent attention that the news media have paid to tattooing speaks volumes to the relevance of this topic. With tattoo shops being ranked among the six fastest growing industries in the nation (Hartford *Courant* 1997), and the recent legalization of tattooing in New York City (Hardt 1997; Kennedy 1997a, 1997b; National Public Radio 1997), we, as sociologists, have a unique opportunity to demystify the processes involved in enacting a cultural phenomenon that is rapidly losing its deviant status.

REFERENCES

Bannatyne, Bryce, ed. 1992. *Forever Yes: Art of the New Tattoo.* Honolulu, HI: Hardy Marks.

Becker, Howard S. 1963. *Outsiders: Studies in the Sociology of Deviance.* New York: Free Press.

Garfinkel, Harold. 1967. *Studies in Ethnomethodology.* Cambridge, MA: Blackwell.

Goffman, Erving. 1963. *Stigma: Notes on the Management of Spoiled Identity.* New York: Touchstone.

Hardt, Robert, Jr. 1997. "City Ends Tattoo Taboo Only Mom Could Love." *New York Post,* February 26, p. 4.

Hartford Courant. 1997. "Have You Heard?" March 1, p. F1.

Kennedy, Randy. 1997a. "Cappuccino with Your Tattoo? Try That on a Sailor." *New York Times,* July 27, pp. 31–2.

———. 1997b. "City Council Gives Tattooing Its Mark of Approval." *New York Times,* February 26, pp. B1–B5.

Matza, David. 1969. *Becoming Deviant.* Englewood Cliffs, NJ: Prentice-Hall.

National Public Radio. 1997. All Things Considered. (Story on legalization of tattooing in New York City). March 16.

Schutz, Alfred. 1962. *Collected Papers.* Vol. I, *The Problem of Social Reality,* edited by Maurice Natanson. Boston: Martinus Nijhoff.

———. 1967. *The Phenomenology of the Social World.* Translated by George Walsh and Frederick Lehnert with an Introduction by George Walsh. Evanston, IL: Northwestern University Press.

Stearns, Michael O. *Tattooing Reality: Hardy & Associates Make Their Marks* (video). San Francisco: Metamorphosis II Productions.

———. 1990. *Frisco Skin and Tattoo Ink.* (video). San Francisco: Metamorphosis II Productions.

Sutherland, Edwin H. 1937. *The Professional Thief* Chicago: University of Chicago Press.

———. 1939. *Principles of Criminology.* 3d ed. New York: Lippincott.

Vail, D. Angus. 1997. "Angels and Dragons: The Social Meanings of Tattoos." Paper presented at the annual meeting of the Popular Culture Association, Arlington, Texas.

50

PANHANDLERS: OVERCOMING THE NONPERSON TREATMENT

STEPHEN E. LANKENAU

Some of the people just walk by and don't say nothin'. I call them zombies [laughs]. You ask them for change and they don't say "yes," "no," or "maybe I be back." They just walk by you like they don't even see you—it's like I'm not even sitting there. They could say "I ain't got none" or "no" or something. They just walk by.

—Alice, a homeless panhandler

We use a variety of ploys to avoid the gaze or overtures extended by panhandlers—we avert our eyes, quicken our pace, increase the volume on our headphones. Some panhandlers manage to capture our attention, less frequently our money, using humor, offering services, telling stories, or by using other dramatic devices. A close examination of the exchanges between panhandler and passersby reveals that these interactions occur within a multilayered, theatrical context; dramas are enacted at the face-to-face level yet display the larger social relations among the poor and nonpoor.

Goffman's (1959) dramaturgical perspective presents social life as a play in which persons or actors conduct themselves before various audiences according to scripted roles. Compared with the exchanges among everyday persons, however, interactions between panhandler and pedestrian more closely resemble the basic structural features of a play. The panhandler, who is the main actor, is like an improvisational performer who uses a repertoire of pieces or numbers to accomplish the act of panhandling. I refer to a panhan-

dler's collection of these actions as his or her panhandling repertoire. Similarly, in reaction to the performer, pedestrians serve as the audience and respond to the panhandling routine by selecting from a menu of responses, like engaging or ignoring the panhandler. Being ignored by a passerby, which Goffman (1963) referred to as the "nonperson treatment," is a primary problem confronted by panhandlers, but one that is directly addressed through a repertoire of panhandling routines.

On the basis of ethnographic observations and interviews of panhandlers on the streets of Washington, DC, I have conceptualized five primary panhandling routines: the entertainer, the greeter, the servicer, the storyteller, and the aggressor. These routines are premised on using various props, manipulating self-presentation, and engaging the sympathies and emotions of passersby. The fact that I am categorizing panhandlers according to various routines, however, does not necessarily imply that certain individuals are acting or feigning need and distress. Rather, panhandling repertoires are one way of describing the public dramas between panhandler and passersby.

THE NONPERSON TREATMENT: A PRIMARY PROBLEM FACING PANHANDLERS

The nonperson treatment of panhandlers, that is, passing by a panhandler as though he or she did not exist, originates in a disposition characterizing many city dwellers, which Simmel ([1903] 1971) called the "blasé attitude." The blasé attitude stems from the constant stimulation found in a city and causes inhabitants to react to new situations with minimal energy or to disregard differences between things. Often, the city commuter's or resident's blasé attitude renders any particular panhandler as an unremarkable or meaningless figure against the backdrop of ubiquitous panhandling and homelessness.

In particular, passersby with the blasé attitude commonly cast panhandlers into the role of the stranger (Simmel [1908] 1971). The stranger is defined by a combination of nearness and remoteness—nearness because one resides within the [same] area and remoteness because one is not integrated into any particular social body. Additionally, the interaction between stranger and other is characterized by various degrees of *strangeness* as a result of this tension between the qualities of nearness and remoteness. Panhandlers resemble the stranger as they, as fellow human beings, stand in close proximity to pedestrians by virtue of asking for money along sidewalks or at subway stations, yet remain distant from these same individuals owing to certain stigmas.

For instance, negative stereotypes of homeless persons, such as being dangerous, dirty, diseased, and mentally ill, are often connected to panhandlers, which then fuels a fearful desire to maintain a certain physical distance from panhandlers (Liebow 1993; Wagner 1993). Similarly, owing to the common associations between poverty and crime in the minds of middle-class persons (Reiman 1970), panhandlers are often merged into the "dangerous class." Additionally, race and gen-

der differences also add strangeness as the great majority of panhandlers in this study are Black and male, whereas the pedestrian population in contact with the panhandling population is much more racially diverse and gender balanced. In particular, because the typical Washington, DC panhandler is a Black man, non-Black panhandlers or female panhandlers who initiate encounters may "break frame" (Goffman 1974)—disrupt the stereotypical racial or gender expectations circumscribing the larger panhandling population. Some passersby may have legitimate reasons for ignoring panhandlers who engage them publicly—regardless of appearances or intentions—on the basis of gender and age mismatches or owing to past violent encounters with strangers.

Hence, a general disposition among urbanites—the blasé attitude—compounded by a variety of stigmas affixed to panhandlers often cause each to be viewed as a stranger. These attitudes and perspectives among passersby typically prompt a particular response toward panhandlers and their overtures for money or food—the nonperson treatment. A person withholding glances or close scrutiny of another and effectively treating the other as though he or she did not exist characterizes the nonperson treatment.

In general, the nonperson treatment is one type of interaction occurring among unfamiliar persons in public places. When approaching a stranger in public, one typically ignores the other completely; provides the other with a subtle, noninvasive form of acknowledgment; or explicitly engages the other in some fashion. Goffman (1963) referred to these three types of interactions, respectively, as the nonperson treatment, civil inattention, and encounter or face engagement.

As suggested earlier by Alice, passersby commonly direct the nonperson treatment toward panhandlers. Pedestrians accomplish the nonperson treatment by effectively using props to pretend that the panhandler is neither seen nor heard or by simply looking down or straight ahead as though the panhandler were an inanimate object, like a tree or statue. From a panhandler's perspective, passersby using these variations of the nonperson treatment appear then as "zombies." Such explicit attempts to avoid and ignore reveal that the nonperson treatment is sometimes a conscious form of interaction rather than a passive or default disposition.

Viewed collectively, actions taken by pedestrians are also drawn from a dramaturgical repertoire of routines; that is, the nonperson treatment, civil inattention, and face engagements constitute routines used by pedestrians to address the encounter treatment initiated by panhandlers. Although not fully developed in this article, the exchanges between pedestrian and panhandler involve the interaction of repertoires. Pedestrians, however, typically control the interaction given their ability to regard the panhandler as a nonperson.

A NEW APPROACH
TO STUDYING PANHANDLERS

I propose that panhandlers devise a repertoire of panhandling routines to break out of the role of stranger or to awaken pedestrians from the blasé state; these dramaturgical actions then minimize the nonperson treatment and pave the way for encounters. Framing panhandling according to a repertoire of actions represents a different analytical approach to the study of panhandler practices and problems. Most prior research on the subject presents typologies that often lack analytical precision. Although these studies offer useful descriptive categories, such as white-collar beggars (Anderson [1923] 1961), child beggars (Freund 1925), store beggars (Gilmore 1940), professional beggars (Wallace 1965), executive beggars (Igbinova 1991), and character beggars (Williams 1995), I argue that they fail to provide a thorough understanding of the phenomenon of panhandling and of the problems faced by panhandlers.

First, past analyses often construct typologies that portray panhandlers not as actors but as types lacking agency and versatility. In contrast, panhandling repertoires highlight the drama and dynamism that often underlay the act of panhandling. I demonstrate how panhandlers confront ambivalent or negative reactions by using one or more routines in a single encounter. Ultimately, framing panhandling in terms of repertoires represents a departure from previous analyses as this strategy typifies action rather than essentializes or rigidifies persons.

Second, prior research typically fails to conceptualize panhandling in terms of interaction between two unequal sets of actors, the panhandler and the passerby. Framing panhandling as a theatrical exchange between two classes of actors with dissimilar material resources, different interactional objectives, and contrasting viewpoints, however, is a critical factor toward understanding the repertoire of routines enacted by panhandlers. Despite these inequalities, this analysis shows that panhandling repertoires lead to exchanges between the zombie and the stranger and thereby foster greater understanding among both classes of actors.

METHOD

I define a panhandler as a person who publicly and regularly requests money or goods for personal use in a face-to-face manner from unfamiliar others without offering a readily identifiable or valued consumer product or service in exchange for items received. Throughout the sampling process, I largely selected panhandlers who appeared mentally and physically fit for regular employment. Among both policymakers and the population at large, these able-bodied, often homeless individuals are generally regarded as the nondeserving poor (Wright 1989), that is, persons viewed as undeserving of sympathy or assistance as they violate basic norms surrounding work. I learned during interviews, however, that these seemingly fit fronts often belied health problems and circumstances that inhibited gainful employment, particularly work requiring physical stamina and strength. For instance, many panhandlers reported mild to serious illnesses and injuries occurring largely before their entry into panhandling, such as back and leg injuries, poorly healed broken bones, knife and gunshot wounds, burns, diabetes, and HIV exposure. Others admitted to past or current drug and alcohol problems, and a few appeared to have mental difficulties. However, no single health factor typically explained entry into panhandling and homelessness. Rather, a constellation of problems, including unemployment, homelessness, family conflicts, or health factors, often characterized each panhandler.

During the data collection period, which spanned from December 1994 to August 1996, I sampled mornings, afternoons, and evenings on both weekdays and weekends within five contiguous neighborhoods or sections of northwest Washington, DC. This area covered a three-mile corridor beginning in a largely White, well-educated, and affluent residential neighborhood at the northern point and terminating in a large downtown business section at the southern end. Both a major avenue and a common subway line connect four of these regions. I undertook about 80 official data collection efforts into this area, which were accomplished largely on foot since I lived in one of the five neighborhoods. Including interviews, each journey usually lasted between two and five hours. At the end of the data collection period in August 1996, I typically was able to identify two out of three panhandlers within this corridor as someone whom I had either interviewed or informally spoken to previously.

Interviews ($N = 37$) were tape recorded and followed a series of open-ended questions focusing on four aspects of the panhandler's experience: street work, relationships, self-issues, and demographics. Panhandlers received $10 for their tape-recorded interviews, which typically lasted between 45 minutes and an hour. On meeting a panhandler for the first time, I usually established basic rapport by giving $0.50, which was then followed by an explanation that I was a student studying panhandling. Other relevant information that may have influenced rapport with each panhandler is that I am White, male, and of a middle-class background. Only a handful of panhandlers, however, refused to be interviewed. In addition to these formal interviews, I informally spoke with dozens of other panhandlers and posed as a panhandler for two consecutive days in downtown Washington, DC.

On the basis of the formal interviews, the profile of the typical panhandler in this sample is as follows: a Black, single, unemployed homeless man in his early 40s who was born into a lower or working-class family in the District of Columbia and who possessed a high school degree or higher. In addition, the typical panhandler began panhandling in his mid-30s or early 40s and had been panhandling consistently for the past five years after losing a job in the construction industry. A negative life event or events, such as an accident, an illness, a spell of homelessness, a layoff, or a drug or alcohol problem generally preceded job losses.

Largely owing to the disproportionate number of male panhandlers, only three female panhandlers were included in the sample of 37 persons. In addition, the city's demographic composition partially explains the high proportion of African American panhandlers in the sample: The District of Columbia is predominantly populated by African Americans (65.8 percent in 1990) and poverty and homelessness are most acute among African Americans (D.C. Government, 1993). When comparing my sample of panhandlers to a study of Washington, DC, homeless individuals conducted by the National Institute on Drug Abuse (NIDA) in 1991, the NIDA sample captured a greater proportion of women, younger persons, White and Hispanic individuals, less educated persons, and employed individuals. Only a small proportion of the NIDA sample reported panhandling on a regular basis.

All quotations in this article are by persons who gave their informed consent to participate in this research. All names in this study are pseudonyms, and certain biographical details have been deleted or altered to protect anonymity.

FINDINGS

Panhandling Repertoires

Panhandlers overcome the nonperson treatment by initiating encounters through the use of dramaturgical techniques, routines, acts, pieces, or numbers, which I collectively call panhandling repertoires. Often enacted in a performancelike manner, repertoires capture the attention and interest of passersby by appealing to a range of emotional qualities, such as amusement, sympathy, and fear.

I have conceptualized five primary panhandling routines: the entertainer, the greeter, the servicer, the storyteller, and the aggressor, along with strategies within certain routines. The entertainer offers music or humor, the greeter provides cordiality and deference, the servicer supplies a kind of service, the storyteller presents a sad or sympathetic tale, and the aggressor deals in fear and intimidation. Generally, the entertainer and greeter attempt to produce enjoyment or good feelings, whereas the storyteller and aggressor elicit more serious or hostile moods. The servicer, who occupies a more neutral position, is focused on providing some sort of utility. Fundamentally, the moods or impressions created by the routines are largely attempts to attenuate strangeness or awaken pedestrians from their blasé condition, which then paves the way for an encounter and possible contributions.

Storyteller

Of all the panhandling routines, the storyteller approach most clearly conveys the dramaturgical nature of panhandling. The storyteller routine is based on using stories to evoke understanding, pity, or guilt from pedestrians. The primary message is need in virtually all cases. Stories consist of various signs, appearances, lines, or narratives that focus on shaking pedestrians from their blasé state. The storyteller routine is then accomplished by means of one or more specific subroutines: the silent storyteller, the sign storyteller, the line storyteller, and the hard luck storyteller. Here, Duane, a long-time homeless panhandler, points to the tactics or arts of capturing the sympathy of passersby with a good story:

What makes my panhandlin' successful and any other panhandlin' successful is the emotions. Now if you were reared in a good moral background and I come up to you [he pulls his face close—about six inches away], "Excuse me sir, I'm really tired. I just moved in and I've got five kids. Me and my wife—we can't get jobs." Now when you say the word kids—"Forget me—I've got babies I'm tryin'

to feed." Or sickness—"I'm dyin' " or "my wife, my mother." More than just I'm givin' them money to get something to eat. These things are tactics. They'll be touched.

In addition to narratives, stories are conveyed symbolically through down-and-out facial expressions, as Ray indicates:

People look at me—the way I talk and you know—feel sorry for me. They know I'm homeless by the way I'm lookin'! And I give them a sad little look.

Clothing, appearances, and presentation of self may also be manipulated or used to tell the desired story. In fact, becoming a successful storyteller is contingent on developing a look that works, as Fox suggests:

When I first started panhandling I couldn't understand why people weren't giving me money—I looked too clean. So I grew this ratty beard and figured so that's the trick of the trade. As long as I was looking presentable like I was doing a 9-to-5 job—say working as a computer specialist—I wasn't getting a dime [laughs].

Hence, storytellers may have to consciously manage their appearance more than others to foster the impression of need. On buying or receiving new or secondhand clothes and shoes, for instance, storytellers find themselves in the difficult position of negotiating those symbols that do not suggest need, as compared with other routines that rely less on a sympathetic or pitiful appearance or story. I now discuss the four storyteller subroutines in greater detail.

The *silent* storyteller relies primarily on symbolic communication rather than verbal exchanges to gain the attention of passersby. The silent storyteller uses attire, expressions, movements, and other props to advertise his or her situation and needs. Movements might entail limping down the street or shivering unprotected in the rain and cold. Props may include crutches, a wheelchair, or other symbols of disability; bags of belongings; or children. Generally, silent storytellers, who often sit with their cup on the sidewalk and refrain from unnecessary interactions, are the most passive of all panhandlers. Harlan, a panhandler for the past six years, explains his silent approach:

> *Over the years I've looked at all the guys' styles and when I first started some of the guys used signs and some of the guys talked, some the guys sing, some of the guys danced, some of the guys do everything—I mean I can do all that too. I don't like to ask people for money so when I first started I used to say "Excuse me sir, can you spare some change?" Then I started to develop my own thing—something told me not to say anything. In other words, I let my cup do the talking. People used to tell me a long time ago, if anyone wants you to have anything they'll give it to you. You know, you don't have to ask. I'm not gonna ask everybody that comes up and down the street to give me a nickel [laughs]. I've tried it, I've done it. You know, I just let my cup do the talking.*

Like the silent storyteller, the *sign* storyteller typically waits passively for a pedestrian to initiate an encounter. A sign is a tool that effectively creates interest and concern within passersby with minimal effort exerted by the panhandler. A sign, as compared with a verbal exchange, reduces the likelihood of being subjected to a negative or humiliating interaction, as explained by Walt:

> *I let the sign do the talking. I don't speak unless I'm spoken to or unless to say "good morning" or something like that or "good afternoon." I just hold a sign and if people want to give me money they give me money and if they don't they walk by and nothing is ever said. There's no dirty looks, no nothin' because you can't look nasty to everyone that doesn't give you money because you'd be looking nasty to 90 percent of the world [chuckles].*

Lou also uses a cardboard sign that reads, "Homeless and Hungry. Please Help. Thank you. God Bless All." He includes his name in the lower right corner of the sign. Lou sits on the sidewalk with his back against a building, his belongings on either side, and his sign and cup positioned in front of him.

Thus, sign storytellers view the sign as an unobtrusive, nonthreatening device but one that still conveys a message of need. Generally, signs protect panhandlers from degrading interactions by

allowing agreeable donors to initiate an exchange without compulsion or intimidation.

The *line* storyteller is the most common among all storytellers and possibly the most ubiquitous routine in the panhandling repertoire. The line storyteller typically remains stationary and simply presents a line to pedestrians as they pass. Almost all lines focus on money in one form or another. The most basic, unadorned money line is "Can you spare some change?" but specific higher amounts, such as a quarter or a dollar are often inserted in place of *change*.

Other lines may refer to "help" rather than money while specifying how the help would be put to good use. In these instances, food is a typical theme, such as "Can you help me get something to eat?" or "Can you spare some change to get a burrito?" In addition to food, transportation needs are another common theme used by line storytellers, such as "Can you spare two or three dollars for bus fare?" Lines invoking transportation may also include a destination and purpose, like returning to the shelter for the evening, buying medication at a hospital, or going to a job interview. Lines also focus on the return from unintended destinations, such as a hospital or jail, which may involve displaying evidence of a stay, like an institutionally marked identification wristband. Beyond money, food, transportation, and destinations, line storytellers focus on innumerable topics, but lines typically center on subjects that a homeless or poor person might realistically need.

The *hard luck* storyteller uses a more direct approach than the teller of a line story and offers an in depth narrative focusing on difficult or unusual circumstances. On gaining the person's attention, the hard luck storyteller then presents an extended narrative to elicit sympathy and a contribution. Often, hard luck storytellers elaborate and combine themes used by line and sign storytellers. Here is an example of a hard luck story told to me one afternoon:

> *I know this is a little unusual but I need you to save me. . . . I almost just committed suicide by jumping off the bridge. You need to help me and my two daughters. We're trying to get a bus ticket to Philadelphia. I've been in prison for the past five*

years and I've been out a month and I'm broke.
When I was in prison my wife was raped and mur-
dered. I need $15—Travelers Aid is going to pay
the rest of the ticket. . . .

In sum, storytellers attempt to negate the
blasé state by emphasizing the apparent disparities between themselves and pedestrians. These
differences then create feelings of sympathy or
pity within passersby and often lead to encounters and contributions. The storyteller's dramatized tales or physical appearance, however, may
actually exacerbate the level of strangeness between panhandler and pedestrian—a result that is
in contrast to more positive routines that neutralize strangeness, such as the entertainer, greeter,
and servicer numbers. Aggravating strangeness
through stories or appearances, though, places
storytellers in the "sick role" (Parsons 1951) or a
position of alienated dependency, which then
paves the way for sympathy and contributions.

Aggressor

The aggressor technique is premised on evoking
guilt and fear in pedestrians by using either real or
feigned aggression. Compared with the storyteller,
the aggressor captures the attention of a pedestrian
in a more pointed and dramatic fashion. Like the
storyteller routine, however, the aggressor increases feelings of strangeness by highlighting disparities and differences. Primarily, the aggressor
obtains food, money, and other items through intimidation, persistence, and shame.

Intimidation is accomplished through sarcastic and abusive comments, or fearful movements,
like walking alongside, grabbing hold of the
pedestrian, or silently using intimidating looks or
stares. *Persistence* entails doggedly pursuing a
contribution after it has been refused or seeking
more money after an initial donation. *Shame* is
evoked by making the donor feel that his or her
quarter or dollar donation is insufficient and cheap
given the vast material discrepancies between
donor and panhandler.

[But the] District of Columbia's Panhandling
Control Act, enacted in 1993, prohibits panhan-

dling in an aggressive manner, which includes
"approaching, speaking to, or following a person
in a manner as would cause a reasonable person to
fear bodily harm" and "continuously asking, begging, or soliciting alms from a person after the person has made a negative response."

Most panhandlers are well aware of this law
and the prohibitions surrounding aggressive panhandling. Consequently, panhandlers often distinguish themselves from other panhandlers who act
in an aggressive fashion, as Lou suggests:

> *You have people out there with the cup going right*
> *up to people and saying "Help me out." That's*
> *what they call aggressive panhandling. That makes*
> *a bad name for me because I use a sign. And I*
> *mean that says it all. I'm not in people's face. I'm*
> *just off on the side. That's how I do it.*

Hence, panhandlers generally understand the
economic and legal imperatives behind remaining
silent when publicly humiliated. Although easier
said than done, managing one's emotions in the
face of rejection or abusive comments is part of
the job, as suggested by Ray:

> *I don't do aggressive panhandling. I don't harass*
> *nobody. If you have a problem with me I have*
> *nothin' to say to you—I'm a panhandler. If people*
> *have something to say I just let it go—words are*
> *words.*

Whereas the aggressor routine is often good at
stirring pedestrians from their blasé condition, such
action runs the risk of furthering strangeness and
alienating potential donors. Particularly among
panhandlers who are tempted to react aggressively
to humiliating interactions with passersby or police, the job of panhandling is akin to service occupations that require emotional labor (Hochschild
1983) or publicly managing one's feelings.

Servicer

In contrast to all other routines, the servicer provides specific services to stimulate social interaction and exchange. Using various dramaturgical
techniques, the servicer transforms the exchange

into something different than merely giving money to a panhandler. The servicer dispels the blasé attitude by ostensibly offering a service while lessening the sense of strangeness by converting the interaction into a kind of business transaction. In other words, giving money to a stranger in public is an unfamiliar practice, whereas being engaged by a salesperson offering a service is a familiar ritual. Regardless of whether a service is desired or not, however, providing a service dampens strangeness by establishing a sense of obligation and reciprocity between panhandler and pedestrian, although this rapport may be contrived in some cases and more akin to "counterfeit intimacy" (Enck and Preston 1988), that is, interaction supporting the illusion that a legitimate service is being performed when both parties know this to be false.

The servicer repertoire consists of a formal, proactive component and an informal, reactive aspect. The formal servicer consciously seeks out situations to provide a service in exchange for a tip, much like a bellhop or bathroom attendant. Roaming the streets in search of an opportunity is a particular characteristic of the formal servicer. In contrast, the informal servicer is more typically sought out by virtue of possessing something desirable, such as information. Additionally, the informal servicer can be viewed as a secondary type of routine that emerges owing to the failure of a primary one or arises when a panhandler is in the right place at the right time.

Car parking, that is, pointing out parking spaces to drivers in exchange for a tip, is the most prevalent type of formal service. This practice, however, is illegal under the Panhandling Control Act. The maximum penalties for violating the statute are a $300 fine and 90 days in jail. Despite its illegality and potential costs, parking cars remains a booming business in certain neighborhoods.

In contrast to the formal servicer, such as the car parker, the informal servicer provides services to pedestrians, vendors, store owners, and the police. These services, which result from a panhandler's propensity of being in the right place at the right time, include offering an umbrella to a soaked pedestrian, giving directions to specific street ad-

dresses, escorting unchaperoned, sometimes inebriated persons to their final destinations, or hailing a taxi for the less streetwise or infirm. These exchanges convert the panhandler into an informal service provider.

Beyond informally offering everyday information and help, panhandlers occasionally encounter more significant and valued news. Owing to their near omnipresence on the streets, panhandlers are frequently knowledgeable of many important happenings. Information absorbed by panhandlers, particularly facts and persons relating to crimes, are sought after by store owners and police, as explained by Vance:

> We provide services to some of the store owners. If there's a break-in or vandalism, we usually know who did it within a 24–48 hour period, whereas it might take the police several days to a week to find out the same information.

In sum, the servicer captures a pedestrian's attention by creating the impression that he or she has some valuable utility to offer in exchange for payment, much like the relationship between salesclerk and patron. Although intimacy or familiarity may increase the likelihood of a pedestrian giving money to a servicer, the quality of strangeness is attenuated by the panhandler's ability to turn the interaction into a kind of neutral business exchange. Because of their presence on the streets, overcoming the nonperson treatment is occasionally a moot point as panhandlers are sometimes actively approached for information or assistance. As indicated, however, panhandlers must intermittently use other dramaturgical routines to avoid encounters (and thereby foster strangeness) with more powerful persons, such as the police, who seek to develop exchanges that may be disadvantageous or detrimental to their existence on the streets.

Greeter

The greeter offers friendliness, respect, flattery, and deference to passersby in exchange for contributions and cordial responses. This routine largely revolves around polite behavior, such as greeting pedestrians with a "hello" or "good morning," quite like department store employees who welcome customers at store entrances. Like these service occupations, the greeter number is firmly rooted in dramaturgically managing emotions. Additionally, the routine is enhanced when a panhandler becomes familiar with a panhandling locale and then remembers faces, names, and biographical facts about contributors. Hence, a command of these more intimate details about passersby allows the greeter to personalize each greeting and devise a more comprehensive panhandling repertoire.

Sanford personifies the greeter number. During numerous observations and encounters, Sanford always offered a pleasant greeting and a distinctive, friendly smile. Sanford typically stands at the top of the Metro (subway) or along a busy side street greeting passersby during their commute or afternoon stroll. As he explains,

> I greet people in the morning—say "good morning" to them—say "hello." I try to make people happy and everything. I generally get a good response—a happy greeting in a happy way especially with a smile. They always like my smile. Everybody has their own different style. My style is my smile. That's how a lot of people remember me you know.

Although some panhandlers possess specific attributes that facilitate the greeter number, such as a friendly smile or a courteous manner, a certain amount of on-the-job learning is usually involved. Wally implicitly describes his evolution from the aggressor to the greeter, which required emotion management skills:

> I always say "good morning" to the people. It makes them feel real good. And most of the time I'm good at it but I was a nasty motherfucker when I came here. But now I've learned my lesson—I've learned from my mistakes. Now that I'm so nice to the people I can get anything I want. When I was nasty and dirty I used the "f" word. Now I think things have changed. Now I just like being friendly with my cup in hand—"Hey, how are you doin'!"

Once a panhandler is known in a certain area and rapport is established with a group of regular contributors, the greeter may be emboldened to mix compliments, such as "You're looking good today," with more conservative salutations, like "good morning." Alternatively, a more confident, forward greeter may deal largely in compliments.

In sum, the greeter deploys pleasantries to maintain friendships with regular contributors or displays politeness and deference to newcomers. Given its versatility, it is a routine used by nearly all panhandlers. Although some use it as a primary part of their repertoire when dealing with large processions of anonymous crowds, storytellers and others typically use it as a secondary routine on encountering persons who give regularly.

Entertainer

The entertainer provides humor and enjoyment and encompasses two more specific numbers: the *joker* and the *musician*. Both typically awaken pedestrians from their blasé state through a benign or positive offering, such as a joke or a song. Strangeness is then reduced by creating rapport or intimacy by performing a familiar tune or by developing an ongoing presence in a particular neighborhood. Generally, the entertainer routine most clearly resembles an actor staging a performance before an audience.

The joker entertains by telling funny stories, making irreverent comments, or offering bizarre appearances. Minimally, the joker's goal is to make an unsuspecting pedestrian smile or laugh. Once the pedestrian is loosened up, it is hoped that a contribution will follow.

For instance, Yancy demonstrates the joker by presenting a strange appearance in conjunction with humorous lines. One evening, I observed Yancy walking along a crowded sidewalk with the collar of his blue shirt pulled over his forehead, exposing only his face and a green leaf drooping over his left eye and cheek. Donning this clownish look and occasionally saying, "Can you help me out? I'm trying to get on the Internet," he moved about holding out an upturned baseball cap. During an interview, Yancy explained how confronting a weary afternoon commuter with a humorous scenario, like the incongruity between a homeless panhandler and the Internet, is a good antidote for the nonperson treatment.

The musician is another variation on the entertainer routine and covers a range of musical acts from polished saxophonist to struggling crooner. Often, musicians play familiar and fun tunes to maximize appeal. Likewise, singers frequently enhance their act by interspersing humorous lines or jokes into songs.

For instance, a companion and I were abruptly accosted one evening by a man standing five-and-a-half feet tall with long sideburns and cowboy boots who introduced himself as "Blelvis"—Black Elvis. Blelvis announced that he could sing over 1,000 Elvis songs and could relate any word to an Elvis song. As we continued walking toward our destination, I mentioned the word *cat* and Blelvis began singing a tuneful Elvis melody containing the word *cat.* Eventually, Blelvis asked for $1.50 for his performance.

This encounter with Blelvis, though largely promoted as a musical/comedy act, also contained elements of the aggressor technique. After initiating the encounter, Blelvis followed close behind and offered us little choice but to engage him. When my companion produced only $0.50 in response to his solicitation, Blelvis deftly grabbed a bottle of beer from the bag I was carrying.

Because many street performers are less aggressive than Blelvis or lack genuine musical talent, contributions may be more linked to sympathy and respect than to performing abilities. For example, late one afternoon, Alvin sat on a milk crate and played a Miles Davis tune, "Solar," on his worn clarinet. Several moments after Alvin ceased his playing, which was inspired but not exceptional, a group of young men walked past, and one dropped a handful of coins into Alvin's green canvas bag. Alvin responded to the contributions by pulling the bag next to his side and reasserting his identity as a musician: "Sometimes people hear me when I'm playing good but give me money when I'm playing bad or just warming up. They might give me money now or later. But I don't want anyone to think I'm a panhandler."

Hence, some ambiguous performers, like Alvin, occasionally struggle to prevent one routine, such as the musician, from being misinterpreted for another act that may be more degrading to the self, like the storyteller.

In sum, entertainers awaken pedestrians from their blasé state through benign or positive offerings, such as a song or a joke. Strangeness is reduced by performing familiar tunes or developing a welcoming presence in a particular neighborhood. Many panhandlers devise a coherent repertoire based largely on the entertainer and greeter routines, given the affinity between these two numbers.

CONCLUSION

I have shown that dramaturgical routines are a useful way of describing and theorizing the interactions and exchanges that constitute panhandling. From this symbolic interactionist perspective, sidewalks serve as stages on which panhandlers confront and overcome the nonperson treatment. Given the numerous contingencies facing panhandlers, the most successful panhandlers devise a repertoire of several routines to stir the blasé attitude, to minimize strangeness, and to maximize contributions.

Fundamentally, however, panhandling and panhandling routines are a response to economic and social marginality. After years of homelessness, joblessness, or health problems, few panhandlers possess the resources or skills necessary to gain stable jobs in the formal economy. Rather than relying exclusively on programs designed for the poor and homeless, such as food stamps, soup kitchens, or shelters (which many view as controlling, humiliating institutions), the individuals described here support themselves by creatively, sometimes desperately, engaging the consciences of passersby. Surviving in this manner is an accomplishment given that the majority of Americans do not believe the homeless should be allowed to panhandle publicly (Link et al. 1995).

In a broader sense, panhandling routines represent general strategies that any person might use to get what he or she wants from reluctant others. For instance, the salesperson who humors her clients to facilitate sales is being the entertainer, whereas the minister who dramatizes the church's financial status to increase contributions is playing the storyteller. Viewed in this manner, panhandler routines perform the same function as those deployed by the salesperson or the minister. When enacted by a panhandler, however, the entertainer, the storyteller, and the other routines appear in their baldest terms; that is, the performing and staging are done in the most unadorned settings and without the protection of position or prestige. In light of such difficulties, panhandlers who devise routines to overcome the nonperson treatment demonstrate a certain resiliency and fortitude, qualities that, were it not for their position as a poor panhandler, might have earned them raises and promotions rather than leftovers and spare change.

REFERENCES

Anderson, Nels. [1923] 1961. *The Hobo: The Sociology of the Homeless Man.* Chicago: University of Chicago Press.

Council of the District of Columbia. 1993. "The Panhandling Control Act." Law No. 10–54. D.C. Register, Washington, DC.

District of Columbia Government. 1993. *Indices: A Statistical Index to District of Columbia Services.* Vol. X. Washington, DC.

Enck, Graves E., and James D. Preston. 1988. "Counterfeit Intimacy: A Dramaturgical Analysis of an Erotic Performance." *Deviant Behavior* 9:369–81.

Freund, Roger Henry. 1925. "Begging in Chicago." Master's thesis, University of Chicago, Chicago, IL.

Gilmore, Harlan W. 1940. *The Beggar.* Chapel Hill: University of North Carolina Press.

Goffman, Erving. 1959. *The Presentation of Self in Everyday Life.* New York: Anchor/Doubleday.

———. 1963. *Behavior in Public Place.* New York: Free Press.

———. 1974. *Frame Analysis: An Essay on the Organization of Experience.* New York: Harper and Row Colophon.

Hochschild, Arlie. 1983. *The Managed Heart: Commercialization of Human Feelings.* Berkeley: University of California Press.

Igbinova, Patrick. 1991. "Begging in Nigeria." *International Journal of Offender Therapy and Comparative Criminology* 35(1):21–33.

Liebow, Elliot. 1993. *Tell Them Who I Am: The Lives of Homeless Women.* New York: Free Press.

Link, Bruce G., Sharon Schwartz, Robert Moore, Jo Phelan, Elmer Struening, Ann Stueve, and Mary Ellen Colten. 1995. "Public Knowledge, Attitudes, and Beliefs About Homeless People: Evidence for Compassion Fatigue." *American Journal of Community Psychology* 23(4):533–55.

Parsons, Talcott. 1951. *The Social System.* New York: Free Press.

Reiman, Jeffrey. 1970. *The Rich Get Richer and the Poor Get Prison.* New York: Simon and Schuster.

Simmel, Georg. [1903] 1971. "Mental Life and the Metropolis." Pp. 324–339 in *On Individuality and Social Forms,* edited by Donald N. Levine. Chicago: University of Chicago Press.

Simmel, Georg. [1908] 1971. "The Stranger." 143–149. in *On Individuality and Social Forms,* edited by Donald N. Levine. Chicago: University of Chicago Press.

Wagner, David. 1993. *Checkerboard Square: Culture and Resistance in a Homeless Community.* Boulder, CO: Westview Press.

Wallace, Samuel. 1965. *Skid Row as a Way of Life.* Totowa, NJ: Bedminister Press.

Williams, Brackette. 1995. "The Public I/Eye: Conducting Fieldwork to Do Homework on Homeless and Begging in Two U.S. Cities." *Current Anthropology* 36(1)25–39.

Wright, James D. 1989. *Address Unknown: The Homeless in America.* New York: Aldine de Gruyter.

CREDITS

1. Stephen Pfohl. "Images of Deviance" is from *Images of Deviance and Social Control,* 2nd ed. (New York: McGraw-Hill, 1994, pp. 1–6), by Stephen Pfohl. Reprinted by permission of The McGraw-Hill Companies.

2. Daniel Patrick Moynihan. "Defining Deviancy Down" is reproduced from *The American Scholar,* Volume 62, Number 1, Winter 1993. Copyright © 1993 by the author.

3. Leon Anderson and Thomas C. Calhoun. "Strategies for Researching Street Deviance," originally titled "Facilitative Aspects of Field Research with Deviant Street Populations," is from *Sociological Inquiry* 62:4, pp. 490–498. Copyright © 1992 by the University of Texas Press. All rights reserved.

4. Erich Goode. "Pleasures and Perils in Deviance Research," originally titled "Sex with Informants as Deviant Behavior: An Account and Commentary," is from *Deviant Behavior,* Vol. 20, 1999, pp. 301–324. Reprinted by permission of Taylor & Francis.

5. Robert K. Merton. "Strain Theory" is reprinted with the permission of The Free Press, a division of Simon & Schuster, from *Social Theory and Social Structure* by Robert K. Merton. Copyright © 1957 by The Free Press; copyright renewed 1985 by Robert K. Merton.

6. Edwin H. Sutherland and Donald R. Cressey. "Differential Association Theory" is from *Criminology,* 9th ed. (Philadelphia: Lippincott, 1974, pp. 75–77). Reprinted by permission of the estate of Donald R. Cressey.

7. Travis Hirschi. "Control Theory" is reprinted from *Causes of Delinquency* (Berkeley: University of California Press, 1969, pp. 16–26) by permission of the author.

8. John Braithwaite. "Shaming Theory" is from *Crime, Shame and Reintegration* (1989, pp. 55–56, 98–102) by John Braithwaite. Copyright © 1989 by Cambridge University Press. Reprinted with the permission of Cambridge University Press.

9. Howard S. Becker. "Labeling Theory" is reprinted with the permission of The Free Press, a division of Simon & Schuster, from *Outsiders: Studies in the Sociology of Deviance* by Howard S. Becker. Copyright © 1963 by The Free Press; copyright renewed 1991 by Howard S. Becker.

10. Jack Katz. "Phenomenological Theory" is from *Seductions of Crime* by Jack Katz. Copyright © 1988 by Jack Katz. Reprinted by permission of Basic Books, a member of Perseus Books, L.L.C.

11. Richard Quinney. "Conflict Theory" is reprinted from *Criminology* (Boston: Little, Brown, 1975, pp. 37–41) by Richard Quinney. Reprinted by permission of the author.

12. Jody Miller. "Feminist Theory" was written specifically for this reader.

13. David O. Friedrichs and Jessica Friedrichs. "Postmodern Theory" was written specifically for this reader, with substantial editing and condensing by Alex Thio.

14. Dane Archer and Patricia McDaniel. "Men and Violence: Is the Pattern Universal?" was written specifically for this reader. The research was supported by a grant from the H. F. Guggenheim Foundation and by the University of California.

15. Martin D. Schwartz. "Date Rape on College Campuses" was written specifically for this reader, though partially based on the author's "Humanist Sociology and Date Rape on the College Campus," *Humanity & Society* 15, 1991, pp. 304–316.

16. Paul Cromwell. "Burglary: The Offender's Perspective" was written specifically for this reader, with portions drawn from *Breaking and Entering: An Ethnographic Analysis of Burglary* (Newbury Park, CA: Sage, 1991) by Paul Cromwell, James N. Olson, and D'Aunn W. Avary.

17. Gilbert Geis. "White-Collar Crime" was written specifically for this reader.

18. Erich Goode. "Drug Use in America: An Overview" was written specifically for this reader.

19. Elliott Currie. "Drug Crisis: The American Nightmare" is excerpted from *Reckoning: Drugs, the Cities, and the American Future* by Elliott Currie. Copyright© 1993 by Elliott Currie. Reprinted by permission of Hill and Wang, a division of Farrar, Straus and Giroux, L.L.C.

20. Erich Goode. "Cigarette Smoking as Deviant Behavior" was written specifically for this reader. Several paragraphs were adapted from *Drugs in American Society,* 5th ed. (New York: McGraw-Hill, 1999, pp. 294–203) by Erich Goode.

21. Thomas A. Workman. "Pleasure versus Public Health: Controlling Collegiate Binge Drinking" was written specifically for this reader.

22. Jody Miller. "Sex Tourism in Southeast Asia" was written specifically for this reader.

23. Marjorie A. Muecke. "Mother Sold Food, Daughter Sells Her Body" is reprinted from *Social Science and Medicine,* Vol. 35, 1992, pp. 891–901, with permission from Elsevier Science.

24. Craig J. Forsyth. "Parade Strippers: Being Naked in Public" is from *Deviant Behavior,* Vol. 13, 1992, pp. 391–403. Reprinted by permission of Taylor & Francis.

25. Thomas C. Calhoun, Julie Ann Harms Cannon, and Rhonda Fisher. "The Naked Body as Site and Sight: Accounting Practices of Amateur Strippers," originally titled "Explorations in Youth Culture: Amateur Stripping: What We Know and What We Don't," is from *Youth Culture Identity in a Postmodern World* (1998, pp. 302–326) edited by Jonathan S. Epstein. Reprinted by permission of Blackwell Publishers, Ltd.

26. Elizabeth Anne Wood. "Strip Club Dancers: Working in the Fantasy Factory" is from the *Journal of Contemporary Ethnography,* February, 2000, pp. 5–31. Copyright © 2000 by Sage Publications, Inc. Reprinted by permission of Sage Publications, Inc.

27. Margaret Cooper. "Rejecting 'Femininity': Gender Identity Development in Lesbians," originally titled "Rejecting 'Femininity': Some Research Notes on Gender Identity Development in Lesbians," is from *Deviant Behavior,* Vol. 11, 1990, pp. 371–380. Reprinted by permission of Taylor & Francis.

28. Bruce Bawer. "Radical Gay Activism: A Critical Gay's View" is reprinted with the permission of Simon & Schuster from *A Place at the Table* by Bruce Bawer. Copyright © 1993 by Bruce Bawer.

29. DeAnn K. Gauthier and Craig J. Forsyth. "Bareback Sex, Bug Chasers, and the Gift of Death" is from *Deviant Behavior,* Vol. 20, 1992, pp. 85–100. Reprinted by permission of Taylor & Francis.

30. Robert P. McNamara. "The Social Organization of Male Prostitution" was written specif- ically for this reader.

31. Andrew S. Walters and David M. Hayes. "Homophobia in Schools," originally titled "Homophobia within Schools: Challenging the Culturally Sanctioned Dismissal of Gay Students and Colleagues," is from the *Journal of Homosexuality,* Vol. 35, No. 2, 1998, pp. 1–20. Copyright © 1998 The Haworth Press, Inc. Reprinted by permission of The Haworth Press, Inc.

32. Emily E. LaBeff, Robert E. Clark, Valerie J. Haines, and George M. Diekhoff. "Situational Ethics and College Student Cheating" is from *Sociological Inquiry 60:2,* pp. 190–198. Copyright © 1990 by the University of Texas Press. All rights reserved.

33. Barbara H. Zaitzow and Matthew B. Robinson. "Criminologists as Criminals" was written specifically for this reader.

34. Mark R. Pogrebin, Eric D. Poole, and Amos Martinez. "Psychotherapists' Accounts of Their Professional Misdeeds," originally titled "Accounts of Professional Misdeeds: The Sexual Exploration of Clients by Psychotherapists," is from *Deviant Behavior,* Vol. 13, 1992, pp. 229–252. Reprinted by permission of Taylor & Francis.

35. Tom Barker and David Carter. "Police Lying: 'Fluffing Up the Evidence and Covering Your Ass,' " originally titled "Fluffing Up the Evidence and Covering Your Ass: Some Conceptual Notes on Police Lying," is from *Deviant Behavior,* Vol. 11, 1990, pp. 61–73. Reprinted by permission of Taylor & Francis.

36. Michael V. Angrosino. "How the Mentally Challenged See Themselves," originally titled "Metaphors of Stigma: How Deinstitutionalized Mentally Retarded Adults See Themselves," is from the *Journal of Contemporary Ethnography,* Vol. 21, No. 2, 1992, pp. 171–199. Copyright © 1992 by Sage Publications, Inc. Reprinted by permission of Sage Publications, Inc.

37. Jennifer E. Pate, Andres J. Pumariega, Colleen Hester, and David M. Garner. "Cross-Cultural Patterns in Eating Disorders," originally titled "Cross-Cultural Patterns in Eating Disorders: A Review," is from the *Journal of American Academy of Child and Adolescent Psychiatry,* Vol. 31, 1992, pp. 802–809. Reprinted by permission of Lippincott Williams & Wilkins.

38. Penelope A. McLorg and Diane E. Taub. "Anorexics and Bulimics: Developing Deviant Identities" was written specifically for this reader.

39. Richard Tewksbury and Deanna McGaughey. "The Stigmatization of Persons with HIV Disease," originally titled "Stigmatization of Persons with HIV Disease: Perceptions, Management, and Consequences of AIDS," is from *Sociological Spectrum,* Vol. 17, 1997, pp. 49–70. Reprinted by permission of Taylor & Francis.

40. Paul A. Taylor. "The Social Construction of Hackers as Deviants" was written specifically for this reader, with most material taken from *Hackers: Crime in the Digital Sublime* (New York: Routledge, 1999) by Paul A. Taylor.

41. Diane Kholos Wysocki. "Let Your Fingers Do the Talking: Sex on an Adult Chat-Line" is from *Sexualities,* Vol. 1, No. 4, 1998, pp. 425–452. Copyright © 1998 by Sage Publications, Inc. Reprinted by permission from Sage Publications, Inc., and the author.

NAME INDEX

SUBJECT INDEX